WHAT WOULD WALLY DO?

Other DILBERT Books from BOXTREE

BUSINESS BOOKS

The Dilbert Principle
TPB ISBN: 0-7522-2470-0
PB ISBN: 0-7522-7220-9

The Way of the Weasel
HB ISBN: 0-7522-6503-2
TPB ISBN: 0-7522-1559-0

The Dilbert Future
TPB ISBN: 0-7522-1161-7
PB ISBN: 0-7522-7221-7

Dogbert's Top Secret Management Handbook
ISBN: 0-7522-1148-X

The Joy of Work
PB ISBN: 0-7522-7222-5

TREASURIES

Fugitive From the Cubicle Police
ISBN: 0-7522-2431-X

Seven Years of Highly Defective People
ISBN: 0-7522-2407-7

Dilbert Gives You the Business
ISBN: 0-7522-2394-1

Dilbert – A Treasury of Sunday Strips: Version 00
ISBN: 0-7522-7232-2

COLLECTIONS

Shave the Whales
ISBN: 0-7522-0849-7

When Did Ignorance Become a Point of View?
ISBN: 0-7522-2412-3

Bring Me the Head of Willy the Mailboy!
ISBN: 0-7522-0136-0

**Words You Don't Want to Hear During Your
Annual Performance Review**
ISBN: 0-7522-2422-0

Always Postpone Meetings with Time-Wasting Morons
ISBN: 0-7522-0854-3

When Body Language Goes Bad
ISBN: 0-7522-2491-3

Another Day In Cubicle Paradise
ISBN: 0-7522-2486-7

Random Acts of Management
ISBN: 0-7522-7174-1

Don't Step in the Leadership
ISBN: 0-7522-2389-5

I'm Not Anti-Business, I'm Anti-Idiot
ISBN: 0-7522-2379-8

Casual Day Has Gone Too Far
ISBN: 0-7522-1119-6

**Don't Stand Where the Comet
is Assumed to Strike Oil**
ISBN: 0-7522-2402-6

Thriving on Vague Objectives
ISBN: 0-7522-2605-3

BEST OF DILBERT

The Best of Dilbert Volume 1
ISBN: 0-7522-6541-5

Best of Dilbert Volume 2
ISBN: 0-7522-1500-0

For ordering information, call +44 01625 677237

WHAT WOULD WALLY DO?

A DILBERT™ BOOK
BY SCOTT ADAMS

BOXTREE

First published by Andrews McMeel Publishing, an Andrews McMeel Universal company,
4520 Main Street, Kansas City, Missouri 64111, USA

First published in Great Britain 2006 by Boxtree
an imprint of Pan Macmillan Ltd
Pan Macmillan, 20 New Wharf Road, London N1 9RR
Basingstoke and Oxford
Associated companies throughout the world
www.panmacmillan.com

ISBN-13: 978-0752-22606-4
ISBN-10: 0-7522-2606-1

DILBERT® is a registered trademark of Scott Adams, Inc. Licensed by United Feature Syndicate, Inc.
DOGBERT® and DILBERT® appear in the comic strip DILBERT®, distributed by United Feature Syndicate, Inc.
and owned by Scott Adams, Inc. Licensed by United Feature Syndicate, Inc.
www.dilbert.com

What Would Wally Do? © by 2006 Scott Adams, Inc.

9 8 7 6 5 4 3 2 1

A CIP catalogue record for this book is available from
the British Library.

Printed by The Bath Press Ltd, Bath

Introduction

You might be aware that Dilbert's coworker Wally was inspired by a real person. Let's call him Wally Version 1.0. He has a fascinating backstory.

One day in the mid '90s, at my old employer Pacific Bell, Wally Version 1.0 made a judgment call that went bad, i.e., he trusted some weasels. Management didn't want to fire him because he had been an excellent employee up to that point. However, they told him that he could never again be promoted, nor would he ever get a raise. It was their subtle way of encouraging him to seek other opportunities.

As fate would have it, somewhere in the bowels of Human Resources, a downsizing scheme was being hatched. The idea was to identify the worst 10 percent of employees and offer them a sizable pot of money to leave peacefully.

Wally Version 1.0 was a brilliant MIT graduate and recognized an opportunity when he saw it. Since he knew he had to leave, he figured it was better to do so with a pot of money than with none. All he had to do was become one of the worst 10 percent of employees.

Now, I don't like to talk smack about my old employer, but I have to tell you that making it into the lowest 10 percent of performers wasn't easy. There was fierce competition for those spots. Luckily, Version 1.0 was up to the challenge.

During the several months it took Version 1.0 to realize his career aspiration of getting laid off with money, he was the most amusing coworker you would ever hope to have. He made his transition gradually so it wouldn't be too obvious. Each day he wore increasingly casual clothes. Toward the end he looked like a blind hobo on laundry day. And it was during this period when he started openly running his side business from his cubicle.

My favorite Wally Version 1.0 experience happened on the day we met our new gaggle of consultants. They were freshly minted MBAs with no experience in the telecommunications field. The idea was that they would learn our entire industry in a few days and then tell us how to do our jobs.

This was no more absurd than anything else the company was doing, so the rest of us accepted it for its entertainment value and went with the flow. Wally Version 1.0 saw more humor potential in the situation and couldn't leave it alone. He stopped the meeting five minutes in and pointedly asked the consultants to defend their qualifications for even being in the room, much less telling us how to do our jobs. The consultant newbies tried their best, but Wally Version 1.0 was on them like a Labrador on a pork chop. He would listen to their explanations about the power of their "process" and then he'd scrunch up his face and ask, "How does that make you qualified to be here?" That question, repeated relentlessly and paired with some head shaking and grimacing, created a humor event that threatened the pants of everyone in the room, excluding the consultants.

Well, maybe you had to be there. Luckily, I was. Soon after, *Dilbert*'s Wally took on this same sociopath personality. The culmination is this book.

Speaking of sociopath culminations, you can join Dogbert's New Ruling Class and be by his side when he conquers the world. All you need to do is sign up for the free *Dilbert Newsletter* that is published approximately whenever I feel like it. To sign up, go to www.dilbert.com and follow the subscription instructions. If that doesn't work for some reason, send e-mail to newsletter@unitedmedia.com.

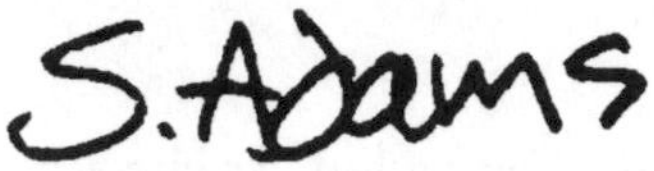

Scott Adams

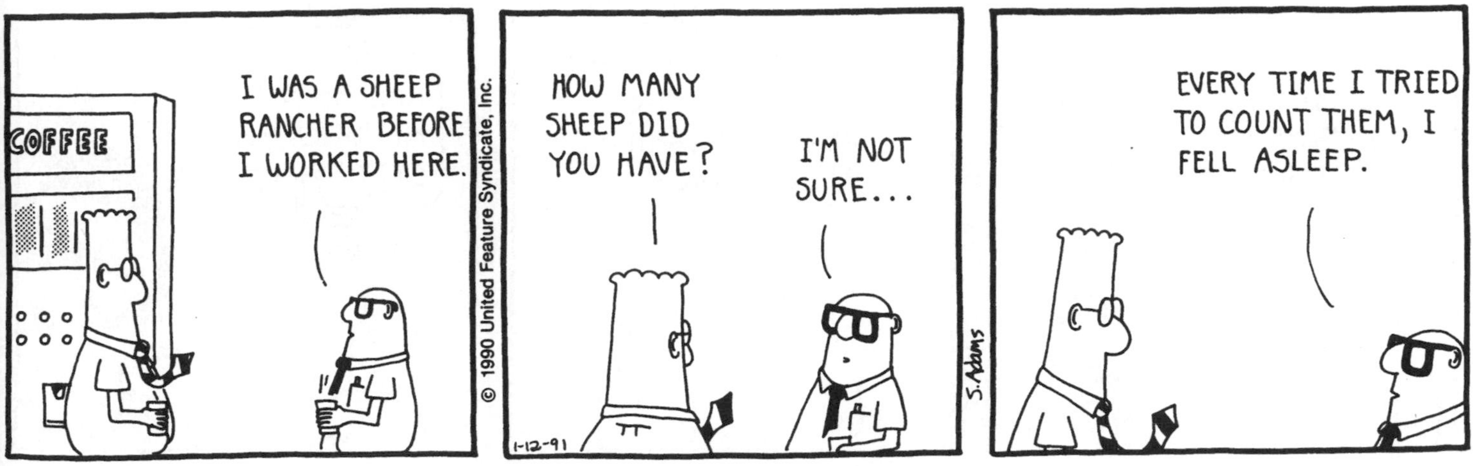
COFFEE
I WAS A SHEEP RANCHER BEFORE I WORKED HERE.
© 1990 United Feature Syndicate, Inc.
HOW MANY SHEEP DID YOU HAVE?
I'M NOT SURE...
1-12-91
S. Adams
EVERY TIME I TRIED TO COUNT THEM, I FELL ASLEEP.

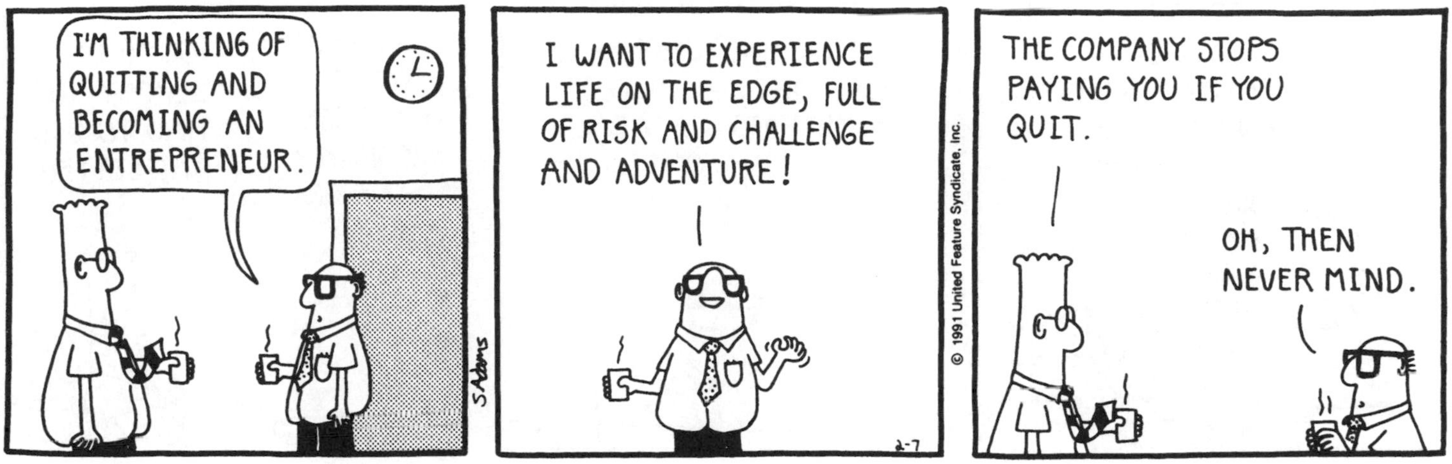
I'M THINKING OF QUITTING AND BECOMING AN ENTREPRENEUR.
S. Adams
I WANT TO EXPERIENCE LIFE ON THE EDGE, FULL OF RISK AND CHALLENGE AND ADVENTURE!
2-7
© 1991 United Feature Syndicate, Inc.
THE COMPANY STOPS PAYING YOU IF YOU QUIT.
OH, THEN NEVER MIND.

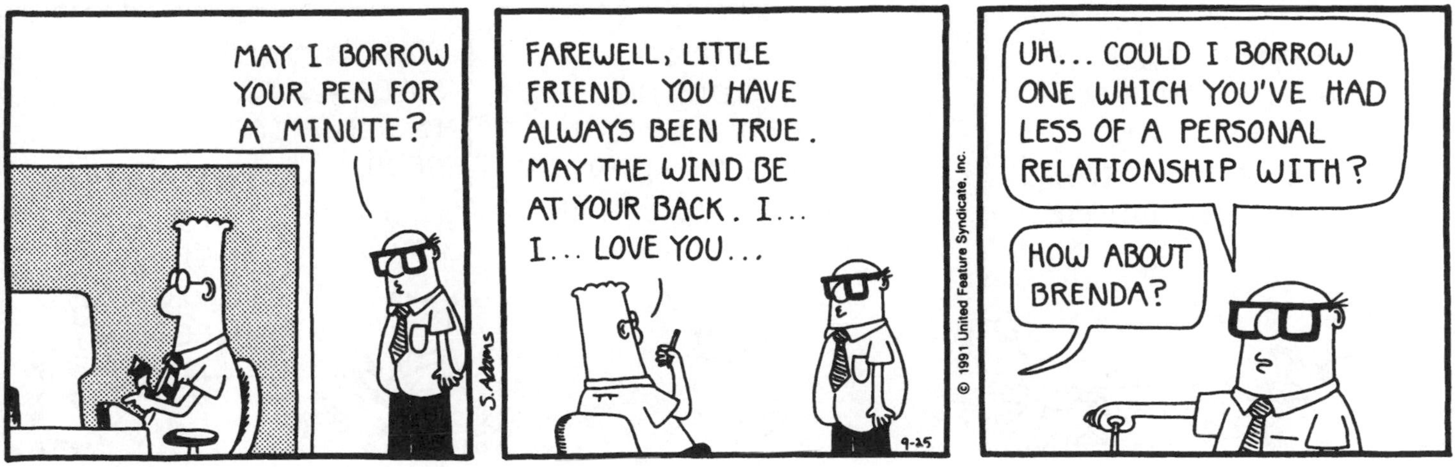
MAY I BORROW YOUR PEN FOR A MINUTE?
S. Adams
FAREWELL, LITTLE FRIEND. YOU HAVE ALWAYS BEEN TRUE. MAY THE WIND BE AT YOUR BACK. I... I... LOVE YOU...
9-25
© 1991 United Feature Syndicate, Inc.
UH... COULD I BORROW ONE WHICH YOU'VE HAD LESS OF A PERSONAL RELATIONSHIP WITH?
HOW ABOUT BRENDA?

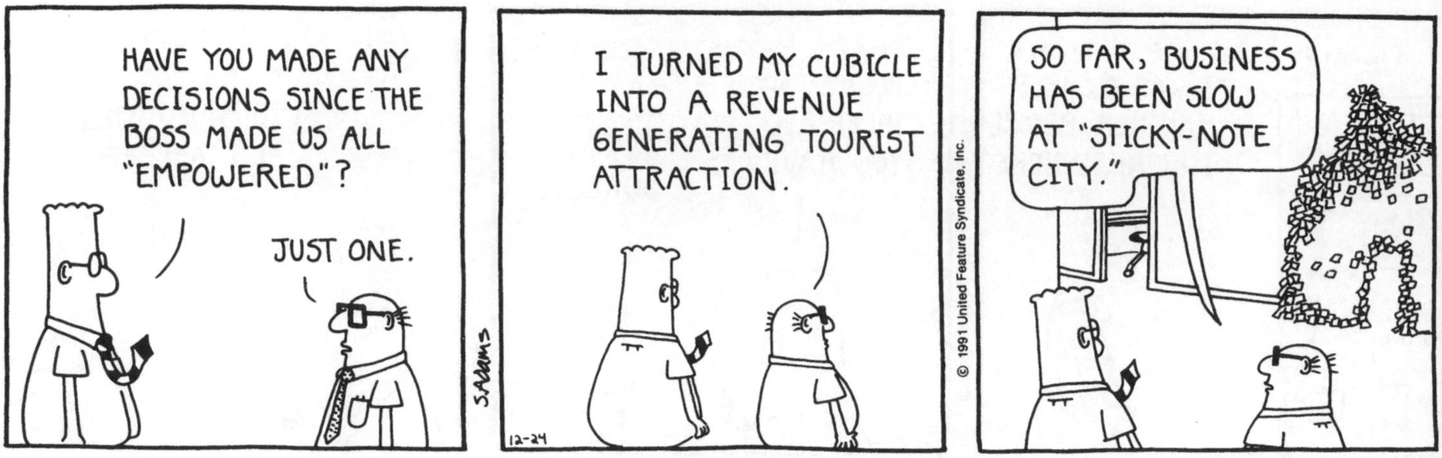
HAVE YOU MADE ANY DECISIONS SINCE THE BOSS MADE US ALL "EMPOWERED"?
JUST ONE.
I TURNED MY CUBICLE INTO A REVENUE GENERATING TOURIST ATTRACTION.
SO FAR, BUSINESS HAS BEEN SLOW AT "STICKY-NOTE CITY."
© 1991 United Feature Syndicate, Inc.

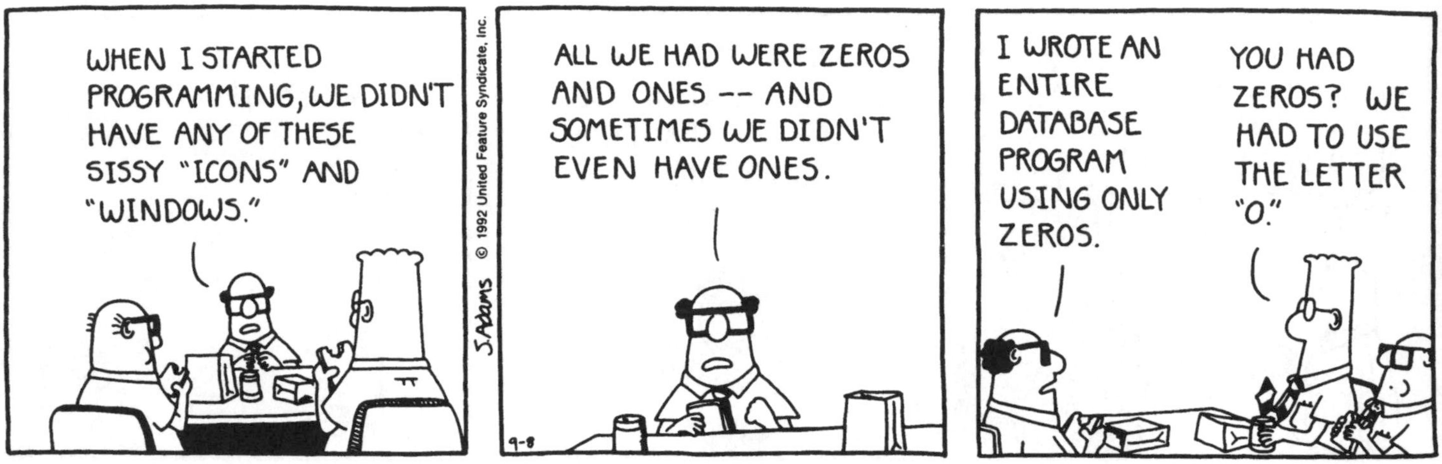
WHEN I STARTED PROGRAMMING, WE DIDN'T HAVE ANY OF THESE SISSY "ICONS" AND "WINDOWS."
ALL WE HAD WERE ZEROS AND ONES -- AND SOMETIMES WE DIDN'T EVEN HAVE ONES.
I WROTE AN ENTIRE DATABASE PROGRAM USING ONLY ZEROS.
YOU HAD ZEROS? WE HAD TO USE THE LETTER "O."
© 1992 United Feature Syndicate, Inc.

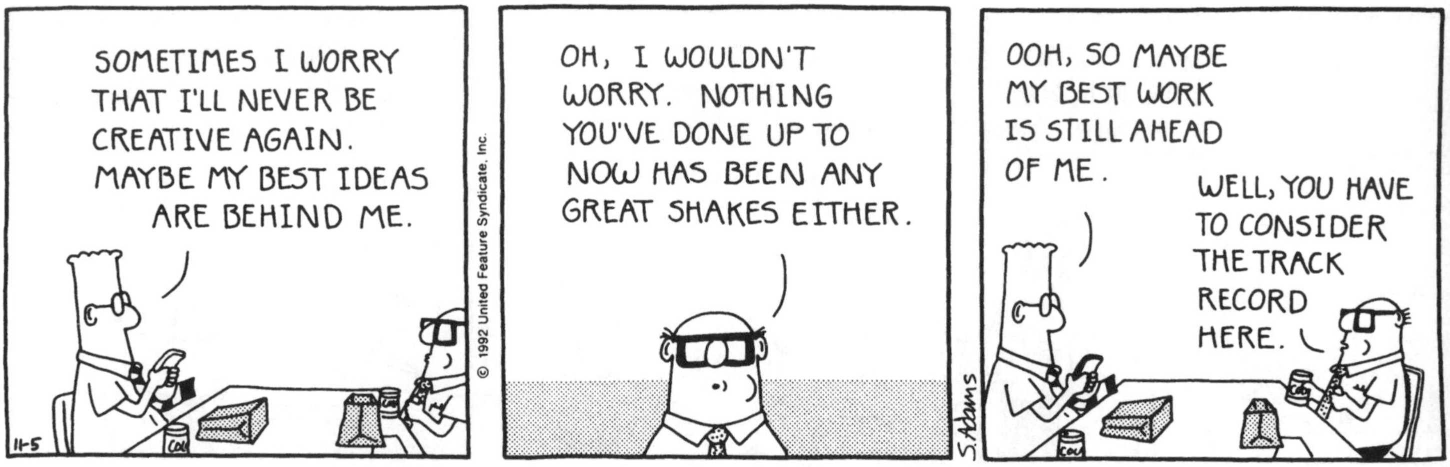
SOMETIMES I WORRY THAT I'LL NEVER BE CREATIVE AGAIN. MAYBE MY BEST IDEAS ARE BEHIND ME.
OH, I WOULDN'T WORRY. NOTHING YOU'VE DONE UP TO NOW HAS BEEN ANY GREAT SHAKES EITHER.
OOH, SO MAYBE MY BEST WORK IS STILL AHEAD OF ME.
WELL, YOU HAVE TO CONSIDER THE TRACK RECORD HERE.
© 1992 United Feature Syndicate, Inc.

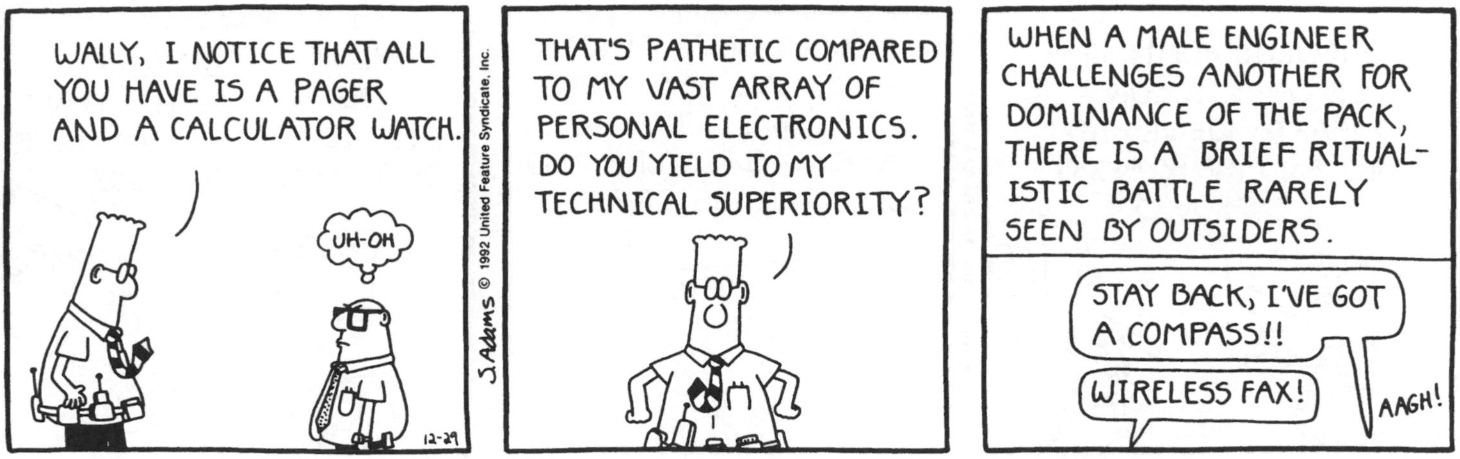
WALLY, I NOTICE THAT ALL YOU HAVE IS A PAGER AND A CALCULATOR WATCH.
UH-OH
S. Adams © 1992 United Feature Syndicate, Inc.
THAT'S PATHETIC COMPARED TO MY VAST ARRAY OF PERSONAL ELECTRONICS. DO YOU YIELD TO MY TECHNICAL SUPERIORITY?
WHEN A MALE ENGINEER CHALLENGES ANOTHER FOR DOMINANCE OF THE PACK, THERE IS A BRIEF RITUALISTIC BATTLE RARELY SEEN BY OUTSIDERS.
STAY BACK, I'VE GOT A COMPASS!!
WIRELESS FAX!
AAGH!

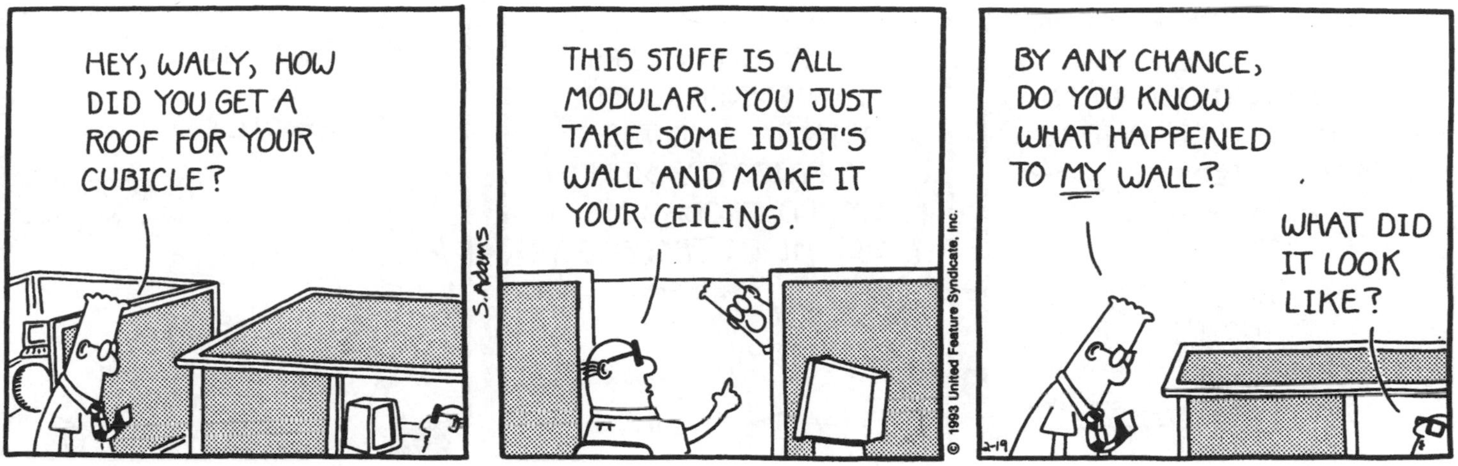
HEY, WALLY, HOW DID YOU GET A ROOF FOR YOUR CUBICLE?
S. Adams
THIS STUFF IS ALL MODULAR. YOU JUST TAKE SOME IDIOT'S WALL AND MAKE IT YOUR CEILING.
© 1993 United Feature Syndicate, Inc.
BY ANY CHANCE, DO YOU KNOW WHAT HAPPENED TO MY WALL?
WHAT DID IT LOOK LIKE?

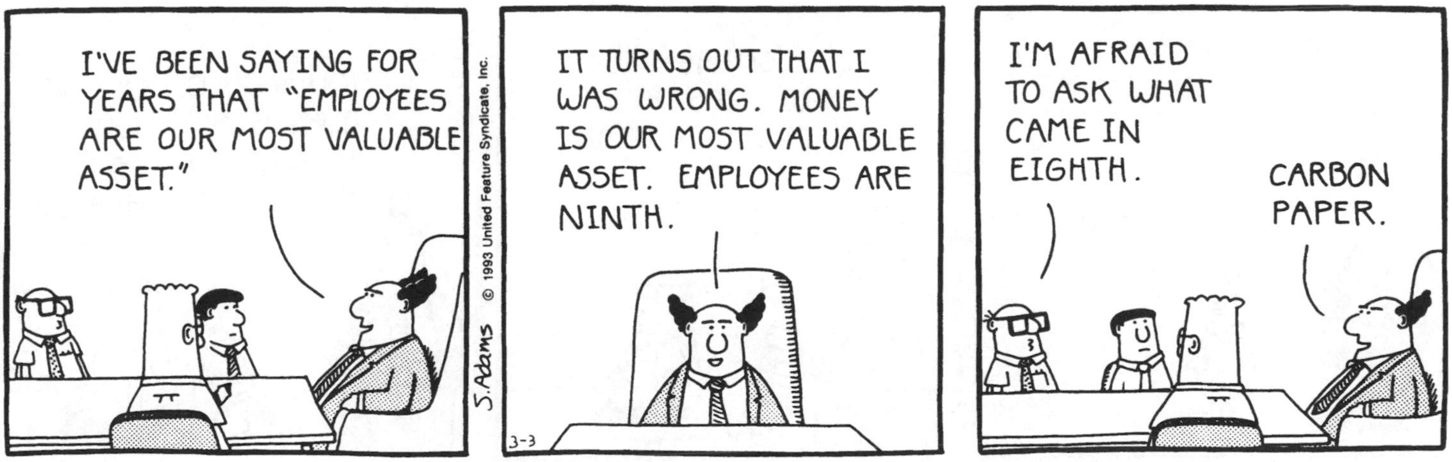
I'VE BEEN SAYING FOR YEARS THAT "EMPLOYEES ARE OUR MOST VALUABLE ASSET."
S. Adams © 1993 United Feature Syndicate, Inc.
IT TURNS OUT THAT I WAS WRONG. MONEY IS OUR MOST VALUABLE ASSET. EMPLOYEES ARE NINTH.
I'M AFRAID TO ASK WHAT CAME IN EIGHTH.
CARBON PAPER.

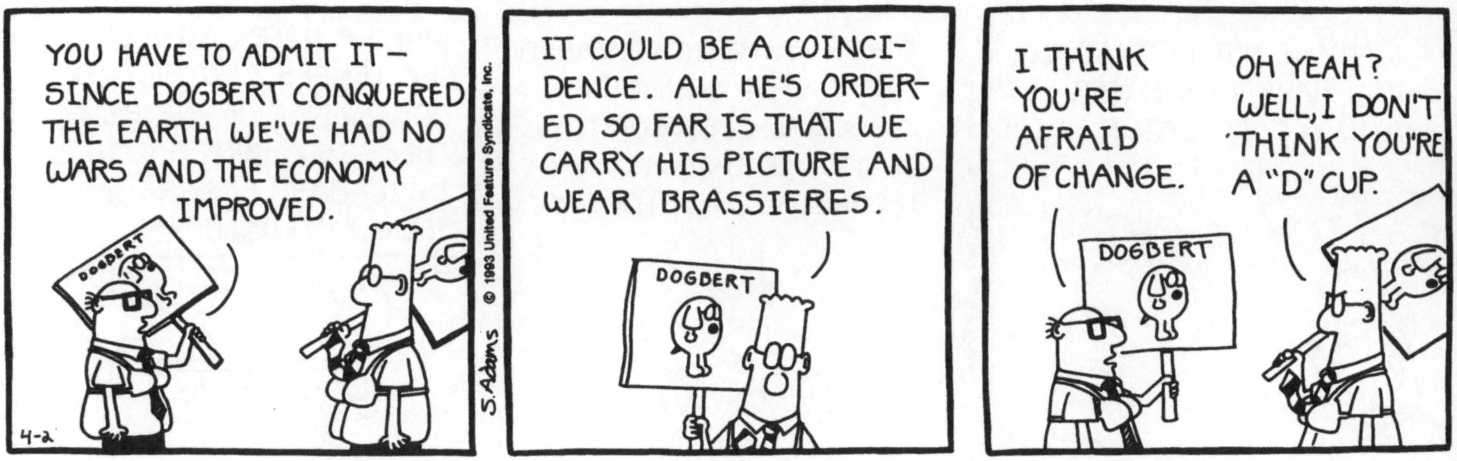
YOU HAVE TO ADMIT IT— SINCE DOGBERT CONQUERED THE EARTH WE'VE HAD NO WARS AND THE ECONOMY IMPROVED.
DOGBERT
4-2
S. Adams
© 1993 United Feature Syndicate, Inc.
IT COULD BE A COINCIDENCE. ALL HE'S ORDERED SO FAR IS THAT WE CARRY HIS PICTURE AND WEAR BRASSIERES.
DOGBERT
I THINK YOU'RE AFRAID OF CHANGE.
DOGBERT
OH YEAH? WELL, I DON'T THINK YOU'RE A "D" CUP.

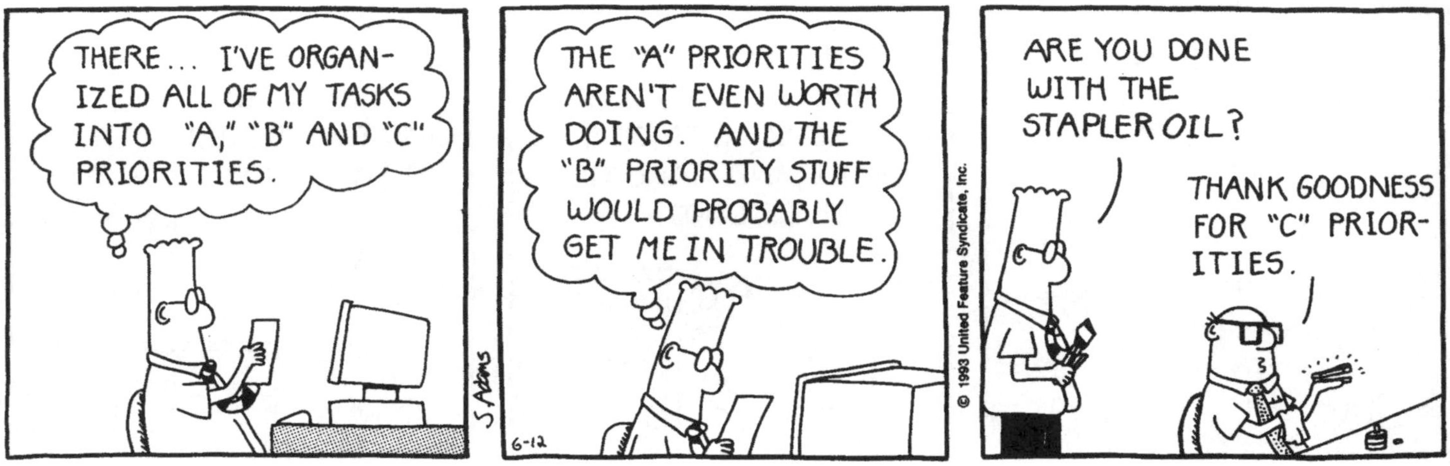
THERE... I'VE ORGANIZED ALL OF MY TASKS INTO "A," "B" AND "C" PRIORITIES.
S. Adams
6-12
THE "A" PRIORITIES AREN'T EVEN WORTH DOING. AND THE "B" PRIORITY STUFF WOULD PROBABLY GET ME IN TROUBLE.
© 1993 United Feature Syndicate, Inc.
ARE YOU DONE WITH THE STAPLER OIL?
THANK GOODNESS FOR "C" PRIORITIES.

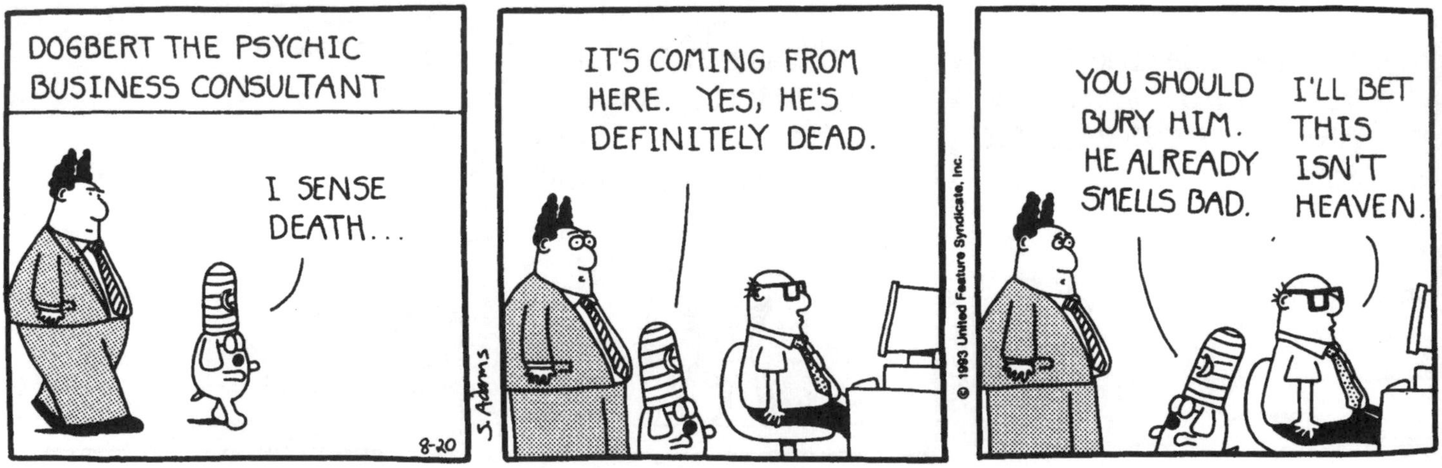
DOGBERT THE PSYCHIC BUSINESS CONSULTANT
I SENSE DEATH...
8-20
S. Adams
IT'S COMING FROM HERE. YES, HE'S DEFINITELY DEAD.
© 1993 United Feature Syndicate, Inc.
YOU SHOULD BURY HIM. HE ALREADY SMELLS BAD.
I'LL BET THIS ISN'T HEAVEN.

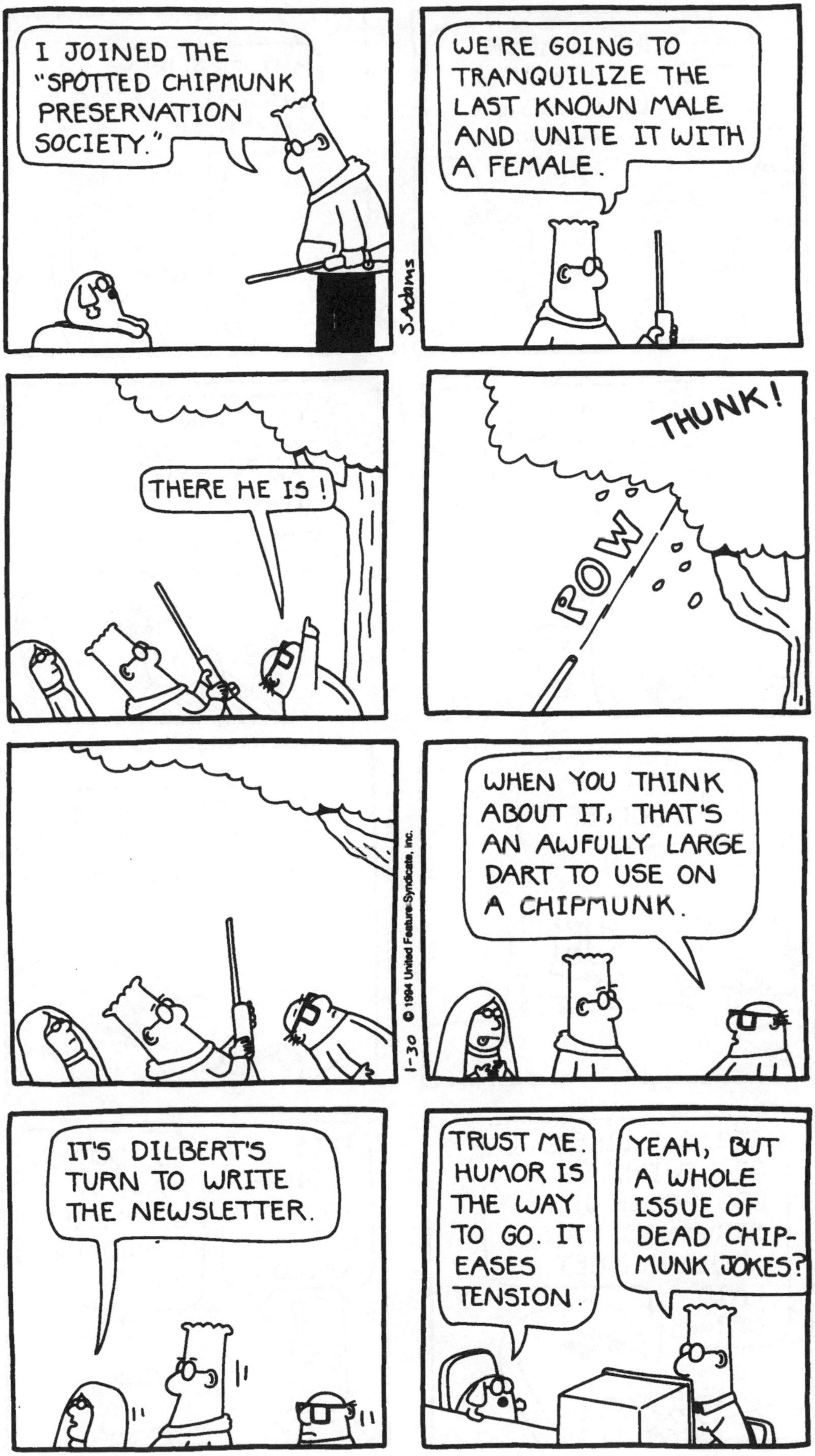
I JOINED THE "SPOTTED CHIPMUNK PRESERVATION SOCIETY."
S. Adams
WE'RE GOING TO TRANQUILIZE THE LAST KNOWN MALE AND UNITE IT WITH A FEMALE.
THERE HE IS!
THUNK!
POW
1-30 © 1994 United Feature Syndicate, Inc.
WHEN YOU THINK ABOUT IT, THAT'S AN AWFULLY LARGE DART TO USE ON A CHIPMUNK.
IT'S DILBERT'S TURN TO WRITE THE NEWSLETTER.
TRUST ME. HUMOR IS THE WAY TO GO. IT EASES TENSION.
YEAH, BUT A WHOLE ISSUE OF DEAD CHIP-MUNK JOKES?

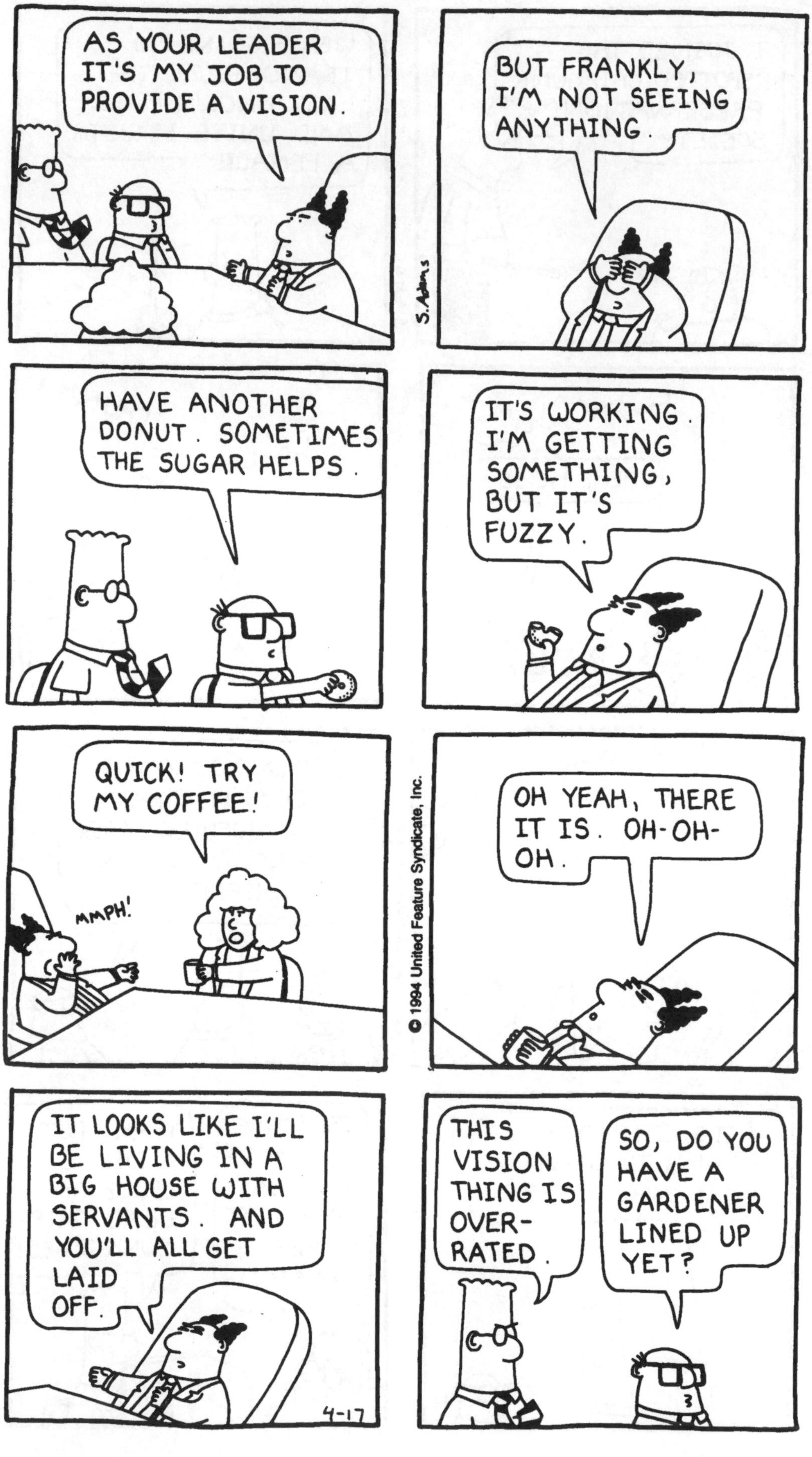
AS YOUR LEADER IT'S MY JOB TO PROVIDE A VISION.
S. Adams
BUT FRANKLY, I'M NOT SEEING ANYTHING.
HAVE ANOTHER DONUT. SOMETIMES THE SUGAR HELPS.
IT'S WORKING. I'M GETTING SOMETHING, BUT IT'S FUZZY.
QUICK! TRY MY COFFEE!
MMPH!
OH YEAH, THERE IT IS. OH-OH-OH.
IT LOOKS LIKE I'LL BE LIVING IN A BIG HOUSE WITH SERVANTS. AND YOU'LL ALL GET LAID OFF.
4-17
THIS VISION THING IS OVER-RATED.
SO, DO YOU HAVE A GARDENER LINED UP YET?

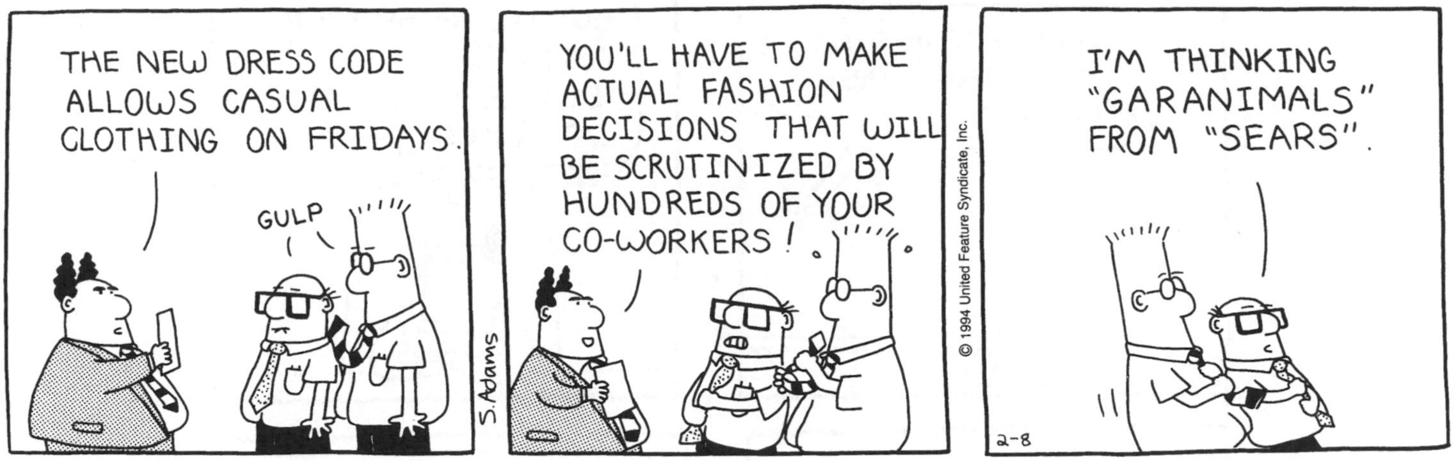
THE NEW DRESS CODE ALLOWS CASUAL CLOTHING ON FRIDAYS.
GULP
S. Adams
YOU'LL HAVE TO MAKE ACTUAL FASHION DECISIONS THAT WILL BE SCRUTINIZED BY HUNDREDS OF YOUR CO-WORKERS!
© 1994 United Feature Syndicate, Inc.
I'M THINKING "GARANIMALS" FROM "SEARS".
2-8

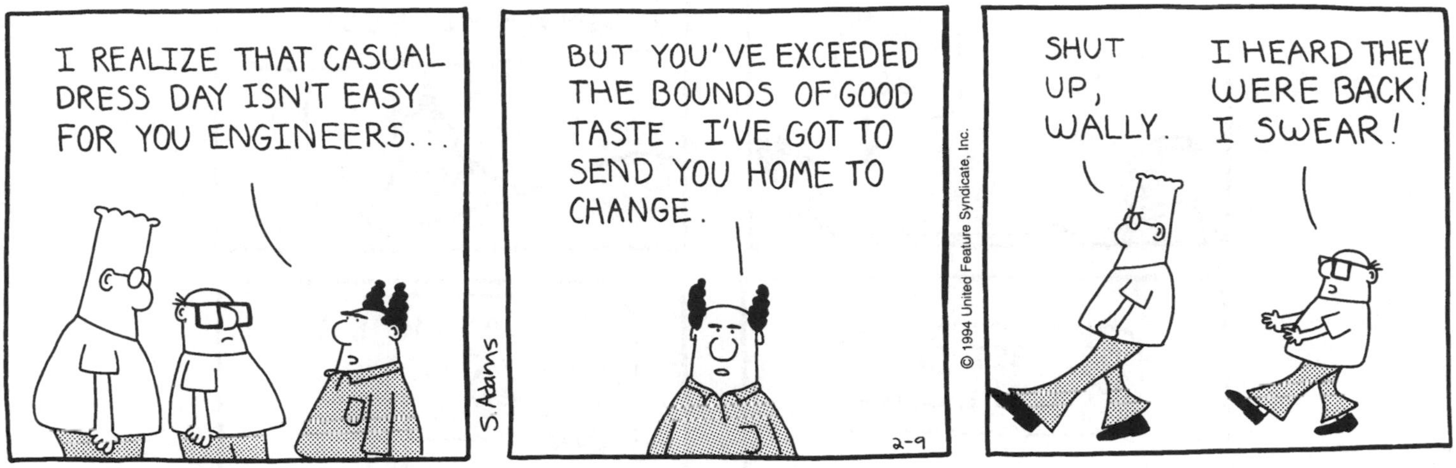
I REALIZE THAT CASUAL DRESS DAY ISN'T EASY FOR YOU ENGINEERS...
S. Adams
BUT YOU'VE EXCEEDED THE BOUNDS OF GOOD TASTE. I'VE GOT TO SEND YOU HOME TO CHANGE.
2-9
© 1994 United Feature Syndicate, Inc.
SHUT UP, WALLY.
I HEARD THEY WERE BACK! I SWEAR!

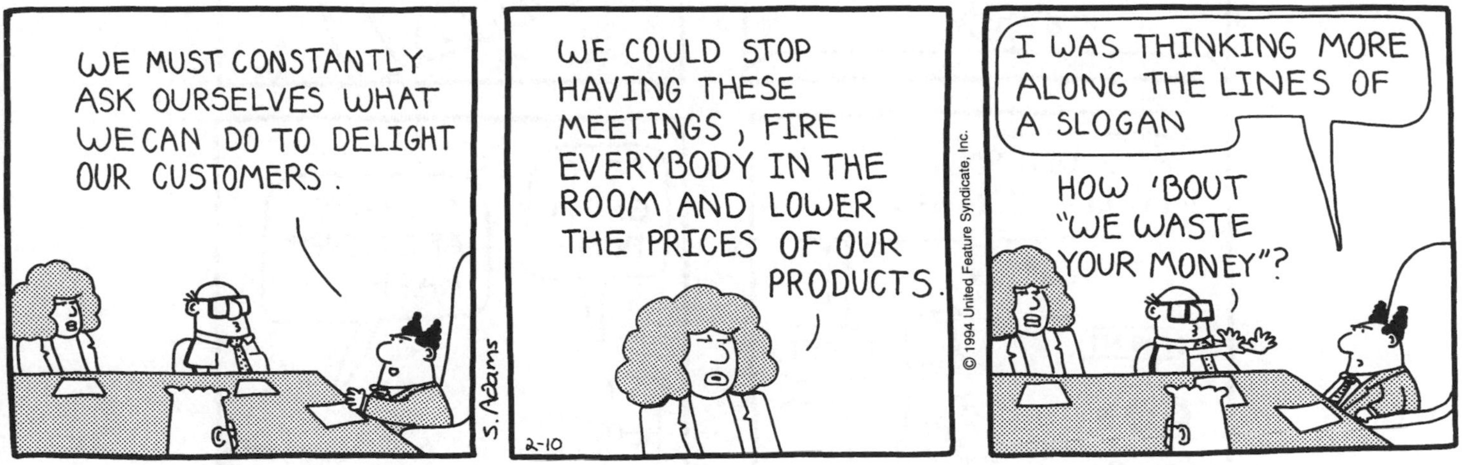
WE MUST CONSTANTLY ASK OURSELVES WHAT WE CAN DO TO DELIGHT OUR CUSTOMERS.
S. Adams
WE COULD STOP HAVING THESE MEETINGS, FIRE EVERYBODY IN THE ROOM AND LOWER THE PRICES OF OUR PRODUCTS.
2-10
© 1994 United Feature Syndicate, Inc.
I WAS THINKING MORE ALONG THE LINES OF A SLOGAN
HOW 'BOUT "WE WASTE YOUR MONEY"?

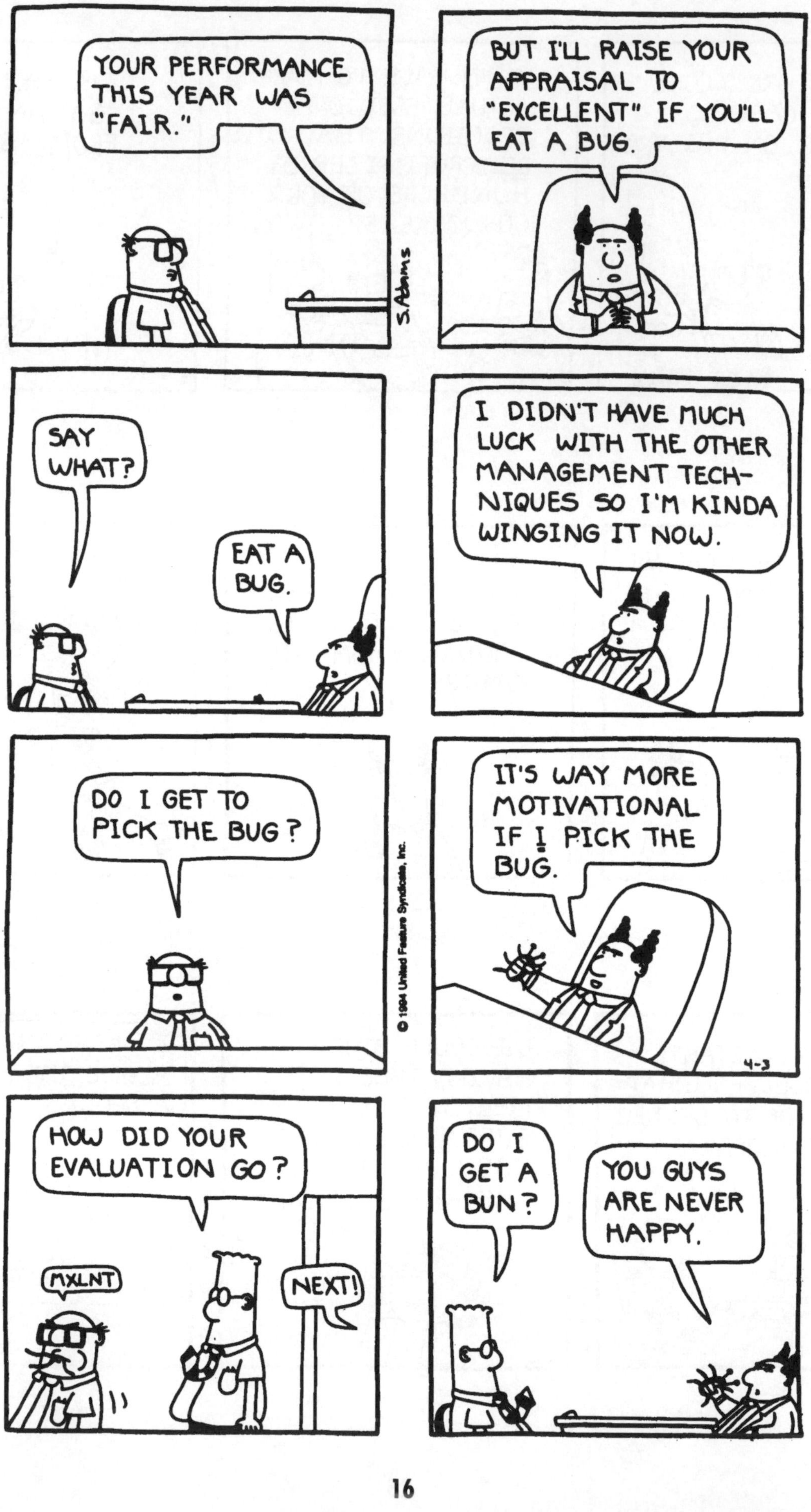
YOUR PERFORMANCE THIS YEAR WAS "FAIR."
S. Adams
BUT I'LL RAISE YOUR APPRAISAL TO "EXCELLENT" IF YOU'LL EAT A BUG.
SAY WHAT?
EAT A BUG.
I DIDN'T HAVE MUCH LUCK WITH THE OTHER MANAGEMENT TECH-NIQUES SO I'M KINDA WINGING IT NOW.
DO I GET TO PICK THE BUG?
© 1994 United Feature Syndicate, Inc.
IT'S WAY MORE MOTIVATIONAL IF I PICK THE BUG.
4-3
HOW DID YOUR EVALUATION GO?
MXLNT
NEXT!
DO I GET A BUN?
YOU GUYS ARE NEVER HAPPY.

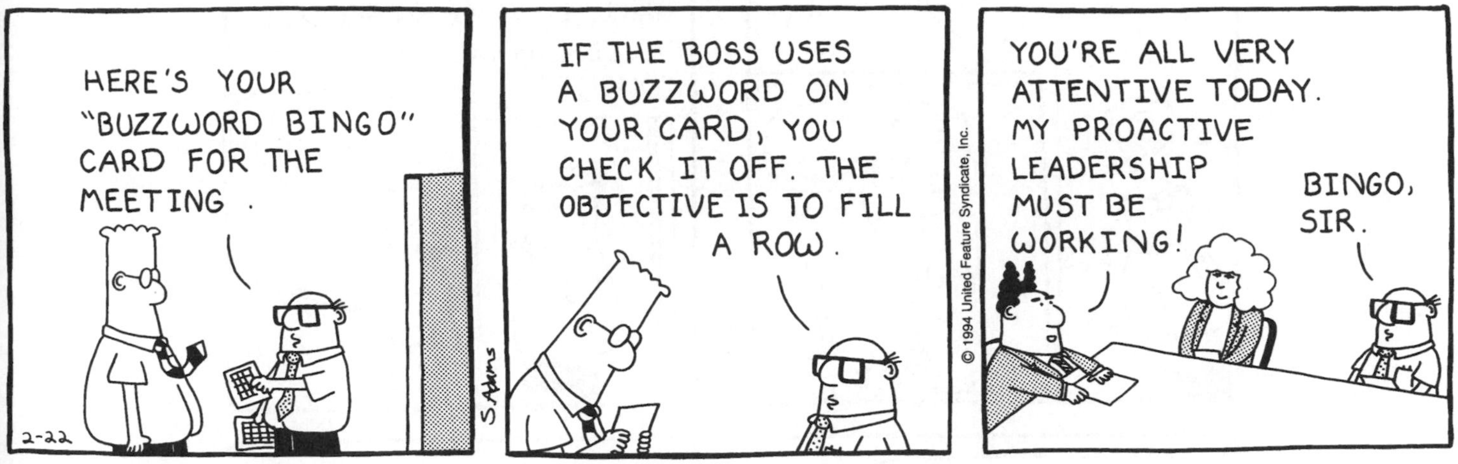
HERE'S YOUR "BUZZWORD BINGO" CARD FOR THE MEETING.
2-22
IF THE BOSS USES A BUZZWORD ON YOUR CARD, YOU CHECK IT OFF. THE OBJECTIVE IS TO FILL A ROW.
S.Adams
© 1994 United Feature Syndicate, Inc.
YOU'RE ALL VERY ATTENTIVE TODAY. MY PROACTIVE LEADERSHIP MUST BE WORKING!
BINGO, SIR.

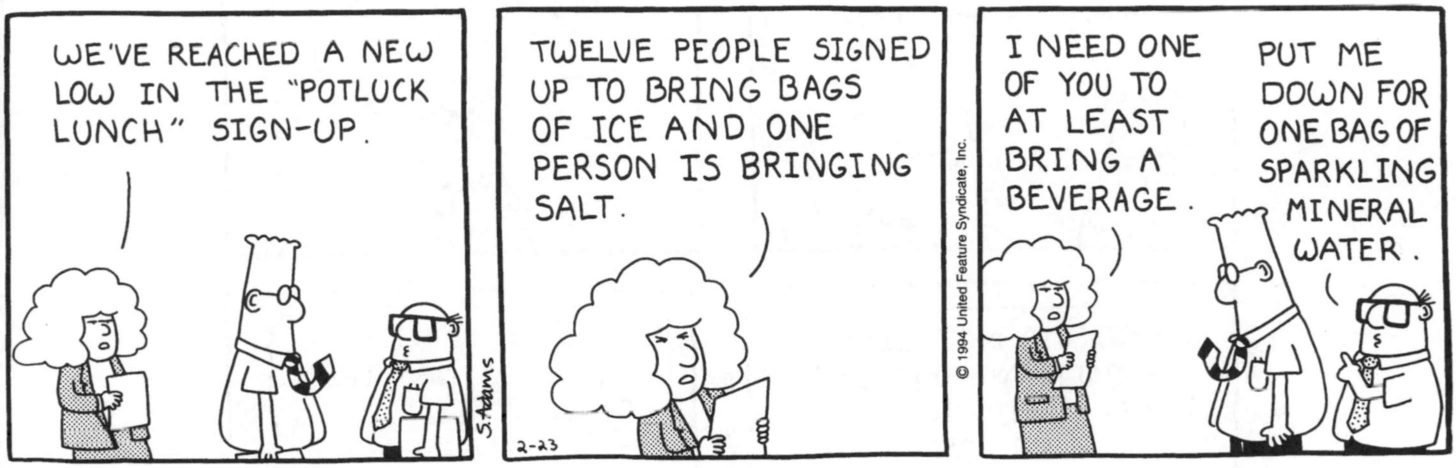
WE'VE REACHED A NEW LOW IN THE "POTLUCK LUNCH" SIGN-UP.
S.Adams
2-23
TWELVE PEOPLE SIGNED UP TO BRING BAGS OF ICE AND ONE PERSON IS BRINGING SALT.
© 1994 United Feature Syndicate, Inc.
I NEED ONE OF YOU TO AT LEAST BRING A BEVERAGE.
PUT ME DOWN FOR ONE BAG OF SPARKLING MINERAL WATER.

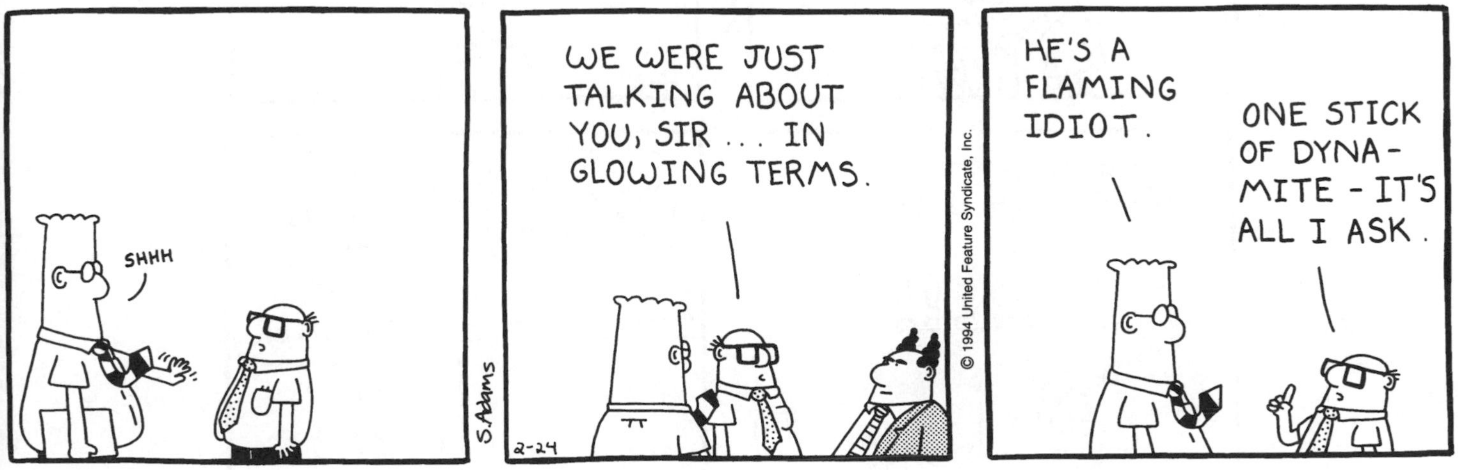
SHHH
S.Adams
2-24
WE WERE JUST TALKING ABOUT YOU, SIR ... IN GLOWING TERMS.
© 1994 United Feature Syndicate, Inc.
HE'S A FLAMING IDIOT.
ONE STICK OF DYNA-MITE - IT'S ALL I ASK.

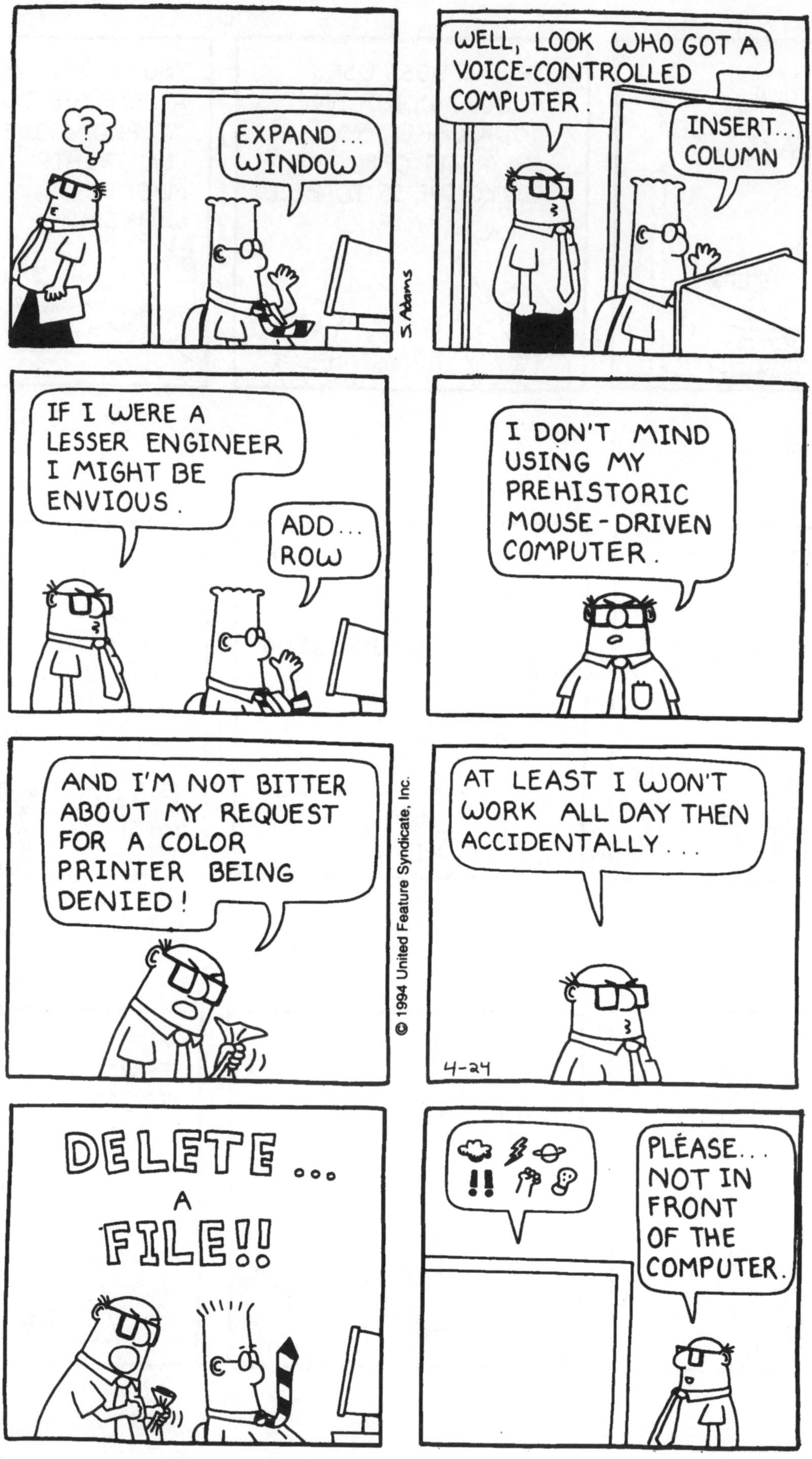
EXPAND... WINDOW
S. Adams
WELL, LOOK WHO GOT A VOICE-CONTROLLED COMPUTER.
INSERT... COLUMN
IF I WERE A LESSER ENGINEER I MIGHT BE ENVIOUS.
ADD... ROW
I DON'T MIND USING MY PREHISTORIC MOUSE-DRIVEN COMPUTER.
AND I'M NOT BITTER ABOUT MY REQUEST FOR A COLOR PRINTER BEING DENIED!
© 1994 United Feature Syndicate, Inc.
AT LEAST I WON'T WORK ALL DAY THEN ACCIDENTALLY...
4-24
DELETE... A FILE!!
!!
PLÉASE... NOT IN FRONT OF THE COMPUTER.

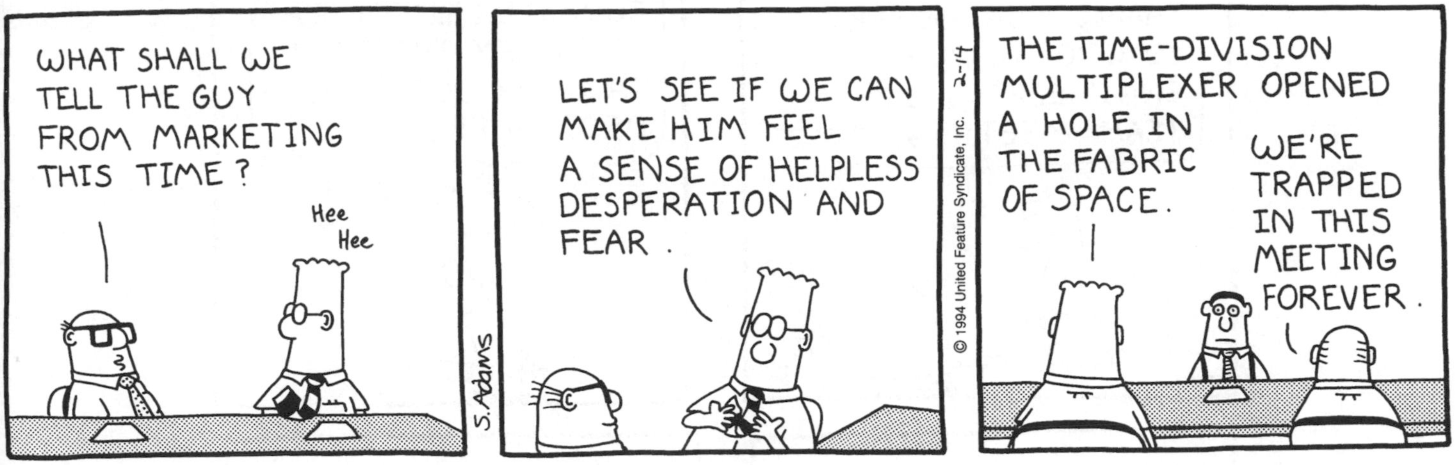
WHAT SHALL WE TELL THE GUY FROM MARKETING THIS TIME?
Hee Hee
S. Adams
LET'S SEE IF WE CAN MAKE HIM FEEL A SENSE OF HELPLESS DESPERATION AND FEAR.
2-14
© 1994 United Feature Syndicate, Inc.
THE TIME-DIVISION MULTIPLEXER OPENED A HOLE IN THE FABRIC OF SPACE.
WE'RE TRAPPED IN THIS MEETING FOREVER.

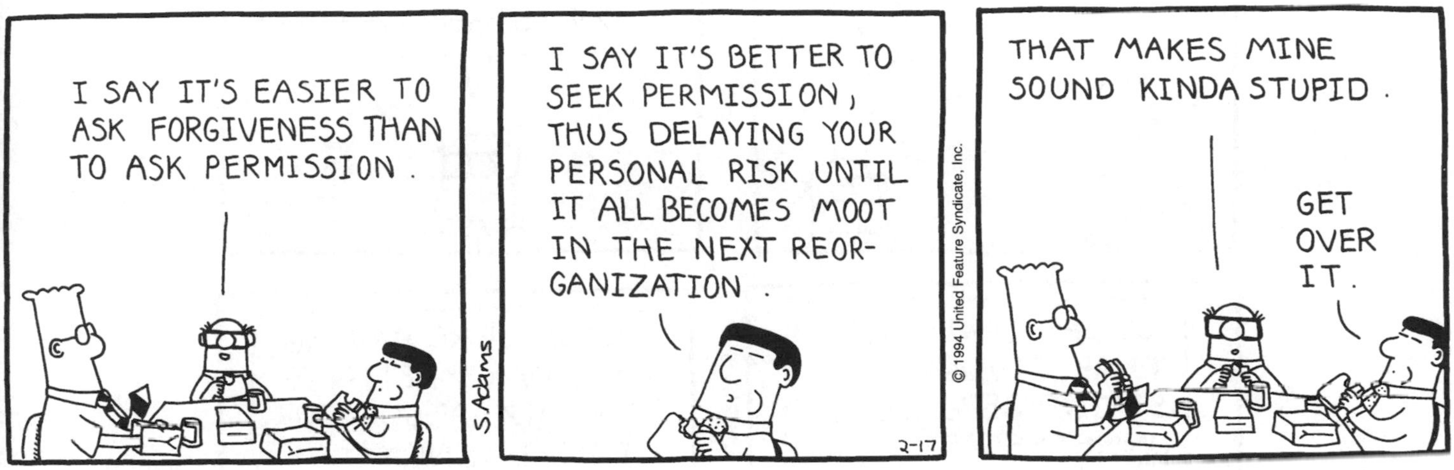
I SAY IT'S EASIER TO ASK FORGIVENESS THAN TO ASK PERMISSION.
S. Adams
I SAY IT'S BETTER TO SEEK PERMISSION, THUS DELAYING YOUR PERSONAL RISK UNTIL IT ALL BECOMES MOOT IN THE NEXT REORGANIZATION.
2-17
© 1994 United Feature Syndicate, Inc.
THAT MAKES MINE SOUND KINDA STUPID.
GET OVER IT.

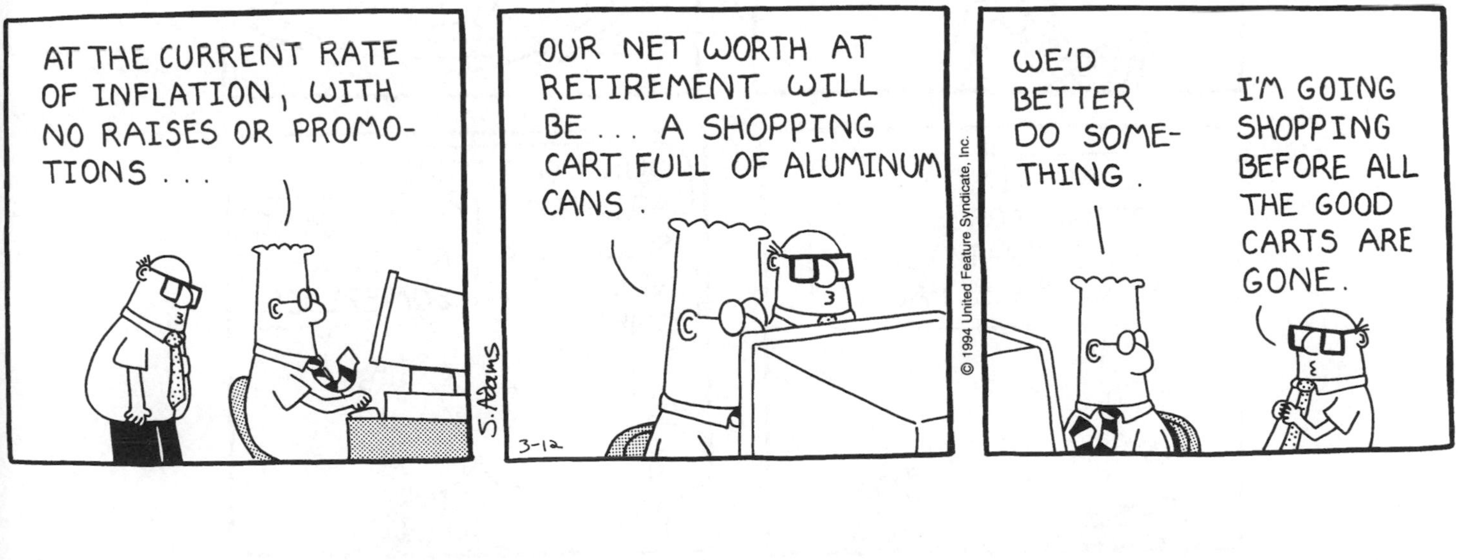
AT THE CURRENT RATE OF INFLATION, WITH NO RAISES OR PROMOTIONS...
S. Adams
OUR NET WORTH AT RETIREMENT WILL BE... A SHOPPING CART FULL OF ALUMINUM CANS.
3-12
© 1994 United Feature Syndicate, Inc.
WE'D BETTER DO SOMETHING.
I'M GOING SHOPPING BEFORE ALL THE GOOD CARTS ARE GONE.

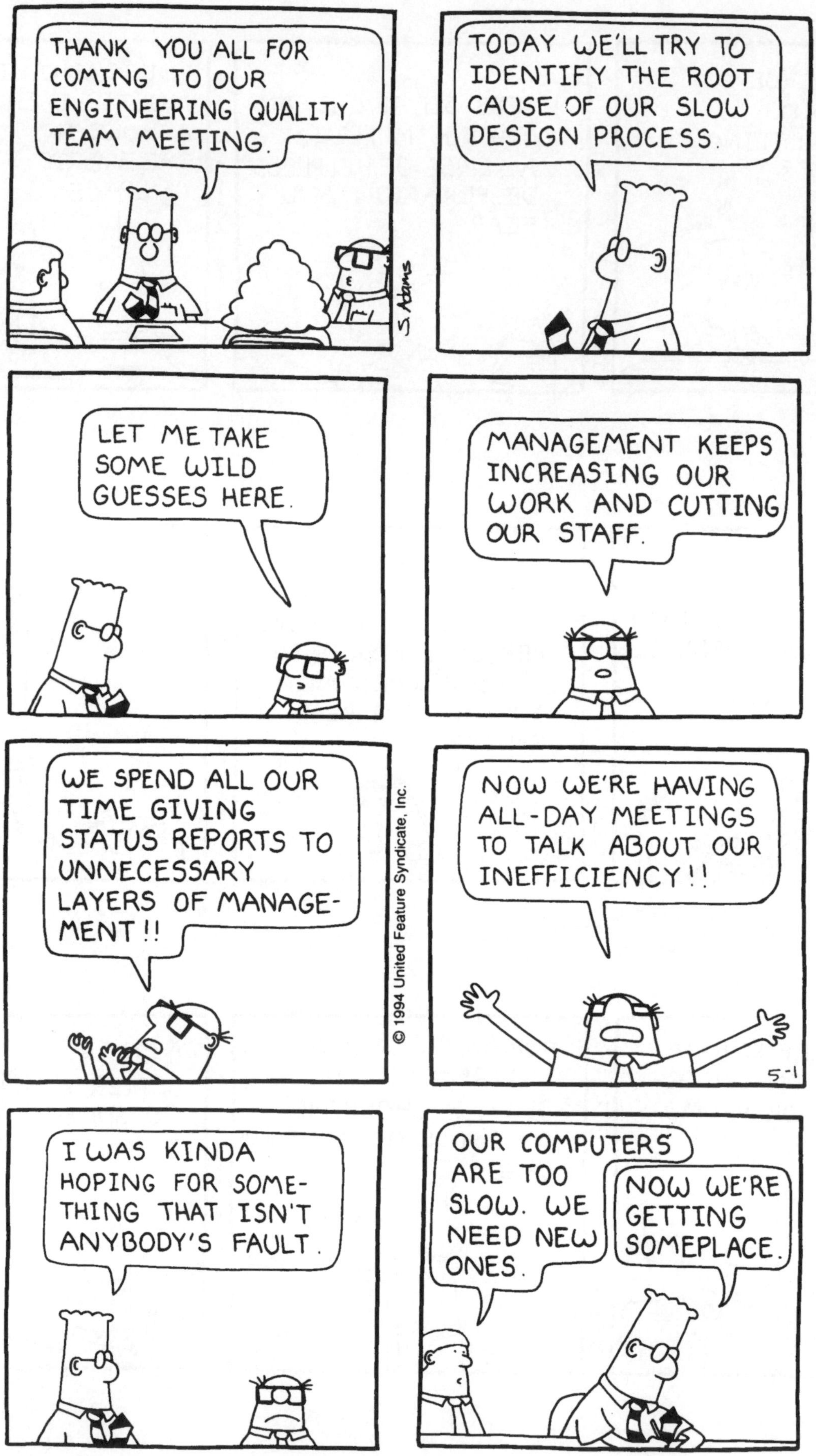
THANK YOU ALL FOR COMING TO OUR ENGINEERING QUALITY TEAM MEETING.
S. Adams
TODAY WE'LL TRY TO IDENTIFY THE ROOT CAUSE OF OUR SLOW DESIGN PROCESS.
LET ME TAKE SOME WILD GUESSES HERE.
MANAGEMENT KEEPS INCREASING OUR WORK AND CUTTING OUR STAFF.
WE SPEND ALL OUR TIME GIVING STATUS REPORTS TO UNNECESSARY LAYERS OF MANAGE-MENT!!
NOW WE'RE HAVING ALL-DAY MEETINGS TO TALK ABOUT OUR INEFFICIENCY!!
5-1
I WAS KINDA HOPING FOR SOME-THING THAT ISN'T ANYBODY'S FAULT.
OUR COMPUTERS ARE TOO SLOW. WE NEED NEW ONES.
NOW WE'RE GETTING SOMEPLACE.

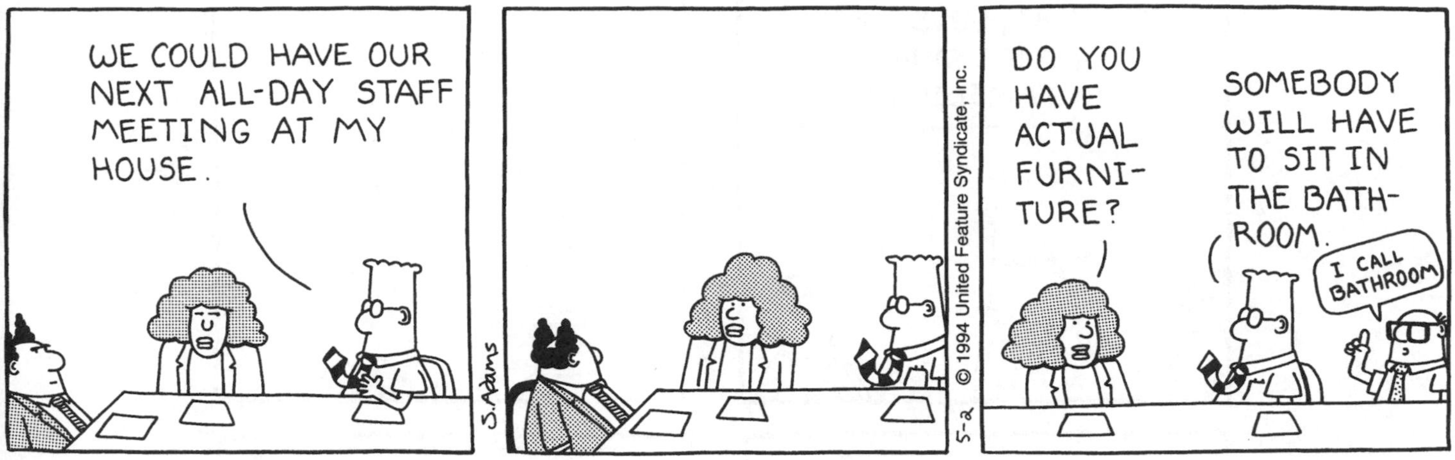
WE COULD HAVE OUR NEXT ALL-DAY STAFF MEETING AT MY HOUSE.
S.Adams
5-2 © 1994 United Feature Syndicate, Inc.
DO YOU HAVE ACTUAL FURNI-TURE?
SOMEBODY WILL HAVE TO SIT IN THE BATH-ROOM.
I CALL BATHROOM

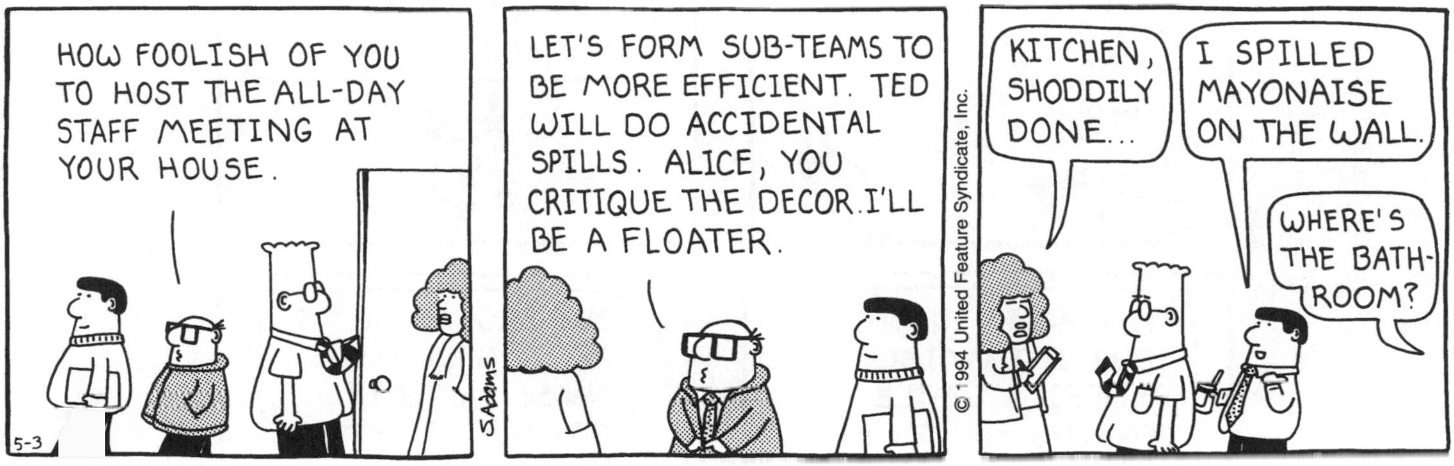
HOW FOOLISH OF YOU TO HOST THE ALL-DAY STAFF MEETING AT YOUR HOUSE.
5-3
S.Adams
LET'S FORM SUB-TEAMS TO BE MORE EFFICIENT. TED WILL DO ACCIDENTAL SPILLS. ALICE, YOU CRITIQUE THE DECOR. I'LL BE A FLOATER.
© 1994 United Feature Syndicate, Inc.
KITCHEN, SHODDILY DONE...
I SPILLED MAYONAISE ON THE WALL.
WHERE'S THE BATH-ROOM?

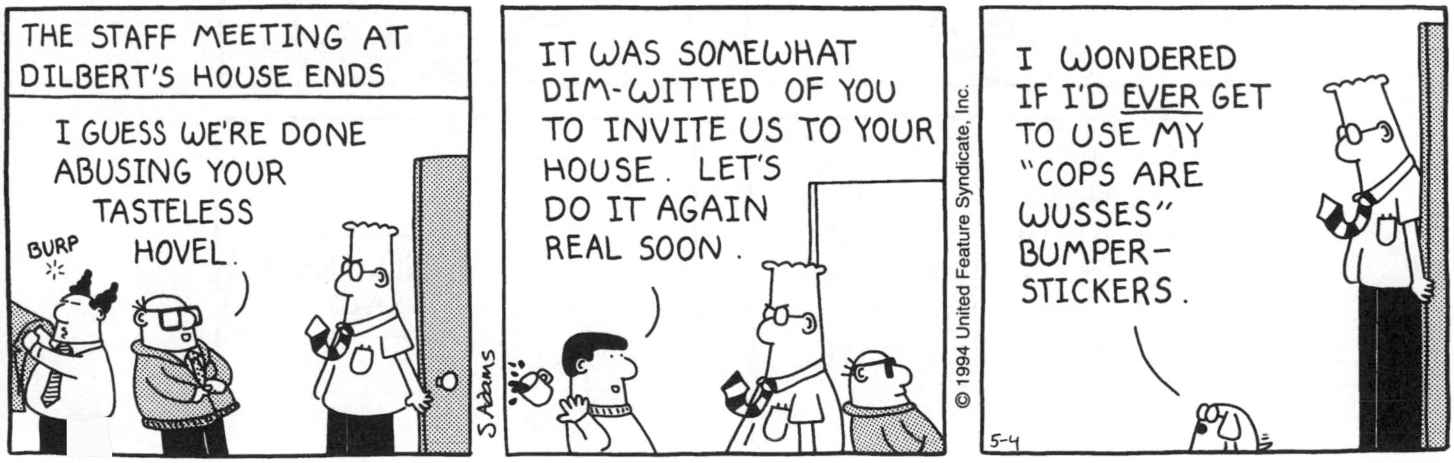
THE STAFF MEETING AT DILBERT'S HOUSE ENDS
I GUESS WE'RE DONE ABUSING YOUR TASTELESS HOVEL.
BURP
S.Adams
IT WAS SOMEWHAT DIM-WITTED OF YOU TO INVITE US TO YOUR HOUSE. LET'S DO IT AGAIN REAL SOON.
© 1994 United Feature Syndicate, Inc.
I WONDERED IF I'D EVER GET TO USE MY "COPS ARE WUSSES" BUMPER-STICKERS.
5-4

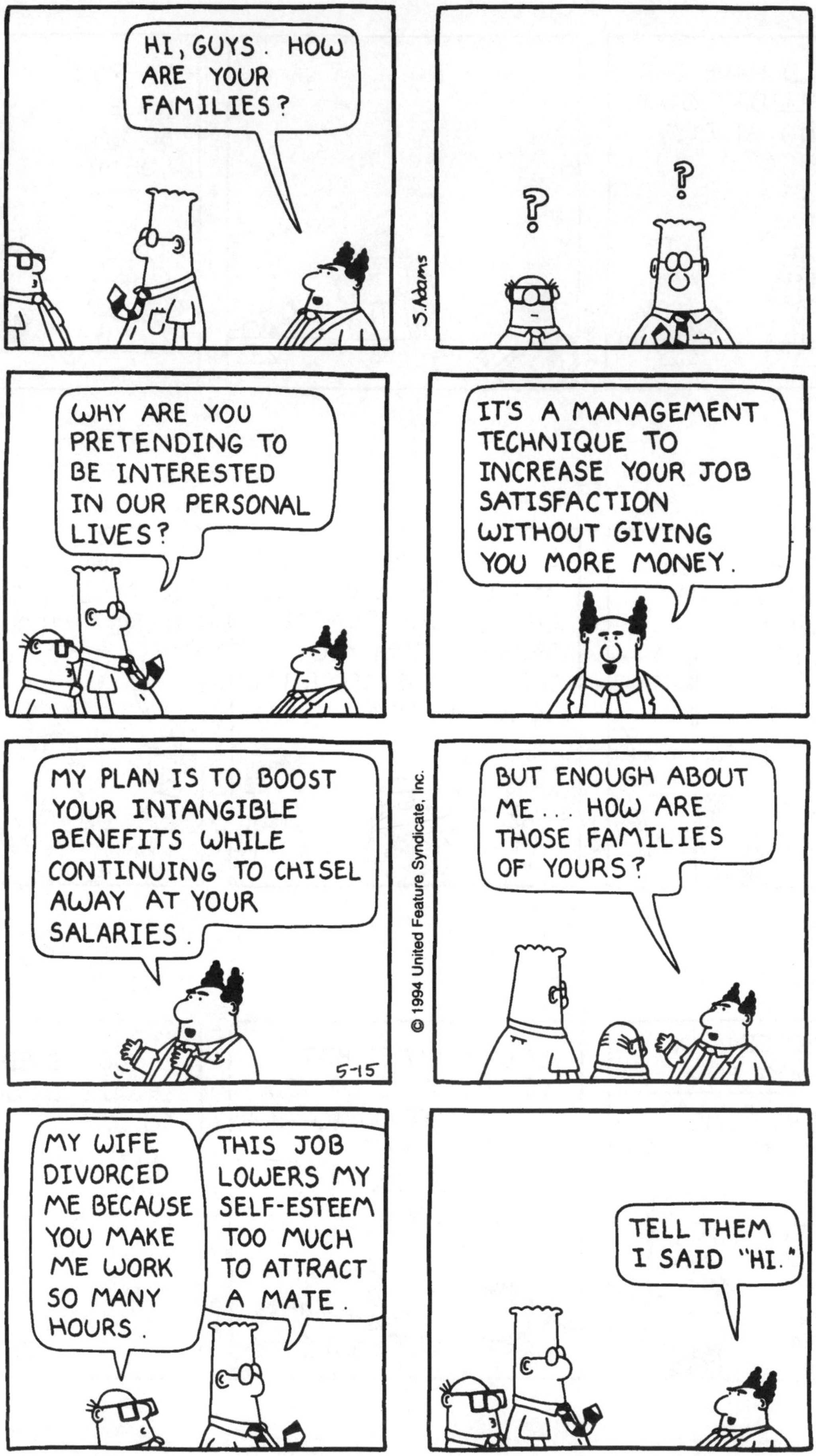
HI, GUYS. HOW ARE YOUR FAMILIES?
S. Adams
?
?
WHY ARE YOU PRETENDING TO BE INTERESTED IN OUR PERSONAL LIVES?
IT'S A MANAGEMENT TECHNIQUE TO INCREASE YOUR JOB SATISFACTION WITHOUT GIVING YOU MORE MONEY.
MY PLAN IS TO BOOST YOUR INTANGIBLE BENEFITS WHILE CONTINUING TO CHISEL AWAY AT YOUR SALARIES.
5-15
© 1994 United Feature Syndicate, Inc.
BUT ENOUGH ABOUT ME... HOW ARE THOSE FAMILIES OF YOURS?
MY WIFE DIVORCED ME BECAUSE YOU MAKE ME WORK SO MANY HOURS.
THIS JOB LOWERS MY SELF-ESTEEM TOO MUCH TO ATTRACT A MATE.
TELL THEM I SAID "HI."

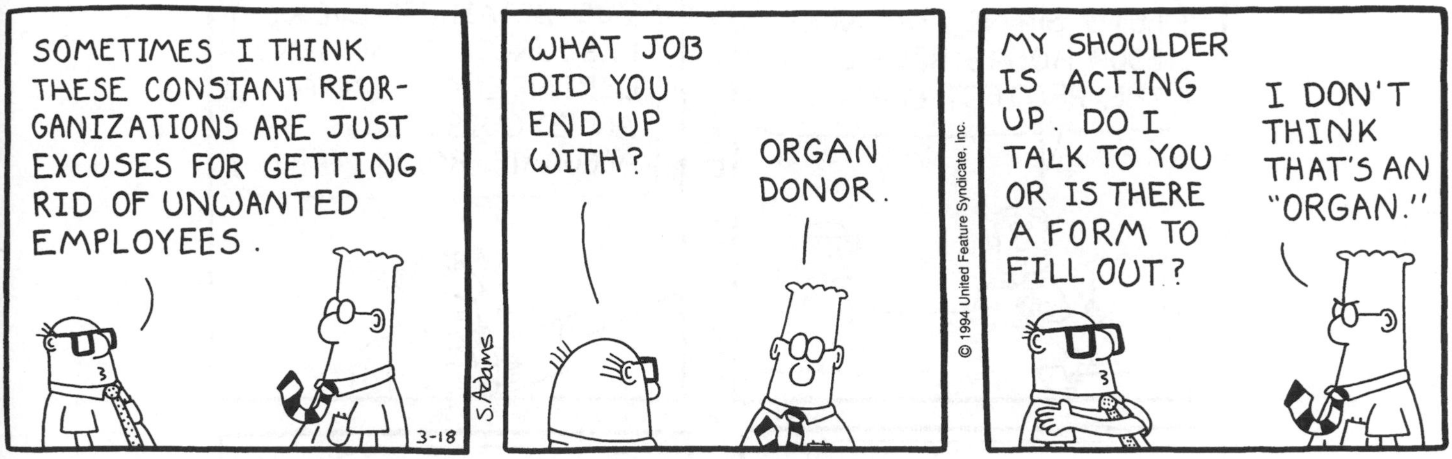
SOMETIMES I THINK THESE CONSTANT REORGANIZATIONS ARE JUST EXCUSES FOR GETTING RID OF UNWANTED EMPLOYEES.
3-18
S. Adams
WHAT JOB DID YOU END UP WITH?
ORGAN DONOR.
© 1994 United Feature Syndicate, Inc.
MY SHOULDER IS ACTING UP. DO I TALK TO YOU OR IS THERE A FORM TO FILL OUT?
I DON'T THINK THAT'S AN "ORGAN."

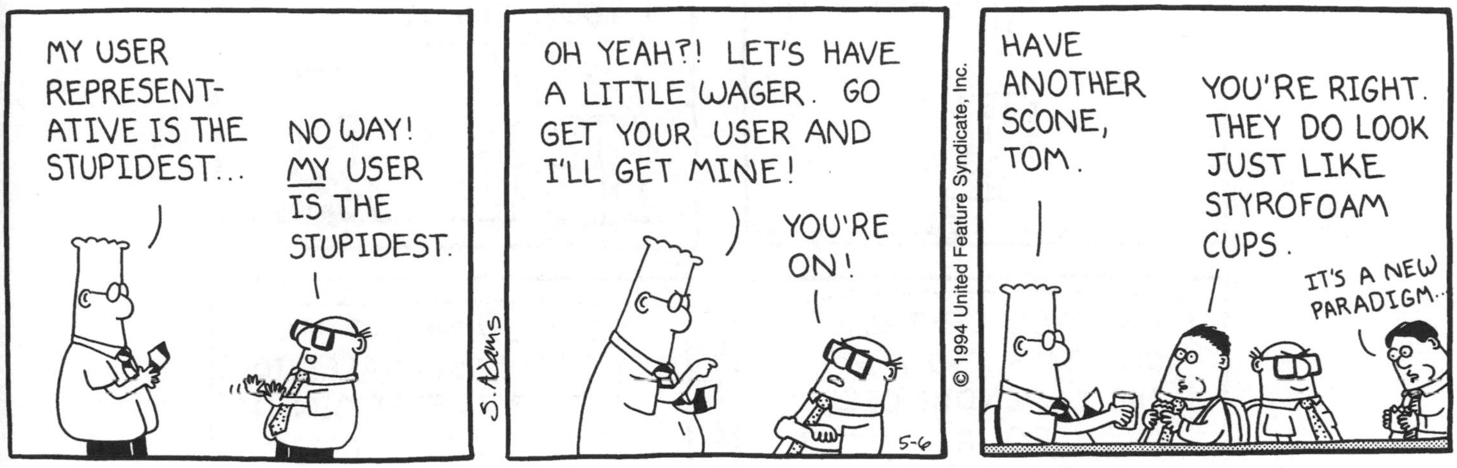
MY USER REPRESENTATIVE IS THE STUPIDEST...
NO WAY! MY USER IS THE STUPIDEST.
S. Adams
OH YEAH?! LET'S HAVE A LITTLE WAGER. GO GET YOUR USER AND I'LL GET MINE!
YOU'RE ON!
5-6
© 1994 United Feature Syndicate, Inc.
HAVE ANOTHER SCONE, TOM.
YOU'RE RIGHT. THEY DO LOOK JUST LIKE STYROFOAM CUPS.
IT'S A NEW PARADIGM...

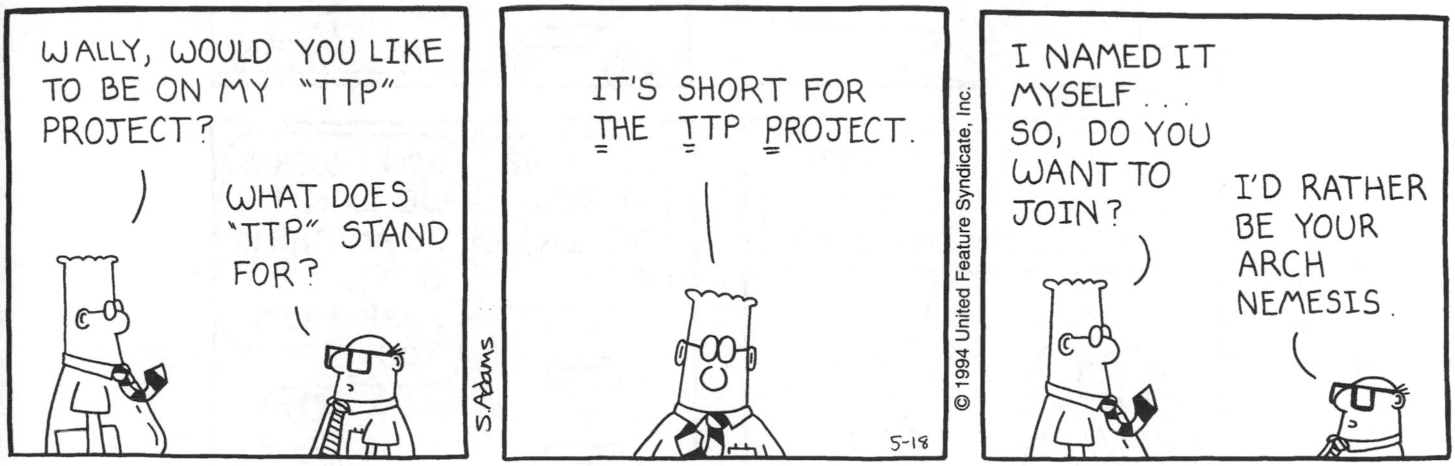
WALLY, WOULD YOU LIKE TO BE ON MY "TTP" PROJECT?
WHAT DOES "TTP" STAND FOR?
S. Adams
IT'S SHORT FOR THE TTP PROJECT.
5-18
© 1994 United Feature Syndicate, Inc.
I NAMED IT MYSELF... SO, DO YOU WANT TO JOIN?
I'D RATHER BE YOUR ARCH NEMESIS.

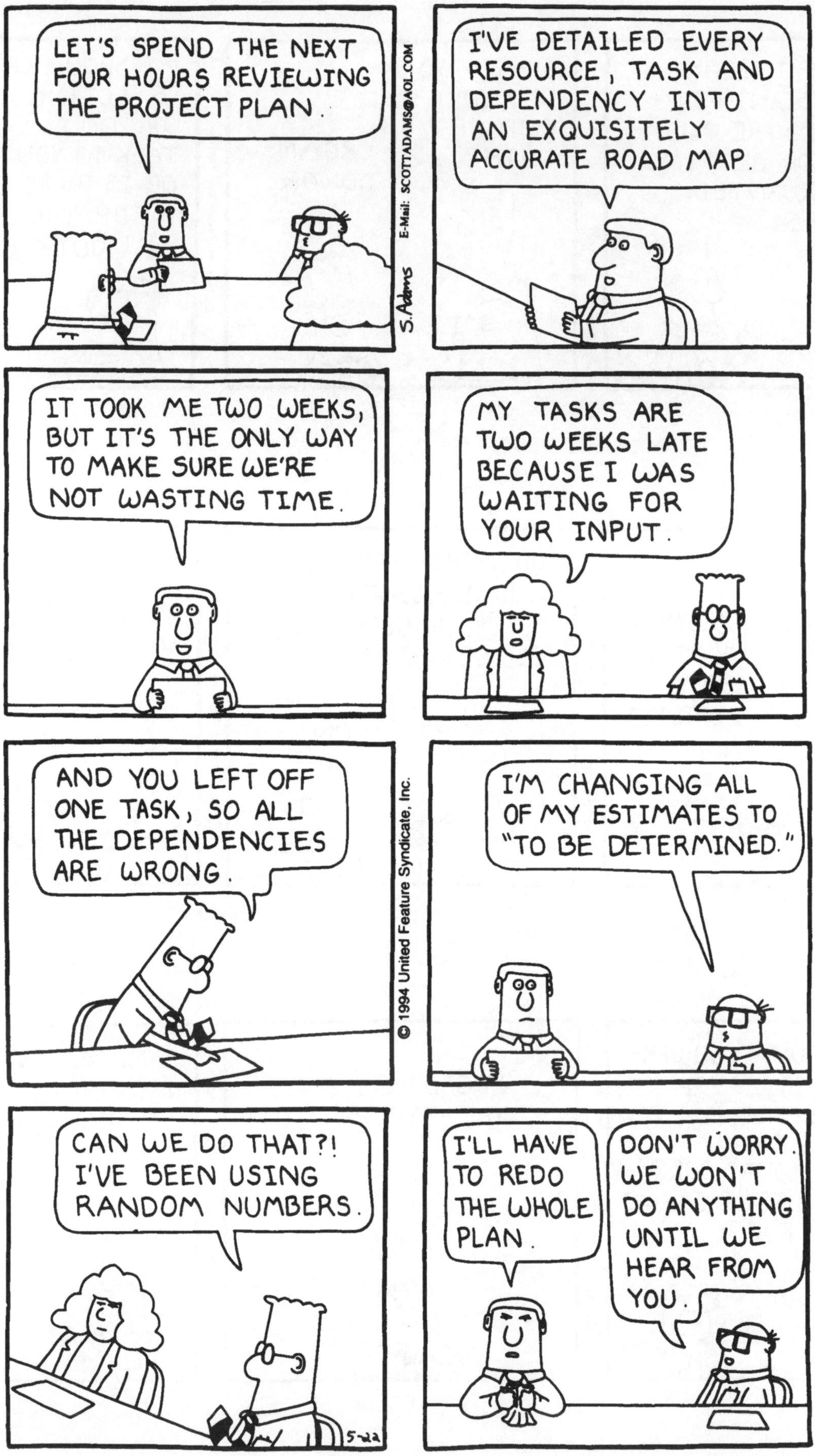
LET'S SPEND THE NEXT FOUR HOURS REVIEWING THE PROJECT PLAN.
I'VE DETAILED EVERY RESOURCE, TASK AND DEPENDENCY INTO AN EXQUISITELY ACCURATE ROAD MAP.
IT TOOK ME TWO WEEKS, BUT IT'S THE ONLY WAY TO MAKE SURE WE'RE NOT WASTING TIME.
MY TASKS ARE TWO WEEKS LATE BECAUSE I WAS WAITING FOR YOUR INPUT.
AND YOU LEFT OFF ONE TASK, SO ALL THE DEPENDENCIES ARE WRONG.
I'M CHANGING ALL OF MY ESTIMATES TO "TO BE DETERMINED."
CAN WE DO THAT?! I'VE BEEN USING RANDOM NUMBERS.
I'LL HAVE TO REDO THE WHOLE PLAN.
DON'T WORRY. WE WON'T DO ANYTHING UNTIL WE HEAR FROM YOU.
S. Adams
E-Mail: SCOTTADAMS@AOL.COM
© 1994 United Feature Syndicate, Inc.
5-22

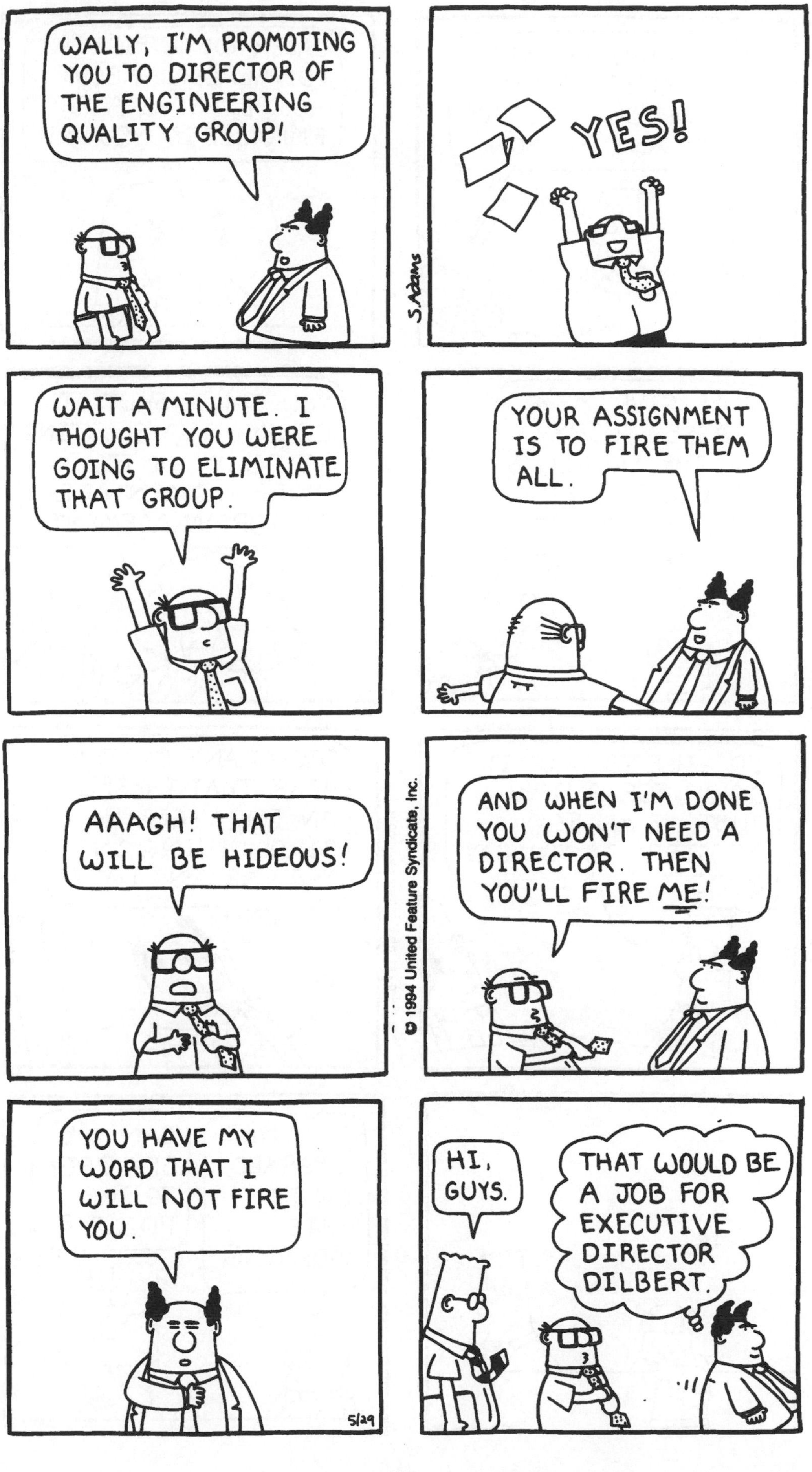
WALLY, I'M PROMOTING YOU TO DIRECTOR OF THE ENGINEERING QUALITY GROUP!
S. Adams
YES!
WAIT A MINUTE. I THOUGHT YOU WERE GOING TO ELIMINATE THAT GROUP.
YOUR ASSIGNMENT IS TO FIRE THEM ALL.
AAAGH! THAT WILL BE HIDEOUS!
© 1994 United Feature Syndicate, Inc.
AND WHEN I'M DONE YOU WON'T NEED A DIRECTOR. THEN YOU'LL FIRE ME!
YOU HAVE MY WORD THAT I WILL NOT FIRE YOU.
5/29
HI, GUYS.
THAT WOULD BE A JOB FOR EXECUTIVE DIRECTOR DILBERT.

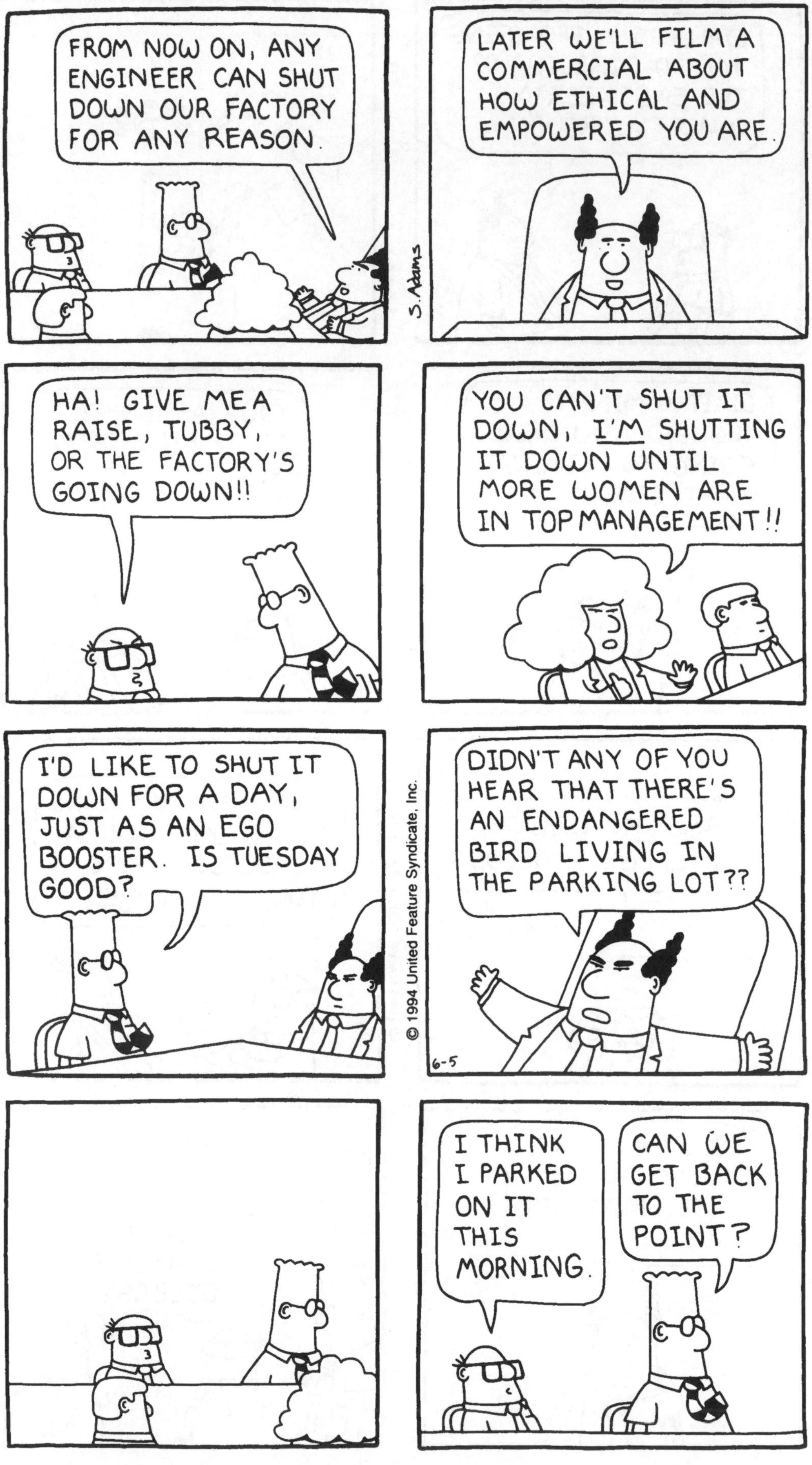
FROM NOW ON, ANY ENGINEER CAN SHUT DOWN OUR FACTORY FOR ANY REASON.
S. Adams
LATER WE'LL FILM A COMMERCIAL ABOUT HOW ETHICAL AND EMPOWERED YOU ARE.
HA! GIVE ME A RAISE, TUBBY, OR THE FACTORY'S GOING DOWN!!
YOU CAN'T SHUT IT DOWN, I'M SHUTTING IT DOWN UNTIL MORE WOMEN ARE IN TOP MANAGEMENT!!
I'D LIKE TO SHUT IT DOWN FOR A DAY, JUST AS AN EGO BOOSTER. IS TUESDAY GOOD?
DIDN'T ANY OF YOU HEAR THAT THERE'S AN ENDANGERED BIRD LIVING IN THE PARKING LOT??
6-5
I THINK I PARKED ON IT THIS MORNING.
CAN WE GET BACK TO THE POINT?

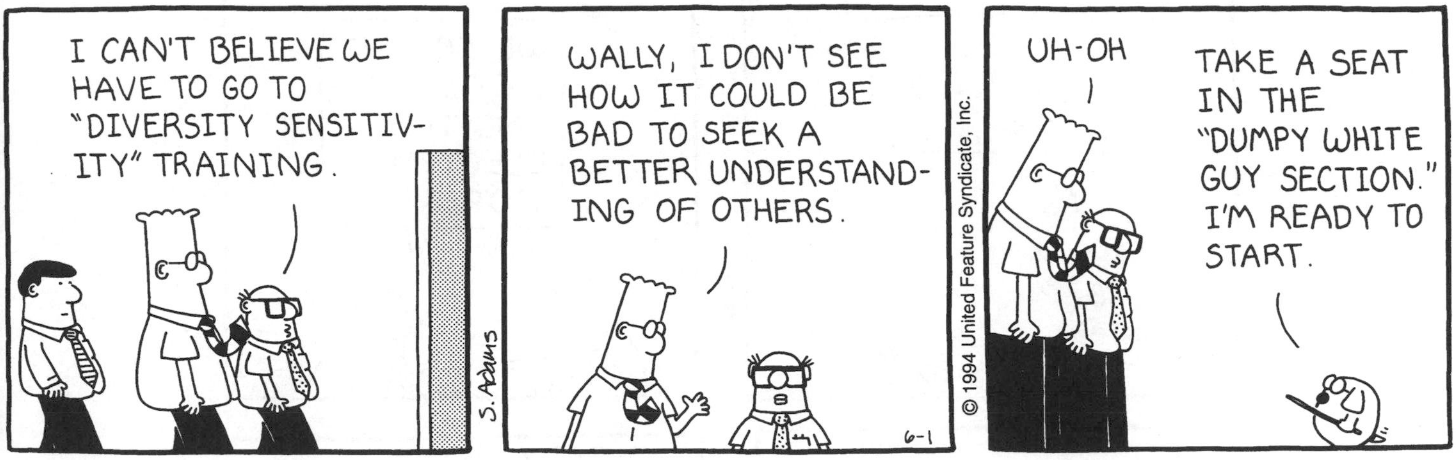
I CAN'T BELIEVE WE HAVE TO GO TO "DIVERSITY SENSITIV-ITY" TRAINING.
S. Adams
WALLY, I DON'T SEE HOW IT COULD BE BAD TO SEEK A BETTER UNDERSTAND-ING OF OTHERS.
6-1
© 1994 United Feature Syndicate, Inc.
UH-OH
TAKE A SEAT IN THE "DUMPY WHITE GUY SECTION." I'M READY TO START.

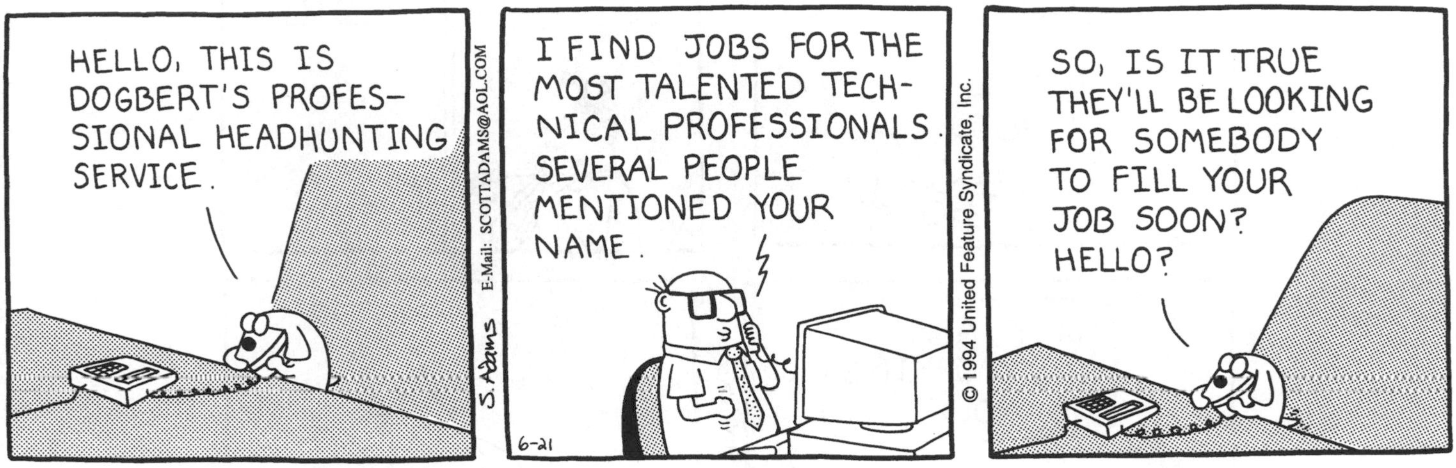
HELLO, THIS IS DOGBERT'S PROFES-SIONAL HEADHUNTING SERVICE.
S. Adams
E-Mail: SCOTTADAMS@AOL.COM
I FIND JOBS FOR THE MOST TALENTED TECH-NICAL PROFESSIONALS. SEVERAL PEOPLE MENTIONED YOUR NAME.
6-21
© 1994 United Feature Syndicate, Inc.
SO, IS IT TRUE THEY'LL BE LOOKING FOR SOMEBODY TO FILL YOUR JOB SOON? HELLO?

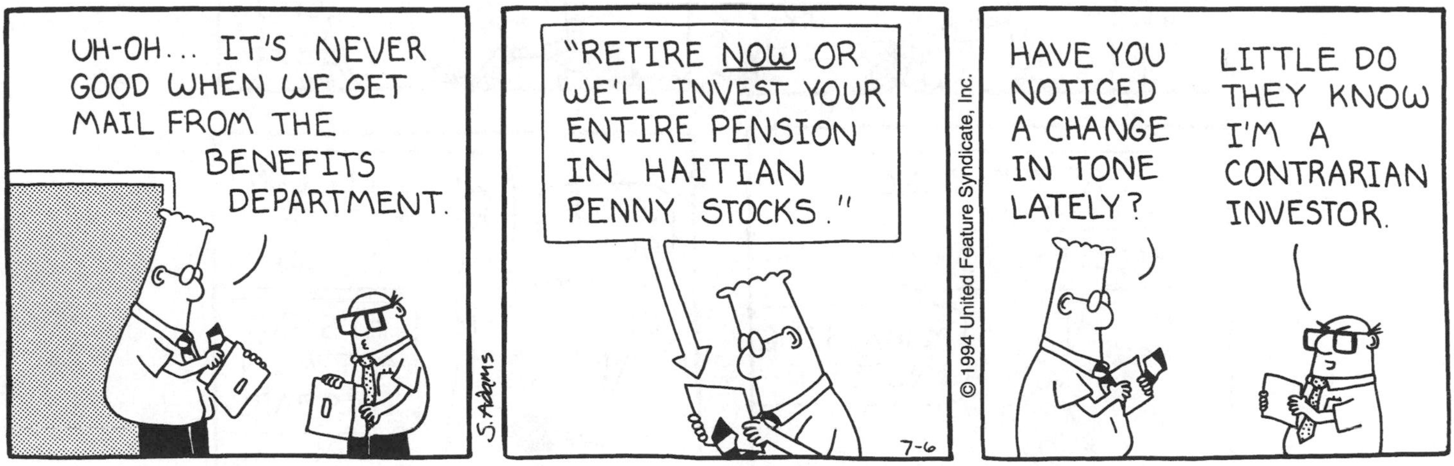
UH-OH... IT'S NEVER GOOD WHEN WE GET MAIL FROM THE BENEFITS DEPARTMENT.
S. Adams
"RETIRE NOW OR WE'LL INVEST YOUR ENTIRE PENSION IN HAITIAN PENNY STOCKS."
7-6
© 1994 United Feature Syndicate, Inc.
HAVE YOU NOTICED A CHANGE IN TONE LATELY?
LITTLE DO THEY KNOW I'M A CONTRARIAN INVESTOR.

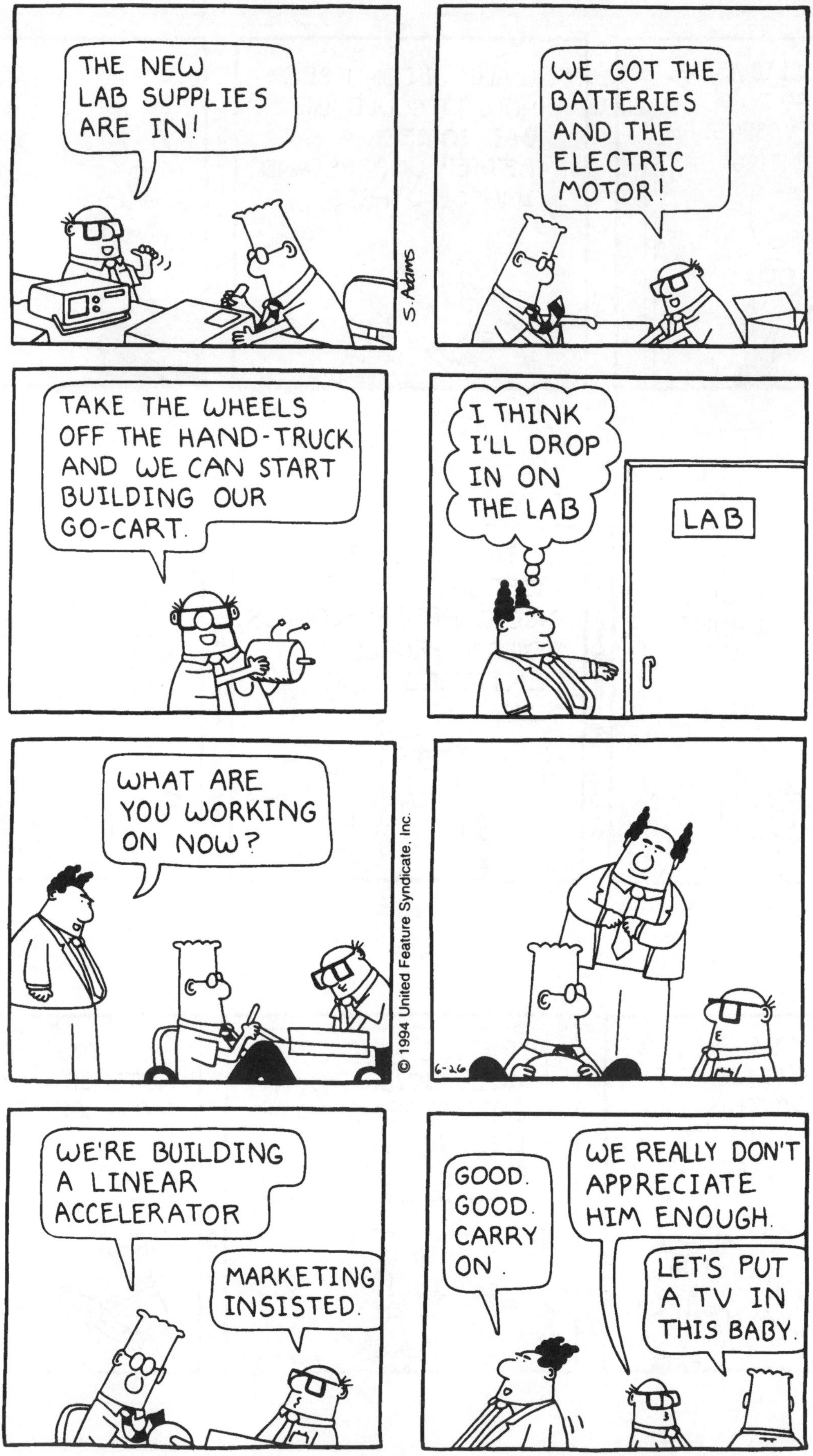
THE NEW LAB SUPPLIES ARE IN!
S. Adams
WE GOT THE BATTERIES AND THE ELECTRIC MOTOR!
TAKE THE WHEELS OFF THE HAND-TRUCK AND WE CAN START BUILDING OUR GO-CART.
I THINK I'LL DROP IN ON THE LAB
LAB
WHAT ARE YOU WORKING ON NOW?
© 1994 United Feature Syndicate, Inc.
6-26
WE'RE BUILDING A LINEAR ACCELERATOR
MARKETING INSISTED.
GOOD. GOOD. CARRY ON.
WE REALLY DON'T APPRECIATE HIM ENOUGH.
LET'S PUT A TV IN THIS BABY.

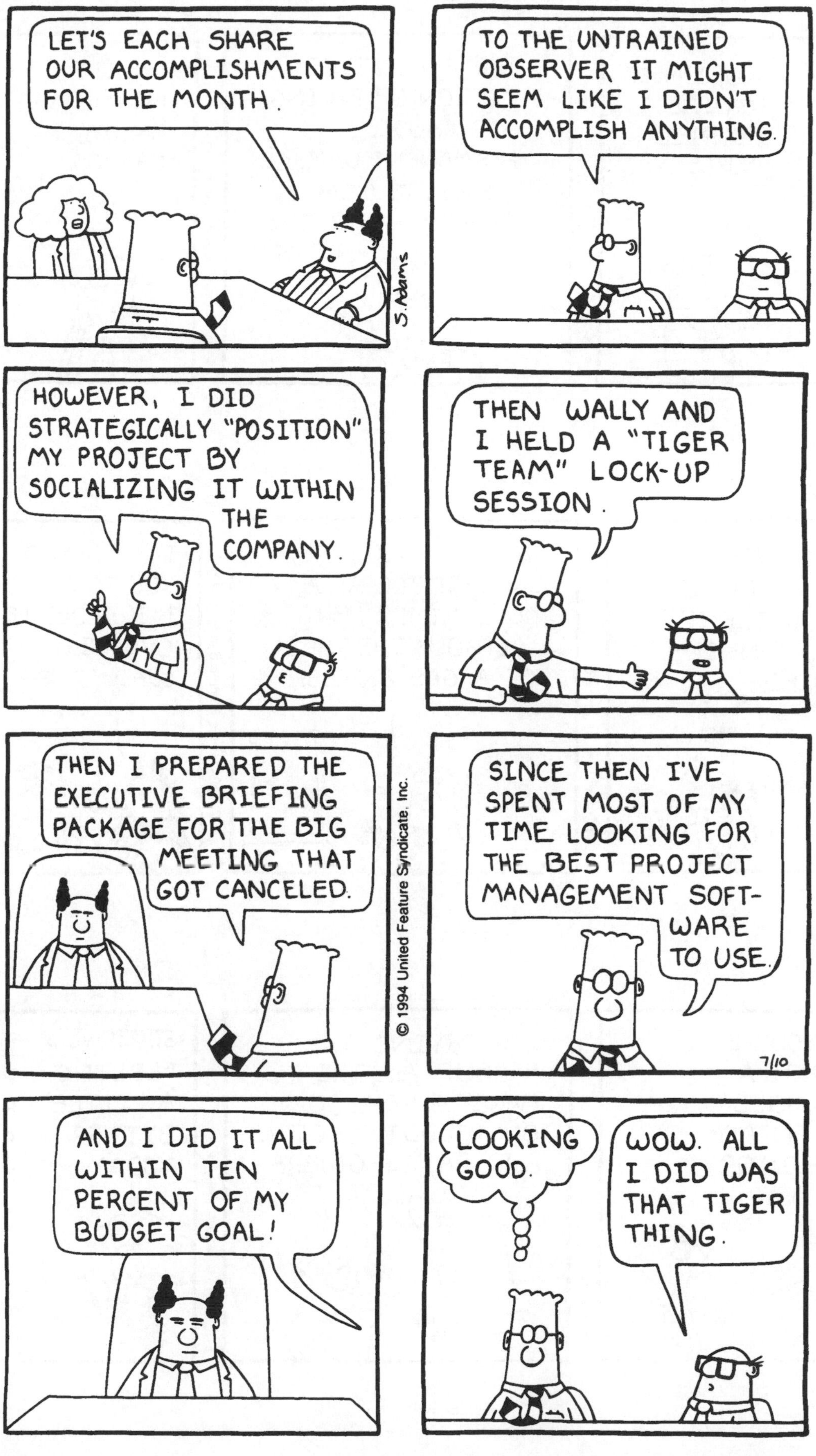
LET'S EACH SHARE OUR ACCOMPLISHMENTS FOR THE MONTH.
S. Adams
TO THE UNTRAINED OBSERVER IT MIGHT SEEM LIKE I DIDN'T ACCOMPLISH ANYTHING.
HOWEVER, I DID STRATEGICALLY "POSITION" MY PROJECT BY SOCIALIZING IT WITHIN THE COMPANY.
THEN WALLY AND I HELD A "TIGER TEAM" LOCK-UP SESSION.
THEN I PREPARED THE EXECUTIVE BRIEFING PACKAGE FOR THE BIG MEETING THAT GOT CANCELED.
© 1994 United Feature Syndicate, Inc.
SINCE THEN I'VE SPENT MOST OF MY TIME LOOKING FOR THE BEST PROJECT MANAGEMENT SOFTWARE TO USE.
7/10
AND I DID IT ALL WITHIN TEN PERCENT OF MY BUDGET GOAL!
LOOKING GOOD.
WOW. ALL I DID WAS THAT TIGER THING.

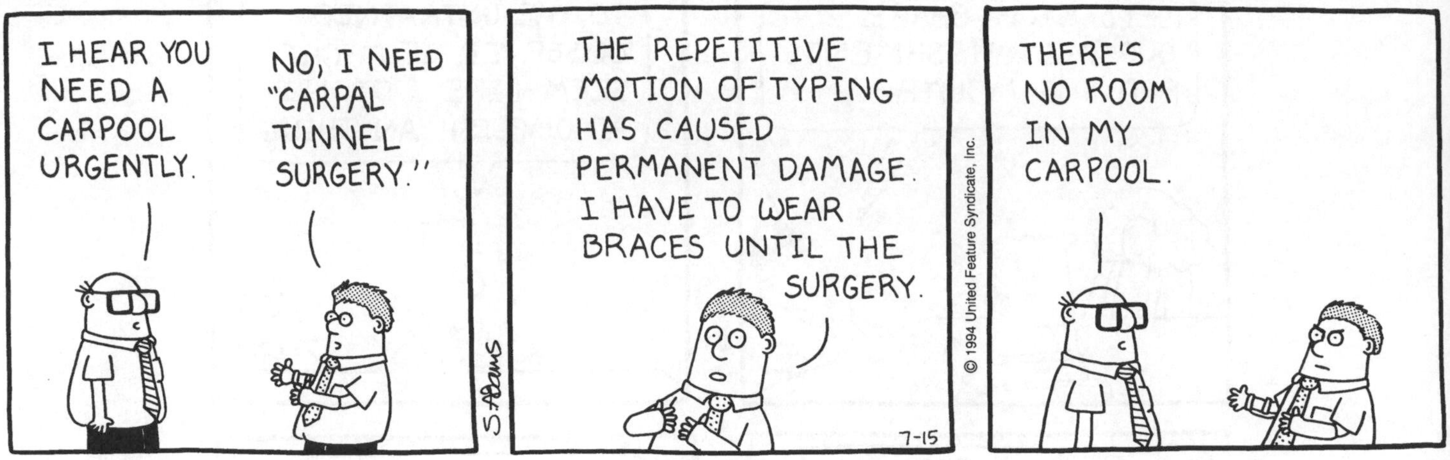
I HEAR YOU NEED A CARPOOL URGENTLY.
NO, I NEED "CARPAL TUNNEL SURGERY."
S. Adams
THE REPETITIVE MOTION OF TYPING HAS CAUSED PERMANENT DAMAGE. I HAVE TO WEAR BRACES UNTIL THE SURGERY.
7-15
© 1994 United Feature Syndicate, Inc.
THERE'S NO ROOM IN MY CARPOOL.

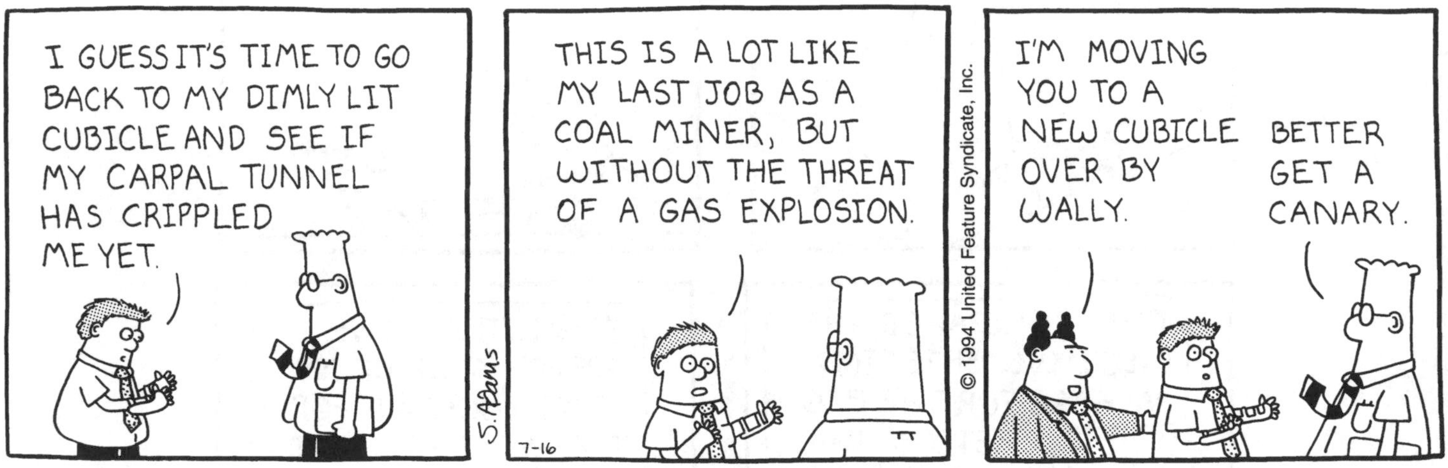
I GUESS IT'S TIME TO GO BACK TO MY DIMLY LIT CUBICLE AND SEE IF MY CARPAL TUNNEL HAS CRIPPLED ME YET.
S. Adams
7-16
THIS IS A LOT LIKE MY LAST JOB AS A COAL MINER, BUT WITHOUT THE THREAT OF A GAS EXPLOSION.
© 1994 United Feature Syndicate, Inc.
I'M MOVING YOU TO A NEW CUBICLE OVER BY WALLY.
BETTER GET A CANARY.

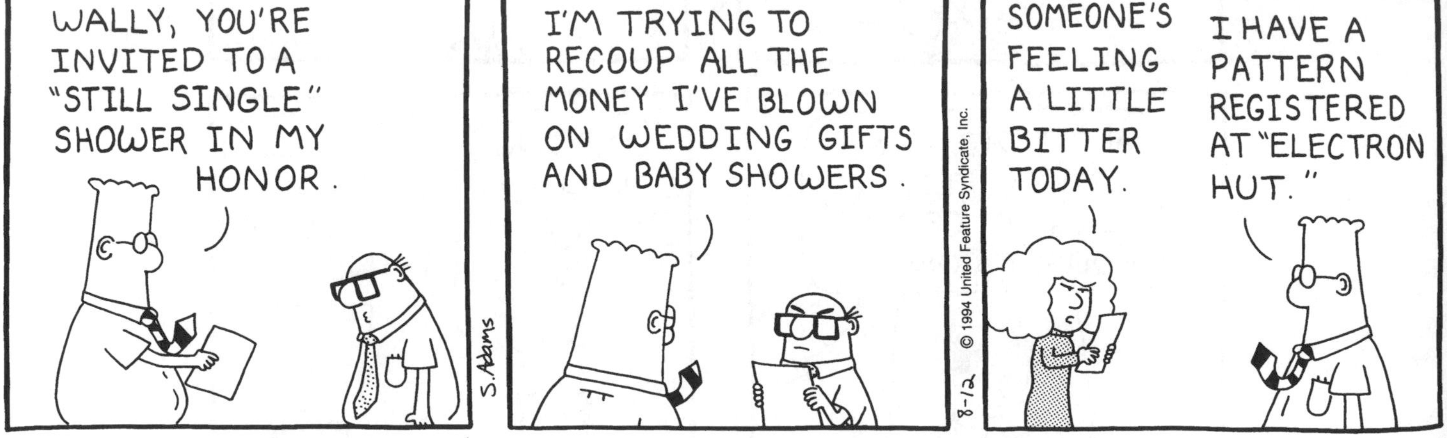
WALLY, YOU'RE INVITED TO A "STILL SINGLE" SHOWER IN MY HONOR.
S. Adams
I'M TRYING TO RECOUP ALL THE MONEY I'VE BLOWN ON WEDDING GIFTS AND BABY SHOWERS.
8-12
© 1994 United Feature Syndicate, Inc.
SOMEONE'S FEELING A LITTLE BITTER TODAY.
I HAVE A PATTERN REGISTERED AT "ELECTRON HUT."

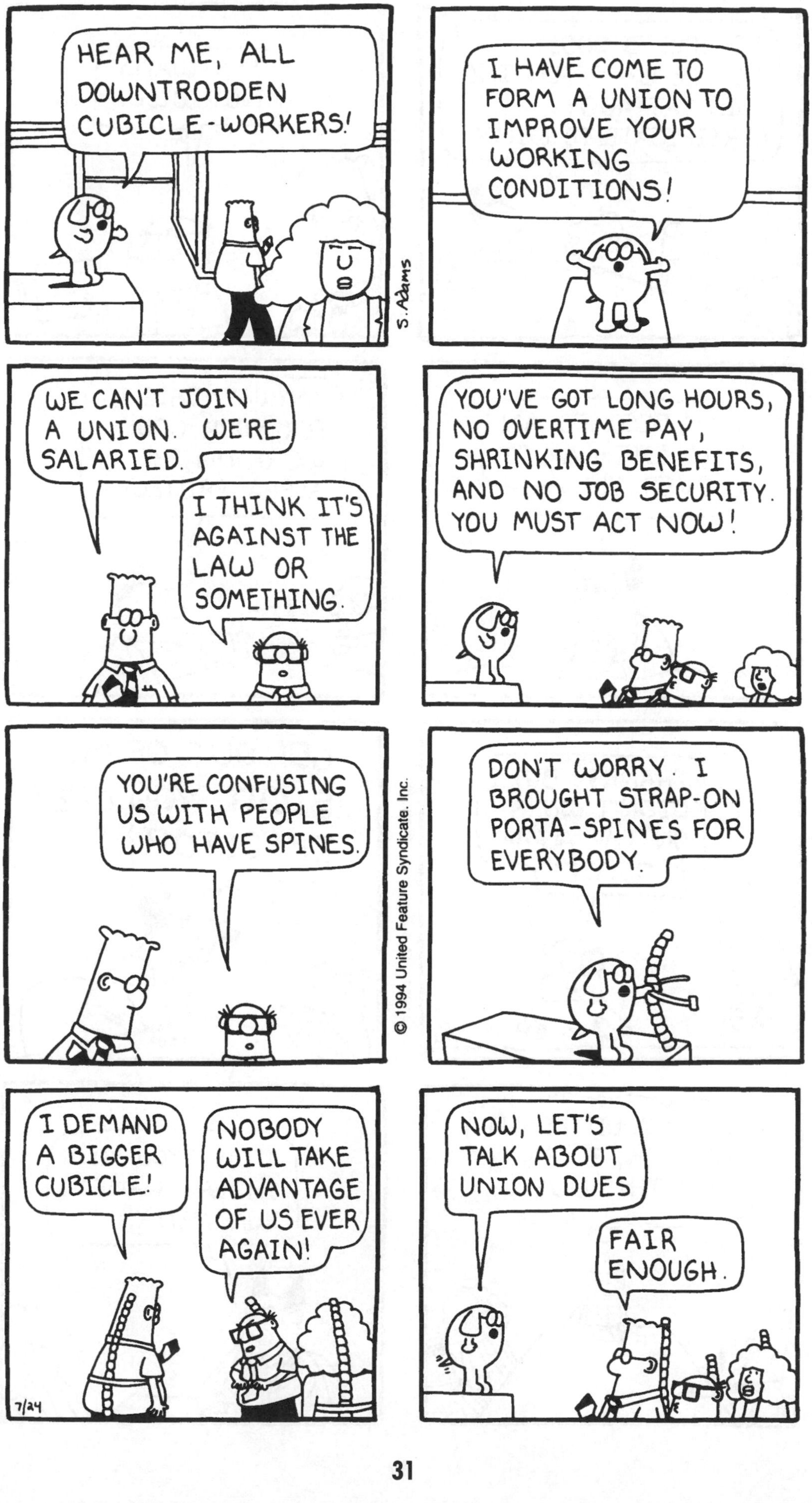

HEAR ME, ALL DOWNTRODDEN CUBICLE-WORKERS!
S. Adams
I HAVE COME TO FORM A UNION TO IMPROVE YOUR WORKING CONDITIONS!
WE CAN'T JOIN A UNION. WE'RE SALARIED.
I THINK IT'S AGAINST THE LAW OR SOMETHING.
YOU'VE GOT LONG HOURS, NO OVERTIME PAY, SHRINKING BENEFITS, AND NO JOB SECURITY. YOU MUST ACT NOW!
YOU'RE CONFUSING US WITH PEOPLE WHO HAVE SPINES.
© 1994 United Feature Syndicate, Inc.
DON'T WORRY. I BROUGHT STRAP-ON PORTA-SPINES FOR EVERYBODY.
I DEMAND A BIGGER CUBICLE!
NOBODY WILL TAKE ADVANTAGE OF US EVER AGAIN!
7/24
NOW, LET'S TALK ABOUT UNION DUES
FAIR ENOUGH.

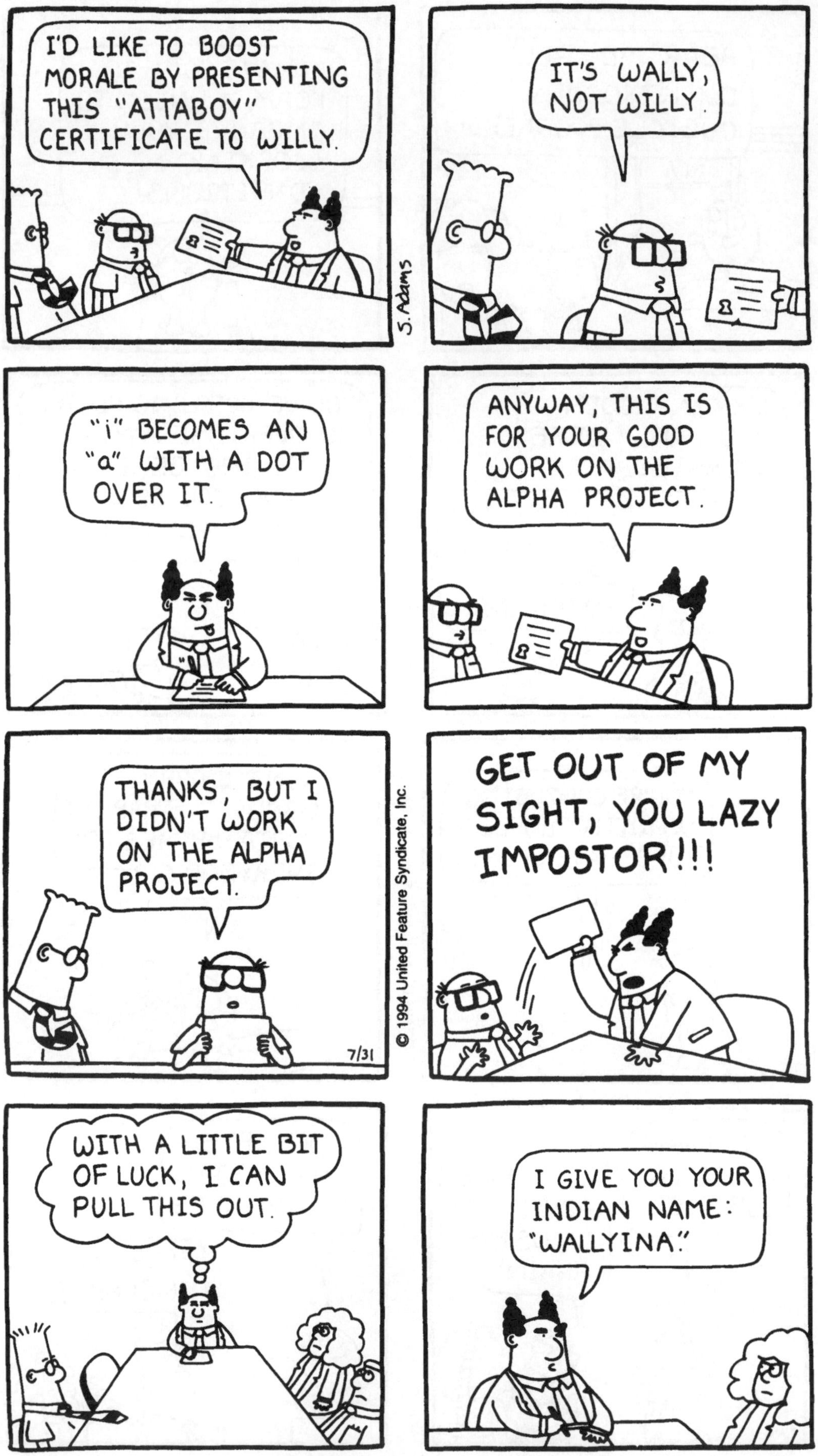

I'D LIKE TO BOOST MORALE BY PRESENTING THIS "ATTABOY" CERTIFICATE TO WILLY.
S. Adams
IT'S WALLY, NOT WILLY.
"i" BECOMES AN "a" WITH A DOT OVER IT.
ANYWAY, THIS IS FOR YOUR GOOD WORK ON THE ALPHA PROJECT.
THANKS, BUT I DIDN'T WORK ON THE ALPHA PROJECT.
7/31
© 1994 United Feature Syndicate, Inc.
GET OUT OF MY SIGHT, YOU LAZY IMPOSTOR!!!
WITH A LITTLE BIT OF LUCK, I CAN PULL THIS OUT.
I GIVE YOU YOUR INDIAN NAME: "WALLYINA."

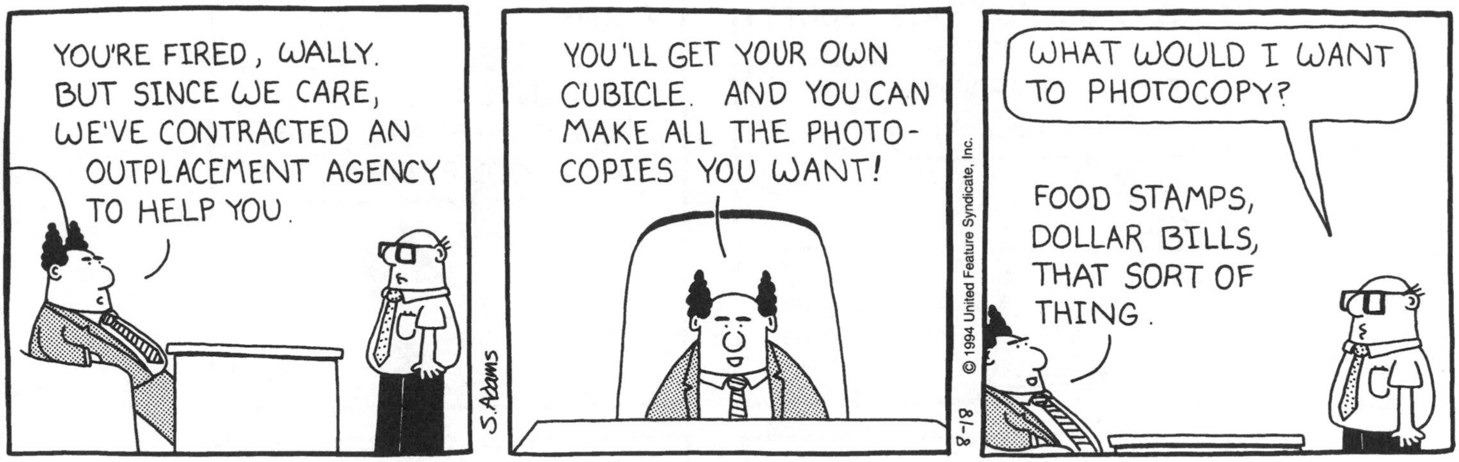
YOU'RE FIRED, WALLY. BUT SINCE WE CARE, WE'VE CONTRACTED AN OUTPLACEMENT AGENCY TO HELP YOU.
YOU'LL GET YOUR OWN CUBICLE. AND YOU CAN MAKE ALL THE PHOTOCOPIES YOU WANT!
WHAT WOULD I WANT TO PHOTOCOPY?
FOOD STAMPS, DOLLAR BILLS, THAT SORT OF THING.
S. Adams
8-18
© 1994 United Feature Syndicate, Inc.

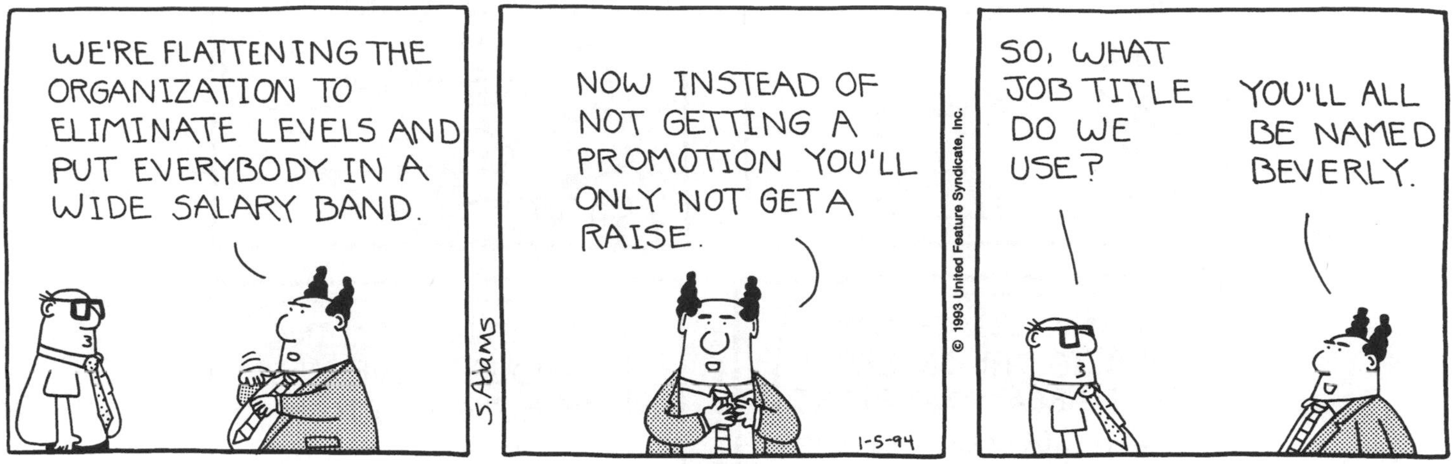
WE'RE FLATTENING THE ORGANIZATION TO ELIMINATE LEVELS AND PUT EVERYBODY IN A WIDE SALARY BAND.
NOW INSTEAD OF NOT GETTING A PROMOTION YOU'LL ONLY NOT GET A RAISE.
SO, WHAT JOB TITLE DO WE USE?
YOU'LL ALL BE NAMED BEVERLY.
S. Adams
1-5-94
© 1993 United Feature Syndicate, Inc.

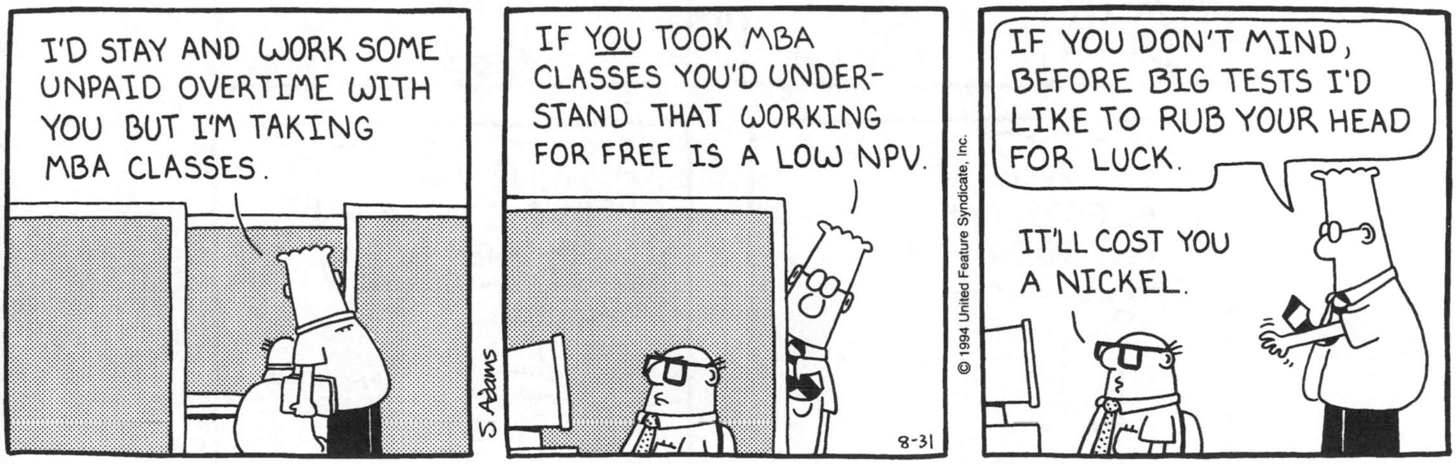
I'D STAY AND WORK SOME UNPAID OVERTIME WITH YOU BUT I'M TAKING MBA CLASSES.
IF YOU TOOK MBA CLASSES YOU'D UNDERSTAND THAT WORKING FOR FREE IS A LOW NPV.
IF YOU DON'T MIND, BEFORE BIG TESTS I'D LIKE TO RUB YOUR HEAD FOR LUCK.
IT'LL COST YOU A NICKEL.
S. Adams
8-31
© 1994 United Feature Syndicate, Inc.

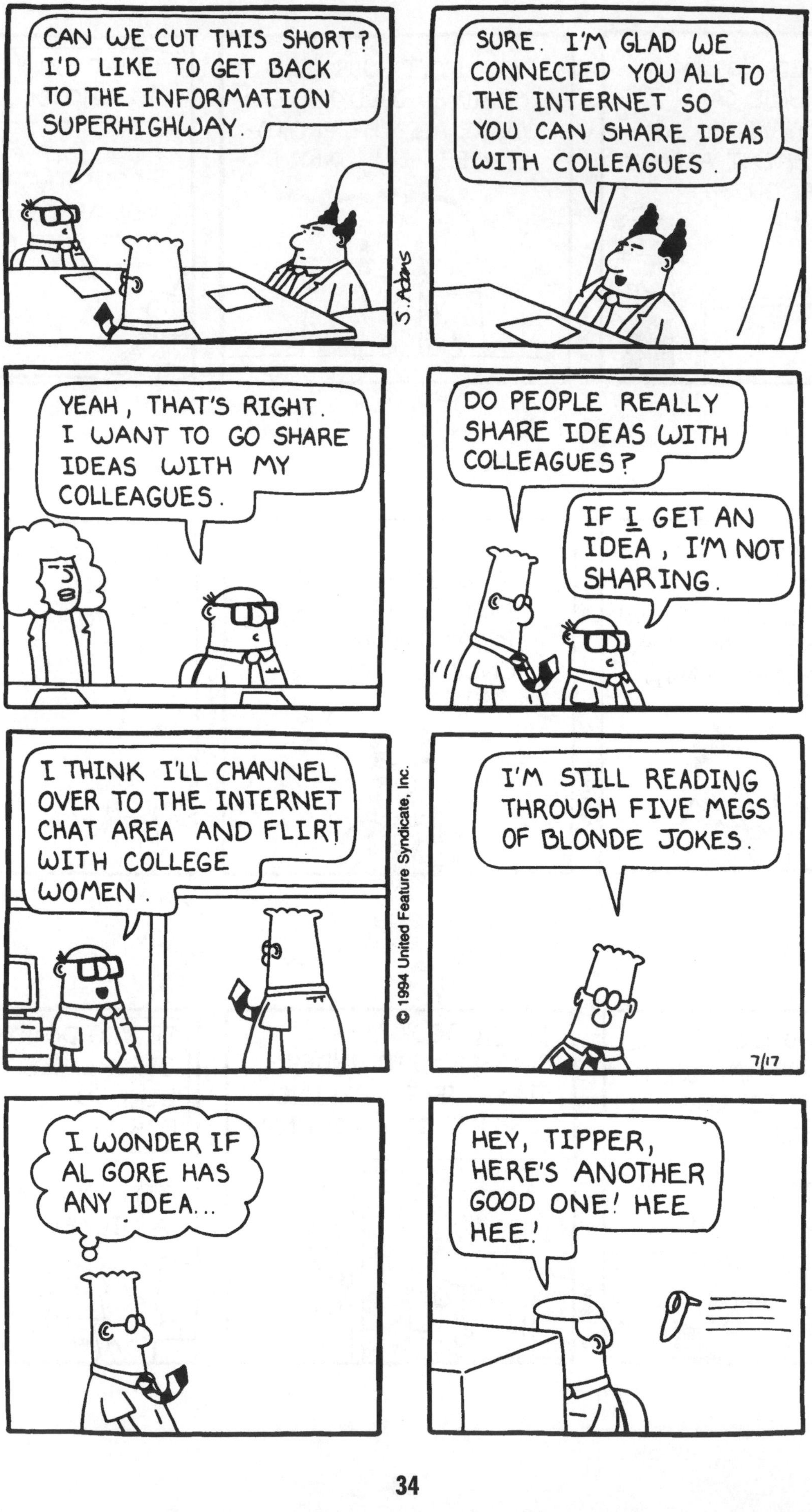
CAN WE CUT THIS SHORT? I'D LIKE TO GET BACK TO THE INFORMATION SUPERHIGHWAY.
S. Adams
SURE. I'M GLAD WE CONNECTED YOU ALL TO THE INTERNET SO YOU CAN SHARE IDEAS WITH COLLEAGUES.
YEAH, THAT'S RIGHT. I WANT TO GO SHARE IDEAS WITH MY COLLEAGUES.
DO PEOPLE REALLY SHARE IDEAS WITH COLLEAGUES?
IF I GET AN IDEA, I'M NOT SHARING.
I THINK I'LL CHANNEL OVER TO THE INTERNET CHAT AREA AND FLIRT WITH COLLEGE WOMEN.
© 1994 United Feature Syndicate, Inc.
I'M STILL READING THROUGH FIVE MEGS OF BLONDE JOKES.
7/17
I WONDER IF AL GORE HAS ANY IDEA...
HEY, TIPPER, HERE'S ANOTHER GOOD ONE! HEE HEE!

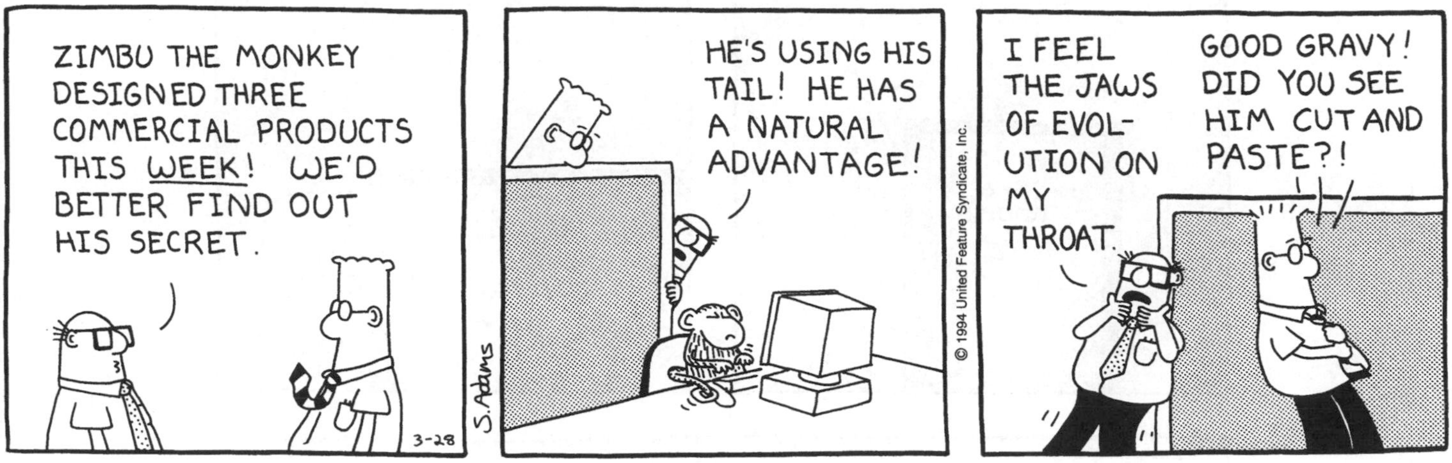
ZIMBU THE MONKEY DESIGNED THREE COMMERCIAL PRODUCTS THIS WEEK! WE'D BETTER FIND OUT HIS SECRET.
S. Adams 3-28
HE'S USING HIS TAIL! HE HAS A NATURAL ADVANTAGE!
© 1994 United Feature Syndicate, Inc.
I FEEL THE JAWS OF EVOL-UTION ON MY THROAT.
GOOD GRAVY! DID YOU SEE HIM CUT AND PASTE?!

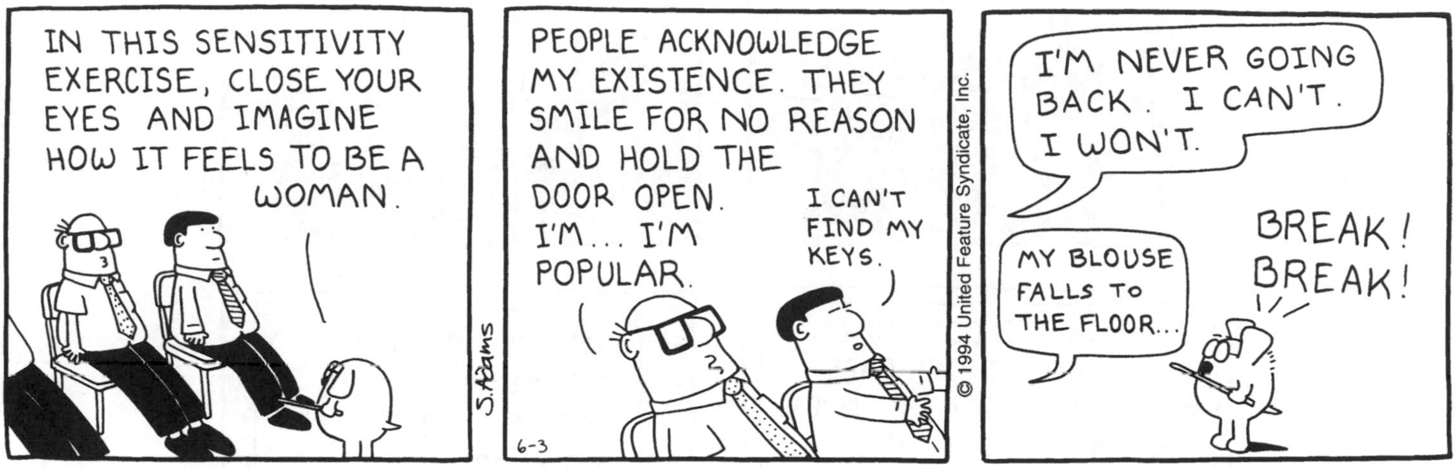
IN THIS SENSITIVITY EXERCISE, CLOSE YOUR EYES AND IMAGINE HOW IT FEELS TO BE A WOMAN.
S. Adams 6-3
PEOPLE ACKNOWLEDGE MY EXISTENCE. THEY SMILE FOR NO REASON AND HOLD THE DOOR OPEN. I'M... I'M POPULAR.
I CAN'T FIND MY KEYS.
© 1994 United Feature Syndicate, Inc.
I'M NEVER GOING BACK. I CAN'T. I WON'T.
MY BLOUSE FALLS TO THE FLOOR...
BREAK! BREAK!

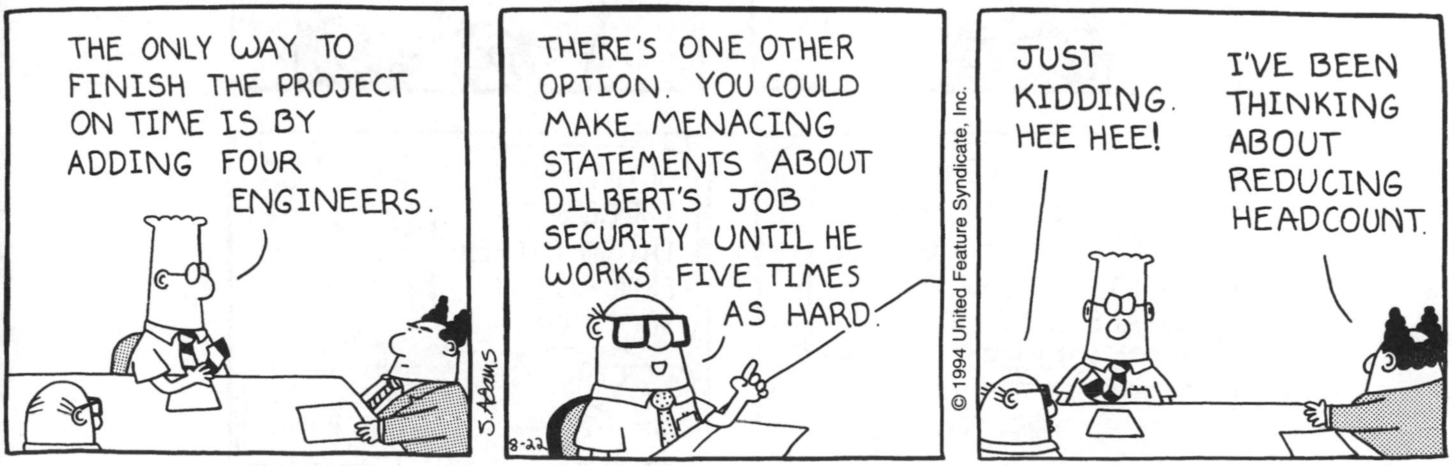
THE ONLY WAY TO FINISH THE PROJECT ON TIME IS BY ADDING FOUR ENGINEERS.
S. Adams 8-22
THERE'S ONE OTHER OPTION. YOU COULD MAKE MENACING STATEMENTS ABOUT DILBERT'S JOB SECURITY UNTIL HE WORKS FIVE TIMES AS HARD.
© 1994 United Feature Syndicate, Inc.
JUST KIDDING. HEE HEE!
I'VE BEEN THINKING ABOUT REDUCING HEADCOUNT.

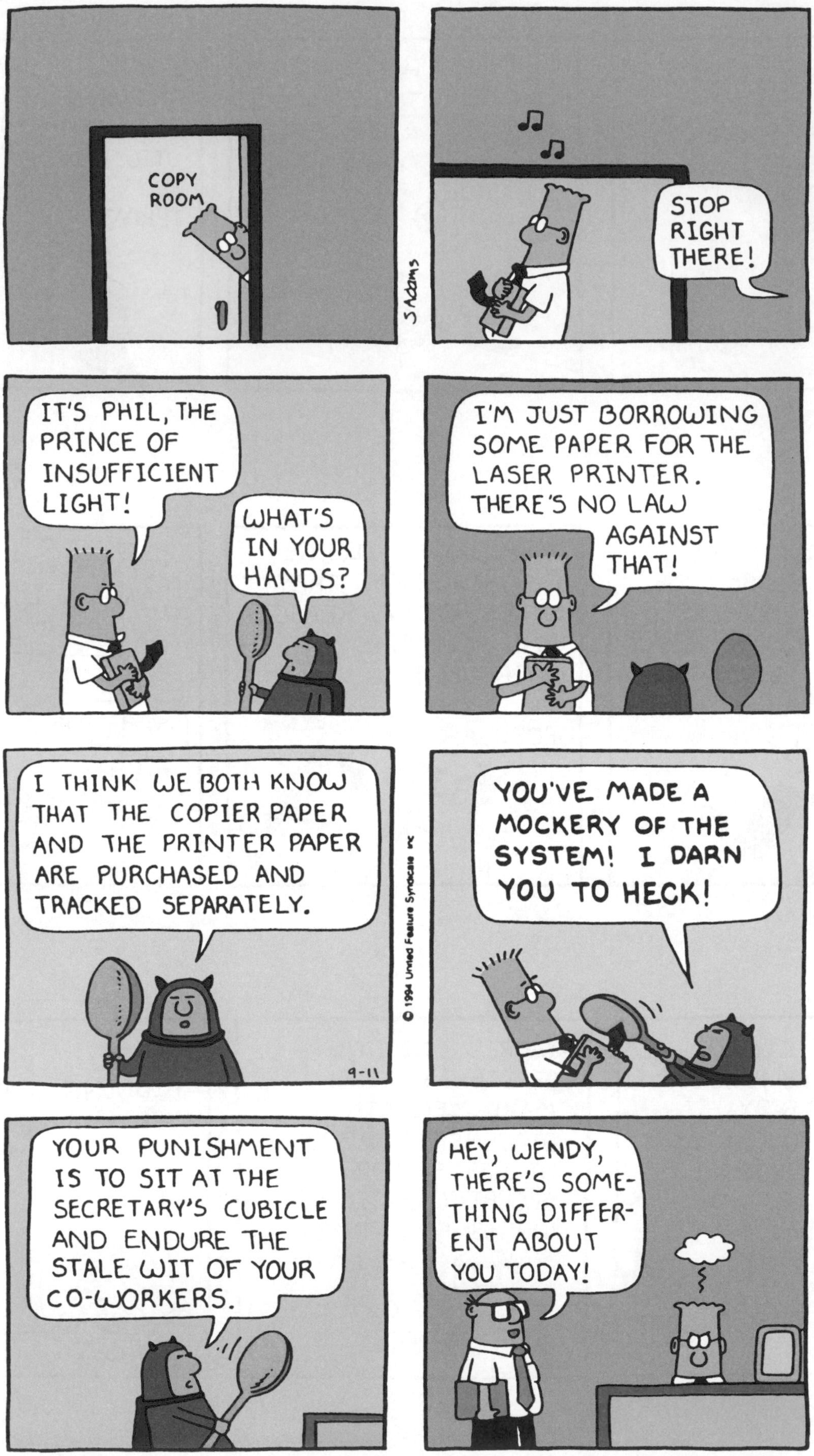
COPY ROOM
S Adams
STOP RIGHT THERE!
IT'S PHIL, THE PRINCE OF INSUFFICIENT LIGHT!
WHAT'S IN YOUR HANDS?
I'M JUST BORROWING SOME PAPER FOR THE LASER PRINTER. THERE'S NO LAW AGAINST THAT!
I THINK WE BOTH KNOW THAT THE COPIER PAPER AND THE PRINTER PAPER ARE PURCHASED AND TRACKED SEPARATELY.
9-11
© 1994 United Feature Syndicate Inc
YOU'VE MADE A MOCKERY OF THE SYSTEM! I DARN YOU TO HECK!
YOUR PUNISHMENT IS TO SIT AT THE SECRETARY'S CUBICLE AND ENDURE THE STALE WIT OF YOUR CO-WORKERS.
HEY, WENDY, THERE'S SOME-THING DIFFER-ENT ABOUT YOU TODAY!

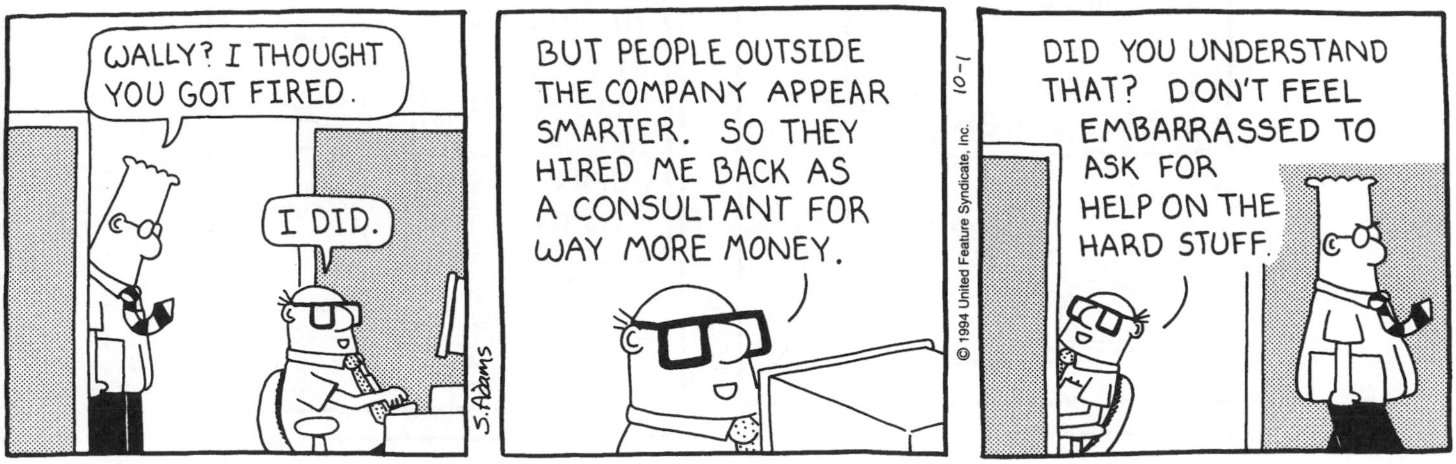
WALLY? I THOUGHT YOU GOT FIRED.
I DID.
S. Adams
BUT PEOPLE OUTSIDE THE COMPANY APPEAR SMARTER. SO THEY HIRED ME BACK AS A CONSULTANT FOR WAY MORE MONEY.
10-1
© 1994 United Feature Syndicate, Inc.
DID YOU UNDERSTAND THAT? DON'T FEEL EMBARRASSED TO ASK FOR HELP ON THE HARD STUFF.

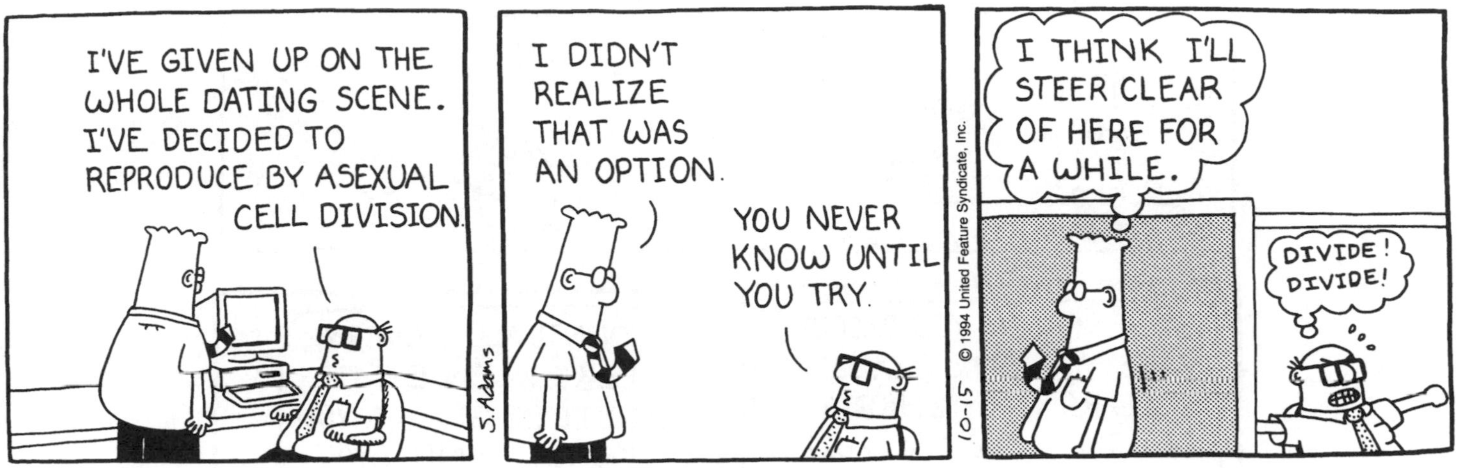
I'VE GIVEN UP ON THE WHOLE DATING SCENE. I'VE DECIDED TO REPRODUCE BY ASEXUAL CELL DIVISION.
S. Adams
I DIDN'T REALIZE THAT WAS AN OPTION.
YOU NEVER KNOW UNTIL YOU TRY.
10-15
© 1994 United Feature Syndicate, Inc.
I THINK I'LL STEER CLEAR OF HERE FOR A WHILE.
DIVIDE! DIVIDE!

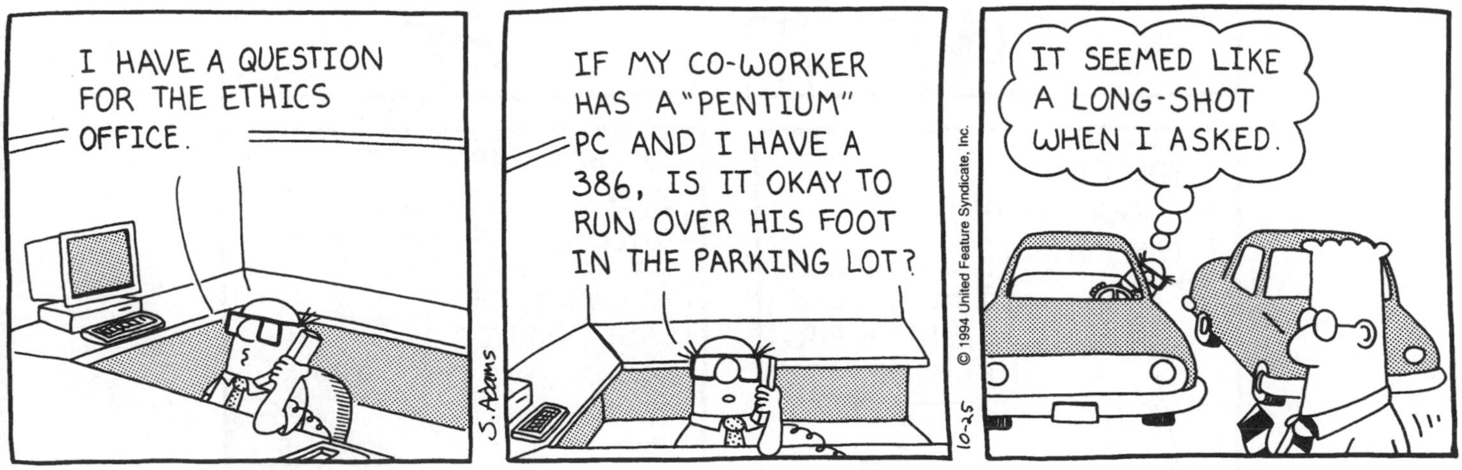
I HAVE A QUESTION FOR THE ETHICS OFFICE.
S. Adams
IF MY CO-WORKER HAS A "PENTIUM" PC AND I HAVE A 386, IS IT OKAY TO RUN OVER HIS FOOT IN THE PARKING LOT?
10-25
© 1994 United Feature Syndicate, Inc.
IT SEEMED LIKE A LONG-SHOT WHEN I ASKED.

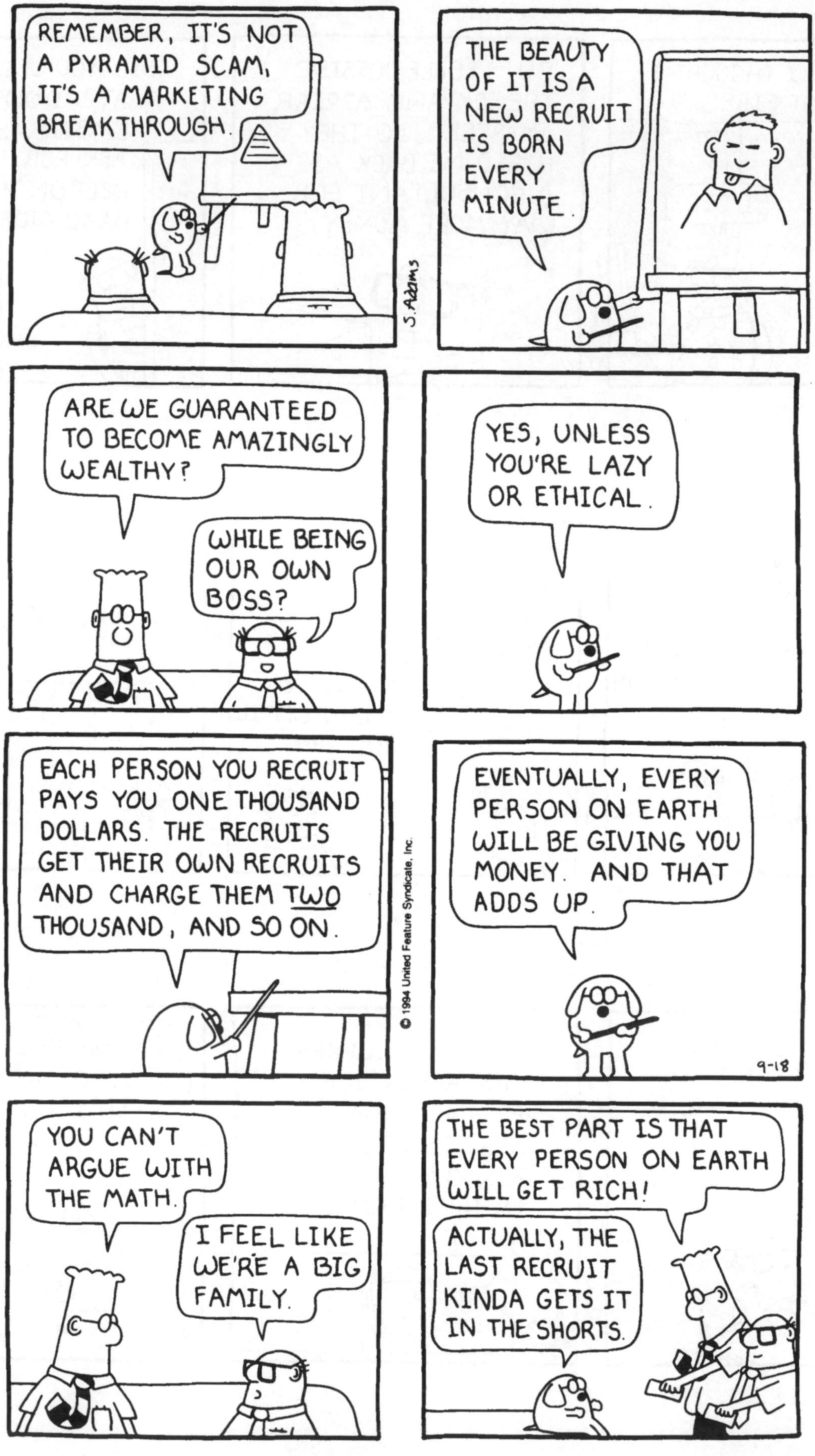
REMEMBER, IT'S NOT A PYRAMID SCAM, IT'S A MARKETING BREAKTHROUGH.
S. ADAMS
THE BEAUTY OF IT IS A NEW RECRUIT IS BORN EVERY MINUTE.
ARE WE GUARANTEED TO BECOME AMAZINGLY WEALTHY?
WHILE BEING OUR OWN BOSS?
YES, UNLESS YOU'RE LAZY OR ETHICAL.
EACH PERSON YOU RECRUIT PAYS YOU ONE THOUSAND DOLLARS. THE RECRUITS GET THEIR OWN RECRUITS AND CHARGE THEM TWO THOUSAND, AND SO ON.
© 1994 United Feature Syndicate, Inc.
EVENTUALLY, EVERY PERSON ON EARTH WILL BE GIVING YOU MONEY. AND THAT ADDS UP.
9-18
YOU CAN'T ARGUE WITH THE MATH.
I FEEL LIKE WE'RE A BIG FAMILY.
THE BEST PART IS THAT EVERY PERSON ON EARTH WILL GET RICH!
ACTUALLY, THE LAST RECRUIT KINDA GETS IT IN THE SHORTS.

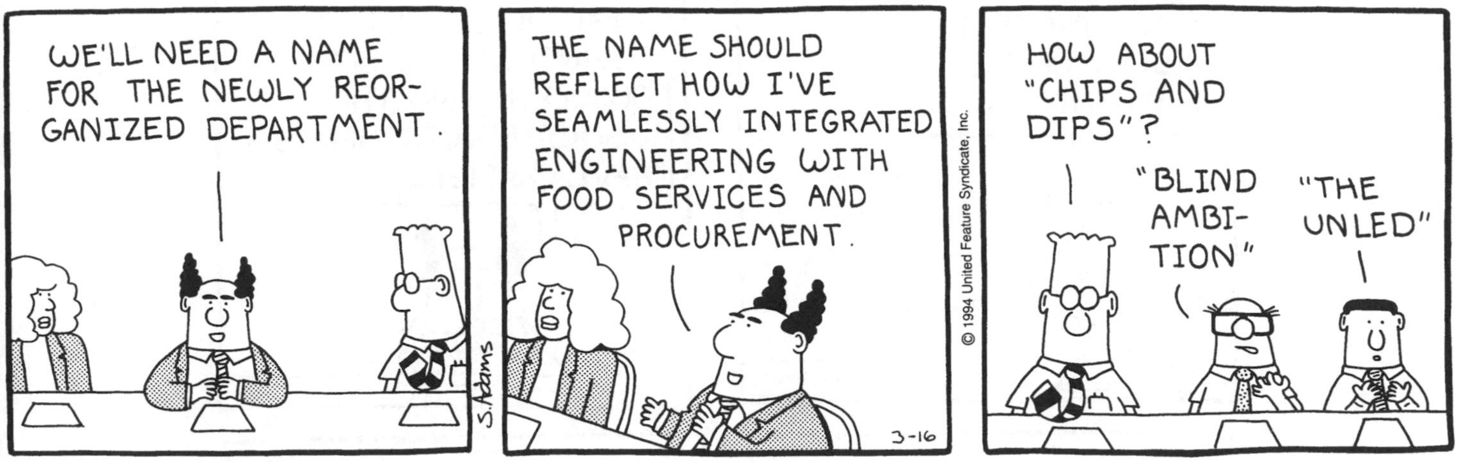
WE'LL NEED A NAME FOR THE NEWLY REORGANIZED DEPARTMENT.
S. Adams
THE NAME SHOULD REFLECT HOW I'VE SEAMLESSLY INTEGRATED ENGINEERING WITH FOOD SERVICES AND PROCUREMENT.
3-16
© 1994 United Feature Syndicate, Inc.
HOW ABOUT "CHIPS AND DIPS"?
"BLIND AMBITION"
"THE UNLED"

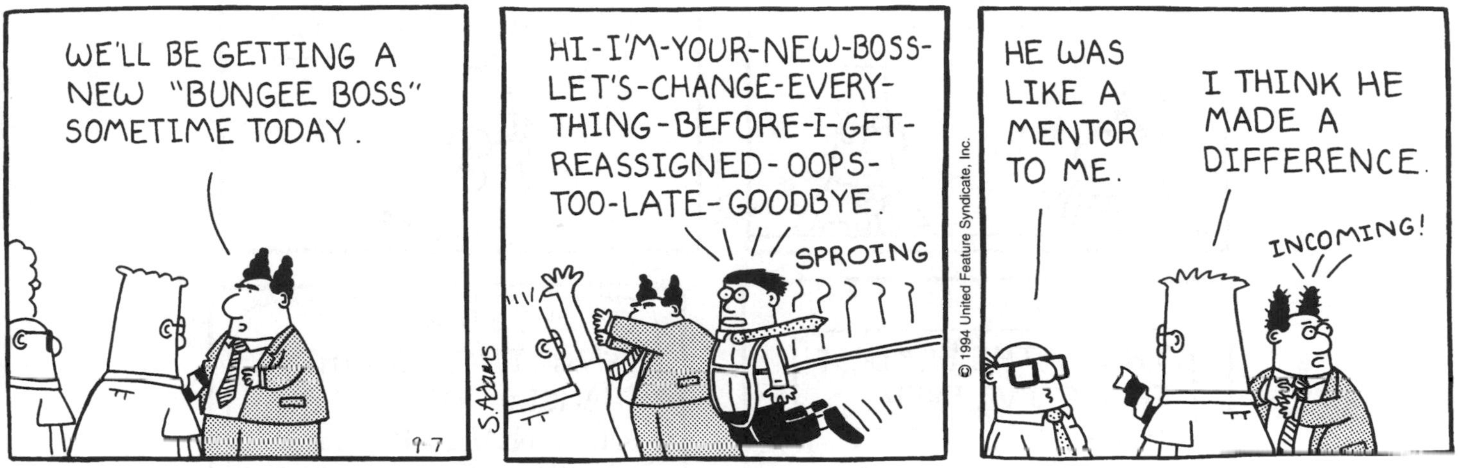
WE'LL BE GETTING A NEW "BUNGEE BOSS" SOMETIME TODAY.
9-7
S. Adams
HI-I'M-YOUR-NEW-BOSS-LET'S-CHANGE-EVERYTHING-BEFORE-I-GET-REASSIGNED-OOPS-TOO-LATE-GOODBYE.
SPROING
© 1994 United Feature Syndicate, Inc.
HE WAS LIKE A MENTOR TO ME.
I THINK HE MADE A DIFFERENCE.
INCOMING!

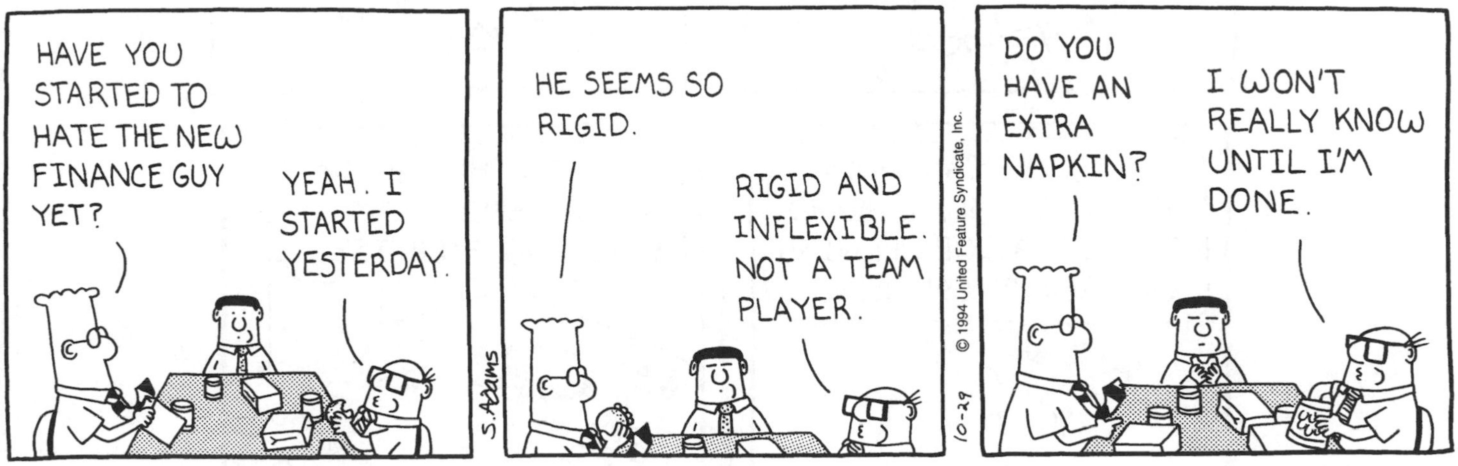
HAVE YOU STARTED TO HATE THE NEW FINANCE GUY YET?
YEAH. I STARTED YESTERDAY.
S. Adams
HE SEEMS SO RIGID.
RIGID AND INFLEXIBLE. NOT A TEAM PLAYER.
10-29
© 1994 United Feature Syndicate, Inc.
DO YOU HAVE AN EXTRA NAPKIN?
I WON'T REALLY KNOW UNTIL I'M DONE.

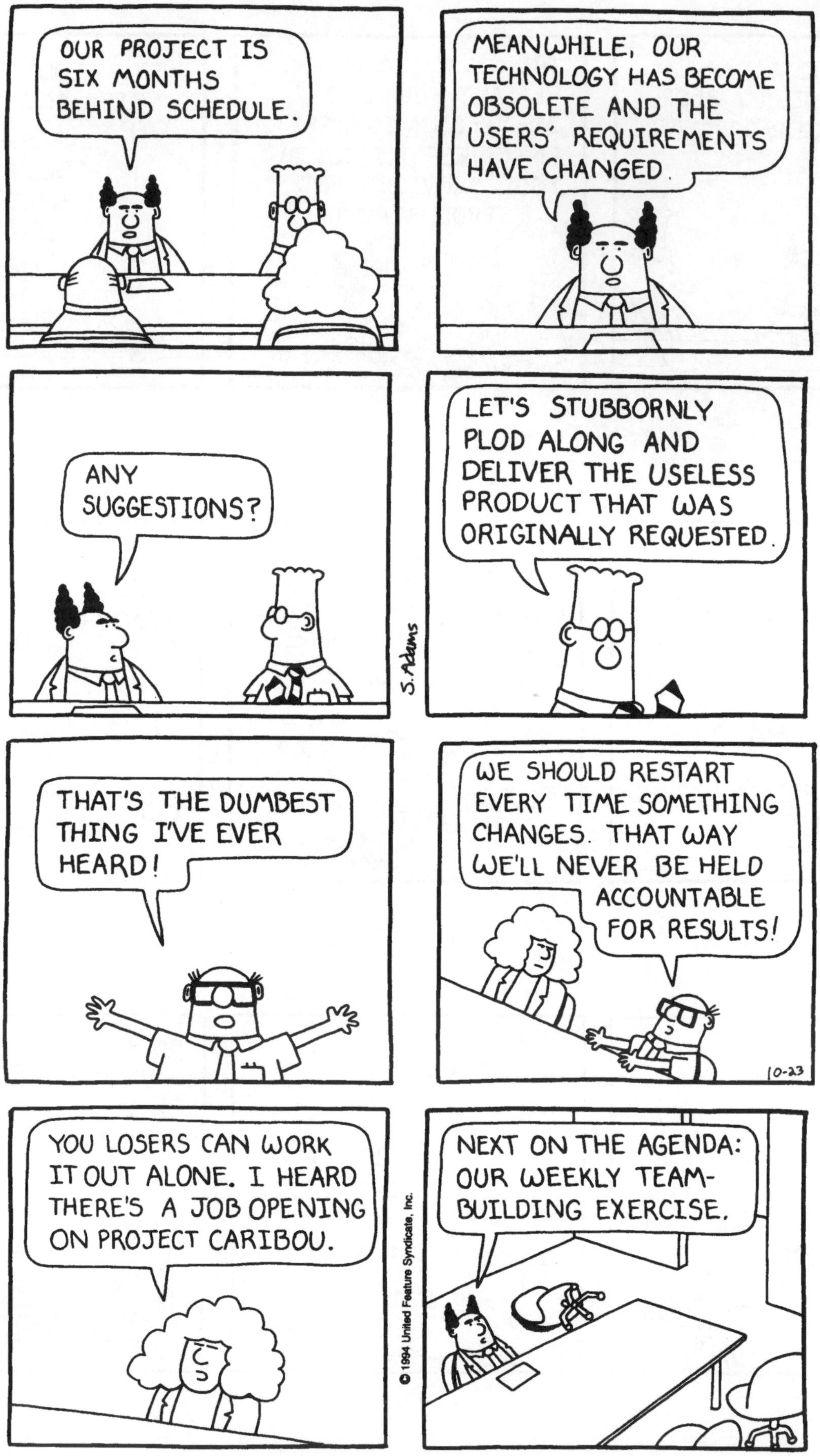
OUR PROJECT IS SIX MONTHS BEHIND SCHEDULE.
MEANWHILE, OUR TECHNOLOGY HAS BECOME OBSOLETE AND THE USERS' REQUIREMENTS HAVE CHANGED.
ANY SUGGESTIONS?
LET'S STUBBORNLY PLOD ALONG AND DELIVER THE USELESS PRODUCT THAT WAS ORIGINALLY REQUESTED.
THAT'S THE DUMBEST THING I'VE EVER HEARD!
WE SHOULD RESTART EVERY TIME SOMETHING CHANGES. THAT WAY WE'LL NEVER BE HELD ACCOUNTABLE FOR RESULTS!
YOU LOSERS CAN WORK IT OUT ALONE. I HEARD THERE'S A JOB OPENING ON PROJECT CARIBOU.
NEXT ON THE AGENDA: OUR WEEKLY TEAM-BUILDING EXERCISE.
S. Adams
10-23

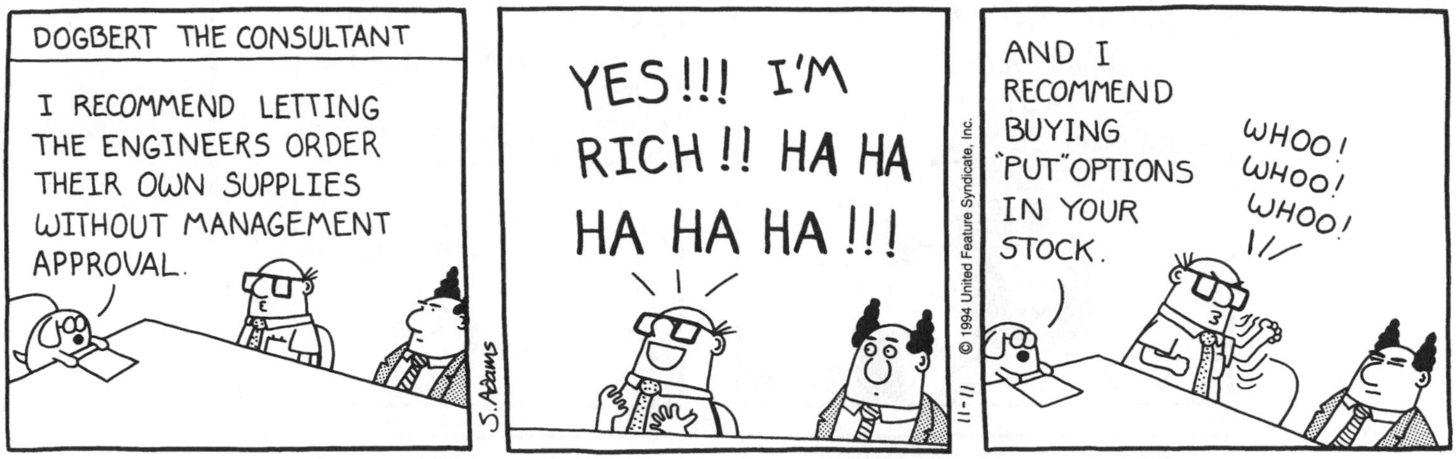
DOGBERT THE CONSULTANT
I RECOMMEND LETTING THE ENGINEERS ORDER THEIR OWN SUPPLIES WITHOUT MANAGEMENT APPROVAL.
S. Adams
YES!!! I'M RICH!! HA HA HA HA HA!!!
11-11
© 1994 United Feature Syndicate, Inc.
AND I RECOMMEND BUYING "PUT" OPTIONS IN YOUR STOCK.
WHOO! WHOO! WHOO!

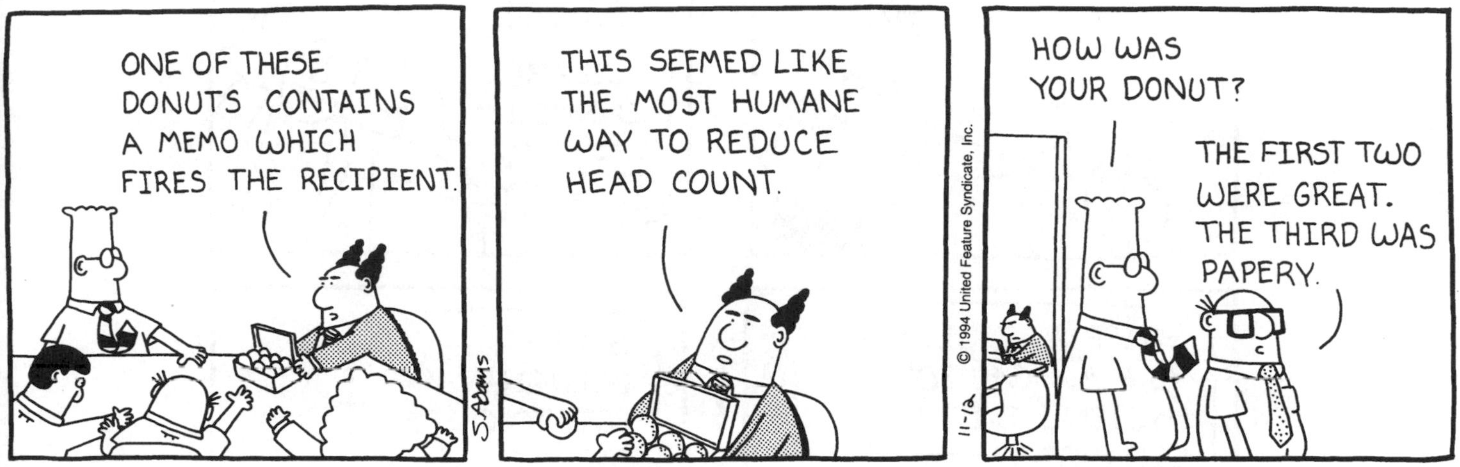
ONE OF THESE DONUTS CONTAINS A MEMO WHICH FIRES THE RECIPIENT.
S. Adams
THIS SEEMED LIKE THE MOST HUMANE WAY TO REDUCE HEAD COUNT.
11-12
© 1994 United Feature Syndicate, Inc.
HOW WAS YOUR DONUT?
THE FIRST TWO WERE GREAT. THE THIRD WAS PAPERY.

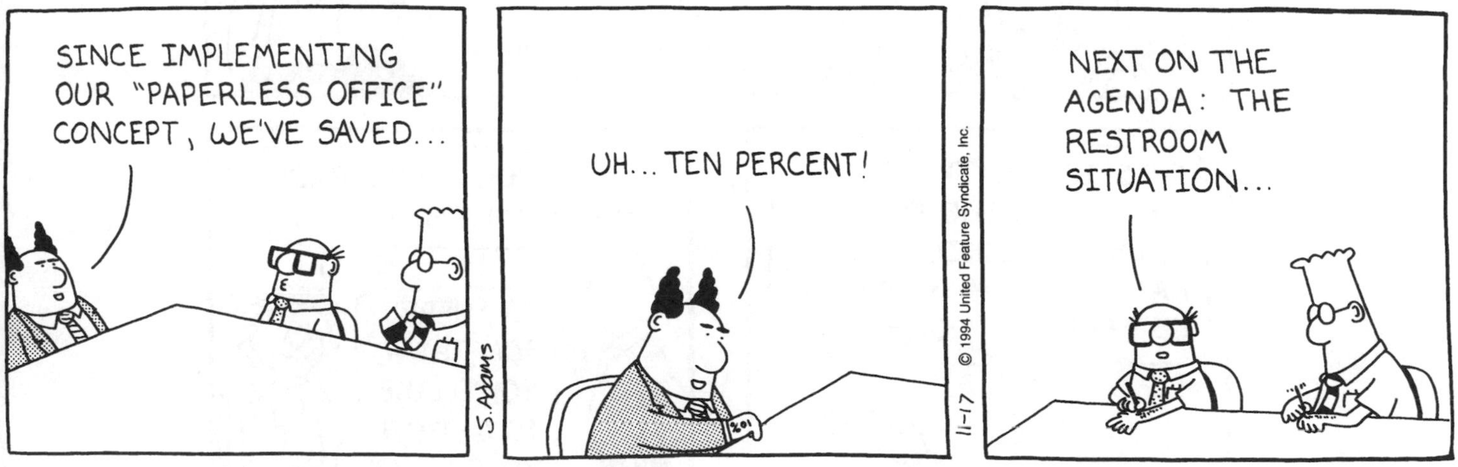
SINCE IMPLEMENTING OUR "PAPERLESS OFFICE" CONCEPT, WE'VE SAVED...
S. Adams
UH... TEN PERCENT!
11-17
© 1994 United Feature Syndicate, Inc.
NEXT ON THE AGENDA: THE RESTROOM SITUATION...

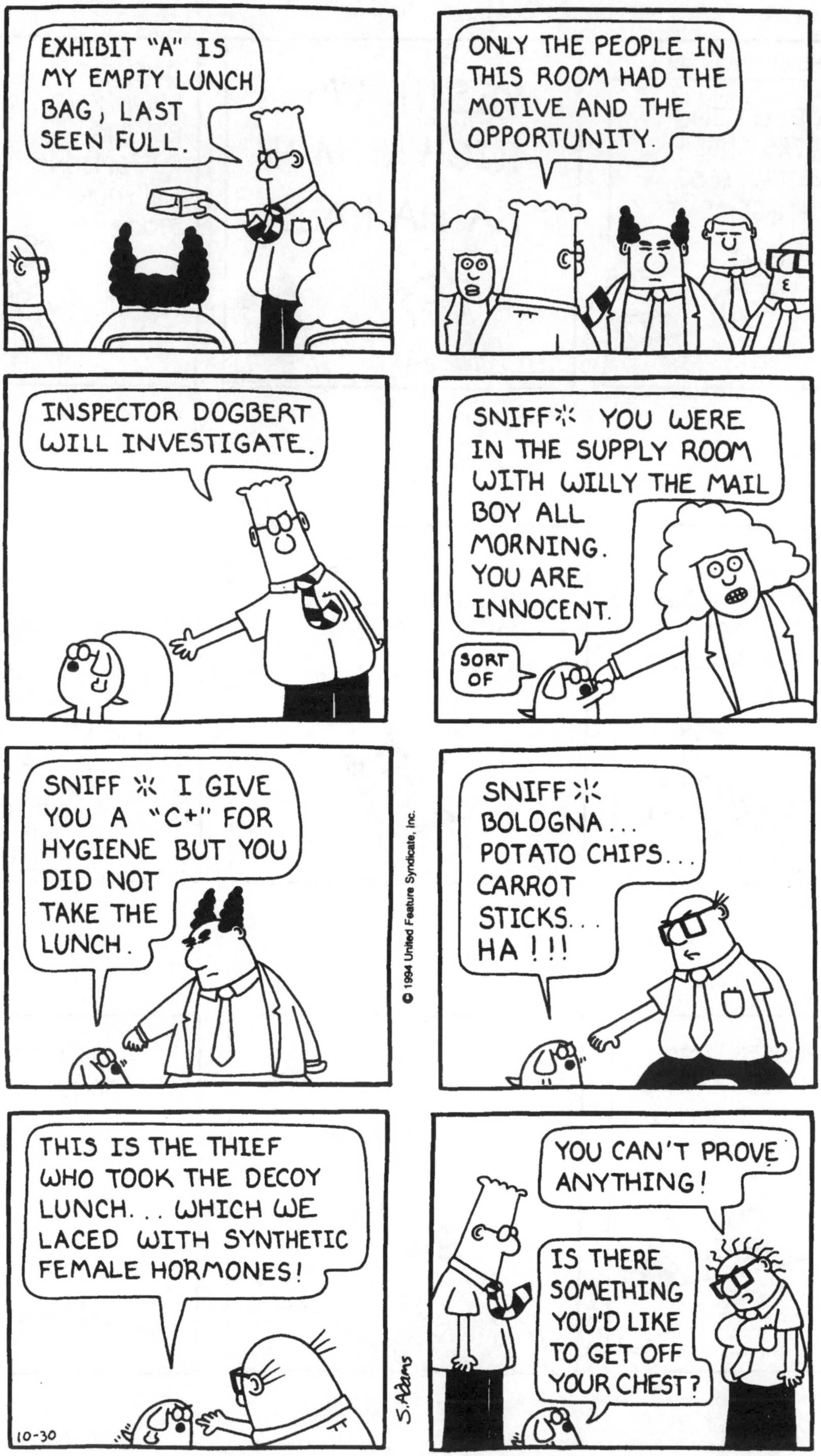
EXHIBIT "A" IS MY EMPTY LUNCH BAG, LAST SEEN FULL.
ONLY THE PEOPLE IN THIS ROOM HAD THE MOTIVE AND THE OPPORTUNITY.
INSPECTOR DOGBERT WILL INVESTIGATE.
SNIFF* YOU WERE IN THE SUPPLY ROOM WITH WILLY THE MAIL BOY ALL MORNING. YOU ARE INNOCENT.
SORT OF
SNIFF* I GIVE YOU A "C+" FOR HYGIENE BUT YOU DID NOT TAKE THE LUNCH.
© 1994 United Feature Syndicate, Inc.
SNIFF* BOLOGNA... POTATO CHIPS... CARROT STICKS... HA!!!
THIS IS THE THIEF WHO TOOK THE DECOY LUNCH... WHICH WE LACED WITH SYNTHETIC FEMALE HORMONES!
10-30
S. Adams
YOU CAN'T PROVE ANYTHING!
IS THERE SOMETHING YOU'D LIKE TO GET OFF YOUR CHEST?

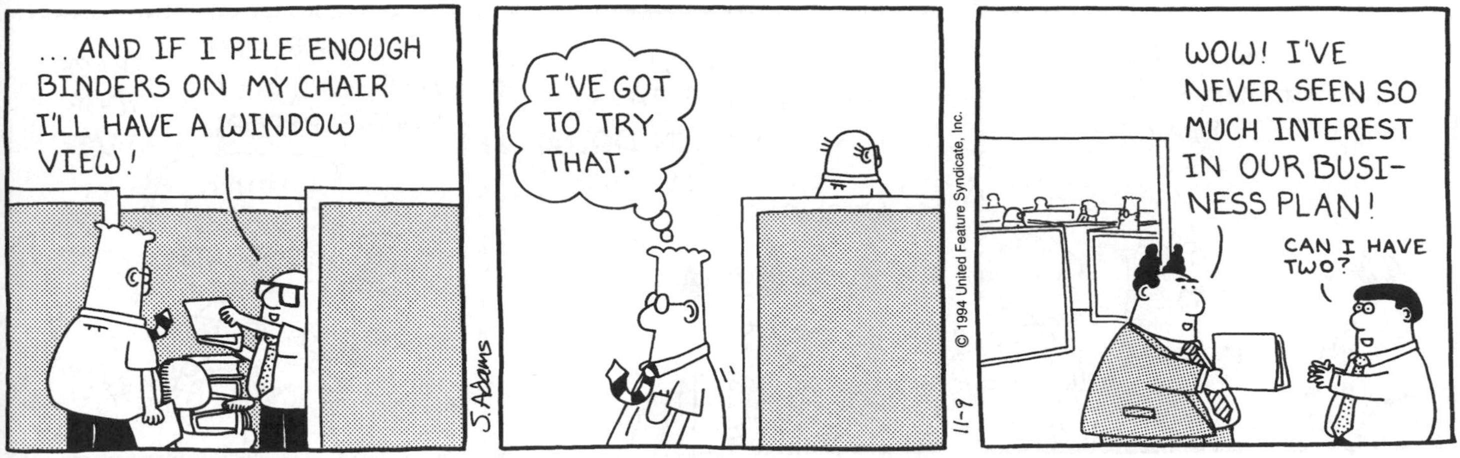
... AND IF I PILE ENOUGH BINDERS ON MY CHAIR I'LL HAVE A WINDOW VIEW!
I'VE GOT TO TRY THAT.
WOW! I'VE NEVER SEEN SO MUCH INTEREST IN OUR BUSINESS PLAN!
CAN I HAVE TWO?
S. Adams
11-9
© 1994 United Feature Syndicate, Inc.

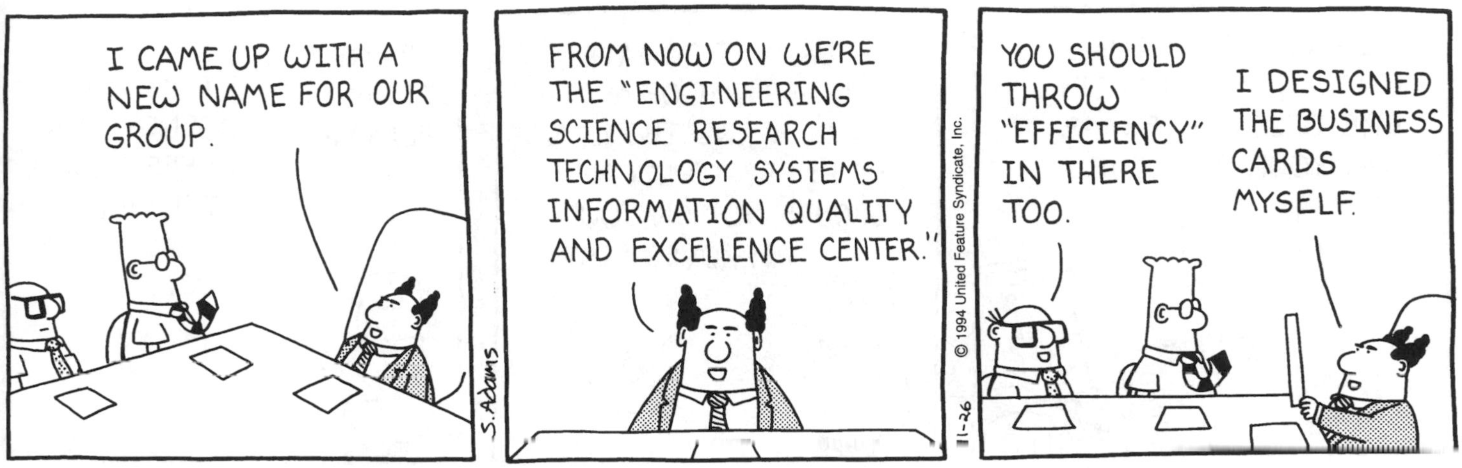
I CAME UP WITH A NEW NAME FOR OUR GROUP.
FROM NOW ON WE'RE THE "ENGINEERING SCIENCE RESEARCH TECHNOLOGY SYSTEMS INFORMATION QUALITY AND EXCELLENCE CENTER."
YOU SHOULD THROW "EFFICIENCY" IN THERE TOO.
I DESIGNED THE BUSINESS CARDS MYSELF.
S. Adams
11-26
© 1994 United Feature Syndicate, Inc.

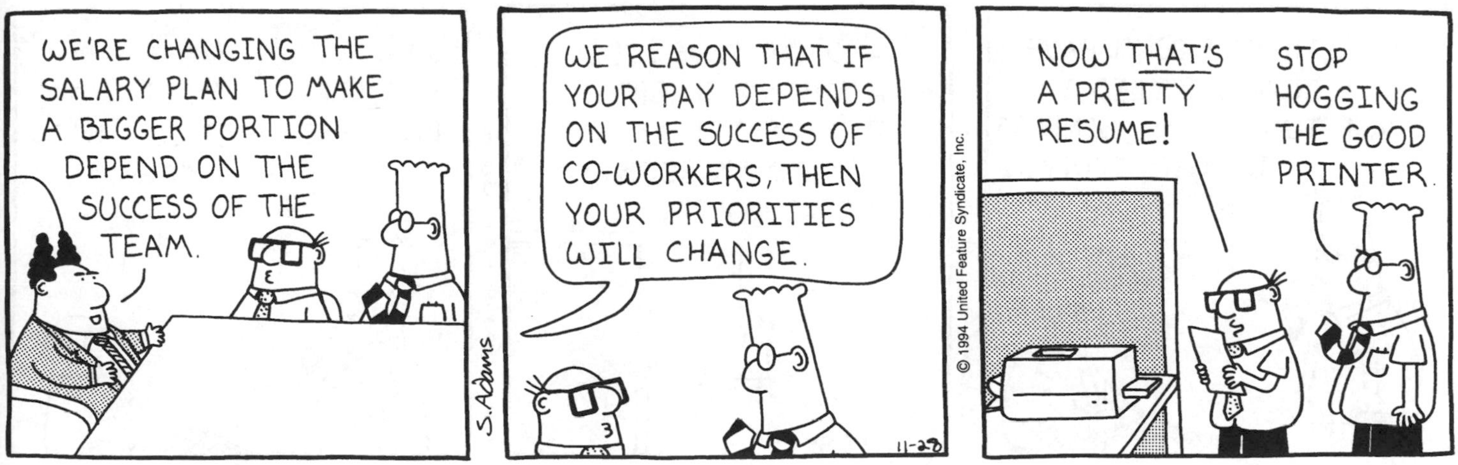
WE'RE CHANGING THE SALARY PLAN TO MAKE A BIGGER PORTION DEPEND ON THE SUCCESS OF THE TEAM.
WE REASON THAT IF YOUR PAY DEPENDS ON THE SUCCESS OF CO-WORKERS, THEN YOUR PRIORITIES WILL CHANGE.
NOW THAT'S A PRETTY RESUME!
STOP HOGGING THE GOOD PRINTER.
S. Adams
11-28
© 1994 United Feature Syndicate, Inc.

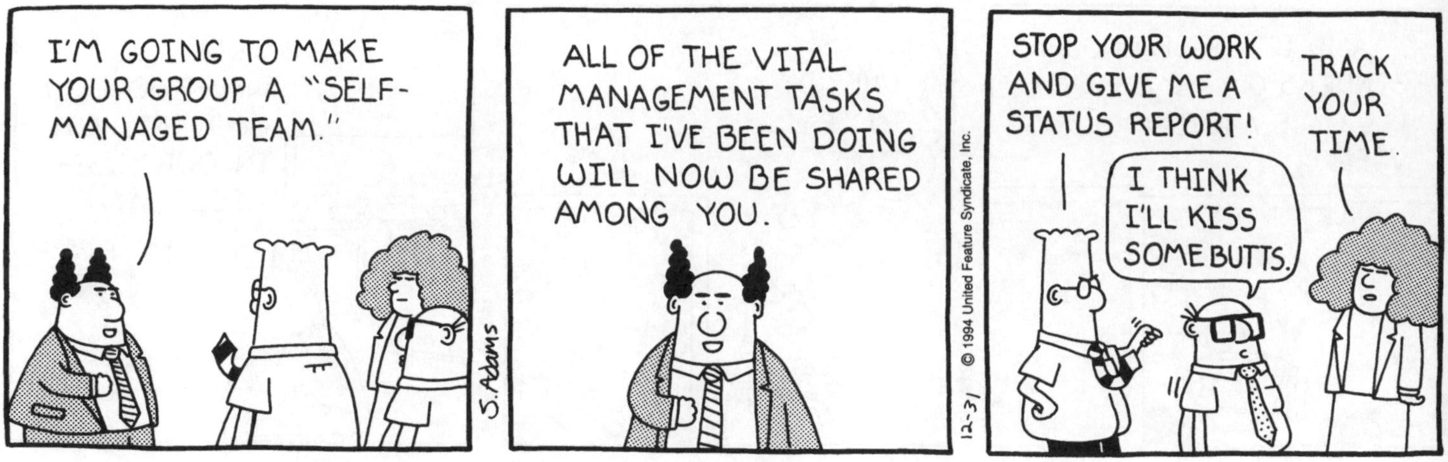
I'M GOING TO MAKE YOUR GROUP A "SELF-MANAGED TEAM."
S. Adams
ALL OF THE VITAL MANAGEMENT TASKS THAT I'VE BEEN DOING WILL NOW BE SHARED AMONG YOU.
12-31
© 1994 United Feature Syndicate, Inc.
STOP YOUR WORK AND GIVE ME A STATUS REPORT!
TRACK YOUR TIME.
I THINK I'LL KISS SOME BUTTS.

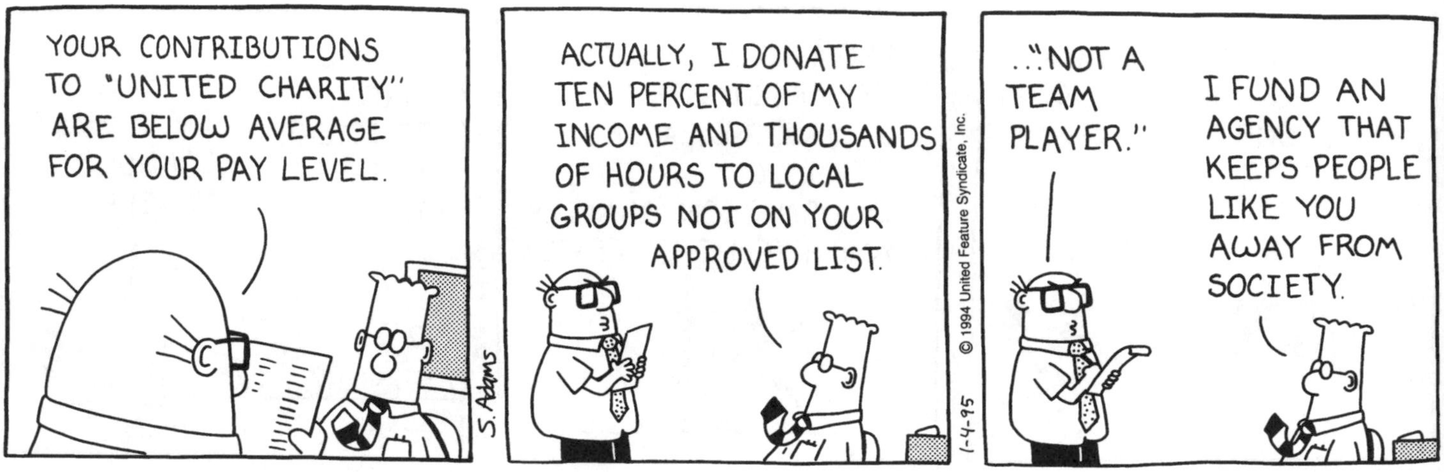
YOUR CONTRIBUTIONS TO "UNITED CHARITY" ARE BELOW AVERAGE FOR YOUR PAY LEVEL.
S. Adams
ACTUALLY, I DONATE TEN PERCENT OF MY INCOME AND THOUSANDS OF HOURS TO LOCAL GROUPS NOT ON YOUR APPROVED LIST.
1-4-95
© 1994 United Feature Syndicate, Inc.
..."NOT A TEAM PLAYER."
I FUND AN AGENCY THAT KEEPS PEOPLE LIKE YOU AWAY FROM SOCIETY.

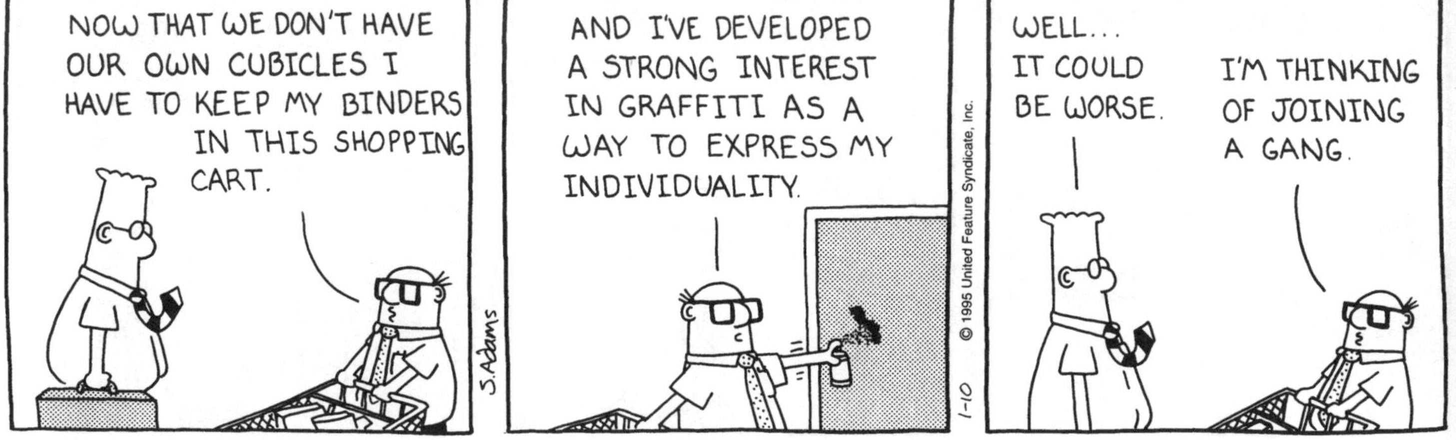
NOW THAT WE DON'T HAVE OUR OWN CUBICLES I HAVE TO KEEP MY BINDERS IN THIS SHOPPING CART.
S. Adams
AND I'VE DEVELOPED A STRONG INTEREST IN GRAFFITI AS A WAY TO EXPRESS MY INDIVIDUALITY.
1-10
© 1995 United Feature Syndicate, Inc.
WELL... IT COULD BE WORSE.
I'M THINKING OF JOINING A GANG.

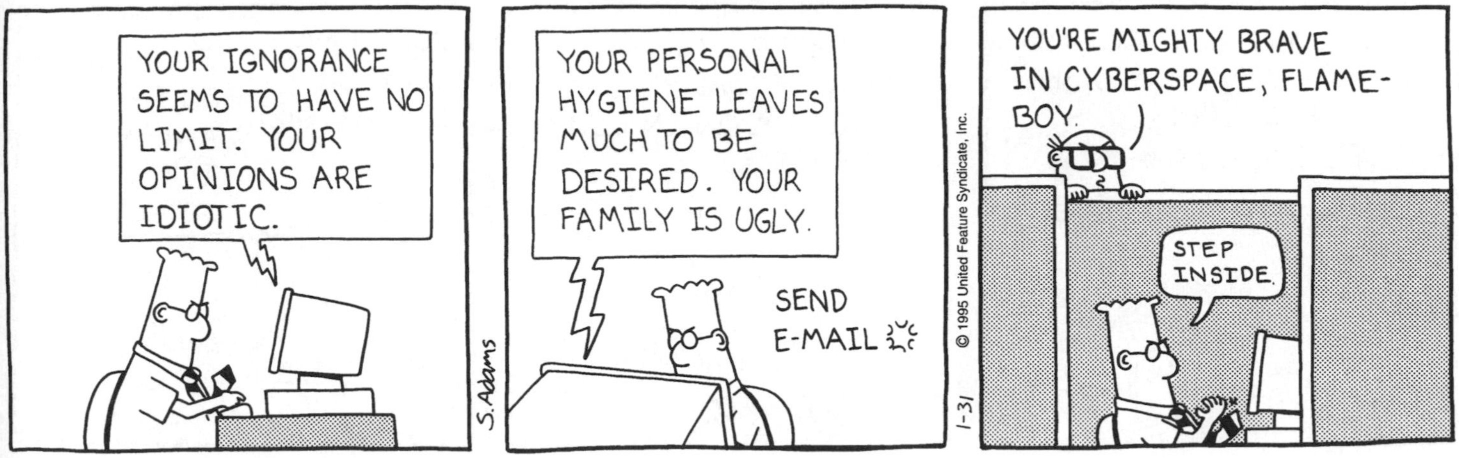

YOUR IGNORANCE SEEMS TO HAVE NO LIMIT. YOUR OPINIONS ARE IDIOTIC.
S. Adams
YOUR PERSONAL HYGIENE LEAVES MUCH TO BE DESIRED. YOUR FAMILY IS UGLY.
SEND E-MAIL
1-31
© 1995 United Feature Syndicate, Inc.
YOU'RE MIGHTY BRAVE IN CYBERSPACE, FLAME-BOY.
STEP INSIDE.

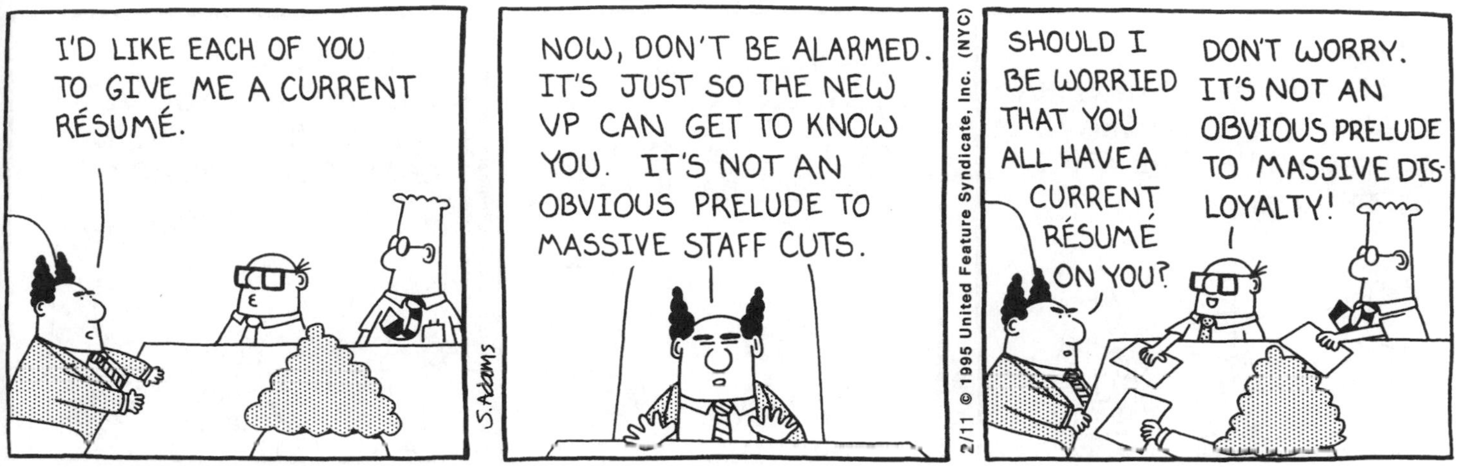

I'D LIKE EACH OF YOU TO GIVE ME A CURRENT RÉSUMÉ.
S. Adams
NOW, DON'T BE ALARMED. IT'S JUST SO THE NEW VP CAN GET TO KNOW YOU. IT'S NOT AN OBVIOUS PRELUDE TO MASSIVE STAFF CUTS.
2/11 © 1995 United Feature Syndicate, Inc. (NYC)
SHOULD I BE WORRIED THAT YOU ALL HAVE A CURRENT RÉSUMÉ ON YOU?
DON'T WORRY. IT'S NOT AN OBVIOUS PRELUDE TO MASSIVE DISLOYALTY!

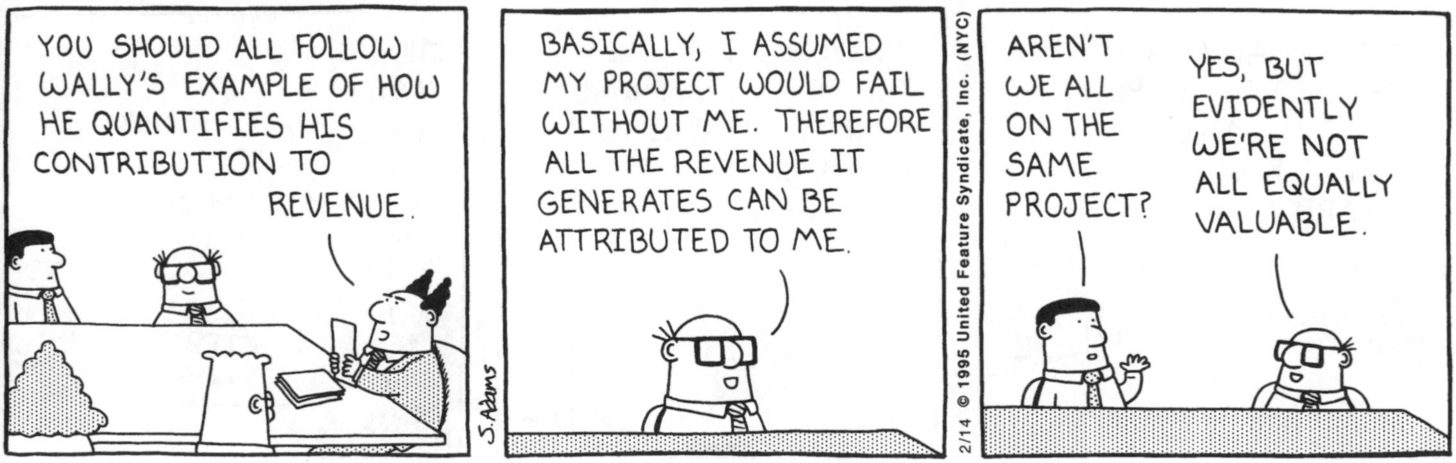

YOU SHOULD ALL FOLLOW WALLY'S EXAMPLE OF HOW HE QUANTIFIES HIS CONTRIBUTION TO REVENUE.
S. Adams
BASICALLY, I ASSUMED MY PROJECT WOULD FAIL WITHOUT ME. THEREFORE ALL THE REVENUE IT GENERATES CAN BE ATTRIBUTED TO ME.
2/14 © 1995 United Feature Syndicate, Inc. (NYC)
AREN'T WE ALL ON THE SAME PROJECT?
YES, BUT EVIDENTLY WE'RE NOT ALL EQUALLY VALUABLE.

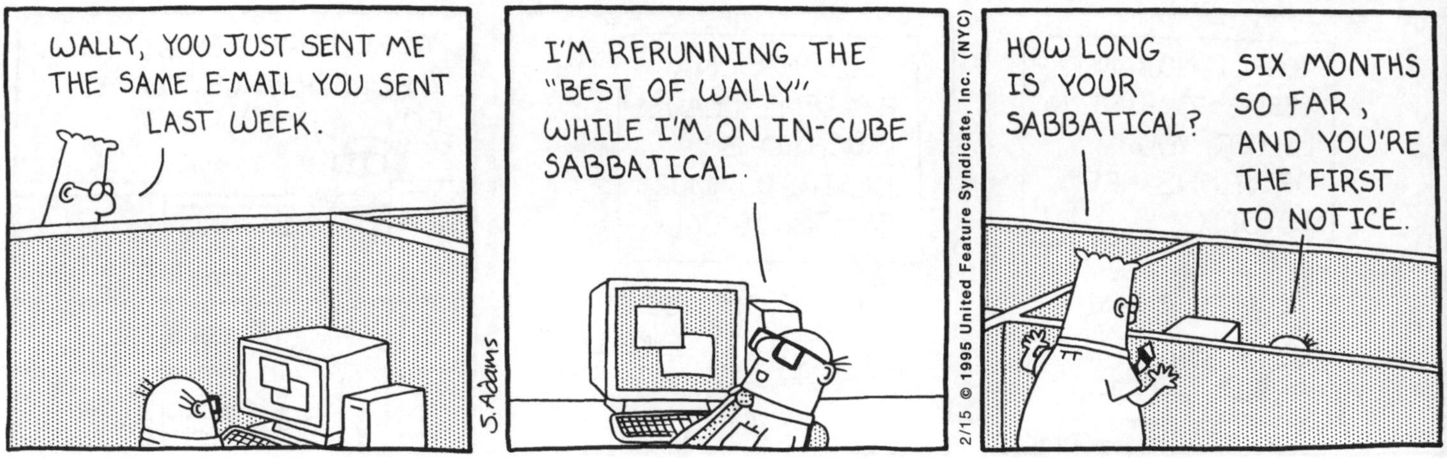
WALLY, YOU JUST SENT ME THE SAME E-MAIL YOU SENT LAST WEEK.
I'M RERUNNING THE "BEST OF WALLY" WHILE I'M ON IN-CUBE SABBATICAL.
HOW LONG IS YOUR SABBATICAL?
SIX MONTHS SO FAR, AND YOU'RE THE FIRST TO NOTICE.
S. Adams
2/15 © 1995 United Feature Syndicate, Inc. (NYC)

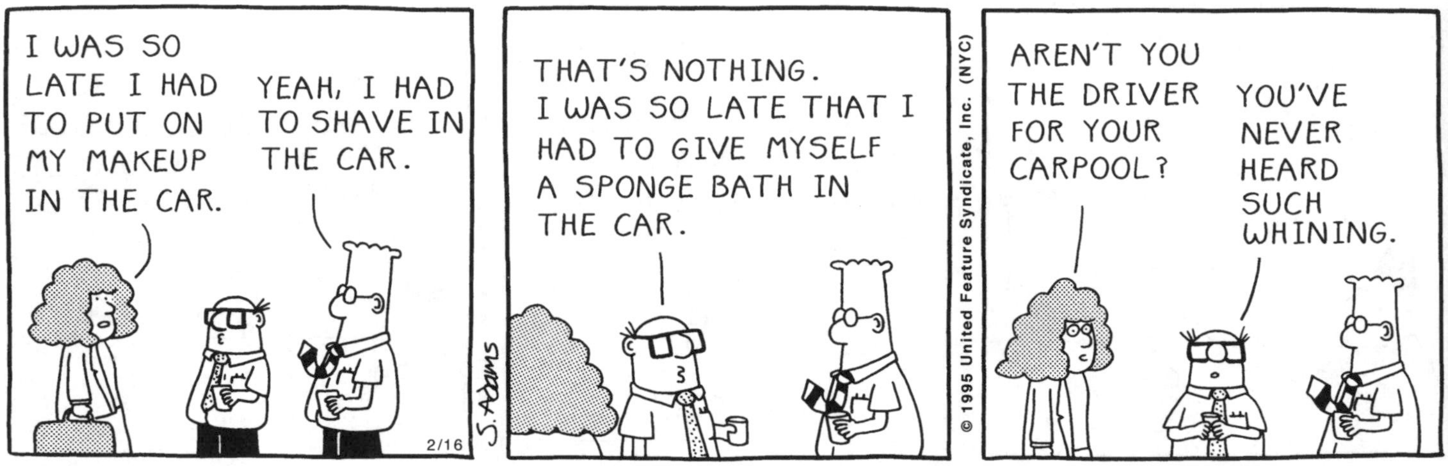
I WAS SO LATE I HAD TO PUT ON MY MAKEUP IN THE CAR.
YEAH, I HAD TO SHAVE IN THE CAR.
2/16
S. Adams
THAT'S NOTHING. I WAS SO LATE THAT I HAD TO GIVE MYSELF A SPONGE BATH IN THE CAR.
© 1995 United Feature Syndicate, Inc. (NYC)
AREN'T YOU THE DRIVER FOR YOUR CARPOOL?
YOU'VE NEVER HEARD SUCH WHINING.

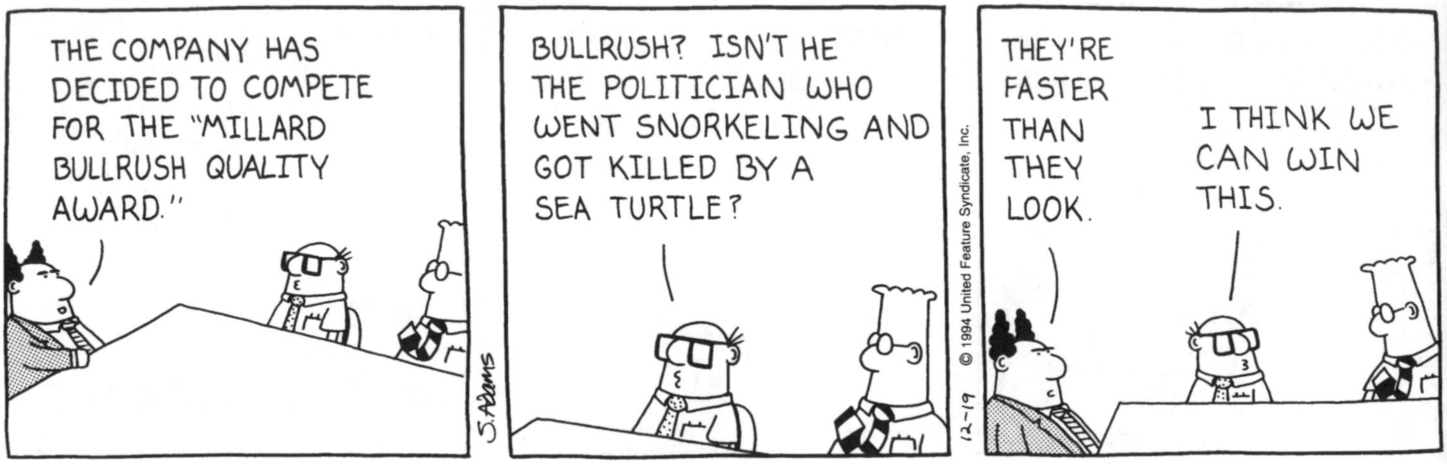
THE COMPANY HAS DECIDED TO COMPETE FOR THE "MILLARD BULLRUSH QUALITY AWARD."
S. Adams
BULLRUSH? ISN'T HE THE POLITICIAN WHO WENT SNORKELING AND GOT KILLED BY A SEA TURTLE?
12-19 © 1994 United Feature Syndicate, Inc.
THEY'RE FASTER THAN THEY LOOK.
I THINK WE CAN WIN THIS.

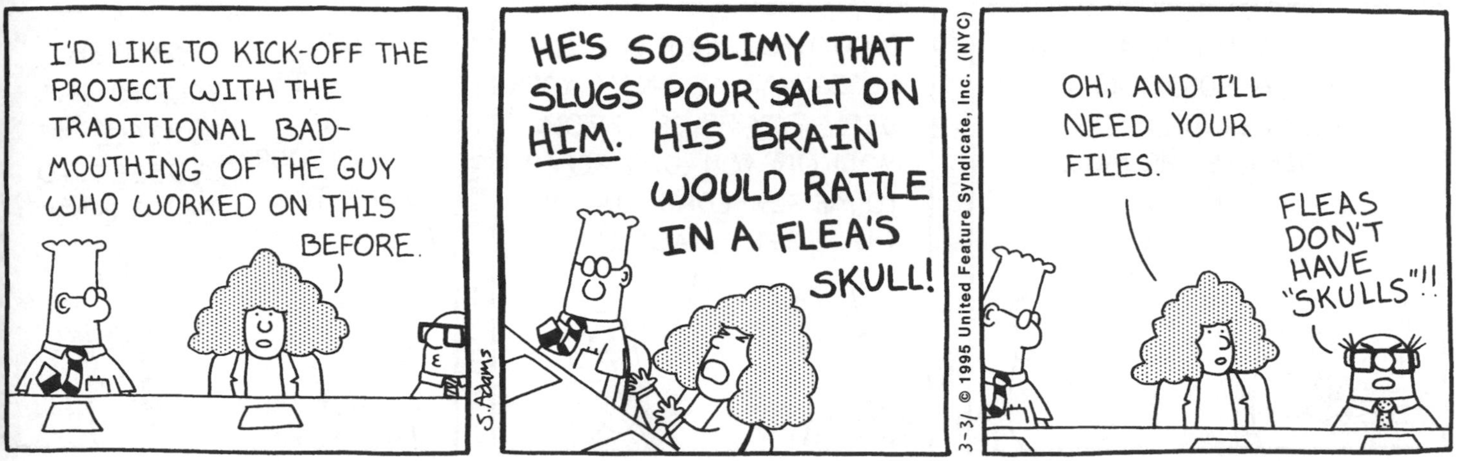
I'D LIKE TO KICK-OFF THE PROJECT WITH THE TRADITIONAL BAD-MOUTHING OF THE GUY WHO WORKED ON THIS BEFORE.
HE'S SO SLIMY THAT SLUGS POUR SALT ON HIM. HIS BRAIN WOULD RATTLE IN A FLEA'S SKULL!
OH, AND I'LL NEED YOUR FILES.
FLEAS DON'T HAVE "SKULLS"!!
S. Adams
3-31 © 1995 United Feature Syndicate, Inc. (NYC)

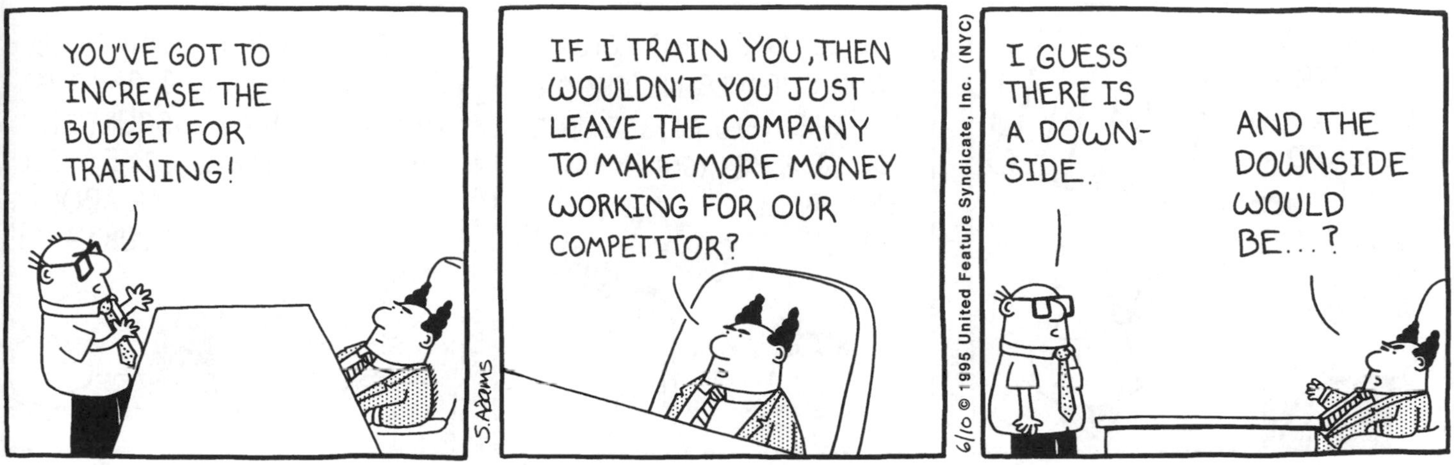
YOU'VE GOT TO INCREASE THE BUDGET FOR TRAINING!
IF I TRAIN YOU, THEN WOULDN'T YOU JUST LEAVE THE COMPANY TO MAKE MORE MONEY WORKING FOR OUR COMPETITOR?
I GUESS THERE IS A DOWN-SIDE.
AND THE DOWNSIDE WOULD BE...?
S. Adams
6/10 © 1995 United Feature Syndicate, Inc. (NYC)

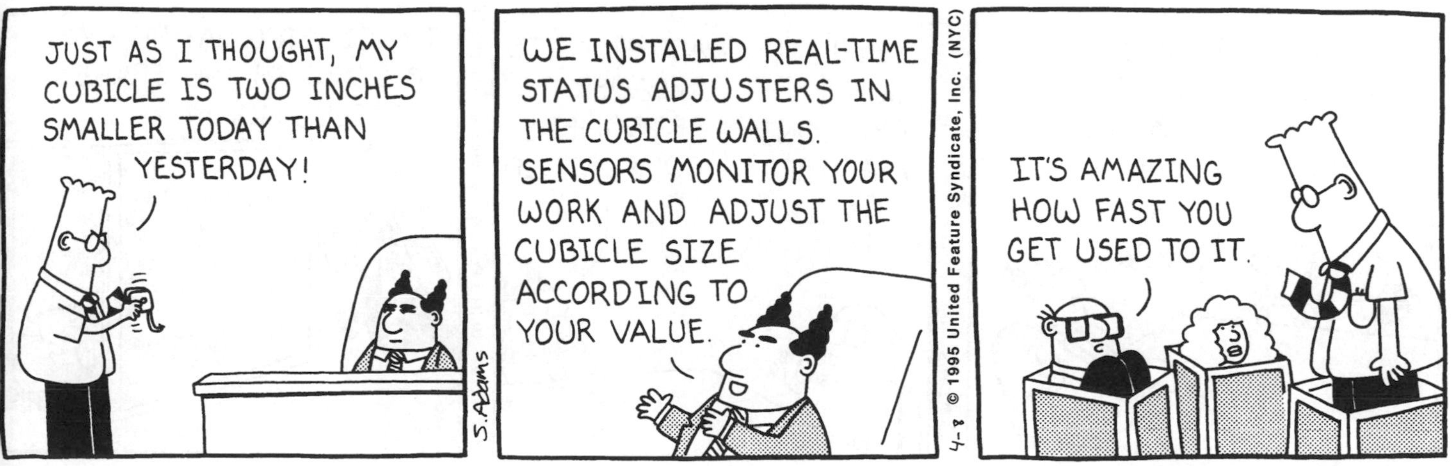
JUST AS I THOUGHT, MY CUBICLE IS TWO INCHES SMALLER TODAY THAN YESTERDAY!
WE INSTALLED REAL-TIME STATUS ADJUSTERS IN THE CUBICLE WALLS. SENSORS MONITOR YOUR WORK AND ADJUST THE CUBICLE SIZE ACCORDING TO YOUR VALUE.
IT'S AMAZING HOW FAST YOU GET USED TO IT.
S. Adams
4-8 © 1995 United Feature Syndicate, Inc. (NYC)

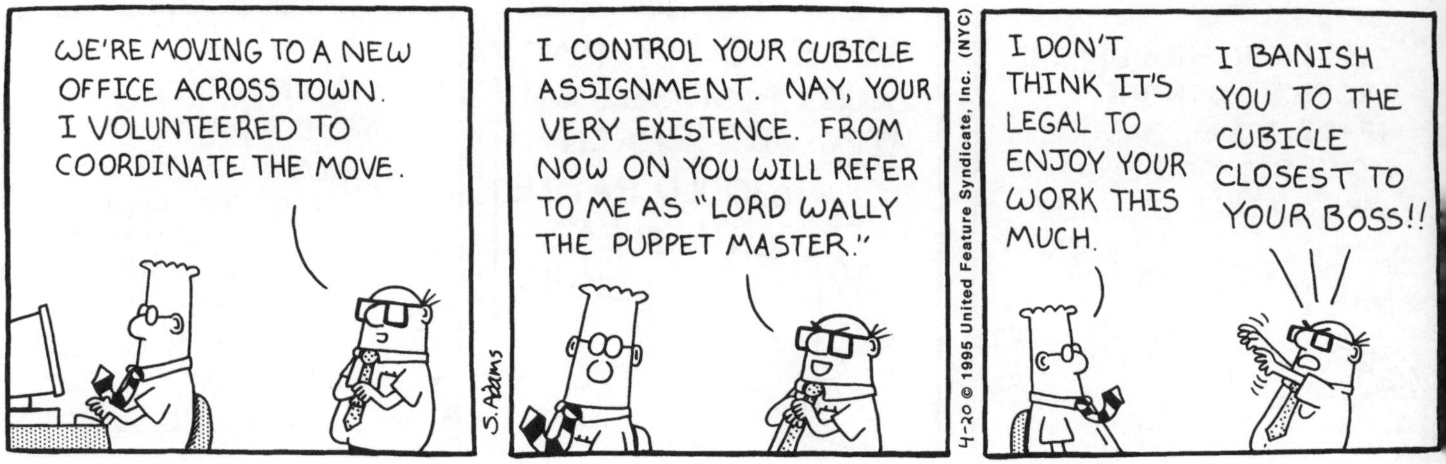
WE'RE MOVING TO A NEW OFFICE ACROSS TOWN. I VOLUNTEERED TO COORDINATE THE MOVE.
S. Adams
I CONTROL YOUR CUBICLE ASSIGNMENT. NAY, YOUR VERY EXISTENCE. FROM NOW ON YOU WILL REFER TO ME AS "LORD WALLY THE PUPPET MASTER."
I DON'T THINK IT'S LEGAL TO ENJOY YOUR WORK THIS MUCH.
I BANISH YOU TO THE CUBICLE CLOSEST TO YOUR BOSS!!

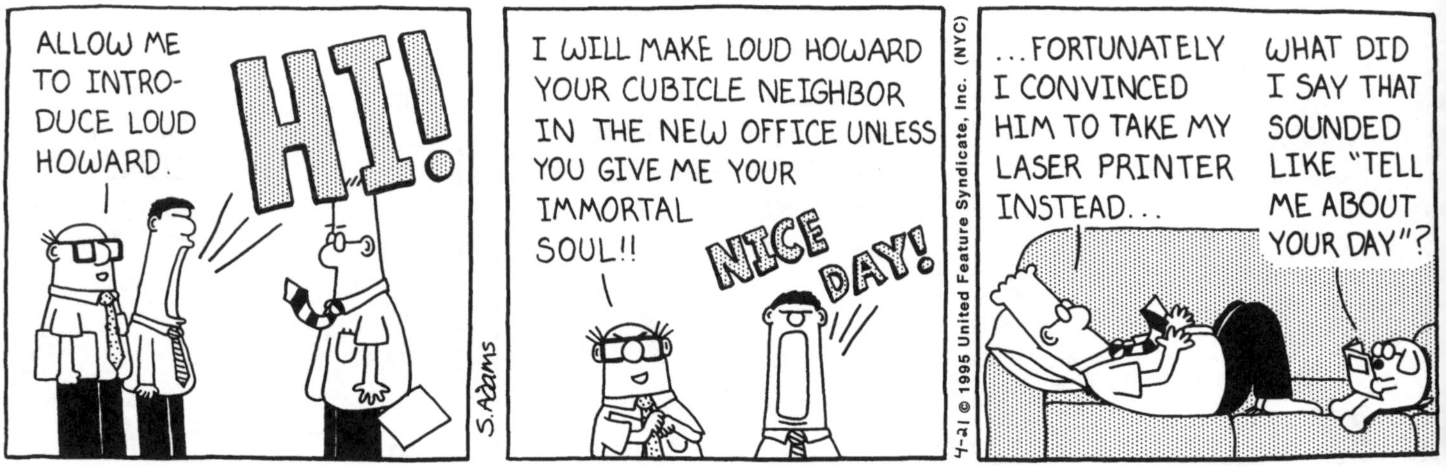
ALLOW ME TO INTRODUCE LOUD HOWARD.
HI!
S. Adams
I WILL MAKE LOUD HOWARD YOUR CUBICLE NEIGHBOR IN THE NEW OFFICE UNLESS YOU GIVE ME YOUR IMMORTAL SOUL!!
NICE DAY!
...FORTUNATELY I CONVINCED HIM TO TAKE MY LASER PRINTER INSTEAD...
WHAT DID I SAY THAT SOUNDED LIKE "TELL ME ABOUT YOUR DAY"?

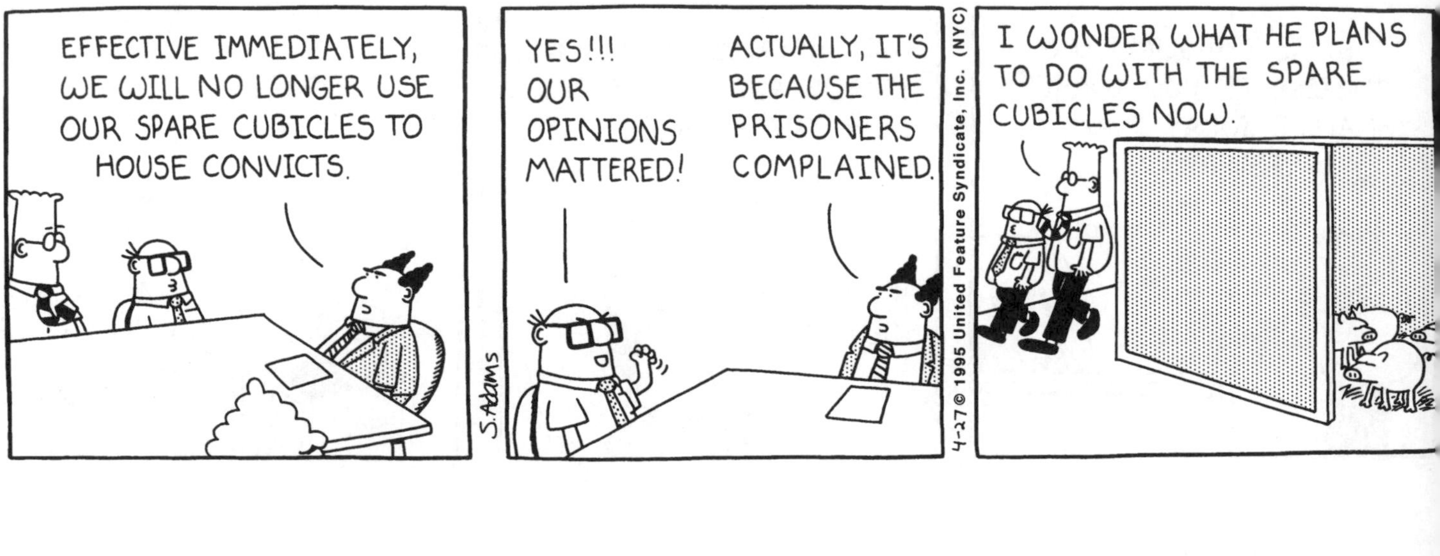
EFFECTIVE IMMEDIATELY, WE WILL NO LONGER USE OUR SPARE CUBICLES TO HOUSE CONVICTS.
S. Adams
YES!!! OUR OPINIONS MATTERED!
ACTUALLY, IT'S BECAUSE THE PRISONERS COMPLAINED.
I WONDER WHAT HE PLANS TO DO WITH THE SPARE CUBICLES NOW.

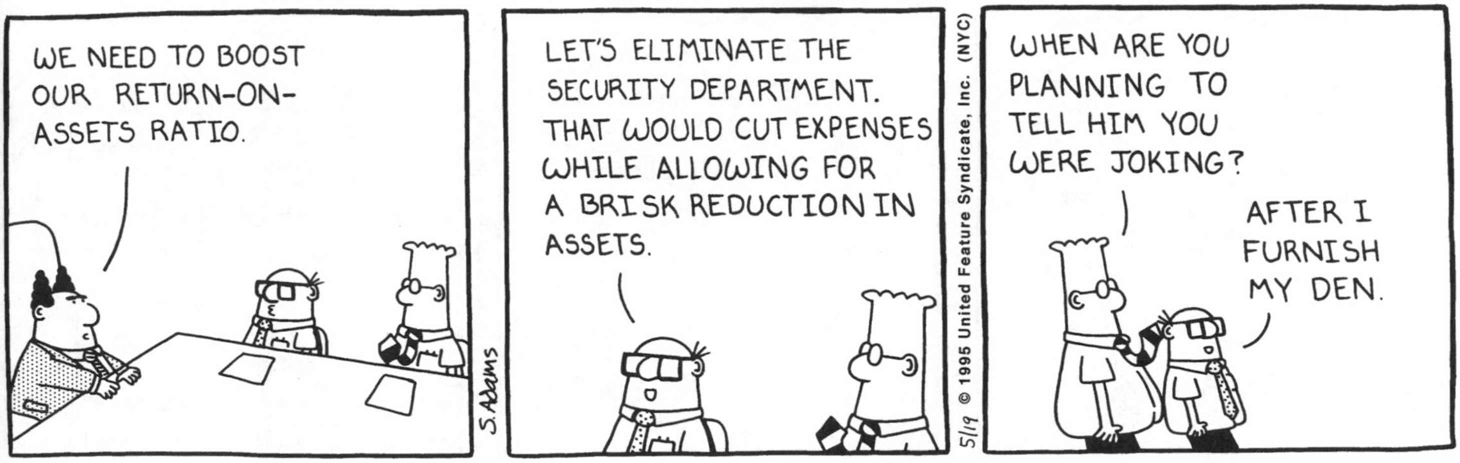
WE NEED TO BOOST OUR RETURN-ON-ASSETS RATIO.
LET'S ELIMINATE THE SECURITY DEPARTMENT. THAT WOULD CUT EXPENSES WHILE ALLOWING FOR A BRISK REDUCTION IN ASSETS.
WHEN ARE YOU PLANNING TO TELL HIM YOU WERE JOKING?
AFTER I FURNISH MY DEN.
S. Adams
5/19 © 1995 United Feature Syndicate, Inc. (NYC)

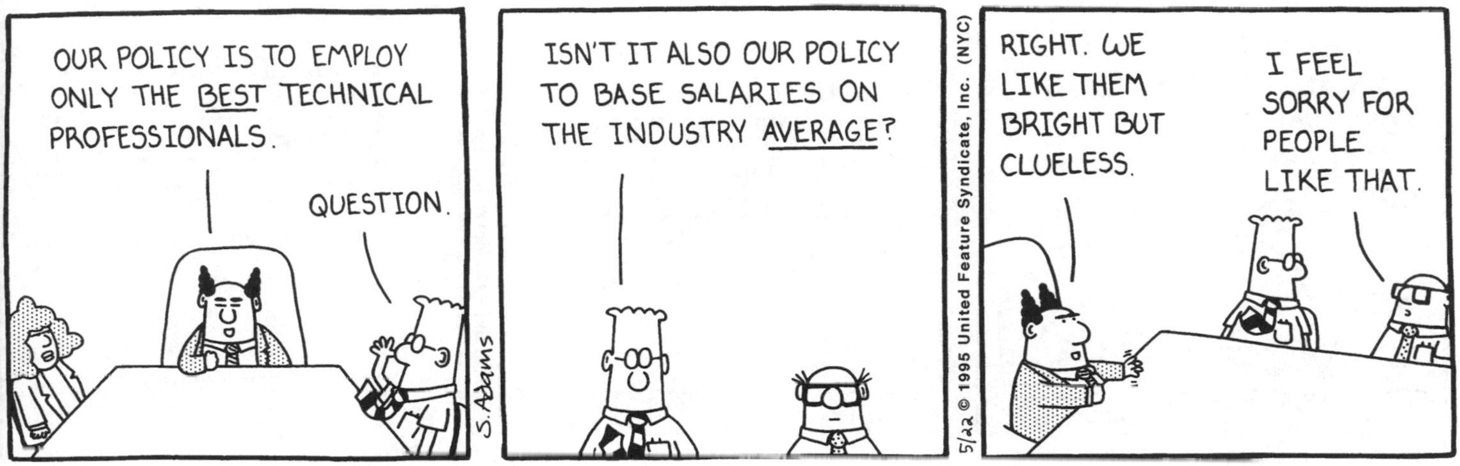
OUR POLICY IS TO EMPLOY ONLY THE BEST TECHNICAL PROFESSIONALS.
QUESTION.
ISN'T IT ALSO OUR POLICY TO BASE SALARIES ON THE INDUSTRY AVERAGE?
RIGHT. WE LIKE THEM BRIGHT BUT CLUELESS.
I FEEL SORRY FOR PEOPLE LIKE THAT.
S. Adams
5/22 © 1995 United Feature Syndicate, Inc. (NYC)

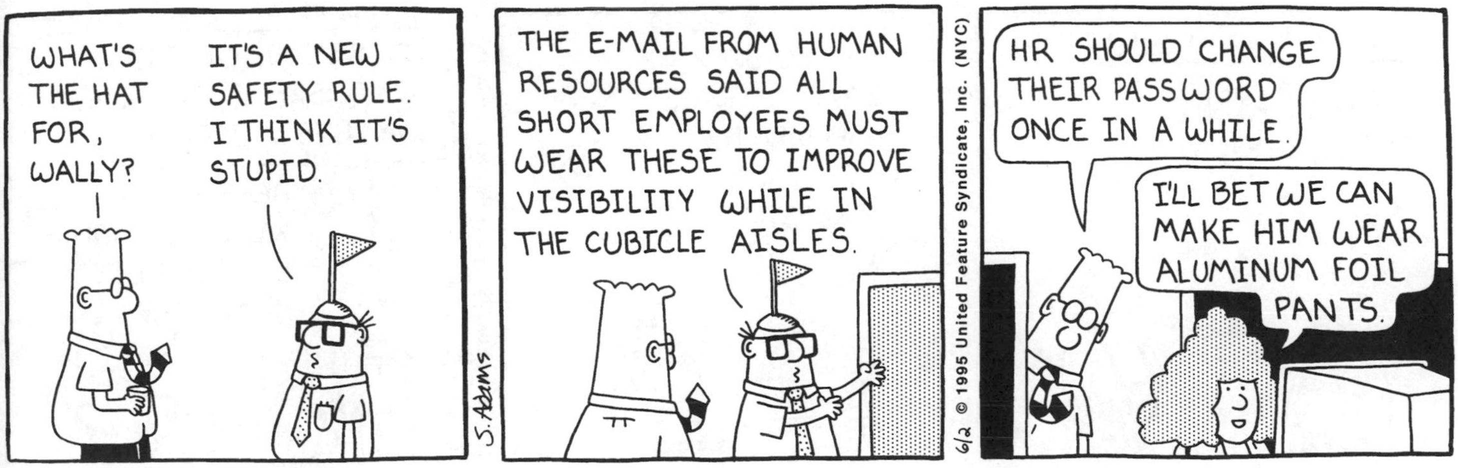
WHAT'S THE HAT FOR, WALLY?
IT'S A NEW SAFETY RULE. I THINK IT'S STUPID.
THE E-MAIL FROM HUMAN RESOURCES SAID ALL SHORT EMPLOYEES MUST WEAR THESE TO IMPROVE VISIBILITY WHILE IN THE CUBICLE AISLES.
HR SHOULD CHANGE THEIR PASSWORD ONCE IN A WHILE.
I'LL BET WE CAN MAKE HIM WEAR ALUMINUM FOIL PANTS.
S. Adams
6/2 © 1995 United Feature Syndicate, Inc. (NYC)

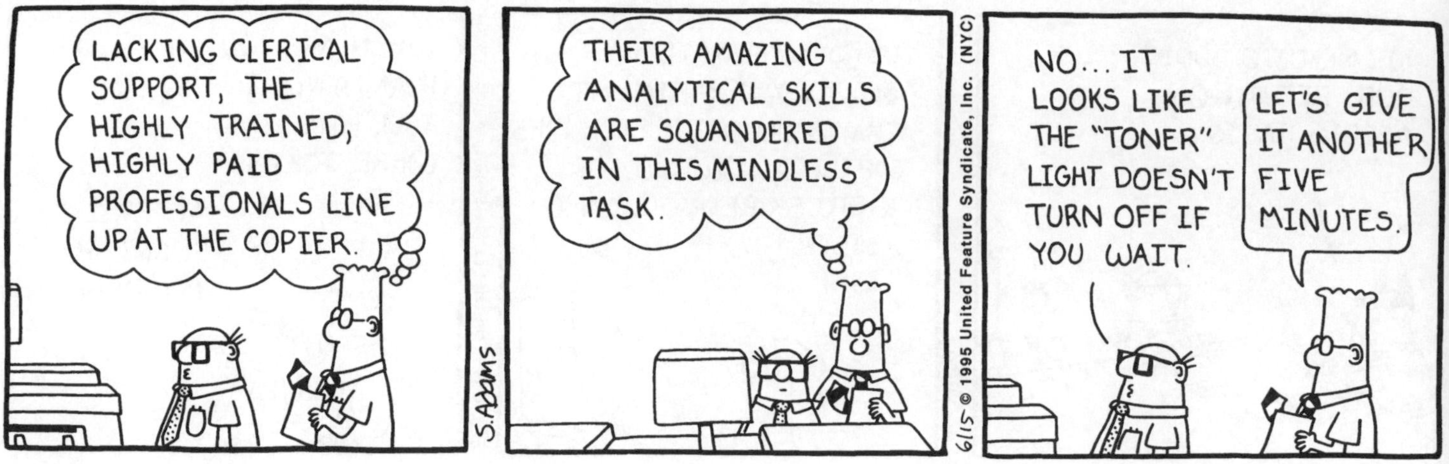
LACKING CLERICAL SUPPORT, THE HIGHLY TRAINED, HIGHLY PAID PROFESSIONALS LINE UP AT THE COPIER.
S. Adams
THEIR AMAZING ANALYTICAL SKILLS ARE SQUANDERED IN THIS MINDLESS TASK.
6/15 © 1995 United Feature Syndicate, Inc. (NYC)
NO... IT LOOKS LIKE THE "TONER" LIGHT DOESN'T TURN OFF IF YOU WAIT.
LET'S GIVE IT ANOTHER FIVE MINUTES.

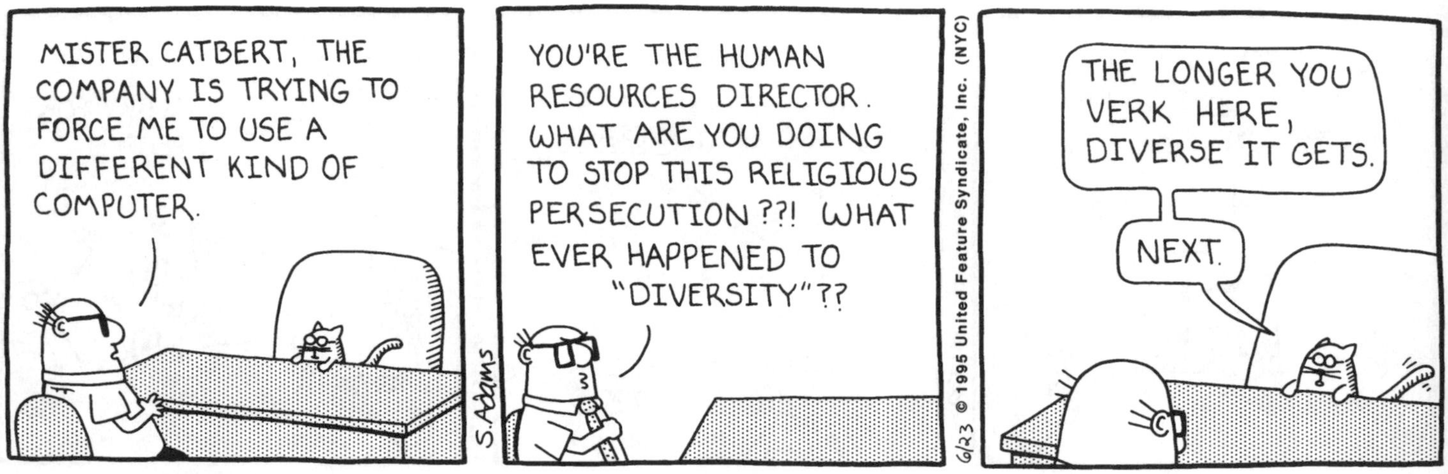
MISTER CATBERT, THE COMPANY IS TRYING TO FORCE ME TO USE A DIFFERENT KIND OF COMPUTER.
S. Adams
YOU'RE THE HUMAN RESOURCES DIRECTOR. WHAT ARE YOU DOING TO STOP THIS RELIGIOUS PERSECUTION??! WHAT EVER HAPPENED TO "DIVERSITY"??
6/23 © 1995 United Feature Syndicate, Inc. (NYC)
THE LONGER YOU VERK HERE, DIVERSE IT GETS.
NEXT.

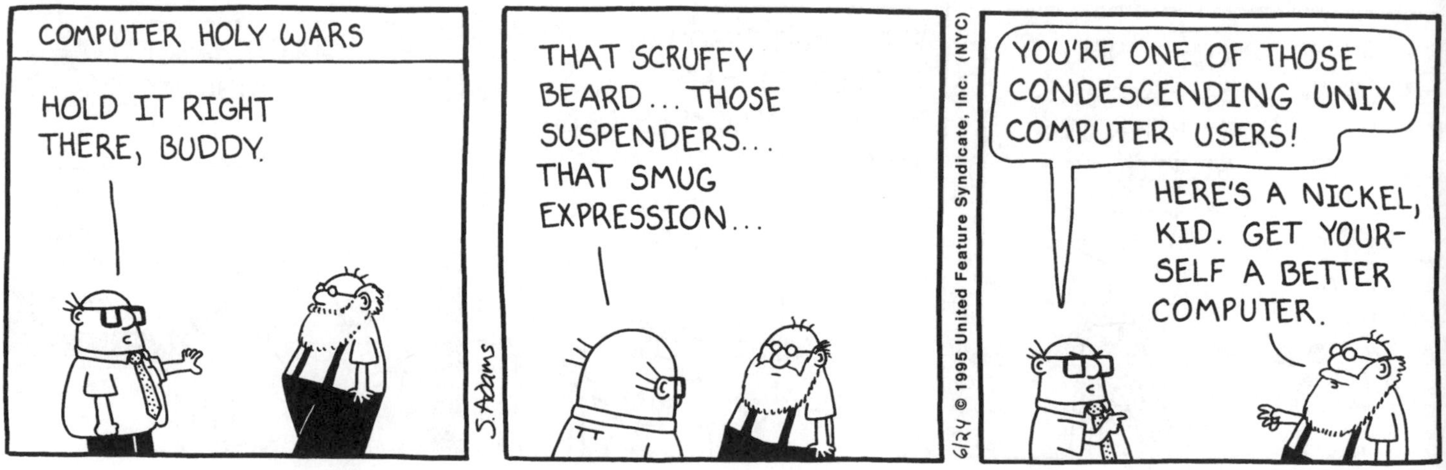
COMPUTER HOLY WARS
HOLD IT RIGHT THERE, BUDDY.
S. Adams
THAT SCRUFFY BEARD... THOSE SUSPENDERS... THAT SMUG EXPRESSION...
6/24 © 1995 United Feature Syndicate, Inc. (NYC)
YOU'RE ONE OF THOSE CONDESCENDING UNIX COMPUTER USERS!
HERE'S A NICKEL, KID. GET YOURSELF A BETTER COMPUTER.

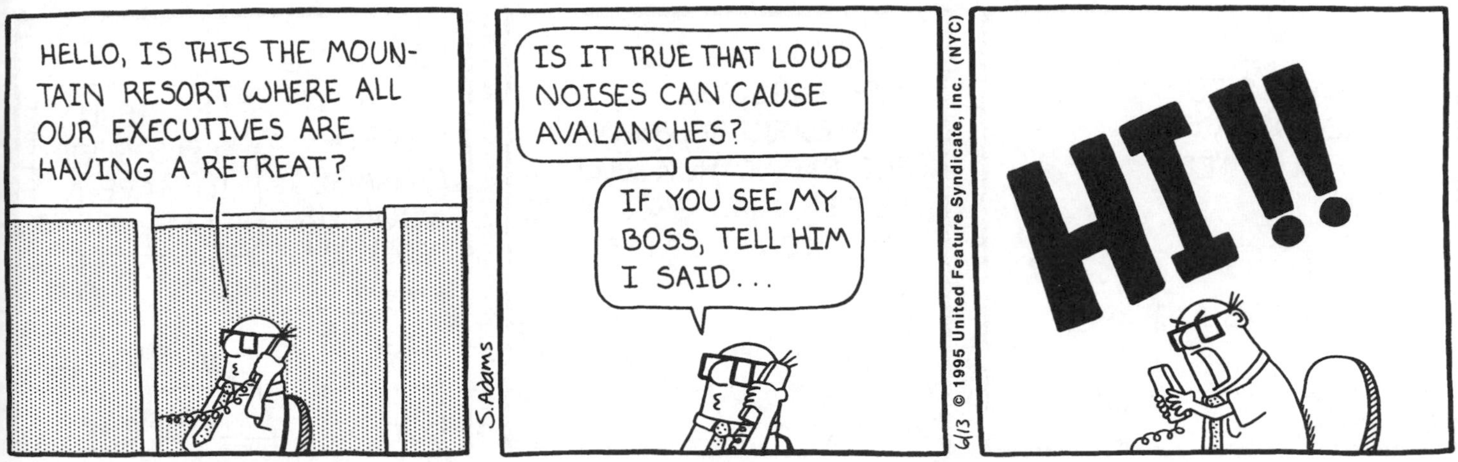
HELLO, IS THIS THE MOUNTAIN RESORT WHERE ALL OUR EXECUTIVES ARE HAVING A RETREAT?
S.Adams
IS IT TRUE THAT LOUD NOISES CAN CAUSE AVALANCHES?
IF YOU SEE MY BOSS, TELL HIM I SAID...
6/13 © 1995 United Feature Syndicate, Inc. (NYC)
HI!!

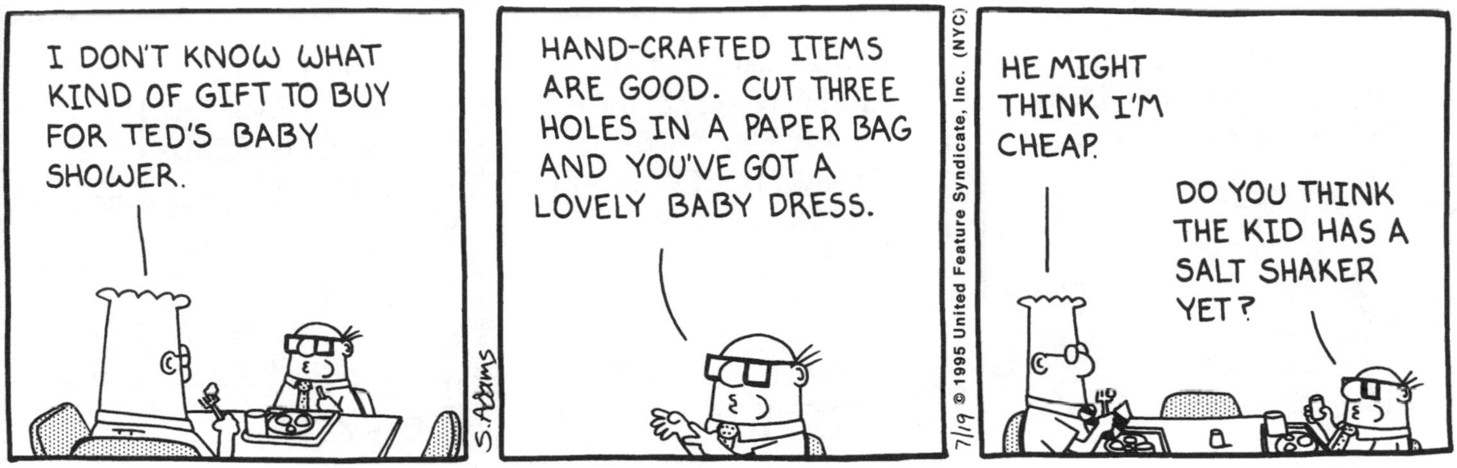
I DON'T KNOW WHAT KIND OF GIFT TO BUY FOR TED'S BABY SHOWER.
S.Adams
HAND-CRAFTED ITEMS ARE GOOD. CUT THREE HOLES IN A PAPER BAG AND YOU'VE GOT A LOVELY BABY DRESS.
7/19 © 1995 United Feature Syndicate, Inc. (NYC)
HE MIGHT THINK I'M CHEAP.
DO YOU THINK THE KID HAS A SALT SHAKER YET?

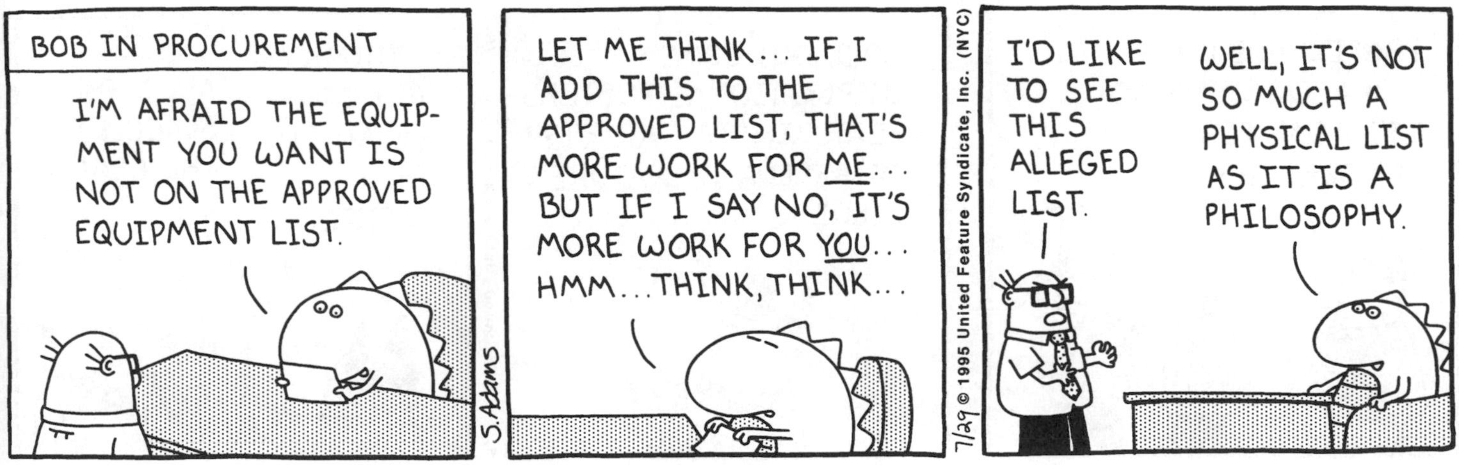
BOB IN PROCUREMENT
I'M AFRAID THE EQUIPMENT YOU WANT IS NOT ON THE APPROVED EQUIPMENT LIST.
S.Adams
LET ME THINK... IF I ADD THIS TO THE APPROVED LIST, THAT'S MORE WORK FOR ME... BUT IF I SAY NO, IT'S MORE WORK FOR YOU... HMM...THINK, THINK...
7/29 © 1995 United Feature Syndicate, Inc. (NYC)
I'D LIKE TO SEE THIS ALLEGED LIST.
WELL, IT'S NOT SO MUCH A PHYSICAL LIST AS IT IS A PHILOSOPHY.

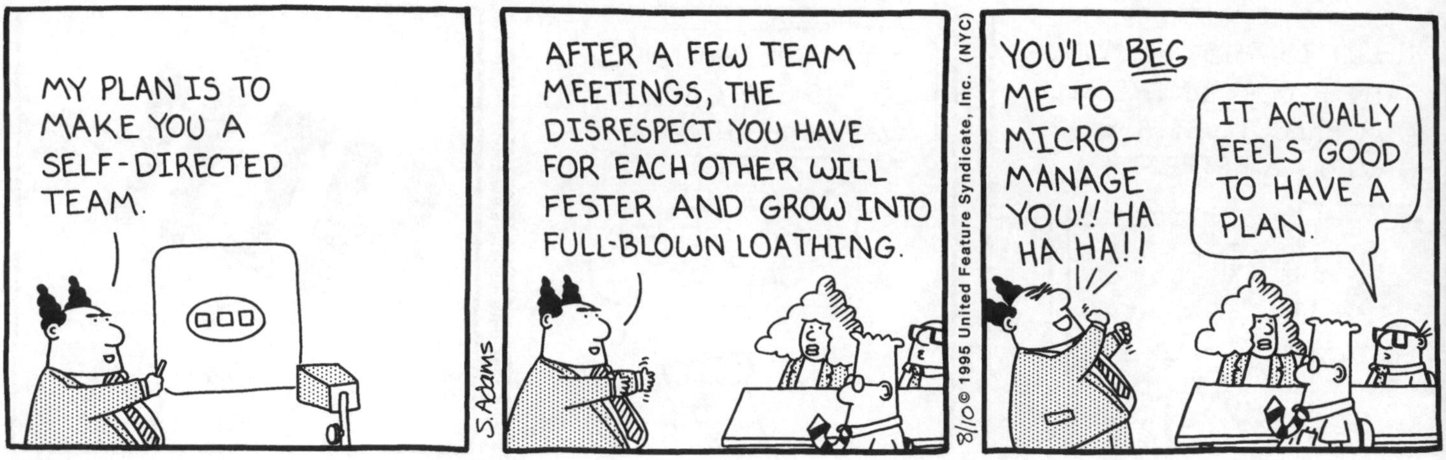
MY PLAN IS TO MAKE YOU A SELF-DIRECTED TEAM.
S.Adams
AFTER A FEW TEAM MEETINGS, THE DISRESPECT YOU HAVE FOR EACH OTHER WILL FESTER AND GROW INTO FULL-BLOWN LOATHING.
8/10 © 1995 United Feature Syndicate, Inc. (NYC)
YOU'LL BEG ME TO MICRO-MANAGE YOU!! HA HA HA!!
IT ACTUALLY FEELS GOOD TO HAVE A PLAN.

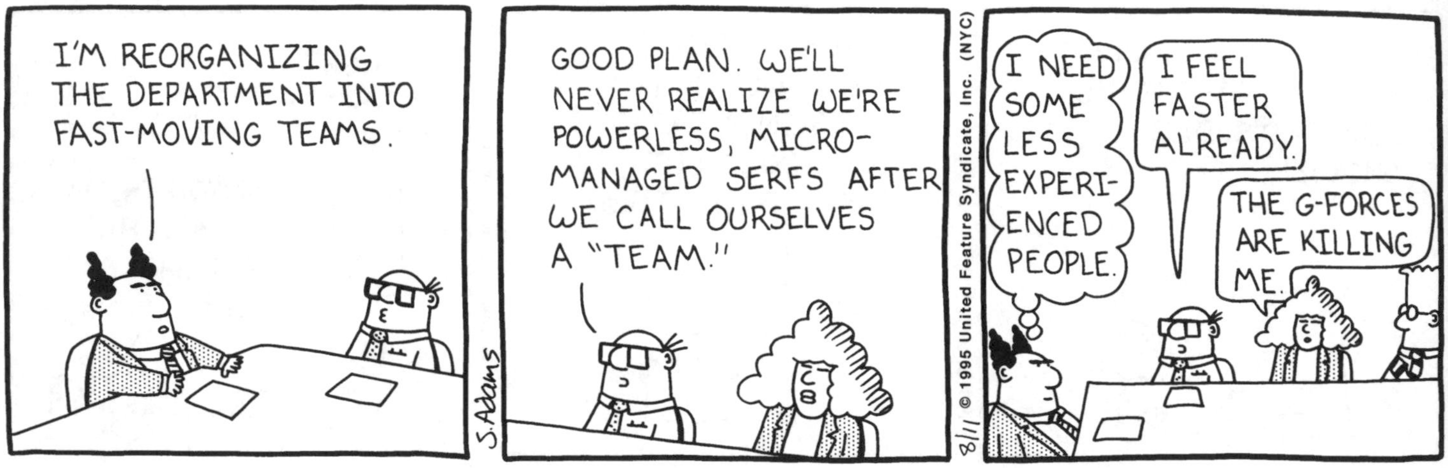
I'M REORGANIZING THE DEPARTMENT INTO FAST-MOVING TEAMS.
S.Adams
GOOD PLAN. WE'LL NEVER REALIZE WE'RE POWERLESS, MICRO-MANAGED SERFS AFTER WE CALL OURSELVES A "TEAM."
8/11 © 1995 United Feature Syndicate, Inc. (NYC)
I NEED SOME LESS EXPERI-ENCED PEOPLE.
I FEEL FASTER ALREADY.
THE G-FORCES ARE KILLING ME.

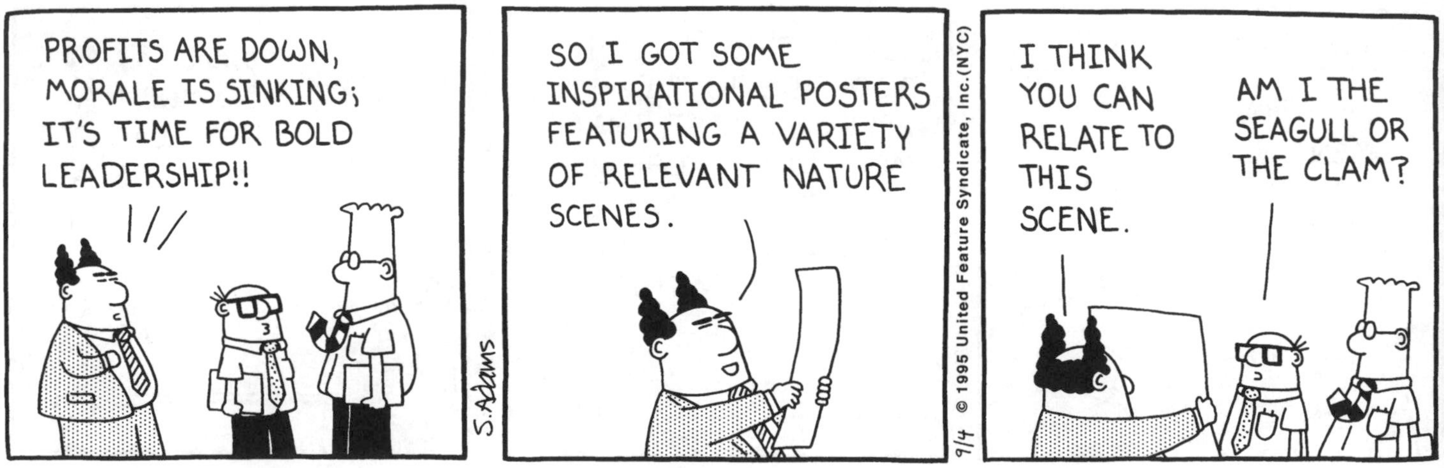
PROFITS ARE DOWN, MORALE IS SINKING; IT'S TIME FOR BOLD LEADERSHIP!!
S.Adams
SO I GOT SOME INSPIRATIONAL POSTERS FEATURING A VARIETY OF RELEVANT NATURE SCENES.
9/4 © 1995 United Feature Syndicate, Inc.(NYC)
I THINK YOU CAN RELATE TO THIS SCENE.
AM I THE SEAGULL OR THE CLAM?

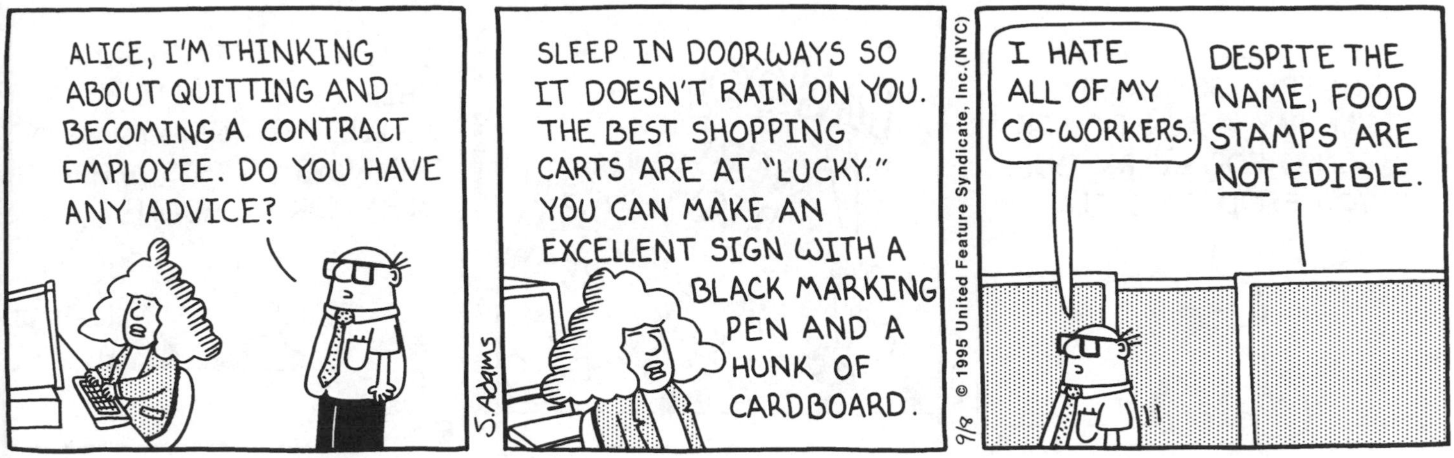
ALICE, I'M THINKING ABOUT QUITTING AND BECOMING A CONTRACT EMPLOYEE. DO YOU HAVE ANY ADVICE?
S. Adams
SLEEP IN DOORWAYS SO IT DOESN'T RAIN ON YOU. THE BEST SHOPPING CARTS ARE AT "LUCKY." YOU CAN MAKE AN EXCELLENT SIGN WITH A BLACK MARKING PEN AND A HUNK OF CARDBOARD.
9/8 © 1995 United Feature Syndicate, Inc.(NYC)
I HATE ALL OF MY CO-WORKERS.
DESPITE THE NAME, FOOD STAMPS ARE NOT EDIBLE.

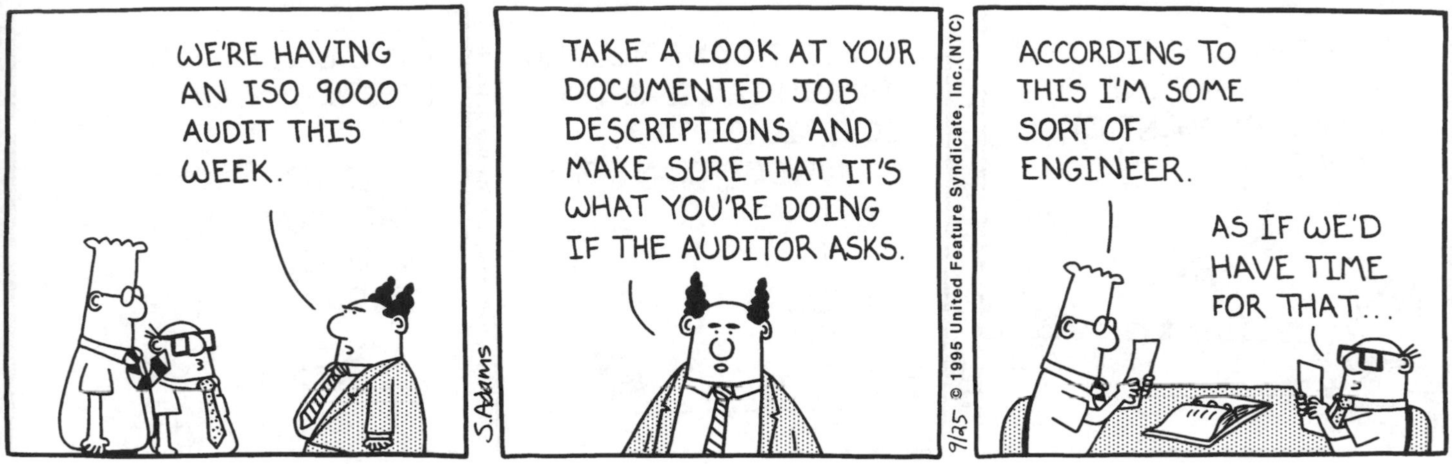
WE'RE HAVING AN ISO 9000 AUDIT THIS WEEK.
S. Adams
TAKE A LOOK AT YOUR DOCUMENTED JOB DESCRIPTIONS AND MAKE SURE THAT IT'S WHAT YOU'RE DOING IF THE AUDITOR ASKS.
9/25 © 1995 United Feature Syndicate, Inc.(NYC)
ACCORDING TO THIS I'M SOME SORT OF ENGINEER.
AS IF WE'D HAVE TIME FOR THAT...

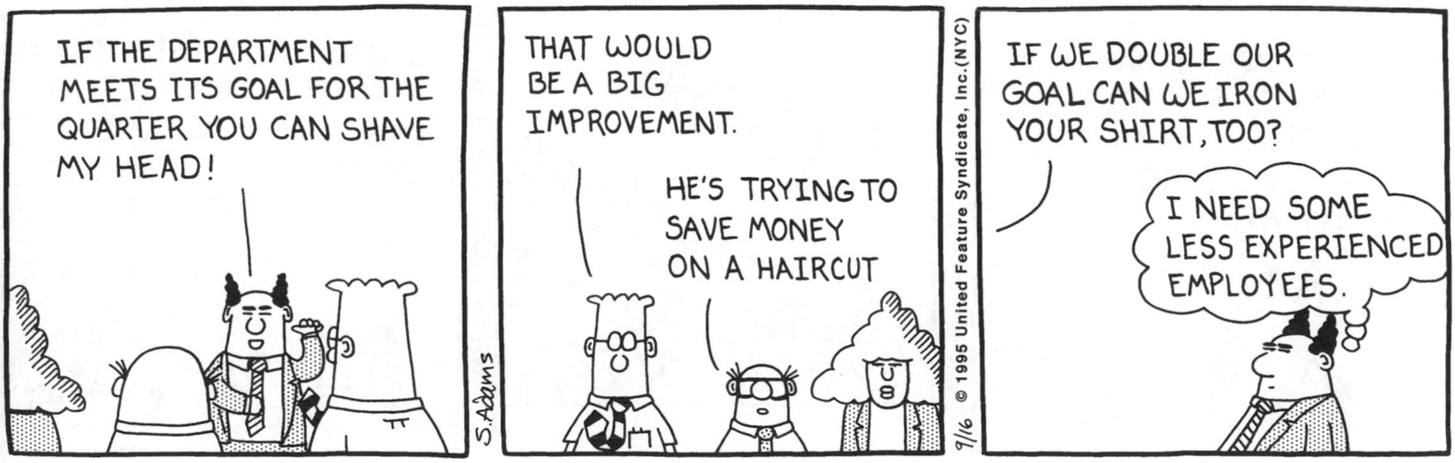
IF THE DEPARTMENT MEETS ITS GOAL FOR THE QUARTER YOU CAN SHAVE MY HEAD!
S. Adams
THAT WOULD BE A BIG IMPROVEMENT.
HE'S TRYING TO SAVE MONEY ON A HAIRCUT
9/16 © 1995 United Feature Syndicate, Inc.(NYC)
IF WE DOUBLE OUR GOAL CAN WE IRON YOUR SHIRT, TOO?
I NEED SOME LESS EXPERIENCED EMPLOYEES.

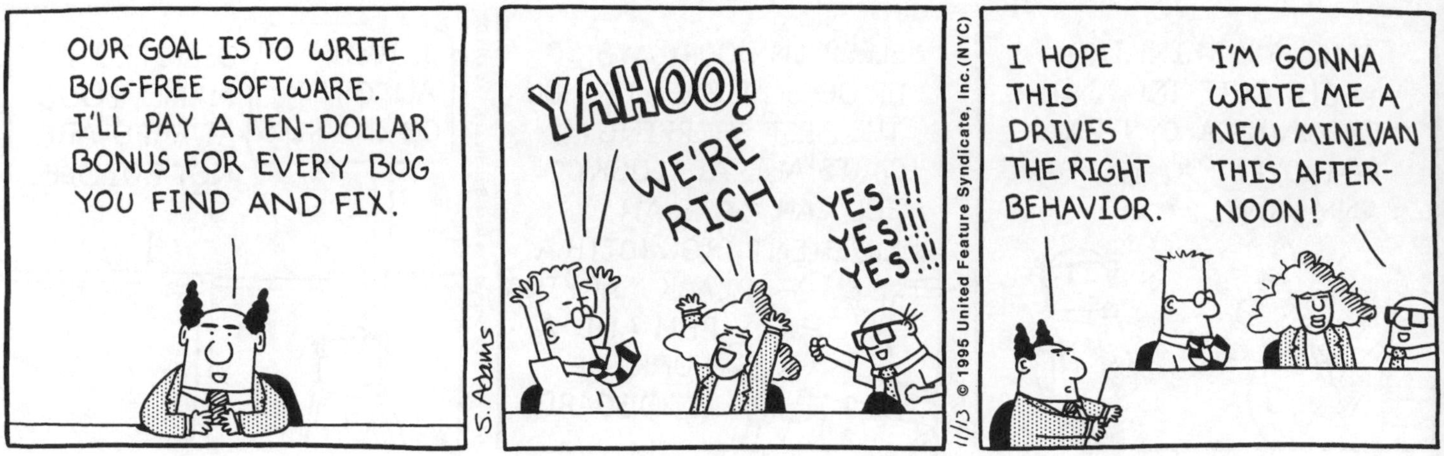
OUR GOAL IS TO WRITE BUG-FREE SOFTWARE. I'LL PAY A TEN-DOLLAR BONUS FOR EVERY BUG YOU FIND AND FIX.
S. Adams
YAHOO!
WE'RE RICH
YES!!! YES!!! YES!!!
11/13 © 1995 United Feature Syndicate, Inc.(NYC)
I HOPE THIS DRIVES THE RIGHT BEHAVIOR.
I'M GONNA WRITE ME A NEW MINIVAN THIS AFTERNOON!

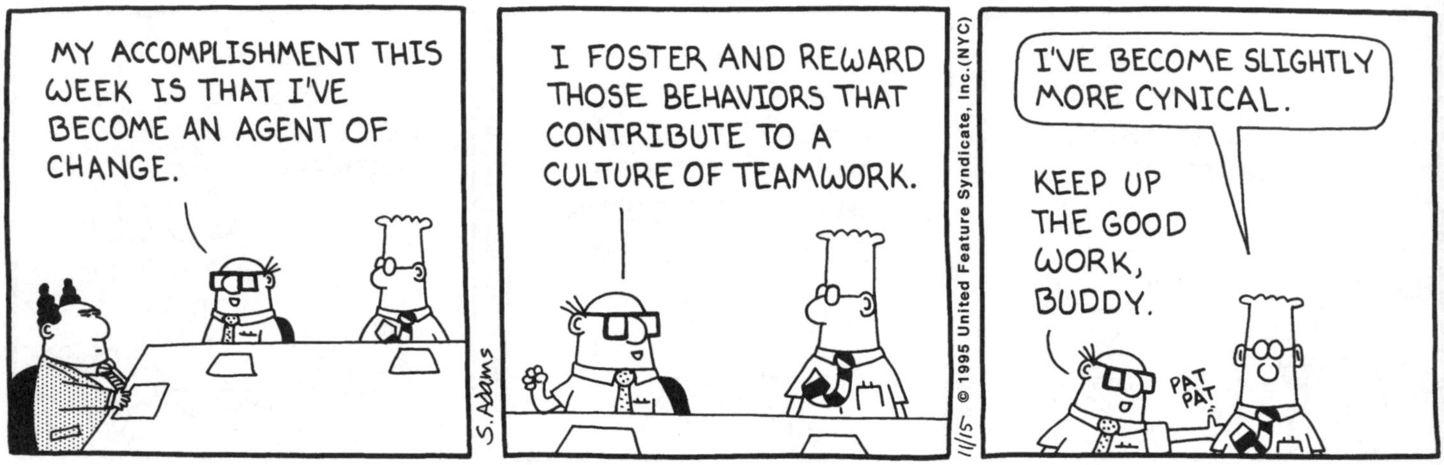
MY ACCOMPLISHMENT THIS WEEK IS THAT I'VE BECOME AN AGENT OF CHANGE.
S. Adams
I FOSTER AND REWARD THOSE BEHAVIORS THAT CONTRIBUTE TO A CULTURE OF TEAMWORK.
11/15 © 1995 United Feature Syndicate, Inc.(NYC)
I'VE BECOME SLIGHTLY MORE CYNICAL.
KEEP UP THE GOOD WORK, BUDDY.
PAT PAT

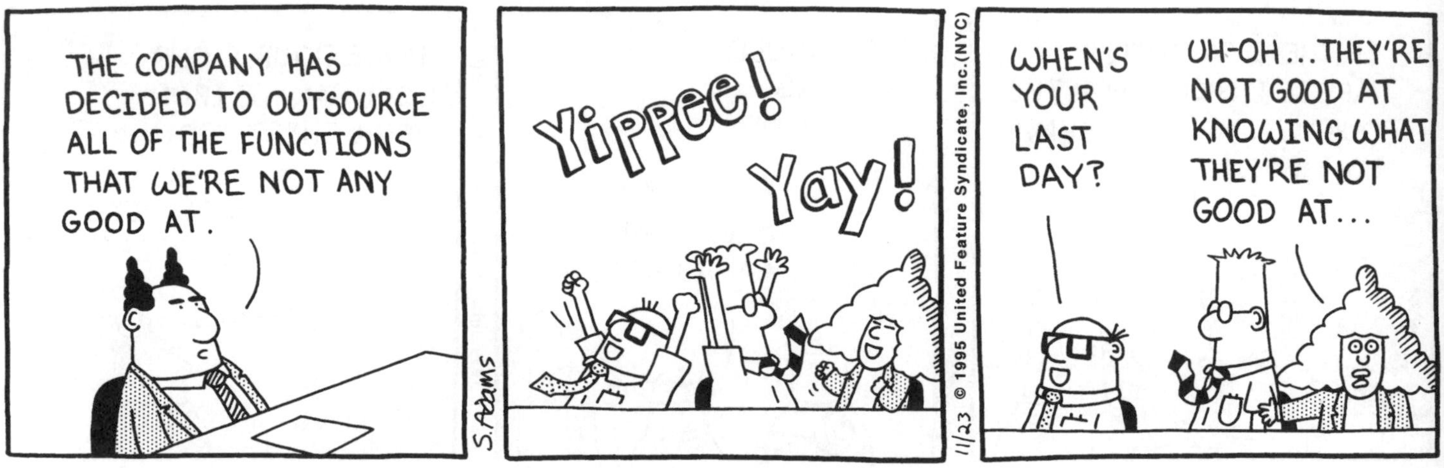
THE COMPANY HAS DECIDED TO OUTSOURCE ALL OF THE FUNCTIONS THAT WE'RE NOT ANY GOOD AT.
S. Adams
Yippee!
Yay!
11/23 © 1995 United Feature Syndicate, Inc.(NYC)
WHEN'S YOUR LAST DAY?
UH-OH... THEY'RE NOT GOOD AT KNOWING WHAT THEY'RE NOT GOOD AT...

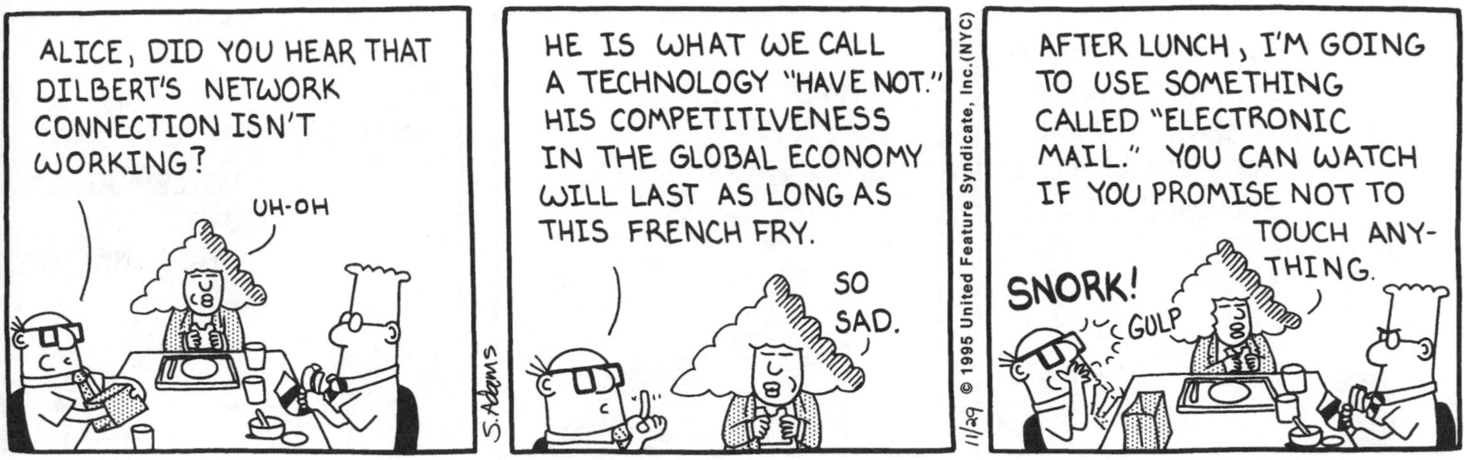
ALICE, DID YOU HEAR THAT DILBERT'S NETWORK CONNECTION ISN'T WORKING?
UH-OH
S. Adams
HE IS WHAT WE CALL A TECHNOLOGY "HAVE NOT." HIS COMPETITIVENESS IN THE GLOBAL ECONOMY WILL LAST AS LONG AS THIS FRENCH FRY.
SO SAD.
11/29 © 1995 United Feature Syndicate, Inc.(NYC)
AFTER LUNCH, I'M GOING TO USE SOMETHING CALLED "ELECTRONIC MAIL." YOU CAN WATCH IF YOU PROMISE NOT TO TOUCH ANYTHING.
SNORK!
GULP

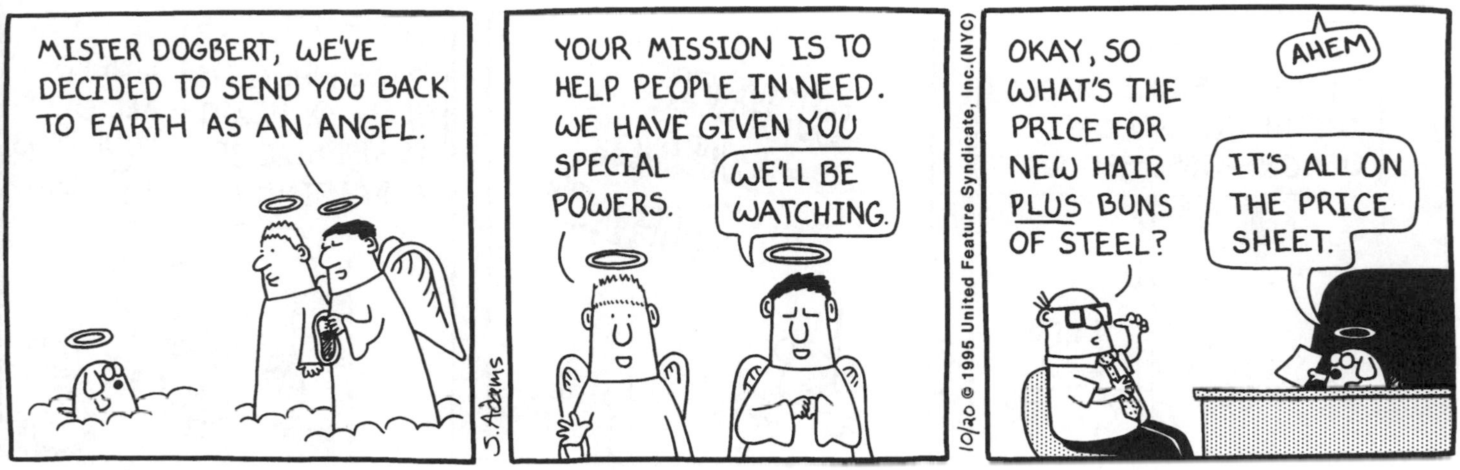
MISTER DOGBERT, WE'VE DECIDED TO SEND YOU BACK TO EARTH AS AN ANGEL.
S. Adams
YOUR MISSION IS TO HELP PEOPLE IN NEED. WE HAVE GIVEN YOU SPECIAL POWERS.
WE'LL BE WATCHING.
10/20 © 1995 United Feature Syndicate, Inc.(NYC)
OKAY, SO WHAT'S THE PRICE FOR NEW HAIR PLUS BUNS OF STEEL?
AHEM
IT'S ALL ON THE PRICE SHEET.

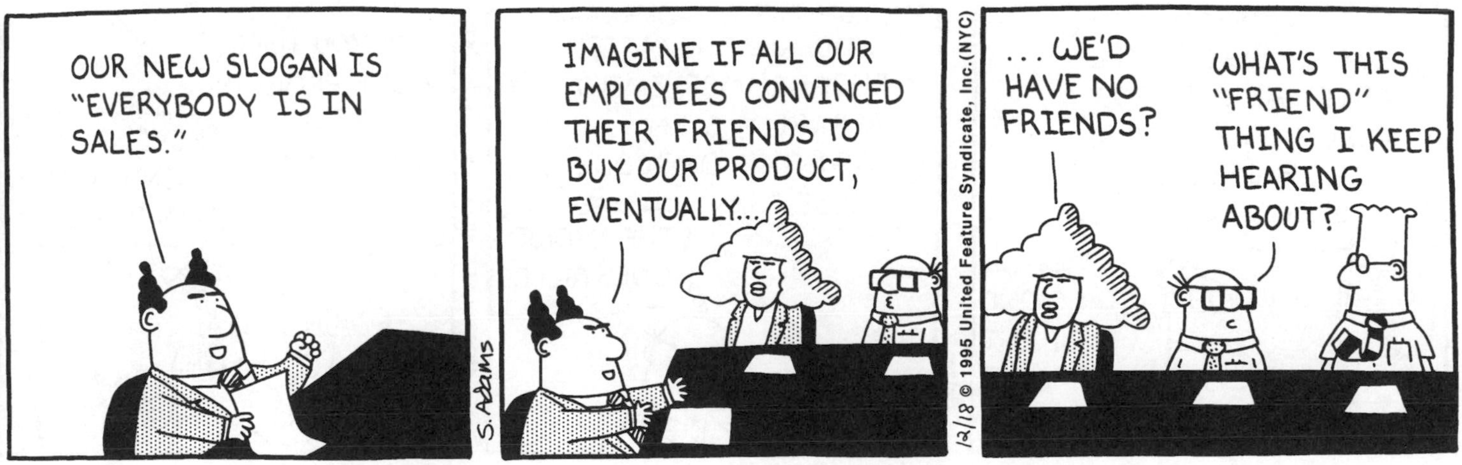
OUR NEW SLOGAN IS "EVERYBODY IS IN SALES."
S. Adams
IMAGINE IF ALL OUR EMPLOYEES CONVINCED THEIR FRIENDS TO BUY OUR PRODUCT, EVENTUALLY...
12/18 © 1995 United Feature Syndicate, Inc.(NYC)
... WE'D HAVE NO FRIENDS?
WHAT'S THIS "FRIEND" THING I KEEP HEARING ABOUT?

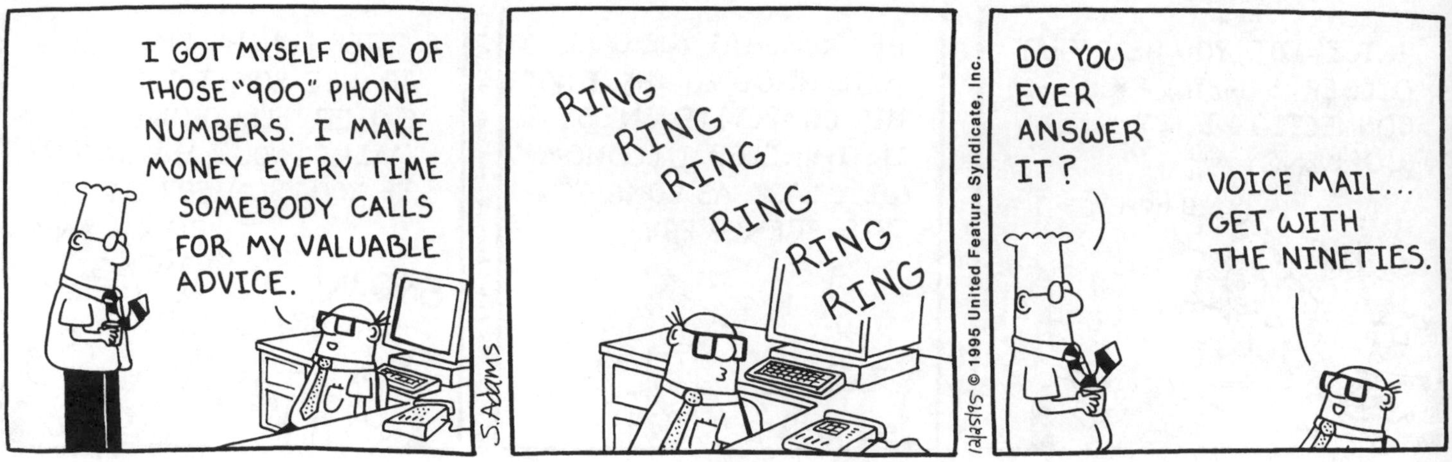
I GOT MYSELF ONE OF THOSE "900" PHONE NUMBERS. I MAKE MONEY EVERY TIME SOMEBODY CALLS FOR MY VALUABLE ADVICE.
S. Adams
RING RING RING RING RING RING
12/25/95 © 1995 United Feature Syndicate, Inc.
DO YOU EVER ANSWER IT?
VOICE MAIL... GET WITH THE NINETIES.

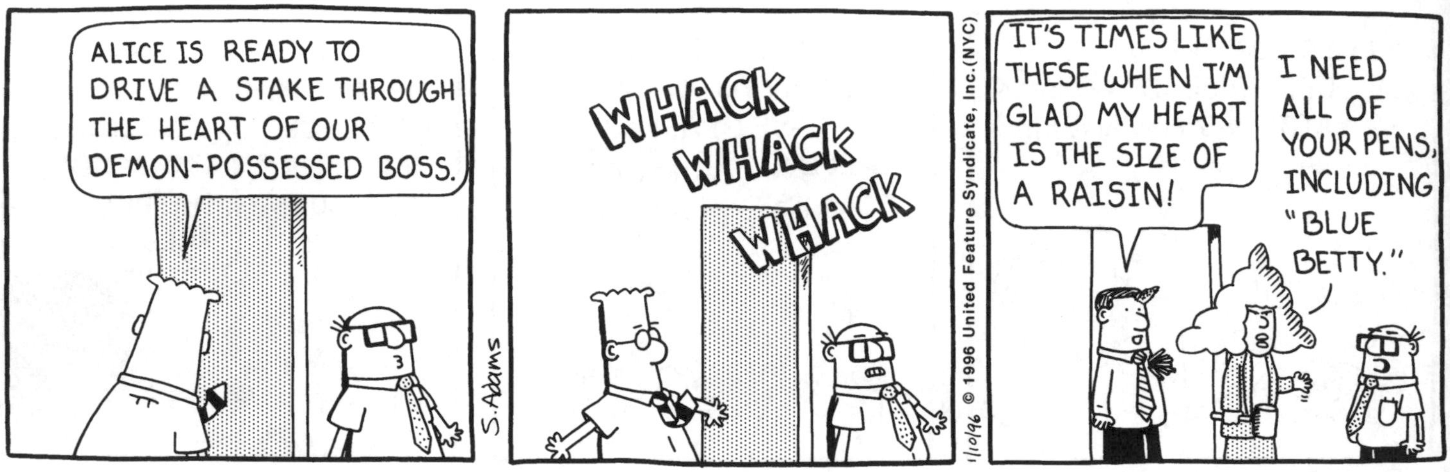
ALICE IS READY TO DRIVE A STAKE THROUGH THE HEART OF OUR DEMON-POSSESSED BOSS.
S. Adams
WHACK WHACK WHACK
1/10/96 © 1996 United Feature Syndicate, Inc.(NYC)
IT'S TIMES LIKE THESE WHEN I'M GLAD MY HEART IS THE SIZE OF A RAISIN!
I NEED ALL OF YOUR PENS, INCLUDING "BLUE BETTY."

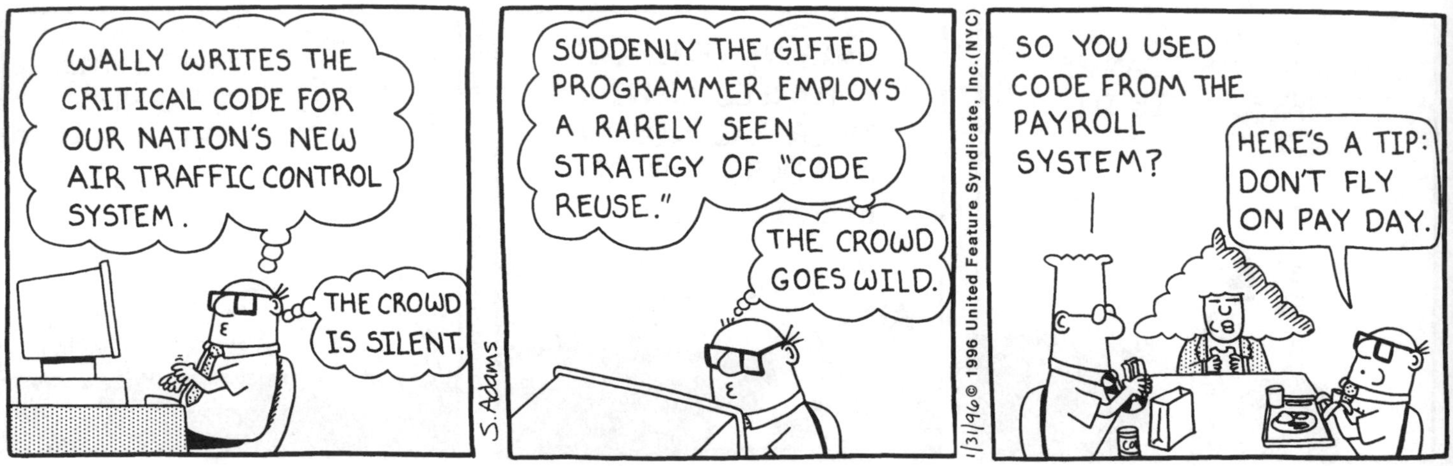
WALLY WRITES THE CRITICAL CODE FOR OUR NATION'S NEW AIR TRAFFIC CONTROL SYSTEM.
THE CROWD IS SILENT.
S. Adams
SUDDENLY THE GIFTED PROGRAMMER EMPLOYS A RARELY SEEN STRATEGY OF "CODE REUSE."
THE CROWD GOES WILD.
1/31/96 © 1996 United Feature Syndicate, Inc.(NYC)
SO YOU USED CODE FROM THE PAYROLL SYSTEM?
HERE'S A TIP: DON'T FLY ON PAY DAY.

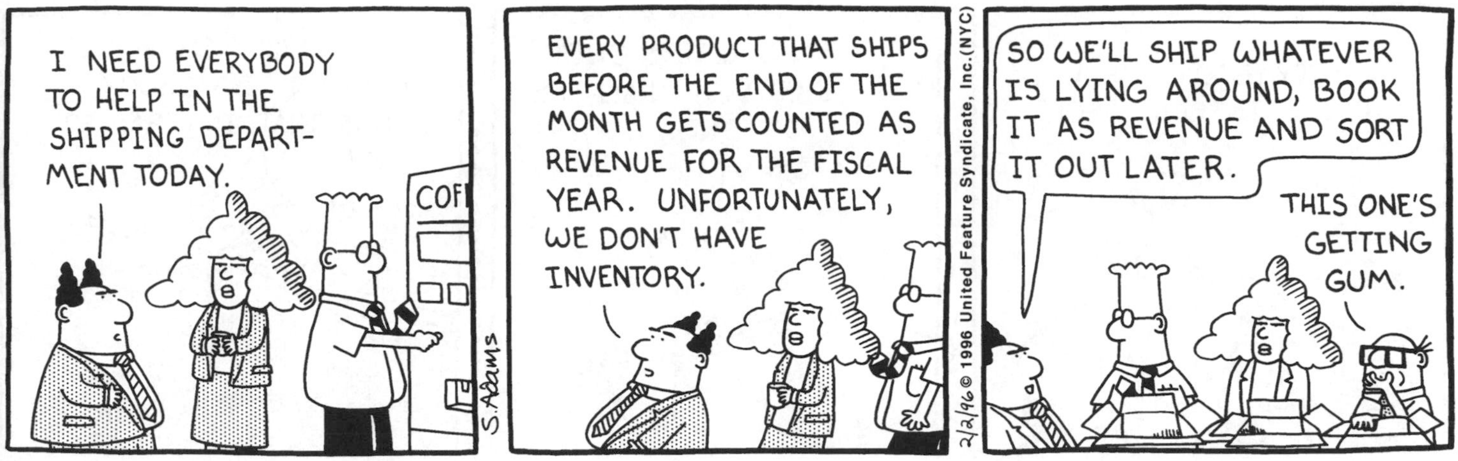
I NEED EVERYBODY TO HELP IN THE SHIPPING DEPARTMENT TODAY.
COF
EVERY PRODUCT THAT SHIPS BEFORE THE END OF THE MONTH GETS COUNTED AS REVENUE FOR THE FISCAL YEAR. UNFORTUNATELY, WE DON'T HAVE INVENTORY.
SO WE'LL SHIP WHATEVER IS LYING AROUND, BOOK IT AS REVENUE AND SORT IT OUT LATER.
THIS ONE'S GETTING GUM.
S. Adams
2/2/96 © 1996 United Feature Syndicate, Inc.(NYC)

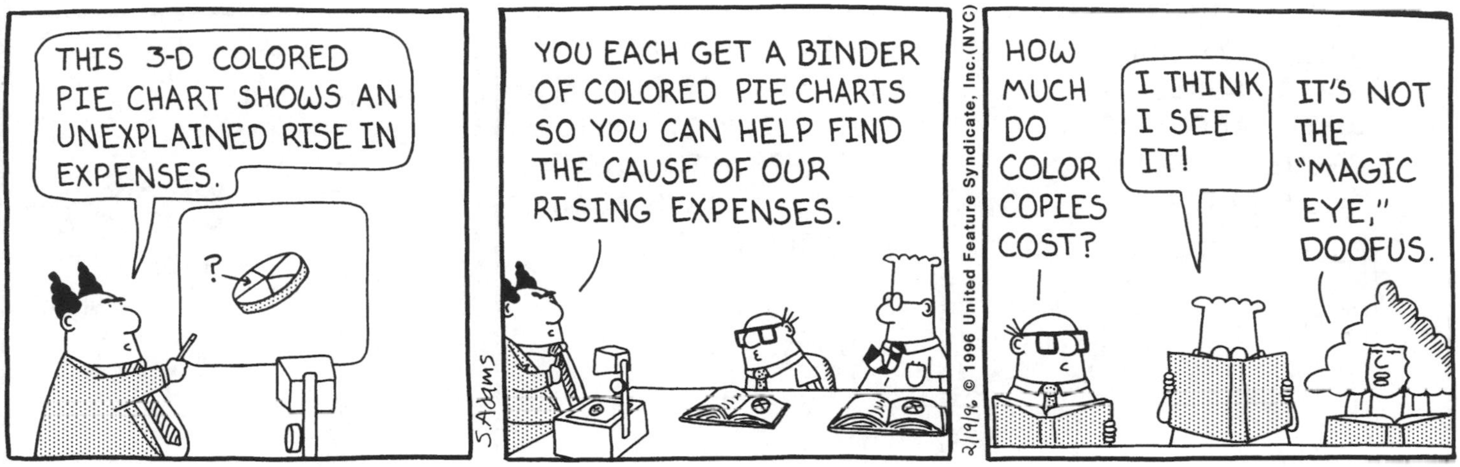
THIS 3-D COLORED PIE CHART SHOWS AN UNEXPLAINED RISE IN EXPENSES.
?
YOU EACH GET A BINDER OF COLORED PIE CHARTS SO YOU CAN HELP FIND THE CAUSE OF OUR RISING EXPENSES.
HOW MUCH DO COLOR COPIES COST?
I THINK I SEE IT!
IT'S NOT THE "MAGIC EYE," DOOFUS.
S. Adams
2/19/96 © 1996 United Feature Syndicate, Inc.(NYC)

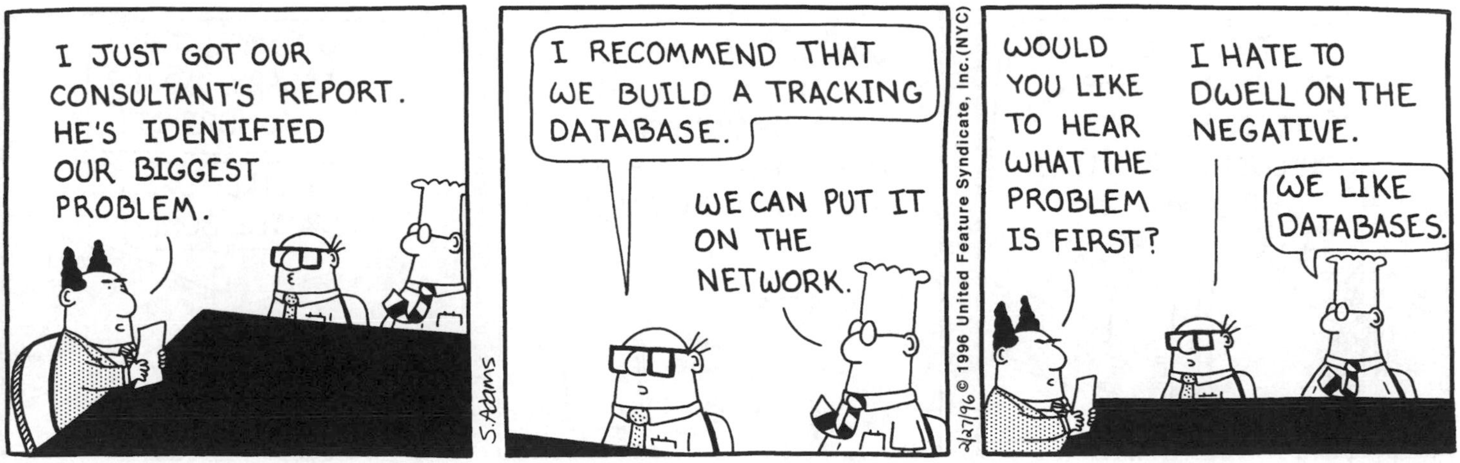
I JUST GOT OUR CONSULTANT'S REPORT. HE'S IDENTIFIED OUR BIGGEST PROBLEM.
I RECOMMEND THAT WE BUILD A TRACKING DATABASE.
WE CAN PUT IT ON THE NETWORK.
WOULD YOU LIKE TO HEAR WHAT THE PROBLEM IS FIRST?
I HATE TO DWELL ON THE NEGATIVE.
WE LIKE DATABASES.
S. Adams
2/27/96 © 1996 United Feature Syndicate, Inc.(NYC)

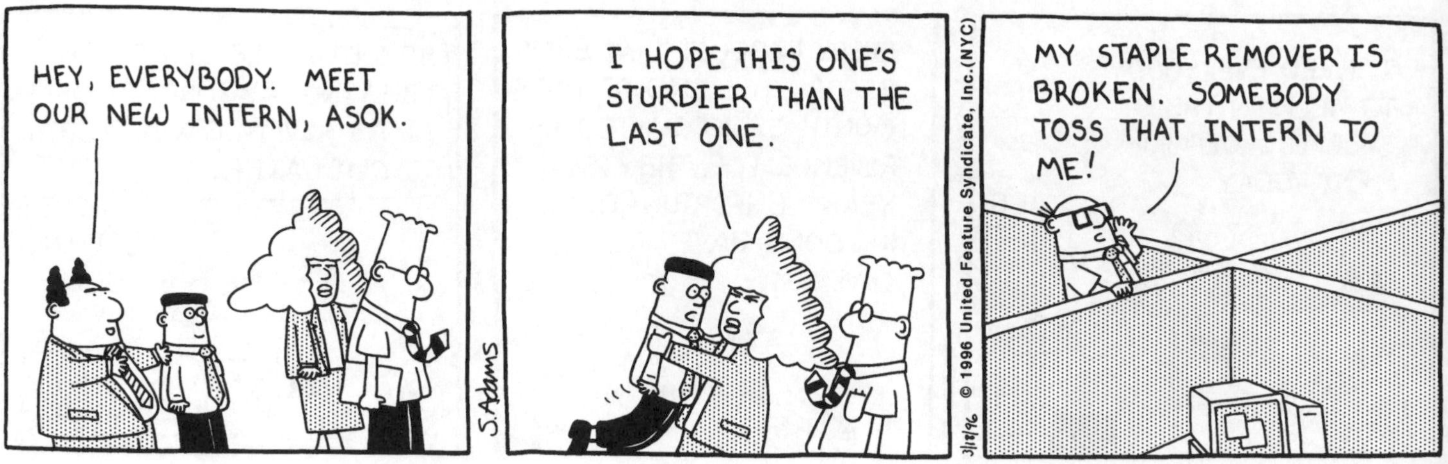
HEY, EVERYBODY. MEET OUR NEW INTERN, ASOK.
S.Adams
I HOPE THIS ONE'S STURDIER THAN THE LAST ONE.
3/18/96 © 1996 United Feature Syndicate, Inc.(NYC)
MY STAPLE REMOVER IS BROKEN. SOMEBODY TOSS THAT INTERN TO ME!

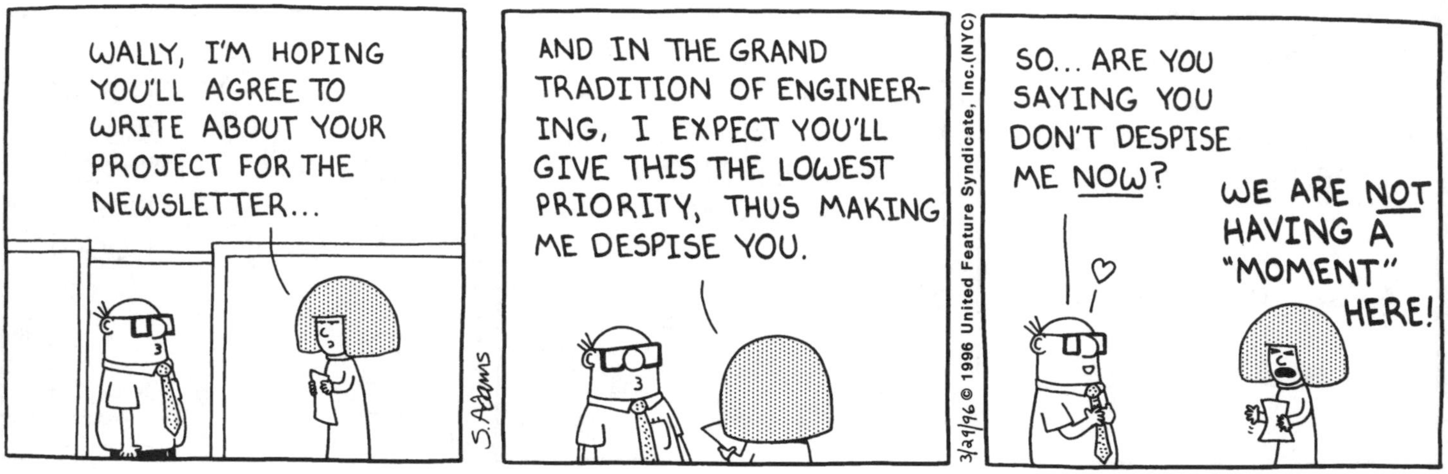
WALLY, I'M HOPING YOU'LL AGREE TO WRITE ABOUT YOUR PROJECT FOR THE NEWSLETTER...
S.Adams
AND IN THE GRAND TRADITION OF ENGINEERING, I EXPECT YOU'LL GIVE THIS THE LOWEST PRIORITY, THUS MAKING ME DESPISE YOU.
3/29/96 © 1996 United Feature Syndicate, Inc.(NYC)
SO... ARE YOU SAYING YOU DON'T DESPISE ME NOW?
WE ARE NOT HAVING A "MOMENT" HERE!

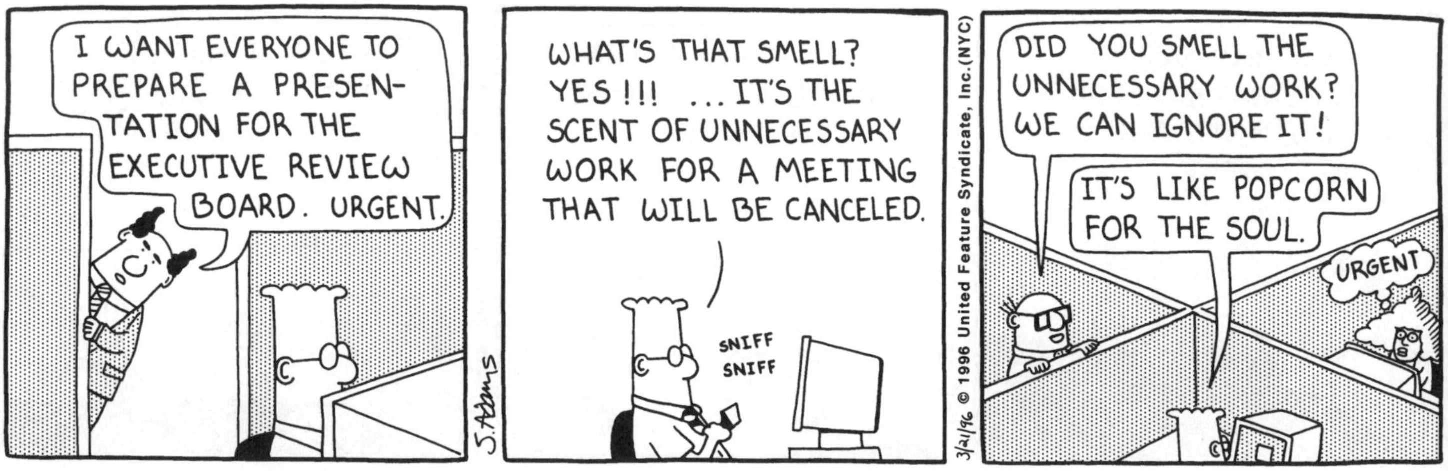
I WANT EVERYONE TO PREPARE A PRESENTATION FOR THE EXECUTIVE REVIEW BOARD. URGENT.
S.Adams
WHAT'S THAT SMELL? YES !!! ...IT'S THE SCENT OF UNNECESSARY WORK FOR A MEETING THAT WILL BE CANCELED.
SNIFF
SNIFF
3/21/96 © 1996 United Feature Syndicate, Inc.(NYC)
DID YOU SMELL THE UNNECESSARY WORK? WE CAN IGNORE IT!
IT'S LIKE POPCORN FOR THE SOUL.
URGENT

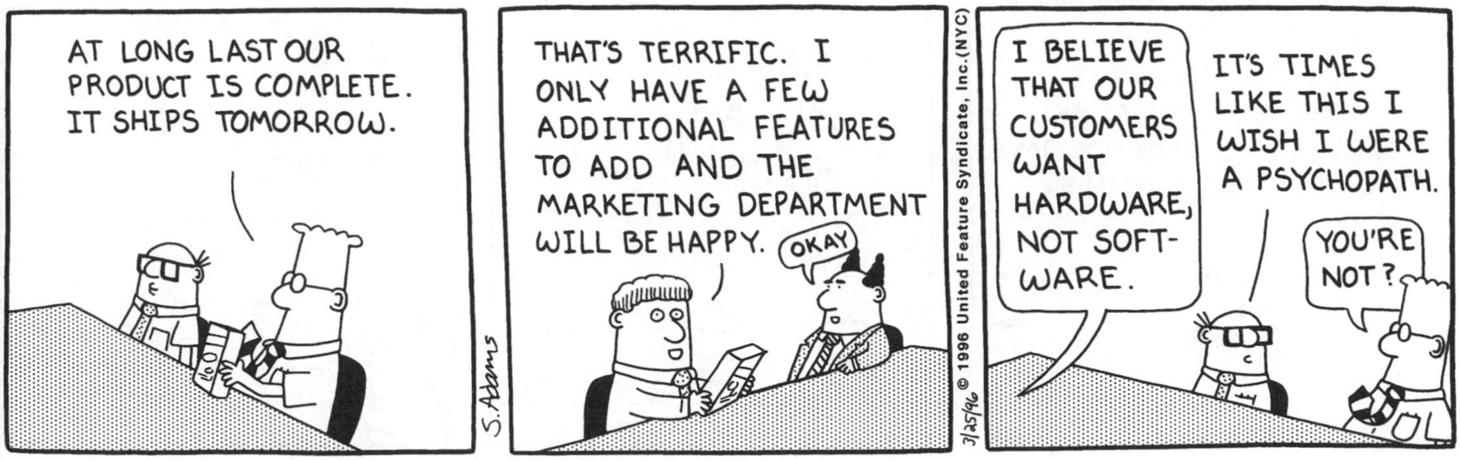
AT LONG LAST OUR PRODUCT IS COMPLETE. IT SHIPS TOMORROW.
S. Adams
THAT'S TERRIFIC. I ONLY HAVE A FEW ADDITIONAL FEATURES TO ADD AND THE MARKETING DEPARTMENT WILL BE HAPPY.
OKAY
3/25/96 © 1996 United Feature Syndicate, Inc.(NYC)
I BELIEVE THAT OUR CUSTOMERS WANT HARDWARE, NOT SOFT-WARE.
IT'S TIMES LIKE THIS I WISH I WERE A PSYCHOPATH.
YOU'RE NOT?

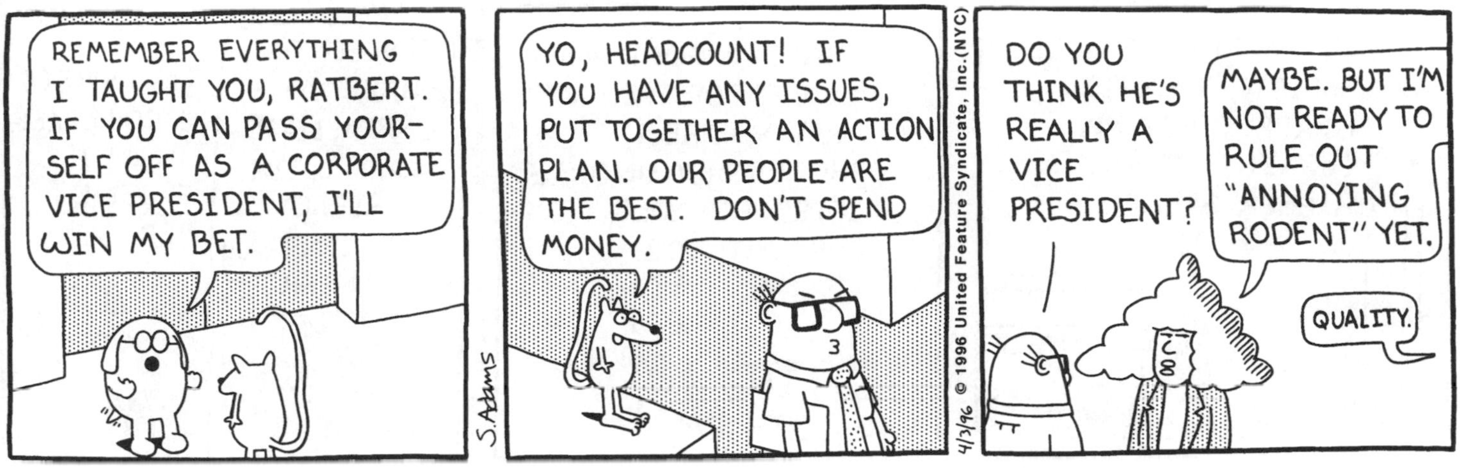
REMEMBER EVERYTHING I TAUGHT YOU, RATBERT. IF YOU CAN PASS YOUR-SELF OFF AS A CORPORATE VICE PRESIDENT, I'LL WIN MY BET.
S. Adams
YO, HEADCOUNT! IF YOU HAVE ANY ISSUES, PUT TOGETHER AN ACTION PLAN. OUR PEOPLE ARE THE BEST. DON'T SPEND MONEY.
4/3/96 © 1996 United Feature Syndicate, Inc.(NYC)
DO YOU THINK HE'S REALLY A VICE PRESIDENT?
MAYBE. BUT I'M NOT READY TO RULE OUT "ANNOYING RODENT" YET.
QUALITY.

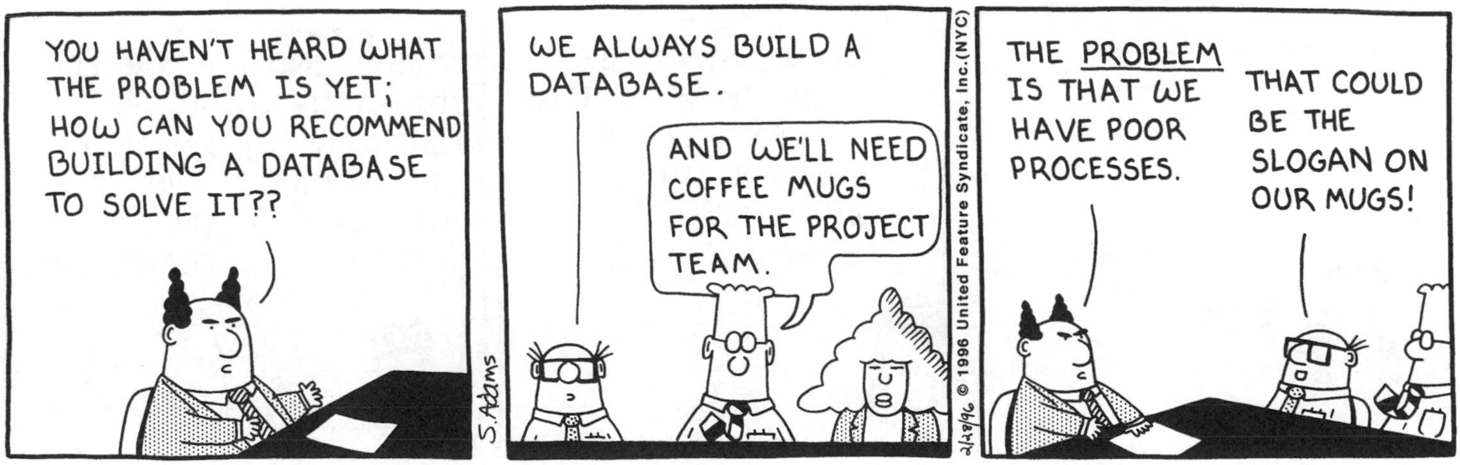
YOU HAVEN'T HEARD WHAT THE PROBLEM IS YET; HOW CAN YOU RECOMMEND BUILDING A DATABASE TO SOLVE IT??
S. Adams
WE ALWAYS BUILD A DATABASE.
AND WE'LL NEED COFFEE MUGS FOR THE PROJECT TEAM.
2/28/96 © 1996 United Feature Syndicate, Inc.(NYC)
THE PROBLEM IS THAT WE HAVE POOR PROCESSES.
THAT COULD BE THE SLOGAN ON OUR MUGS!

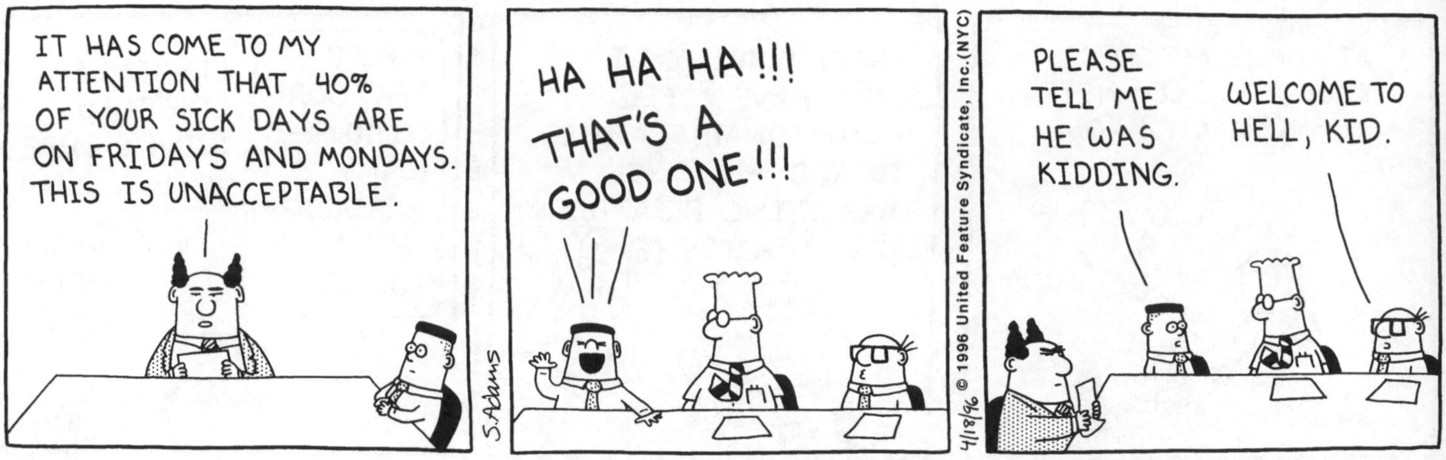
IT HAS COME TO MY ATTENTION THAT 40% OF YOUR SICK DAYS ARE ON FRIDAYS AND MONDAYS. THIS IS UNACCEPTABLE.
HA HA HA !!! THAT'S A GOOD ONE !!!
PLEASE TELL ME HE WAS KIDDING.
WELCOME TO HELL, KID.
S. Adams
4/18/96 © 1996 United Feature Syndicate, Inc.(NYC)

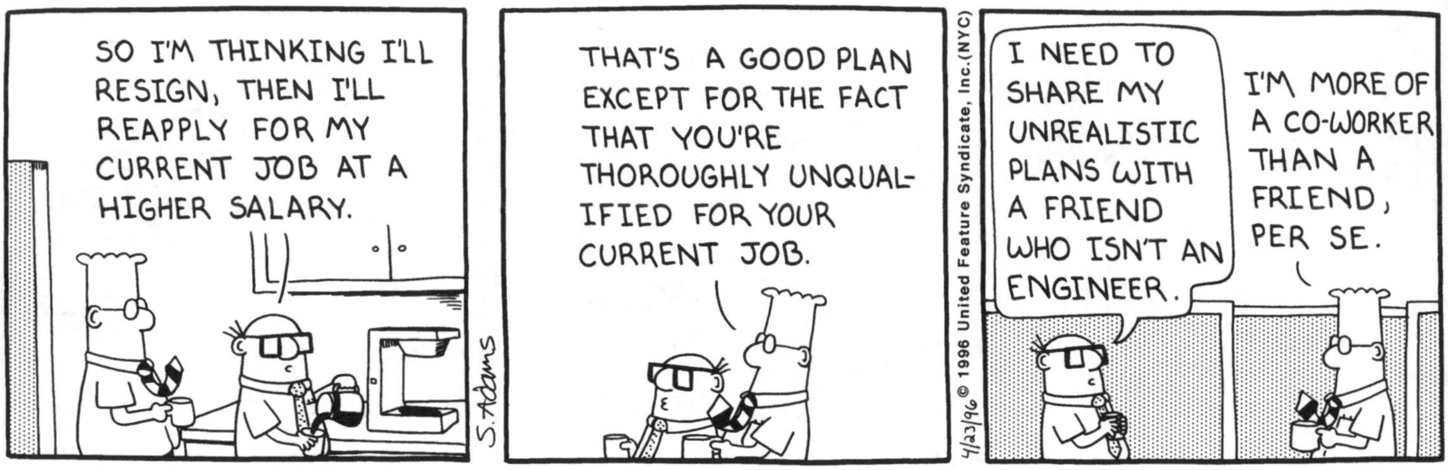
SO I'M THINKING I'LL RESIGN, THEN I'LL REAPPLY FOR MY CURRENT JOB AT A HIGHER SALARY.
THAT'S A GOOD PLAN EXCEPT FOR THE FACT THAT YOU'RE THOROUGHLY UNQUALIFIED FOR YOUR CURRENT JOB.
I NEED TO SHARE MY UNREALISTIC PLANS WITH A FRIEND WHO ISN'T AN ENGINEER.
I'M MORE OF A CO-WORKER THAN A FRIEND, PER SE.
S. Adams
4/23/96 © 1996 United Feature Syndicate, Inc.(NYC)

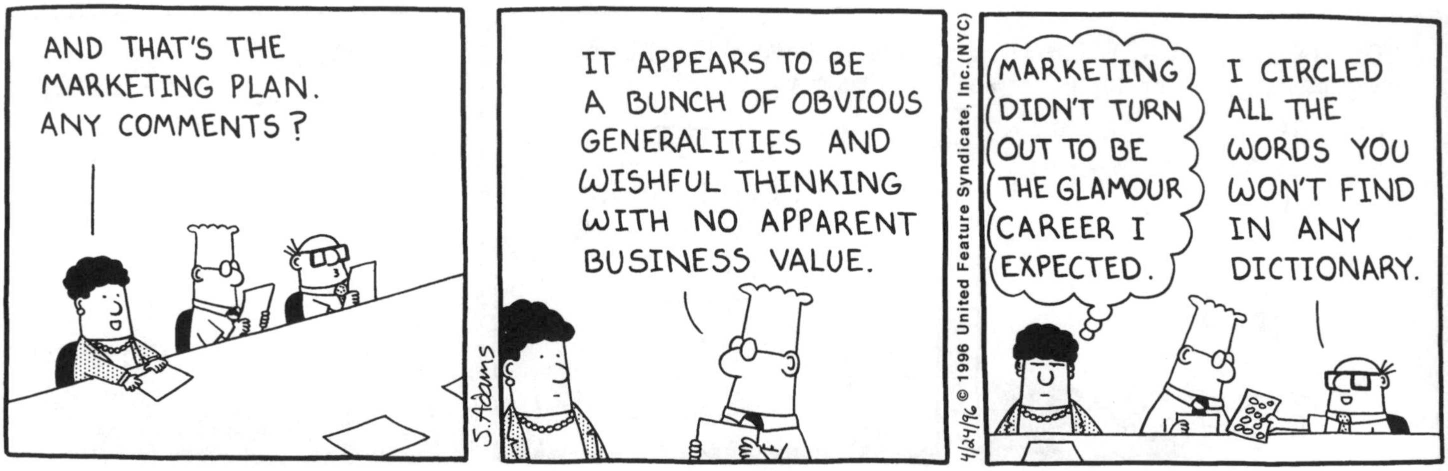
AND THAT'S THE MARKETING PLAN. ANY COMMENTS ?
IT APPEARS TO BE A BUNCH OF OBVIOUS GENERALITIES AND WISHFUL THINKING WITH NO APPARENT BUSINESS VALUE.
MARKETING DIDN'T TURN OUT TO BE THE GLAMOUR CAREER I EXPECTED.
I CIRCLED ALL THE WORDS YOU WON'T FIND IN ANY DICTIONARY.
S. Adams
4/24/96 © 1996 United Feature Syndicate, Inc.(NYC)

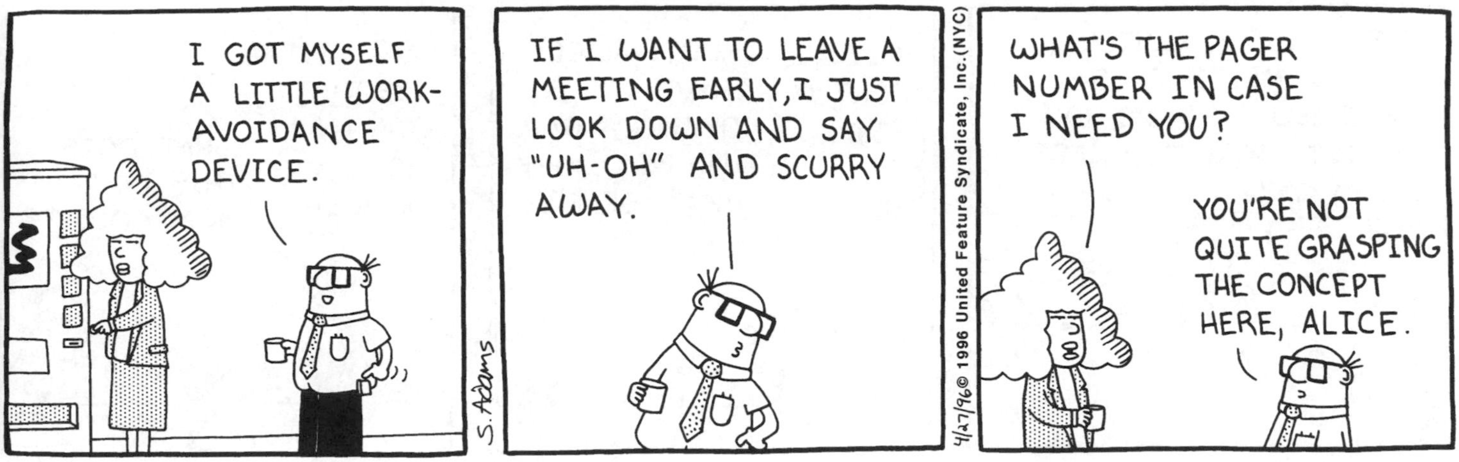
I GOT MYSELF A LITTLE WORK-AVOIDANCE DEVICE.
S. Adams
IF I WANT TO LEAVE A MEETING EARLY, I JUST LOOK DOWN AND SAY "UH-OH" AND SCURRY AWAY.
4/27/96 © 1996 United Feature Syndicate, Inc.(NYC)
WHAT'S THE PAGER NUMBER IN CASE I NEED YOU?
YOU'RE NOT QUITE GRASPING THE CONCEPT HERE, ALICE.

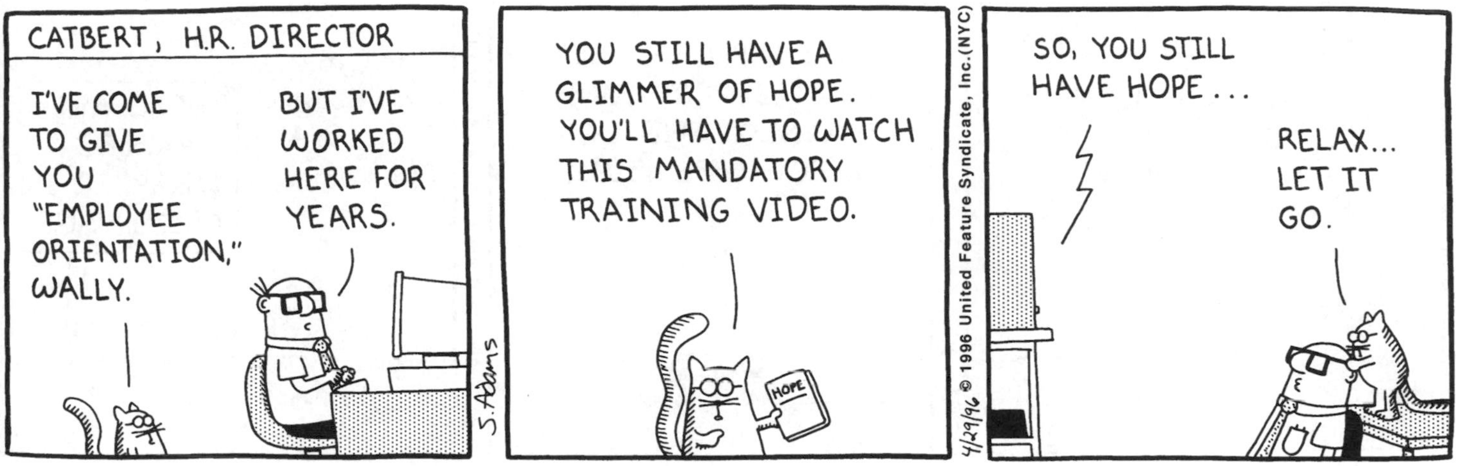
CATBERT, H.R. DIRECTOR
I'VE COME TO GIVE YOU "EMPLOYEE ORIENTATION," WALLY.
BUT I'VE WORKED HERE FOR YEARS.
S. Adams
YOU STILL HAVE A GLIMMER OF HOPE. YOU'LL HAVE TO WATCH THIS MANDATORY TRAINING VIDEO.
HOPE
4/29/96 © 1996 United Feature Syndicate, Inc.(NYC)
SO, YOU STILL HAVE HOPE...
RELAX... LET IT GO.

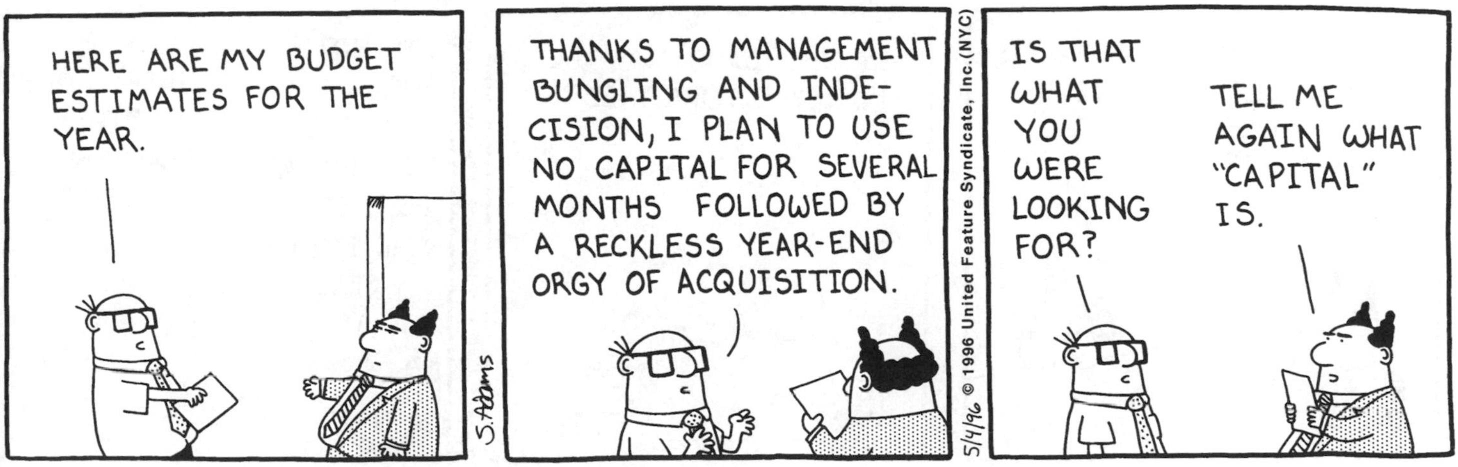
HERE ARE MY BUDGET ESTIMATES FOR THE YEAR.
S. Adams
THANKS TO MANAGEMENT BUNGLING AND INDECISION, I PLAN TO USE NO CAPITAL FOR SEVERAL MONTHS FOLLOWED BY A RECKLESS YEAR-END ORGY OF ACQUISITION.
5/4/96 © 1996 United Feature Syndicate, Inc.(NYC)
IS THAT WHAT YOU WERE LOOKING FOR?
TELL ME AGAIN WHAT "CAPITAL" IS.

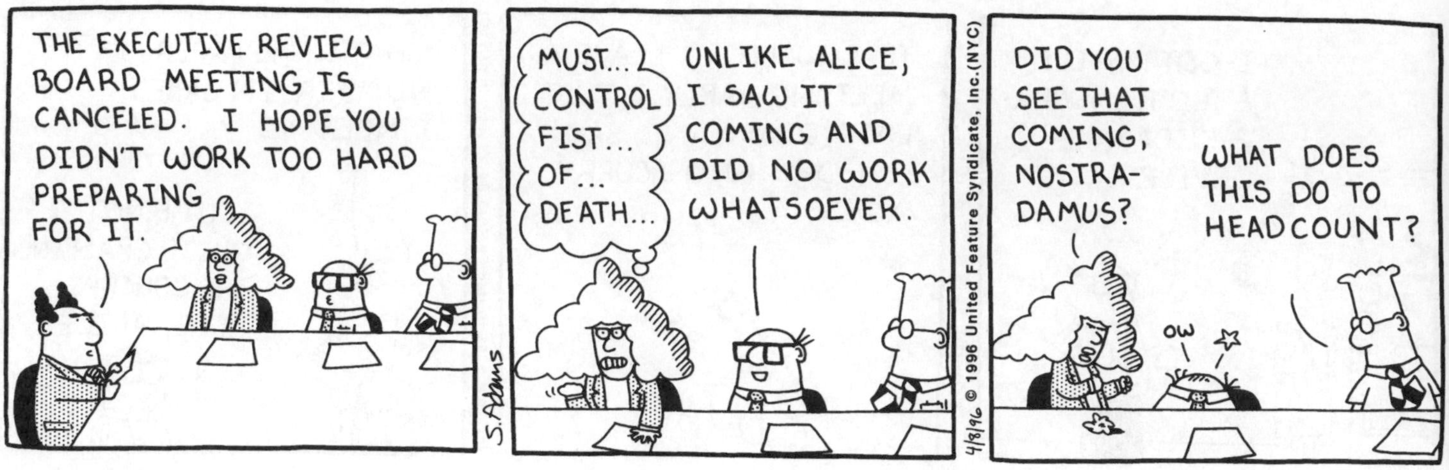
THE EXECUTIVE REVIEW BOARD MEETING IS CANCELED. I HOPE YOU DIDN'T WORK TOO HARD PREPARING FOR IT.
S. Adams
MUST... CONTROL FIST... OF... DEATH...
UNLIKE ALICE, I SAW IT COMING AND DID NO WORK WHATSOEVER.
4/8/96 © 1996 United Feature Syndicate, Inc.(NYC)
DID YOU SEE THAT COMING, NOSTRA-DAMUS?
OW
WHAT DOES THIS DO TO HEADCOUNT?

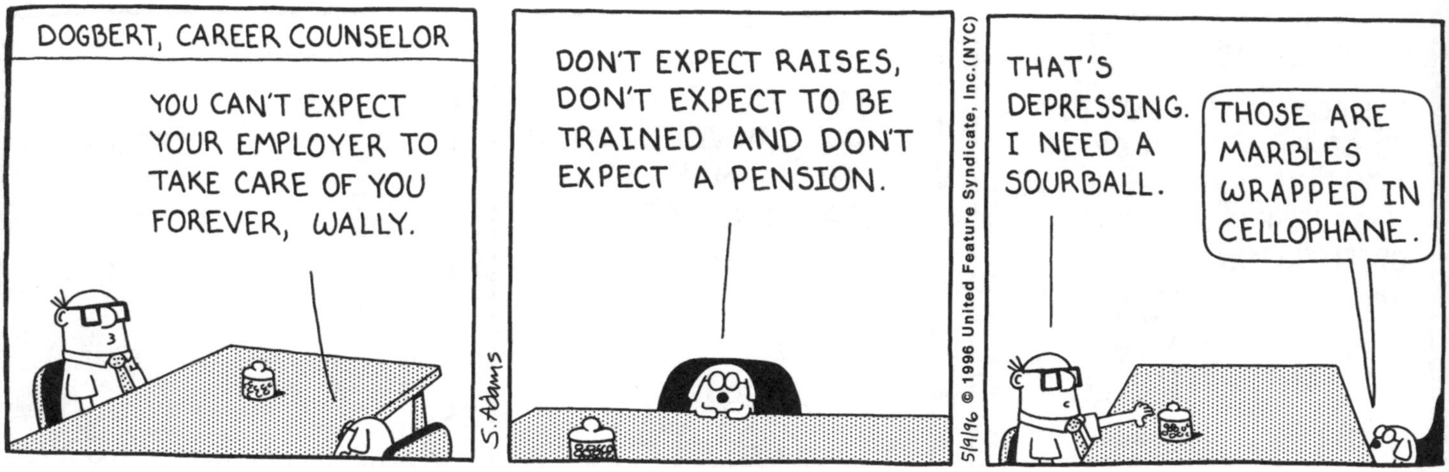
DOGBERT, CAREER COUNSELOR
YOU CAN'T EXPECT YOUR EMPLOYER TO TAKE CARE OF YOU FOREVER, WALLY.
S. Adams
DON'T EXPECT RAISES, DON'T EXPECT TO BE TRAINED AND DON'T EXPECT A PENSION.
5/9/96 © 1996 United Feature Syndicate, Inc.(NYC)
THAT'S DEPRESSING. I NEED A SOURBALL.
THOSE ARE MARBLES WRAPPED IN CELLOPHANE.

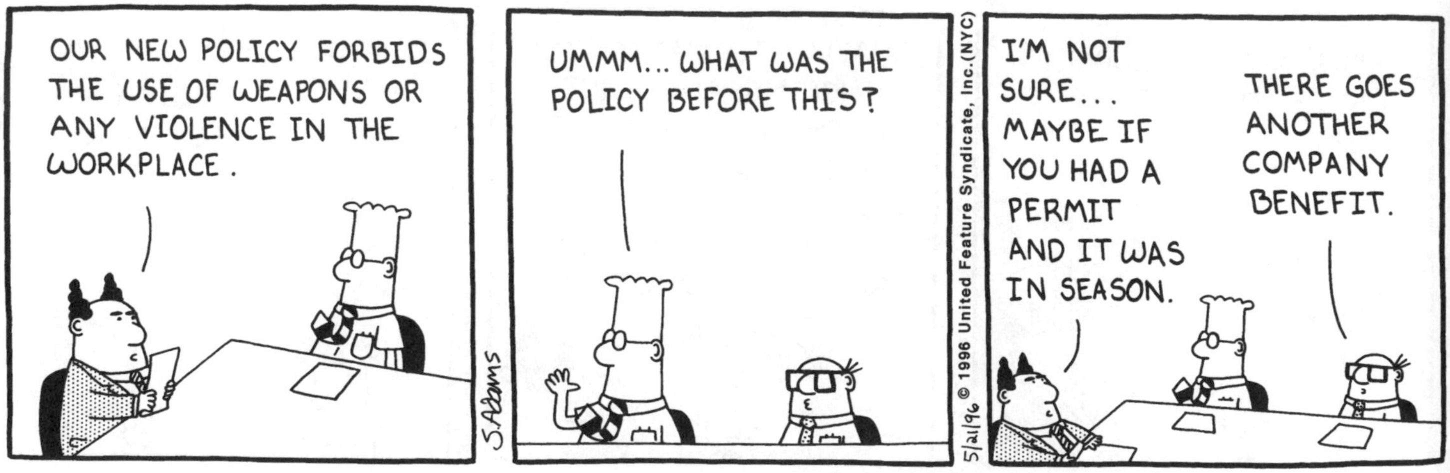
OUR NEW POLICY FORBIDS THE USE OF WEAPONS OR ANY VIOLENCE IN THE WORKPLACE.
S. Adams
UMMM... WHAT WAS THE POLICY BEFORE THIS?
5/21/96 © 1996 United Feature Syndicate, Inc.(NYC)
I'M NOT SURE... MAYBE IF YOU HAD A PERMIT AND IT WAS IN SEASON.
THERE GOES ANOTHER COMPANY BENEFIT.

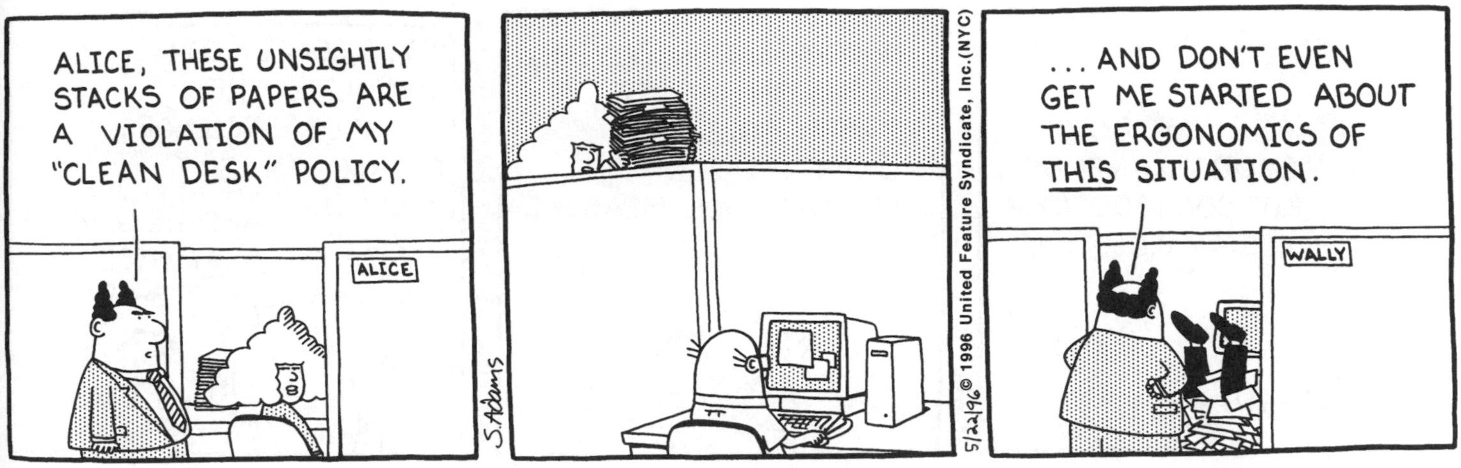
ALICE, THESE UNSIGHTLY STACKS OF PAPERS ARE A VIOLATION OF MY "CLEAN DESK" POLICY.
ALICE
S. Adams
5/22/96 © 1996 United Feature Syndicate, Inc.(NYC)
... AND DON'T EVEN GET ME STARTED ABOUT THE ERGONOMICS OF THIS SITUATION.
WALLY

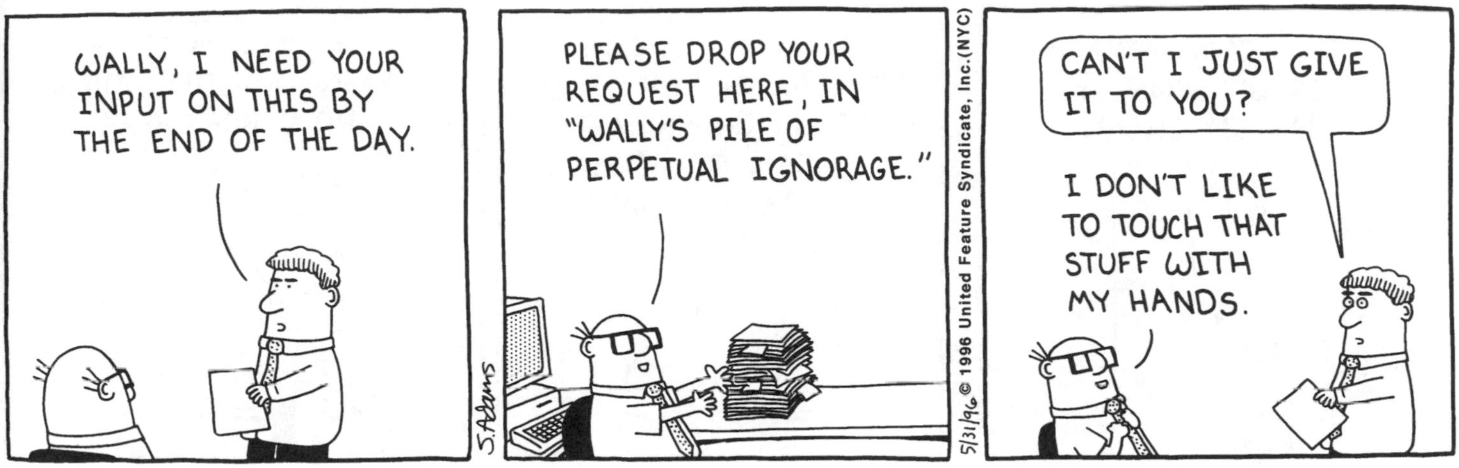
WALLY, I NEED YOUR INPUT ON THIS BY THE END OF THE DAY.
PLEASE DROP YOUR REQUEST HERE, IN "WALLY'S PILE OF PERPETUAL IGNORAGE."
S. Adams
5/31/96 © 1996 United Feature Syndicate, Inc.(NYC)
CAN'T I JUST GIVE IT TO YOU?
I DON'T LIKE TO TOUCH THAT STUFF WITH MY HANDS.

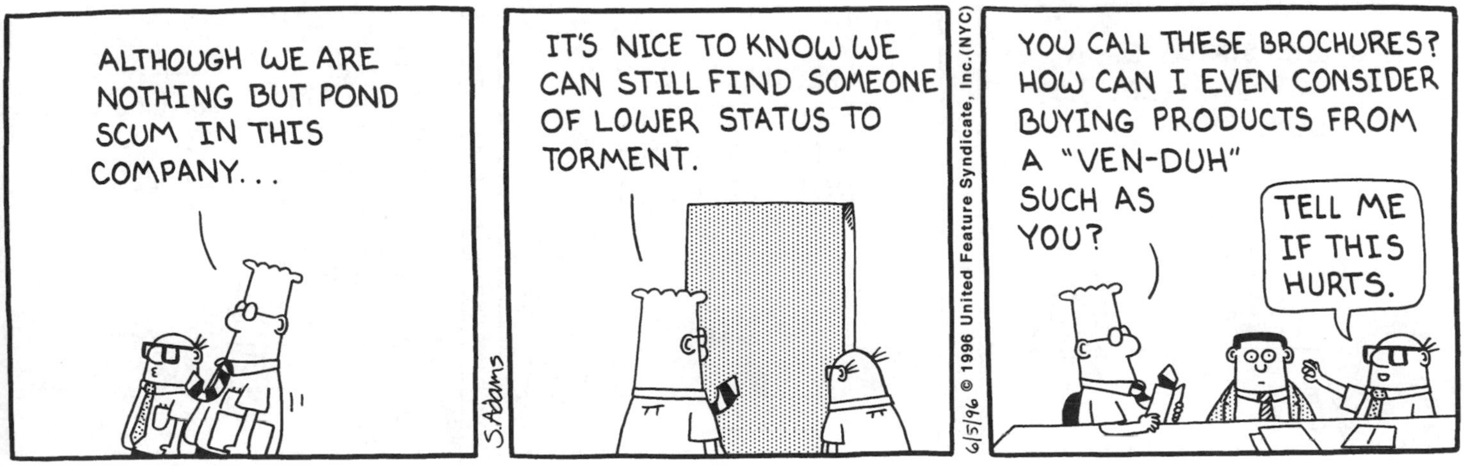
ALTHOUGH WE ARE NOTHING BUT POND SCUM IN THIS COMPANY...
IT'S NICE TO KNOW WE CAN STILL FIND SOMEONE OF LOWER STATUS TO TORMENT.
S. Adams
6/5/96 © 1996 United Feature Syndicate, Inc.(NYC)
YOU CALL THESE BROCHURES? HOW CAN I EVEN CONSIDER BUYING PRODUCTS FROM A "VEN-DUH" SUCH AS YOU?
TELL ME IF THIS HURTS.

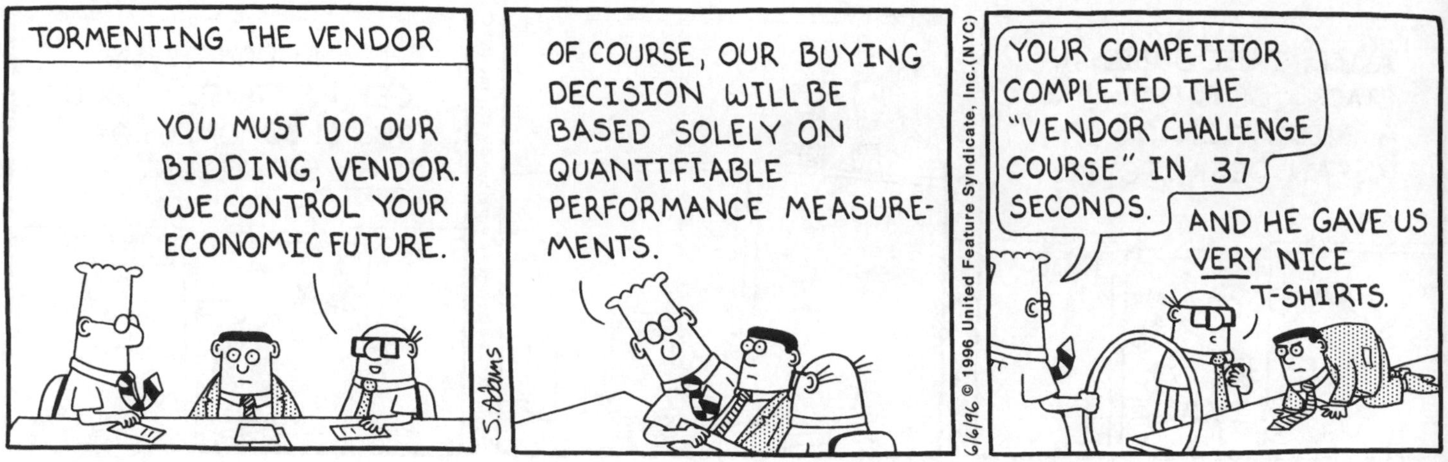
TORMENTING THE VENDOR
YOU MUST DO OUR BIDDING, VENDOR. WE CONTROL YOUR ECONOMIC FUTURE.
S. Adams
OF COURSE, OUR BUYING DECISION WILL BE BASED SOLELY ON QUANTIFIABLE PERFORMANCE MEASUREMENTS.
6/6/96 © 1996 United Feature Syndicate, Inc.(NYC)
YOUR COMPETITOR COMPLETED THE "VENDOR CHALLENGE COURSE" IN 37 SECONDS.
AND HE GAVE US VERY NICE T-SHIRTS.

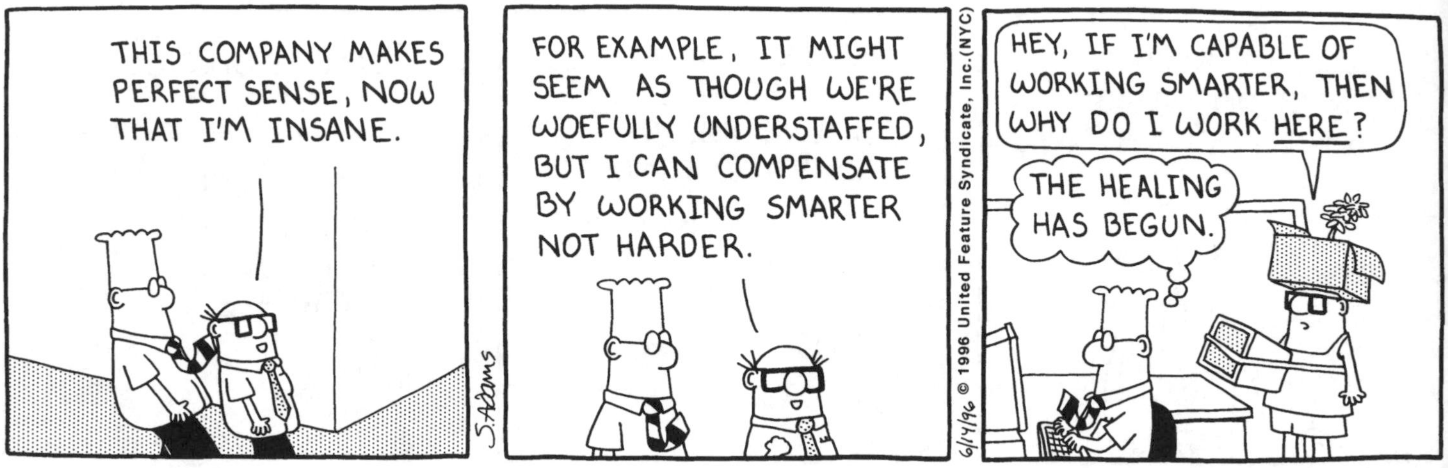
THIS COMPANY MAKES PERFECT SENSE, NOW THAT I'M INSANE.
S. Adams
FOR EXAMPLE, IT MIGHT SEEM AS THOUGH WE'RE WOEFULLY UNDERSTAFFED, BUT I CAN COMPENSATE BY WORKING SMARTER NOT HARDER.
6/14/96 © 1996 United Feature Syndicate, Inc.(NYC)
HEY, IF I'M CAPABLE OF WORKING SMARTER, THEN WHY DO I WORK HERE?
THE HEALING HAS BEGUN.

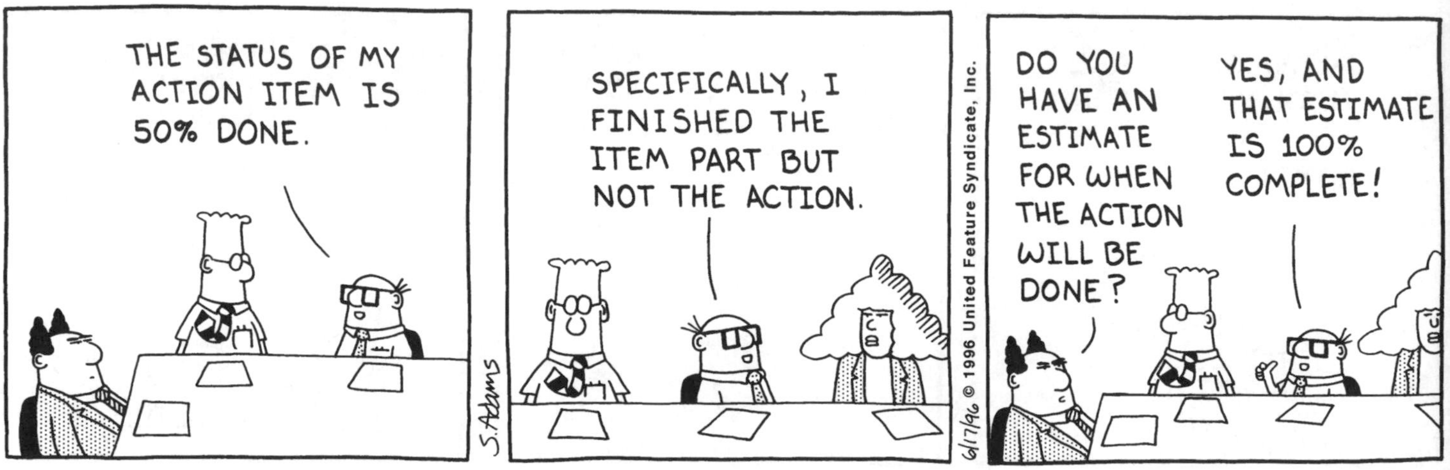
THE STATUS OF MY ACTION ITEM IS 50% DONE.
S. Adams
SPECIFICALLY, I FINISHED THE ITEM PART BUT NOT THE ACTION.
6/17/96 © 1996 United Feature Syndicate, Inc.
DO YOU HAVE AN ESTIMATE FOR WHEN THE ACTION WILL BE DONE?
YES, AND THAT ESTIMATE IS 100% COMPLETE!

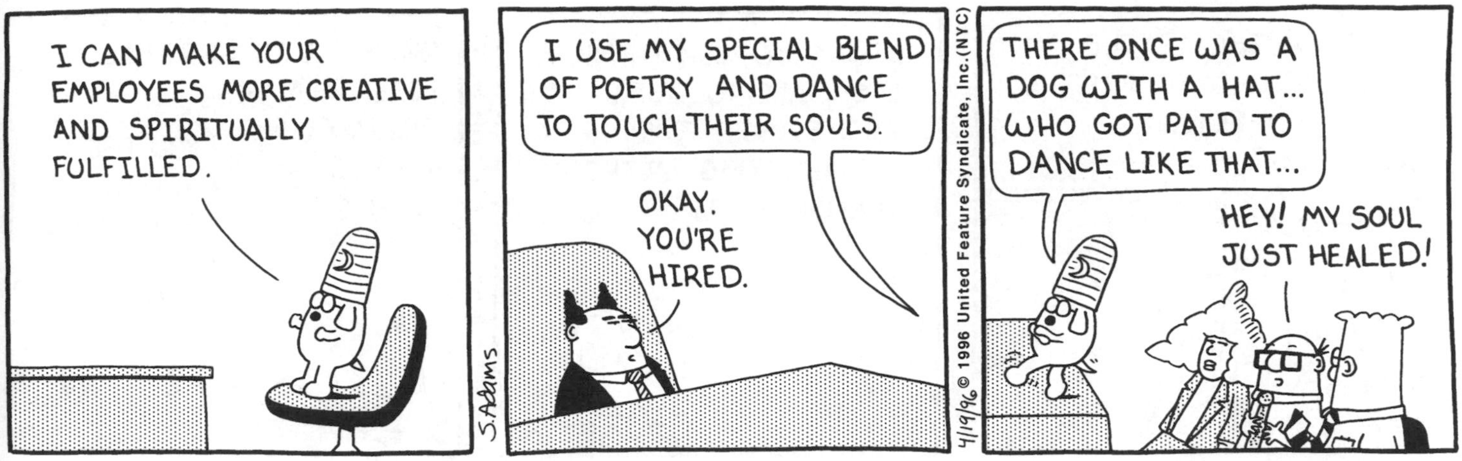
I CAN MAKE YOUR EMPLOYEES MORE CREATIVE AND SPIRITUALLY FULFILLED.
S. Adams
I USE MY SPECIAL BLEND OF POETRY AND DANCE TO TOUCH THEIR SOULS.
OKAY. YOU'RE HIRED.
4/19/96 © 1996 United Feature Syndicate, Inc.(NYC)
THERE ONCE WAS A DOG WITH A HAT... WHO GOT PAID TO DANCE LIKE THAT...
HEY! MY SOUL JUST HEALED!

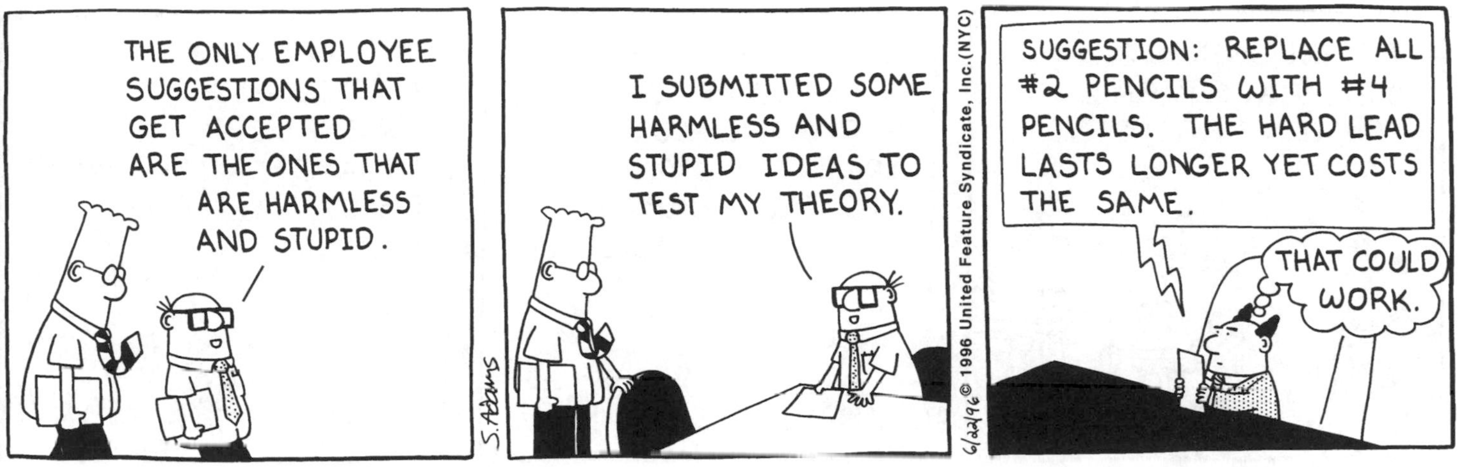
THE ONLY EMPLOYEE SUGGESTIONS THAT GET ACCEPTED ARE THE ONES THAT ARE HARMLESS AND STUPID.
S. Adams
I SUBMITTED SOME HARMLESS AND STUPID IDEAS TO TEST MY THEORY.
6/22/96 © 1996 United Feature Syndicate, Inc.(NYC)
SUGGESTION: REPLACE ALL #2 PENCILS WITH #4 PENCILS. THE HARD LEAD LASTS LONGER YET COSTS THE SAME.
THAT COULD WORK.

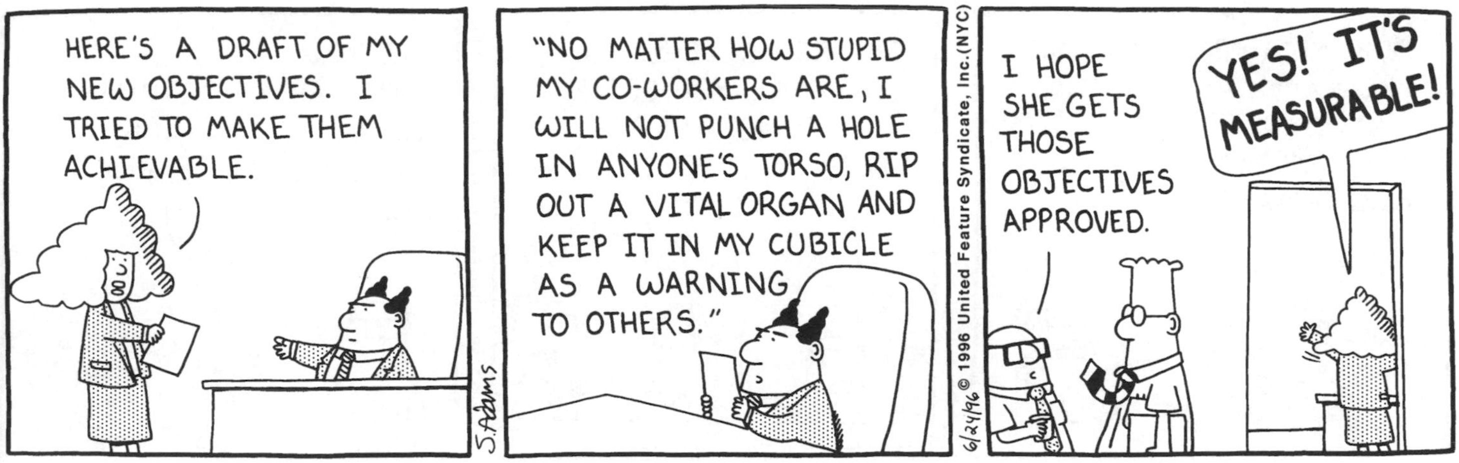
HERE'S A DRAFT OF MY NEW OBJECTIVES. I TRIED TO MAKE THEM ACHIEVABLE.
S. Adams
"NO MATTER HOW STUPID MY CO-WORKERS ARE, I WILL NOT PUNCH A HOLE IN ANYONE'S TORSO, RIP OUT A VITAL ORGAN AND KEEP IT IN MY CUBICLE AS A WARNING TO OTHERS."
6/24/96 © 1996 United Feature Syndicate, Inc.(NYC)
I HOPE SHE GETS THOSE OBJECTIVES APPROVED.
YES! IT'S MEASURABLE!

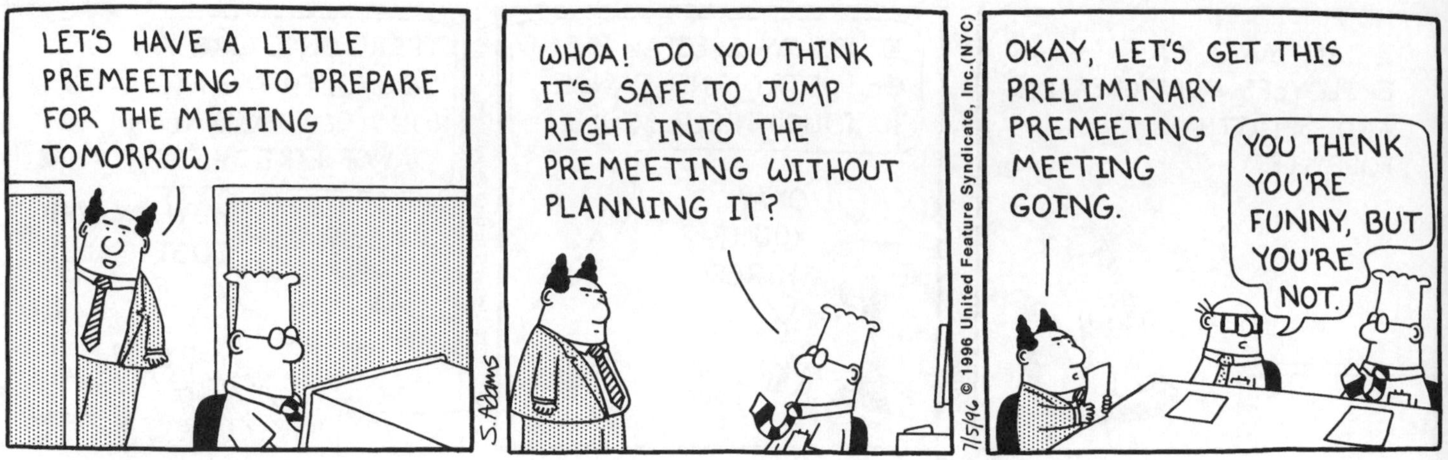
LET'S HAVE A LITTLE PREMEETING TO PREPARE FOR THE MEETING TOMORROW.
WHOA! DO YOU THINK IT'S SAFE TO JUMP RIGHT INTO THE PREMEETING WITHOUT PLANNING IT?
OKAY, LET'S GET THIS PRELIMINARY PREMEETING MEETING GOING.
YOU THINK YOU'RE FUNNY, BUT YOU'RE NOT.
S. Adams
7/5/96 © 1996 United Feature Syndicate, Inc.(NYC)

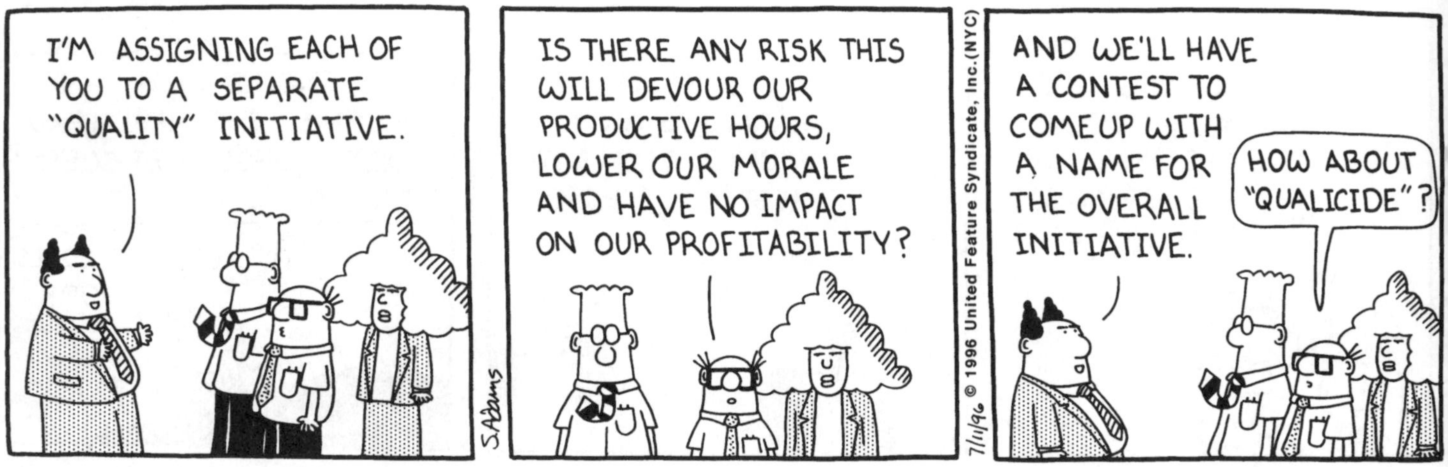
I'M ASSIGNING EACH OF YOU TO A SEPARATE "QUALITY" INITIATIVE.
IS THERE ANY RISK THIS WILL DEVOUR OUR PRODUCTIVE HOURS, LOWER OUR MORALE AND HAVE NO IMPACT ON OUR PROFITABILITY?
AND WE'LL HAVE A CONTEST TO COME UP WITH A NAME FOR THE OVERALL INITIATIVE.
HOW ABOUT "QUALICIDE"?
S. Adams
7/11/96 © 1996 United Feature Syndicate, Inc.(NYC)

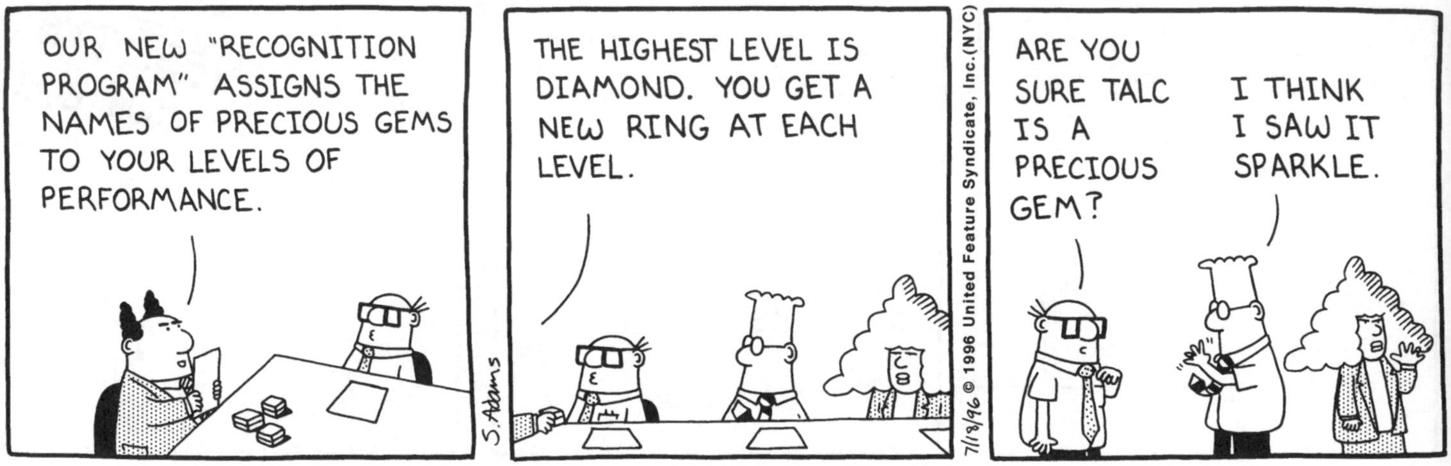
OUR NEW "RECOGNITION PROGRAM" ASSIGNS THE NAMES OF PRECIOUS GEMS TO YOUR LEVELS OF PERFORMANCE.
THE HIGHEST LEVEL IS DIAMOND. YOU GET A NEW RING AT EACH LEVEL.
ARE YOU SURE TALC IS A PRECIOUS GEM?
I THINK I SAW IT SPARKLE.
S. Adams
7/8/96 © 1996 United Feature Syndicate, Inc.(NYC)

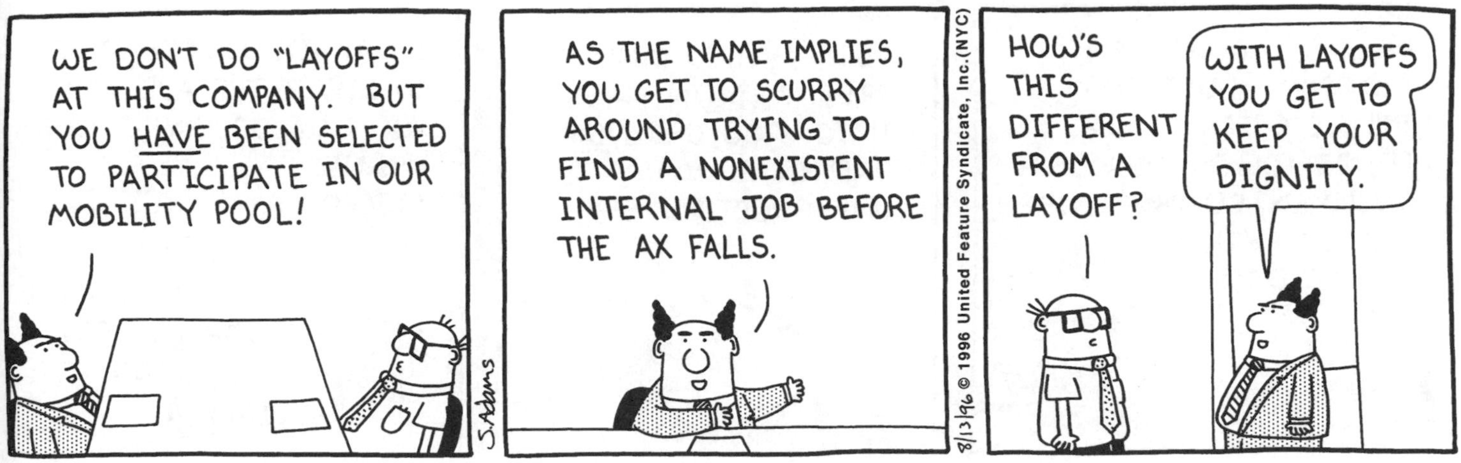
WE DON'T DO "LAYOFFS" AT THIS COMPANY. BUT YOU HAVE BEEN SELECTED TO PARTICIPATE IN OUR MOBILITY POOL!
S. Adams
AS THE NAME IMPLIES, YOU GET TO SCURRY AROUND TRYING TO FIND A NONEXISTENT INTERNAL JOB BEFORE THE AX FALLS.
8/13/96 © 1996 United Feature Syndicate, Inc.(NYC)
HOW'S THIS DIFFERENT FROM A LAYOFF?
WITH LAYOFFS YOU GET TO KEEP YOUR DIGNITY.

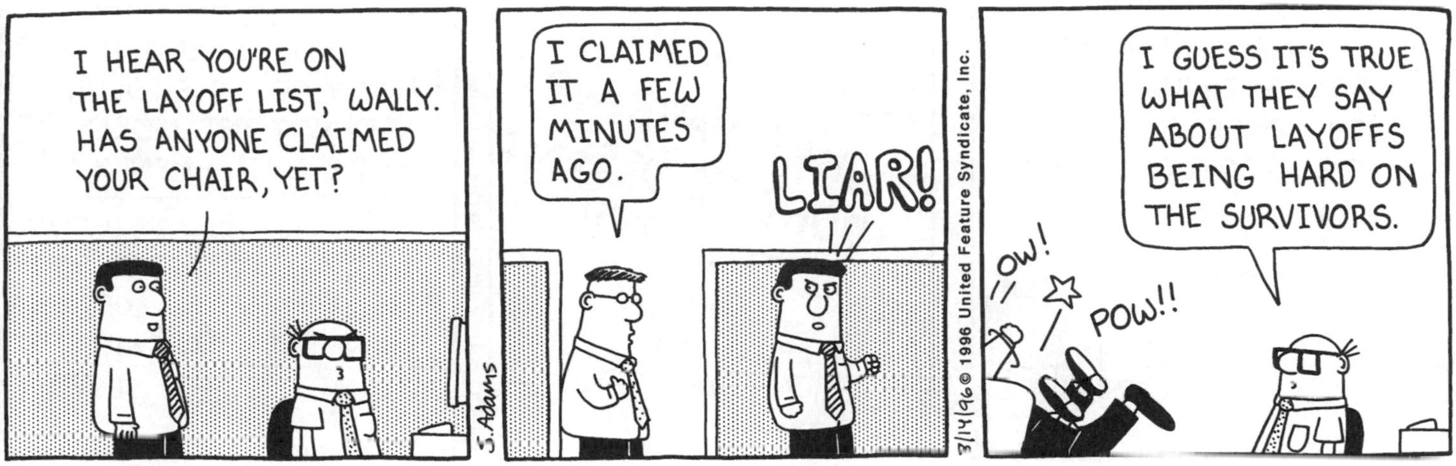
I HEAR YOU'RE ON THE LAYOFF LIST, WALLY. HAS ANYONE CLAIMED YOUR CHAIR, YET?
S. Adams
I CLAIMED IT A FEW MINUTES AGO.
LIAR!
8/14/96 © 1996 United Feature Syndicate, Inc.
OW!
POW!!
I GUESS IT'S TRUE WHAT THEY SAY ABOUT LAYOFFS BEING HARD ON THE SURVIVORS.

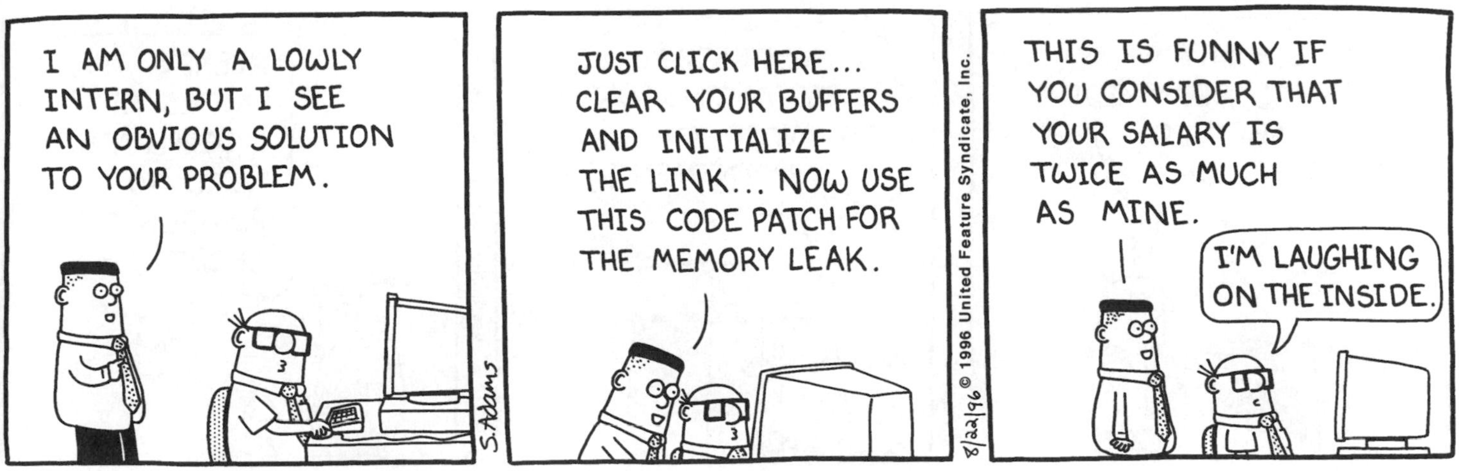
I AM ONLY A LOWLY INTERN, BUT I SEE AN OBVIOUS SOLUTION TO YOUR PROBLEM.
S. Adams
JUST CLICK HERE... CLEAR YOUR BUFFERS AND INITIALIZE THE LINK... NOW USE THIS CODE PATCH FOR THE MEMORY LEAK.
8/22/96 © 1996 United Feature Syndicate, Inc.
THIS IS FUNNY IF YOU CONSIDER THAT YOUR SALARY IS TWICE AS MUCH AS MINE.
I'M LAUGHING ON THE INSIDE.

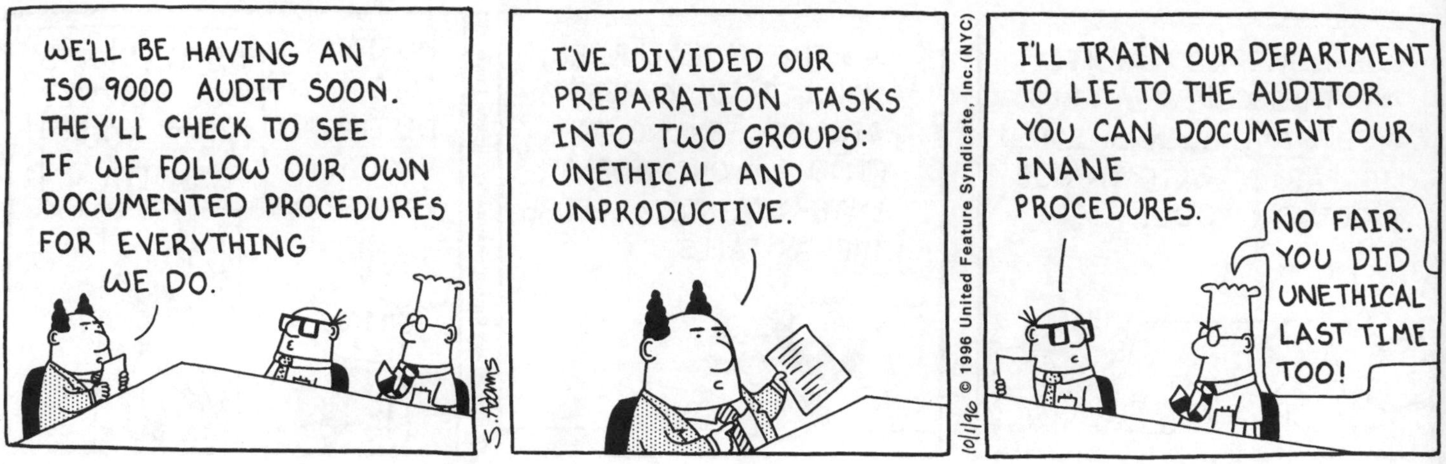
WE'LL BE HAVING AN ISO 9000 AUDIT SOON. THEY'LL CHECK TO SEE IF WE FOLLOW OUR OWN DOCUMENTED PROCEDURES FOR EVERYTHING WE DO.
S. Adams
I'VE DIVIDED OUR PREPARATION TASKS INTO TWO GROUPS: UNETHICAL AND UNPRODUCTIVE.
10/1/96 © 1996 United Feature Syndicate, Inc.(NYC)
I'LL TRAIN OUR DEPARTMENT TO LIE TO THE AUDITOR. YOU CAN DOCUMENT OUR INANE PROCEDURES.
NO FAIR. YOU DID UNETHICAL LAST TIME TOO!

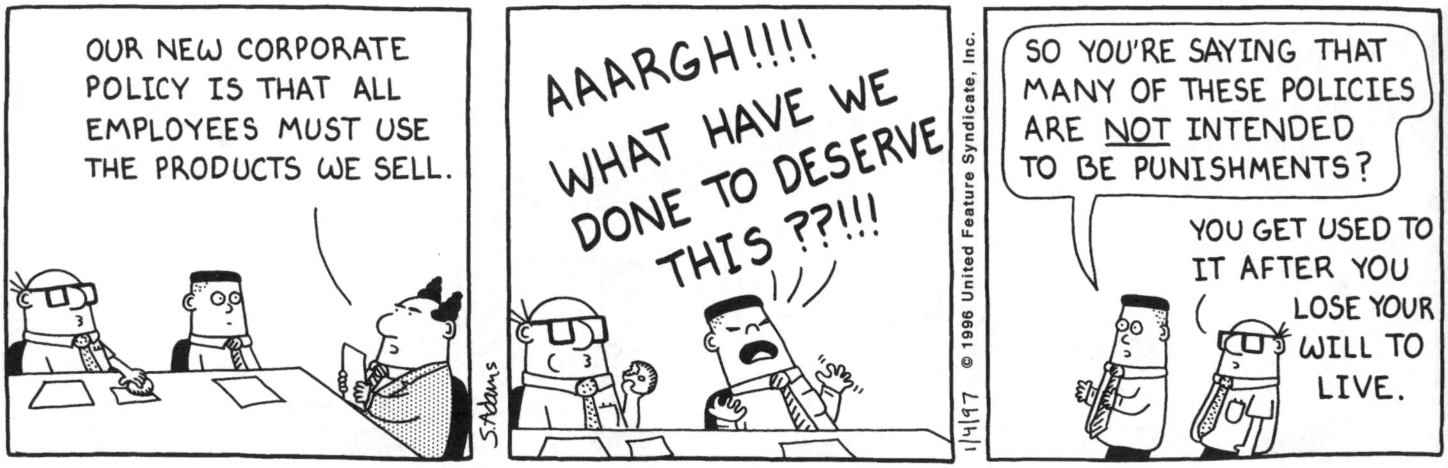
OUR NEW CORPORATE POLICY IS THAT ALL EMPLOYEES MUST USE THE PRODUCTS WE SELL.
S. Adams
AAARGH!!!! WHAT HAVE WE DONE TO DESERVE THIS ??!!!
1/4/97 © 1996 United Feature Syndicate, Inc.
SO YOU'RE SAYING THAT MANY OF THESE POLICIES ARE NOT INTENDED TO BE PUNISHMENTS?
YOU GET USED TO IT AFTER YOU LOSE YOUR WILL TO LIVE.

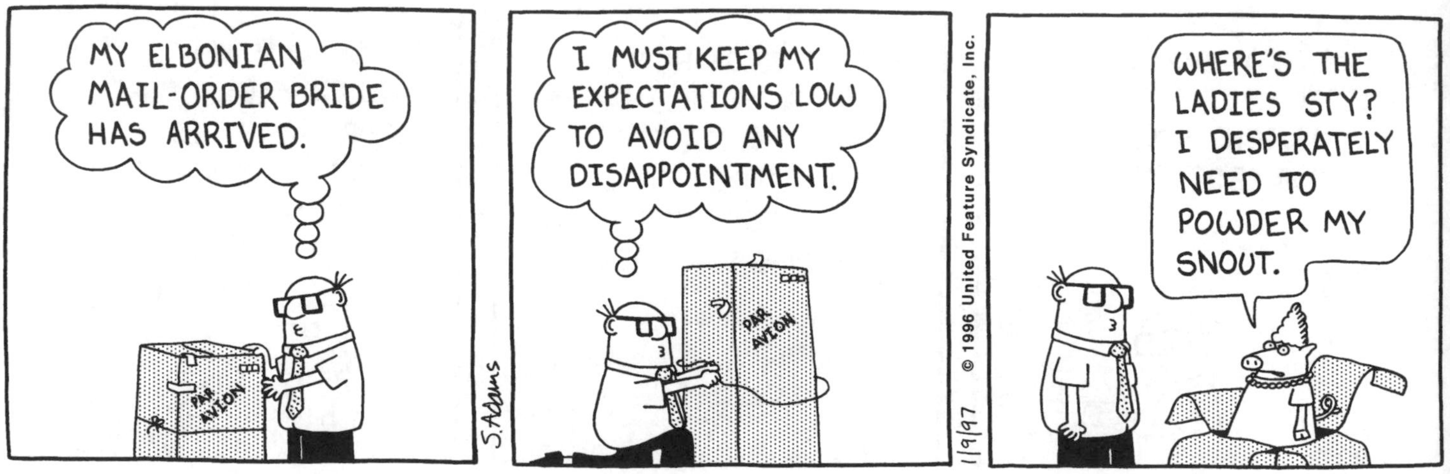
MY ELBONIAN MAIL-ORDER BRIDE HAS ARRIVED.
PAR AVION
S. Adams
I MUST KEEP MY EXPECTATIONS LOW TO AVOID ANY DISAPPOINTMENT.
PAR AVION
1/9/97 © 1996 United Feature Syndicate, Inc.
WHERE'S THE LADIES STY? I DESPERATELY NEED TO POWDER MY SNOUT.

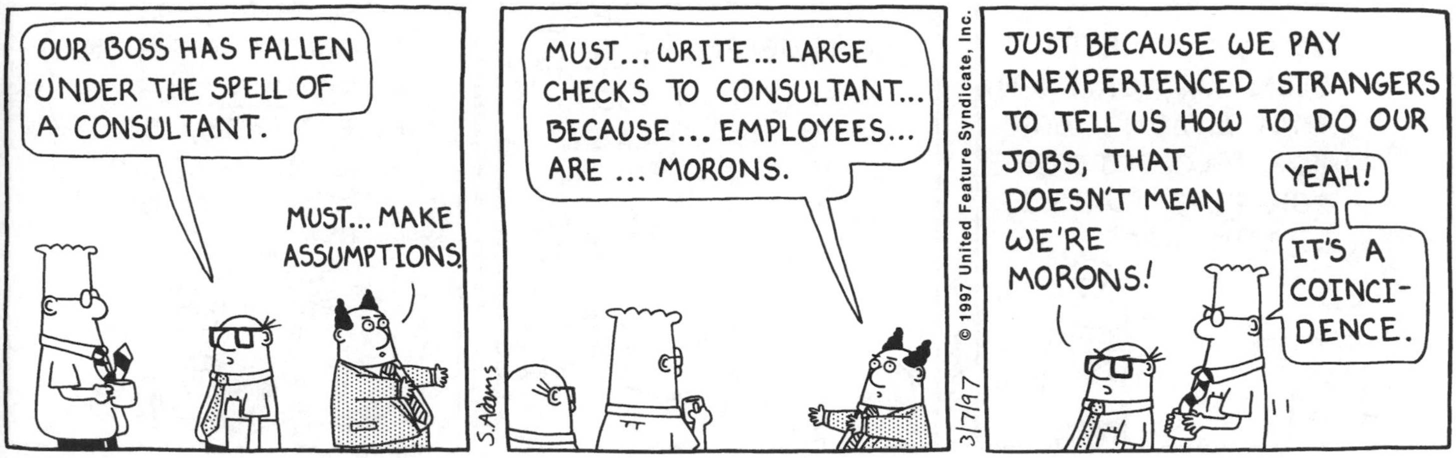

OUR BOSS HAS FALLEN UNDER THE SPELL OF A CONSULTANT.
MUST... MAKE ASSUMPTIONS.
S. Adams
MUST... WRITE... LARGE CHECKS TO CONSULTANT... BECAUSE... EMPLOYEES... ARE ... MORONS.
3/7/97 © 1997 United Feature Syndicate, Inc.
JUST BECAUSE WE PAY INEXPERIENCED STRANGERS TO TELL US HOW TO DO OUR JOBS, THAT DOESN'T MEAN WE'RE MORONS!
YEAH!
IT'S A COINCIDENCE.

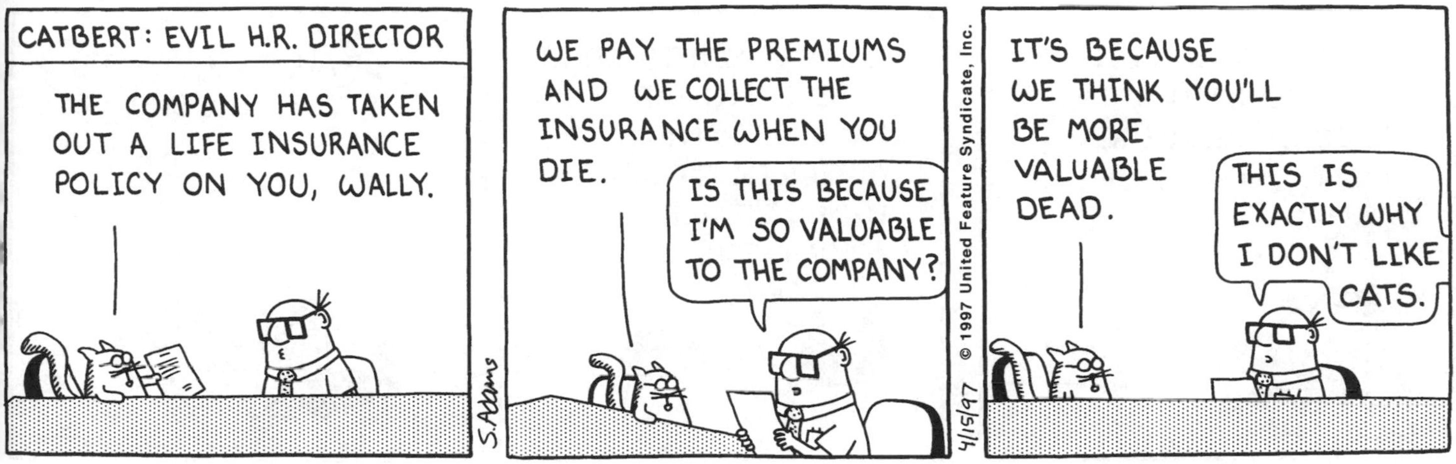

CATBERT: EVIL H.R. DIRECTOR
THE COMPANY HAS TAKEN OUT A LIFE INSURANCE POLICY ON YOU, WALLY.
S. Adams
WE PAY THE PREMIUMS AND WE COLLECT THE INSURANCE WHEN YOU DIE.
IS THIS BECAUSE I'M SO VALUABLE TO THE COMPANY?
4/15/97 © 1997 United Feature Syndicate, Inc.
IT'S BECAUSE WE THINK YOU'LL BE MORE VALUABLE DEAD.
THIS IS EXACTLY WHY I DON'T LIKE CATS.

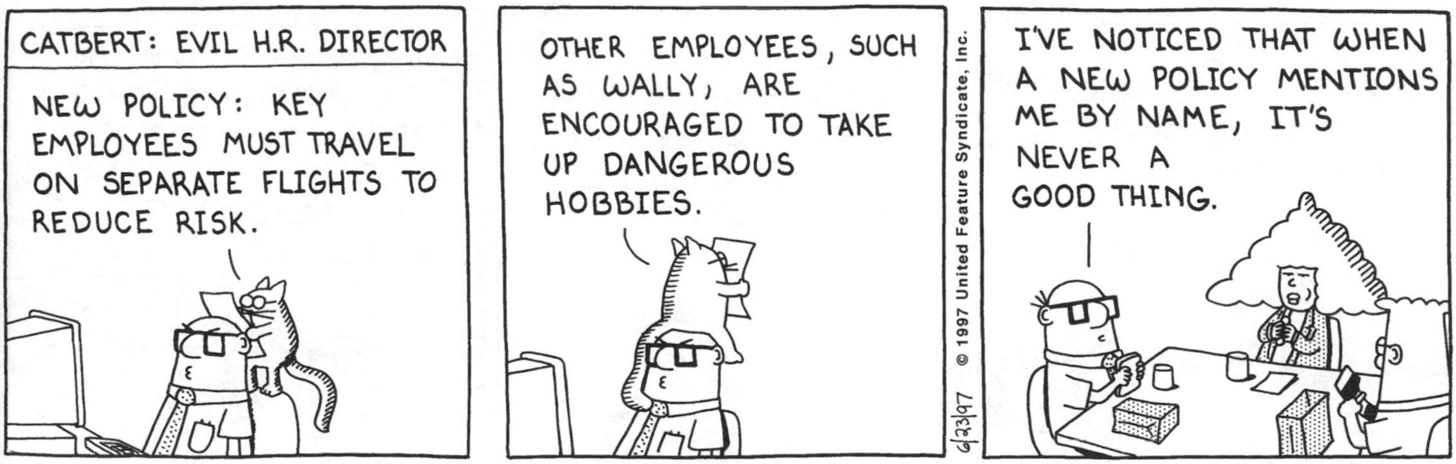

CATBERT: EVIL H.R. DIRECTOR
NEW POLICY: KEY EMPLOYEES MUST TRAVEL ON SEPARATE FLIGHTS TO REDUCE RISK.
OTHER EMPLOYEES, SUCH AS WALLY, ARE ENCOURAGED TO TAKE UP DANGEROUS HOBBIES.
6/23/97 © 1997 United Feature Syndicate, Inc.
I'VE NOTICED THAT WHEN A NEW POLICY MENTIONS ME BY NAME, IT'S NEVER A GOOD THING.

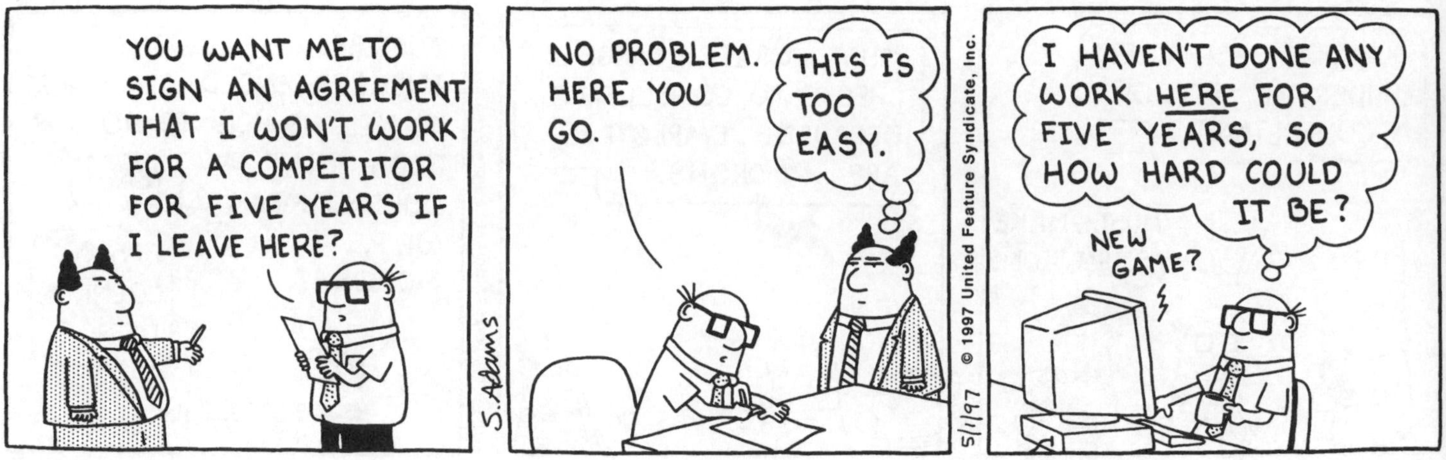
YOU WANT ME TO SIGN AN AGREEMENT THAT I WON'T WORK FOR A COMPETITOR FOR FIVE YEARS IF I LEAVE HERE?
S. Adams
NO PROBLEM. HERE YOU GO.
THIS IS TOO EASY.
5/1/97 © 1997 United Feature Syndicate, Inc.
I HAVEN'T DONE ANY WORK HERE FOR FIVE YEARS, SO HOW HARD COULD IT BE?
NEW GAME?

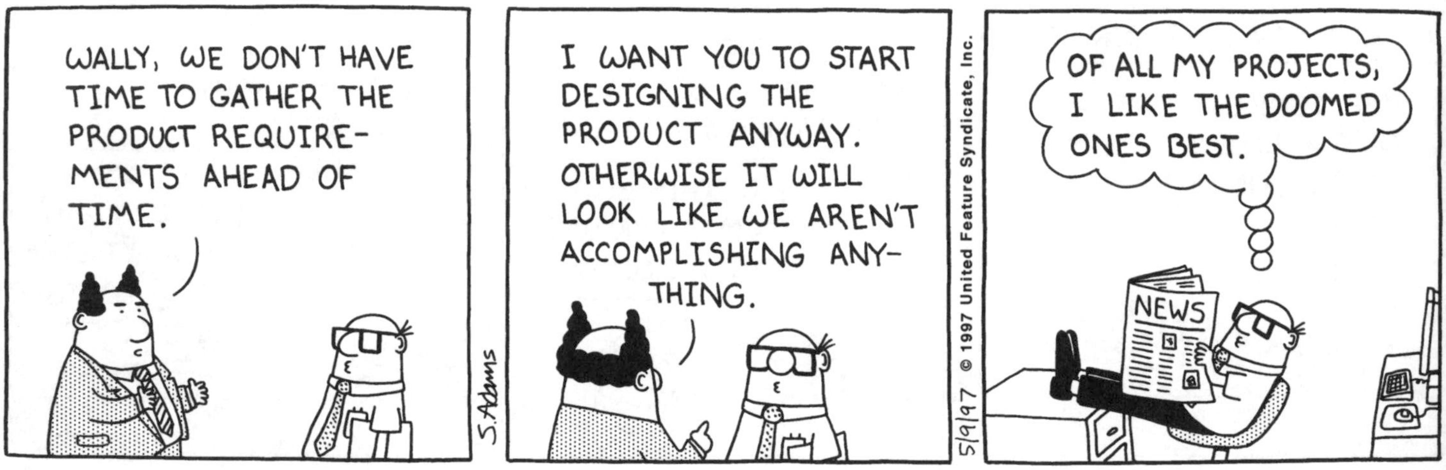
WALLY, WE DON'T HAVE TIME TO GATHER THE PRODUCT REQUIRE-MENTS AHEAD OF TIME.
S. Adams
I WANT YOU TO START DESIGNING THE PRODUCT ANYWAY. OTHERWISE IT WILL LOOK LIKE WE AREN'T ACCOMPLISHING ANY-THING.
5/9/97 © 1997 United Feature Syndicate, Inc.
OF ALL MY PROJECTS, I LIKE THE DOOMED ONES BEST.
NEWS

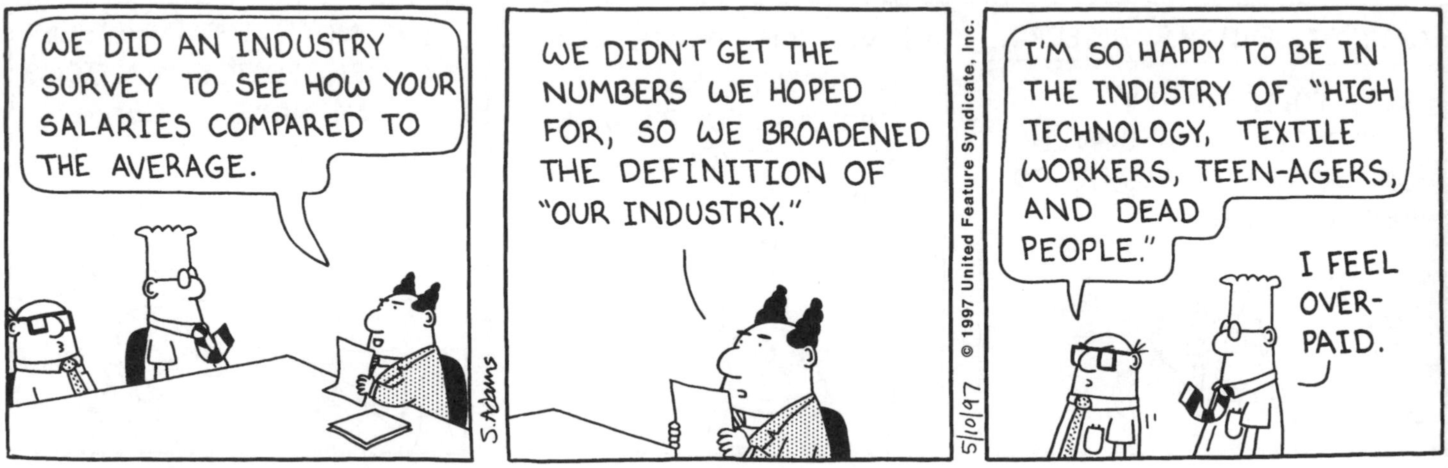
WE DID AN INDUSTRY SURVEY TO SEE HOW YOUR SALARIES COMPARED TO THE AVERAGE.
S. Adams
WE DIDN'T GET THE NUMBERS WE HOPED FOR, SO WE BROADENED THE DEFINITION OF "OUR INDUSTRY."
5/10/97 © 1997 United Feature Syndicate, Inc.
I'M SO HAPPY TO BE IN THE INDUSTRY OF "HIGH TECHNOLOGY, TEXTILE WORKERS, TEEN-AGERS, AND DEAD PEOPLE."
I FEEL OVER-PAID.

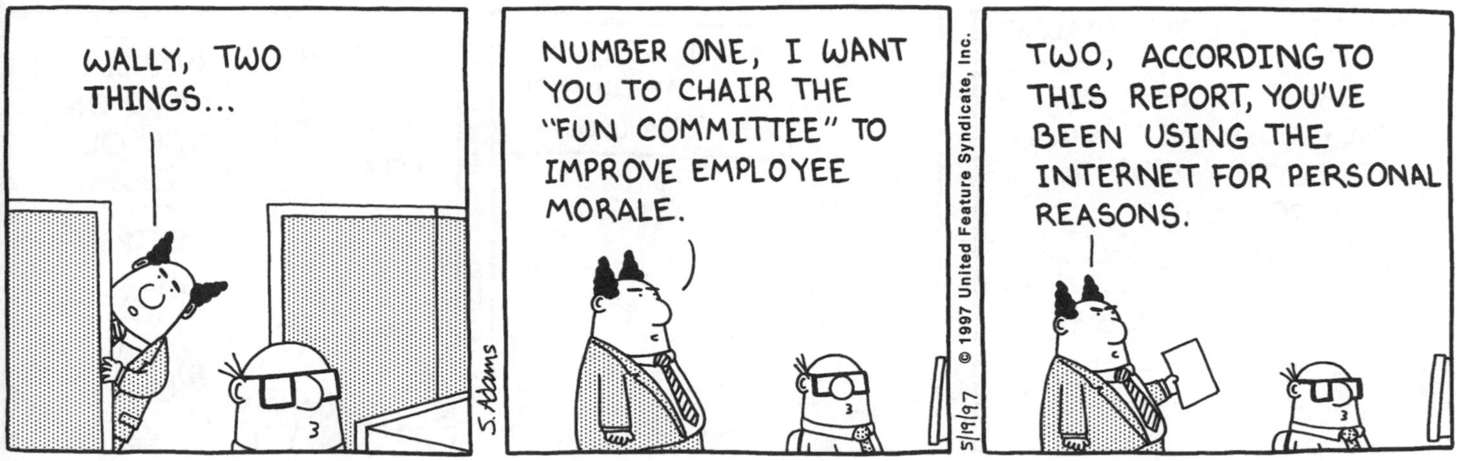
WALLY, TWO THINGS...
NUMBER ONE, I WANT YOU TO CHAIR THE "FUN COMMITTEE" TO IMPROVE EMPLOYEE MORALE.
TWO, ACCORDING TO THIS REPORT, YOU'VE BEEN USING THE INTERNET FOR PERSONAL REASONS.
S. Adams
5/19/97 © 1997 United Feature Syndicate, Inc.

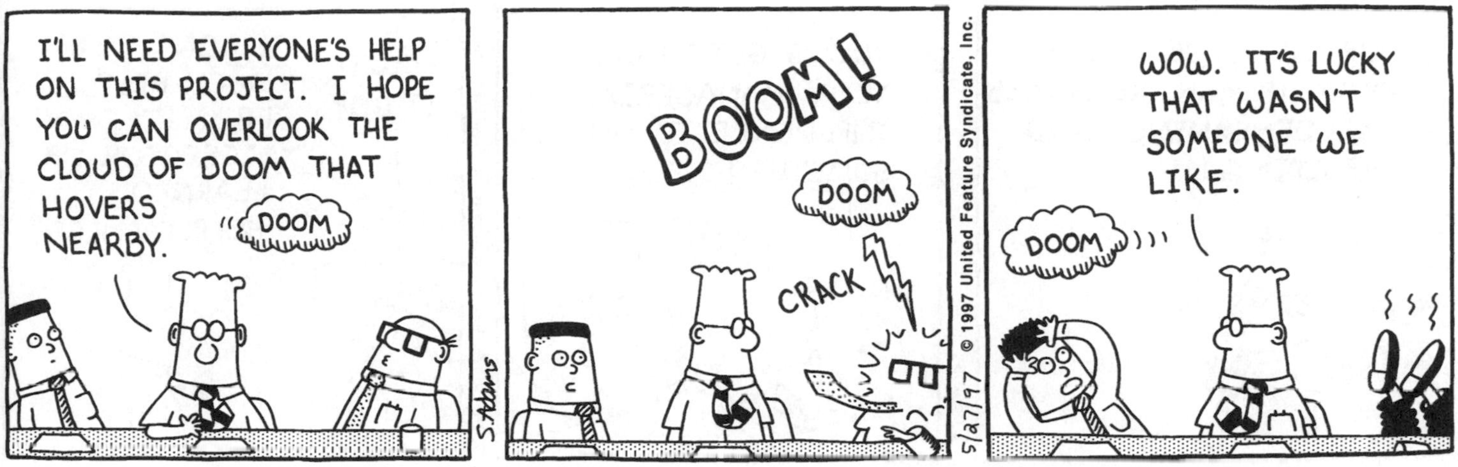
I'LL NEED EVERYONE'S HELP ON THIS PROJECT. I HOPE YOU CAN OVERLOOK THE CLOUD OF DOOM THAT HOVERS NEARBY.
DOOM
BOOM!
DOOM
CRACK
WOW. IT'S LUCKY THAT WASN'T SOMEONE WE LIKE.
DOOM
S. Adams
5/27/97 © 1997 United Feature Syndicate, Inc.

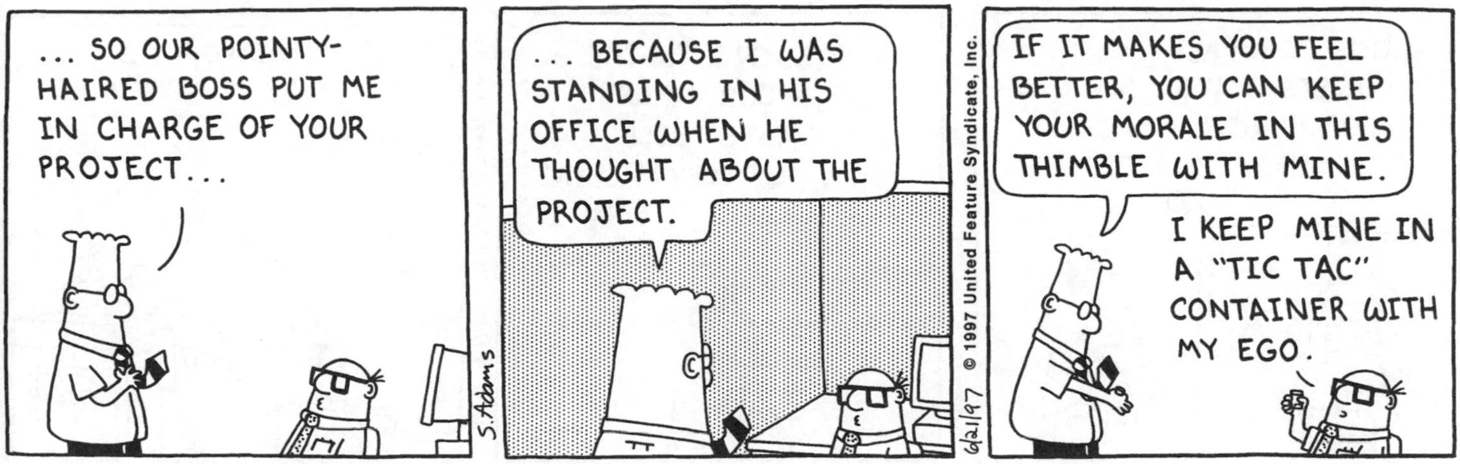
... SO OUR POINTY-HAIRED BOSS PUT ME IN CHARGE OF YOUR PROJECT...
... BECAUSE I WAS STANDING IN HIS OFFICE WHEN HE THOUGHT ABOUT THE PROJECT.
IF IT MAKES YOU FEEL BETTER, YOU CAN KEEP YOUR MORALE IN THIS THIMBLE WITH MINE.
I KEEP MINE IN A "TIC TAC" CONTAINER WITH MY EGO.
S. Adams
6/2/97 © 1997 United Feature Syndicate, Inc.

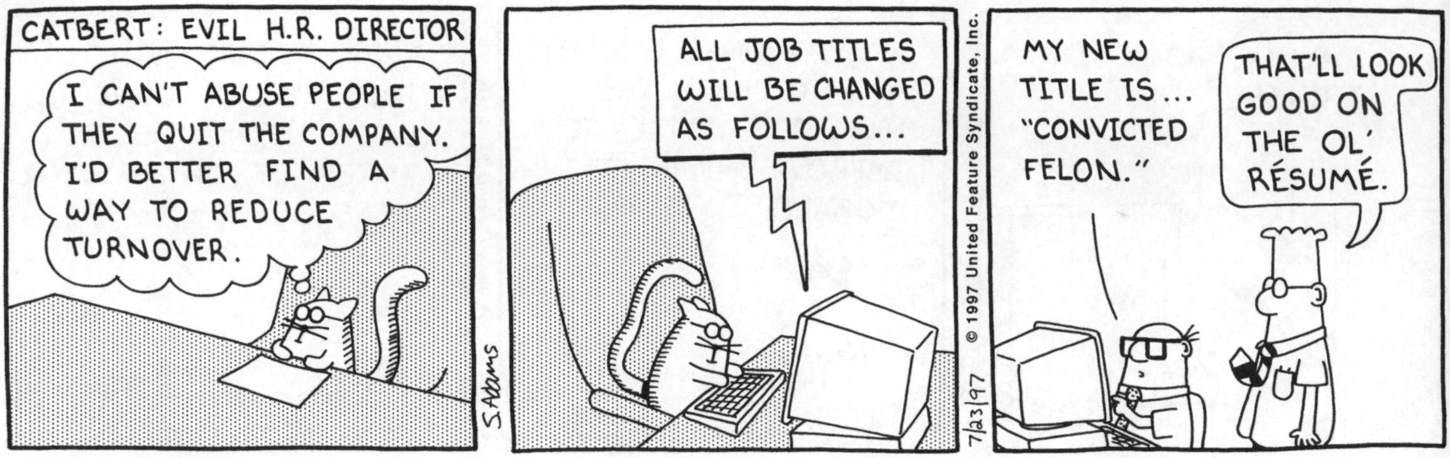
CATBERT: EVIL H.R. DIRECTOR
I CAN'T ABUSE PEOPLE IF THEY QUIT THE COMPANY. I'D BETTER FIND A WAY TO REDUCE TURNOVER.
ALL JOB TITLES WILL BE CHANGED AS FOLLOWS...
MY NEW TITLE IS... "CONVICTED FELON."
THAT'LL LOOK GOOD ON THE OL' RÉSUMÉ.
S. Adams
7/23/97
© 1997 United Feature Syndicate, Inc.

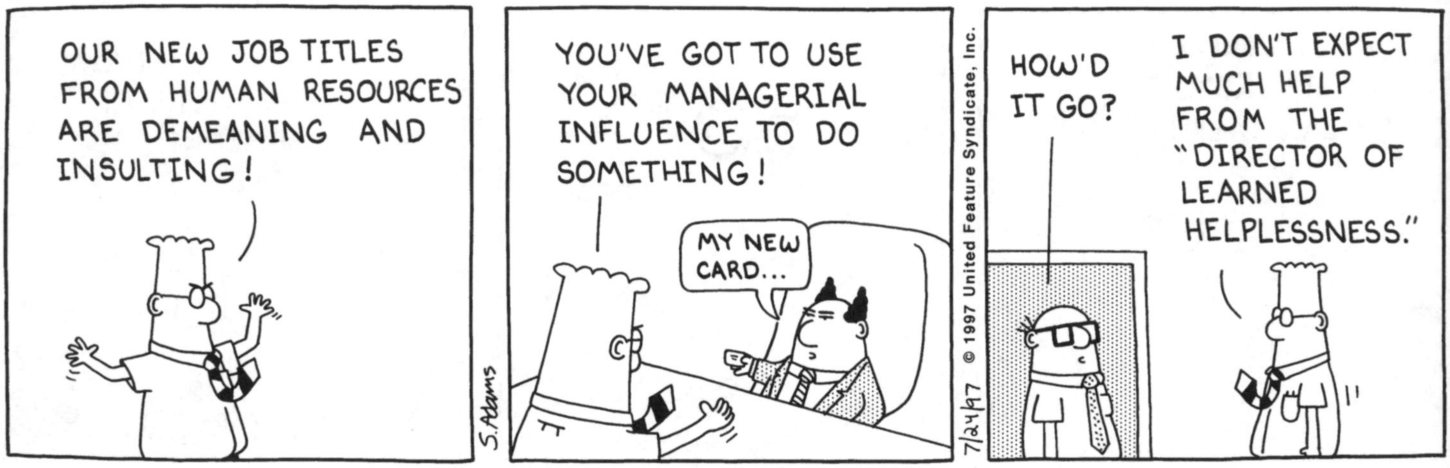
OUR NEW JOB TITLES FROM HUMAN RESOURCES ARE DEMEANING AND INSULTING!
YOU'VE GOT TO USE YOUR MANAGERIAL INFLUENCE TO DO SOMETHING!
MY NEW CARD...
HOW'D IT GO?
I DON'T EXPECT MUCH HELP FROM THE "DIRECTOR OF LEARNED HELPLESSNESS."
S. Adams
7/24/97
© 1997 United Feature Syndicate, Inc.

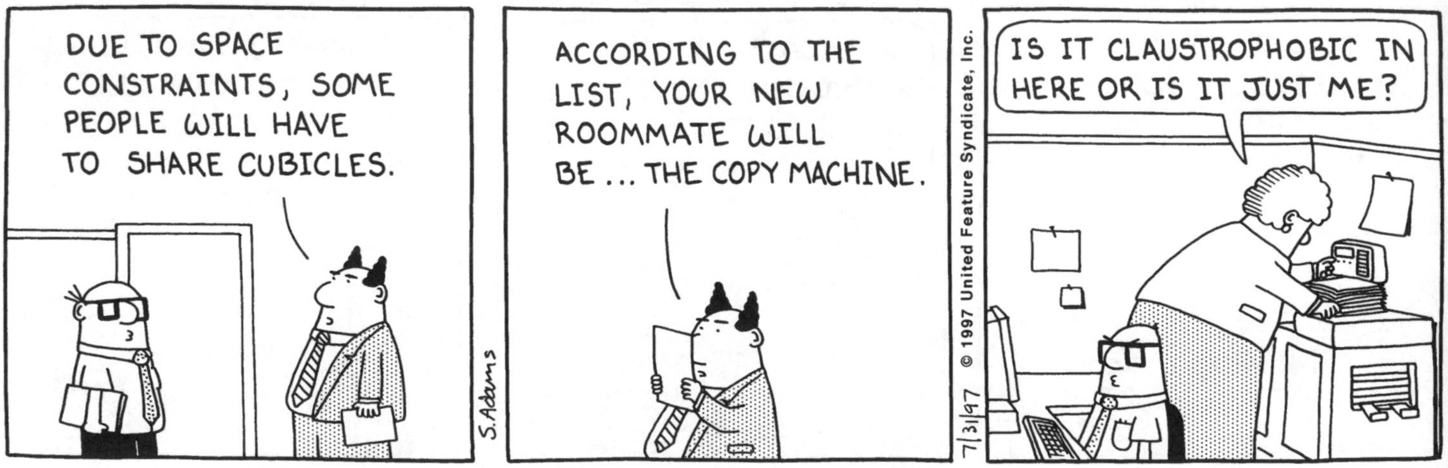
DUE TO SPACE CONSTRAINTS, SOME PEOPLE WILL HAVE TO SHARE CUBICLES.
ACCORDING TO THE LIST, YOUR NEW ROOMMATE WILL BE... THE COPY MACHINE.
IS IT CLAUSTROPHOBIC IN HERE OR IS IT JUST ME?
S. Adams
7/31/97
© 1997 United Feature Syndicate, Inc.

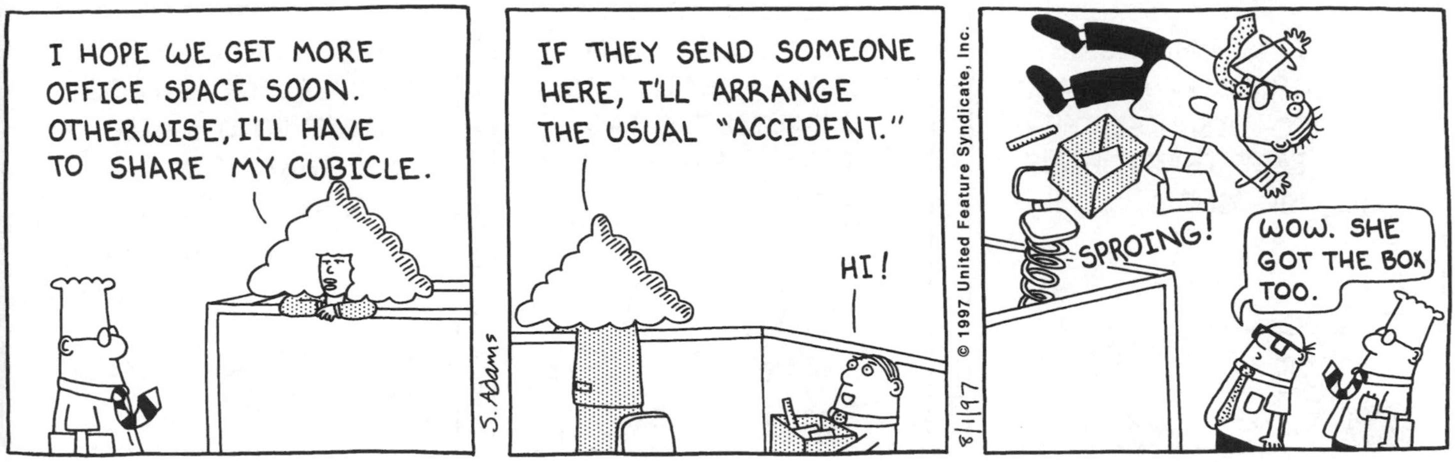
I HOPE WE GET MORE OFFICE SPACE SOON. OTHERWISE, I'LL HAVE TO SHARE MY CUBICLE.
IF THEY SEND SOMEONE HERE, I'LL ARRANGE THE USUAL "ACCIDENT."
HI!
SPROING!
WOW. SHE GOT THE BOX TOO.
S. Adams

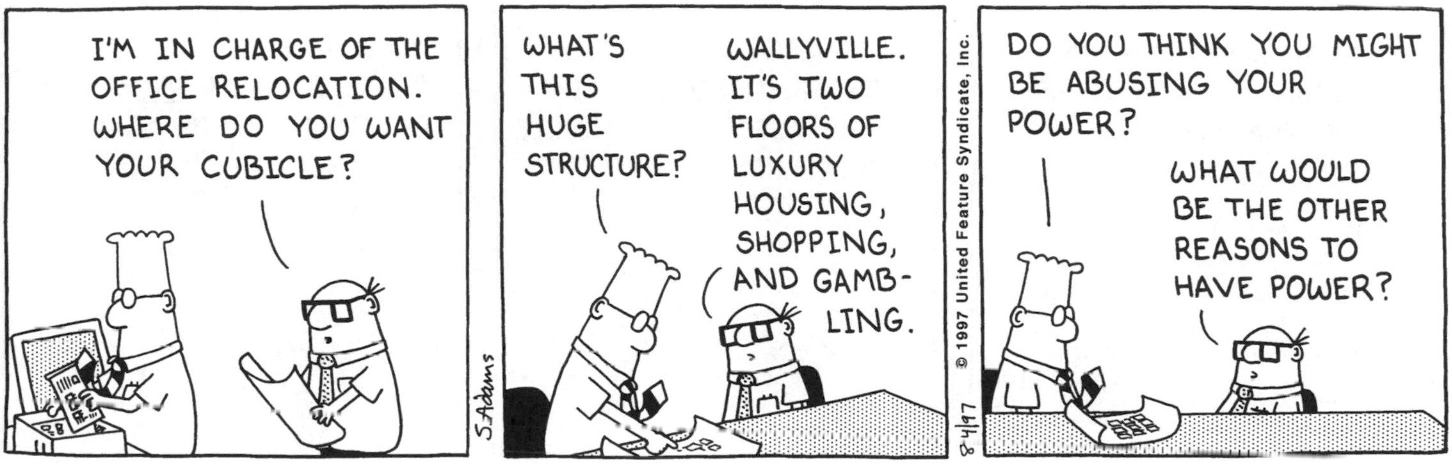
I'M IN CHARGE OF THE OFFICE RELOCATION. WHERE DO YOU WANT YOUR CUBICLE?
WHAT'S THIS HUGE STRUCTURE?
WALLYVILLE. IT'S TWO FLOORS OF LUXURY HOUSING, SHOPPING, AND GAMBLING.
DO YOU THINK YOU MIGHT BE ABUSING YOUR POWER?
WHAT WOULD BE THE OTHER REASONS TO HAVE POWER?
S. Adams

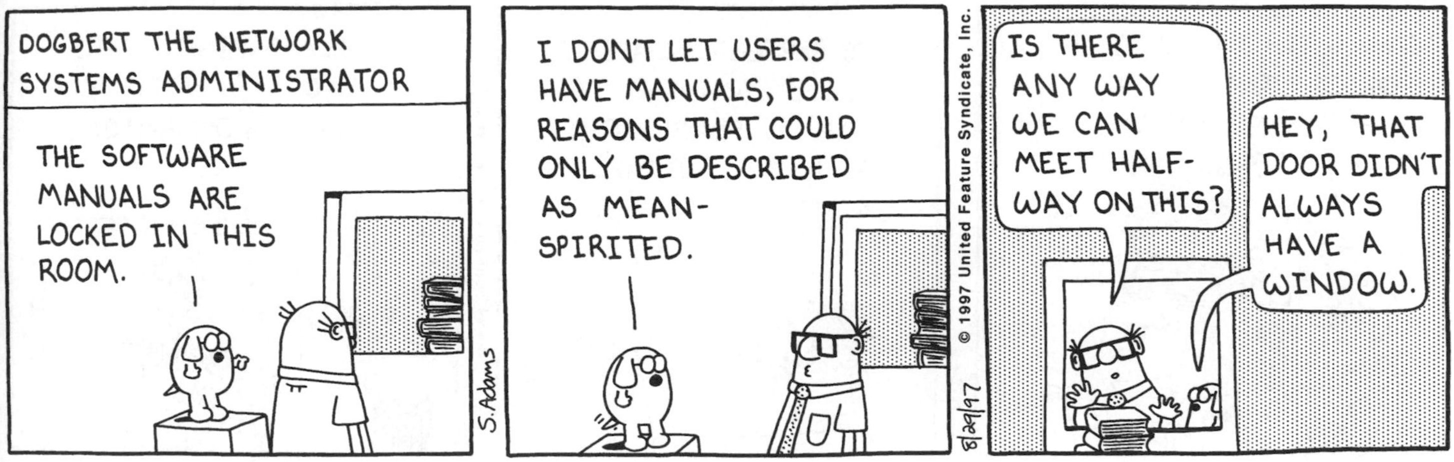
DOGBERT THE NETWORK SYSTEMS ADMINISTRATOR
THE SOFTWARE MANUALS ARE LOCKED IN THIS ROOM.
I DON'T LET USERS HAVE MANUALS, FOR REASONS THAT COULD ONLY BE DESCRIBED AS MEAN-SPIRITED.
IS THERE ANY WAY WE CAN MEET HALF-WAY ON THIS?
HEY, THAT DOOR DIDN'T ALWAYS HAVE A WINDOW.
S. Adams

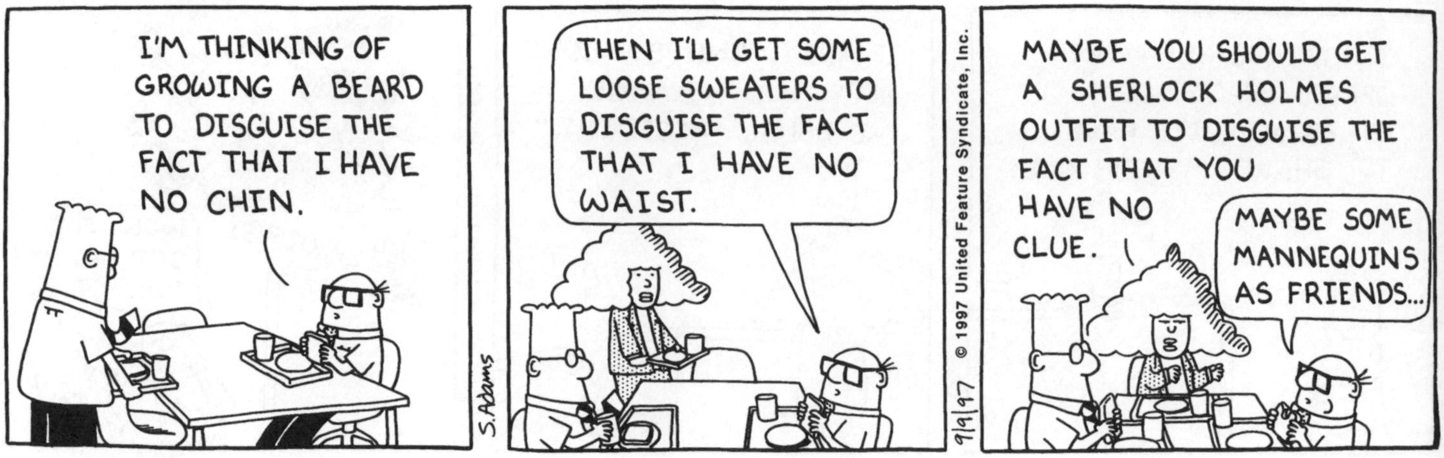
I'M THINKING OF GROWING A BEARD TO DISGUISE THE FACT THAT I HAVE NO CHIN.
THEN I'LL GET SOME LOOSE SWEATERS TO DISGUISE THE FACT THAT I HAVE NO WAIST.
MAYBE YOU SHOULD GET A SHERLOCK HOLMES OUTFIT TO DISGUISE THE FACT THAT YOU HAVE NO CLUE.
MAYBE SOME MANNEQUINS AS FRIENDS...
S. Adams
9/9/97
© 1997 United Feature Syndicate, Inc.

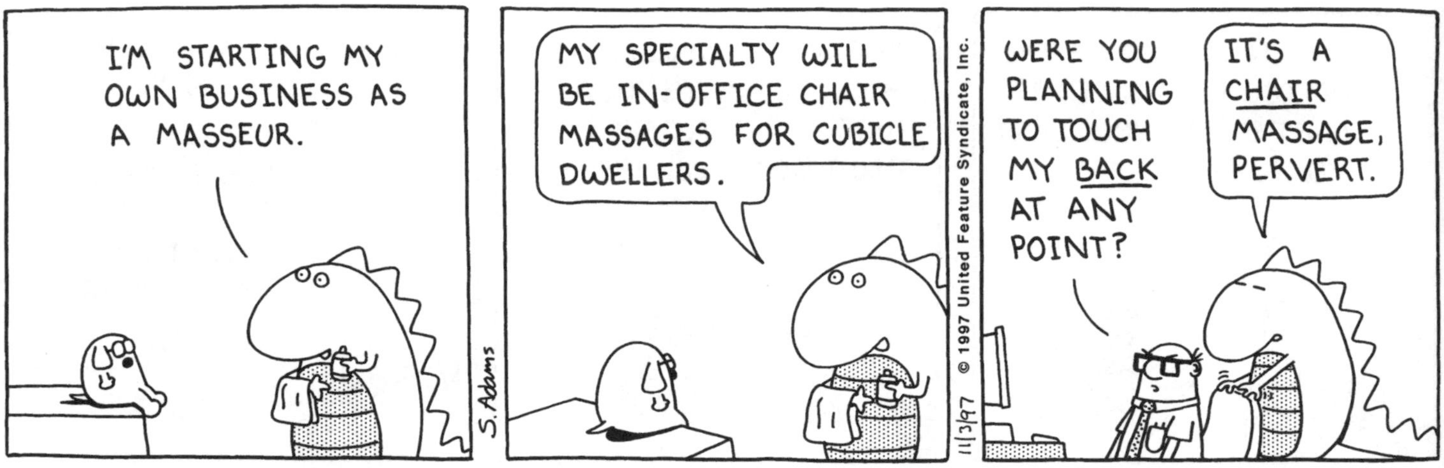
I'M STARTING MY OWN BUSINESS AS A MASSEUR.
MY SPECIALTY WILL BE IN-OFFICE CHAIR MASSAGES FOR CUBICLE DWELLERS.
WERE YOU PLANNING TO TOUCH MY BACK AT ANY POINT?
IT'S A CHAIR MASSAGE, PERVERT.
S. Adams
11/3/97
© 1997 United Feature Syndicate, Inc.

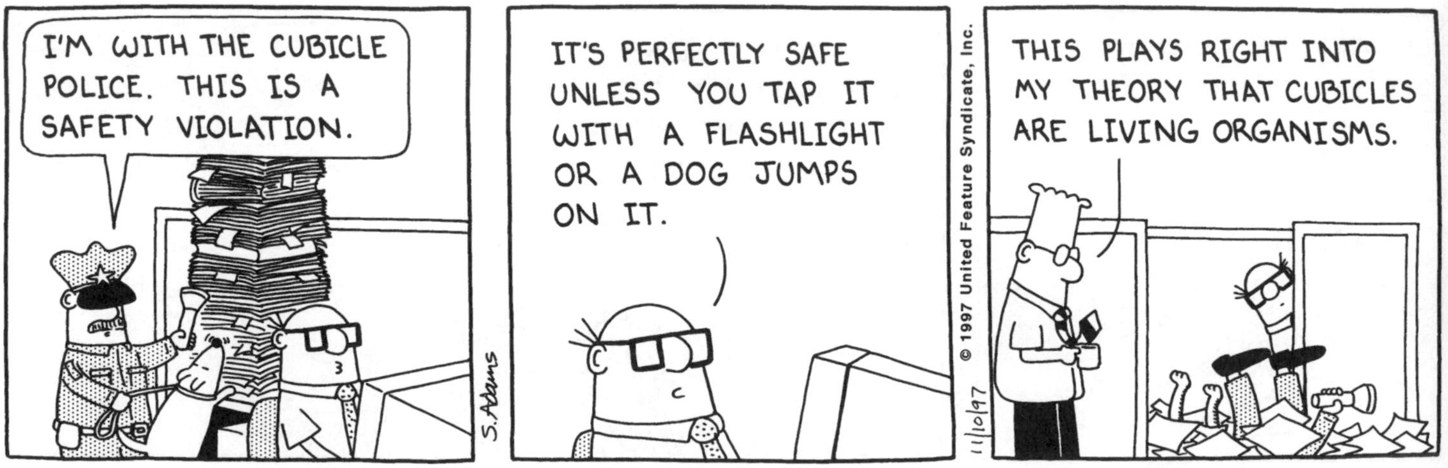
I'M WITH THE CUBICLE POLICE. THIS IS A SAFETY VIOLATION.
IT'S PERFECTLY SAFE UNLESS YOU TAP IT WITH A FLASHLIGHT OR A DOG JUMPS ON IT.
THIS PLAYS RIGHT INTO MY THEORY THAT CUBICLES ARE LIVING ORGANISMS.
S. Adams
11/10/97
© 1997 United Feature Syndicate, Inc.

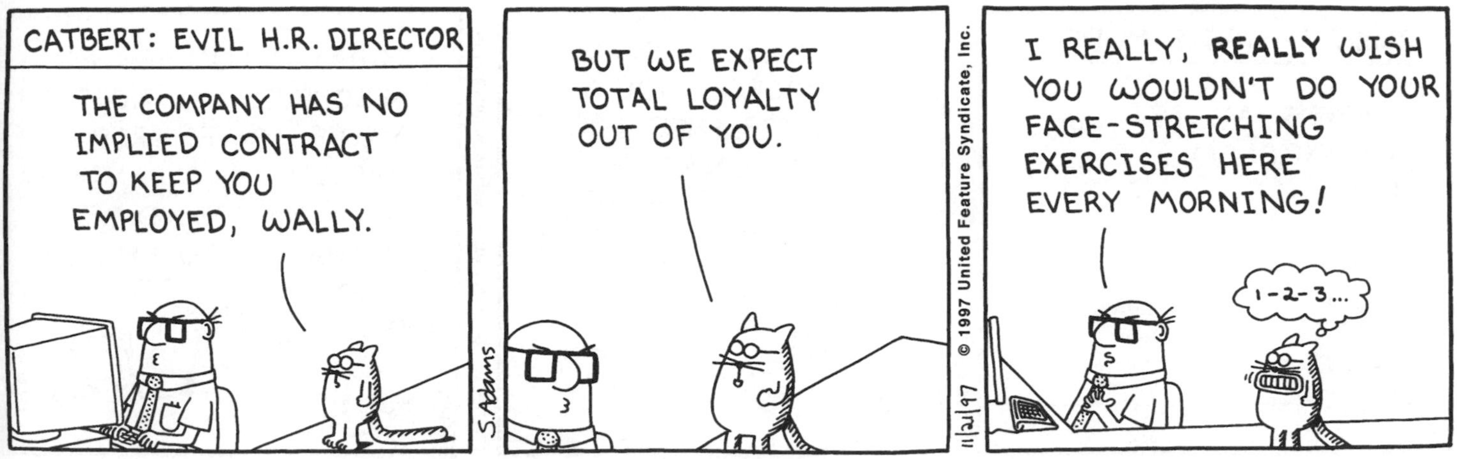
CATBERT: EVIL H.R. DIRECTOR
THE COMPANY HAS NO IMPLIED CONTRACT TO KEEP YOU EMPLOYED, WALLY.
BUT WE EXPECT TOTAL LOYALTY OUT OF YOU.
I REALLY, **REALLY** WISH YOU WOULDN'T DO YOUR FACE-STRETCHING EXERCISES HERE EVERY MORNING!
1-2-3...
S. Adams
11/21/97
© 1997 United Feature Syndicate, Inc.

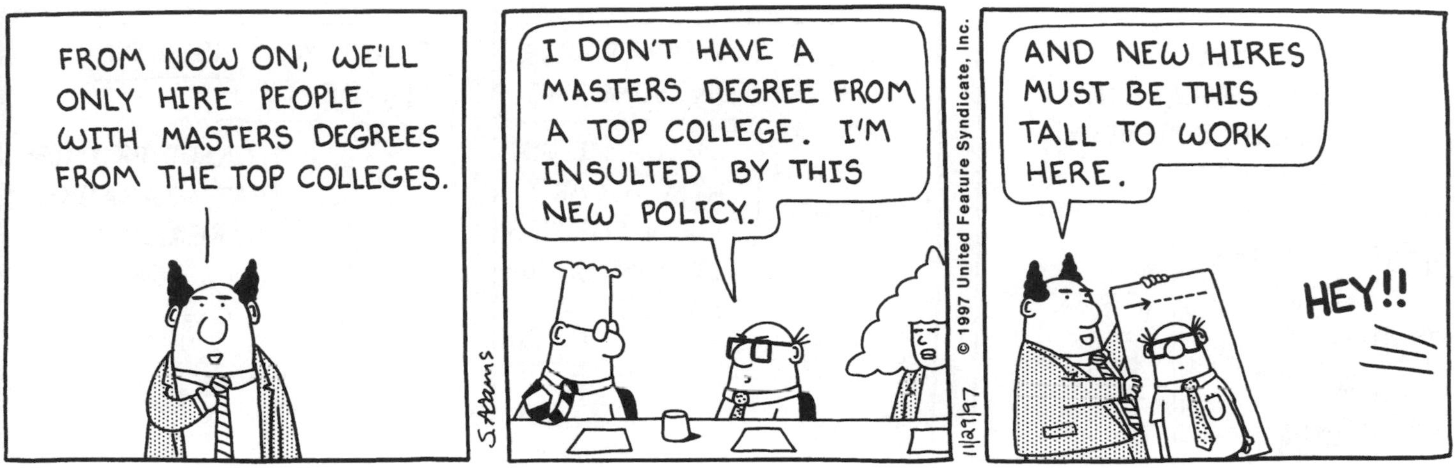
FROM NOW ON, WE'LL ONLY HIRE PEOPLE WITH MASTERS DEGREES FROM THE TOP COLLEGES.
I DON'T HAVE A MASTERS DEGREE FROM A TOP COLLEGE. I'M INSULTED BY THIS NEW POLICY.
AND NEW HIRES MUST BE THIS TALL TO WORK HERE.
HEY!!
S. Adams
11/29/97
© 1997 United Feature Syndicate, Inc.

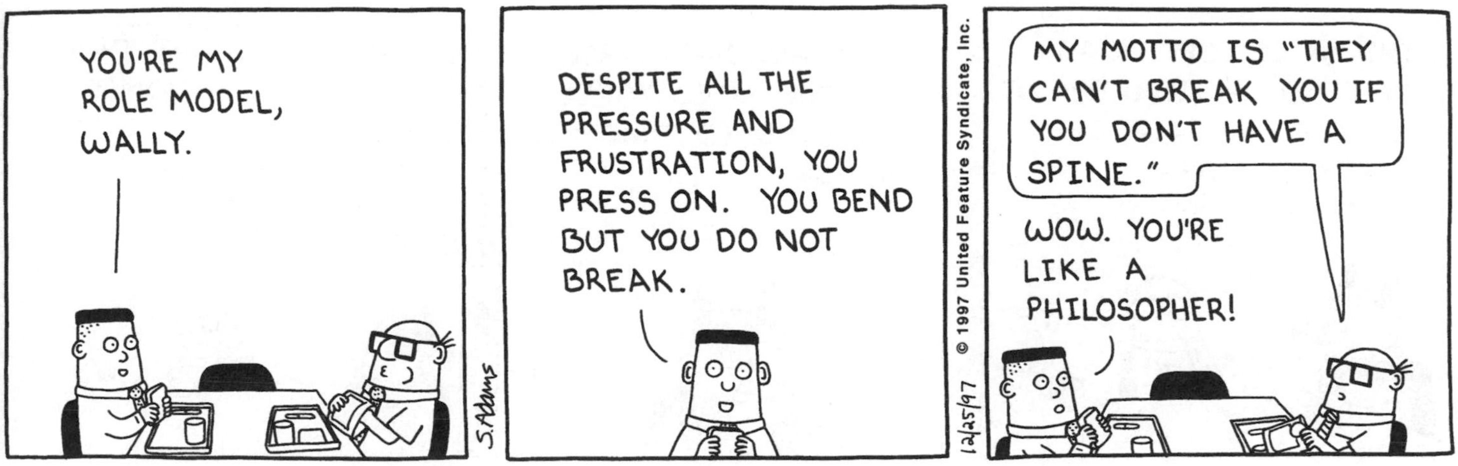
YOU'RE MY ROLE MODEL, WALLY.
DESPITE ALL THE PRESSURE AND FRUSTRATION, YOU PRESS ON. YOU BEND BUT YOU DO NOT BREAK.
MY MOTTO IS "THEY CAN'T BREAK YOU IF YOU DON'T HAVE A SPINE."
WOW. YOU'RE LIKE A PHILOSOPHER!
S. Adams
12/25/97
© 1997 United Feature Syndicate, Inc.

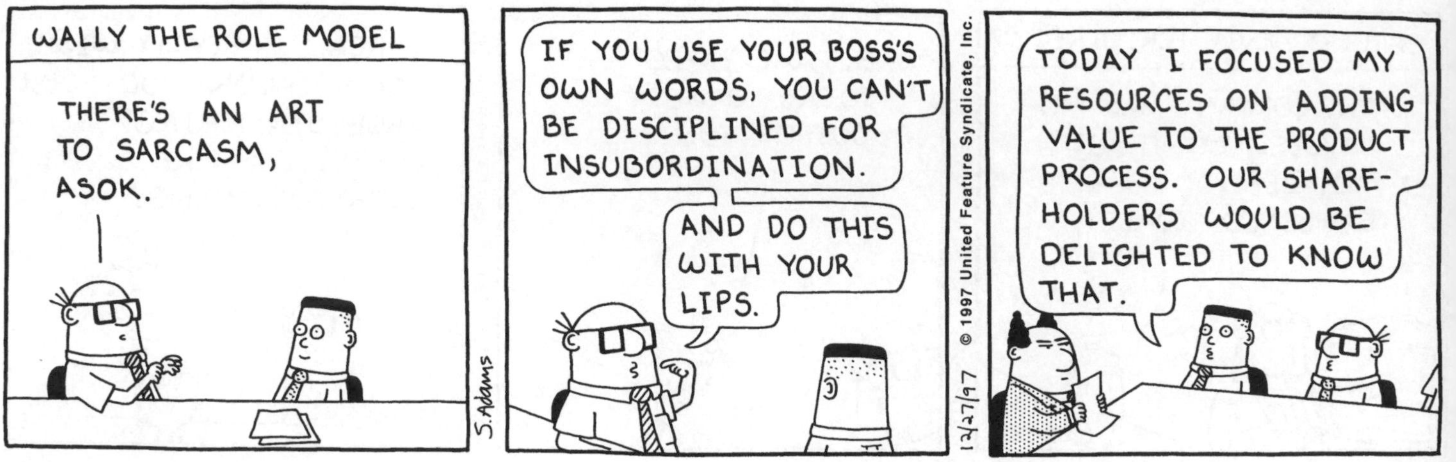
WALLY THE ROLE MODEL
THERE'S AN ART TO SARCASM, ASOK.
S. Adams
IF YOU USE YOUR BOSS'S OWN WORDS, YOU CAN'T BE DISCIPLINED FOR INSUBORDINATION.
AND DO THIS WITH YOUR LIPS.
12/27/97
© 1997 United Feature Syndicate, Inc.
TODAY I FOCUSED MY RESOURCES ON ADDING VALUE TO THE PRODUCT PROCESS. OUR SHARE-HOLDERS WOULD BE DELIGHTED TO KNOW THAT.

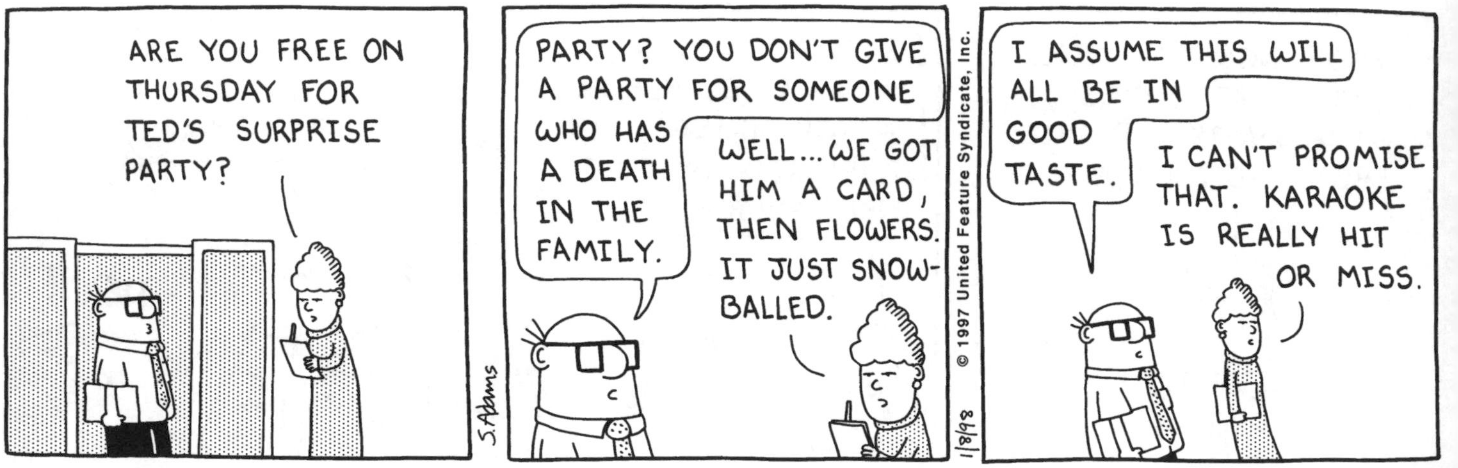
ARE YOU FREE ON THURSDAY FOR TED'S SURPRISE PARTY?
S. Adams
PARTY? YOU DON'T GIVE A PARTY FOR SOMEONE WHO HAS A DEATH IN THE FAMILY.
WELL... WE GOT HIM A CARD, THEN FLOWERS. IT JUST SNOW-BALLED.
1/8/98
© 1997 United Feature Syndicate, Inc.
I ASSUME THIS WILL ALL BE IN GOOD TASTE.
I CAN'T PROMISE THAT. KARAOKE IS REALLY HIT OR MISS.

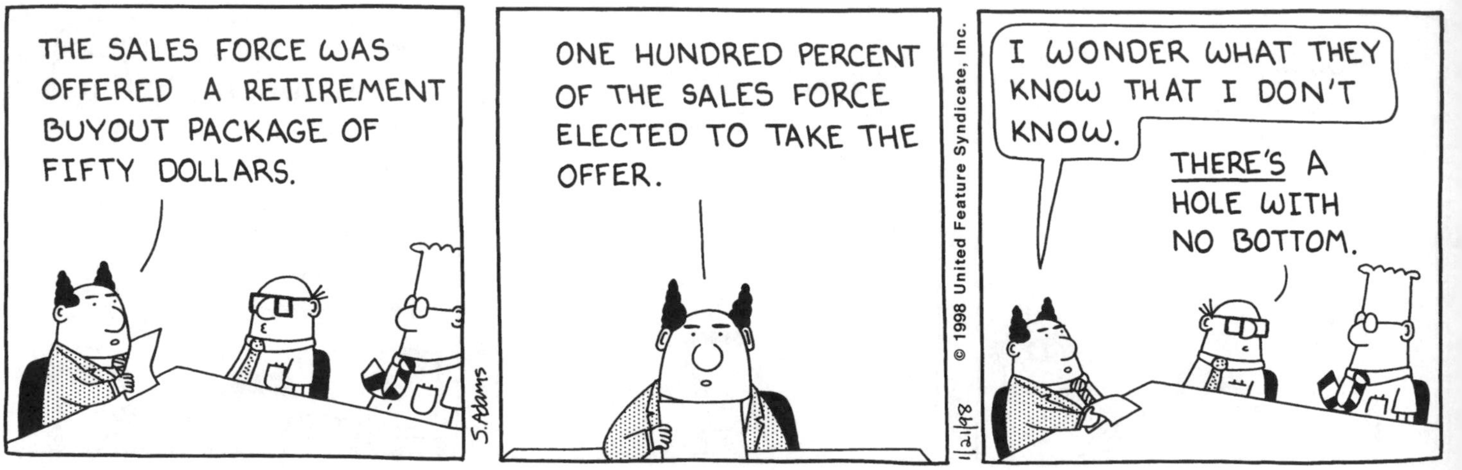
THE SALES FORCE WAS OFFERED A RETIREMENT BUYOUT PACKAGE OF FIFTY DOLLARS.
S. Adams
ONE HUNDRED PERCENT OF THE SALES FORCE ELECTED TO TAKE THE OFFER.
1/21/98
© 1998 United Feature Syndicate, Inc.
I WONDER WHAT THEY KNOW THAT I DON'T KNOW.
THERE'S A HOLE WITH NO BOTTOM.

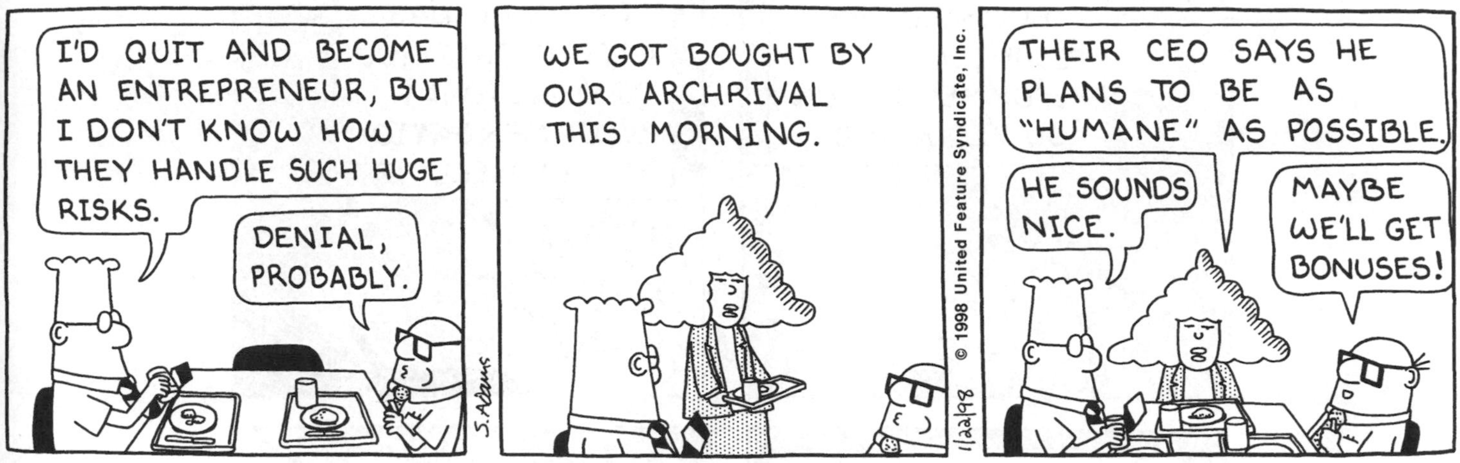
I'D QUIT AND BECOME AN ENTREPRENEUR, BUT I DON'T KNOW HOW THEY HANDLE SUCH HUGE RISKS.
DENIAL, PROBABLY.
WE GOT BOUGHT BY OUR ARCHRIVAL THIS MORNING.
THEIR CEO SAYS HE PLANS TO BE AS "HUMANE" AS POSSIBLE.
HE SOUNDS NICE.
MAYBE WE'LL GET BONUSES!
S. Adams
1/22/98
© 1998 United Feature Syndicate, Inc.

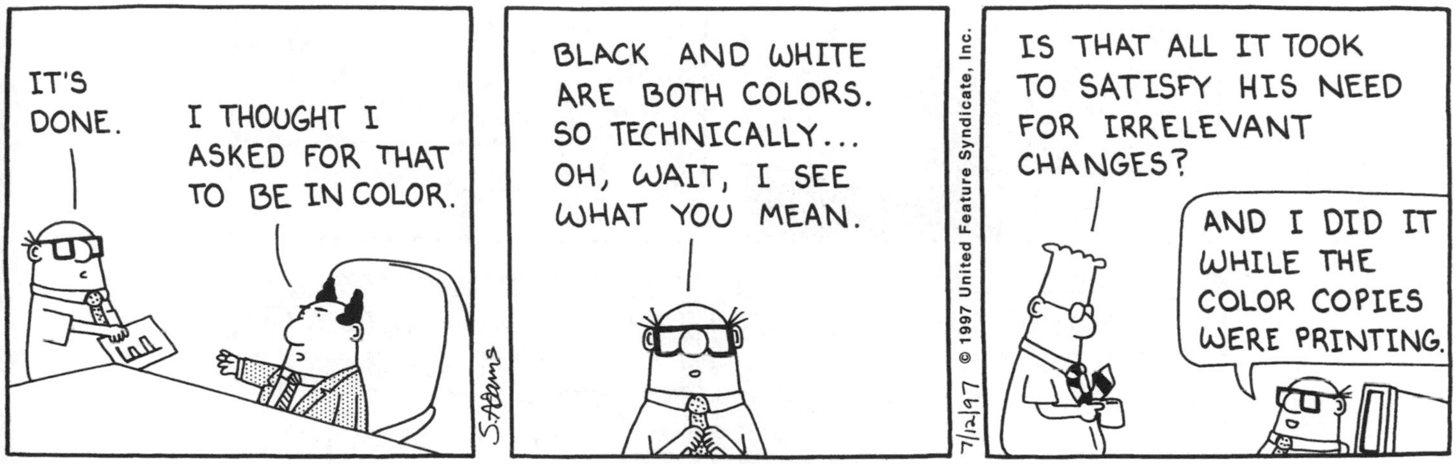
IT'S DONE.
I THOUGHT I ASKED FOR THAT TO BE IN COLOR.
BLACK AND WHITE ARE BOTH COLORS. SO TECHNICALLY... OH, WAIT, I SEE WHAT YOU MEAN.
IS THAT ALL IT TOOK TO SATISFY HIS NEED FOR IRRELEVANT CHANGES?
AND I DID IT WHILE THE COLOR COPIES WERE PRINTING.
S. Adams
7/12/97
© 1997 United Feature Syndicate, Inc.

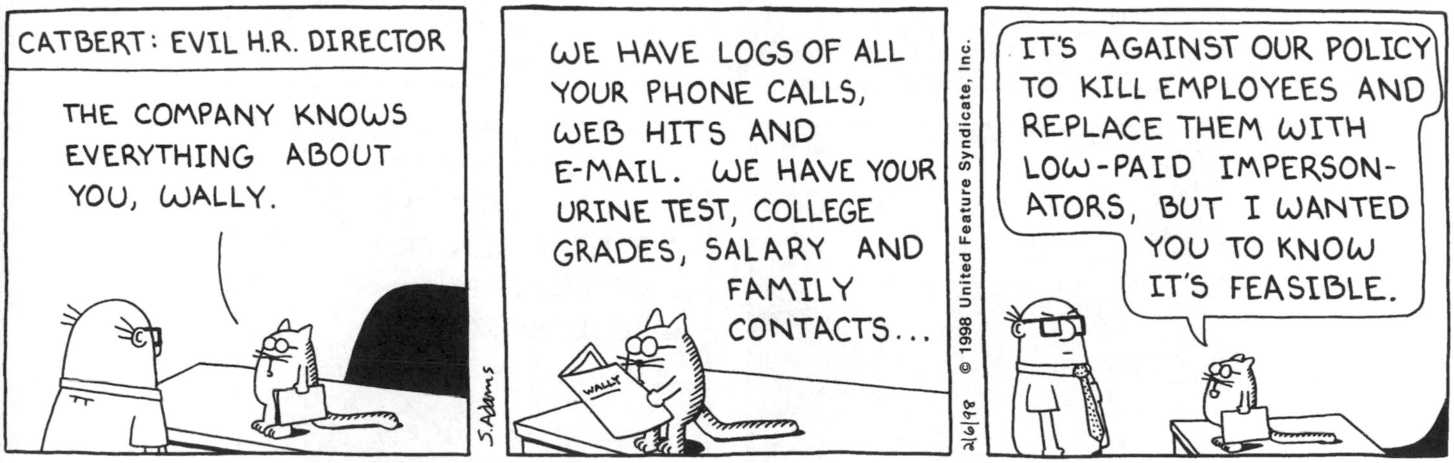
CATBERT: EVIL H.R. DIRECTOR
THE COMPANY KNOWS EVERYTHING ABOUT YOU, WALLY.
WE HAVE LOGS OF ALL YOUR PHONE CALLS, WEB HITS AND E-MAIL. WE HAVE YOUR URINE TEST, COLLEGE GRADES, SALARY AND FAMILY CONTACTS...
WALLY
IT'S AGAINST OUR POLICY TO KILL EMPLOYEES AND REPLACE THEM WITH LOW-PAID IMPERSON-ATORS, BUT I WANTED YOU TO KNOW IT'S FEASIBLE.
S. Adams
2/6/98
© 1998 United Feature Syndicate, Inc.

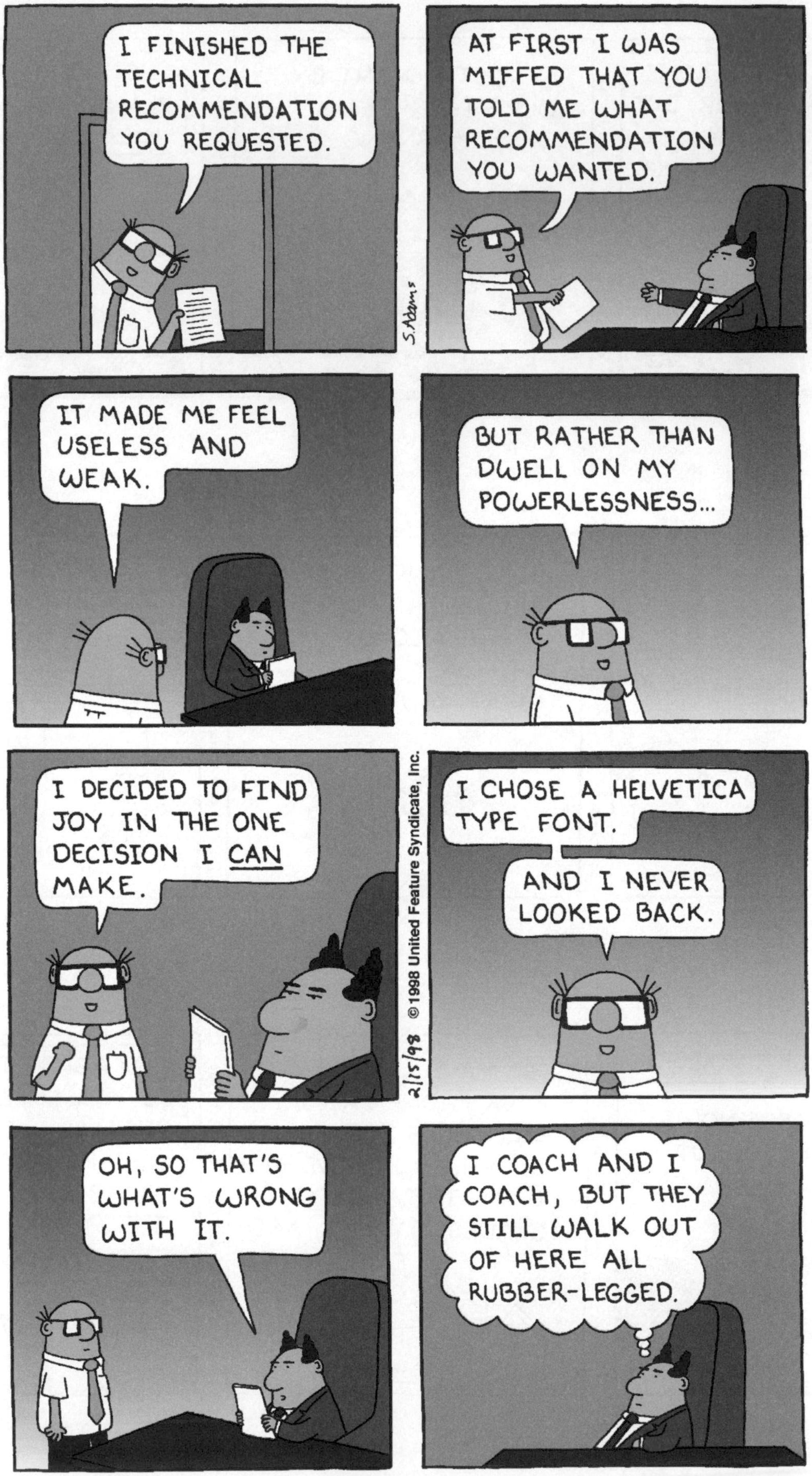
I FINISHED THE TECHNICAL RECOMMENDATION YOU REQUESTED.
AT FIRST I WAS MIFFED THAT YOU TOLD ME WHAT RECOMMENDATION YOU WANTED.
IT MADE ME FEEL USELESS AND WEAK.
BUT RATHER THAN DWELL ON MY POWERLESSNESS...
I DECIDED TO FIND JOY IN THE ONE DECISION I CAN MAKE.
I CHOSE A HELVETICA TYPE FONT.
AND I NEVER LOOKED BACK.
OH, SO THAT'S WHAT'S WRONG WITH IT.
I COACH AND I COACH, BUT THEY STILL WALK OUT OF HERE ALL RUBBER-LEGGED.
S. Adams
2/15/98 © 1998 United Feature Syndicate, Inc.

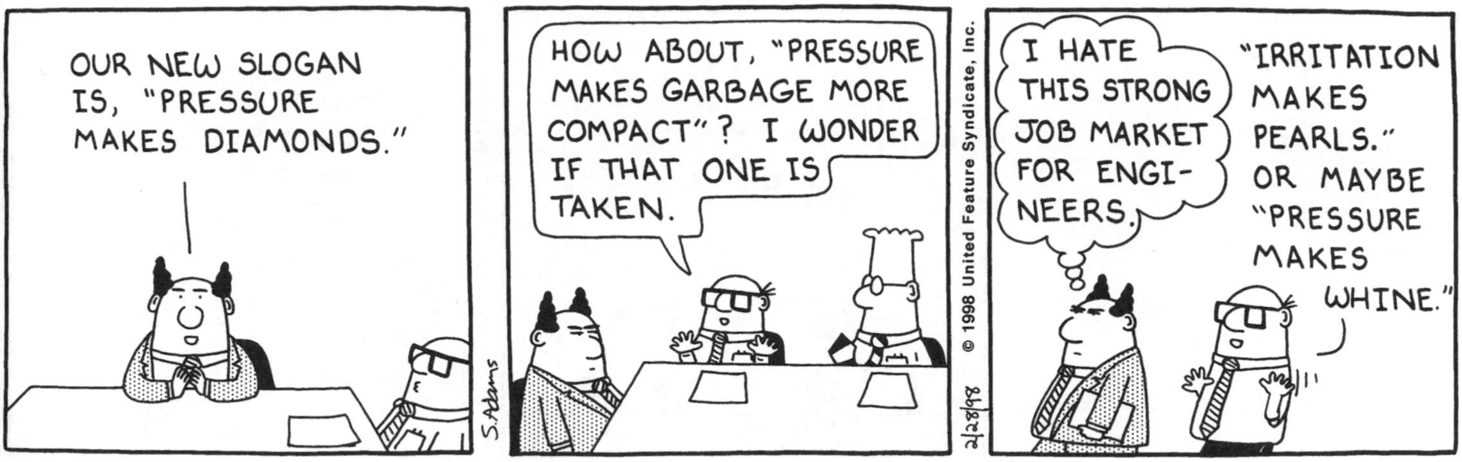
OUR NEW SLOGAN IS, "PRESSURE MAKES DIAMONDS."
HOW ABOUT, "PRESSURE MAKES GARBAGE MORE COMPACT"? I WONDER IF THAT ONE IS TAKEN.
I HATE THIS STRONG JOB MARKET FOR ENGINEERS.
"IRRITATION MAKES PEARLS." OR MAYBE "PRESSURE MAKES WHINE."
S. Adams
2/28/98
© 1998 United Feature Syndicate, Inc.

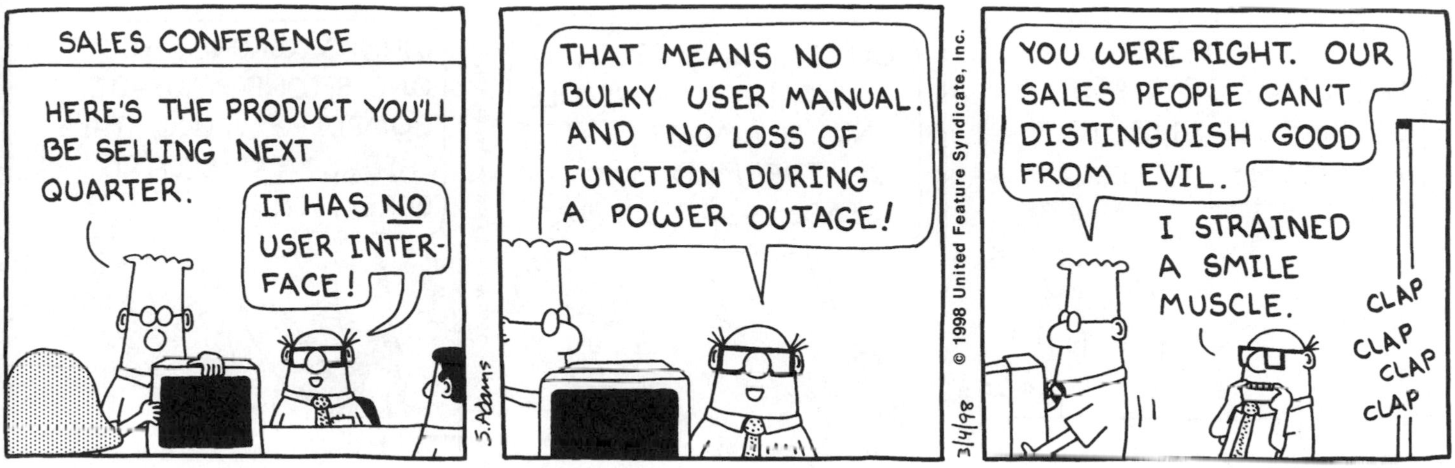
SALES CONFERENCE
HERE'S THE PRODUCT YOU'LL BE SELLING NEXT QUARTER.
IT HAS NO USER INTERFACE!
THAT MEANS NO BULKY USER MANUAL. AND NO LOSS OF FUNCTION DURING A POWER OUTAGE!
YOU WERE RIGHT. OUR SALES PEOPLE CAN'T DISTINGUISH GOOD FROM EVIL.
I STRAINED A SMILE MUSCLE.
CLAP CLAP CLAP CLAP
S. Adams
3/4/98
© 1998 United Feature Syndicate, Inc.

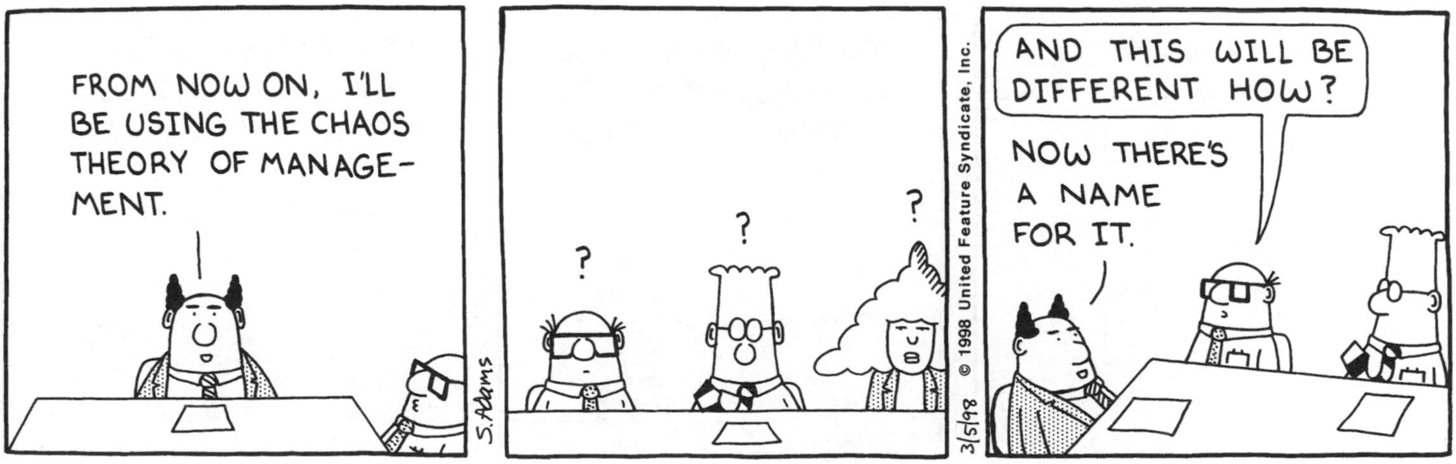
FROM NOW ON, I'LL BE USING THE CHAOS THEORY OF MANAGEMENT.
? ? ?
AND THIS WILL BE DIFFERENT HOW?
NOW THERE'S A NAME FOR IT.
S. Adams
3/5/98
© 1998 United Feature Syndicate, Inc.

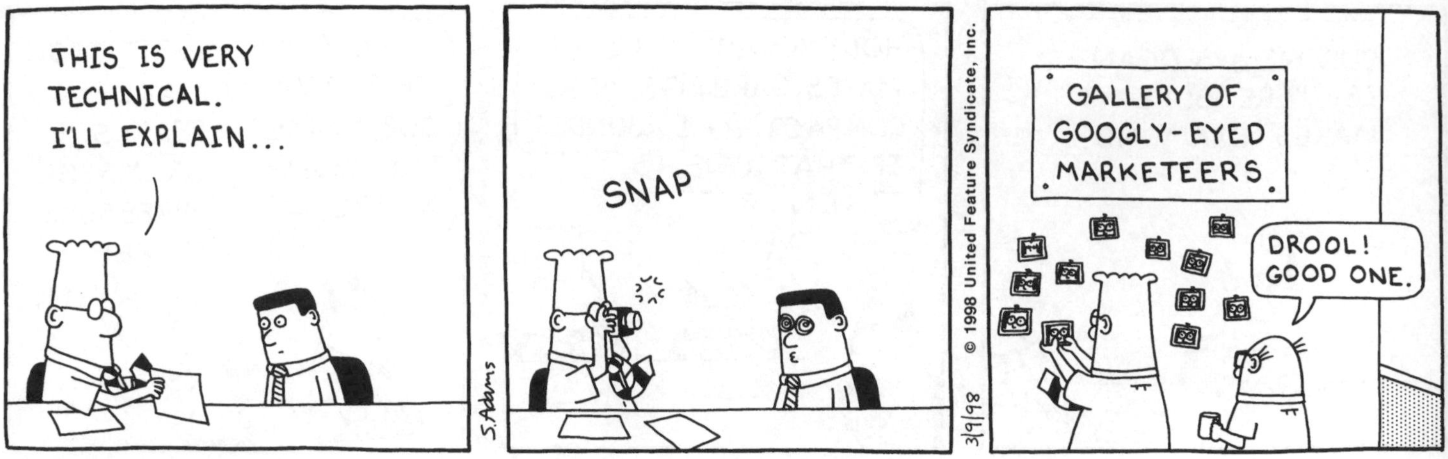
THIS IS VERY TECHNICAL. I'LL EXPLAIN...
S. Adams
SNAP
3/9/98
© 1998 United Feature Syndicate, Inc.
GALLERY OF GOOGLY-EYED MARKETEERS
DROOL! GOOD ONE.

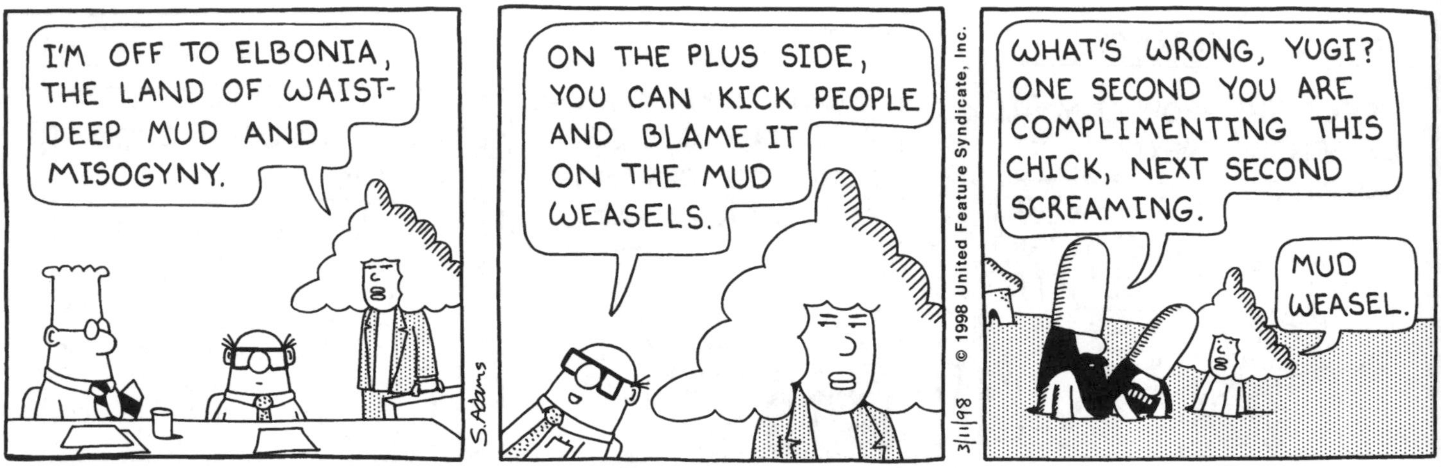
I'M OFF TO ELBONIA, THE LAND OF WAIST-DEEP MUD AND MISOGYNY.
S. Adams
ON THE PLUS SIDE, YOU CAN KICK PEOPLE AND BLAME IT ON THE MUD WEASELS.
3/1/98
© 1998 United Feature Syndicate, Inc.
WHAT'S WRONG, YUGI? ONE SECOND YOU ARE COMPLIMENTING THIS CHICK, NEXT SECOND SCREAMING.
MUD WEASEL.

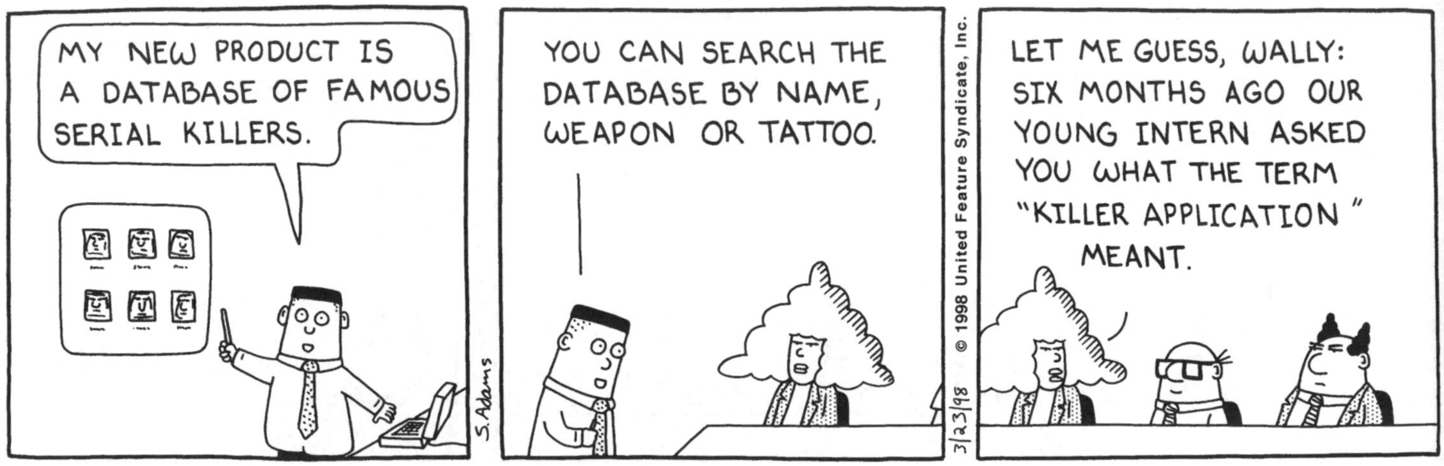
MY NEW PRODUCT IS A DATABASE OF FAMOUS SERIAL KILLERS.
S. Adams
YOU CAN SEARCH THE DATABASE BY NAME, WEAPON OR TATTOO.
3/23/98
© 1998 United Feature Syndicate, Inc.
LET ME GUESS, WALLY: SIX MONTHS AGO OUR YOUNG INTERN ASKED YOU WHAT THE TERM "KILLER APPLICATION" MEANT.

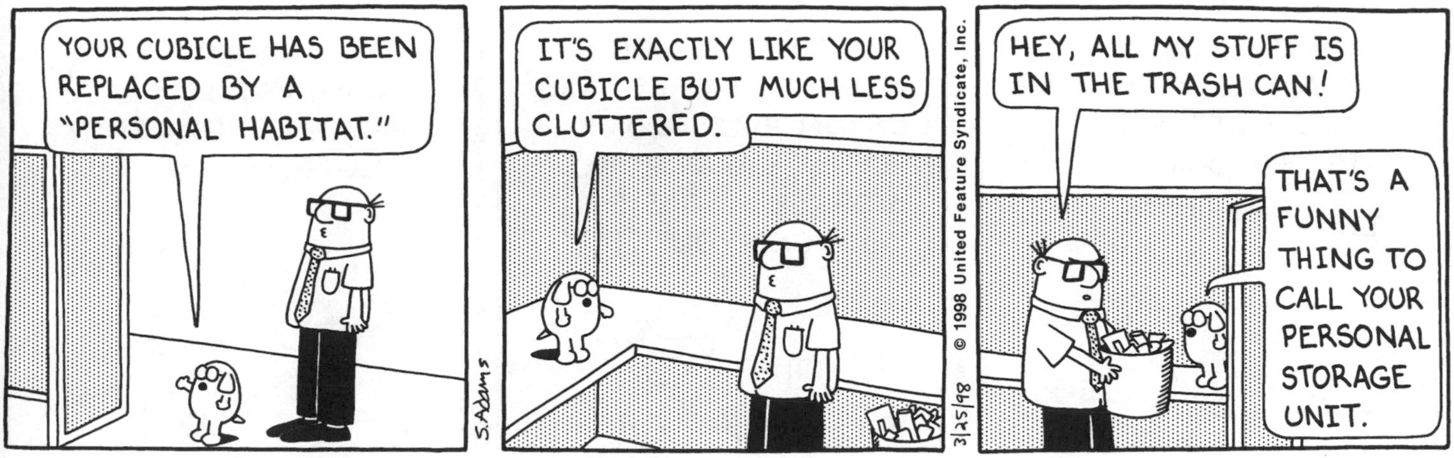
YOUR CUBICLE HAS BEEN REPLACED BY A "PERSONAL HABITAT."
IT'S EXACTLY LIKE YOUR CUBICLE BUT MUCH LESS CLUTTERED.
S. Adams 3/25/98 © 1998 United Feature Syndicate, Inc.
HEY, ALL MY STUFF IS IN THE TRASH CAN!
THAT'S A FUNNY THING TO CALL YOUR PERSONAL STORAGE UNIT.

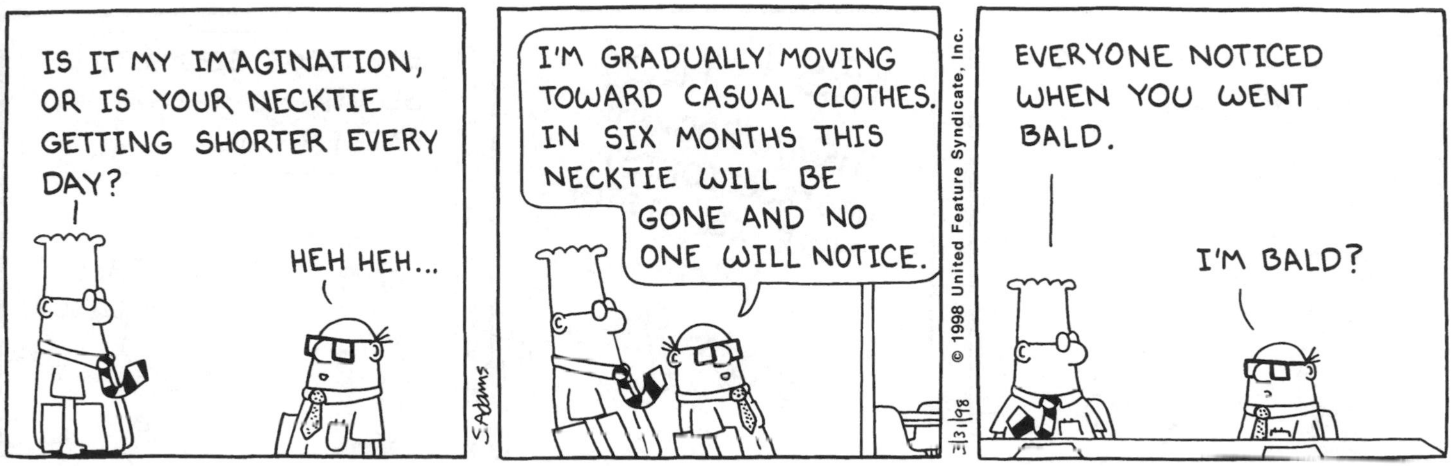
IS IT MY IMAGINATION, OR IS YOUR NECKTIE GETTING SHORTER EVERY DAY?
HEH HEH...
I'M GRADUALLY MOVING TOWARD CASUAL CLOTHES. IN SIX MONTHS THIS NECKTIE WILL BE GONE AND NO ONE WILL NOTICE.
S. Adams 3/31/98 © 1998 United Feature Syndicate, Inc.
EVERYONE NOTICED WHEN YOU WENT BALD.
I'M BALD?

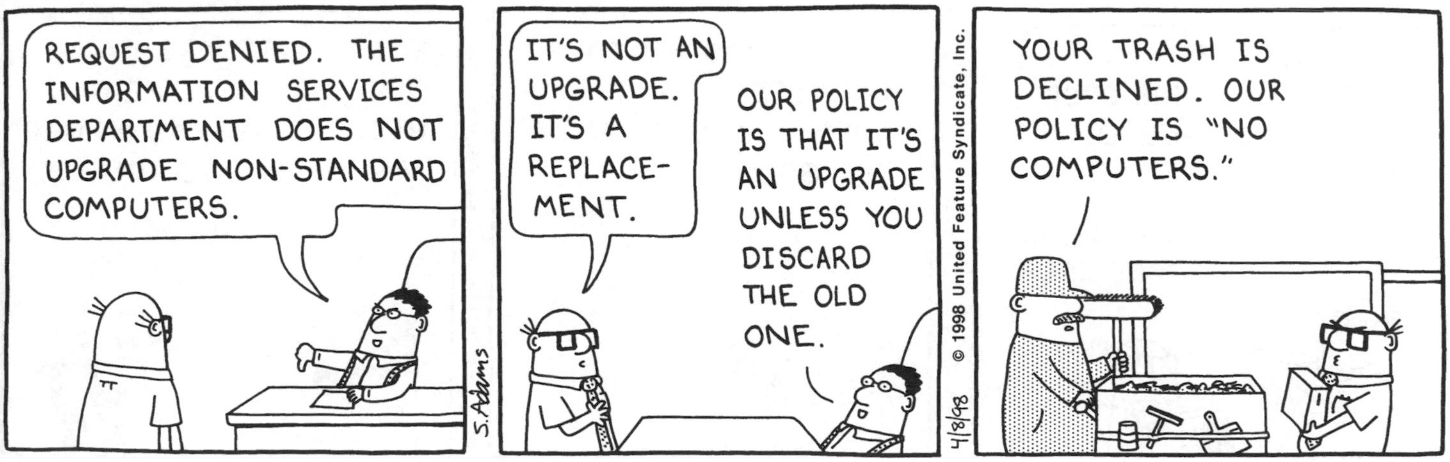
REQUEST DENIED. THE INFORMATION SERVICES DEPARTMENT DOES NOT UPGRADE NON-STANDARD COMPUTERS.
IT'S NOT AN UPGRADE. IT'S A REPLACE-MENT.
OUR POLICY IS THAT IT'S AN UPGRADE UNLESS YOU DISCARD THE OLD ONE.
S. Adams 4/8/98 © 1998 United Feature Syndicate, Inc.
YOUR TRASH IS DECLINED. OUR POLICY IS "NO COMPUTERS."

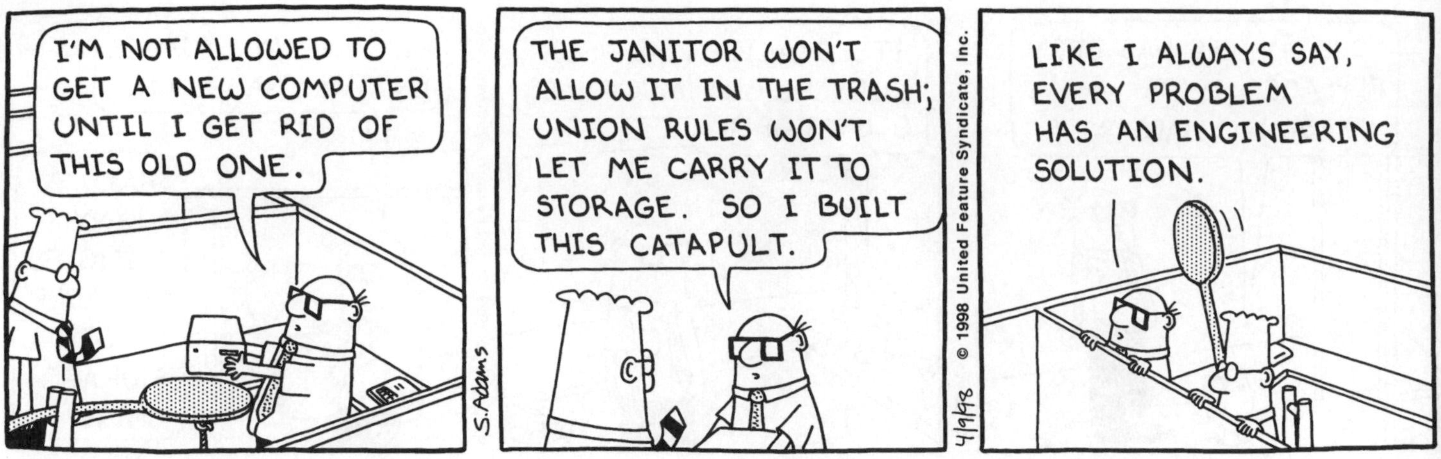
I'M NOT ALLOWED TO GET A NEW COMPUTER UNTIL I GET RID OF THIS OLD ONE.
S.Adams
THE JANITOR WON'T ALLOW IT IN THE TRASH; UNION RULES WON'T LET ME CARRY IT TO STORAGE. SO I BUILT THIS CATAPULT.
4/9/98 © 1998 United Feature Syndicate, Inc.
LIKE I ALWAYS SAY, EVERY PROBLEM HAS AN ENGINEERING SOLUTION.

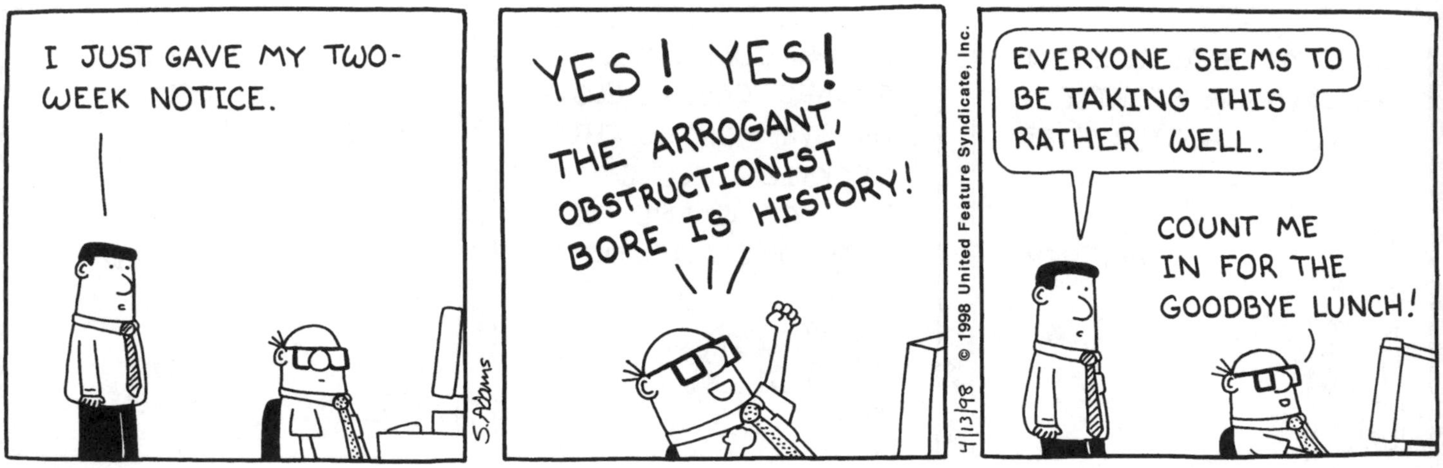
I JUST GAVE MY TWO-WEEK NOTICE.
S.Adams
YES! YES!
THE ARROGANT, OBSTRUCTIONIST BORE IS HISTORY!
4/13/98 © 1998 United Feature Syndicate, Inc.
EVERYONE SEEMS TO BE TAKING THIS RATHER WELL.
COUNT ME IN FOR THE GOODBYE LUNCH!

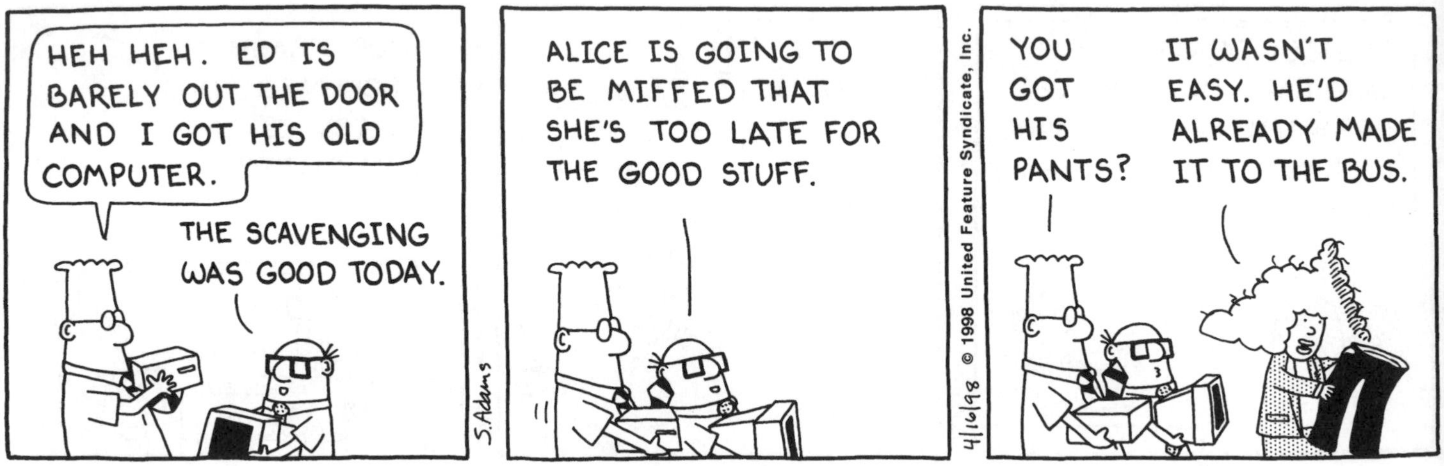
HEH HEH. ED IS BARELY OUT THE DOOR AND I GOT HIS OLD COMPUTER.
THE SCAVENGING WAS GOOD TODAY.
S.Adams
ALICE IS GOING TO BE MIFFED THAT SHE'S TOO LATE FOR THE GOOD STUFF.
4/16/98 © 1998 United Feature Syndicate, Inc.
YOU GOT HIS PANTS?
IT WASN'T EASY. HE'D ALREADY MADE IT TO THE BUS.

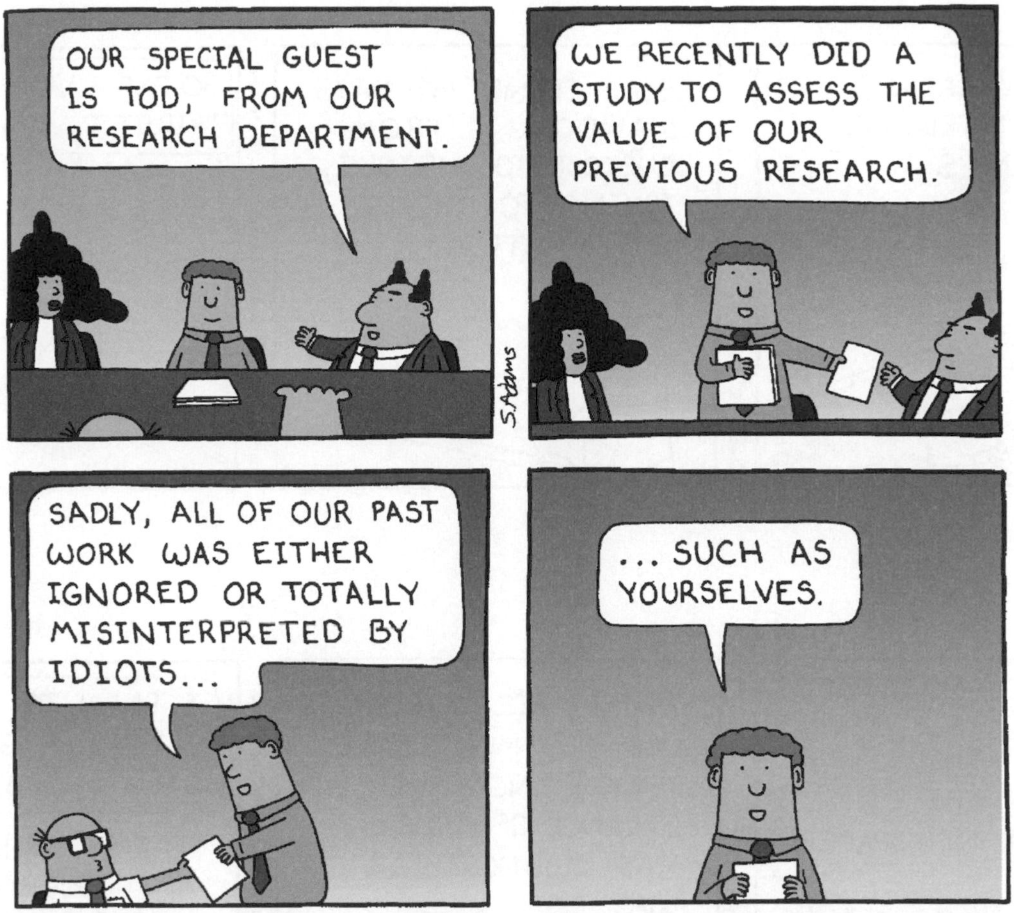
OUR SPECIAL GUEST IS TOD, FROM OUR RESEARCH DEPARTMENT.
WE RECENTLY DID A STUDY TO ASSESS THE VALUE OF OUR PREVIOUS RESEARCH.
SADLY, ALL OF OUR PAST WORK WAS EITHER IGNORED OR TOTALLY MISINTERPRETED BY IDIOTS...
... SUCH AS YOURSELVES.
S. Adams

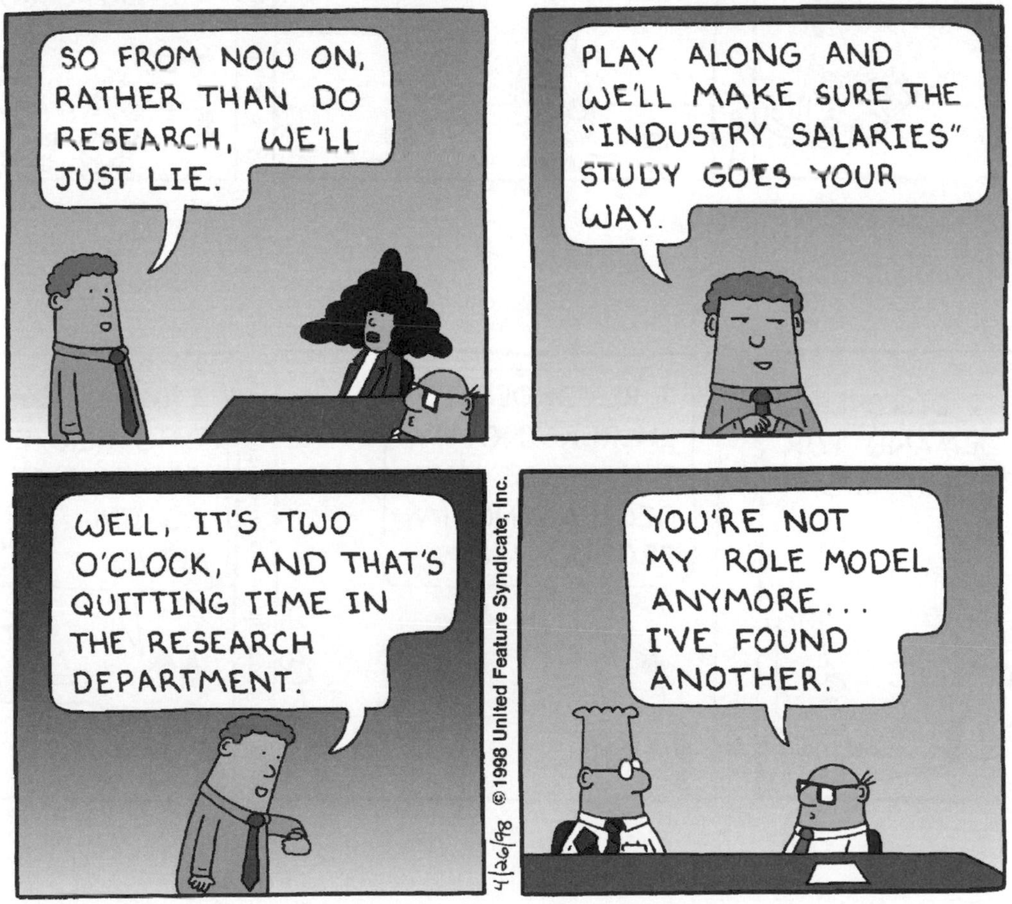
SO FROM NOW ON, RATHER THAN DO RESEARCH, WE'LL JUST LIE.
PLAY ALONG AND WE'LL MAKE SURE THE "INDUSTRY SALARIES" STUDY GOES YOUR WAY.
WELL, IT'S TWO O'CLOCK, AND THAT'S QUITTING TIME IN THE RESEARCH DEPARTMENT.
YOU'RE NOT MY ROLE MODEL ANYMORE... I'VE FOUND ANOTHER.
4/26/98 © 1998 United Feature Syndicate, Inc.

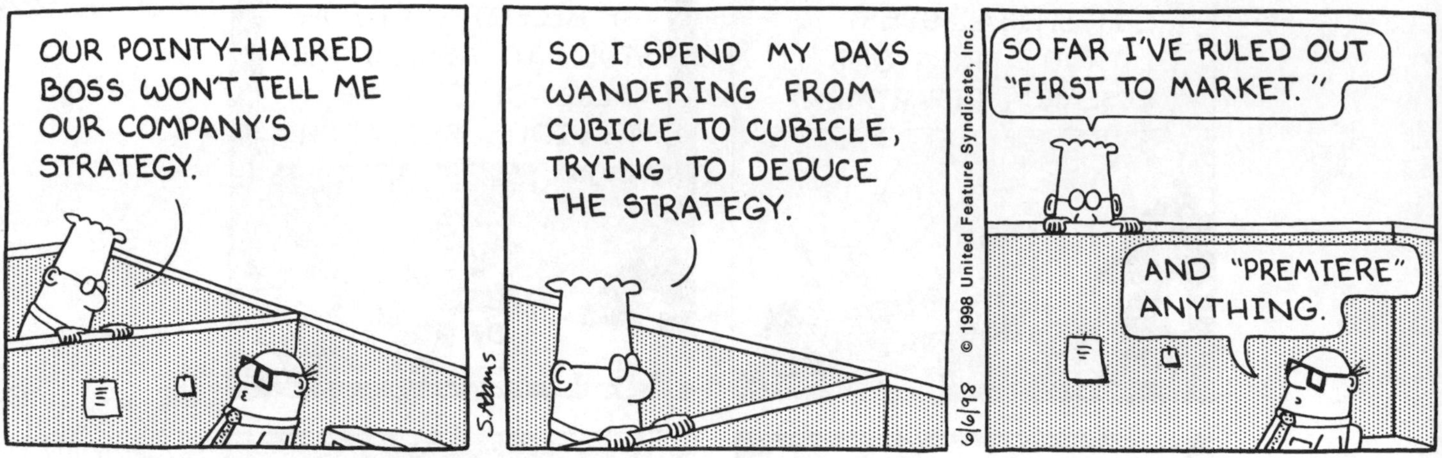
OUR POINTY-HAIRED BOSS WON'T TELL ME OUR COMPANY'S STRATEGY.
SO I SPEND MY DAYS WANDERING FROM CUBICLE TO CUBICLE, TRYING TO DEDUCE THE STRATEGY.
S. Adams
6/6/98 © 1998 United Feature Syndicate, Inc.
SO FAR I'VE RULED OUT "FIRST TO MARKET."
AND "PREMIERE" ANYTHING.

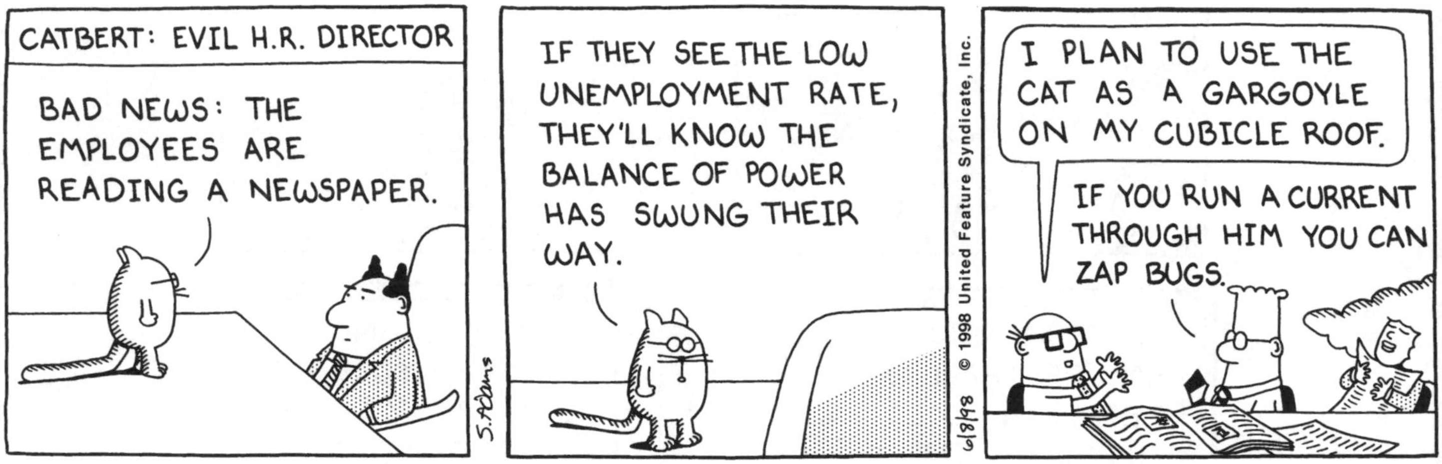
CATBERT: EVIL H.R. DIRECTOR
BAD NEWS: THE EMPLOYEES ARE READING A NEWSPAPER.
IF THEY SEE THE LOW UNEMPLOYMENT RATE, THEY'LL KNOW THE BALANCE OF POWER HAS SWUNG THEIR WAY.
S. Adams
6/8/98 © 1998 United Feature Syndicate, Inc.
I PLAN TO USE THE CAT AS A GARGOYLE ON MY CUBICLE ROOF.
IF YOU RUN A CURRENT THROUGH HIM YOU CAN ZAP BUGS.

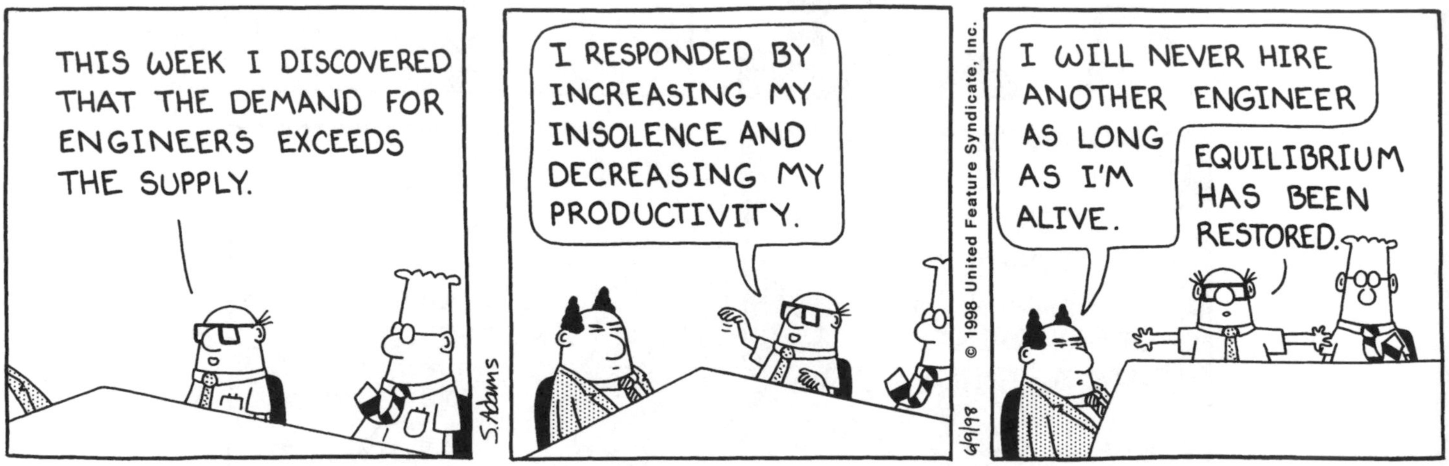
THIS WEEK I DISCOVERED THAT THE DEMAND FOR ENGINEERS EXCEEDS THE SUPPLY.
I RESPONDED BY INCREASING MY INSOLENCE AND DECREASING MY PRODUCTIVITY.
S. Adams
6/9/98 © 1998 United Feature Syndicate, Inc.
I WILL NEVER HIRE ANOTHER ENGINEER AS LONG AS I'M ALIVE.
EQUILIBRIUM HAS BEEN RESTORED.

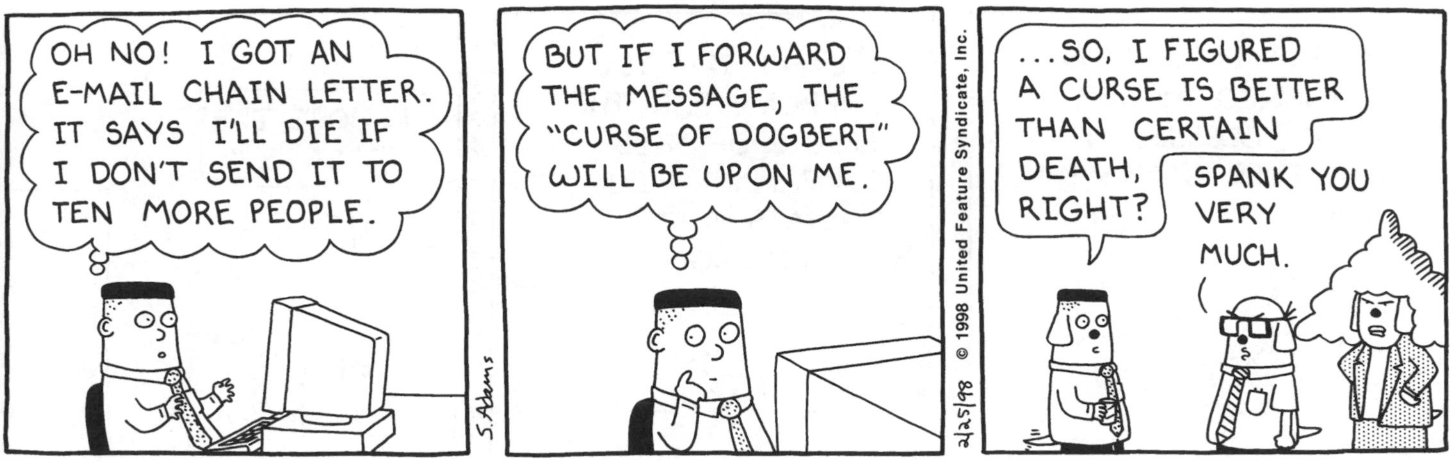
OH NO! I GOT AN E-MAIL CHAIN LETTER. IT SAYS I'LL DIE IF I DON'T SEND IT TO TEN MORE PEOPLE.
BUT IF I FORWARD THE MESSAGE, THE "CURSE OF DOGBERT" WILL BE UPON ME.
...SO, I FIGURED A CURSE IS BETTER THAN CERTAIN DEATH, RIGHT?
SPANK YOU VERY MUCH.
S. Adams
2/25/98
© 1998 United Feature Syndicate, Inc.

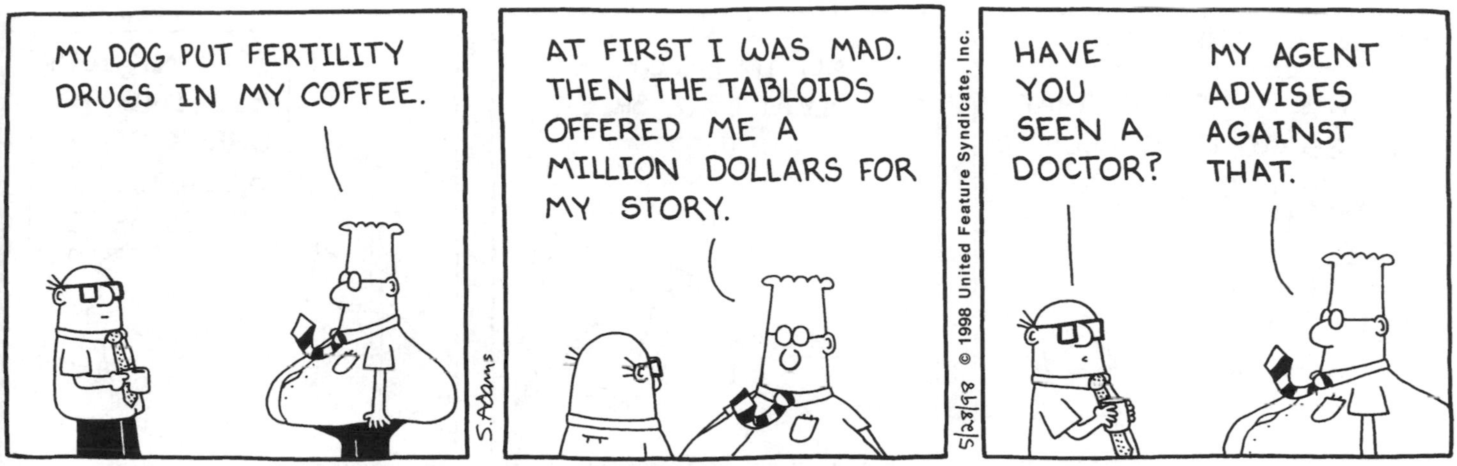
MY DOG PUT FERTILITY DRUGS IN MY COFFEE.
AT FIRST I WAS MAD. THEN THE TABLOIDS OFFERED ME A MILLION DOLLARS FOR MY STORY.
HAVE YOU SEEN A DOCTOR?
MY AGENT ADVISES AGAINST THAT.
S. Adams
5/28/98
© 1998 United Feature Syndicate, Inc.

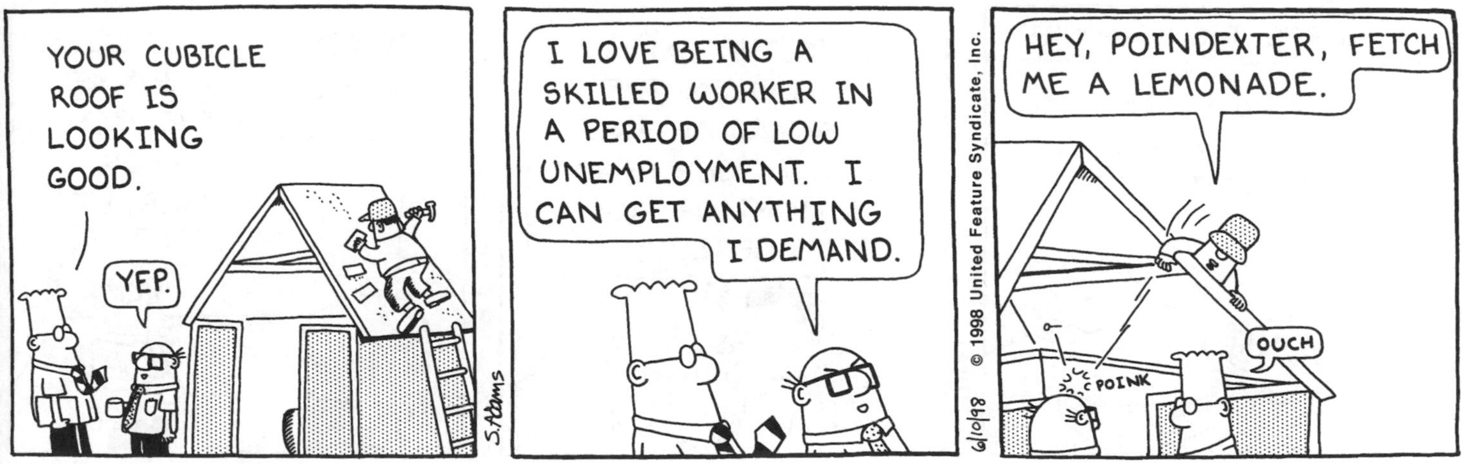
YOUR CUBICLE ROOF IS LOOKING GOOD.
YEP.
I LOVE BEING A SKILLED WORKER IN A PERIOD OF LOW UNEMPLOYMENT. I CAN GET ANYTHING I DEMAND.
HEY, POINDEXTER, FETCH ME A LEMONADE.
POINK
OUCH
S. Adams
6/10/98
© 1998 United Feature Syndicate, Inc.

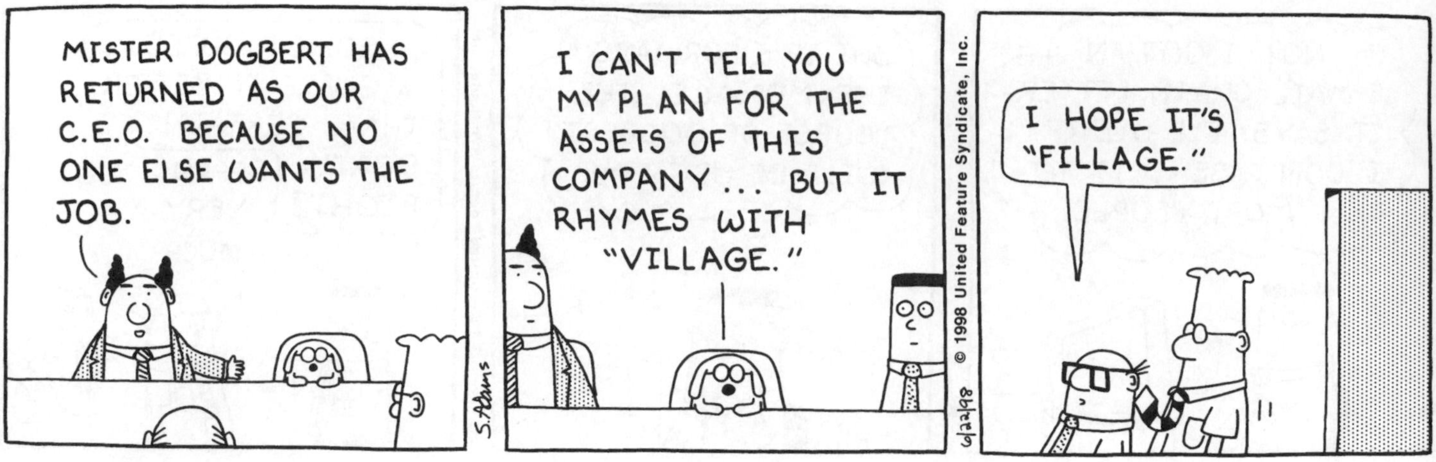
MISTER DOGBERT HAS RETURNED AS OUR C.E.O. BECAUSE NO ONE ELSE WANTS THE JOB.
I CAN'T TELL YOU MY PLAN FOR THE ASSETS OF THIS COMPANY ... BUT IT RHYMES WITH "VILLAGE."
© 1998 United Feature Syndicate, Inc.
I HOPE IT'S "FILLAGE."

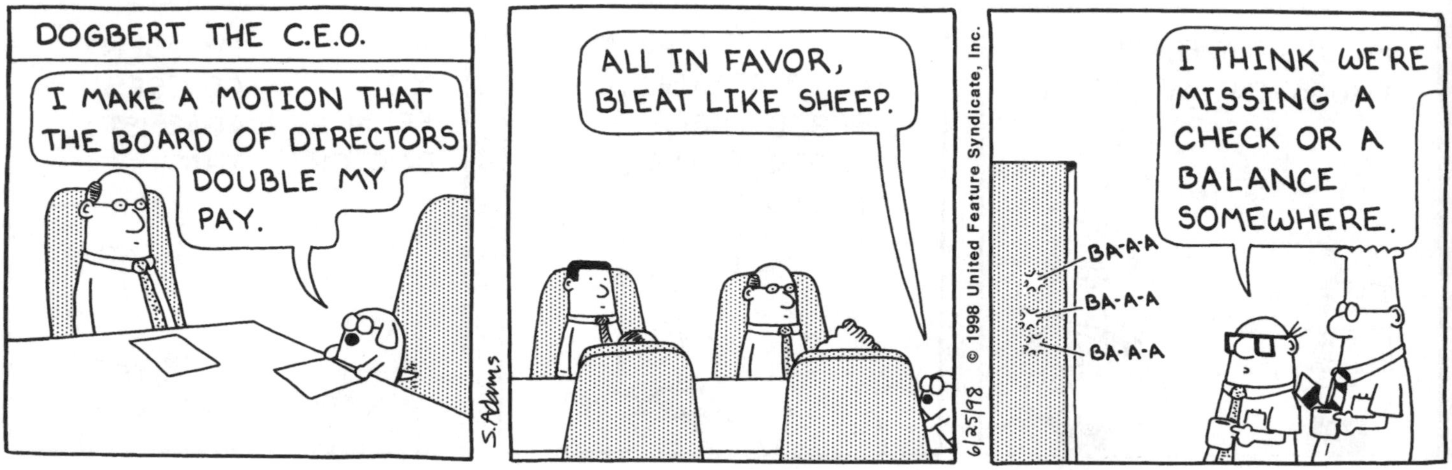
DOGBERT THE C.E.O.
I MAKE A MOTION THAT THE BOARD OF DIRECTORS DOUBLE MY PAY.
ALL IN FAVOR, BLEAT LIKE SHEEP.
© 1998 United Feature Syndicate, Inc.
BA-A-A
BA-A-A
BA-A-A
I THINK WE'RE MISSING A CHECK OR A BALANCE SOMEWHERE.

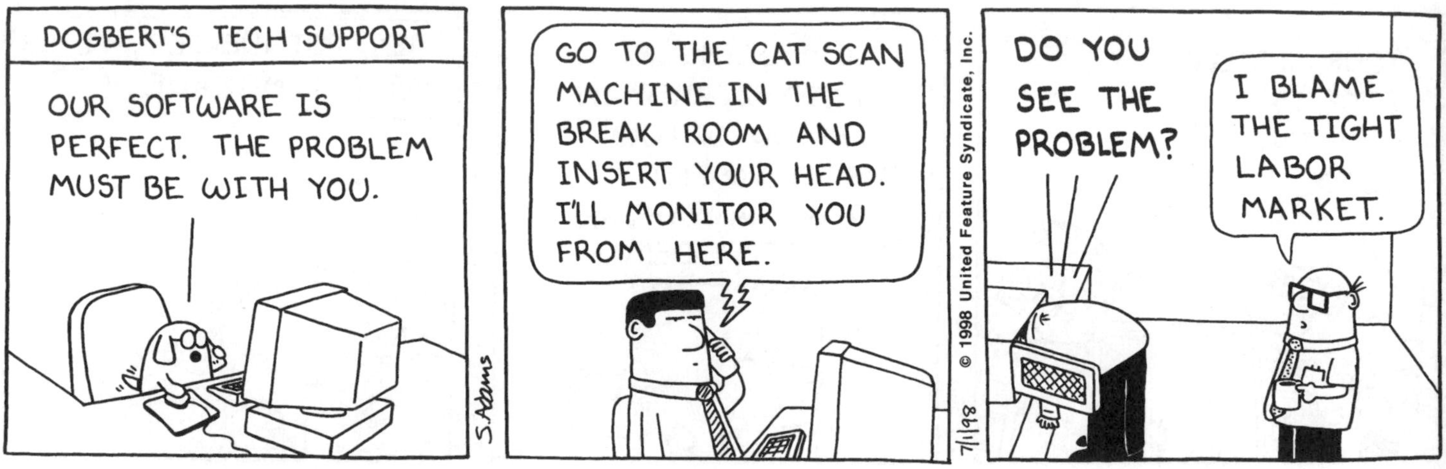
DOGBERT'S TECH SUPPORT
OUR SOFTWARE IS PERFECT. THE PROBLEM MUST BE WITH YOU.
GO TO THE CAT SCAN MACHINE IN THE BREAK ROOM AND INSERT YOUR HEAD. I'LL MONITOR YOU FROM HERE.
© 1998 United Feature Syndicate, Inc.
DO YOU SEE THE PROBLEM?
I BLAME THE TIGHT LABOR MARKET.

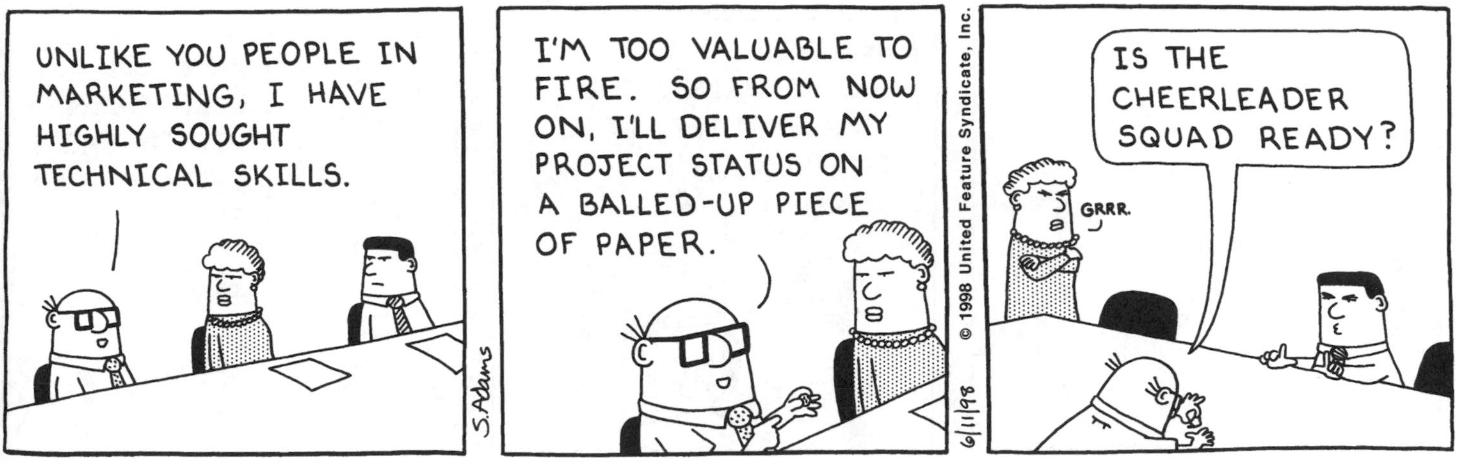
UNLIKE YOU PEOPLE IN MARKETING, I HAVE HIGHLY SOUGHT TECHNICAL SKILLS.
S. Adams
I'M TOO VALUABLE TO FIRE. SO FROM NOW ON, I'LL DELIVER MY PROJECT STATUS ON A BALLED-UP PIECE OF PAPER.
6/1/98
© 1998 United Feature Syndicate, Inc.
IS THE CHEERLEADER SQUAD READY?
GRRR.

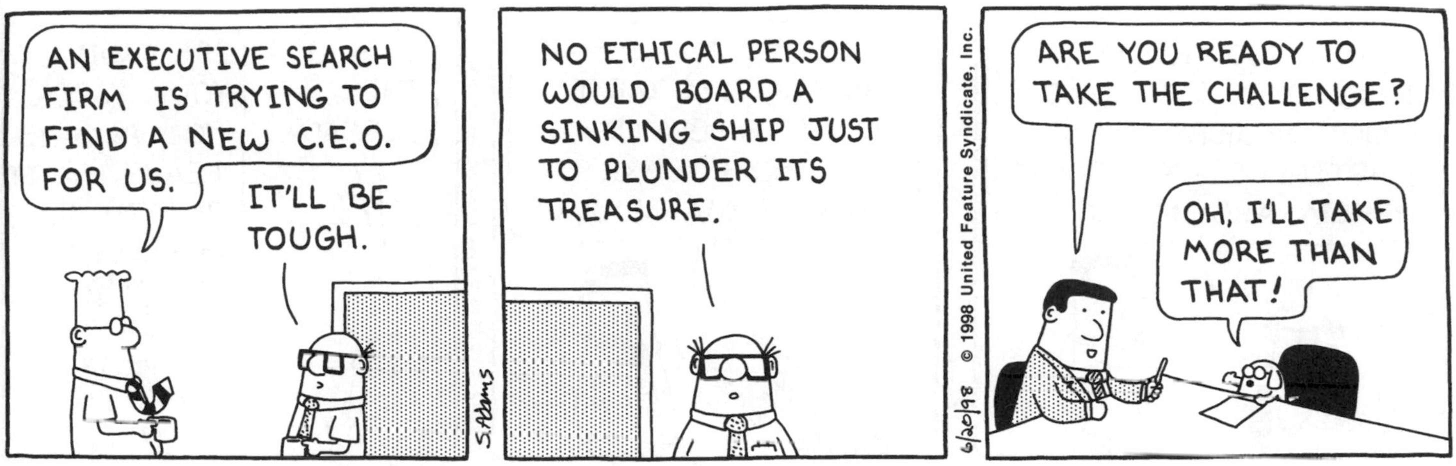
AN EXECUTIVE SEARCH FIRM IS TRYING TO FIND A NEW C.E.O. FOR US.
IT'LL BE TOUGH.
S. Adams
NO ETHICAL PERSON WOULD BOARD A SINKING SHIP JUST TO PLUNDER ITS TREASURE.
6/20/98
© 1998 United Feature Syndicate, Inc.
ARE YOU READY TO TAKE THE CHALLENGE?
OH, I'LL TAKE MORE THAN THAT!

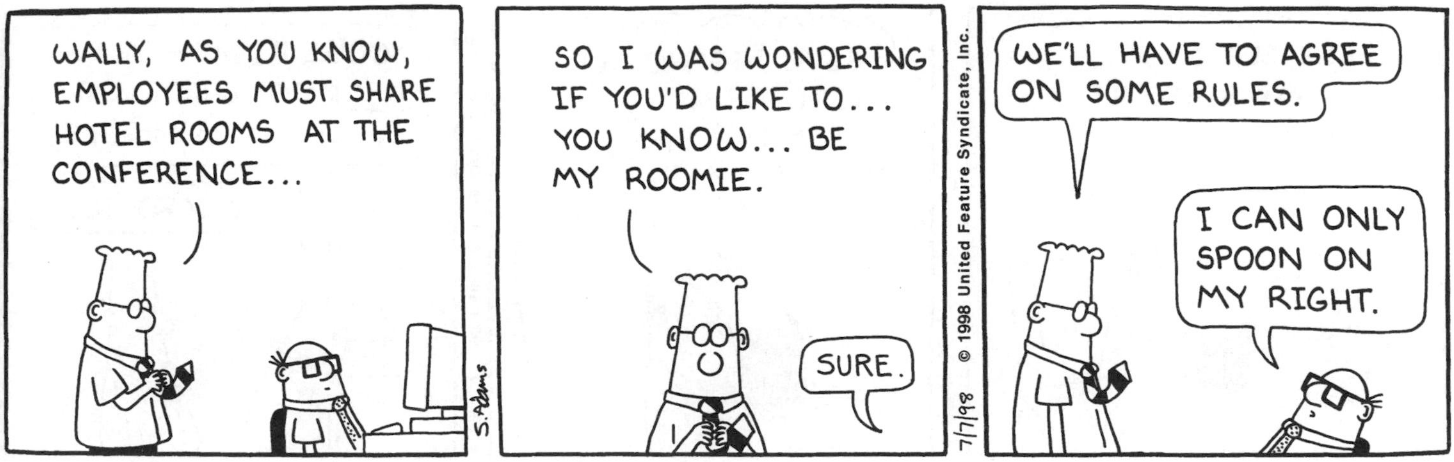
WALLY, AS YOU KNOW, EMPLOYEES MUST SHARE HOTEL ROOMS AT THE CONFERENCE...
S. Adams
SO I WAS WONDERING IF YOU'D LIKE TO... YOU KNOW... BE MY ROOMIE.
SURE.
7/7/98
© 1998 United Feature Syndicate, Inc.
WE'LL HAVE TO AGREE ON SOME RULES.
I CAN ONLY SPOON ON MY RIGHT.

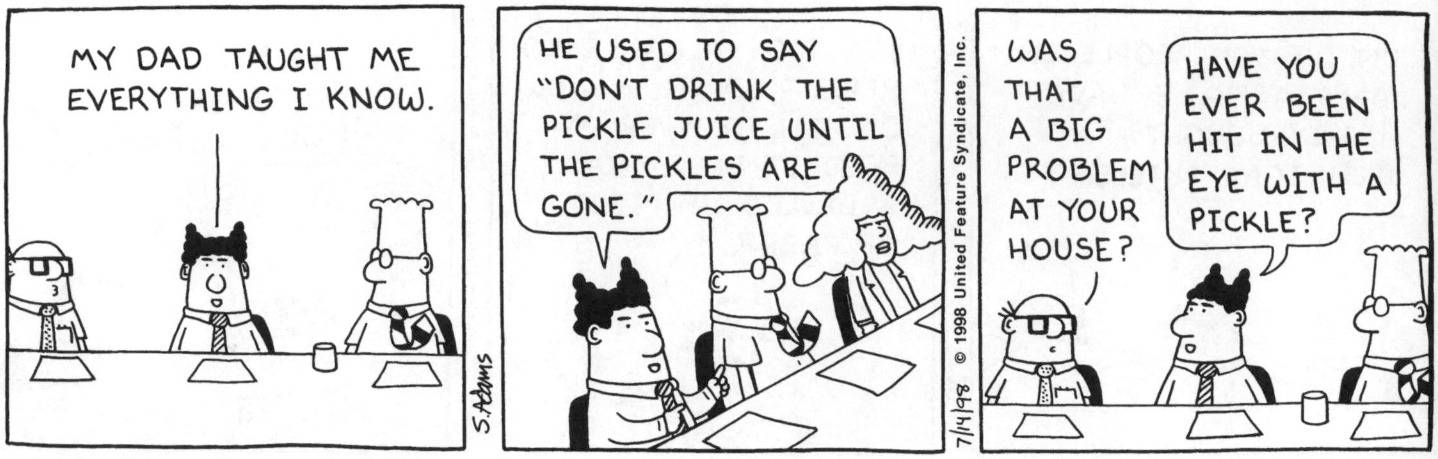
MY DAD TAUGHT ME EVERYTHING I KNOW.
S. Adams
HE USED TO SAY "DON'T DRINK THE PICKLE JUICE UNTIL THE PICKLES ARE GONE."
7/14/98 © 1998 United Feature Syndicate, Inc.
WAS THAT A BIG PROBLEM AT YOUR HOUSE?
HAVE YOU EVER BEEN HIT IN THE EYE WITH A PICKLE?

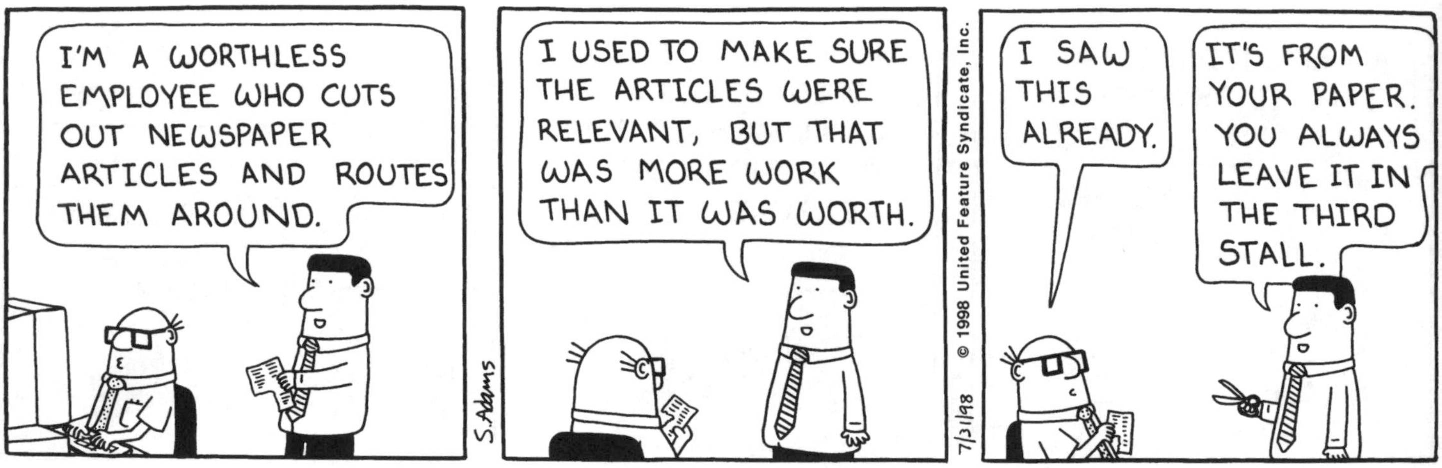
I'M A WORTHLESS EMPLOYEE WHO CUTS OUT NEWSPAPER ARTICLES AND ROUTES THEM AROUND.
S. Adams
I USED TO MAKE SURE THE ARTICLES WERE RELEVANT, BUT THAT WAS MORE WORK THAN IT WAS WORTH.
7/31/98 © 1998 United Feature Syndicate, Inc.
I SAW THIS ALREADY.
IT'S FROM YOUR PAPER. YOU ALWAYS LEAVE IT IN THE THIRD STALL.

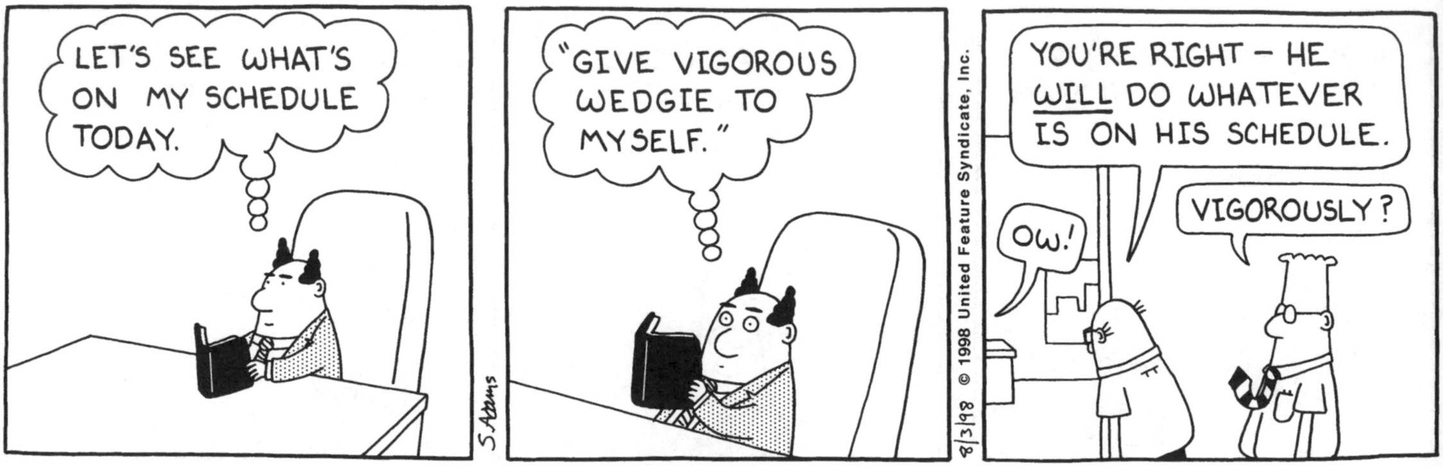
LET'S SEE WHAT'S ON MY SCHEDULE TODAY.
S. Adams
"GIVE VIGOROUS WEDGIE TO MYSELF."
8/3/98 © 1998 United Feature Syndicate, Inc.
YOU'RE RIGHT – HE WILL DO WHATEVER IS ON HIS SCHEDULE.
OW!
VIGOROUSLY?

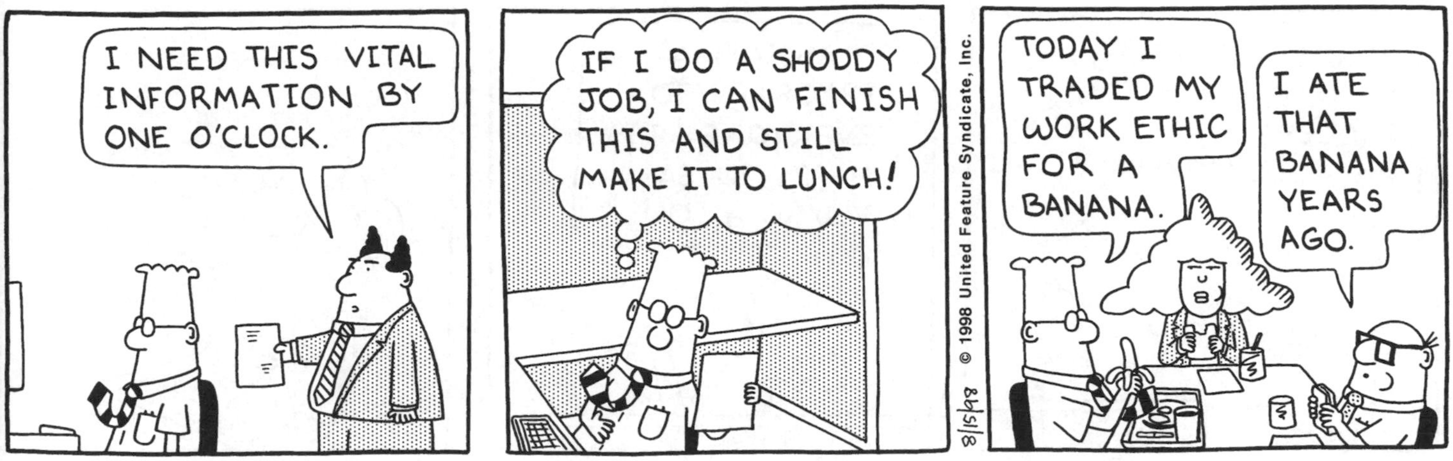
I NEED THIS VITAL INFORMATION BY ONE O'CLOCK.
IF I DO A SHODDY JOB, I CAN FINISH THIS AND STILL MAKE IT TO LUNCH!
© 1998 United Feature Syndicate, Inc.
8/15/98
TODAY I TRADED MY WORK ETHIC FOR A BANANA.
I ATE THAT BANANA YEARS AGO.

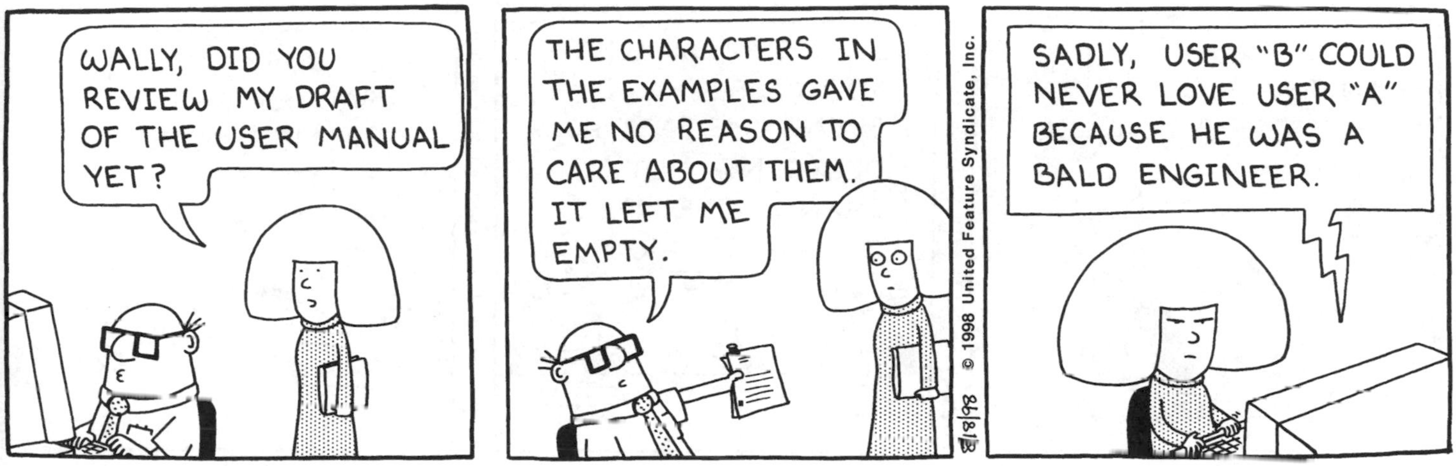
WALLY, DID YOU REVIEW MY DRAFT OF THE USER MANUAL YET?
THE CHARACTERS IN THE EXAMPLES GAVE ME NO REASON TO CARE ABOUT THEM. IT LEFT ME EMPTY.
© 1998 United Feature Syndicate, Inc.
SADLY, USER "B" COULD NEVER LOVE USER "A" BECAUSE HE WAS A BALD ENGINEER.

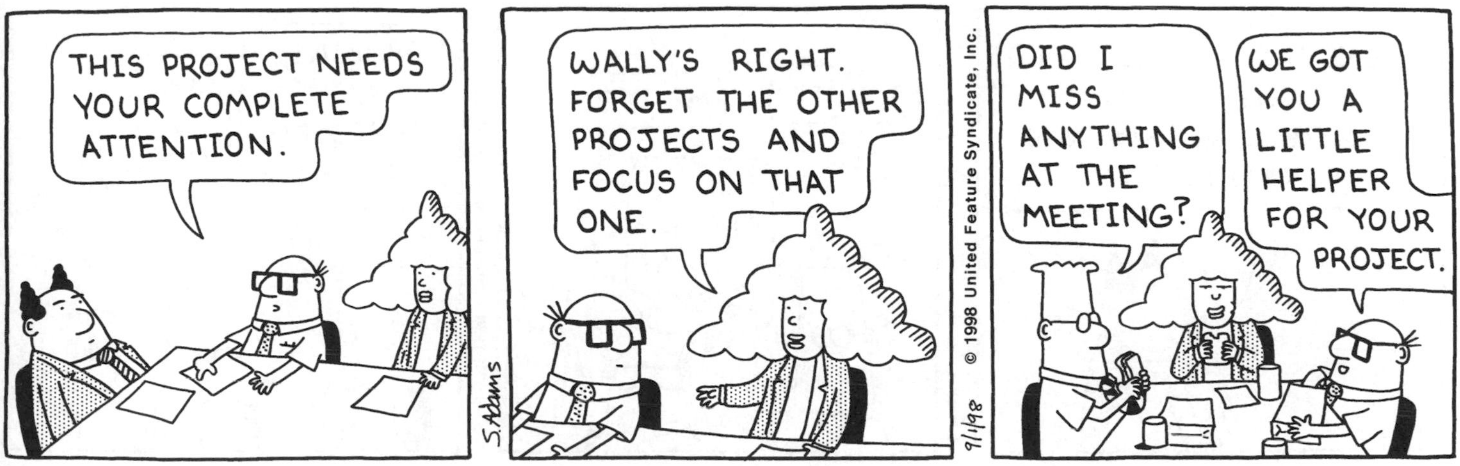
THIS PROJECT NEEDS YOUR COMPLETE ATTENTION.
S. Adams
WALLY'S RIGHT. FORGET THE OTHER PROJECTS AND FOCUS ON THAT ONE.
9/1/98
© 1998 United Feature Syndicate, Inc.
DID I MISS ANYTHING AT THE MEETING?
WE GOT YOU A LITTLE HELPER FOR YOUR PROJECT.

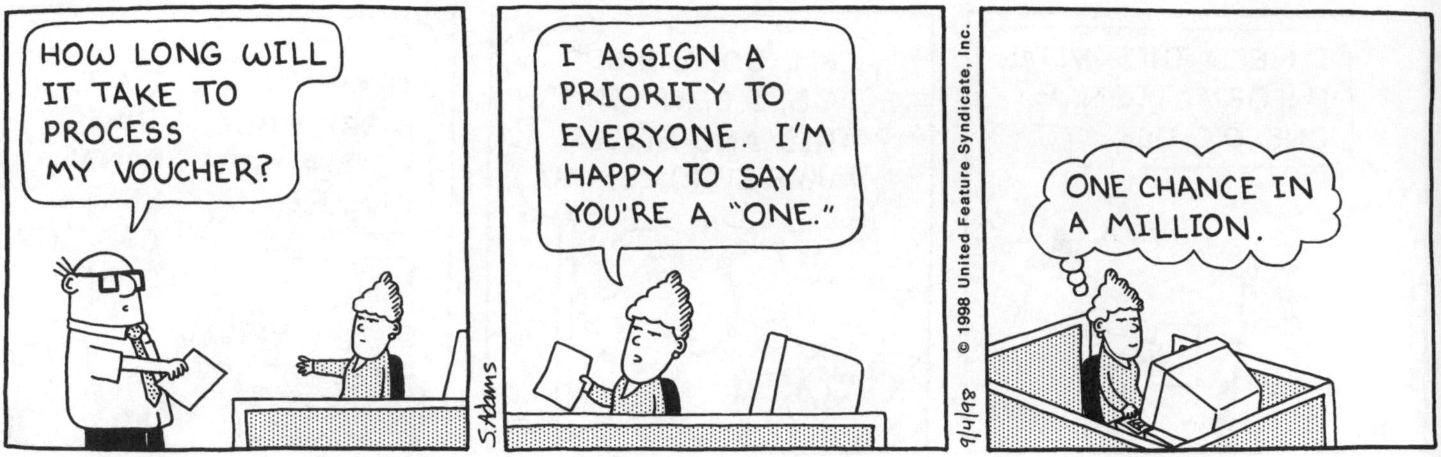
HOW LONG WILL IT TAKE TO PROCESS MY VOUCHER?
I ASSIGN A PRIORITY TO EVERYONE. I'M HAPPY TO SAY YOU'RE A "ONE."
ONE CHANCE IN A MILLION.
S.Adams
9/4/98
© 1998 United Feature Syndicate, Inc.

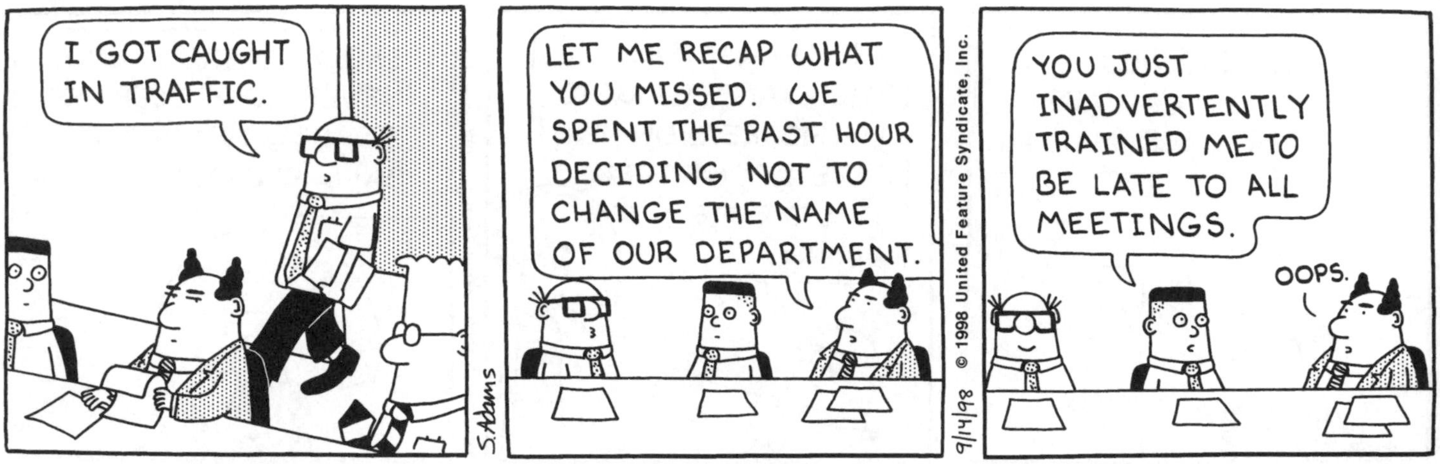
I GOT CAUGHT IN TRAFFIC.
LET ME RECAP WHAT YOU MISSED. WE SPENT THE PAST HOUR DECIDING NOT TO CHANGE THE NAME OF OUR DEPARTMENT.
YOU JUST INADVERTENTLY TRAINED ME TO BE LATE TO ALL MEETINGS.
OOPS.
S.Adams
9/14/98
© 1998 United Feature Syndicate, Inc.

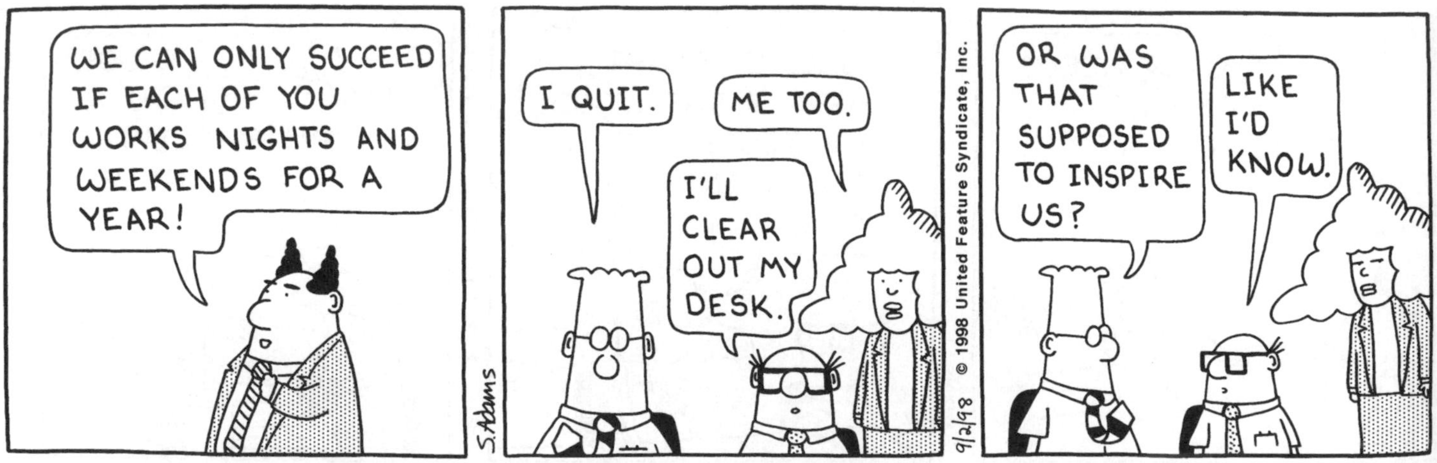
WE CAN ONLY SUCCEED IF EACH OF YOU WORKS NIGHTS AND WEEKENDS FOR A YEAR!
I QUIT.
ME TOO.
I'LL CLEAR OUT MY DESK.
OR WAS THAT SUPPOSED TO INSPIRE US?
LIKE I'D KNOW.
S.Adams
9/2/98
© 1998 United Feature Syndicate, Inc.

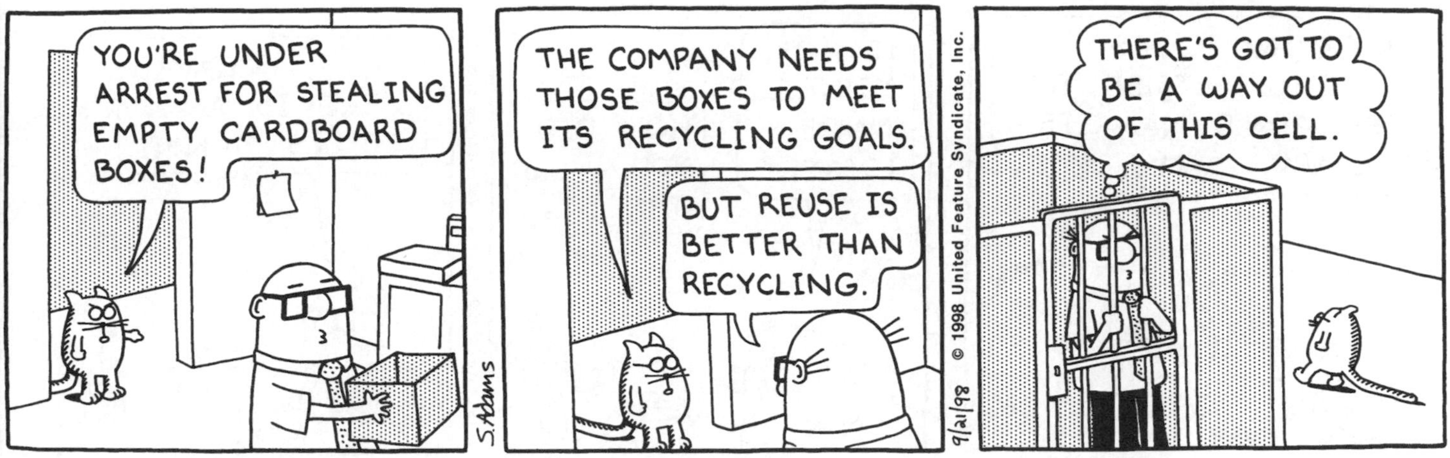
YOU'RE UNDER ARREST FOR STEALING EMPTY CARDBOARD BOXES!
S.Adams
THE COMPANY NEEDS THOSE BOXES TO MEET ITS RECYCLING GOALS.
BUT REUSE IS BETTER THAN RECYCLING.
9/21/98 © 1998 United Feature Syndicate, Inc.
THERE'S GOT TO BE A WAY OUT OF THIS CELL.

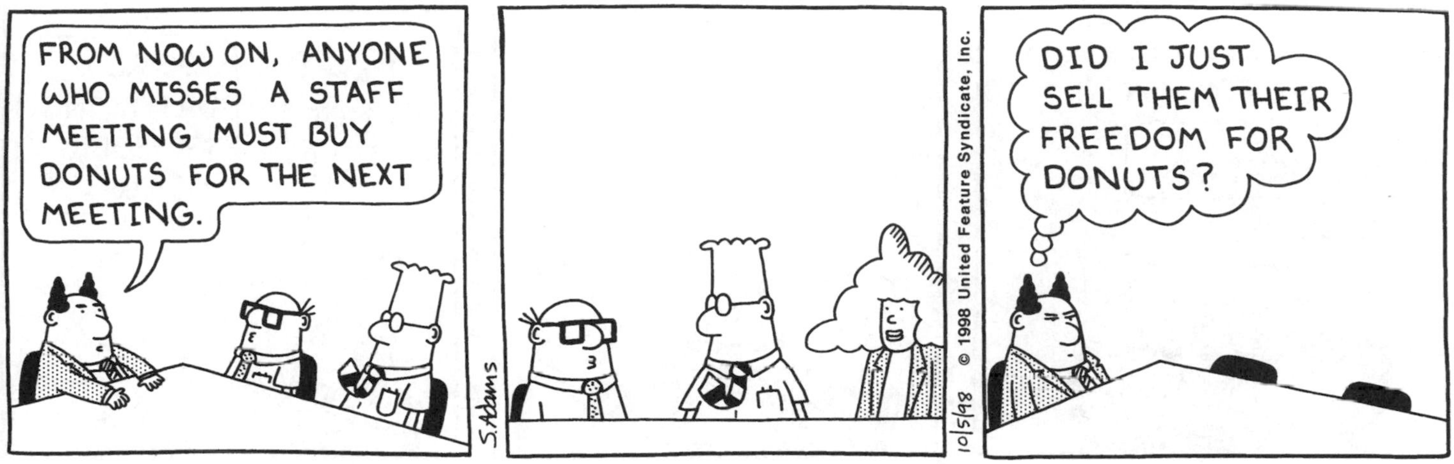
FROM NOW ON, ANYONE WHO MISSES A STAFF MEETING MUST BUY DONUTS FOR THE NEXT MEETING.
S.Adams
10/5/98 © 1998 United Feature Syndicate, Inc.
DID I JUST SELL THEM THEIR FREEDOM FOR DONUTS?

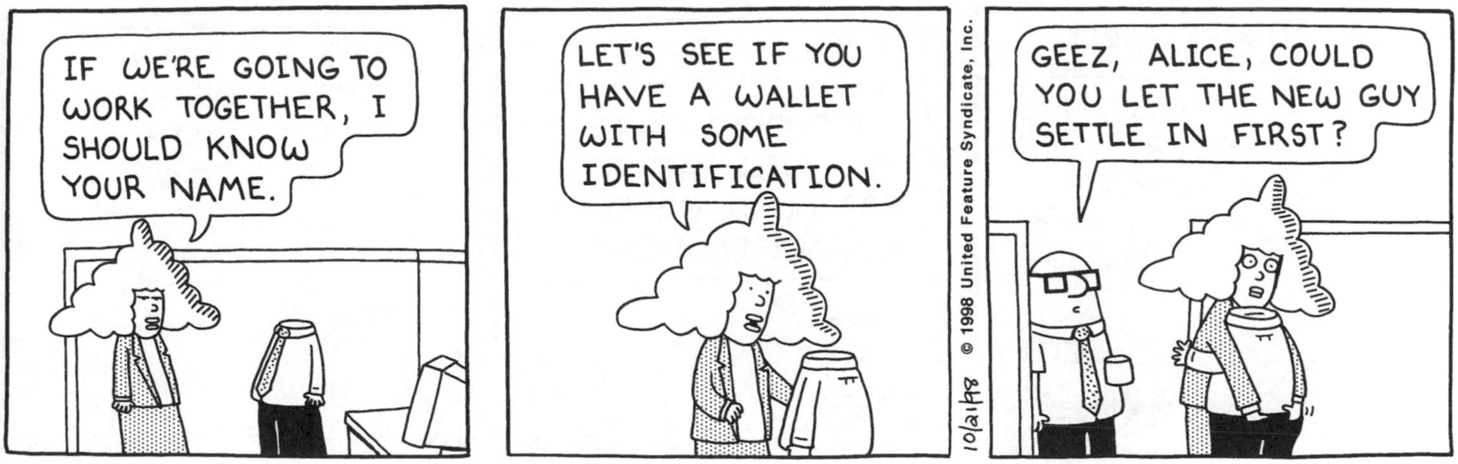
IF WE'RE GOING TO WORK TOGETHER, I SHOULD KNOW YOUR NAME.
LET'S SEE IF YOU HAVE A WALLET WITH SOME IDENTIFICATION.
10/21/98 © 1998 United Feature Syndicate, Inc.
GEEZ, ALICE, COULD YOU LET THE NEW GUY SETTLE IN FIRST?

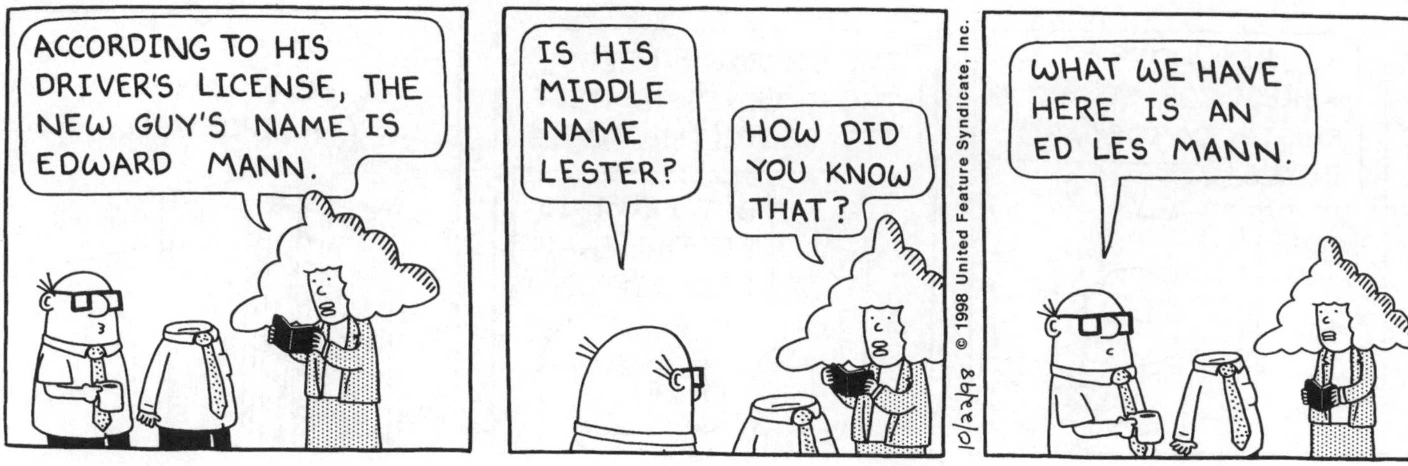
ACCORDING TO HIS DRIVER'S LICENSE, THE NEW GUY'S NAME IS EDWARD MANN.
IS HIS MIDDLE NAME LESTER?
HOW DID YOU KNOW THAT?
WHAT WE HAVE HERE IS AN ED LES MANN.
10/22/98 © 1998 United Feature Syndicate, Inc.

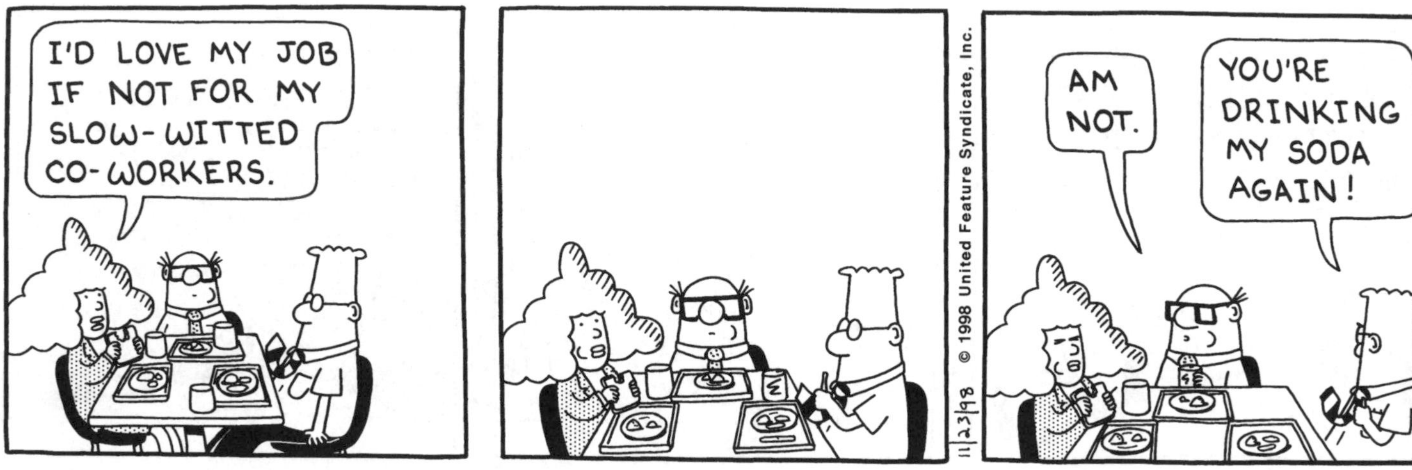
I'D LOVE MY JOB IF NOT FOR MY SLOW-WITTED CO-WORKERS.
YOU'RE DRINKING MY SODA AGAIN!
AM NOT.
11/23/98 © 1998 United Feature Syndicate, Inc.

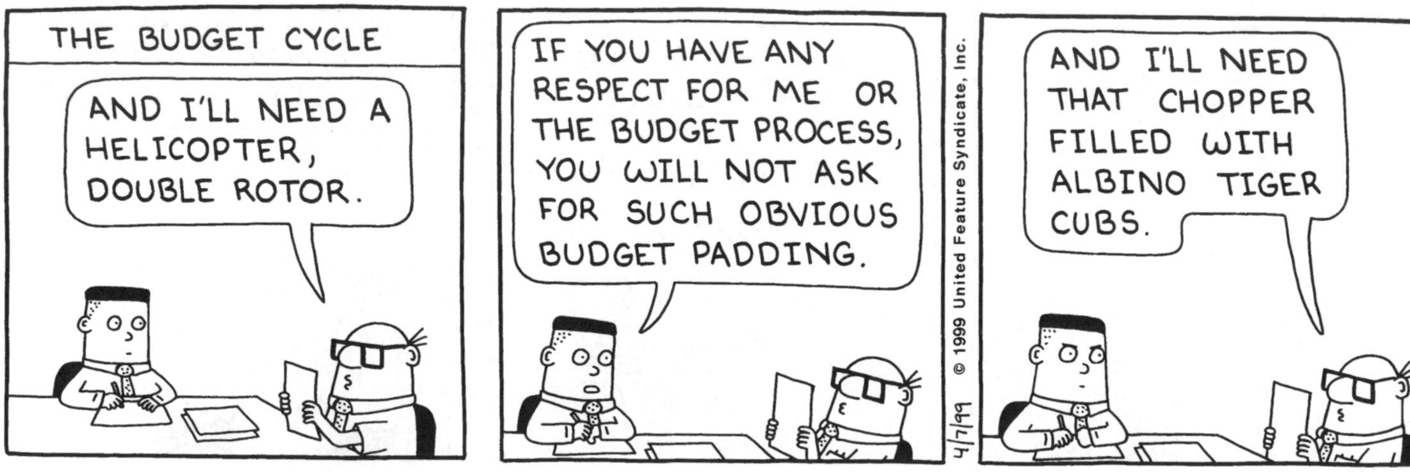
THE BUDGET CYCLE
AND I'LL NEED A HELICOPTER, DOUBLE ROTOR.
IF YOU HAVE ANY RESPECT FOR ME OR THE BUDGET PROCESS, YOU WILL NOT ASK FOR SUCH OBVIOUS BUDGET PADDING.
AND I'LL NEED THAT CHOPPER FILLED WITH ALBINO TIGER CUBS.
4/7/99 © 1999 United Feature Syndicate, Inc.

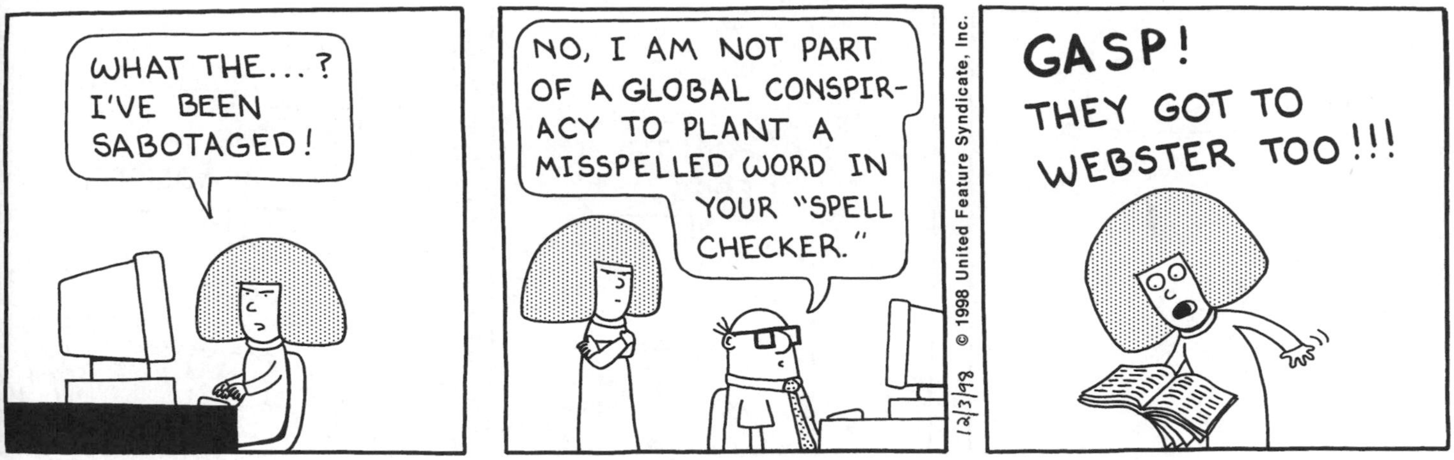
WHAT THE...? I'VE BEEN SABOTAGED!
NO, I AM NOT PART OF A GLOBAL CONSPIR-ACY TO PLANT A MISSPELLED WORD IN YOUR "SPELL CHECKER."
12/3/98 © 1998 United Feature Syndicate, Inc.
GASP! THEY GOT TO WEBSTER TOO!!!

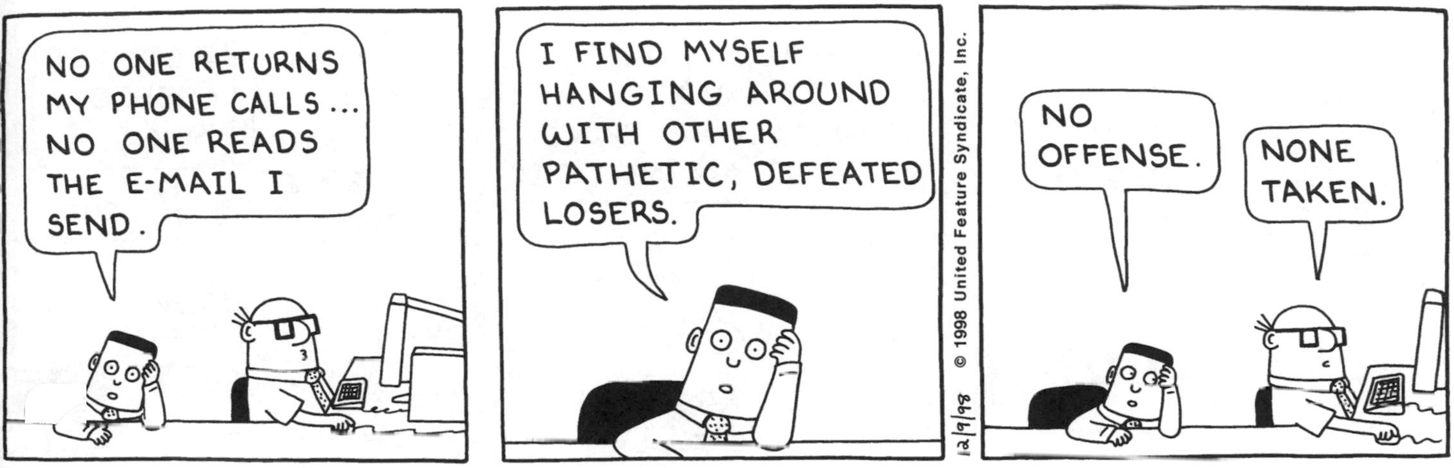
NO ONE RETURNS MY PHONE CALLS... NO ONE READS THE E-MAIL I SEND.
I FIND MYSELF HANGING AROUND WITH OTHER PATHETIC, DEFEATED LOSERS.
12/9/98 © 1998 United Feature Syndicate, Inc.
NO OFFENSE.
NONE TAKEN.

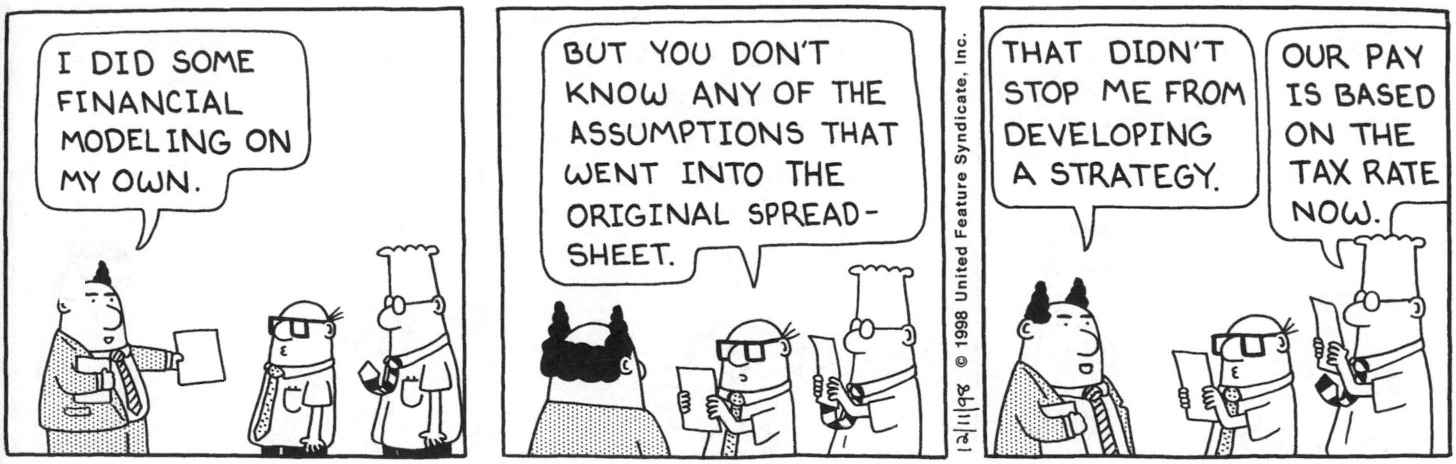
I DID SOME FINANCIAL MODELING ON MY OWN.
BUT YOU DON'T KNOW ANY OF THE ASSUMPTIONS THAT WENT INTO THE ORIGINAL SPREAD-SHEET.
12/11/98 © 1998 United Feature Syndicate, Inc.
THAT DIDN'T STOP ME FROM DEVELOPING A STRATEGY.
OUR PAY IS BASED ON THE TAX RATE NOW.

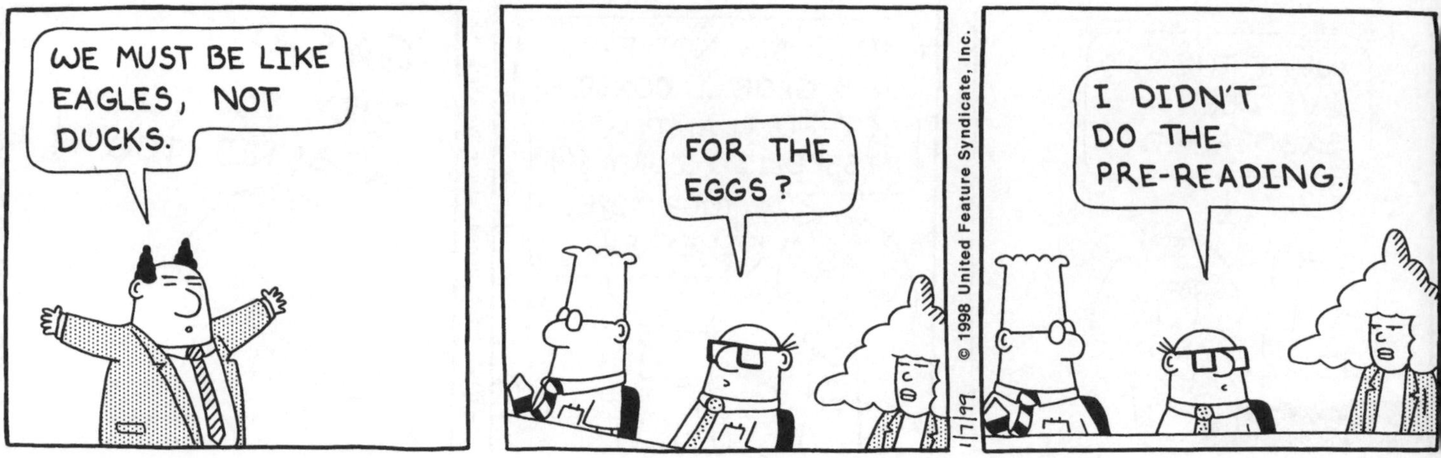
WE MUST BE LIKE EAGLES, NOT DUCKS.
FOR THE EGGS?
© 1998 United Feature Syndicate, Inc.
1/7/99
I DIDN'T DO THE PRE-READING.

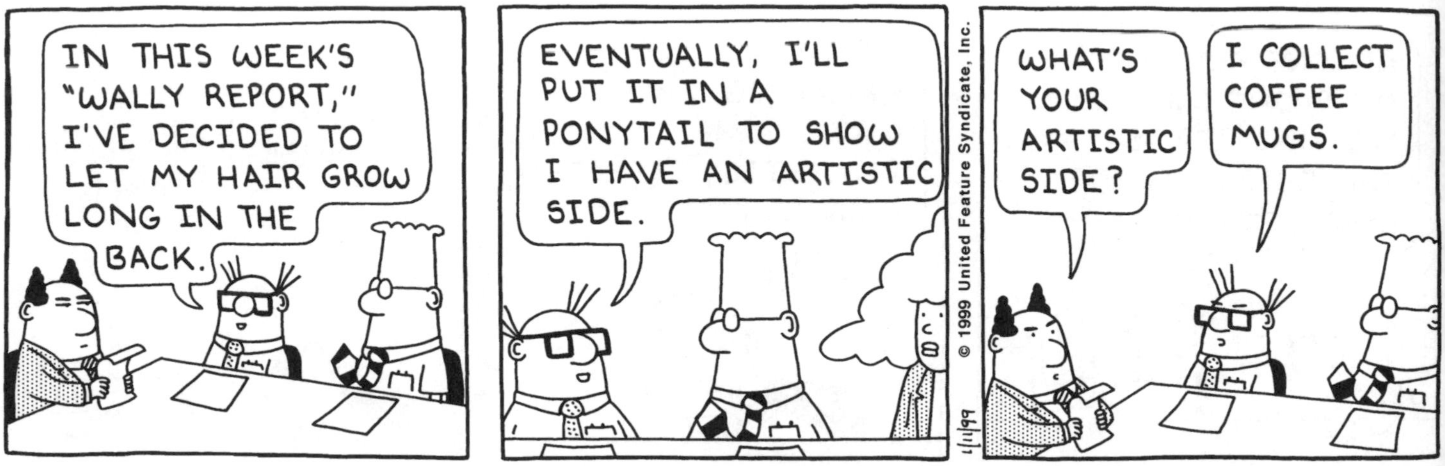
IN THIS WEEK'S "WALLY REPORT," I'VE DECIDED TO LET MY HAIR GROW LONG IN THE BACK.
EVENTUALLY, I'LL PUT IT IN A PONYTAIL TO SHOW I HAVE AN ARTISTIC SIDE.
© 1999 United Feature Syndicate, Inc.
1/11/99
WHAT'S YOUR ARTISTIC SIDE?
I COLLECT COFFEE MUGS.

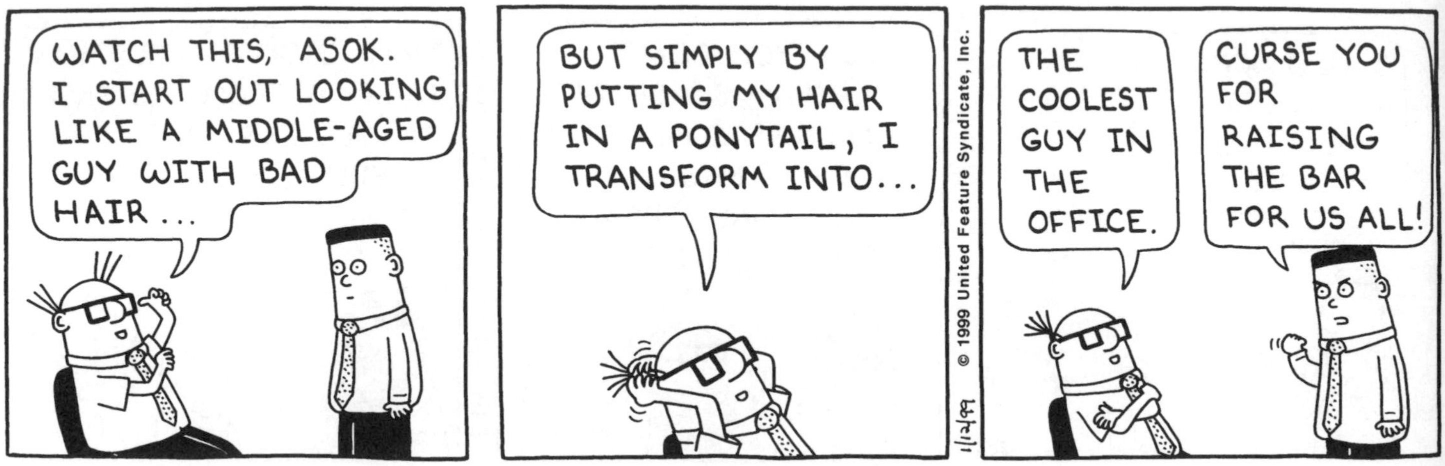
WATCH THIS, ASOK. I START OUT LOOKING LIKE A MIDDLE-AGED GUY WITH BAD HAIR...
BUT SIMPLY BY PUTTING MY HAIR IN A PONYTAIL, I TRANSFORM INTO...
© 1999 United Feature Syndicate, Inc.
1/12/99
THE COOLEST GUY IN THE OFFICE.
CURSE YOU FOR RAISING THE BAR FOR US ALL!

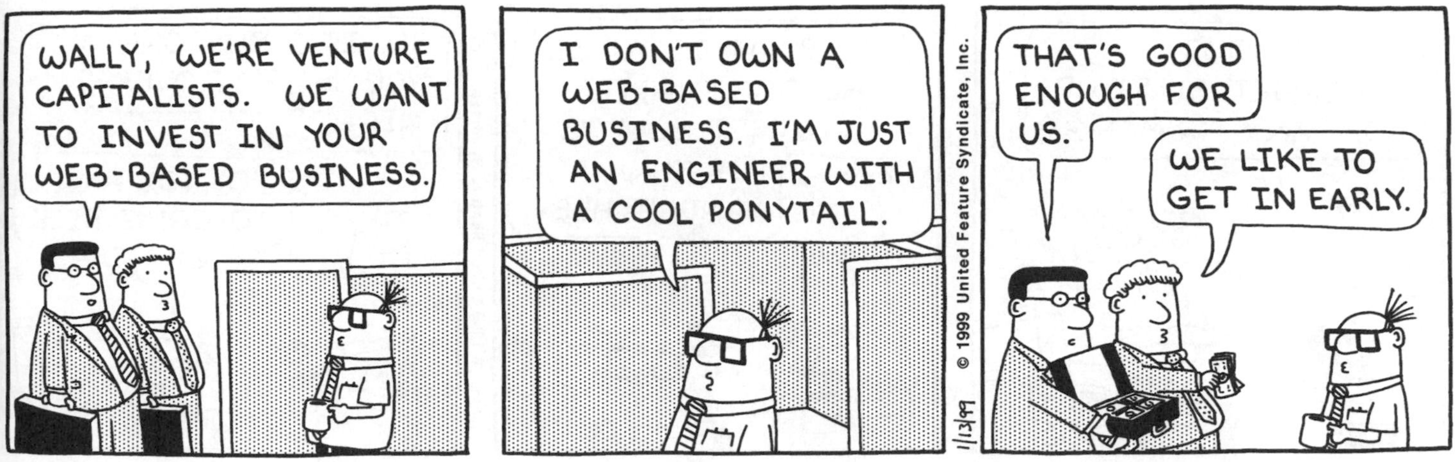
WALLY, WE'RE VENTURE CAPITALISTS. WE WANT TO INVEST IN YOUR WEB-BASED BUSINESS.
I DON'T OWN A WEB-BASED BUSINESS. I'M JUST AN ENGINEER WITH A COOL PONYTAIL.
1/13/99 © 1999 United Feature Syndicate, Inc.
THAT'S GOOD ENOUGH FOR US.
WE LIKE TO GET IN EARLY.

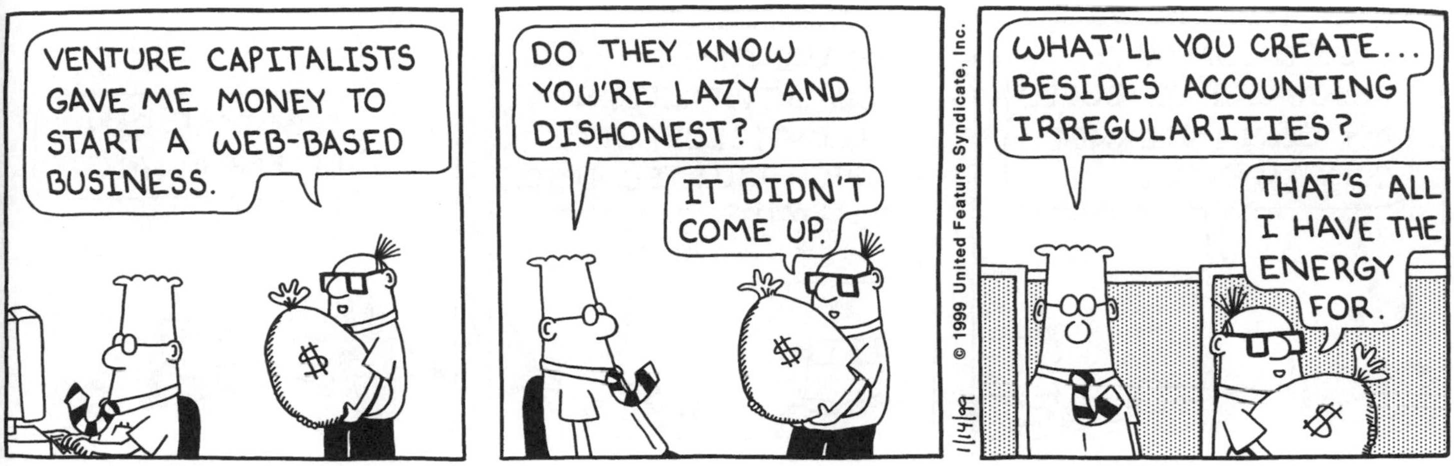
VENTURE CAPITALISTS GAVE ME MONEY TO START A WEB-BASED BUSINESS.
DO THEY KNOW YOU'RE LAZY AND DISHONEST?
IT DIDN'T COME UP.
1/14/99 © 1999 United Feature Syndicate, Inc.
WHAT'LL YOU CREATE... BESIDES ACCOUNTING IRREGULARITIES?
THAT'S ALL I HAVE THE ENERGY FOR.

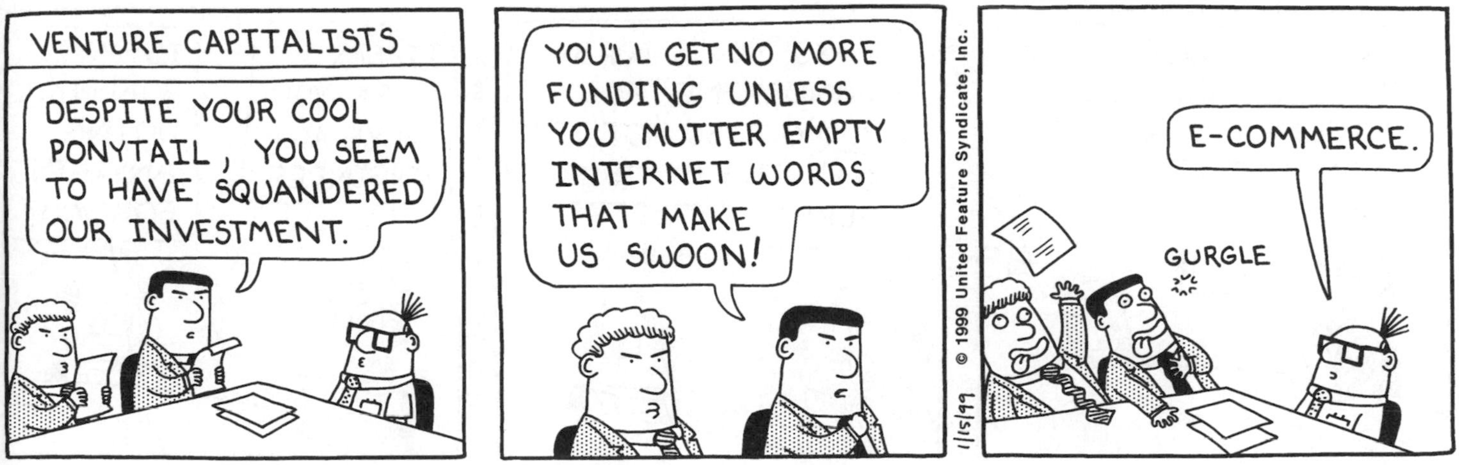
VENTURE CAPITALISTS
DESPITE YOUR COOL PONYTAIL, YOU SEEM TO HAVE SQUANDERED OUR INVESTMENT.
YOU'LL GET NO MORE FUNDING UNLESS YOU MUTTER EMPTY INTERNET WORDS THAT MAKE US SWOON!
1/15/99 © 1999 United Feature Syndicate, Inc.
E-COMMERCE.
GURGLE

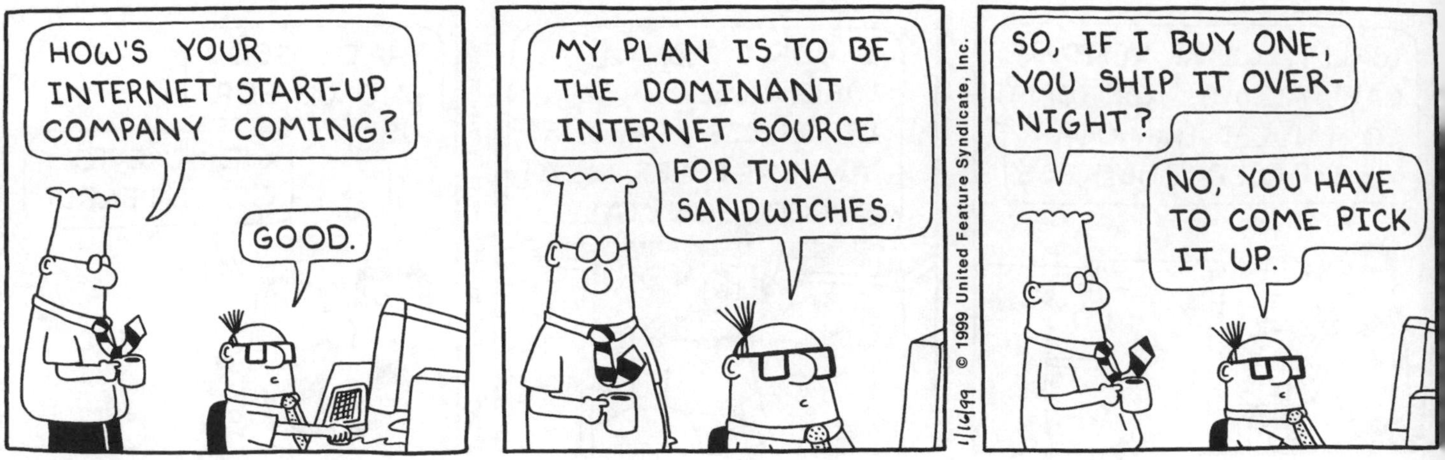
HOW'S YOUR INTERNET START-UP COMPANY COMING?
GOOD.
MY PLAN IS TO BE THE DOMINANT INTERNET SOURCE FOR TUNA SANDWICHES.
1/16/99 © 1999 United Feature Syndicate, Inc.
SO, IF I BUY ONE, YOU SHIP IT OVER-NIGHT?
NO, YOU HAVE TO COME PICK IT UP.

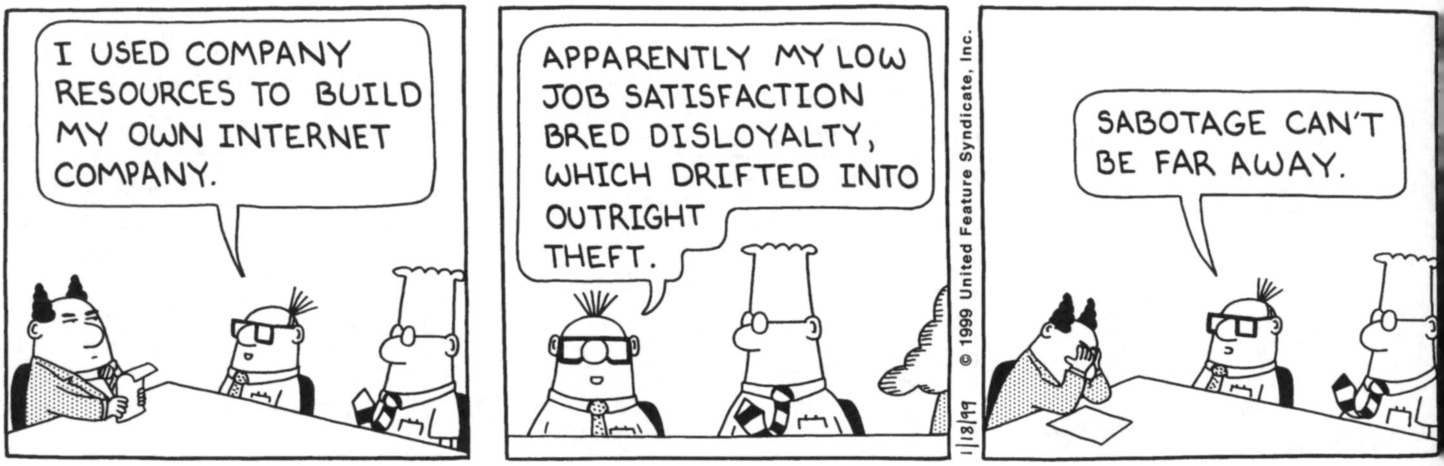
I USED COMPANY RESOURCES TO BUILD MY OWN INTERNET COMPANY.
APPARENTLY MY LOW JOB SATISFACTION BRED DISLOYALTY, WHICH DRIFTED INTO OUTRIGHT THEFT.
1/18/99 © 1999 United Feature Syndicate, Inc.
SABOTAGE CAN'T BE FAR AWAY.

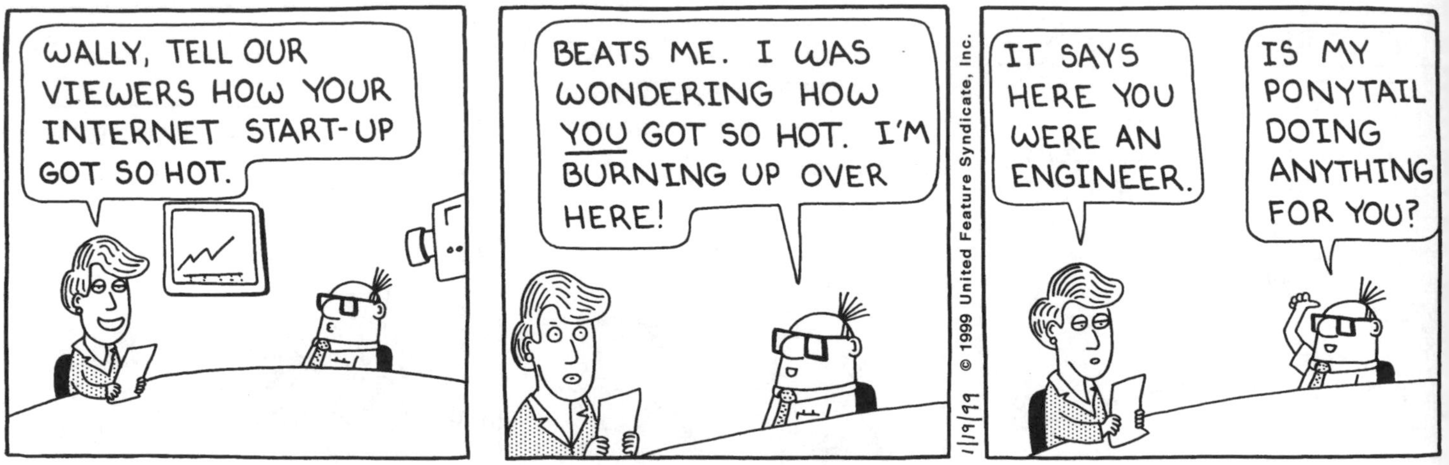
WALLY, TELL OUR VIEWERS HOW YOUR INTERNET START-UP GOT SO HOT.
BEATS ME. I WAS WONDERING HOW YOU GOT SO HOT. I'M BURNING UP OVER HERE!
1/19/99 © 1999 United Feature Syndicate, Inc.
IT SAYS HERE YOU WERE AN ENGINEER.
IS MY PONYTAIL DOING ANYTHING FOR YOU?

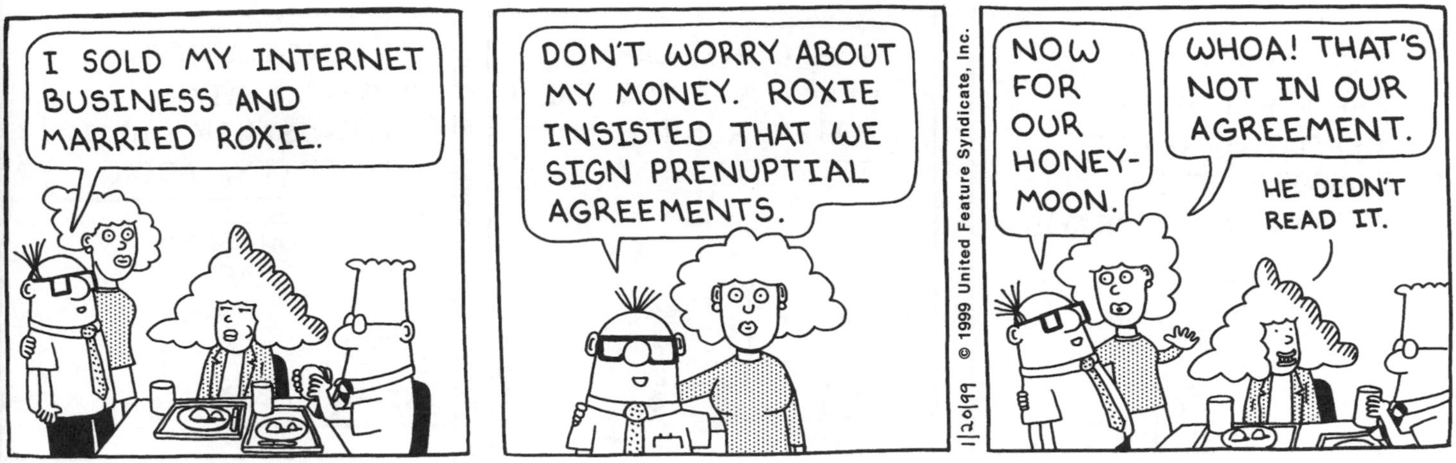

I SOLD MY INTERNET BUSINESS AND MARRIED ROXIE.
DON'T WORRY ABOUT MY MONEY. ROXIE INSISTED THAT WE SIGN PRENUPTIAL AGREEMENTS.
1/20/99 © 1999 United Feature Syndicate, Inc.
NOW FOR OUR HONEY-MOON.
WHOA! THAT'S NOT IN OUR AGREEMENT.
HE DIDN'T READ IT.

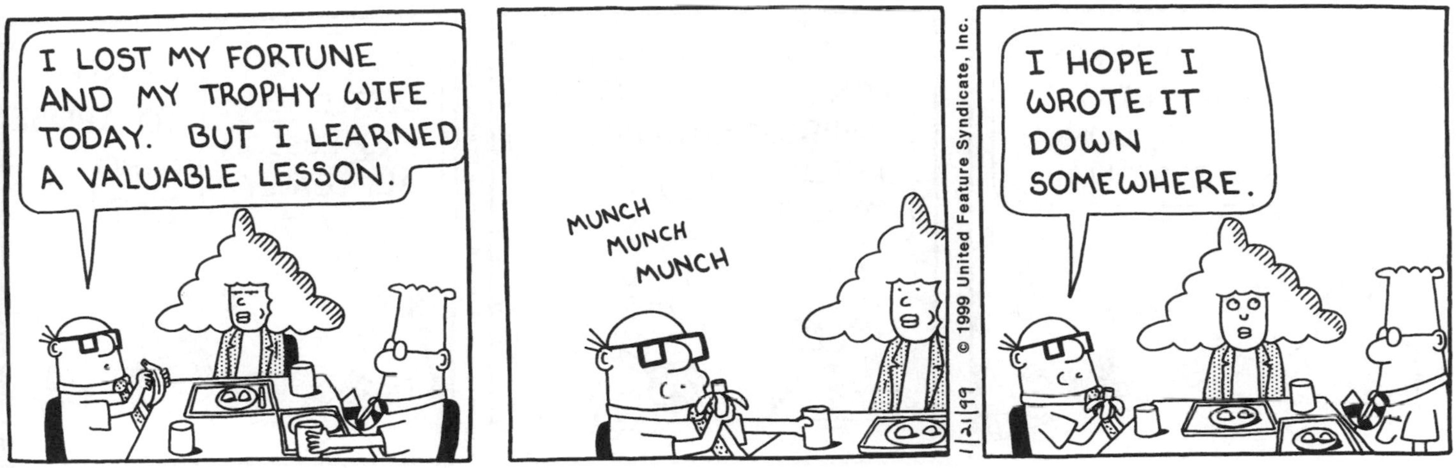

I LOST MY FORTUNE AND MY TROPHY WIFE TODAY. BUT I LEARNED A VALUABLE LESSON.
MUNCH MUNCH MUNCH
1/21/99 © 1999 United Feature Syndicate, Inc.
I HOPE I WROTE IT DOWN SOMEWHERE.

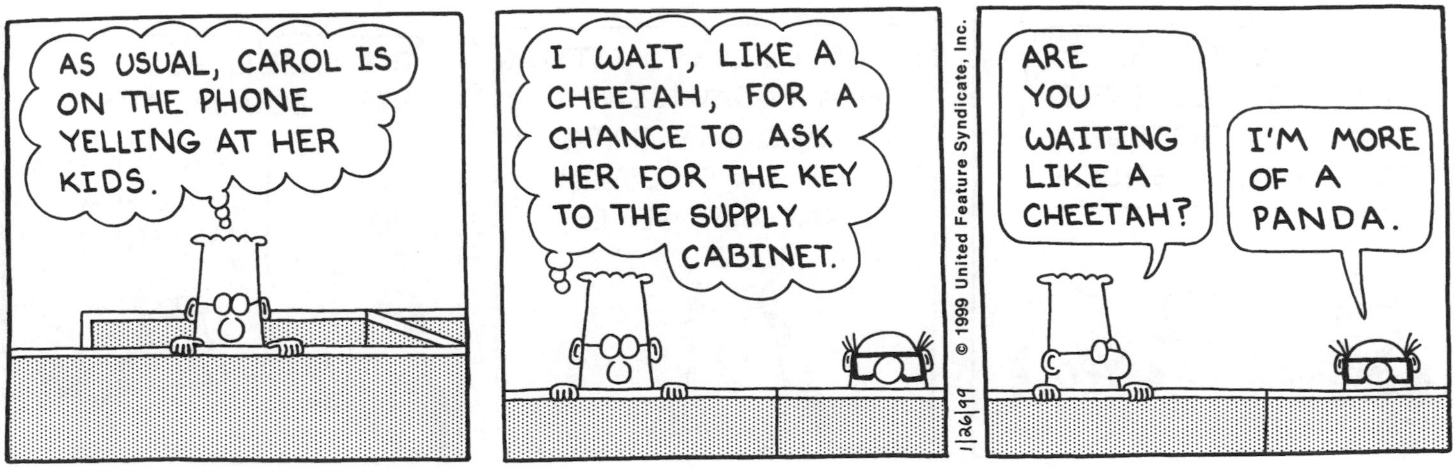

AS USUAL, CAROL IS ON THE PHONE YELLING AT HER KIDS.
I WAIT, LIKE A CHEETAH, FOR A CHANCE TO ASK HER FOR THE KEY TO THE SUPPLY CABINET.
1/26/99 © 1999 United Feature Syndicate, Inc.
ARE YOU WAITING LIKE A CHEETAH?
I'M MORE OF A PANDA.

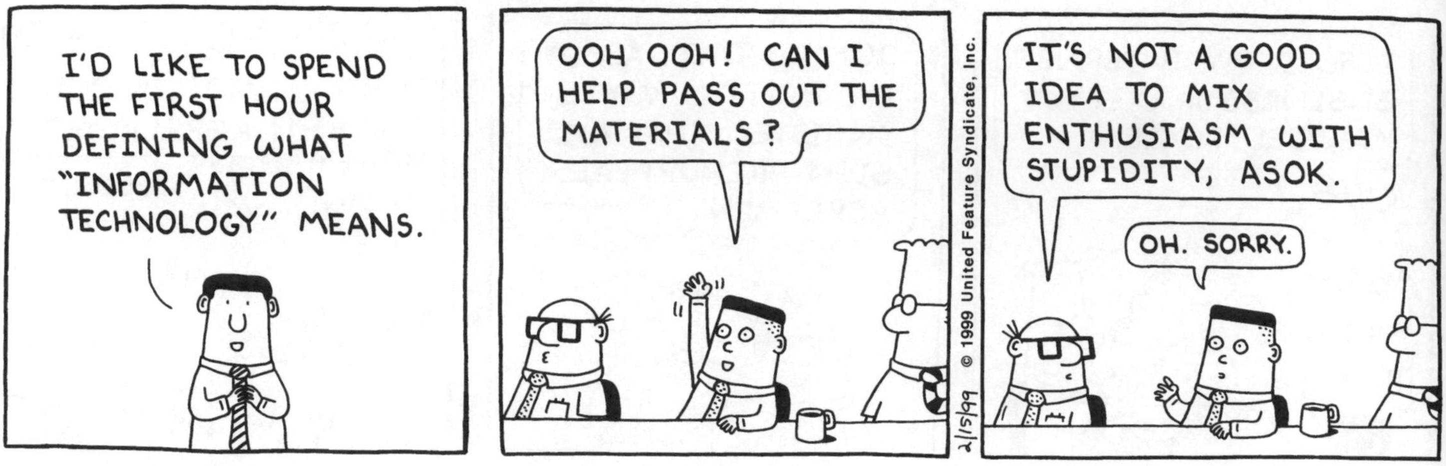
I'D LIKE TO SPEND THE FIRST HOUR DEFINING WHAT "INFORMATION TECHNOLOGY" MEANS.
OOH OOH! CAN I HELP PASS OUT THE MATERIALS?
2/15/99 © 1999 United Feature Syndicate, Inc.
IT'S NOT A GOOD IDEA TO MIX ENTHUSIASM WITH STUPIDITY, ASOK.
OH. SORRY.

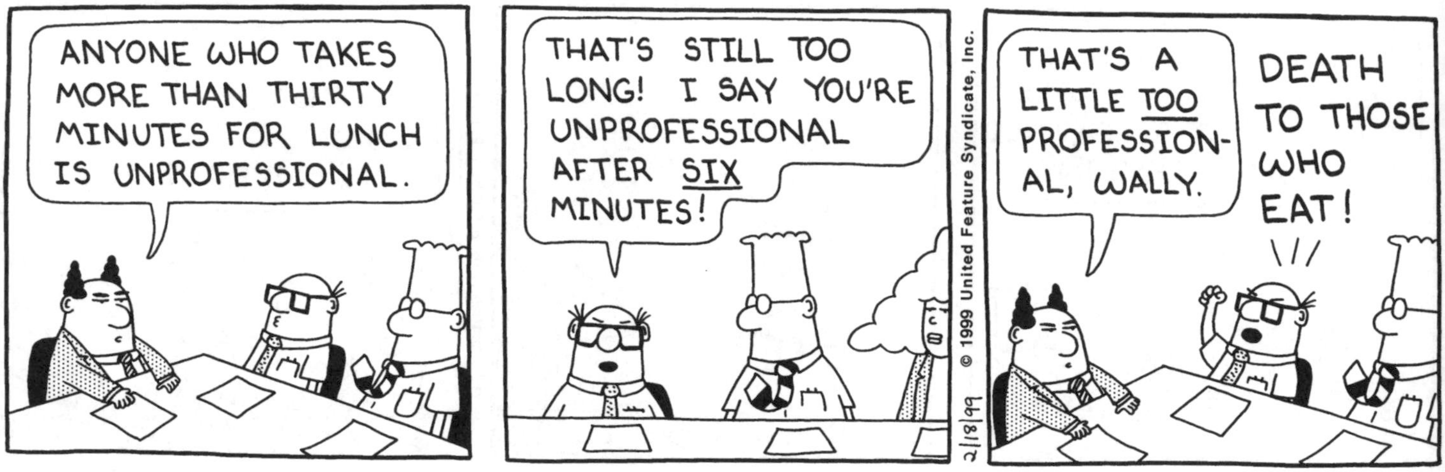
ANYONE WHO TAKES MORE THAN THIRTY MINUTES FOR LUNCH IS UNPROFESSIONAL.
THAT'S STILL TOO LONG! I SAY YOU'RE UNPROFESSIONAL AFTER SIX MINUTES!
2/18/99 © 1999 United Feature Syndicate, Inc.
THAT'S A LITTLE TOO PROFESSION-AL, WALLY.
DEATH TO THOSE WHO EAT!

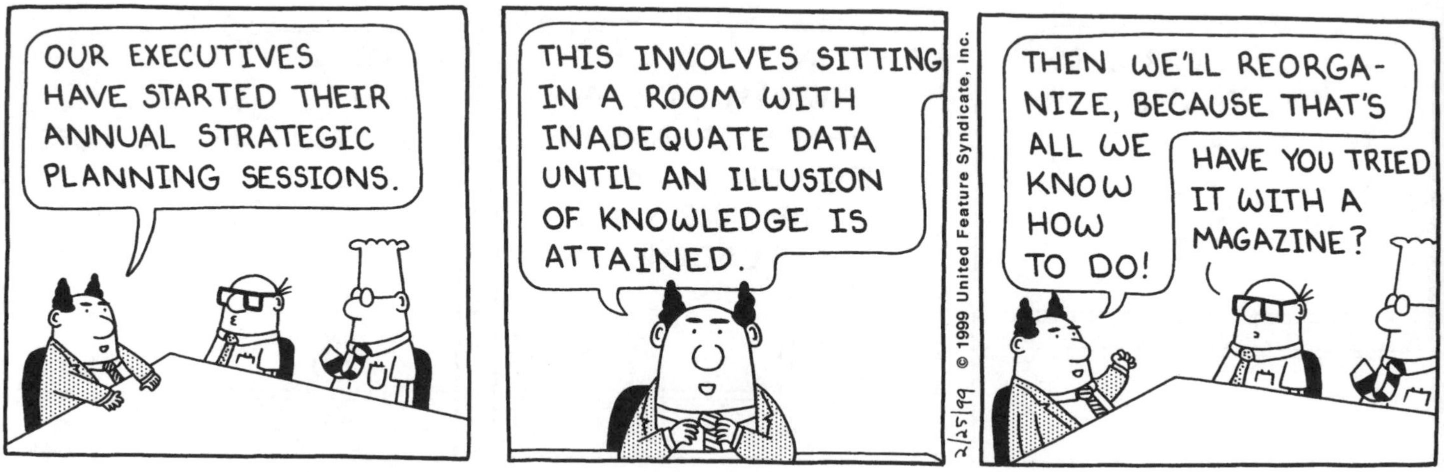
OUR EXECUTIVES HAVE STARTED THEIR ANNUAL STRATEGIC PLANNING SESSIONS.
THIS INVOLVES SITTING IN A ROOM WITH INADEQUATE DATA UNTIL AN ILLUSION OF KNOWLEDGE IS ATTAINED.
2/25/99 © 1999 United Feature Syndicate, Inc.
THEN WE'LL REORGA-NIZE, BECAUSE THAT'S ALL WE KNOW HOW TO DO!
HAVE YOU TRIED IT WITH A MAGAZINE?

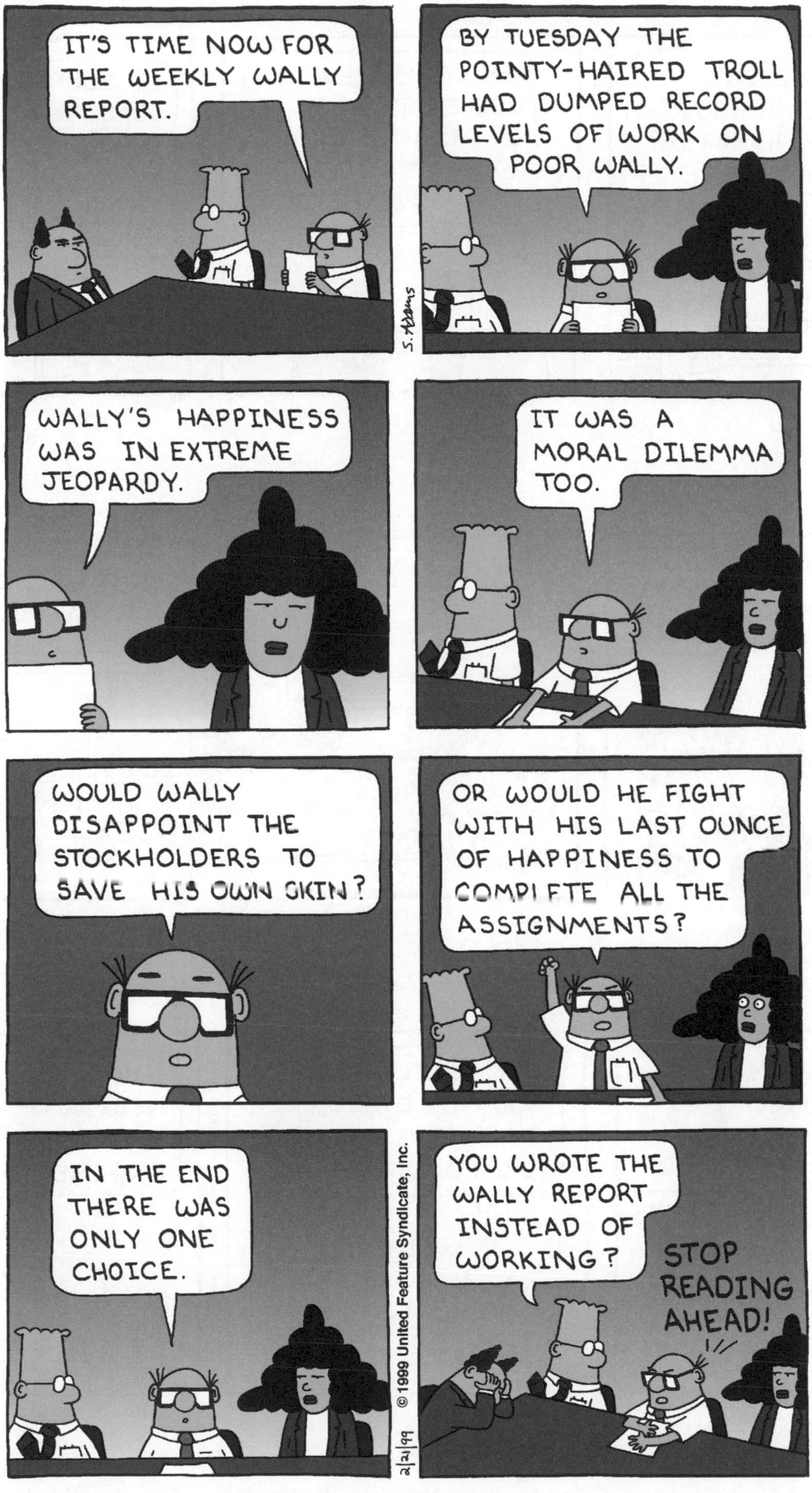
IT'S TIME NOW FOR THE WEEKLY WALLY REPORT.
BY TUESDAY THE POINTY-HAIRED TROLL HAD DUMPED RECORD LEVELS OF WORK ON POOR WALLY.
S. Adams
WALLY'S HAPPINESS WAS IN EXTREME JEOPARDY.
IT WAS A MORAL DILEMMA TOO.
WOULD WALLY DISAPPOINT THE STOCKHOLDERS TO SAVE HIS OWN SKIN?
OR WOULD HE FIGHT WITH HIS LAST OUNCE OF HAPPINESS TO COMPLETE ALL THE ASSIGNMENTS?
IN THE END THERE WAS ONLY ONE CHOICE.
© 1999 United Feature Syndicate, Inc.
2/21/99
YOU WROTE THE WALLY REPORT INSTEAD OF WORKING?
STOP READING AHEAD!

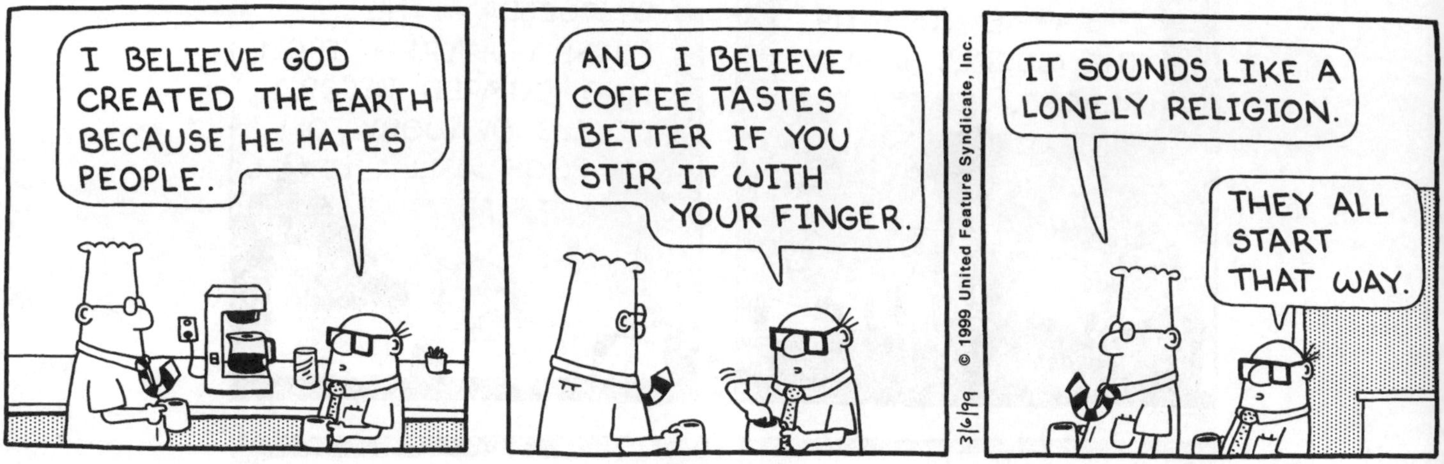
I BELIEVE GOD CREATED THE EARTH BECAUSE HE HATES PEOPLE.
AND I BELIEVE COFFEE TASTES BETTER IF YOU STIR IT WITH YOUR FINGER.
3/6/99 © 1999 United Feature Syndicate, Inc.
IT SOUNDS LIKE A LONELY RELIGION.
THEY ALL START THAT WAY.

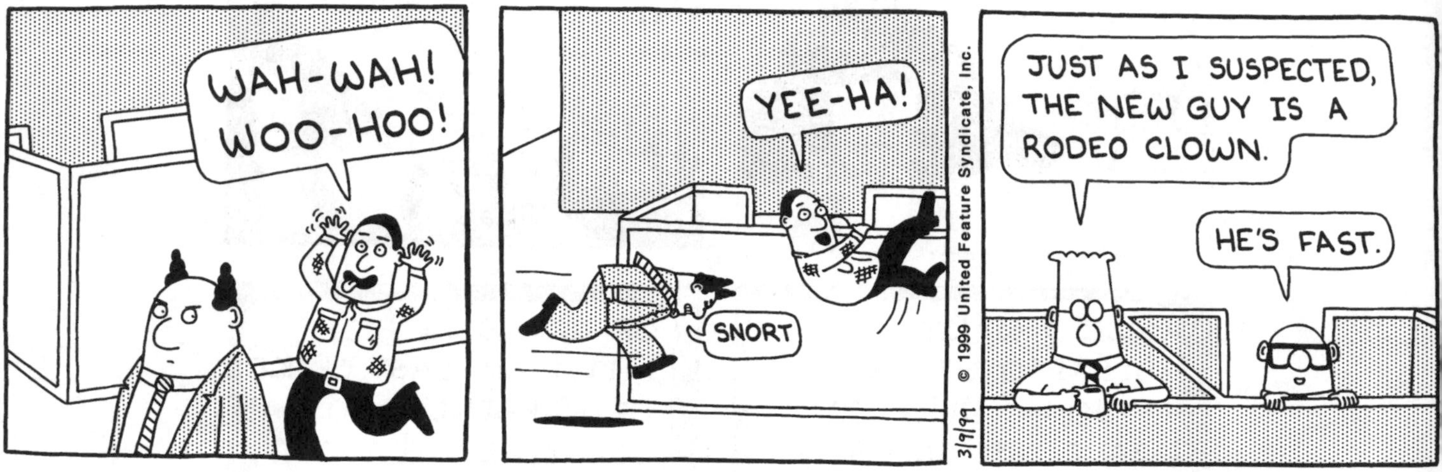
WAH-WAH! WOO-HOO!
YEE-HA!
SNORT
3/9/99 © 1999 United Feature Syndicate, Inc.
JUST AS I SUSPECTED, THE NEW GUY IS A RODEO CLOWN.
HE'S FAST.

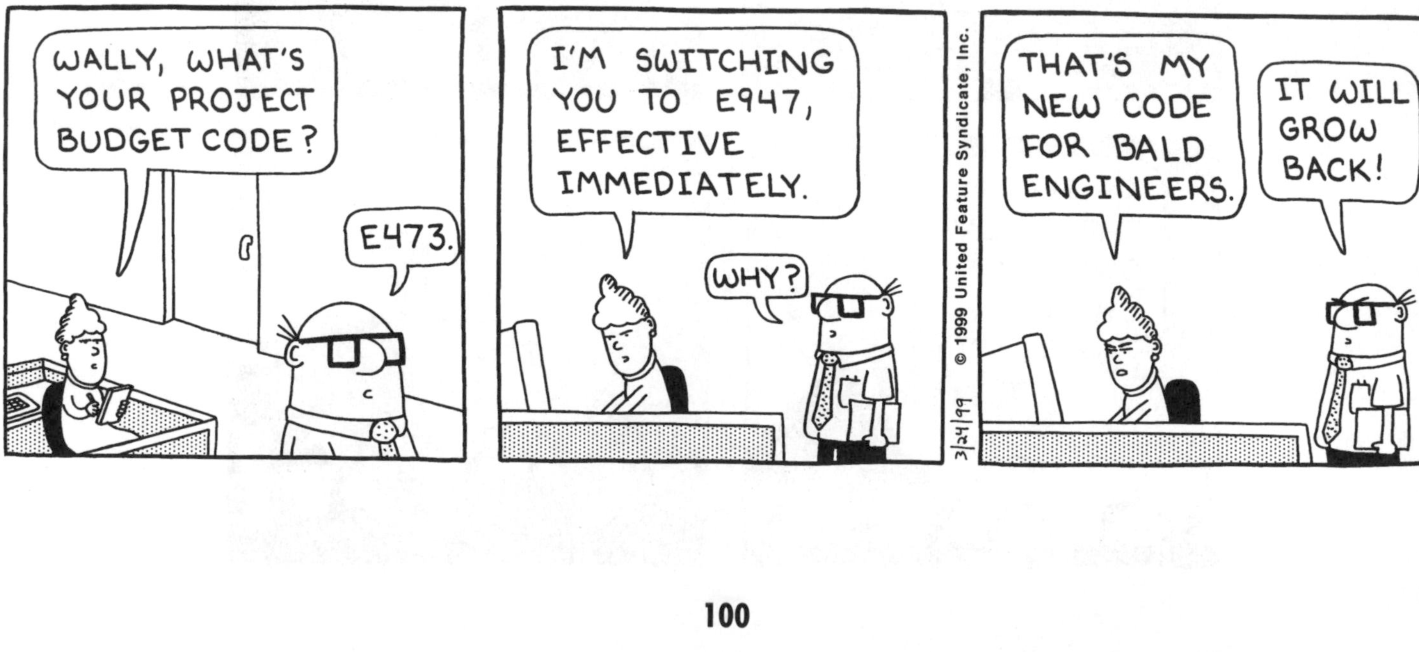
WALLY, WHAT'S YOUR PROJECT BUDGET CODE?
E473.
I'M SWITCHING YOU TO E947, EFFECTIVE IMMEDIATELY.
WHY?
3/24/99 © 1999 United Feature Syndicate, Inc.
THAT'S MY NEW CODE FOR BALD ENGINEERS.
IT WILL GROW BACK!

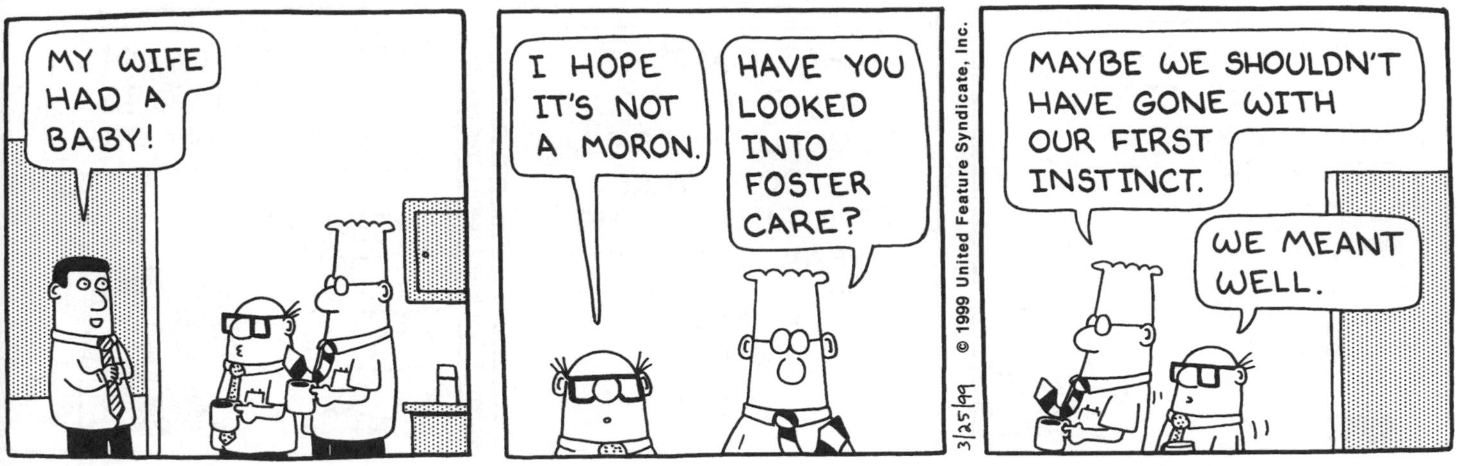
MY WIFE HAD A BABY!
I HOPE IT'S NOT A MORON.
HAVE YOU LOOKED INTO FOSTER CARE?
MAYBE WE SHOULDN'T HAVE GONE WITH OUR FIRST INSTINCT.
WE MEANT WELL.
3/25/99
© 1999 United Feature Syndicate, Inc.

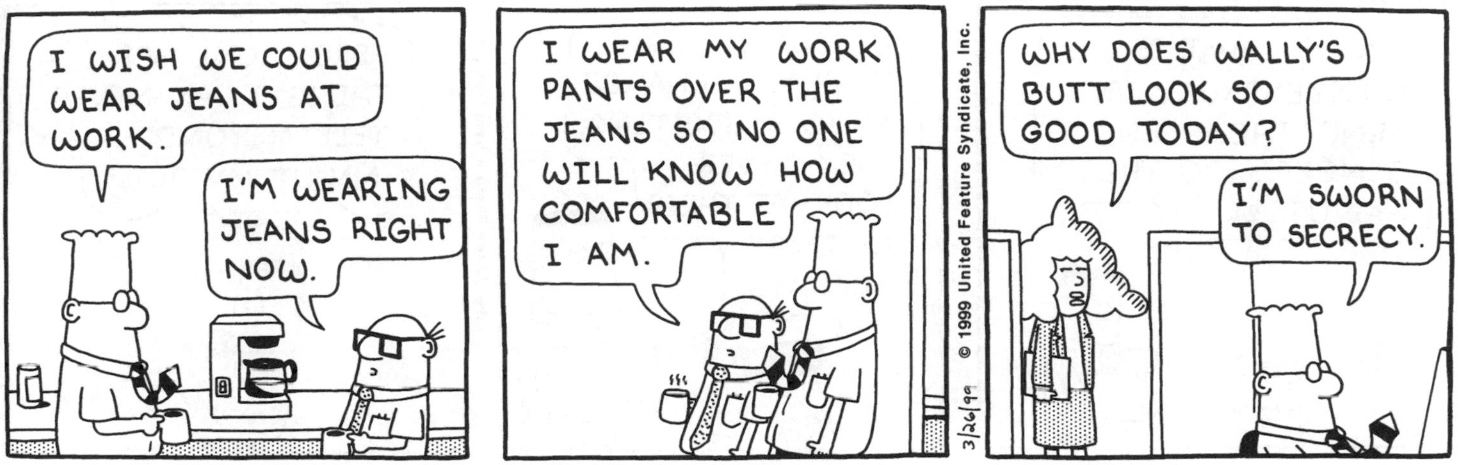
I WISH WE COULD WEAR JEANS AT WORK.
I'M WEARING JEANS RIGHT NOW.
I WEAR MY WORK PANTS OVER THE JEANS SO NO ONE WILL KNOW HOW COMFORTABLE I AM.
WHY DOES WALLY'S BUTT LOOK SO GOOD TODAY?
I'M SWORN TO SECRECY.
3/26/99
© 1999 United Feature Syndicate, Inc.

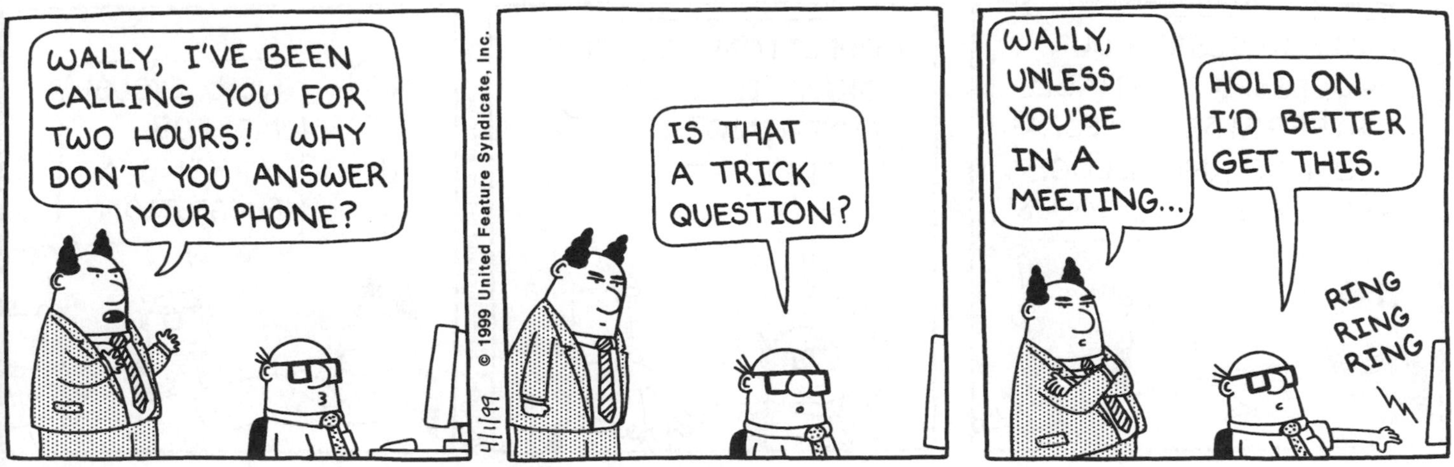
WALLY, I'VE BEEN CALLING YOU FOR TWO HOURS! WHY DON'T YOU ANSWER YOUR PHONE?
IS THAT A TRICK QUESTION?
WALLY, UNLESS YOU'RE IN A MEETING...
HOLD ON. I'D BETTER GET THIS.
RING RING RING
4/1/99
© 1999 United Feature Syndicate, Inc.

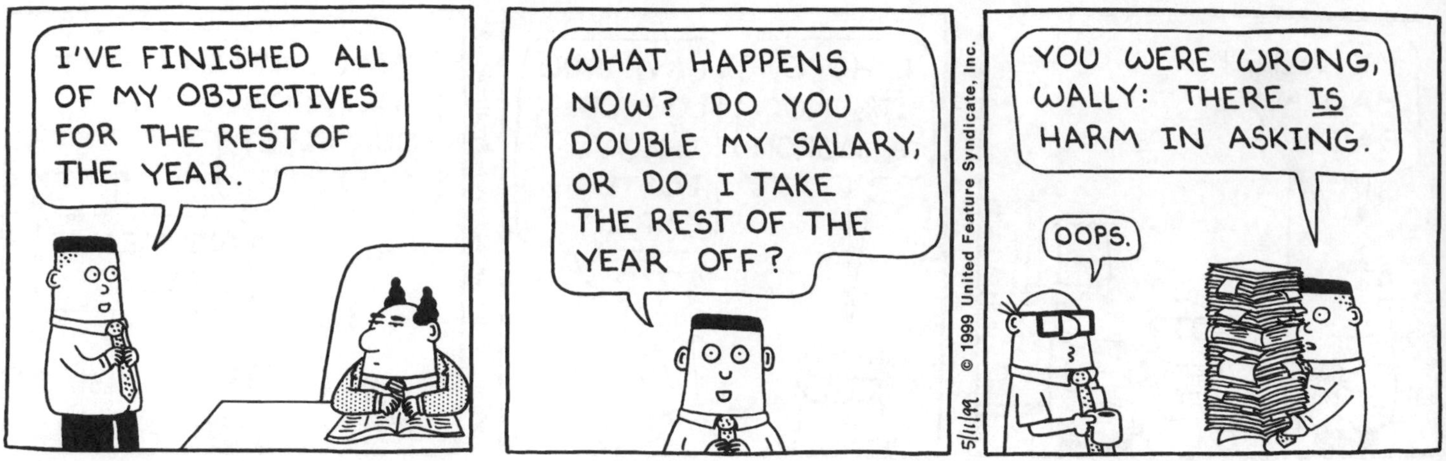
I'VE FINISHED ALL OF MY OBJECTIVES FOR THE REST OF THE YEAR.
WHAT HAPPENS NOW? DO YOU DOUBLE MY SALARY, OR DO I TAKE THE REST OF THE YEAR OFF?
5/11/99 © 1999 United Feature Syndicate, Inc.
YOU WERE WRONG, WALLY: THERE IS HARM IN ASKING.
OOPS.

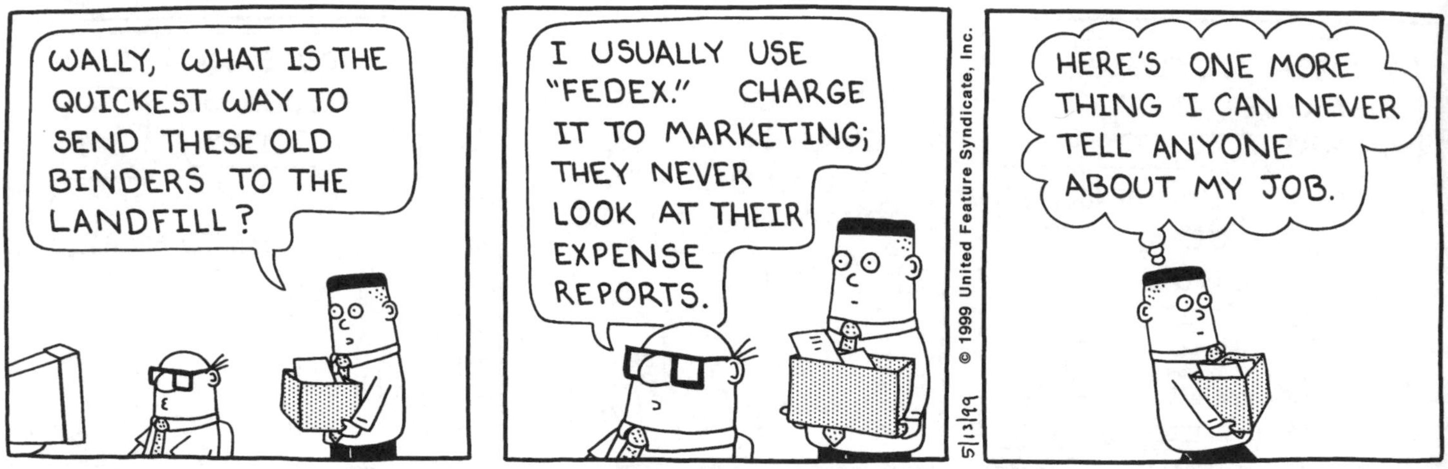
WALLY, WHAT IS THE QUICKEST WAY TO SEND THESE OLD BINDERS TO THE LANDFILL?
I USUALLY USE "FEDEX." CHARGE IT TO MARKETING; THEY NEVER LOOK AT THEIR EXPENSE REPORTS.
5/13/99 © 1999 United Feature Syndicate, Inc.
HERE'S ONE MORE THING I CAN NEVER TELL ANYONE ABOUT MY JOB.

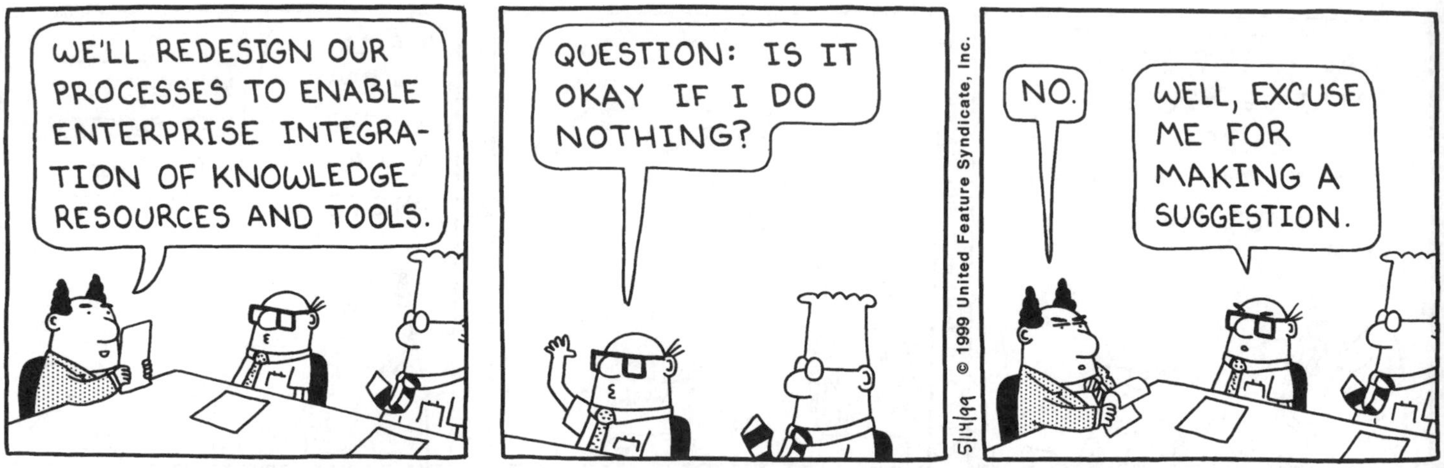
WE'LL REDESIGN OUR PROCESSES TO ENABLE ENTERPRISE INTEGRATION OF KNOWLEDGE RESOURCES AND TOOLS.
QUESTION: IS IT OKAY IF I DO NOTHING?
5/14/99 © 1999 United Feature Syndicate, Inc.
NO.
WELL, EXCUSE ME FOR MAKING A SUGGESTION.

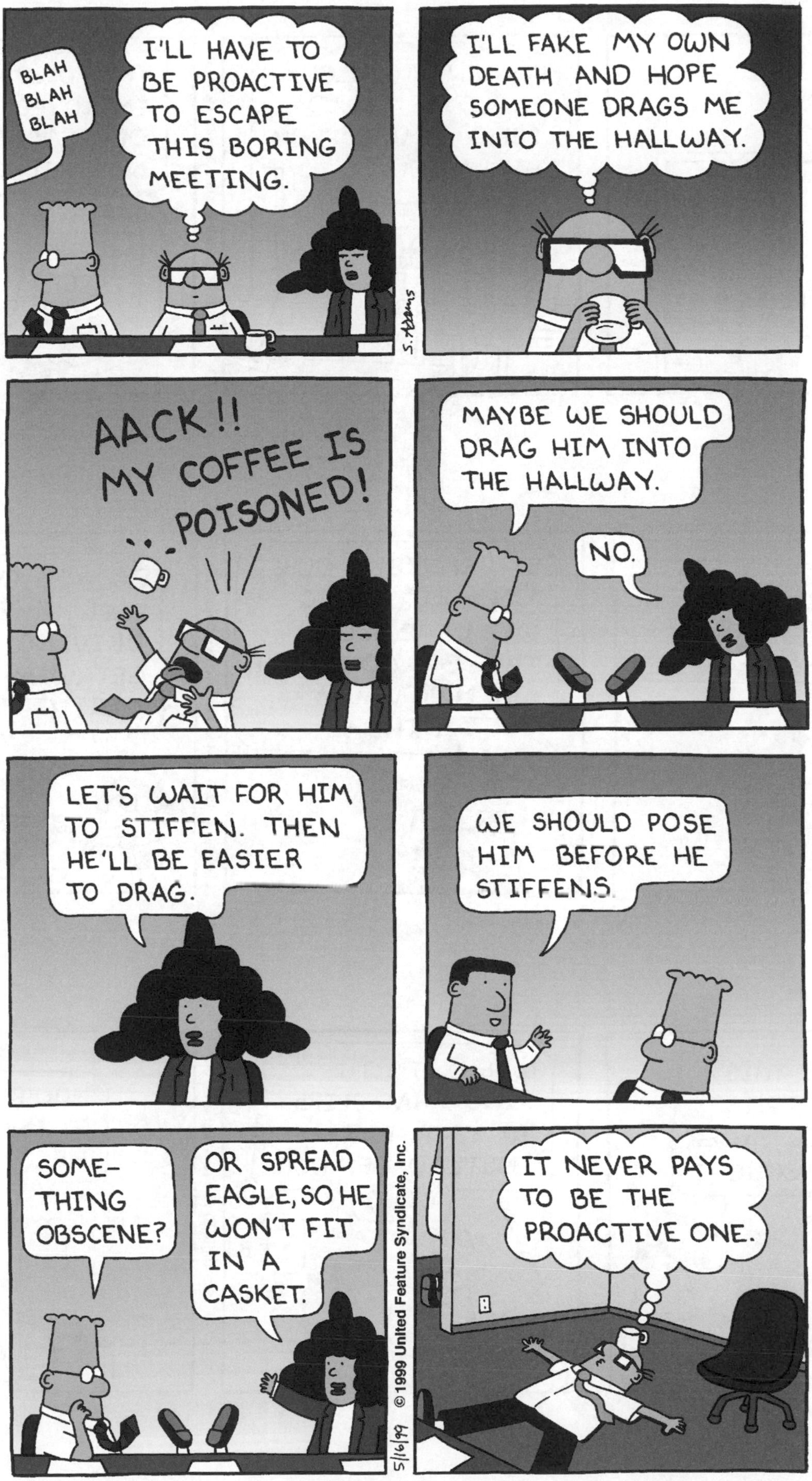
BLAH BLAH BLAH
I'LL HAVE TO BE PROACTIVE TO ESCAPE THIS BORING MEETING.
S. Adams
I'LL FAKE MY OWN DEATH AND HOPE SOMEONE DRAGS ME INTO THE HALLWAY.
AACK!! MY COFFEE IS POISONED!
MAYBE WE SHOULD DRAG HIM INTO THE HALLWAY.
NO.
LET'S WAIT FOR HIM TO STIFFEN. THEN HE'LL BE EASIER TO DRAG.
WE SHOULD POSE HIM BEFORE HE STIFFENS.
SOME-THING OBSCENE?
OR SPREAD EAGLE, SO HE WON'T FIT IN A CASKET.
5/16/99 © 1999 United Feature Syndicate, Inc.
IT NEVER PAYS TO BE THE PROACTIVE ONE.

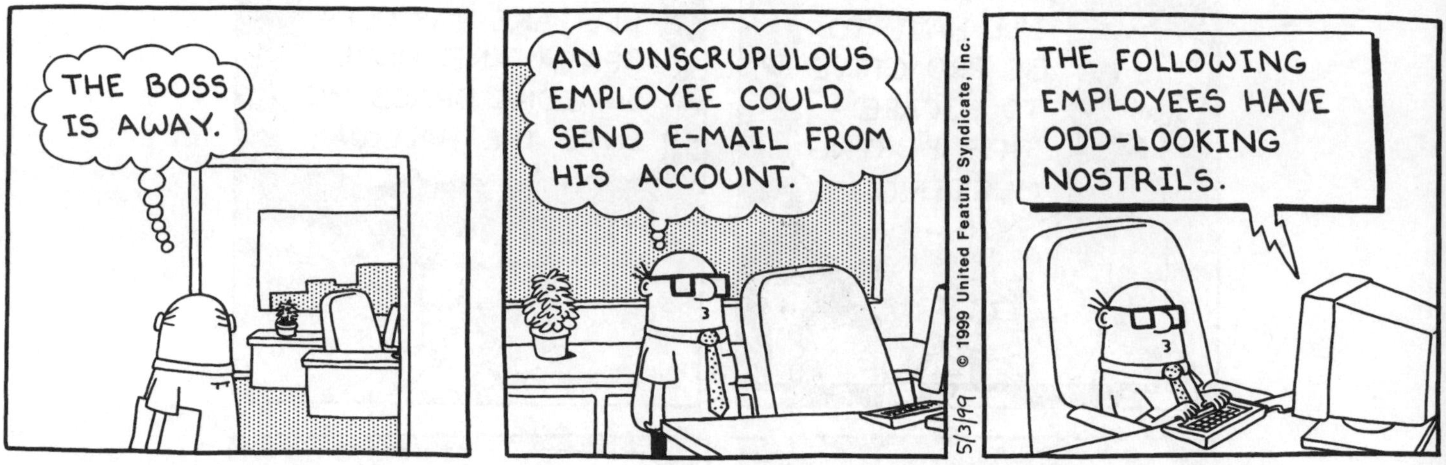
THE BOSS IS AWAY.
AN UNSCRUPULOUS EMPLOYEE COULD SEND E-MAIL FROM HIS ACCOUNT.
5/3/99 © 1999 United Feature Syndicate, Inc.
THE FOLLOWING EMPLOYEES HAVE ODD-LOOKING NOSTRILS.

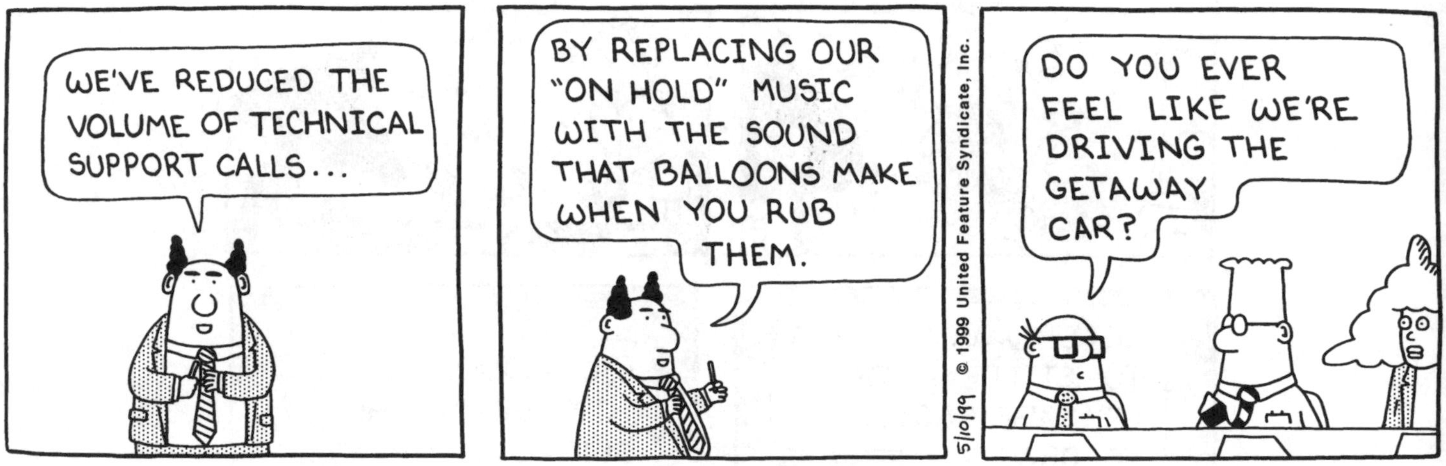
WE'VE REDUCED THE VOLUME OF TECHNICAL SUPPORT CALLS...
BY REPLACING OUR "ON HOLD" MUSIC WITH THE SOUND THAT BALLOONS MAKE WHEN YOU RUB THEM.
5/10/99 © 1999 United Feature Syndicate, Inc.
DO YOU EVER FEEL LIKE WE'RE DRIVING THE GETAWAY CAR?

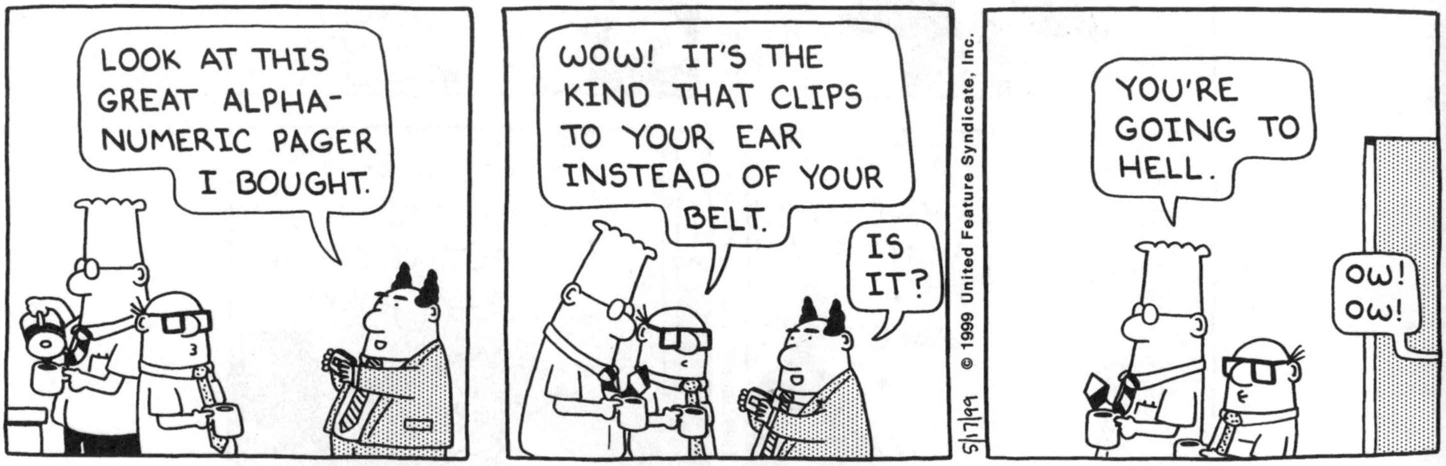
LOOK AT THIS GREAT ALPHA-NUMERIC PAGER I BOUGHT.
WOW! IT'S THE KIND THAT CLIPS TO YOUR EAR INSTEAD OF YOUR BELT.
IS IT?
5/17/99 © 1999 United Feature Syndicate, Inc.
YOU'RE GOING TO HELL.
OW! OW!

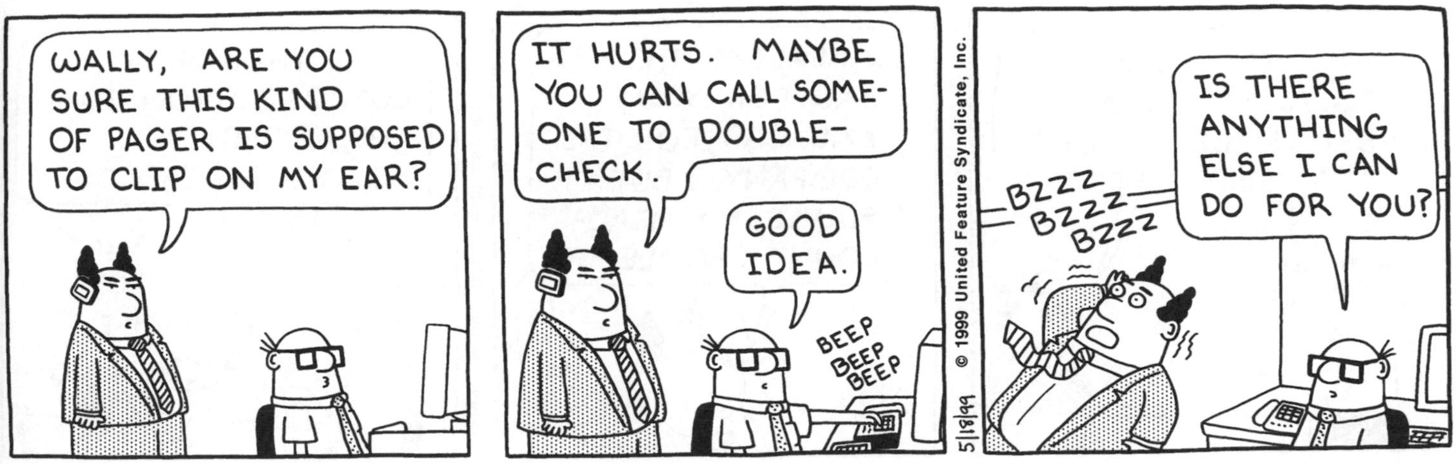
WALLY, ARE YOU SURE THIS KIND OF PAGER IS SUPPOSED TO CLIP ON MY EAR?
IT HURTS. MAYBE YOU CAN CALL SOMEONE TO DOUBLE-CHECK.
GOOD IDEA.
BEEP BEEP BEEP
BZZZ BZZZ BZZZ
IS THERE ANYTHING ELSE I CAN DO FOR YOU?

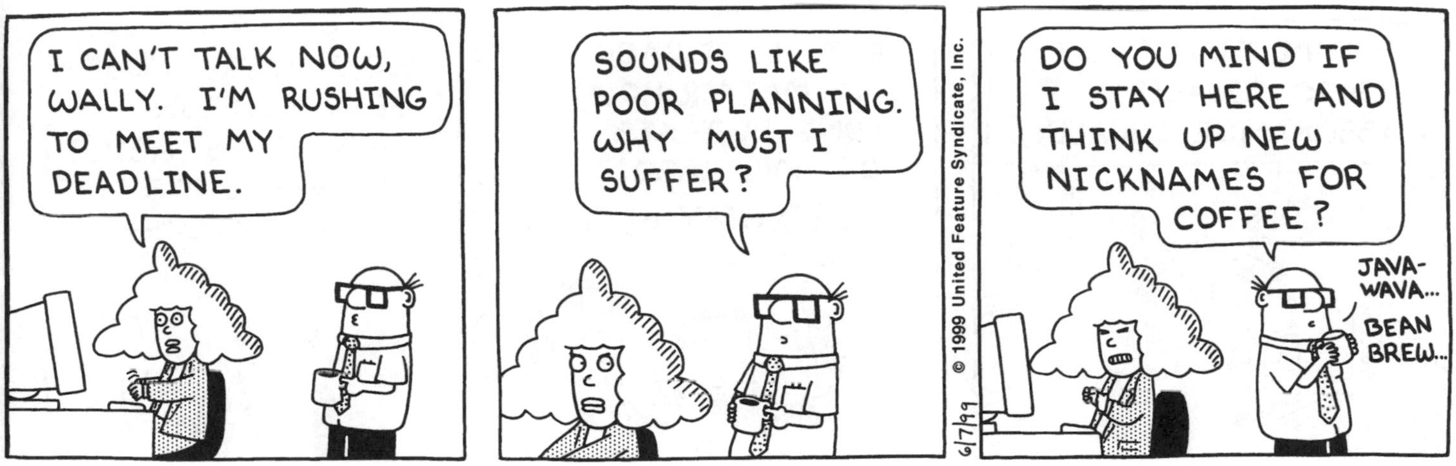
I CAN'T TALK NOW, WALLY. I'M RUSHING TO MEET MY DEADLINE.
SOUNDS LIKE POOR PLANNING. WHY MUST I SUFFER?
DO YOU MIND IF I STAY HERE AND THINK UP NEW NICKNAMES FOR COFFEE?
JAVA-WAVA...
BEAN BREW...

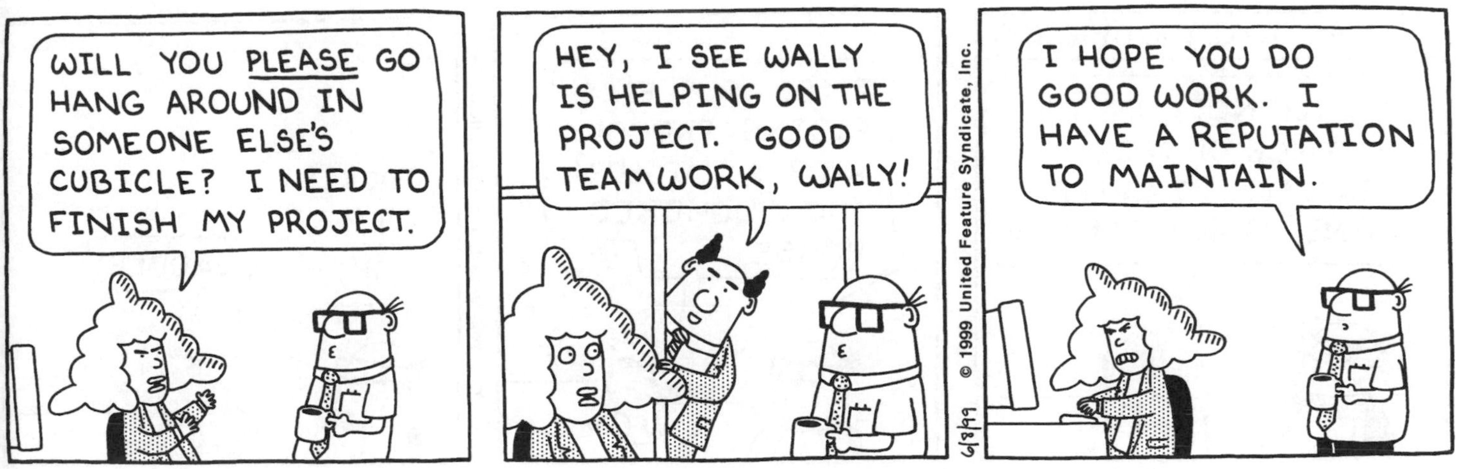
WILL YOU PLEASE GO HANG AROUND IN SOMEONE ELSE'S CUBICLE? I NEED TO FINISH MY PROJECT.
HEY, I SEE WALLY IS HELPING ON THE PROJECT. GOOD TEAMWORK, WALLY!
I HOPE YOU DO GOOD WORK. I HAVE A REPUTATION TO MAINTAIN.

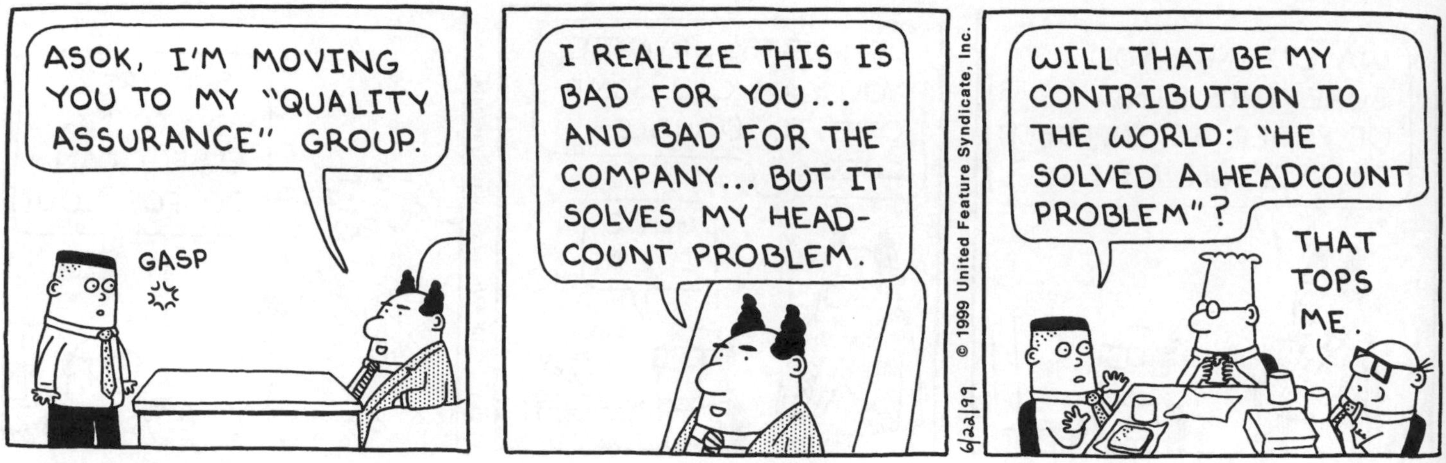
ASOK, I'M MOVING YOU TO MY "QUALITY ASSURANCE" GROUP.
GASP
I REALIZE THIS IS BAD FOR YOU... AND BAD FOR THE COMPANY... BUT IT SOLVES MY HEAD-COUNT PROBLEM.
© 1999 United Feature Syndicate, Inc.
6/22/99
WILL THAT BE MY CONTRIBUTION TO THE WORLD: "HE SOLVED A HEADCOUNT PROBLEM"?
THAT TOPS ME.

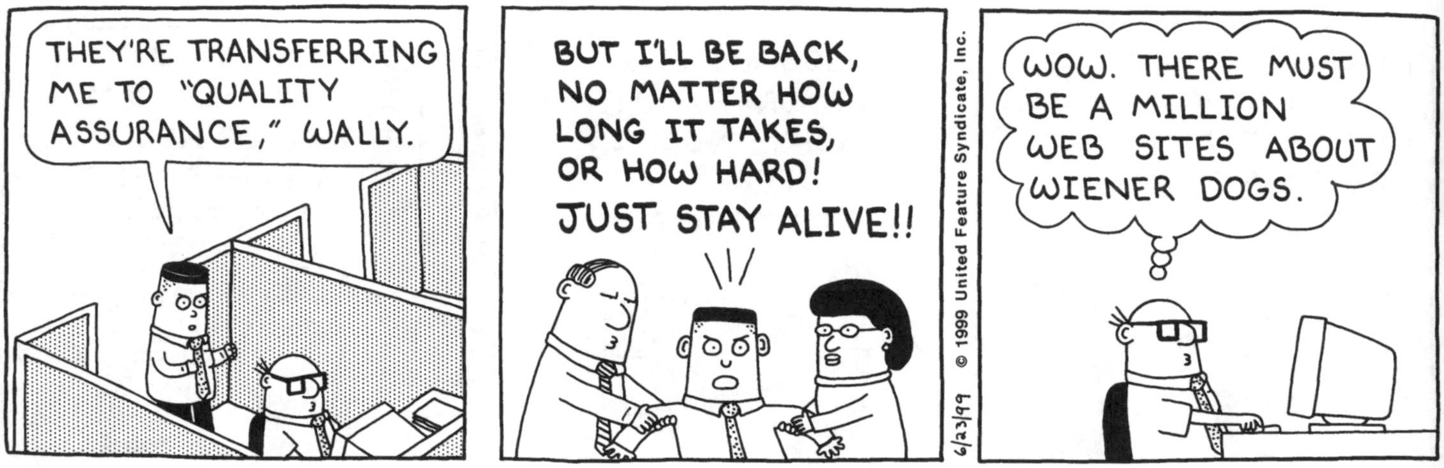
THEY'RE TRANSFERRING ME TO "QUALITY ASSURANCE," WALLY.
BUT I'LL BE BACK, NO MATTER HOW LONG IT TAKES, OR HOW HARD!
JUST STAY ALIVE!!
© 1999 United Feature Syndicate, Inc.
6/23/99
WOW. THERE MUST BE A MILLION WEB SITES ABOUT WIENER DOGS.

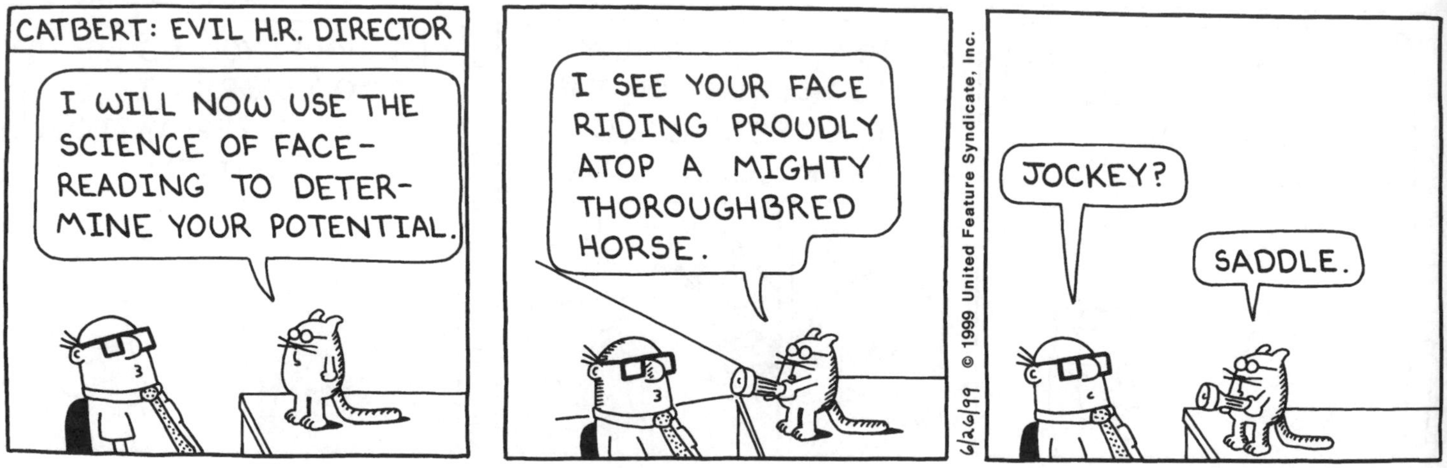
CATBERT: EVIL H.R. DIRECTOR
I WILL NOW USE THE SCIENCE OF FACE-READING TO DETER-MINE YOUR POTENTIAL.
I SEE YOUR FACE RIDING PROUDLY ATOP A MIGHTY THOROUGHBRED HORSE.
© 1999 United Feature Syndicate, Inc.
6/26/99
JOCKEY?
SADDLE.

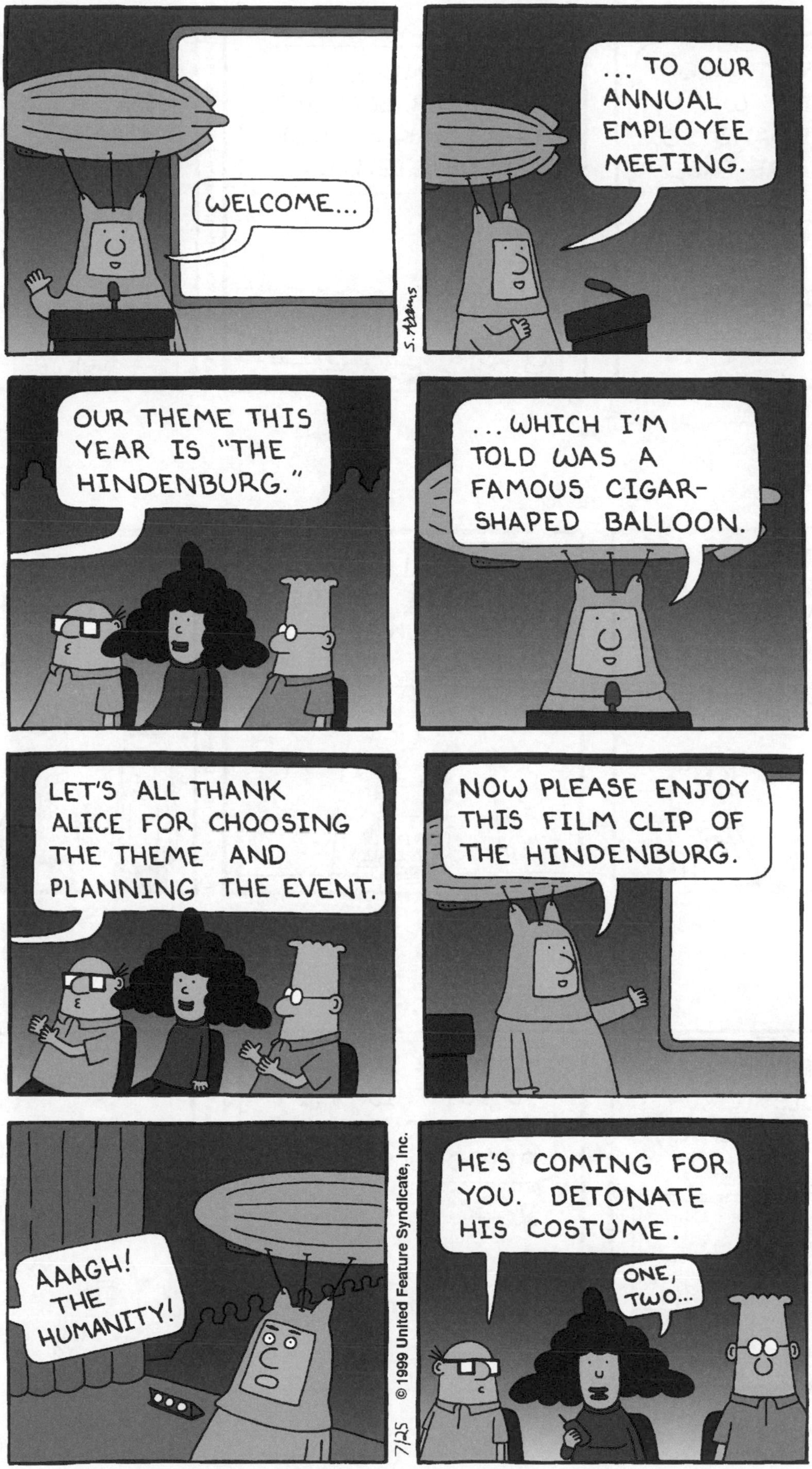
WELCOME...
... TO OUR ANNUAL EMPLOYEE MEETING.
S. Adams
OUR THEME THIS YEAR IS "THE HINDENBURG."
... WHICH I'M TOLD WAS A FAMOUS CIGAR-SHAPED BALLOON.
LET'S ALL THANK ALICE FOR CHOOSING THE THEME AND PLANNING THE EVENT.
NOW PLEASE ENJOY THIS FILM CLIP OF THE HINDENBURG.
AAAGH! THE HUMANITY!
7/25 © 1999 United Feature Syndicate, Inc.
HE'S COMING FOR YOU. DETONATE HIS COSTUME.
ONE, TWO...

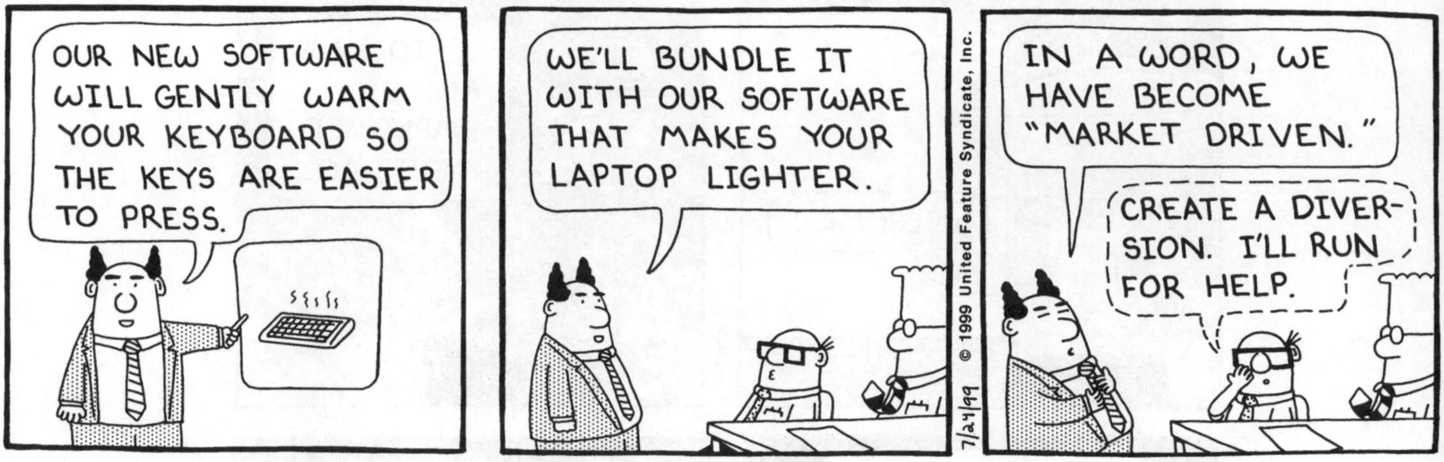
OUR NEW SOFTWARE WILL GENTLY WARM YOUR KEYBOARD SO THE KEYS ARE EASIER TO PRESS.
WE'LL BUNDLE IT WITH OUR SOFTWARE THAT MAKES YOUR LAPTOP LIGHTER.
7/24/99 © 1999 United Feature Syndicate, Inc.
IN A WORD, WE HAVE BECOME "MARKET DRIVEN."
CREATE A DIVERSION. I'LL RUN FOR HELP.

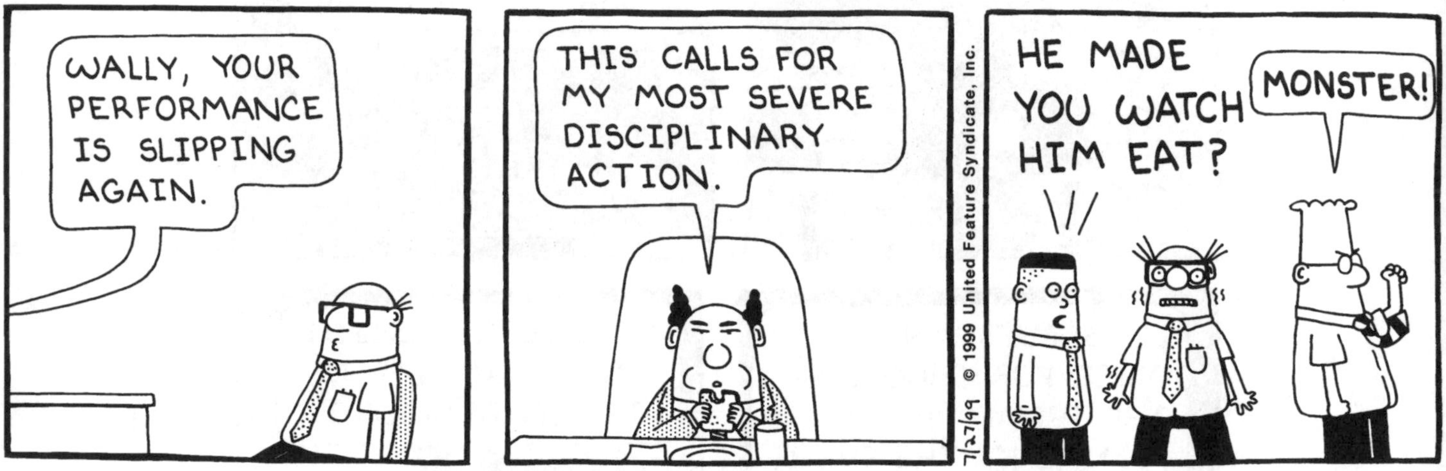
WALLY, YOUR PERFORMANCE IS SLIPPING AGAIN.
THIS CALLS FOR MY MOST SEVERE DISCIPLINARY ACTION.
7/27/99 © 1999 United Feature Syndicate, Inc.
HE MADE YOU WATCH HIM EAT?
MONSTER!

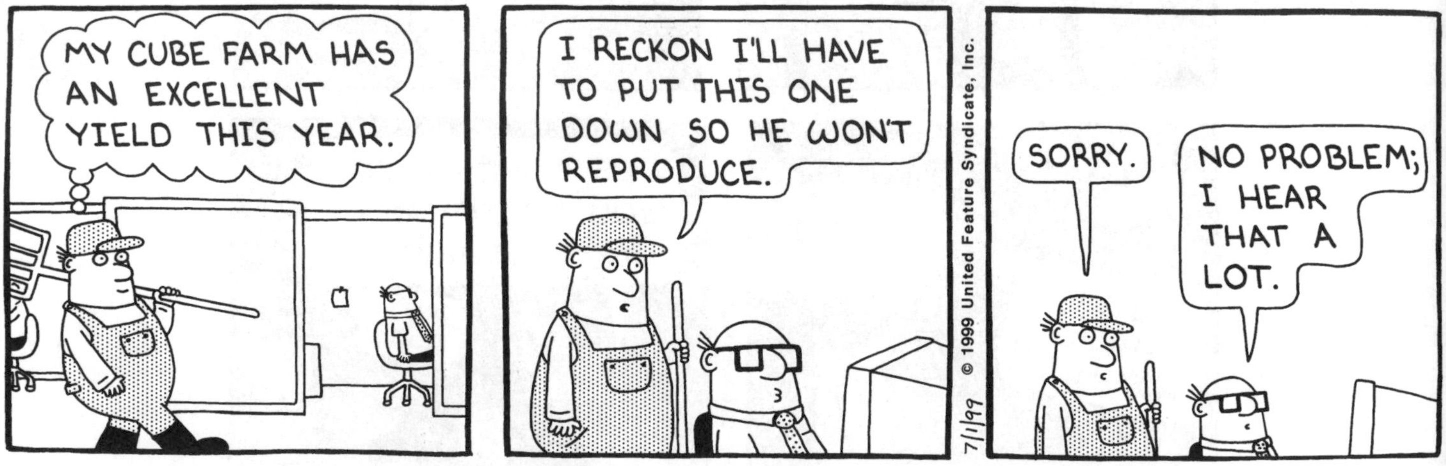
MY CUBE FARM HAS AN EXCELLENT YIELD THIS YEAR.
I RECKON I'LL HAVE TO PUT THIS ONE DOWN SO HE WON'T REPRODUCE.
7/1/99 © 1999 United Feature Syndicate, Inc.
SORRY.
NO PROBLEM; I HEAR THAT A LOT.

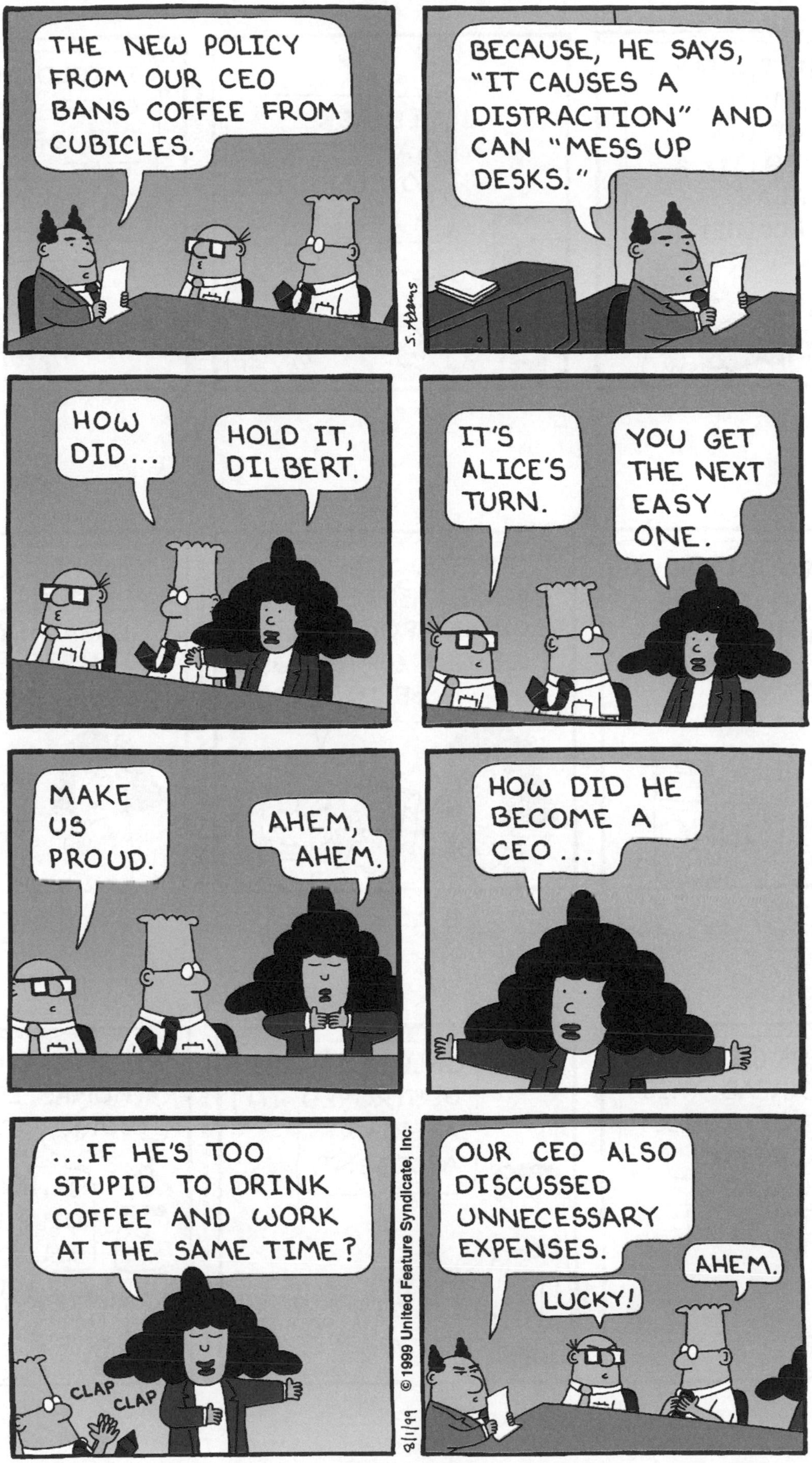
THE NEW POLICY FROM OUR CEO BANS COFFEE FROM CUBICLES.
S. Adams
BECAUSE, HE SAYS, "IT CAUSES A DISTRACTION" AND CAN "MESS UP DESKS."
HOW DID...
HOLD IT, DILBERT.
IT'S ALICE'S TURN.
YOU GET THE NEXT EASY ONE.
MAKE US PROUD.
AHEM, AHEM.
HOW DID HE BECOME A CEO...
...IF HE'S TOO STUPID TO DRINK COFFEE AND WORK AT THE SAME TIME?
CLAP CLAP
8/1/99 © 1999 United Feature Syndicate, Inc.
OUR CEO ALSO DISCUSSED UNNECESSARY EXPENSES.
LUCKY!
AHEM.

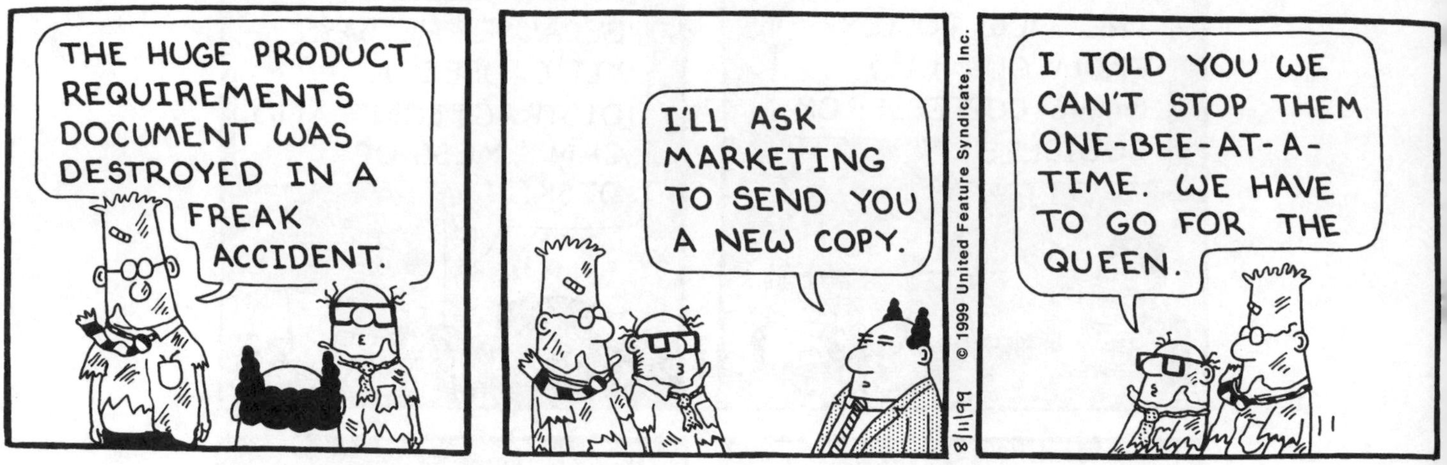
THE HUGE PRODUCT REQUIREMENTS DOCUMENT WAS DESTROYED IN A FREAK ACCIDENT.
I'LL ASK MARKETING TO SEND YOU A NEW COPY.
8/11/99 © 1999 United Feature Syndicate, Inc.
I TOLD YOU WE CAN'T STOP THEM ONE-BEE-AT-A-TIME. WE HAVE TO GO FOR THE QUEEN.

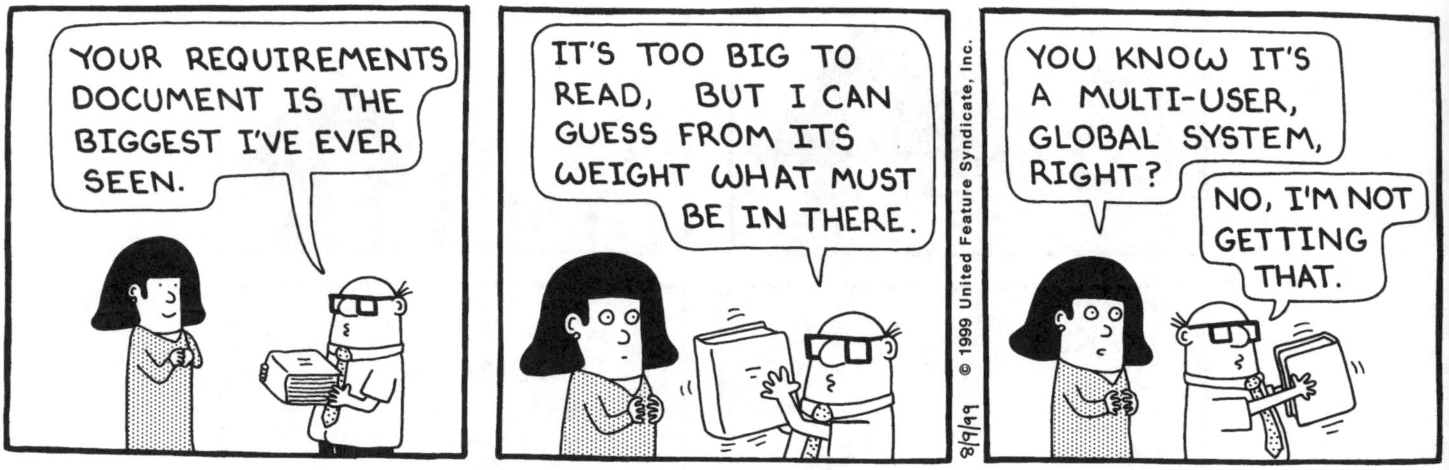
YOUR REQUIREMENTS DOCUMENT IS THE BIGGEST I'VE EVER SEEN.
IT'S TOO BIG TO READ, BUT I CAN GUESS FROM ITS WEIGHT WHAT MUST BE IN THERE.
8/9/99 © 1999 United Feature Syndicate, Inc.
YOU KNOW IT'S A MULTI-USER, GLOBAL SYSTEM, RIGHT?
NO, I'M NOT GETTING THAT.

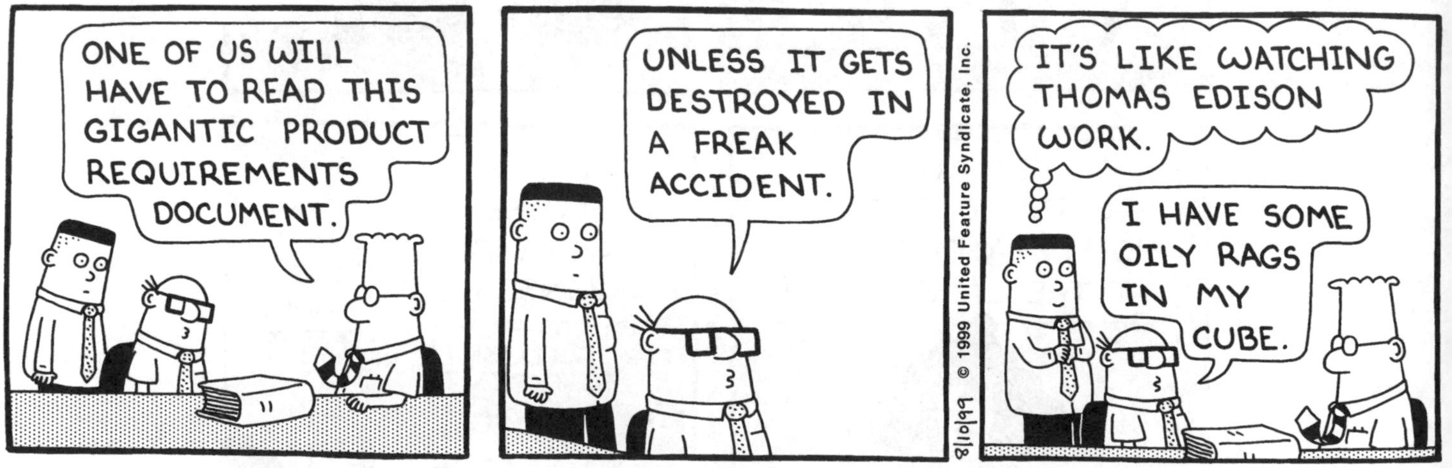
ONE OF US WILL HAVE TO READ THIS GIGANTIC PRODUCT REQUIREMENTS DOCUMENT.
UNLESS IT GETS DESTROYED IN A FREAK ACCIDENT.
8/10/99 © 1999 United Feature Syndicate, Inc.
IT'S LIKE WATCHING THOMAS EDISON WORK.
I HAVE SOME OILY RAGS IN MY CUBE.

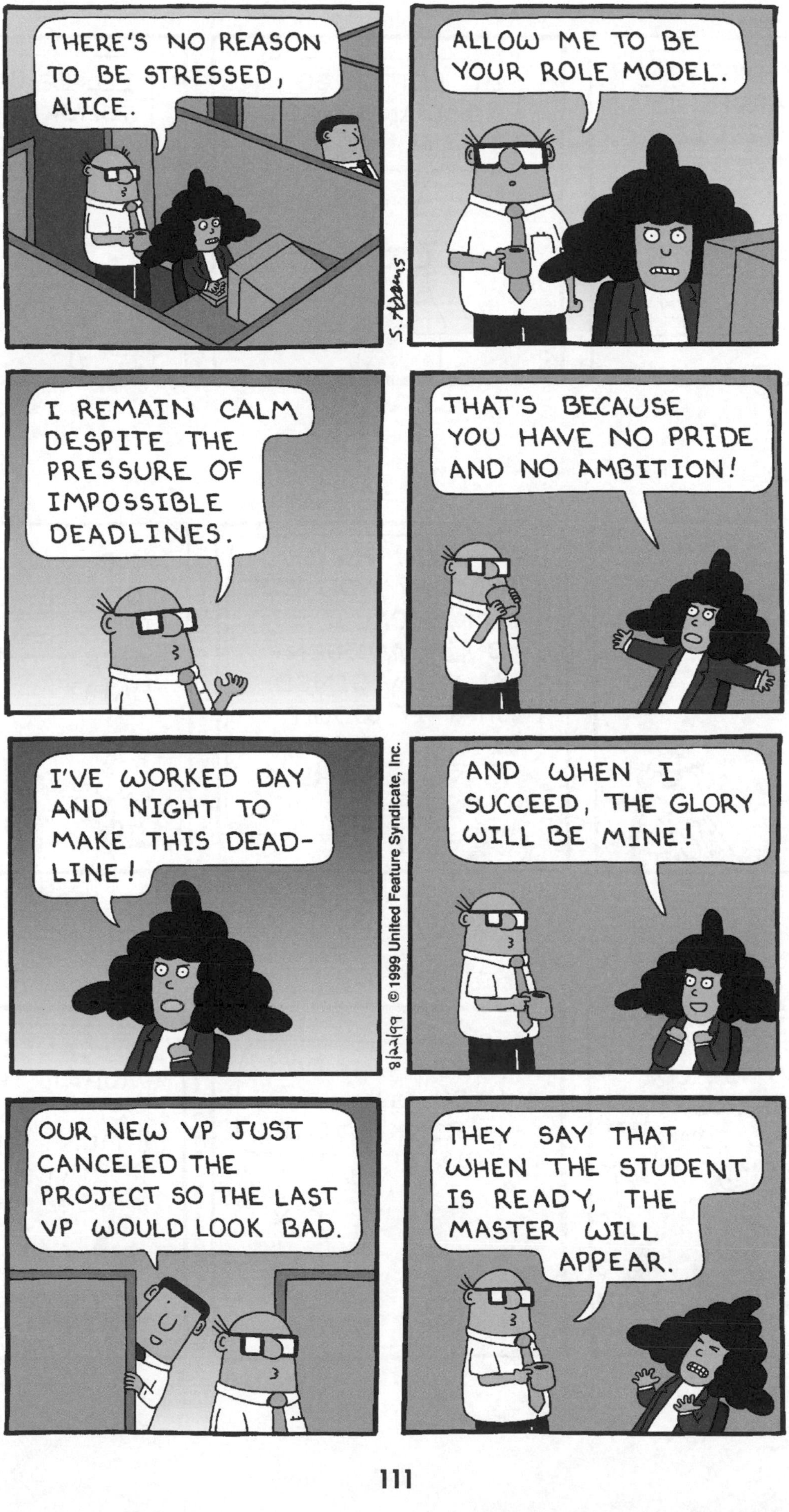
THERE'S NO REASON TO BE STRESSED, ALICE.
ALLOW ME TO BE YOUR ROLE MODEL.
S. ADAMS
I REMAIN CALM DESPITE THE PRESSURE OF IMPOSSIBLE DEADLINES.
THAT'S BECAUSE YOU HAVE NO PRIDE AND NO AMBITION!
I'VE WORKED DAY AND NIGHT TO MAKE THIS DEAD-LINE!
AND WHEN I SUCCEED, THE GLORY WILL BE MINE!
© 1999 United Feature Syndicate, Inc.
8/22/99
OUR NEW VP JUST CANCELED THE PROJECT SO THE LAST VP WOULD LOOK BAD.
THEY SAY THAT WHEN THE STUDENT IS READY, THE MASTER WILL APPEAR.

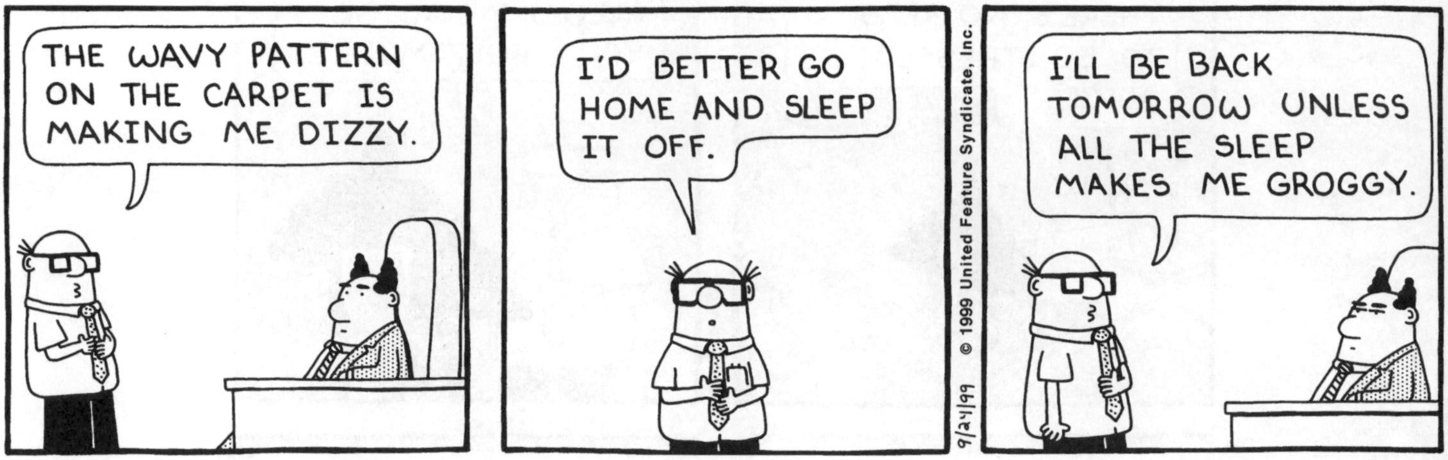
THE WAVY PATTERN ON THE CARPET IS MAKING ME DIZZY.
I'D BETTER GO HOME AND SLEEP IT OFF.
9/24/99 © 1999 United Feature Syndicate, Inc.
I'LL BE BACK TOMORROW UNLESS ALL THE SLEEP MAKES ME GROGGY.

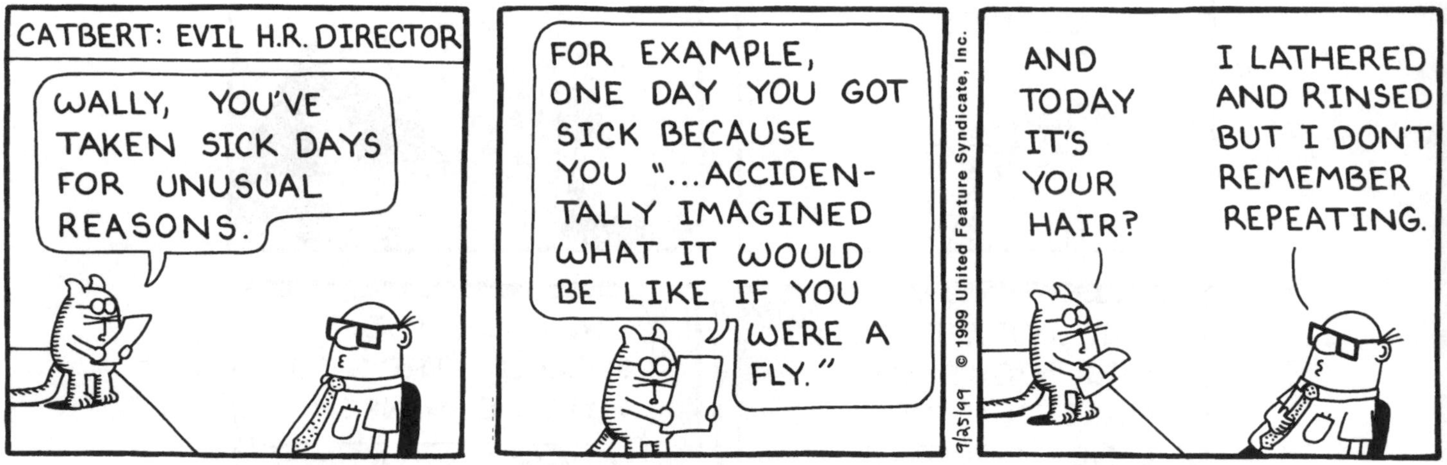
CATBERT: EVIL H.R. DIRECTOR
WALLY, YOU'VE TAKEN SICK DAYS FOR UNUSUAL REASONS.
FOR EXAMPLE, ONE DAY YOU GOT SICK BECAUSE YOU "...ACCIDENTALLY IMAGINED WHAT IT WOULD BE LIKE IF YOU WERE A FLY."
9/25/99 © 1999 United Feature Syndicate, Inc.
AND TODAY IT'S YOUR HAIR?
I LATHERED AND RINSED BUT I DON'T REMEMBER REPEATING.

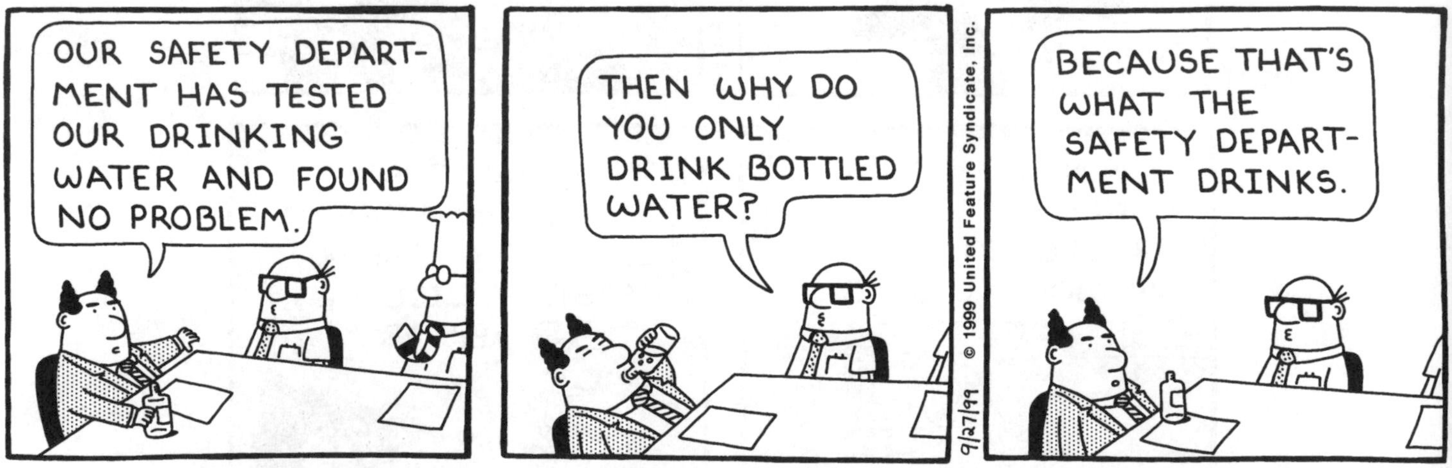
OUR SAFETY DEPARTMENT HAS TESTED OUR DRINKING WATER AND FOUND NO PROBLEM.
THEN WHY DO YOU ONLY DRINK BOTTLED WATER?
9/27/99 © 1999 United Feature Syndicate, Inc.
BECAUSE THAT'S WHAT THE SAFETY DEPARTMENT DRINKS.

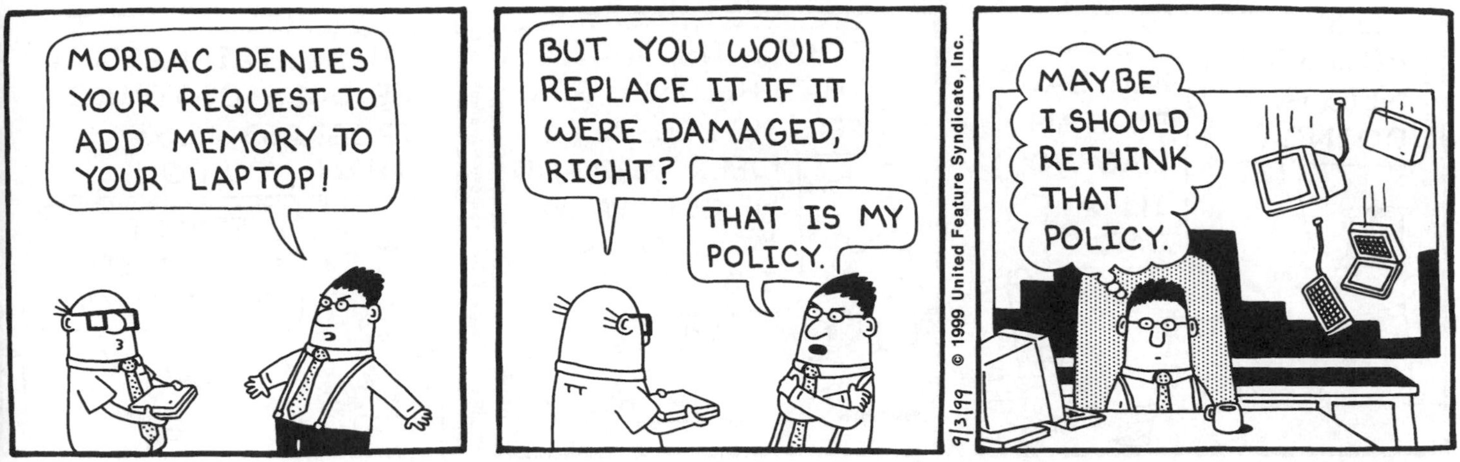
MORDAC DENIES YOUR REQUEST TO ADD MEMORY TO YOUR LAPTOP!
BUT YOU WOULD REPLACE IT IF IT WERE DAMAGED, RIGHT?
THAT IS MY POLICY.
9/3/99 © 1999 United Feature Syndicate, Inc.
MAYBE I SHOULD RETHINK THAT POLICY.

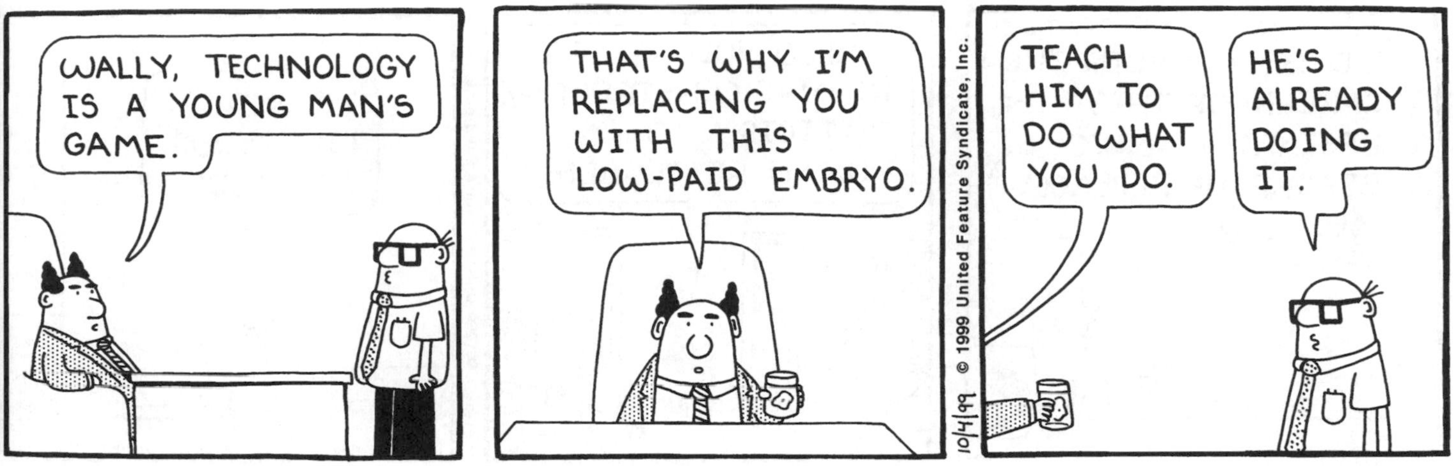
WALLY, TECHNOLOGY IS A YOUNG MAN'S GAME.
THAT'S WHY I'M REPLACING YOU WITH THIS LOW-PAID EMBRYO.
10/4/99 © 1999 United Feature Syndicate, Inc.
TEACH HIM TO DO WHAT YOU DO.
HE'S ALREADY DOING IT.

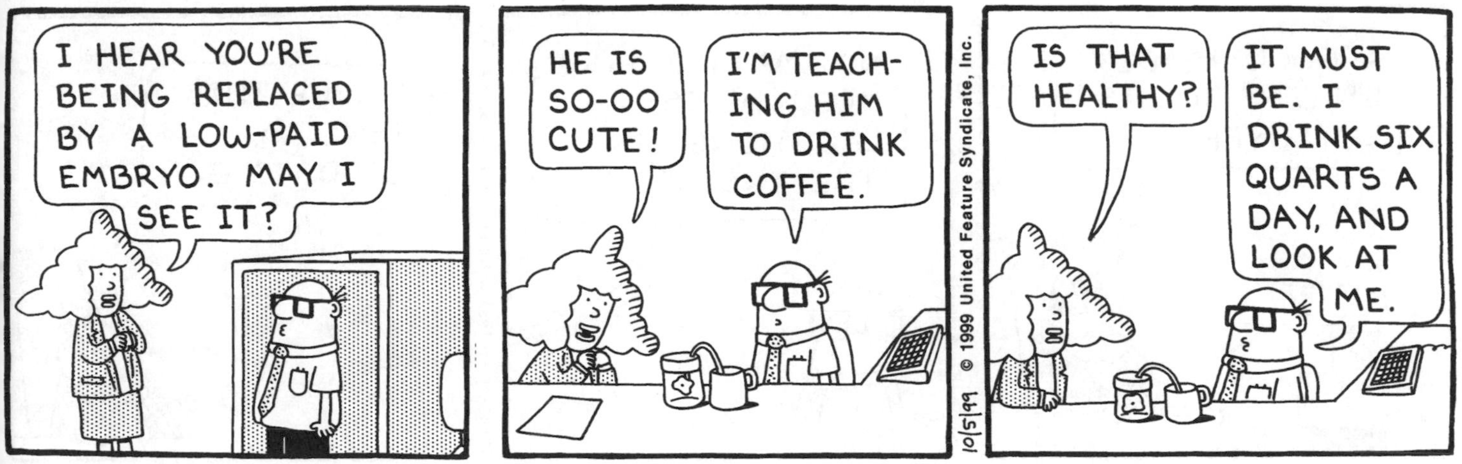
I HEAR YOU'RE BEING REPLACED BY A LOW-PAID EMBRYO. MAY I SEE IT?
HE IS SO-OO CUTE!
I'M TEACH-ING HIM TO DRINK COFFEE.
10/5/99 © 1999 United Feature Syndicate, Inc.
IS THAT HEALTHY?
IT MUST BE. I DRINK SIX QUARTS A DAY, AND LOOK AT ME.

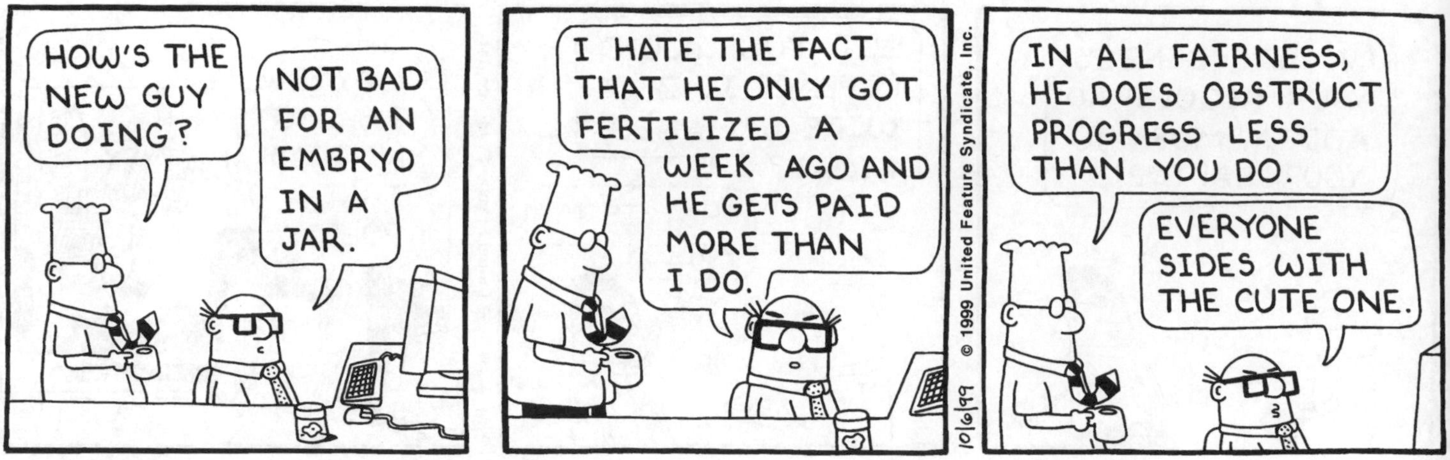
HOW'S THE NEW GUY DOING?
NOT BAD FOR AN EMBRYO IN A JAR.
I HATE THE FACT THAT HE ONLY GOT FERTILIZED A WEEK AGO AND HE GETS PAID MORE THAN I DO.
10/6/99 © 1999 United Feature Syndicate, Inc.
IN ALL FAIRNESS, HE DOES OBSTRUCT PROGRESS LESS THAN YOU DO.
EVERYONE SIDES WITH THE CUTE ONE.

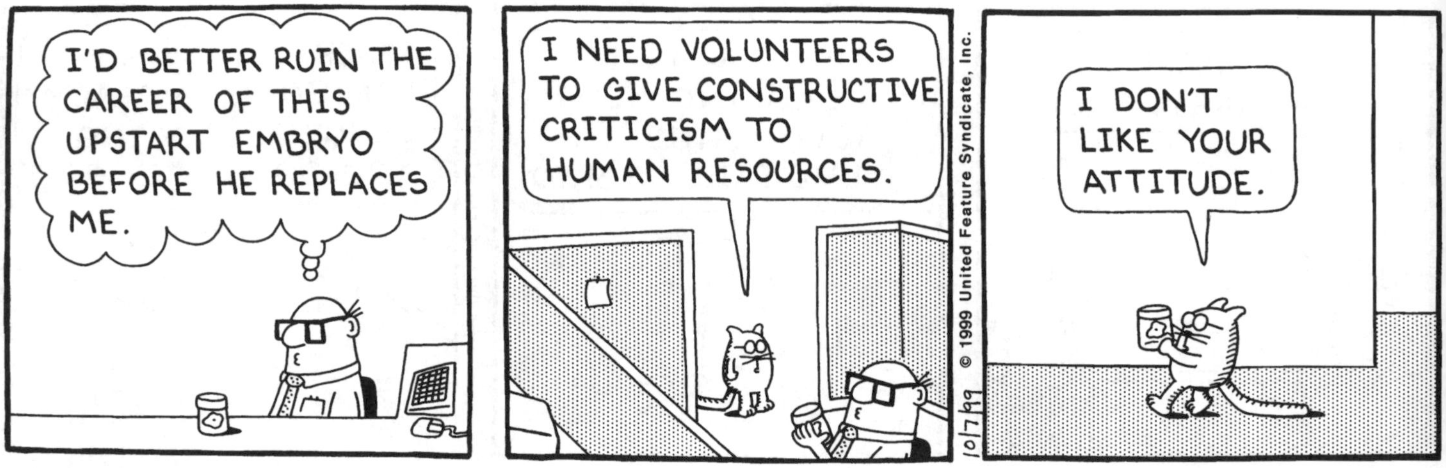
I'D BETTER RUIN THE CAREER OF THIS UPSTART EMBRYO BEFORE HE REPLACES ME.
I NEED VOLUNTEERS TO GIVE CONSTRUCTIVE CRITICISM TO HUMAN RESOURCES.
10/7/99 © 1999 United Feature Syndicate, Inc.
I DON'T LIKE YOUR ATTITUDE.

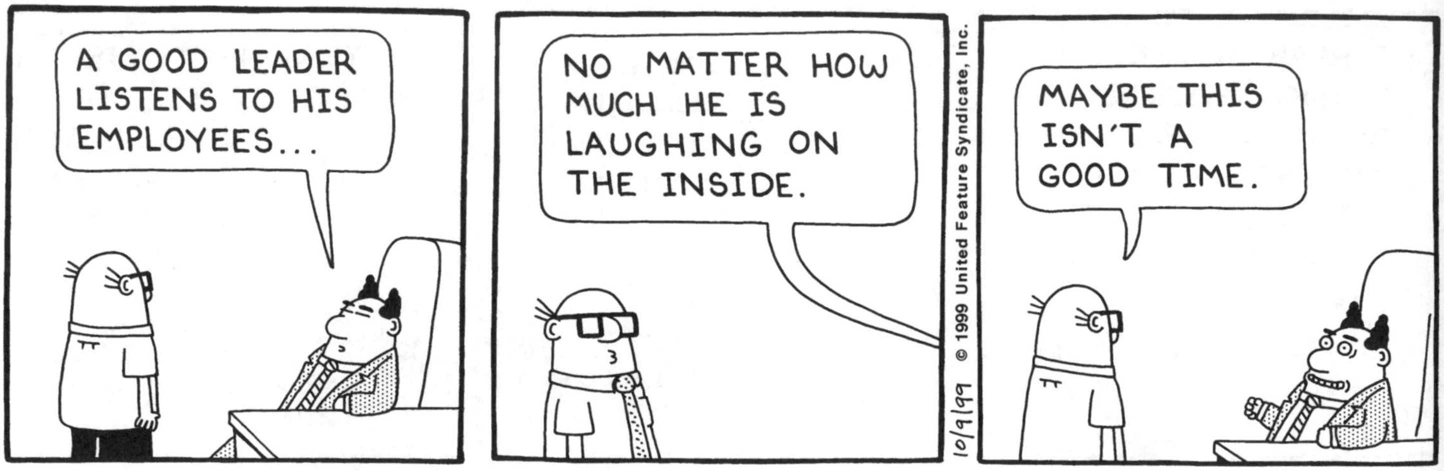
A GOOD LEADER LISTENS TO HIS EMPLOYEES...
NO MATTER HOW MUCH HE IS LAUGHING ON THE INSIDE.
10/9/99 © 1999 United Feature Syndicate, Inc.
MAYBE THIS ISN'T A GOOD TIME.

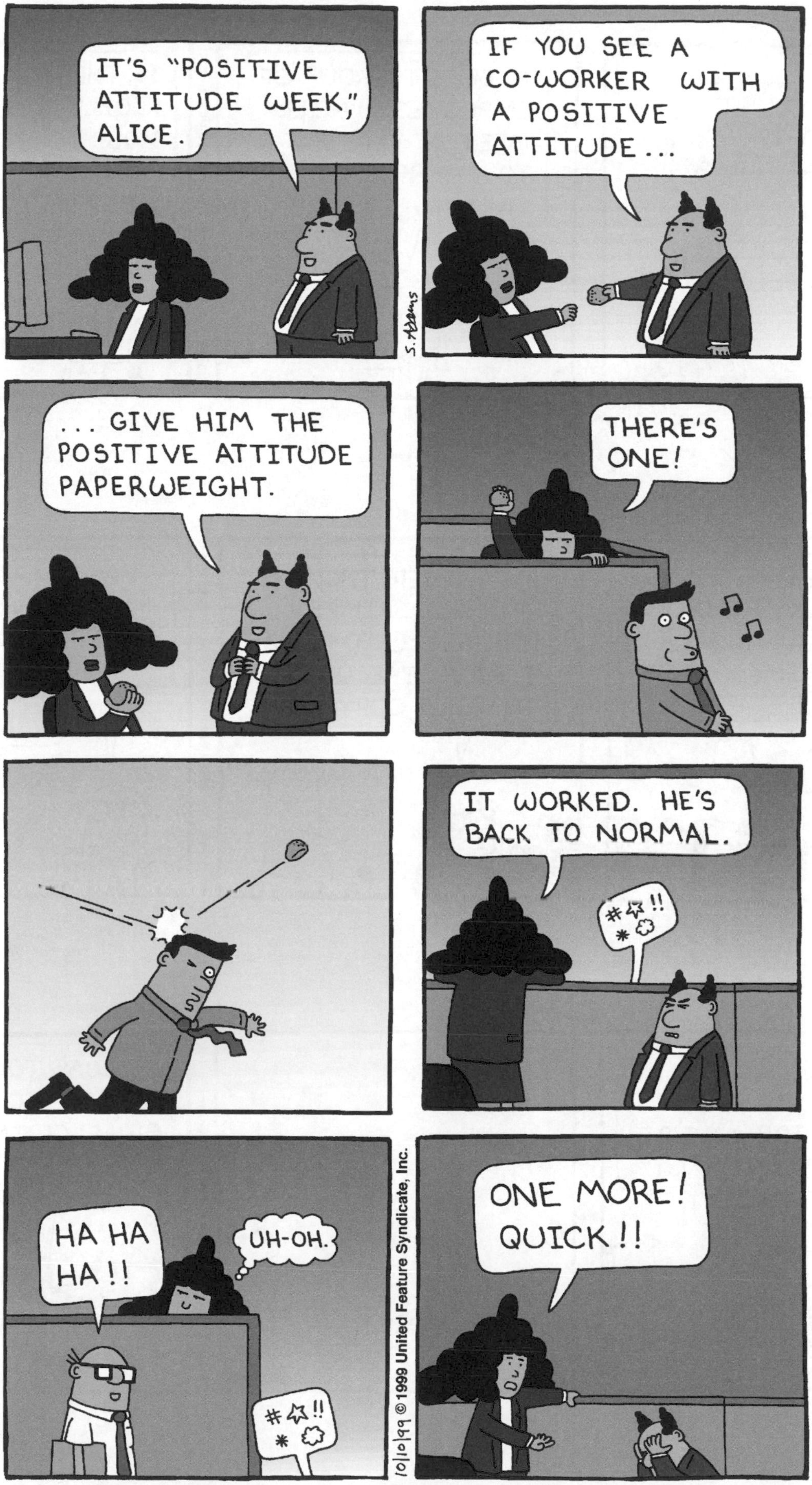
IT'S "POSITIVE ATTITUDE WEEK," ALICE.
S. Adams
IF YOU SEE A CO-WORKER WITH A POSITIVE ATTITUDE...
... GIVE HIM THE POSITIVE ATTITUDE PAPERWEIGHT.
THERE'S ONE!
IT WORKED. HE'S BACK TO NORMAL.
#☆!! * ✿
HA HA HA!!
UH-OH.
#☆!! * ✿
10/10/99 © 1999 United Feature Syndicate, Inc.
ONE MORE! QUICK!!

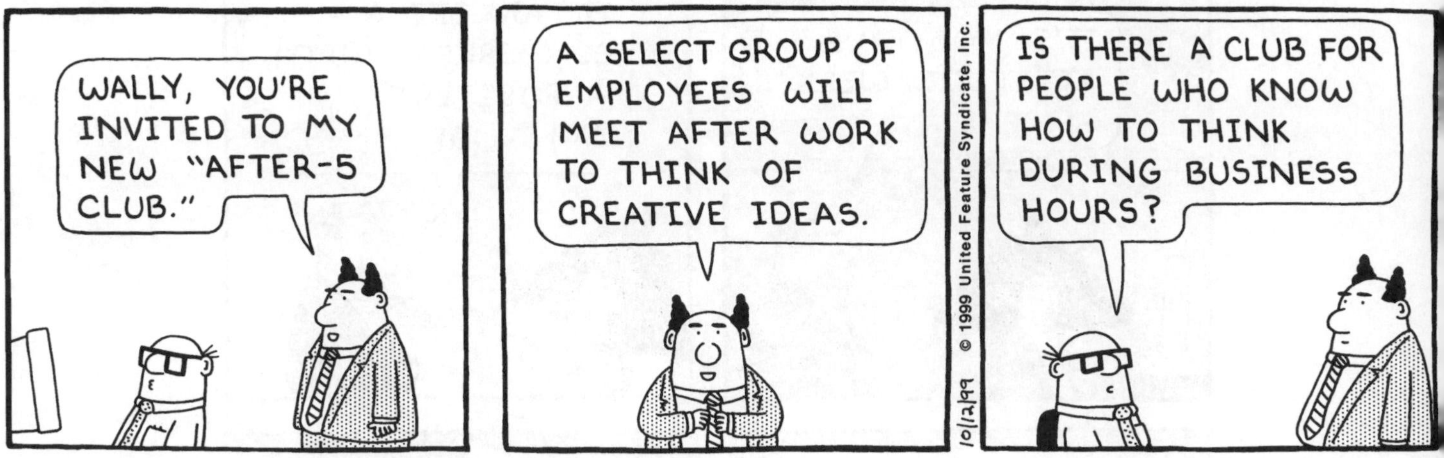

WALLY, YOU'RE INVITED TO MY NEW "AFTER-5 CLUB."
A SELECT GROUP OF EMPLOYEES WILL MEET AFTER WORK TO THINK OF CREATIVE IDEAS.
10/12/99 © 1999 United Feature Syndicate, Inc.
IS THERE A CLUB FOR PEOPLE WHO KNOW HOW TO THINK DURING BUSINESS HOURS?

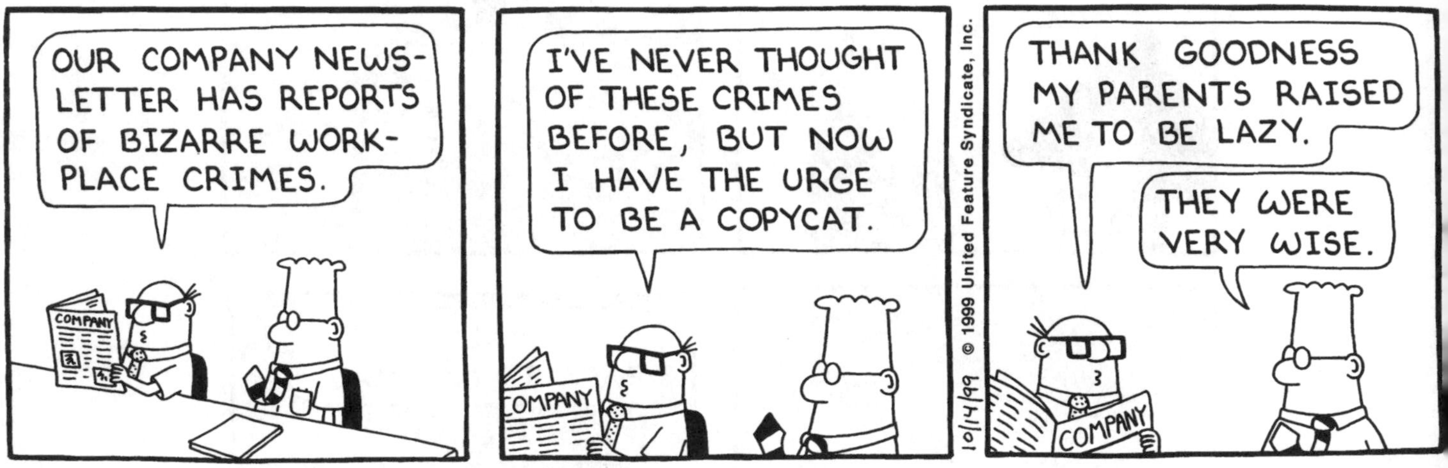

OUR COMPANY NEWSLETTER HAS REPORTS OF BIZARRE WORKPLACE CRIMES.
COMPANY
I'VE NEVER THOUGHT OF THESE CRIMES BEFORE, BUT NOW I HAVE THE URGE TO BE A COPYCAT.
COMPANY
10/14/99 © 1999 United Feature Syndicate, Inc.
THANK GOODNESS MY PARENTS RAISED ME TO BE LAZY.
THEY WERE VERY WISE.
COMPANY

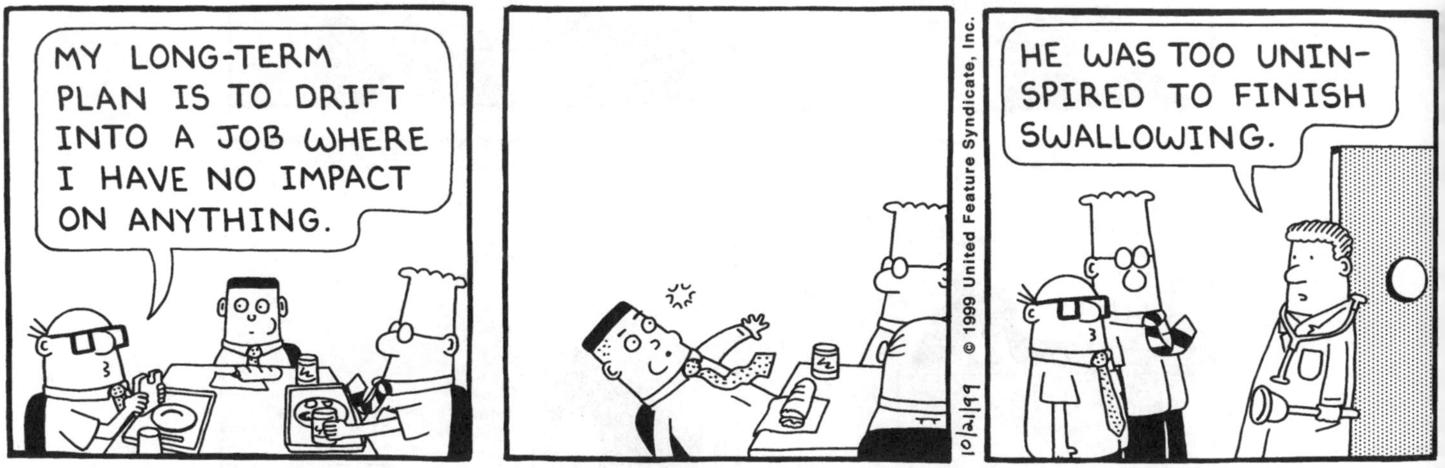

MY LONG-TERM PLAN IS TO DRIFT INTO A JOB WHERE I HAVE NO IMPACT ON ANYTHING.
10/21/99 © 1999 United Feature Syndicate, Inc.
HE WAS TOO UNINSPIRED TO FINISH SWALLOWING.

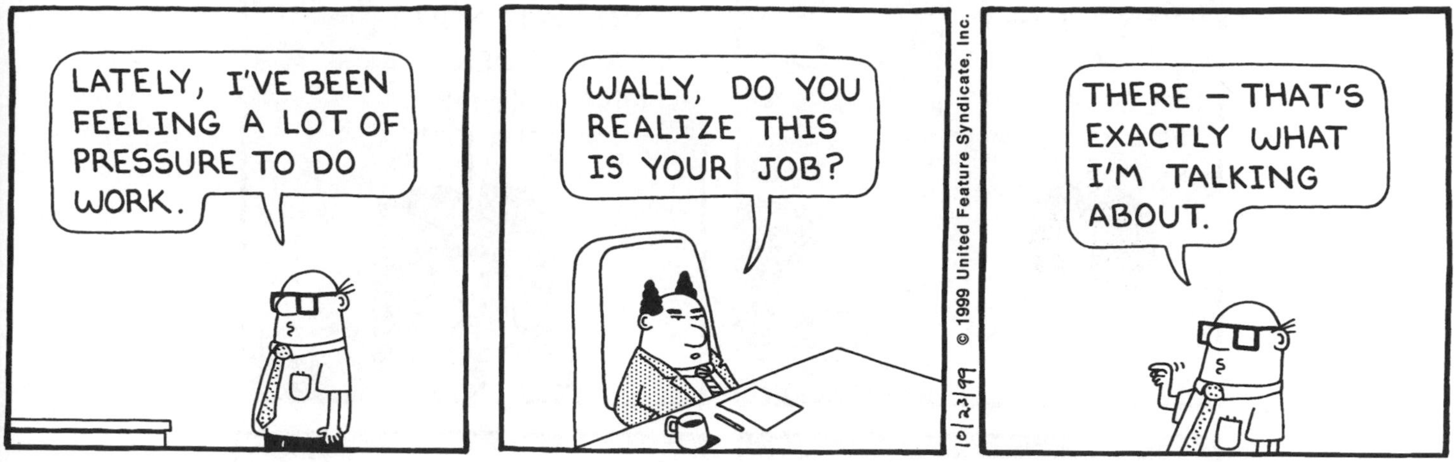
LATELY, I'VE BEEN FEELING A LOT OF PRESSURE TO DO WORK.
WALLY, DO YOU REALIZE THIS IS YOUR JOB?
10/23/99 © 1999 United Feature Syndicate, Inc.
THERE — THAT'S EXACTLY WHAT I'M TALKING ABOUT.

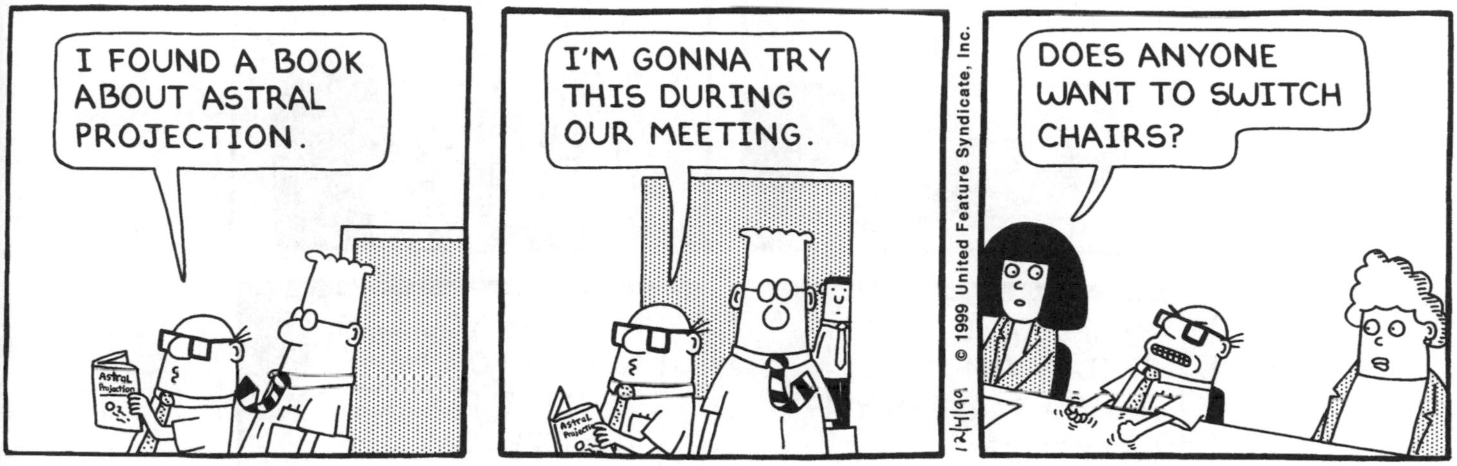
I FOUND A BOOK ABOUT ASTRAL PROJECTION.
Astral Projection
I'M GONNA TRY THIS DURING OUR MEETING.
Astral Projection
12/4/99 © 1999 United Feature Syndicate, Inc.
DOES ANYONE WANT TO SWITCH CHAIRS?

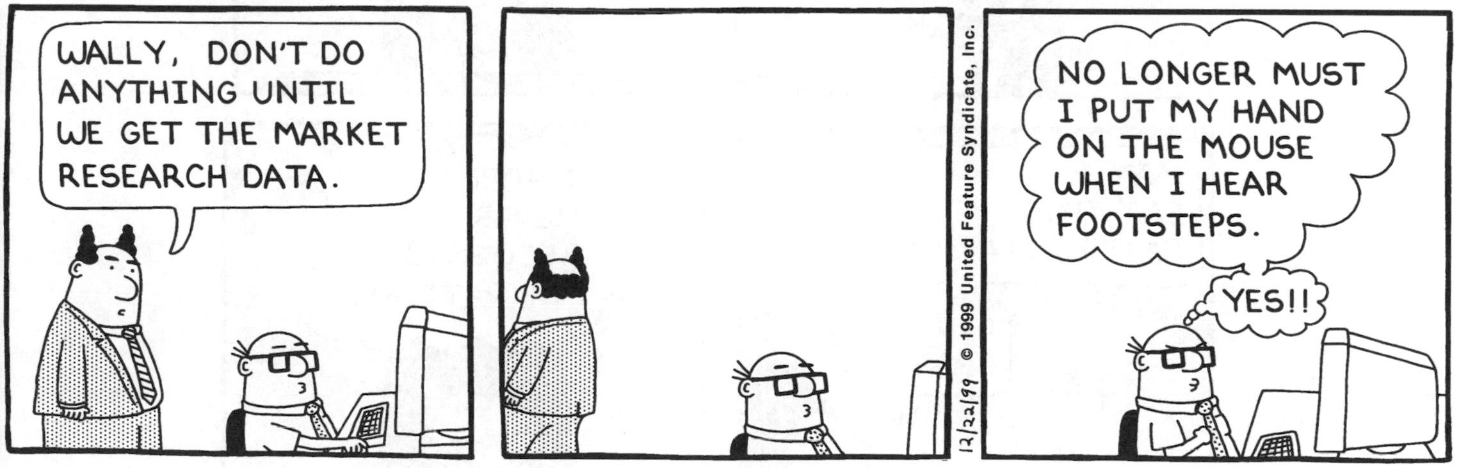
WALLY, DON'T DO ANYTHING UNTIL WE GET THE MARKET RESEARCH DATA.
12/22/99 © 1999 United Feature Syndicate, Inc.
NO LONGER MUST I PUT MY HAND ON THE MOUSE WHEN I HEAR FOOTSTEPS.
YES!!

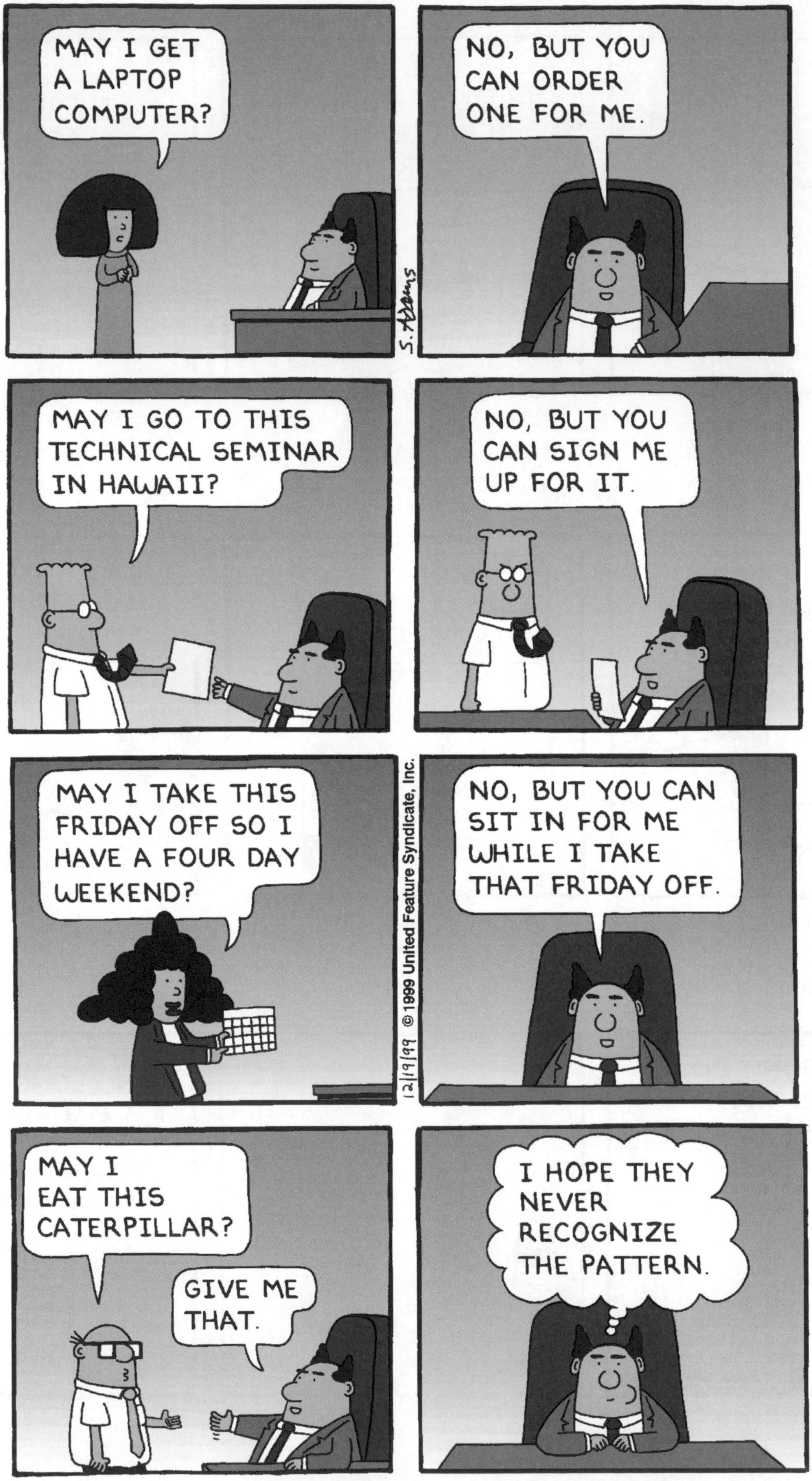
MAY I GET A LAPTOP COMPUTER?
NO, BUT YOU CAN ORDER ONE FOR ME.
S. Adams
MAY I GO TO THIS TECHNICAL SEMINAR IN HAWAII?
NO, BUT YOU CAN SIGN ME UP FOR IT.
MAY I TAKE THIS FRIDAY OFF SO I HAVE A FOUR DAY WEEKEND?
NO, BUT YOU CAN SIT IN FOR ME WHILE I TAKE THAT FRIDAY OFF.
12/19/99 © 1999 United Feature Syndicate, Inc.
MAY I EAT THIS CATERPILLAR?
GIVE ME THAT.
I HOPE THEY NEVER RECOGNIZE THE PATTERN.

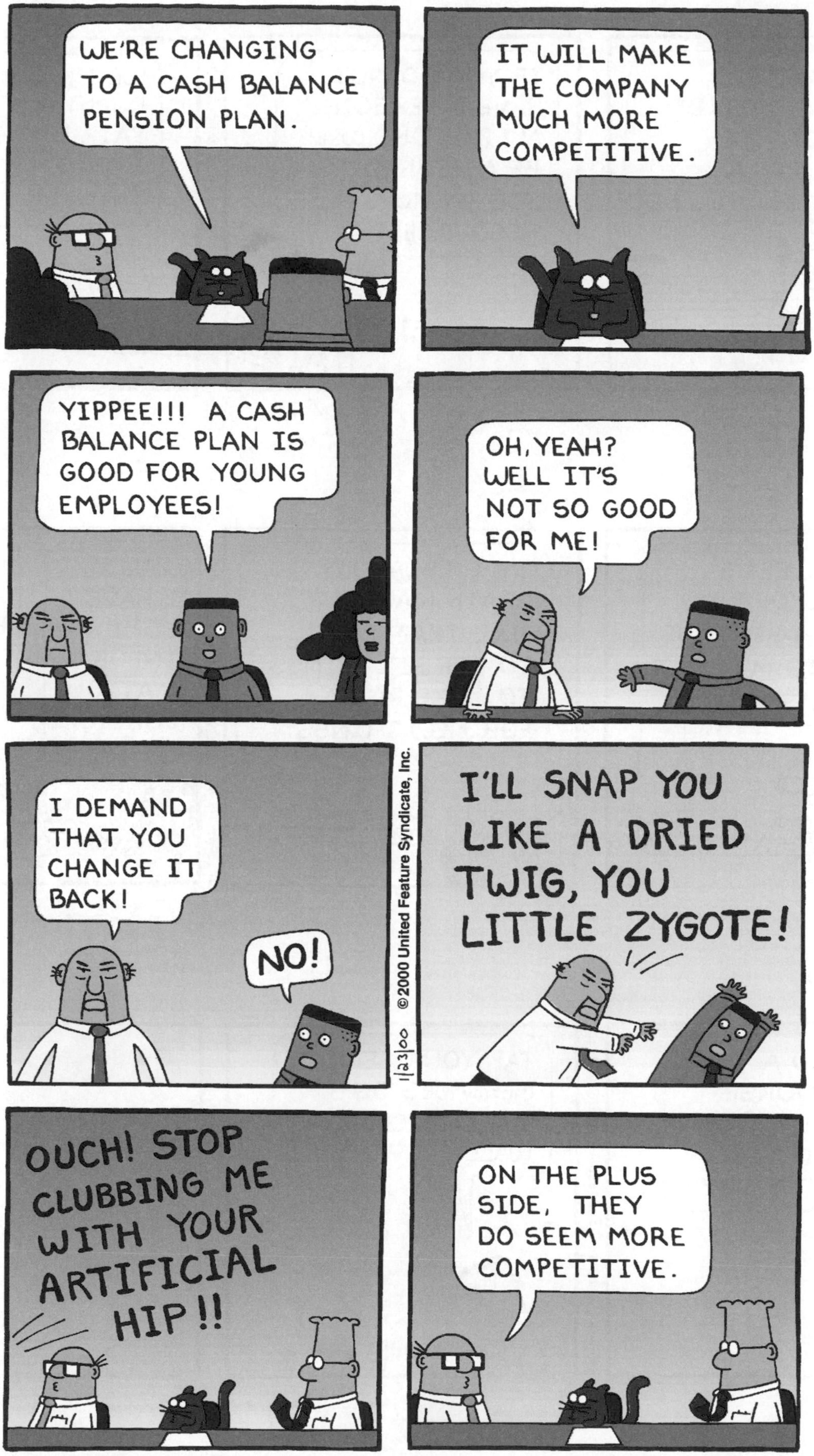
WE'RE CHANGING TO A CASH BALANCE PENSION PLAN.
IT WILL MAKE THE COMPANY MUCH MORE COMPETITIVE.
YIPPEE!!! A CASH BALANCE PLAN IS GOOD FOR YOUNG EMPLOYEES!
OH, YEAH? WELL IT'S NOT SO GOOD FOR ME!
I DEMAND THAT YOU CHANGE IT BACK!
NO!
©2000 United Feature Syndicate, Inc.
1/23/00
I'LL SNAP YOU LIKE A DRIED TWIG, YOU LITTLE ZYGOTE!
OUCH! STOP CLUBBING ME WITH YOUR ARTIFICIAL HIP!!
ON THE PLUS SIDE, THEY DO SEEM MORE COMPETITIVE.

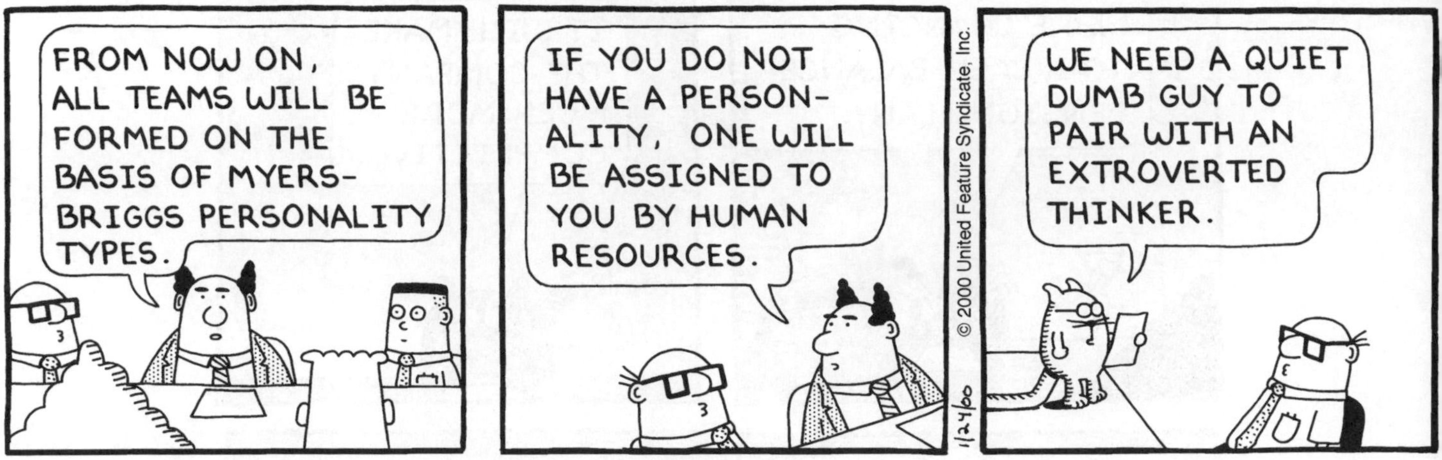
FROM NOW ON, ALL TEAMS WILL BE FORMED ON THE BASIS OF MYERS-BRIGGS PERSONALITY TYPES.
IF YOU DO NOT HAVE A PERSON-ALITY, ONE WILL BE ASSIGNED TO YOU BY HUMAN RESOURCES.
© 2000 United Feature Syndicate, Inc.
1/24/00
WE NEED A QUIET DUMB GUY TO PAIR WITH AN EXTROVERTED THINKER.

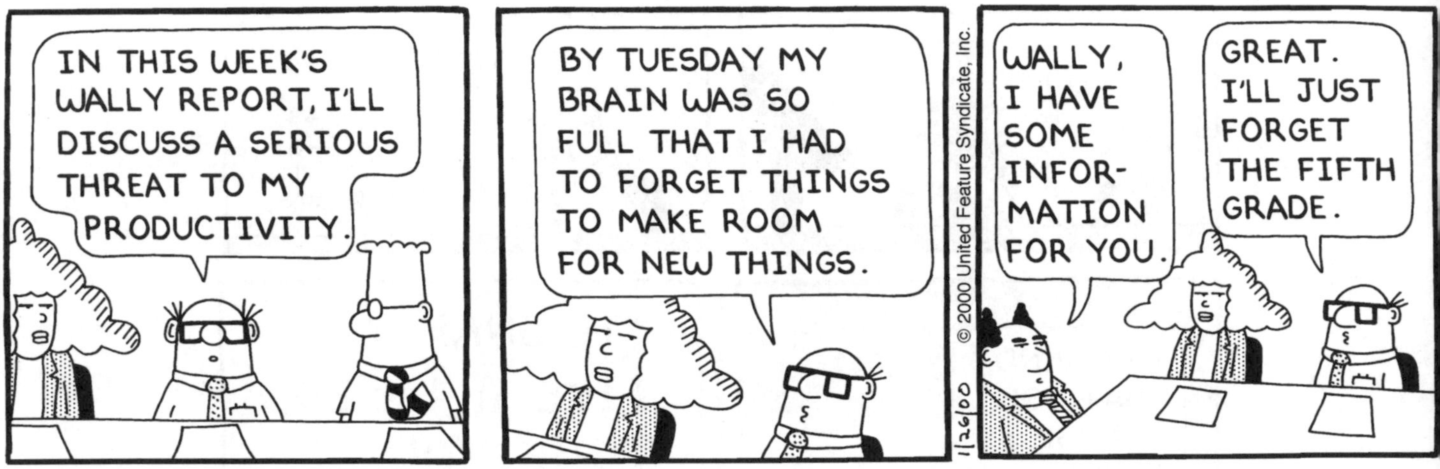
IN THIS WEEK'S WALLY REPORT, I'LL DISCUSS A SERIOUS THREAT TO MY PRODUCTIVITY.
BY TUESDAY MY BRAIN WAS SO FULL THAT I HAD TO FORGET THINGS TO MAKE ROOM FOR NEW THINGS.
© 2000 United Feature Syndicate, Inc.
1/26/00
WALLY, I HAVE SOME INFOR-MATION FOR YOU.
GREAT. I'LL JUST FORGET THE FIFTH GRADE.

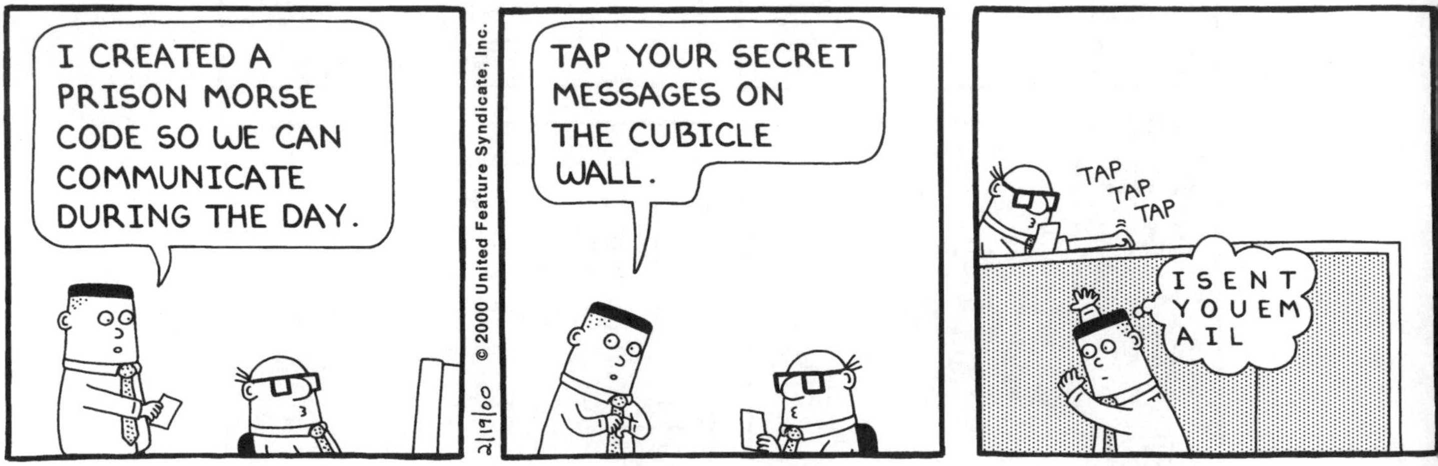
I CREATED A PRISON MORSE CODE SO WE CAN COMMUNICATE DURING THE DAY.
© 2000 United Feature Syndicate, Inc.
2/19/00
TAP YOUR SECRET MESSAGES ON THE CUBICLE WALL.
TAP
TAP
TAP
I S E N T
Y O U E M
A I L

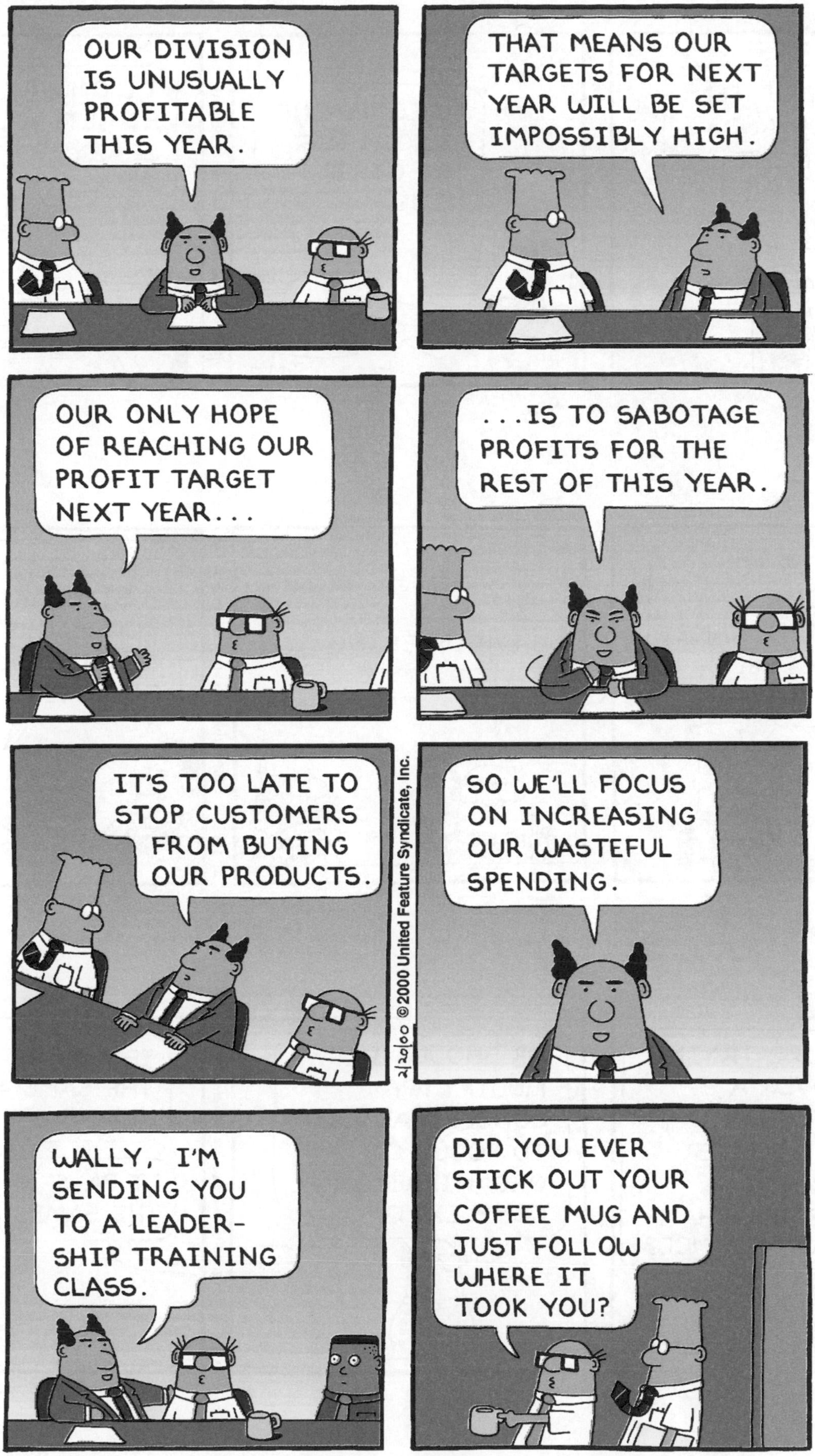
OUR DIVISION IS UNUSUALLY PROFITABLE THIS YEAR.
THAT MEANS OUR TARGETS FOR NEXT YEAR WILL BE SET IMPOSSIBLY HIGH.
OUR ONLY HOPE OF REACHING OUR PROFIT TARGET NEXT YEAR...
...IS TO SABOTAGE PROFITS FOR THE REST OF THIS YEAR.
IT'S TOO LATE TO STOP CUSTOMERS FROM BUYING OUR PRODUCTS.
2/20/00 © 2000 United Feature Syndicate, Inc.
SO WE'LL FOCUS ON INCREASING OUR WASTEFUL SPENDING.
WALLY, I'M SENDING YOU TO A LEADER-SHIP TRAINING CLASS.
DID YOU EVER STICK OUT YOUR COFFEE MUG AND JUST FOLLOW WHERE IT TOOK YOU?

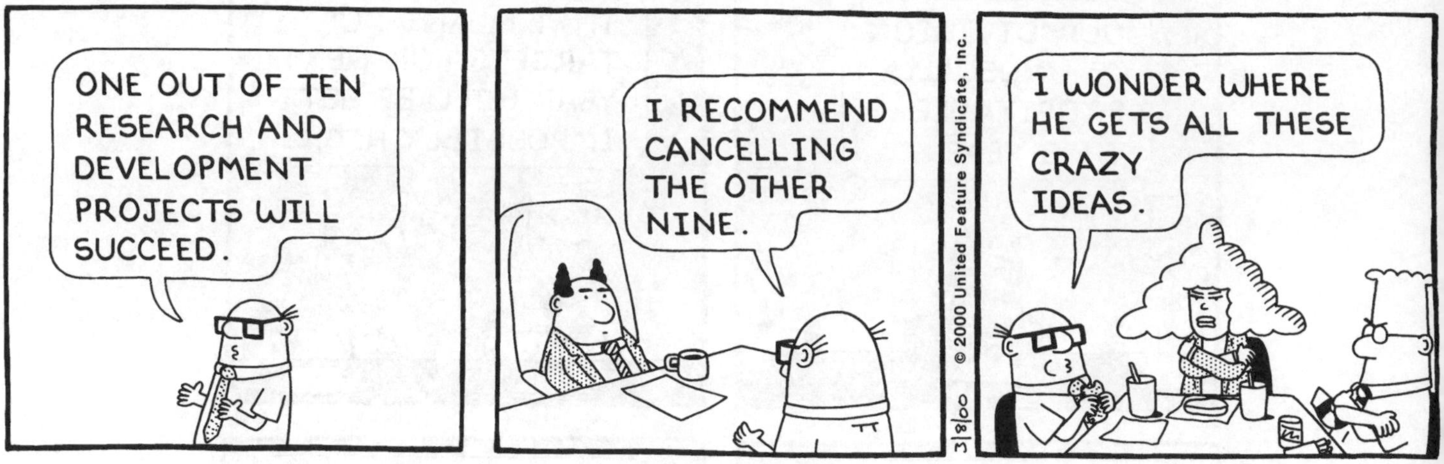
ONE OUT OF TEN RESEARCH AND DEVELOPMENT PROJECTS WILL SUCCEED.
I RECOMMEND CANCELLING THE OTHER NINE.
I WONDER WHERE HE GETS ALL THESE CRAZY IDEAS.
3/8/00 © 2000 United Feature Syndicate, Inc.

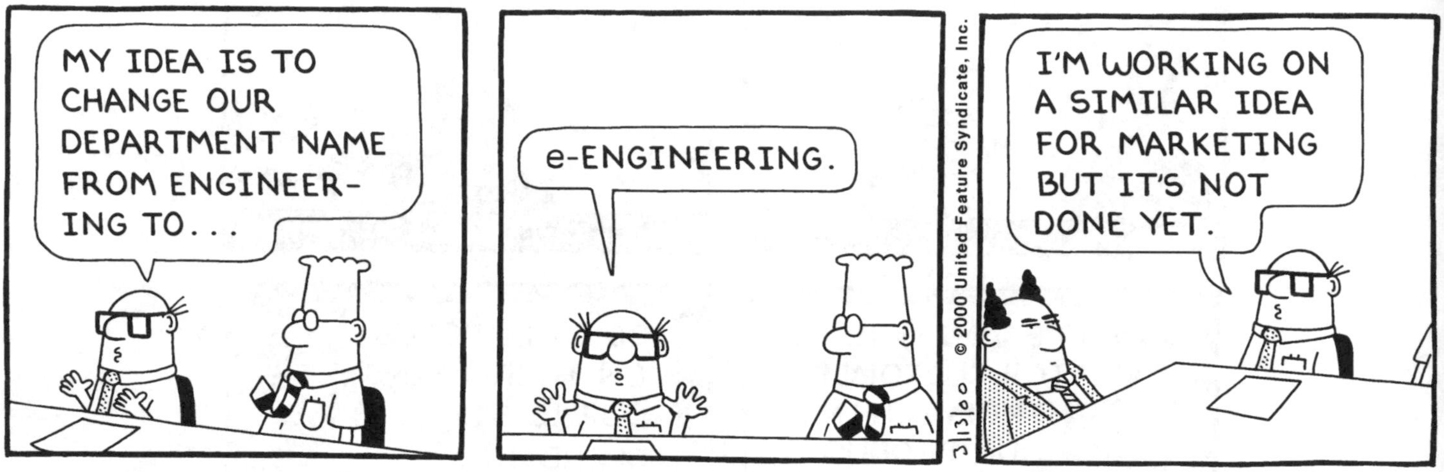
MY IDEA IS TO CHANGE OUR DEPARTMENT NAME FROM ENGINEER-ING TO . . .
e-ENGINEERING.
I'M WORKING ON A SIMILAR IDEA FOR MARKETING BUT IT'S NOT DONE YET.
3/13/00 © 2000 United Feature Syndicate, Inc.

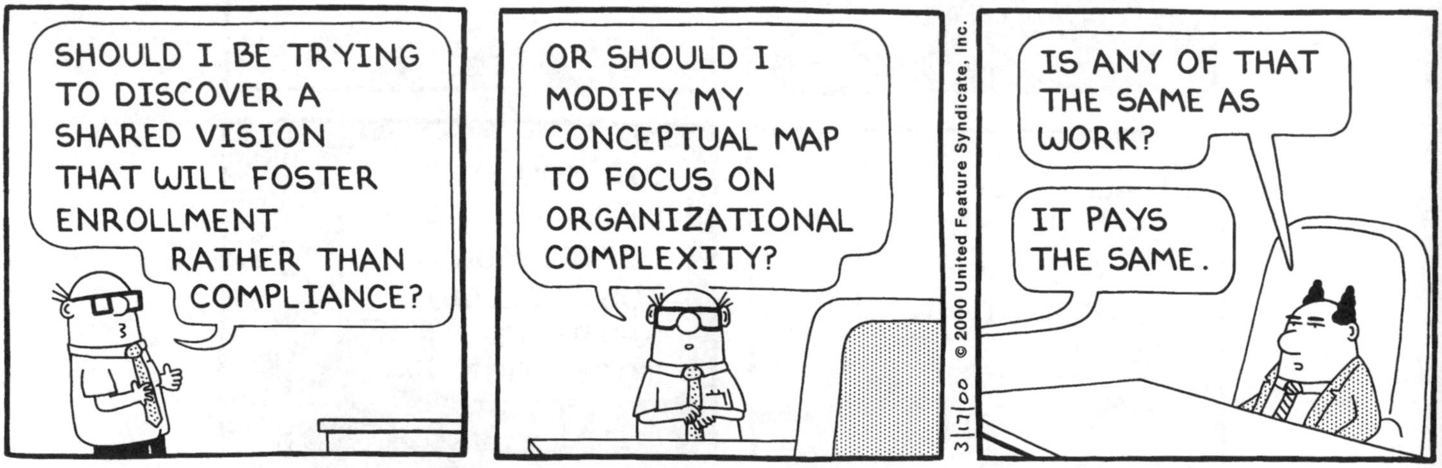
SHOULD I BE TRYING TO DISCOVER A SHARED VISION THAT WILL FOSTER ENROLLMENT RATHER THAN COMPLIANCE?
OR SHOULD I MODIFY MY CONCEPTUAL MAP TO FOCUS ON ORGANIZATIONAL COMPLEXITY?
IS ANY OF THAT THE SAME AS WORK?
IT PAYS THE SAME.
3/7/00 © 2000 United Feature Syndicate, Inc.

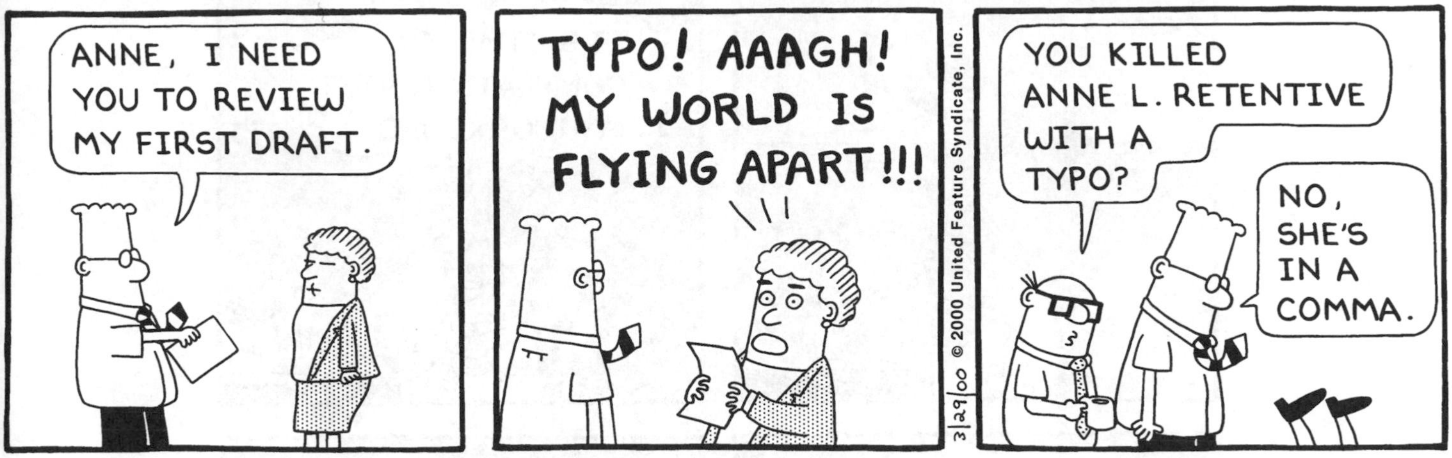
ANNE, I NEED YOU TO REVIEW MY FIRST DRAFT.
TYPO! AAAGH! MY WORLD IS FLYING APART!!!
3/29/00 © 2000 United Feature Syndicate, Inc.
YOU KILLED ANNE L. RETENTIVE WITH A TYPO?
NO, SHE'S IN A COMMA.

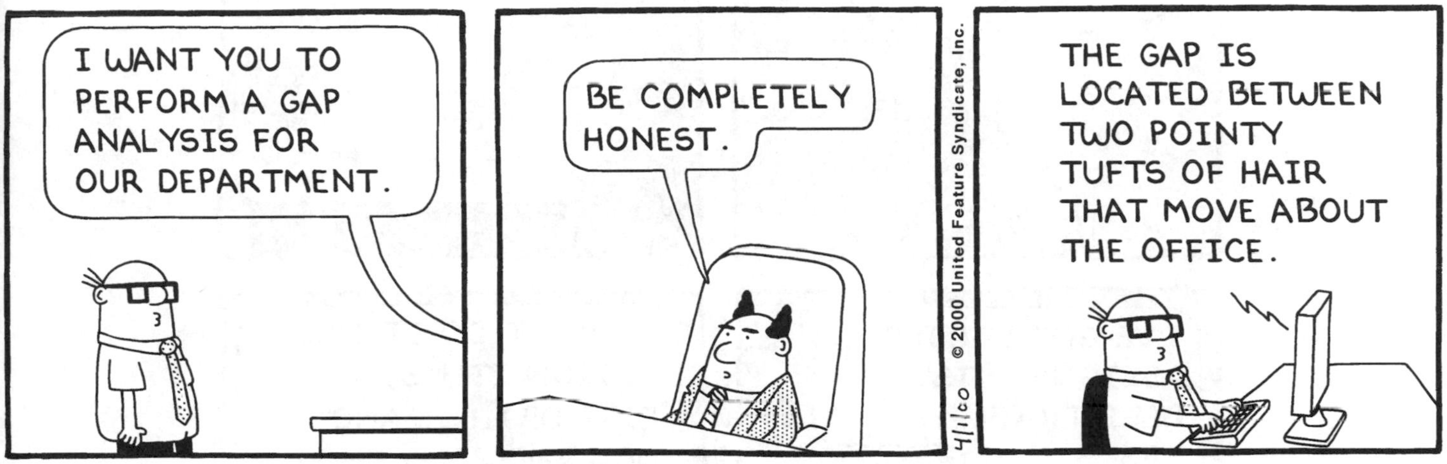
I WANT YOU TO PERFORM A GAP ANALYSIS FOR OUR DEPARTMENT.
BE COMPLETELY HONEST.
4/1/00 © 2000 United Feature Syndicate, Inc.
THE GAP IS LOCATED BETWEEN TWO POINTY TUFTS OF HAIR THAT MOVE ABOUT THE OFFICE.

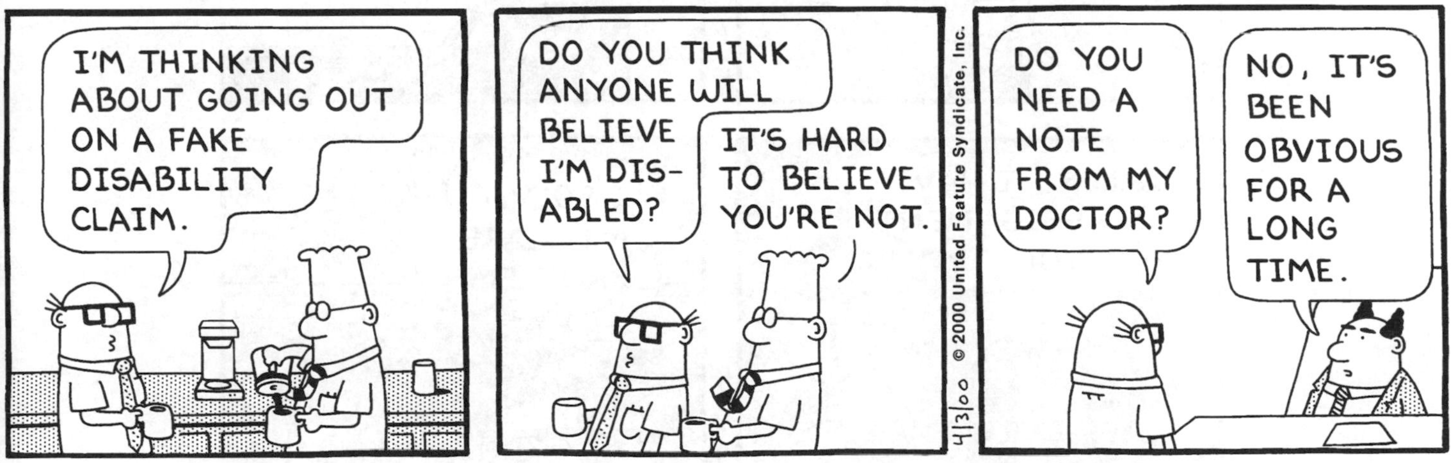
I'M THINKING ABOUT GOING OUT ON A FAKE DISABILITY CLAIM.
DO YOU THINK ANYONE WILL BELIEVE I'M DIS-ABLED?
IT'S HARD TO BELIEVE YOU'RE NOT.
4/3/00 © 2000 United Feature Syndicate, Inc.
DO YOU NEED A NOTE FROM MY DOCTOR?
NO, IT'S BEEN OBVIOUS FOR A LONG TIME.

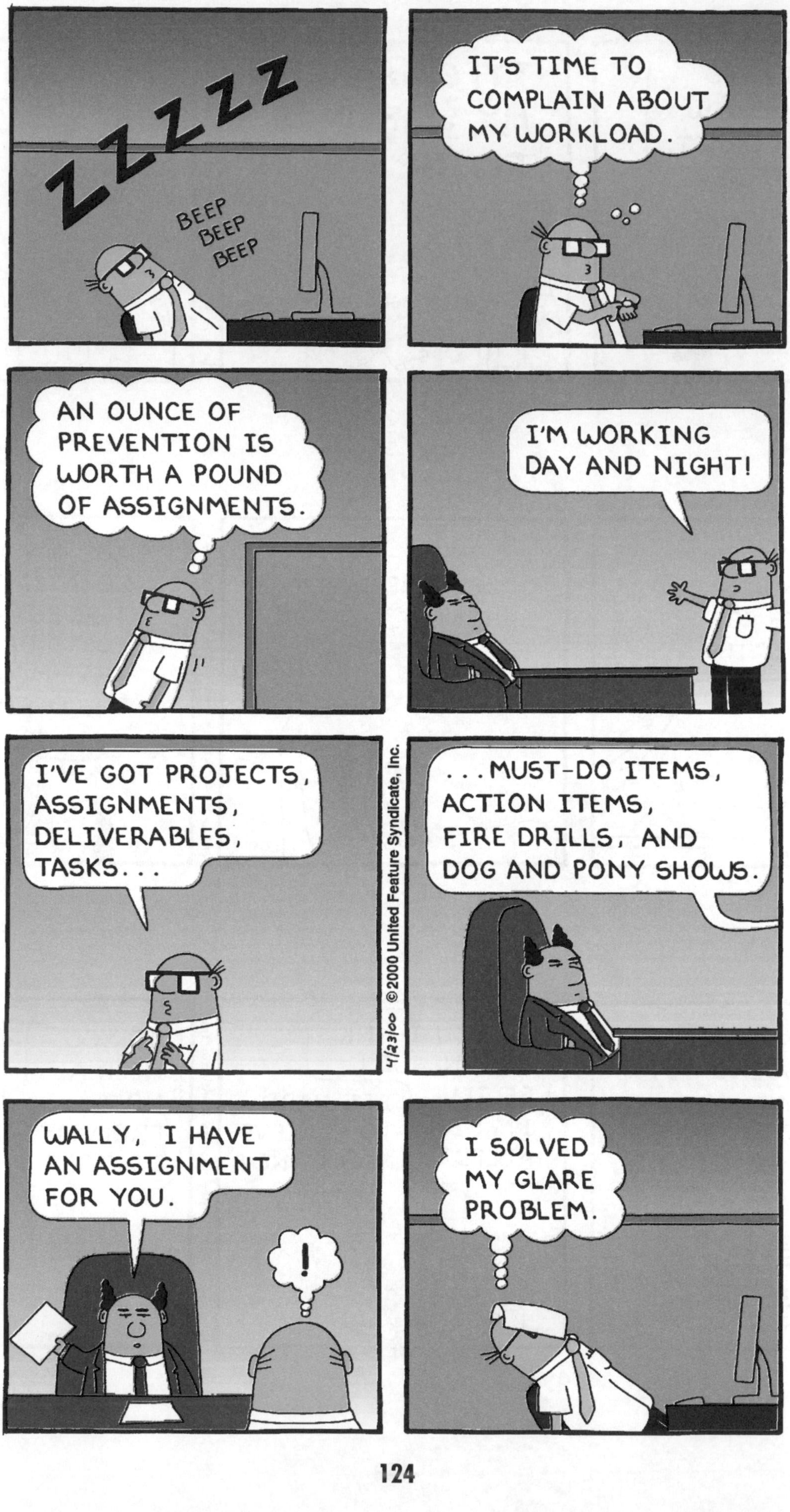
ZZZZZ
BEEP
BEEP
BEEP
IT'S TIME TO COMPLAIN ABOUT MY WORKLOAD.
AN OUNCE OF PREVENTION IS WORTH A POUND OF ASSIGNMENTS.
I'M WORKING DAY AND NIGHT!
I'VE GOT PROJECTS, ASSIGNMENTS, DELIVERABLES, TASKS...
...MUST-DO ITEMS, ACTION ITEMS, FIRE DRILLS, AND DOG AND PONY SHOWS.
4/23/00 © 2000 United Feature Syndicate, Inc.
WALLY, I HAVE AN ASSIGNMENT FOR YOU.
!
I SOLVED MY GLARE PROBLEM.

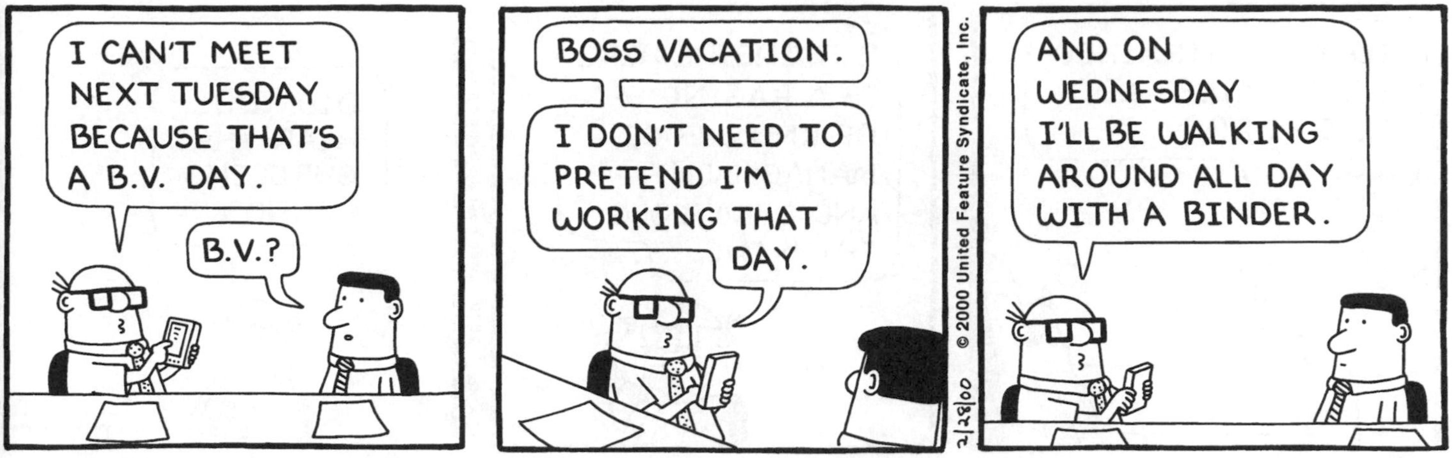
I CAN'T MEET NEXT TUESDAY BECAUSE THAT'S A B.V. DAY.
B.V.?
BOSS VACATION.
I DON'T NEED TO PRETEND I'M WORKING THAT DAY.
AND ON WEDNESDAY I'LL BE WALKING AROUND ALL DAY WITH A BINDER.
2/28/00 © 2000 United Feature Syndicate, Inc.

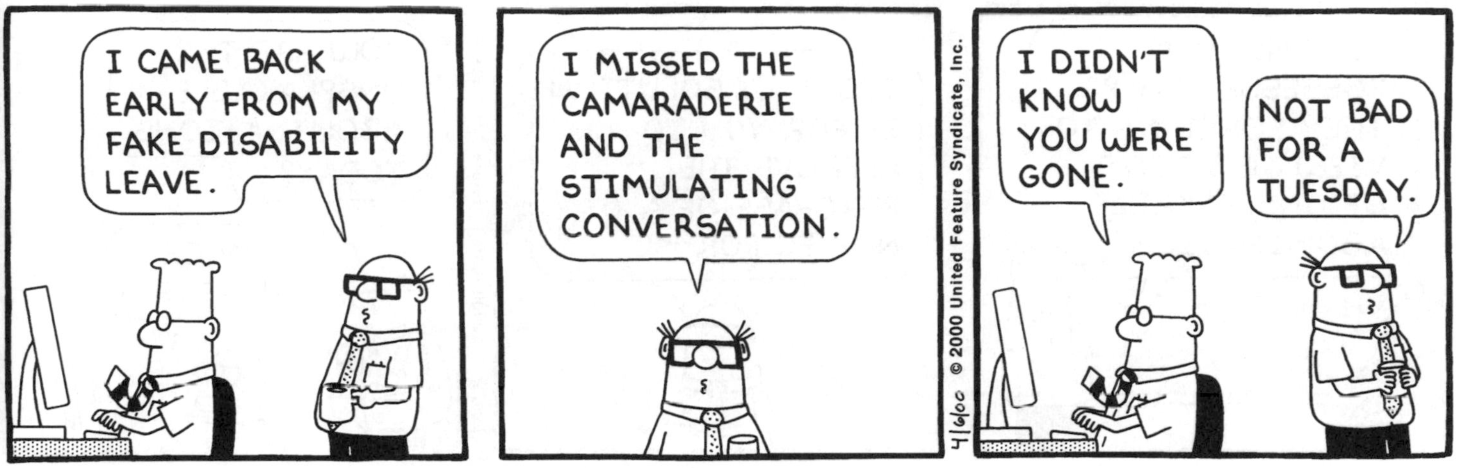
I CAME BACK EARLY FROM MY FAKE DISABILITY LEAVE.
I MISSED THE CAMARADERIE AND THE STIMULATING CONVERSATION.
I DIDN'T KNOW YOU WERE GONE.
NOT BAD FOR A TUESDAY.
4/6/00 © 2000 United Feature Syndicate, Inc.

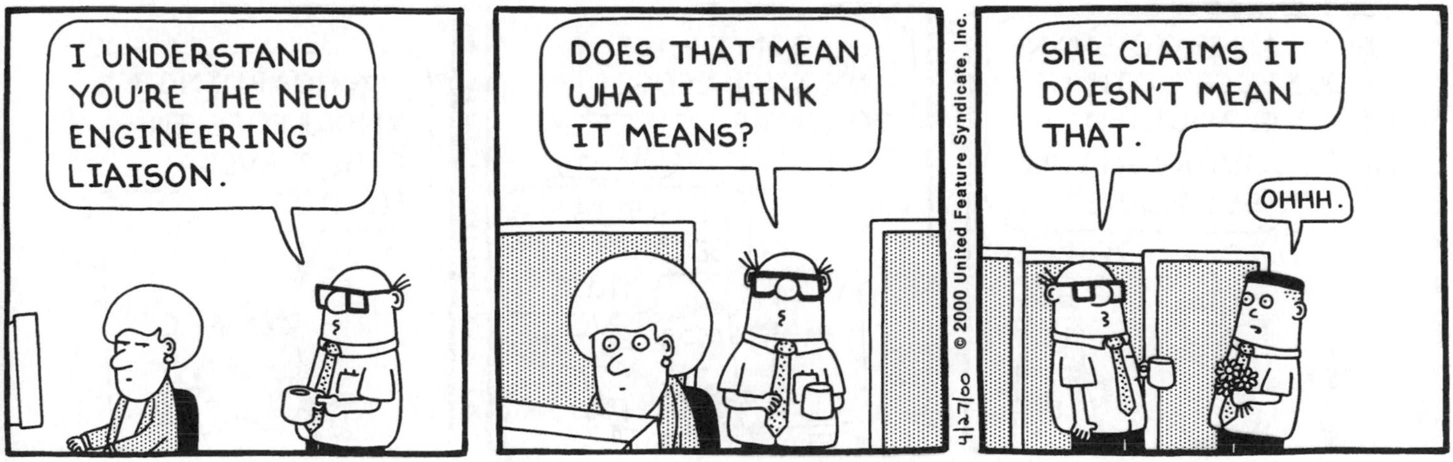
I UNDERSTAND YOU'RE THE NEW ENGINEERING LIAISON.
DOES THAT MEAN WHAT I THINK IT MEANS?
SHE CLAIMS IT DOESN'T MEAN THAT.
OHHH.
4/27/00 © 2000 United Feature Syndicate, Inc.

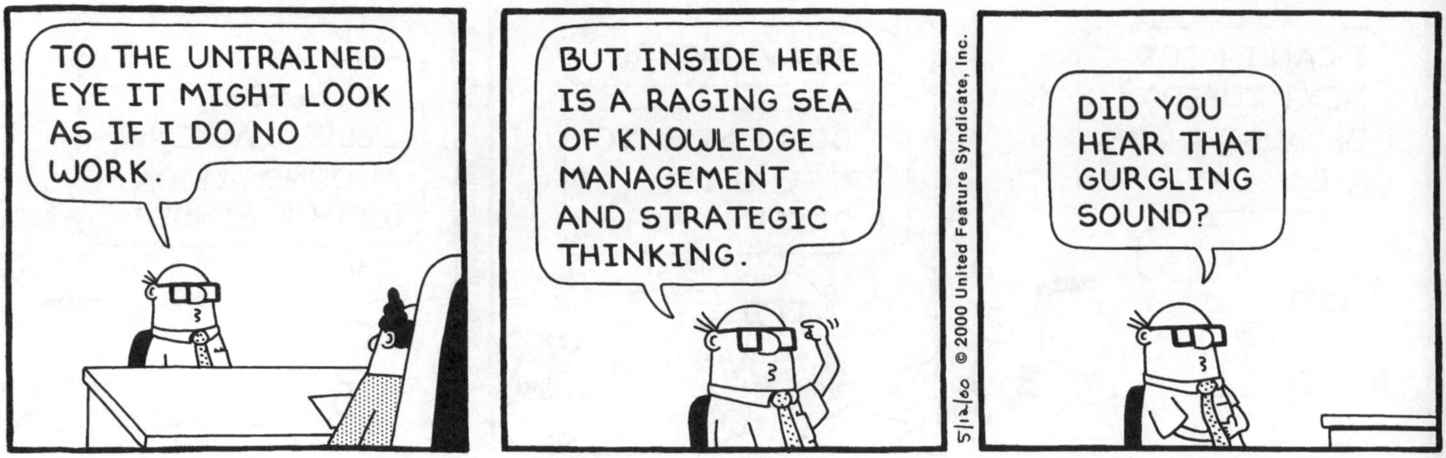
TO THE UNTRAINED EYE IT MIGHT LOOK AS IF I DO NO WORK.
BUT INSIDE HERE IS A RAGING SEA OF KNOWLEDGE MANAGEMENT AND STRATEGIC THINKING.
5/12/00 © 2000 United Feature Syndicate, Inc.
DID YOU HEAR THAT GURGLING SOUND?

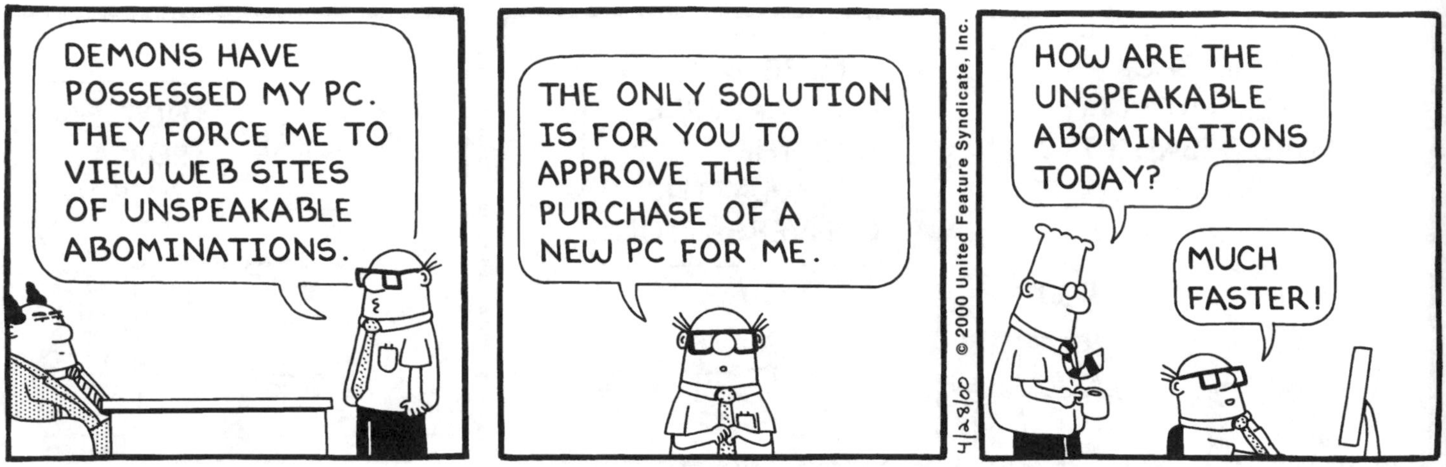
DEMONS HAVE POSSESSED MY PC. THEY FORCE ME TO VIEW WEB SITES OF UNSPEAKABLE ABOMINATIONS.
THE ONLY SOLUTION IS FOR YOU TO APPROVE THE PURCHASE OF A NEW PC FOR ME.
4/28/00 © 2000 United Feature Syndicate, Inc.
HOW ARE THE UNSPEAKABLE ABOMINATIONS TODAY?
MUCH FASTER!

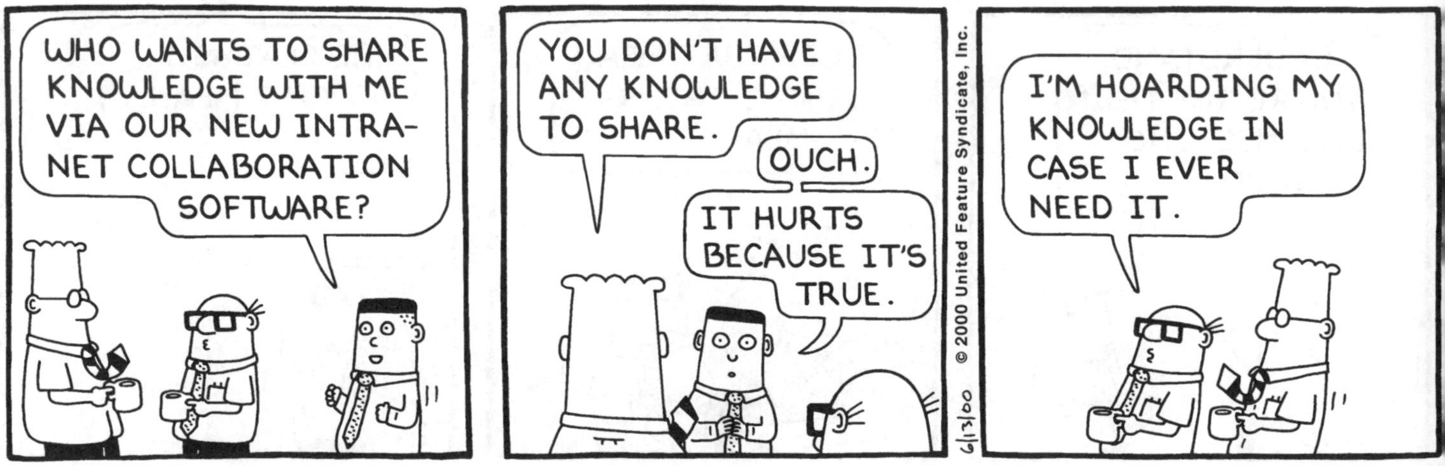
WHO WANTS TO SHARE KNOWLEDGE WITH ME VIA OUR NEW INTRA-NET COLLABORATION SOFTWARE?
YOU DON'T HAVE ANY KNOWLEDGE TO SHARE.
OUCH.
IT HURTS BECAUSE IT'S TRUE.
6/13/00 © 2000 United Feature Syndicate, Inc.
I'M HOARDING MY KNOWLEDGE IN CASE I EVER NEED IT.

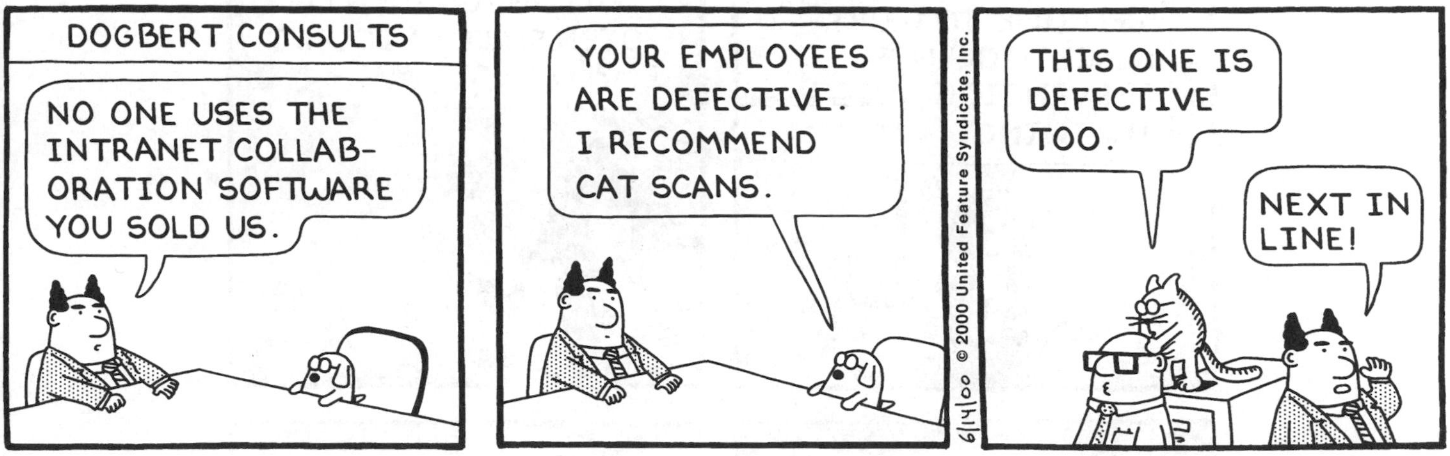
DOGBERT CONSULTS
NO ONE USES THE INTRANET COLLAB-ORATION SOFTWARE YOU SOLD US.
YOUR EMPLOYEES ARE DEFECTIVE. I RECOMMEND CAT SCANS.
6/14/00 © 2000 United Feature Syndicate, Inc.
THIS ONE IS DEFECTIVE TOO.
NEXT IN LINE!

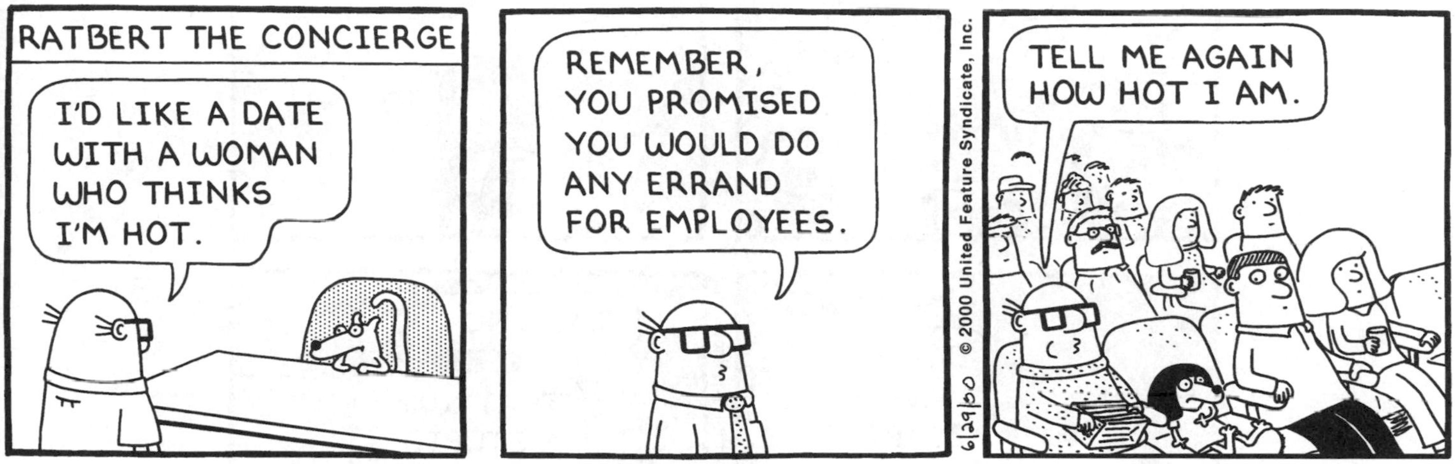
RATBERT THE CONCIERGE
I'D LIKE A DATE WITH A WOMAN WHO THINKS I'M HOT.
REMEMBER, YOU PROMISED YOU WOULD DO ANY ERRAND FOR EMPLOYEES.
6/29/00 © 2000 United Feature Syndicate, Inc.
TELL ME AGAIN HOW HOT I AM.

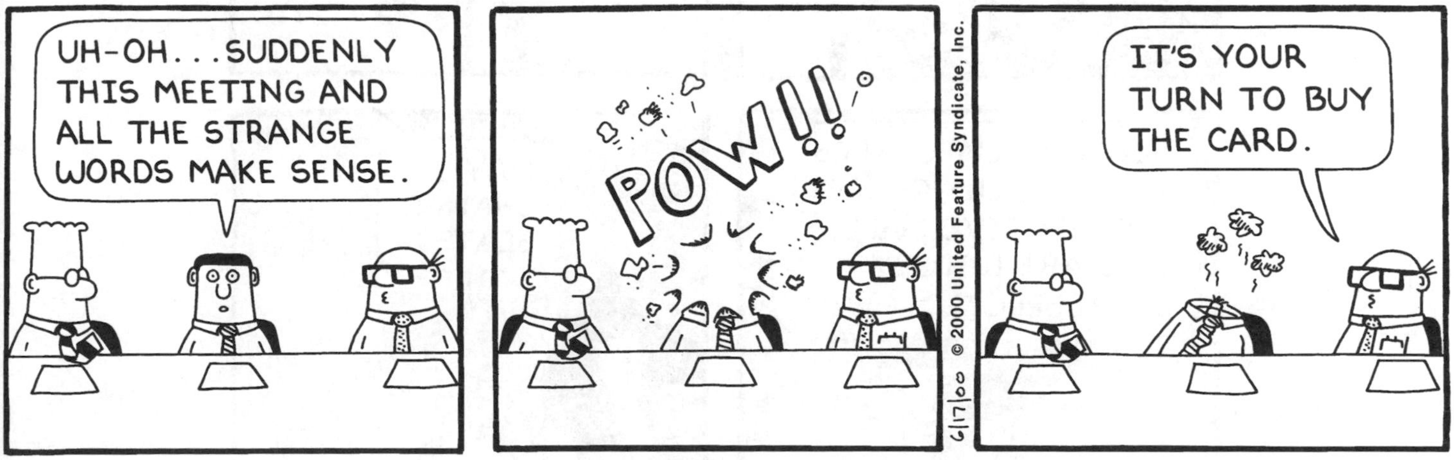
UH-OH...SUDDENLY THIS MEETING AND ALL THE STRANGE WORDS MAKE SENSE.
POW!!
6/17/00 © 2000 United Feature Syndicate, Inc.
IT'S YOUR TURN TO BUY THE CARD.

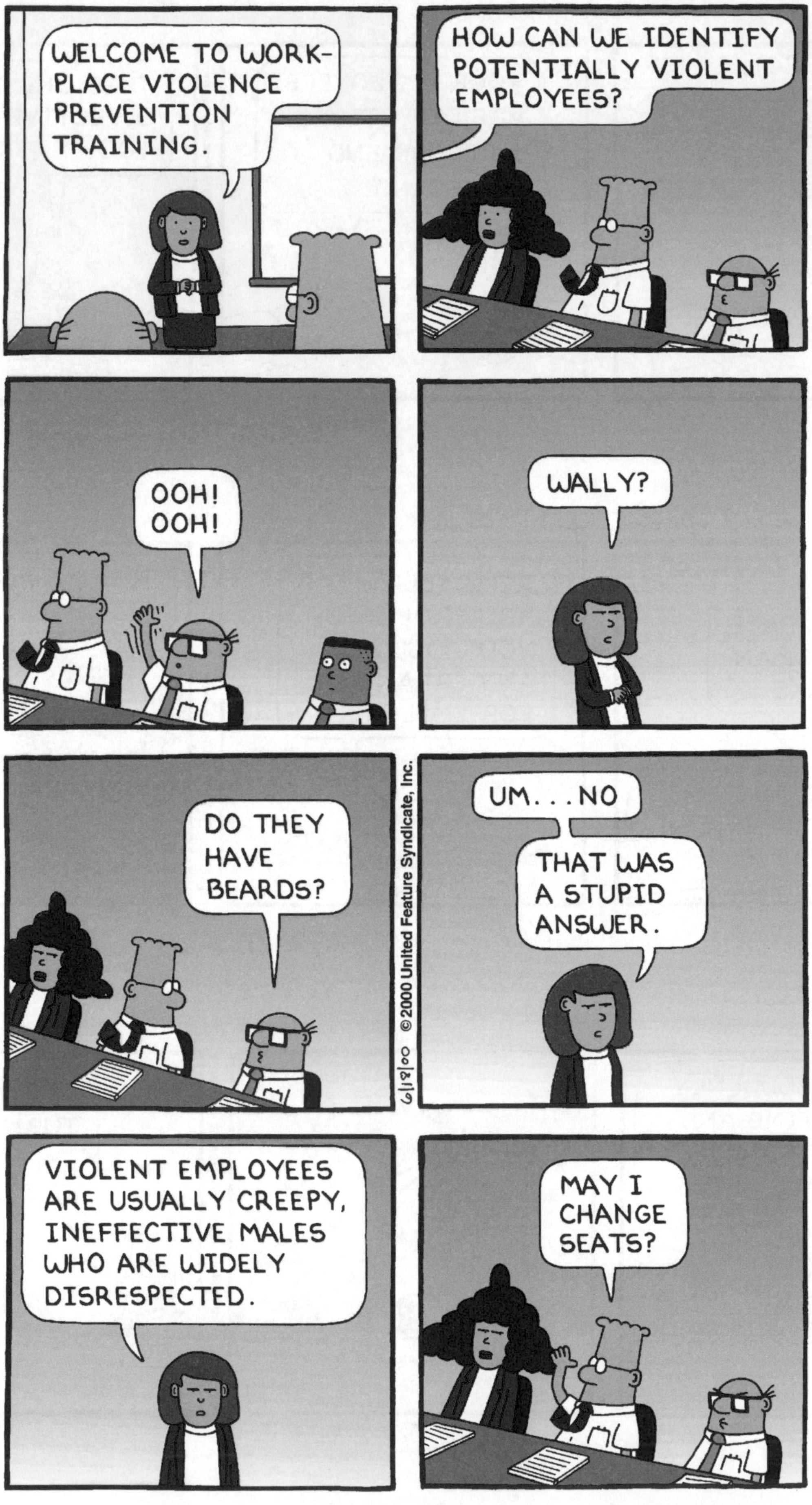
WELCOME TO WORK-PLACE VIOLENCE PREVENTION TRAINING.
HOW CAN WE IDENTIFY POTENTIALLY VIOLENT EMPLOYEES?
OOH! OOH!
WALLY?
DO THEY HAVE BEARDS?
UM...NO
THAT WAS A STUPID ANSWER.
VIOLENT EMPLOYEES ARE USUALLY CREEPY, INEFFECTIVE MALES WHO ARE WIDELY DISRESPECTED.
MAY I CHANGE SEATS?
6/18/00 © 2000 United Feature Syndicate, Inc.

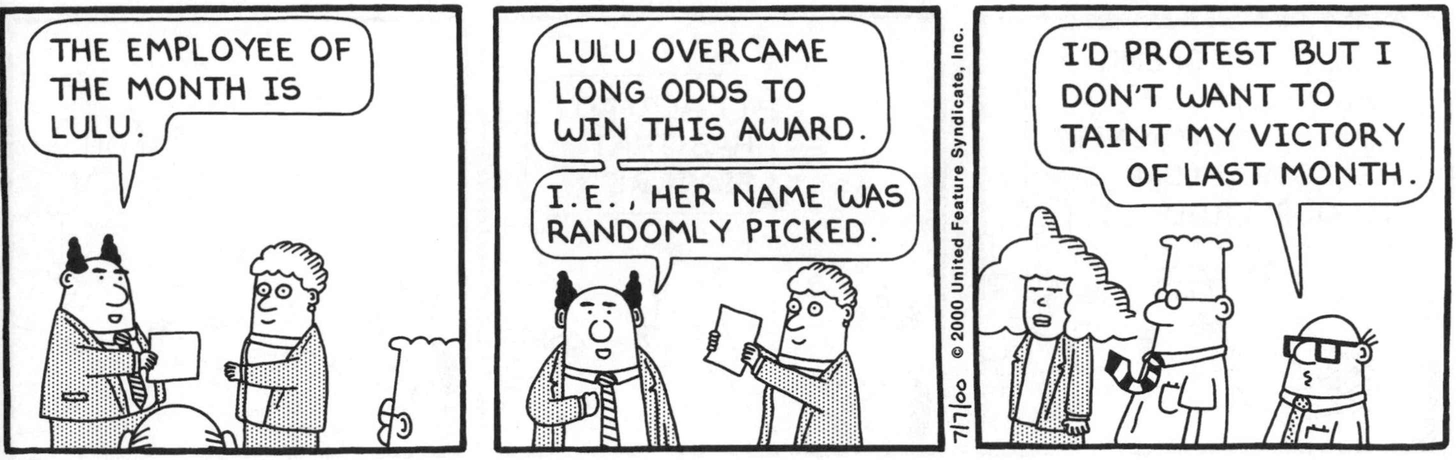
THE EMPLOYEE OF THE MONTH IS LULU.
LULU OVERCAME LONG ODDS TO WIN THIS AWARD.
I.E., HER NAME WAS RANDOMLY PICKED.
7/7/00
© 2000 United Feature Syndicate, Inc.
I'D PROTEST BUT I DON'T WANT TO TAINT MY VICTORY OF LAST MONTH.

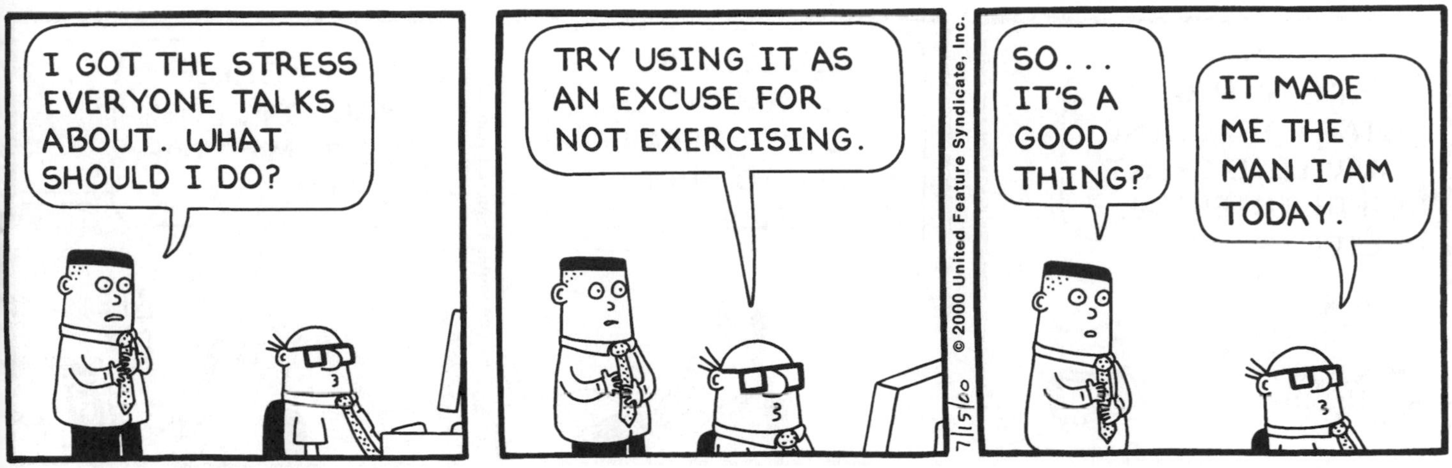
I GOT THE STRESS EVERYONE TALKS ABOUT. WHAT SHOULD I DO?
TRY USING IT AS AN EXCUSE FOR NOT EXERCISING.
7/15/00
© 2000 United Feature Syndicate, Inc.
SO... IT'S A GOOD THING?
IT MADE ME THE MAN I AM TODAY.

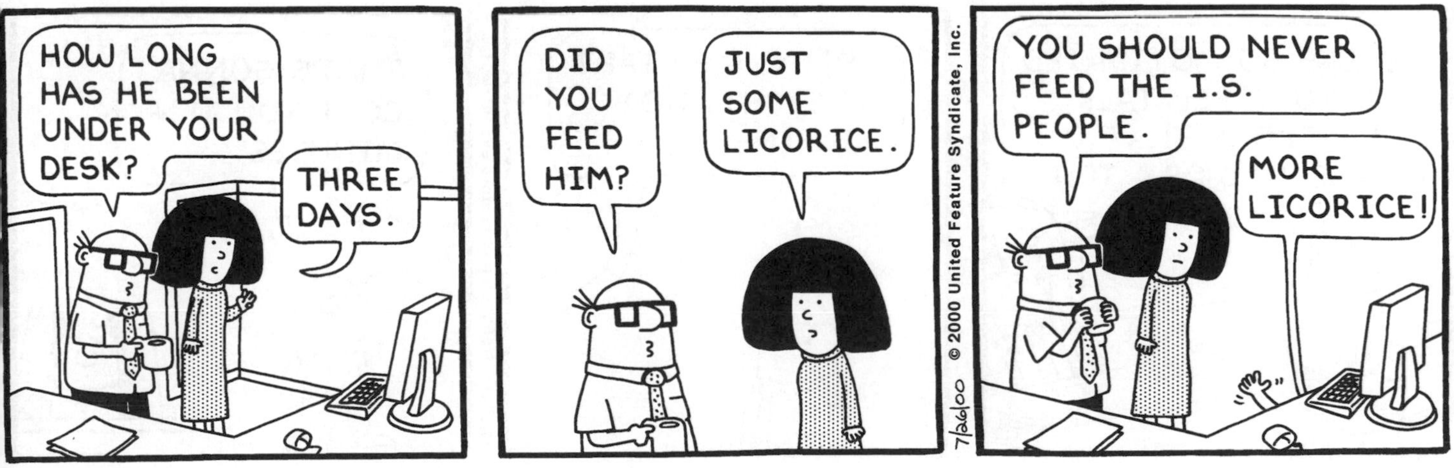
HOW LONG HAS HE BEEN UNDER YOUR DESK?
THREE DAYS.
DID YOU FEED HIM?
JUST SOME LICORICE.
7/26/00
© 2000 United Feature Syndicate, Inc.
YOU SHOULD NEVER FEED THE I.S. PEOPLE.
MORE LICORICE!

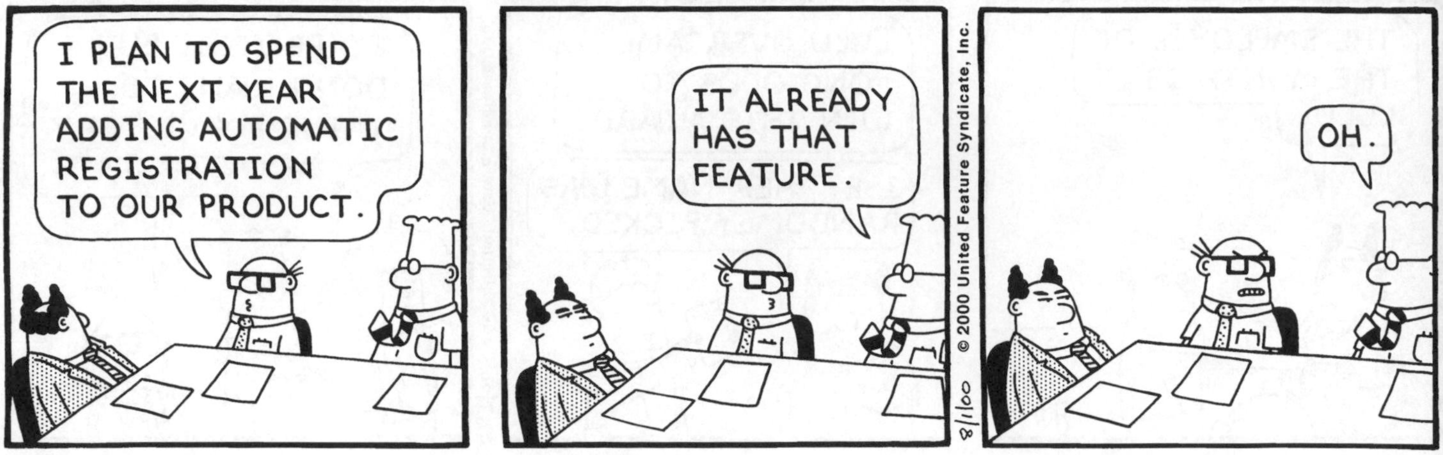
I PLAN TO SPEND THE NEXT YEAR ADDING AUTOMATIC REGISTRATION TO OUR PRODUCT.
IT ALREADY HAS THAT FEATURE.
OH.
© 2000 United Feature Syndicate, Inc.
8/1/00

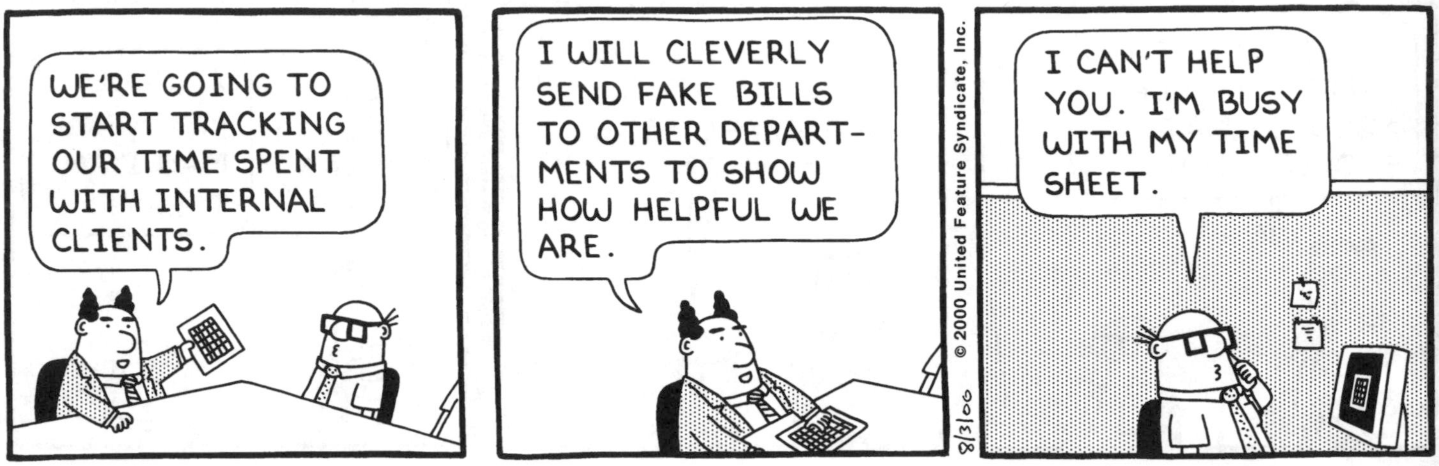
WE'RE GOING TO START TRACKING OUR TIME SPENT WITH INTERNAL CLIENTS.
I WILL CLEVERLY SEND FAKE BILLS TO OTHER DEPART-MENTS TO SHOW HOW HELPFUL WE ARE.
I CAN'T HELP YOU. I'M BUSY WITH MY TIME SHEET.
© 2000 United Feature Syndicate, Inc.
8/3/00

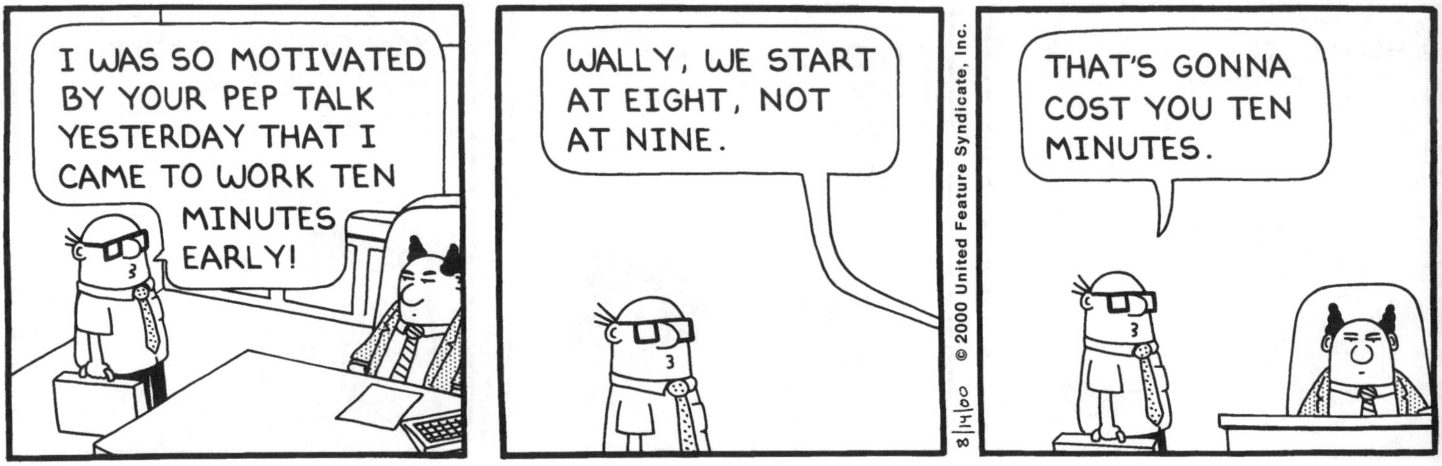
I WAS SO MOTIVATED BY YOUR PEP TALK YESTERDAY THAT I CAME TO WORK TEN MINUTES EARLY!
WALLY, WE START AT EIGHT, NOT AT NINE.
THAT'S GONNA COST YOU TEN MINUTES.
© 2000 United Feature Syndicate, Inc.
8/14/00

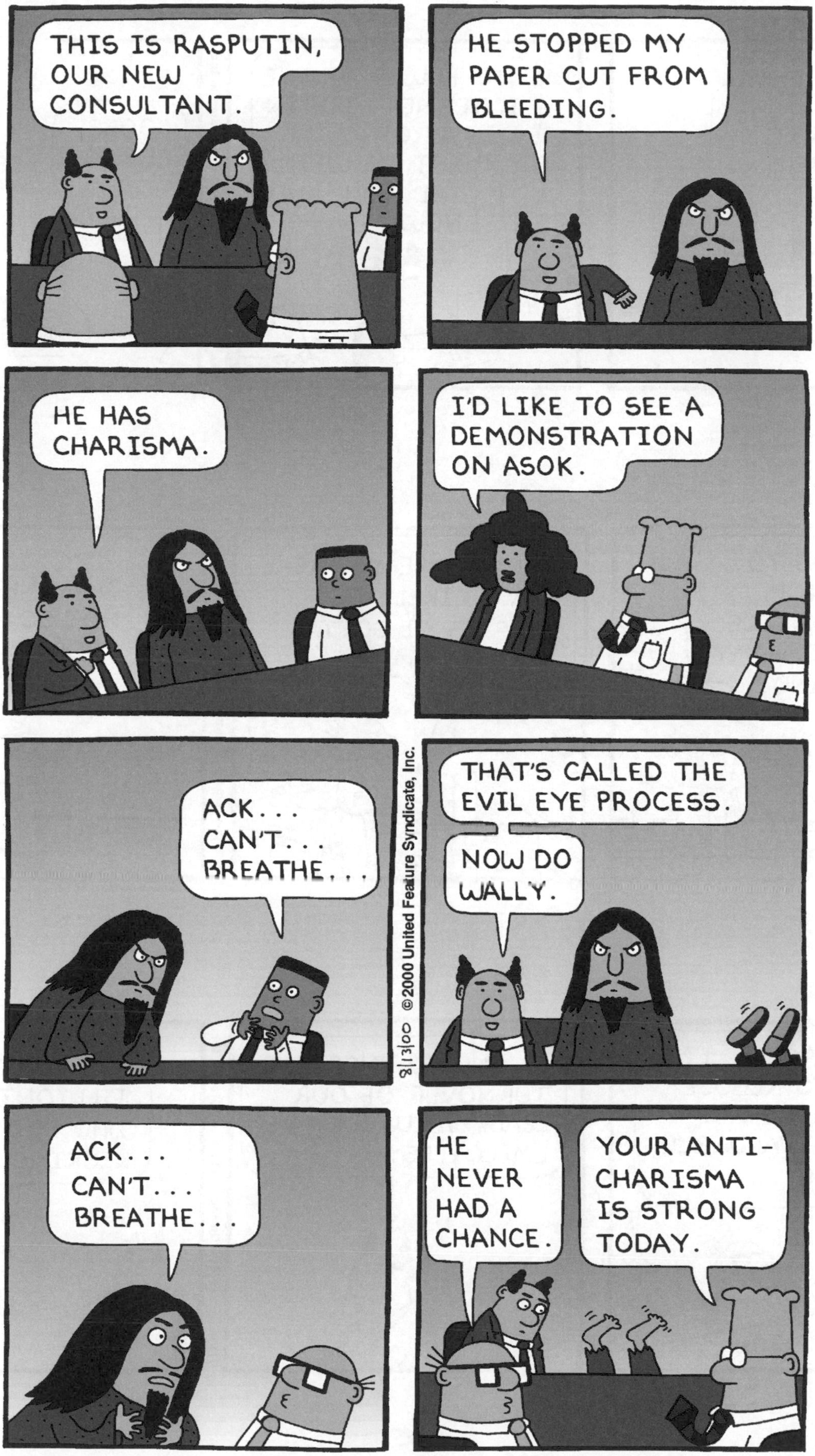
THIS IS RASPUTIN, OUR NEW CONSULTANT.
HE STOPPED MY PAPER CUT FROM BLEEDING.
HE HAS CHARISMA.
I'D LIKE TO SEE A DEMONSTRATION ON ASOK.
ACK... CAN'T... BREATHE...
THAT'S CALLED THE EVIL EYE PROCESS.
NOW DO WALLY.
ACK... CAN'T... BREATHE...
HE NEVER HAD A CHANCE.
YOUR ANTI-CHARISMA IS STRONG TODAY.
©2000 United Feature Syndicate, Inc.
8/13/00

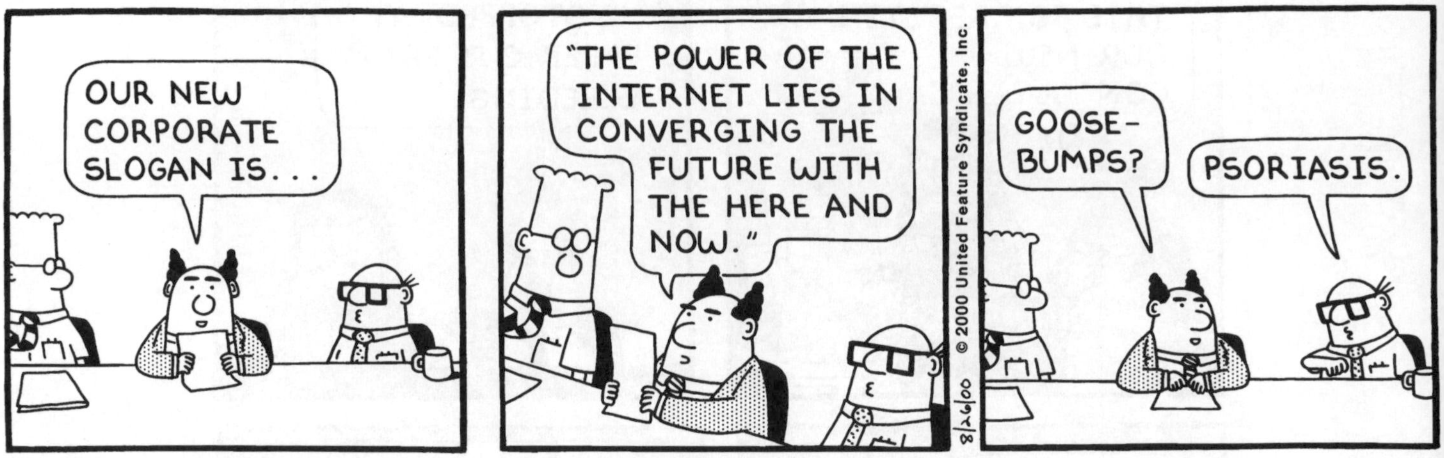
OUR NEW CORPORATE SLOGAN IS...
"THE POWER OF THE INTERNET LIES IN CONVERGING THE FUTURE WITH THE HERE AND NOW."
8/26/00 © 2000 United Feature Syndicate, Inc.
GOOSE-BUMPS?
PSORIASIS.

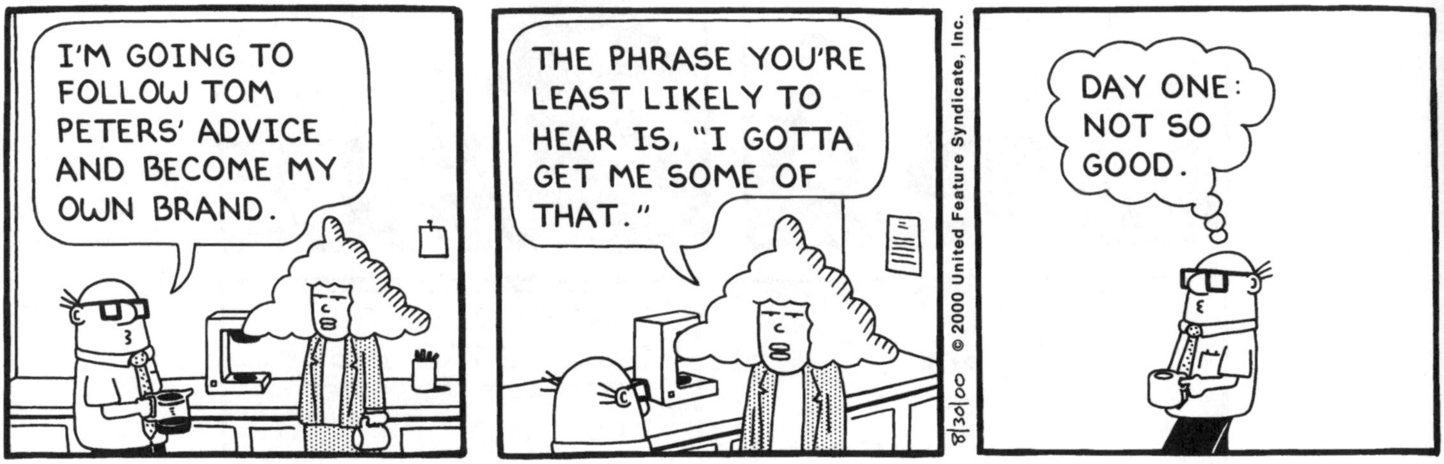
I'M GOING TO FOLLOW TOM PETERS' ADVICE AND BECOME MY OWN BRAND.
THE PHRASE YOU'RE LEAST LIKELY TO HEAR IS, "I GOTTA GET ME SOME OF THAT."
8/30/00 © 2000 United Feature Syndicate, Inc.
DAY ONE: NOT SO GOOD.

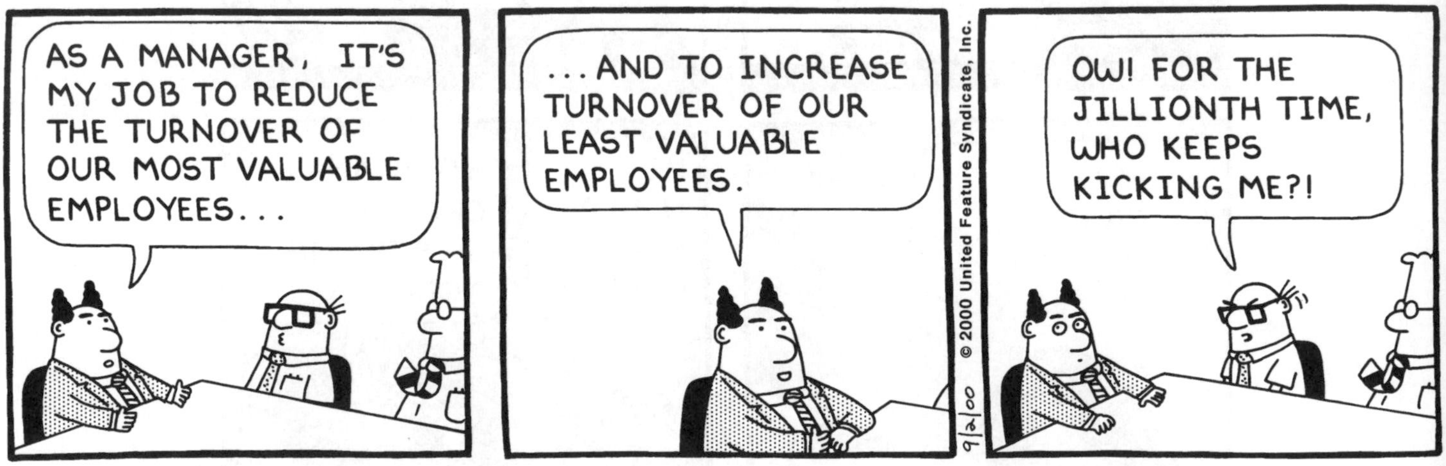
AS A MANAGER, IT'S MY JOB TO REDUCE THE TURNOVER OF OUR MOST VALUABLE EMPLOYEES...
...AND TO INCREASE TURNOVER OF OUR LEAST VALUABLE EMPLOYEES.
9/2/00 © 2000 United Feature Syndicate, Inc.
OW! FOR THE JILLIONTH TIME, WHO KEEPS KICKING ME?!

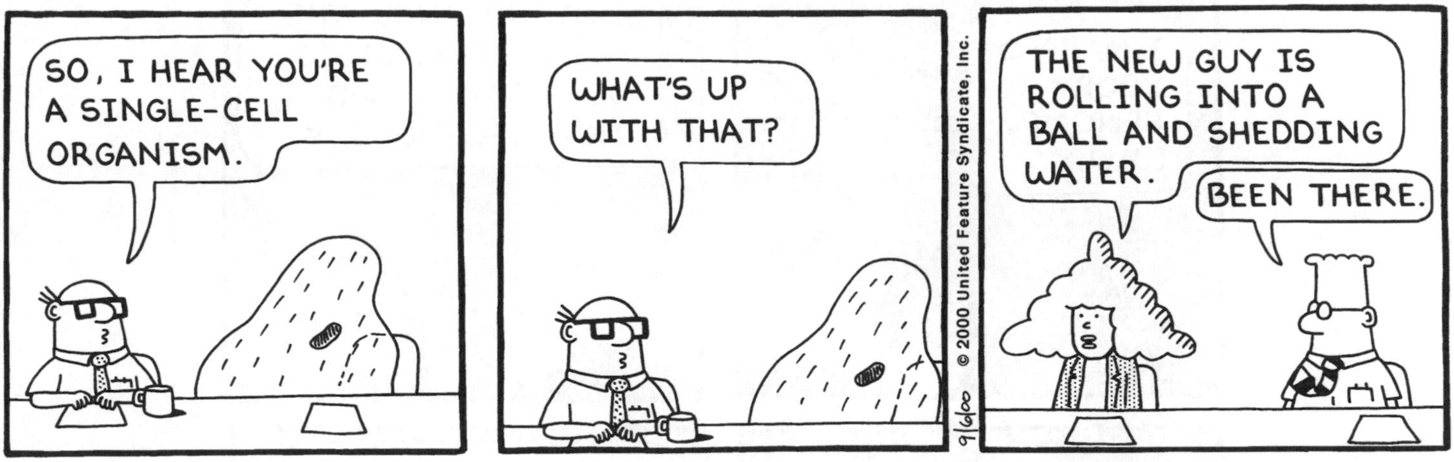
SO, I HEAR YOU'RE A SINGLE-CELL ORGANISM.
WHAT'S UP WITH THAT?
9/6/00
© 2000 United Feature Syndicate, Inc.
THE NEW GUY IS ROLLING INTO A BALL AND SHEDDING WATER.
BEEN THERE.

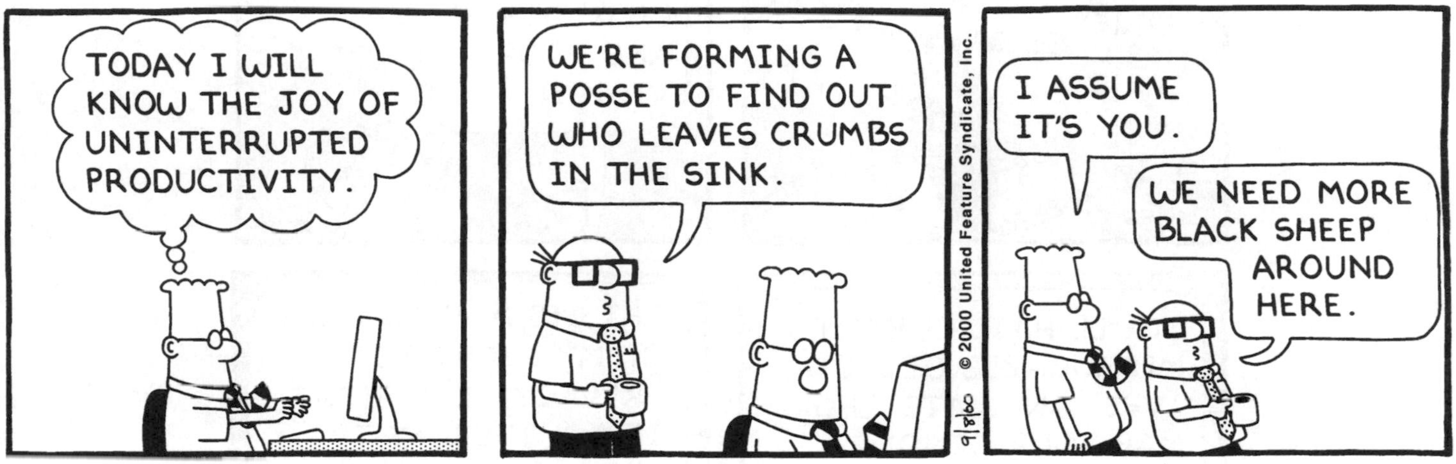
TODAY I WILL KNOW THE JOY OF UNINTERRUPTED PRODUCTIVITY.
WE'RE FORMING A POSSE TO FIND OUT WHO LEAVES CRUMBS IN THE SINK.
9/8/00
© 2000 United Feature Syndicate, Inc.
I ASSUME IT'S YOU.
WE NEED MORE BLACK SHEEP AROUND HERE.

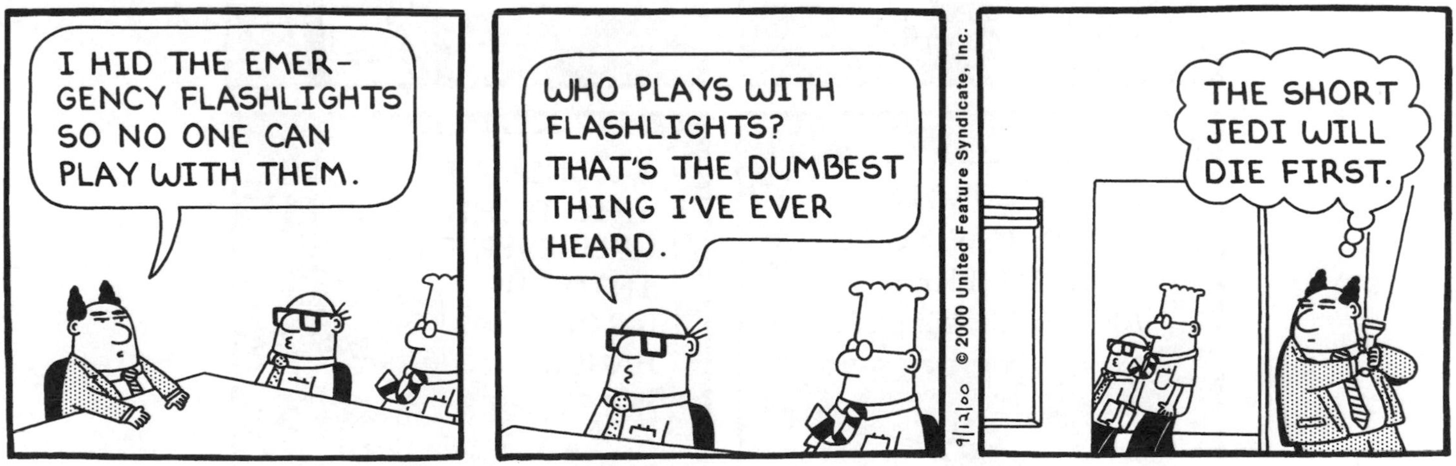
I HID THE EMER-GENCY FLASHLIGHTS SO NO ONE CAN PLAY WITH THEM.
WHO PLAYS WITH FLASHLIGHTS? THAT'S THE DUMBEST THING I'VE EVER HEARD.
9/12/00
© 2000 United Feature Syndicate, Inc.
THE SHORT JEDI WILL DIE FIRST.

I MAPPED YOUR GENOME, WALLY.
I DIDN'T KNOW THE HUMAN RESOURCES DEPARTMENT HAD THAT TECHNOLOGY.
I USED A PENCIL.
YOUR GENES PREDICT THAT YOU WILL BE A BITTER, LAZY, CAUCASIAN GUY WITH SIX HAIRS AND POOR VISION.
YOU'LL HATE CUBICLES, MEASURABLE OBJECTIVES, AND CATS WHO MAP YOUR GENOME.
©2000 United Feature Syndicate, Inc.
9/10/00
THIS IS A VIOLATION OF MY RIGHT TO PRIVACY! I'LL FIGHT IT ALL THE WAY TO THE SUPREME COURT!
NO, ACCORDING TO MY MAP, YOU'LL LOSE INTEREST AND FALL ASLEEP.
I WONDER IF THIS TECHNOLOGY WILL EVER FALL INTO THE WRONG HANDS.
ZZZZZ

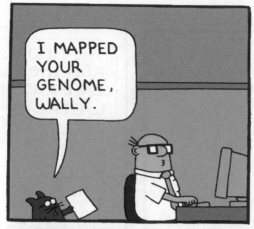

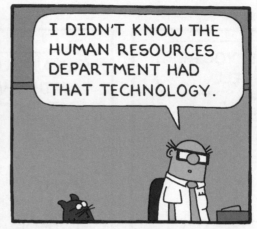

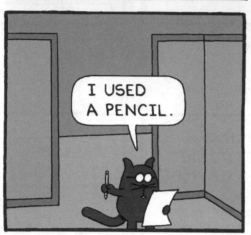

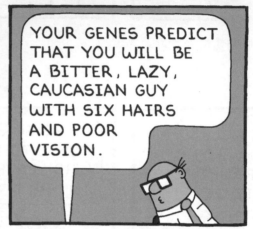

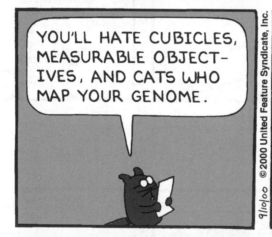

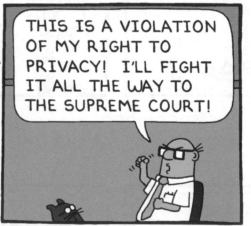

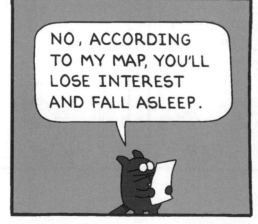

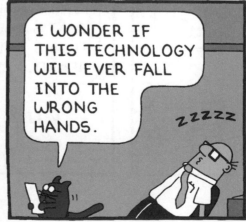

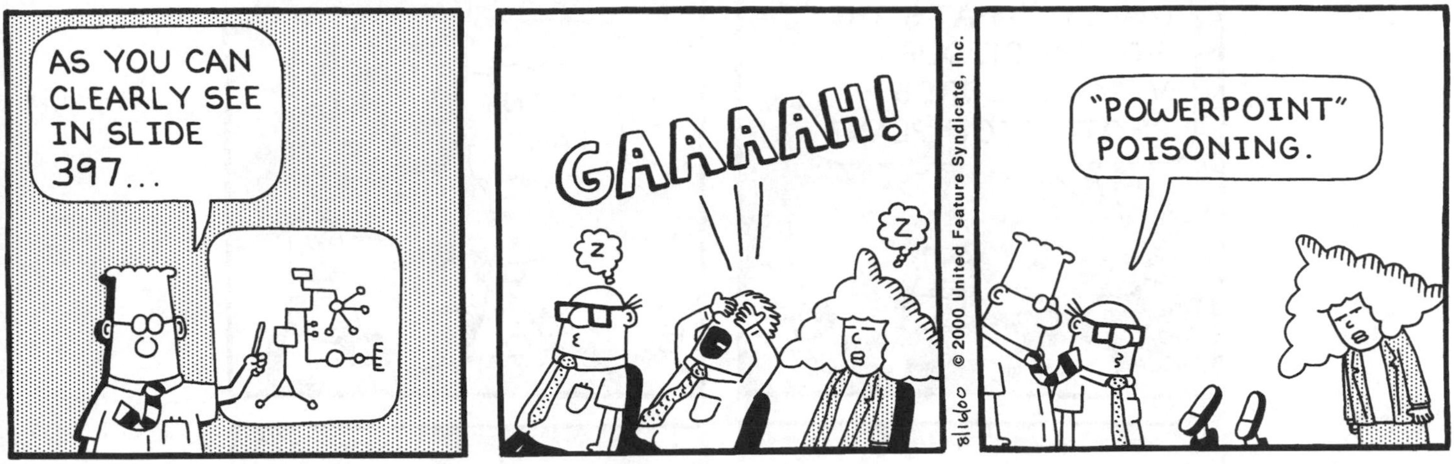
AS YOU CAN CLEARLY SEE IN SLIDE 397...
GAAAAH!
"POWERPOINT" POISONING.
8/16/00 © 2000 United Feature Syndicate, Inc.

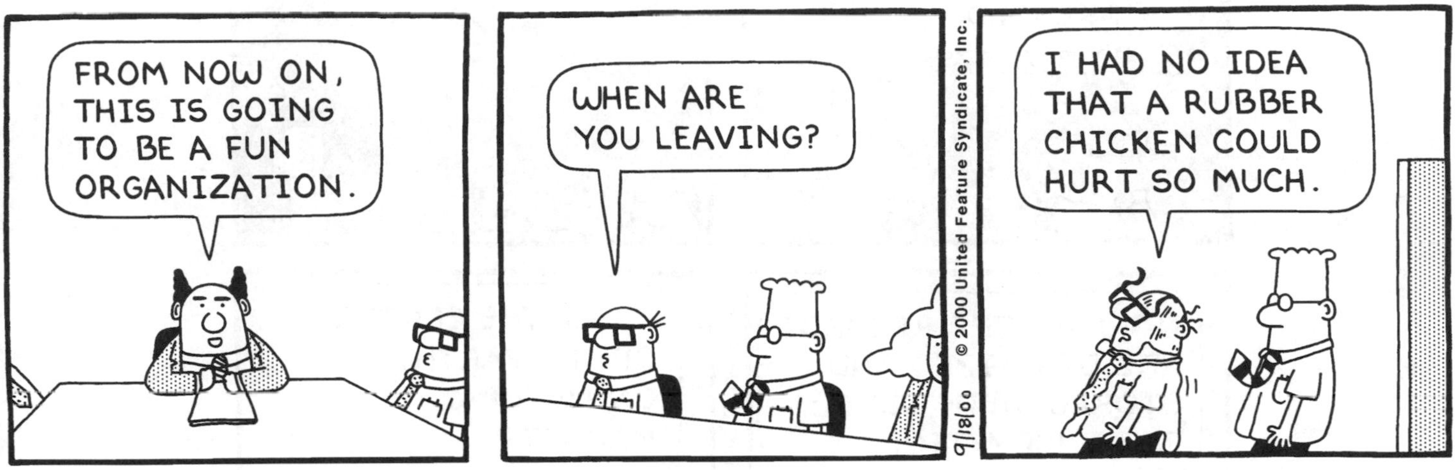
FROM NOW ON, THIS IS GOING TO BE A FUN ORGANIZATION.
WHEN ARE YOU LEAVING?
I HAD NO IDEA THAT A RUBBER CHICKEN COULD HURT SO MUCH.
9/18/00 © 2000 United Feature Syndicate, Inc.

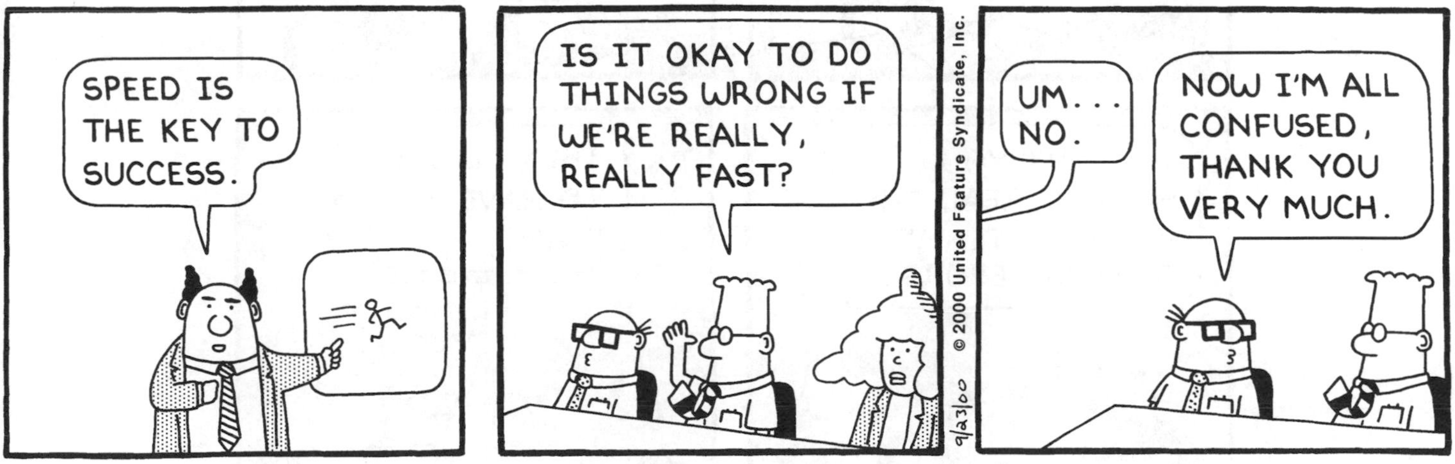
SPEED IS THE KEY TO SUCCESS.
IS IT OKAY TO DO THINGS WRONG IF WE'RE REALLY, REALLY FAST?
UM... NO.
NOW I'M ALL CONFUSED, THANK YOU VERY MUCH.
9/23/00 © 2000 United Feature Syndicate, Inc.

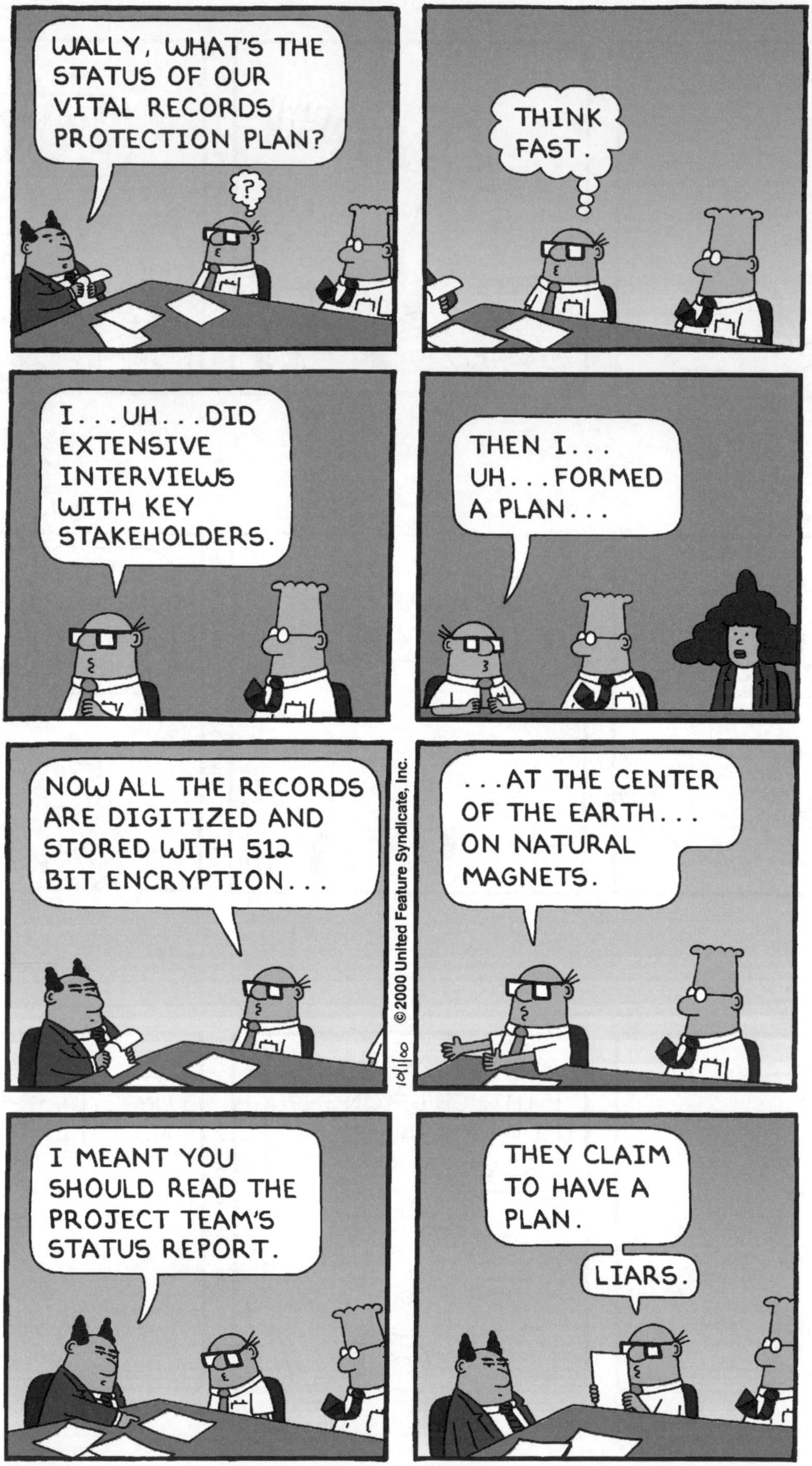
WALLY, WHAT'S THE STATUS OF OUR VITAL RECORDS PROTECTION PLAN?
?
THINK FAST.
I . . . UH . . . DID EXTENSIVE INTERVIEWS WITH KEY STAKEHOLDERS.
THEN I . . . UH . . . FORMED A PLAN . . .
NOW ALL THE RECORDS ARE DIGITIZED AND STORED WITH 512 BIT ENCRYPTION . . .
©2000 United Feature Syndicate, Inc.
10/1/00
. . . AT THE CENTER OF THE EARTH . . . ON NATURAL MAGNETS.
I MEANT YOU SHOULD READ THE PROJECT TEAM'S STATUS REPORT.
THEY CLAIM TO HAVE A PLAN.
LIARS.

THE INSPIRATIONAL CEO

OUR COMPANY IS TOO GOOD TO HAVE RESULTS THIS POOR.

QUESTION.

%#!* ENGINEERS.

WHAT?

ARE YOU SAYING THE LAWS OF CAUSE AND EFFECT DO NOT APPLY?

LOGICALLY, IF WE WERE GOOD, WE WOULD GENERATE GOOD RESULTS.

© 2000 United Feature Syndicate, Inc.

IS IT NOT MORE LIKELY THAT WE ARE PATHETIC LOSERS WHO GET EXACTLY WHAT WE DESERVE?

YES, INDIVIDUALLY YOU'RE ALL LOSERS. BUT TOGETHER WE'RE A GREAT COMPANY.

THANKS TO MY LEADER-SHIP.

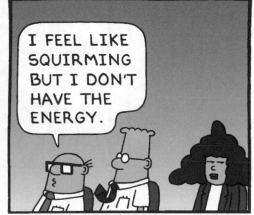

I FEEL LIKE SQUIRMING BUT I DON'T HAVE THE ENERGY.

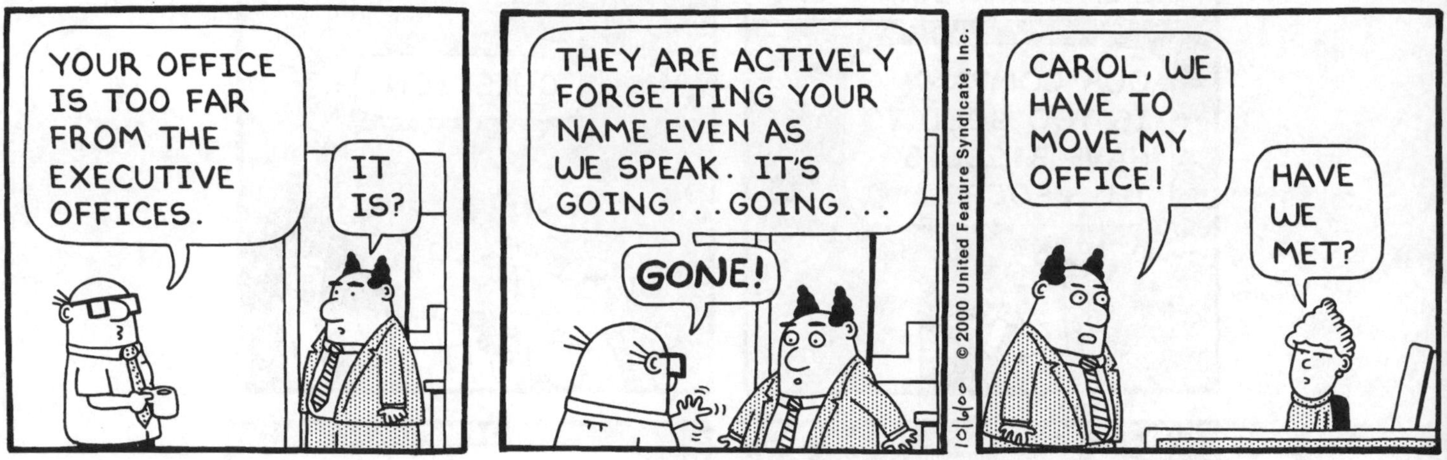
YOUR OFFICE IS TOO FAR FROM THE EXECUTIVE OFFICES.
IT IS?
THEY ARE ACTIVELY FORGETTING YOUR NAME EVEN AS WE SPEAK. IT'S GOING...GOING...
GONE!
10/6/00 © 2000 United Feature Syndicate, Inc.
CAROL, WE HAVE TO MOVE MY OFFICE!
HAVE WE MET?

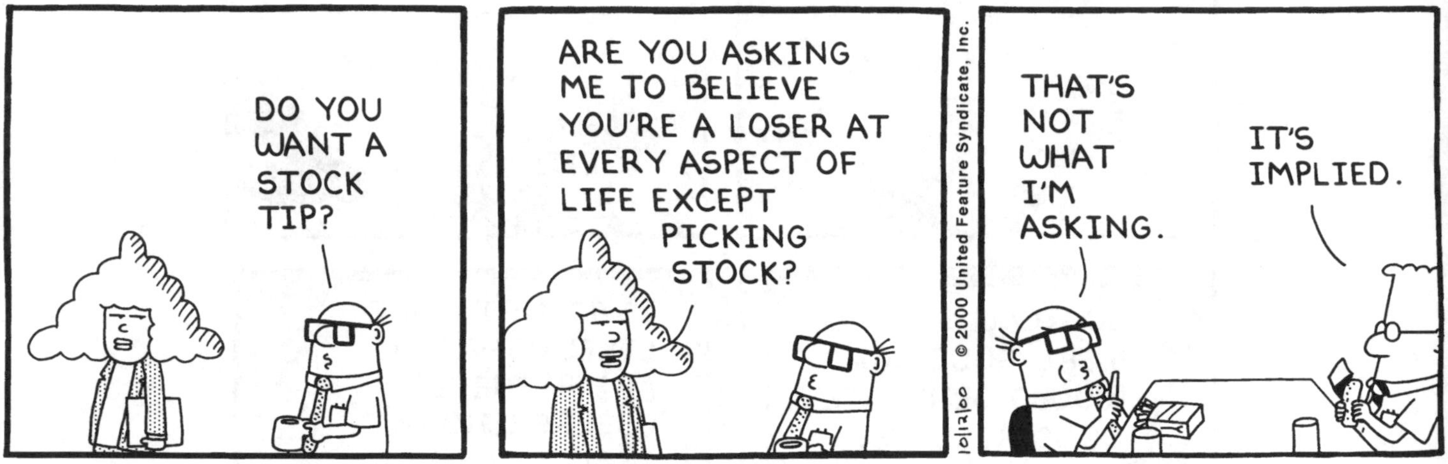
DO YOU WANT A STOCK TIP?
ARE YOU ASKING ME TO BELIEVE YOU'RE A LOSER AT EVERY ASPECT OF LIFE EXCEPT PICKING STOCK?
10/12/00 © 2000 United Feature Syndicate, Inc.
THAT'S NOT WHAT I'M ASKING.
IT'S IMPLIED.

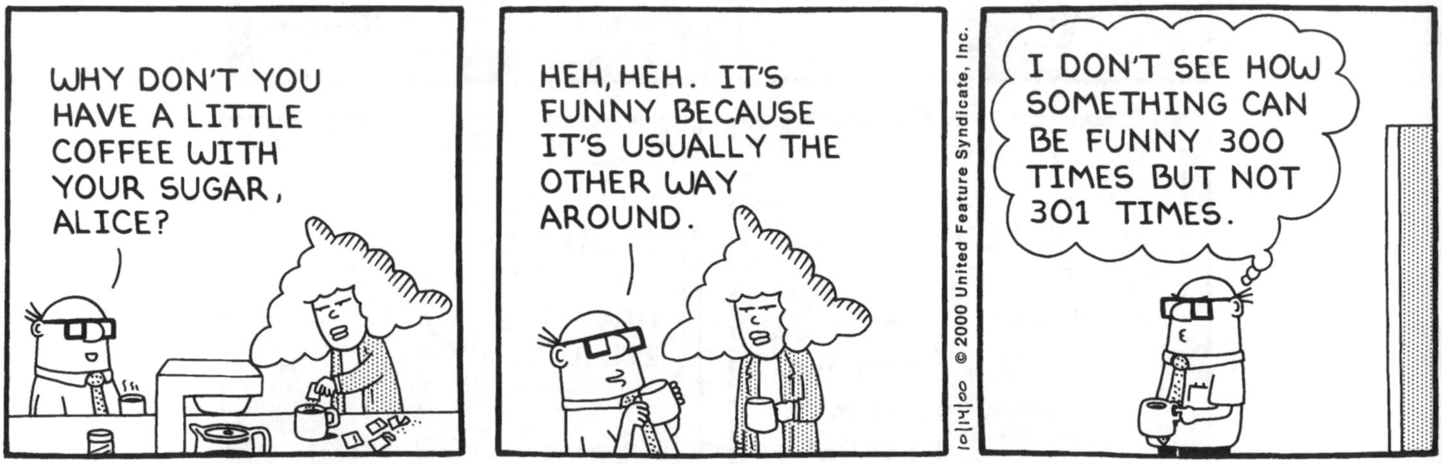
WHY DON'T YOU HAVE A LITTLE COFFEE WITH YOUR SUGAR, ALICE?
HEH, HEH. IT'S FUNNY BECAUSE IT'S USUALLY THE OTHER WAY AROUND.
10/14/00 © 2000 United Feature Syndicate, Inc.
I DON'T SEE HOW SOMETHING CAN BE FUNNY 300 TIMES BUT NOT 301 TIMES.

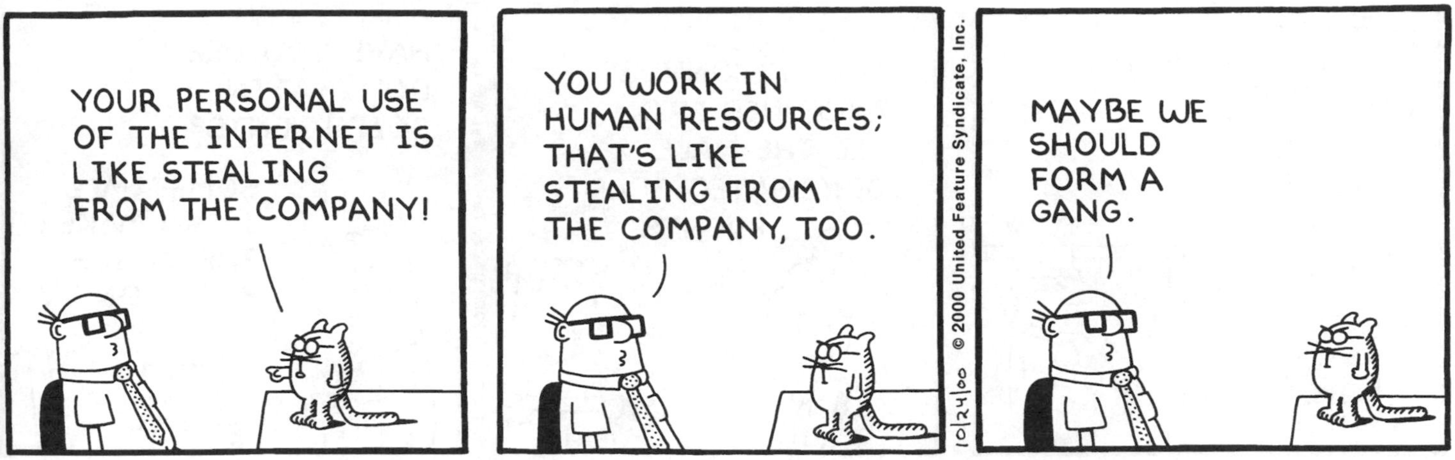
YOUR PERSONAL USE OF THE INTERNET IS LIKE STEALING FROM THE COMPANY!
YOU WORK IN HUMAN RESOURCES; THAT'S LIKE STEALING FROM THE COMPANY, TOO.
© 2000 United Feature Syndicate, Inc.
10/24/00
MAYBE WE SHOULD FORM A GANG.

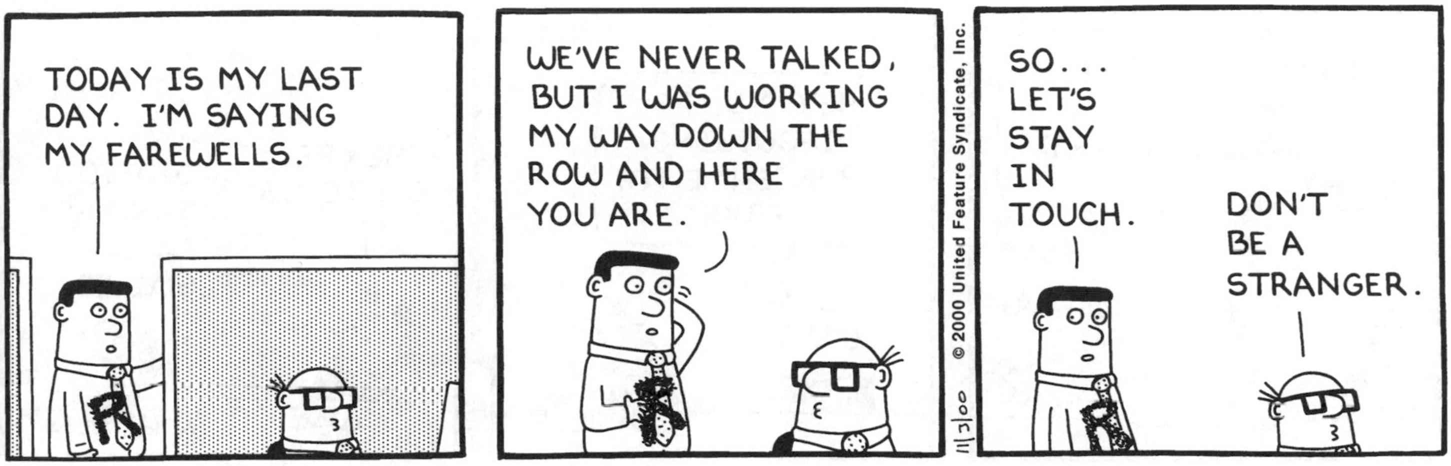
TODAY IS MY LAST DAY. I'M SAYING MY FAREWELLS.
WE'VE NEVER TALKED, BUT I WAS WORKING MY WAY DOWN THE ROW AND HERE YOU ARE.
© 2000 United Feature Syndicate, Inc.
11/3/00
SO... LET'S STAY IN TOUCH.
DON'T BE A STRANGER.

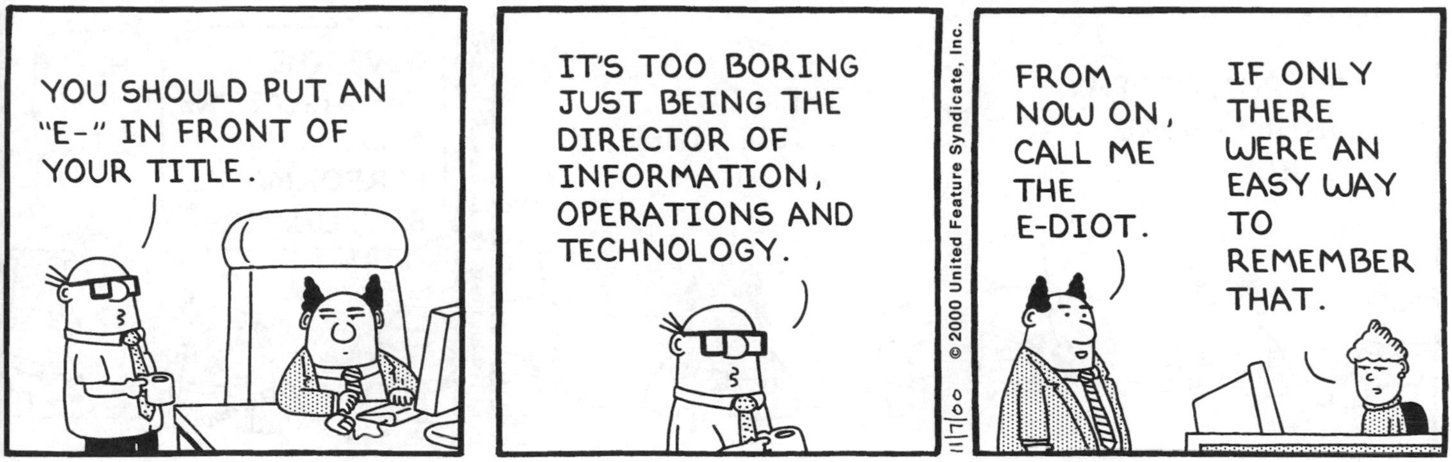
YOU SHOULD PUT AN "E-" IN FRONT OF YOUR TITLE.
IT'S TOO BORING JUST BEING THE DIRECTOR OF INFORMATION, OPERATIONS AND TECHNOLOGY.
© 2000 United Feature Syndicate, Inc.
11/7/00
FROM NOW ON, CALL ME THE E-DIOT.
IF ONLY THERE WERE AN EASY WAY TO REMEMBER THAT.

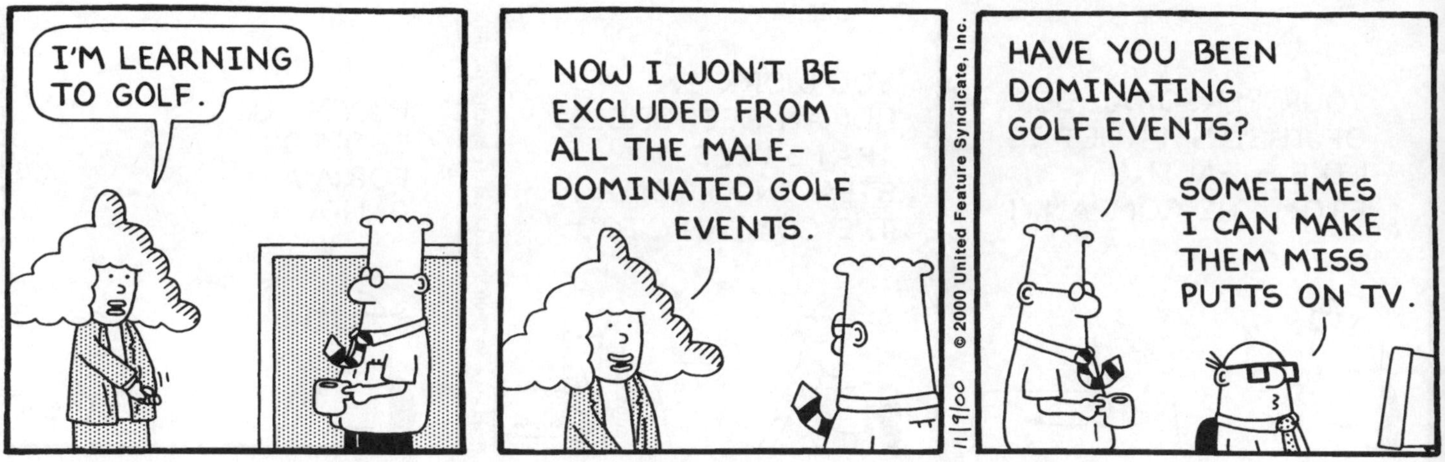
I'M LEARNING TO GOLF.
NOW I WON'T BE EXCLUDED FROM ALL THE MALE-DOMINATED GOLF EVENTS.
11/9/00 © 2000 United Feature Syndicate, Inc.
HAVE YOU BEEN DOMINATING GOLF EVENTS?
SOMETIMES I CAN MAKE THEM MISS PUTTS ON TV.

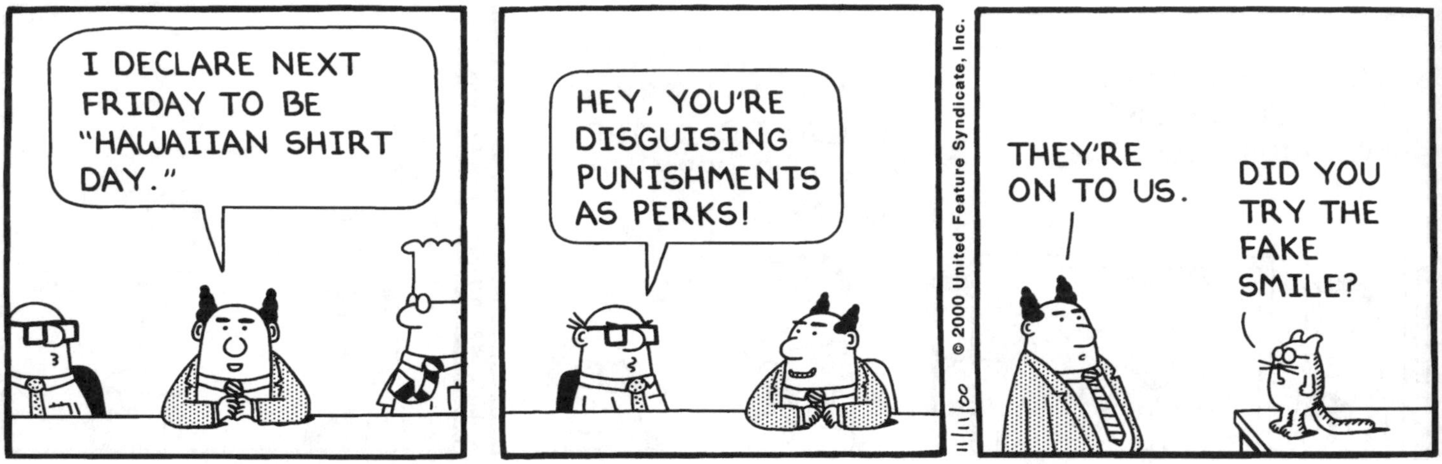
I DECLARE NEXT FRIDAY TO BE "HAWAIIAN SHIRT DAY."
HEY, YOU'RE DISGUISING PUNISHMENTS AS PERKS!
11/11/00 © 2000 United Feature Syndicate, Inc.
THEY'RE ON TO US.
DID YOU TRY THE FAKE SMILE?

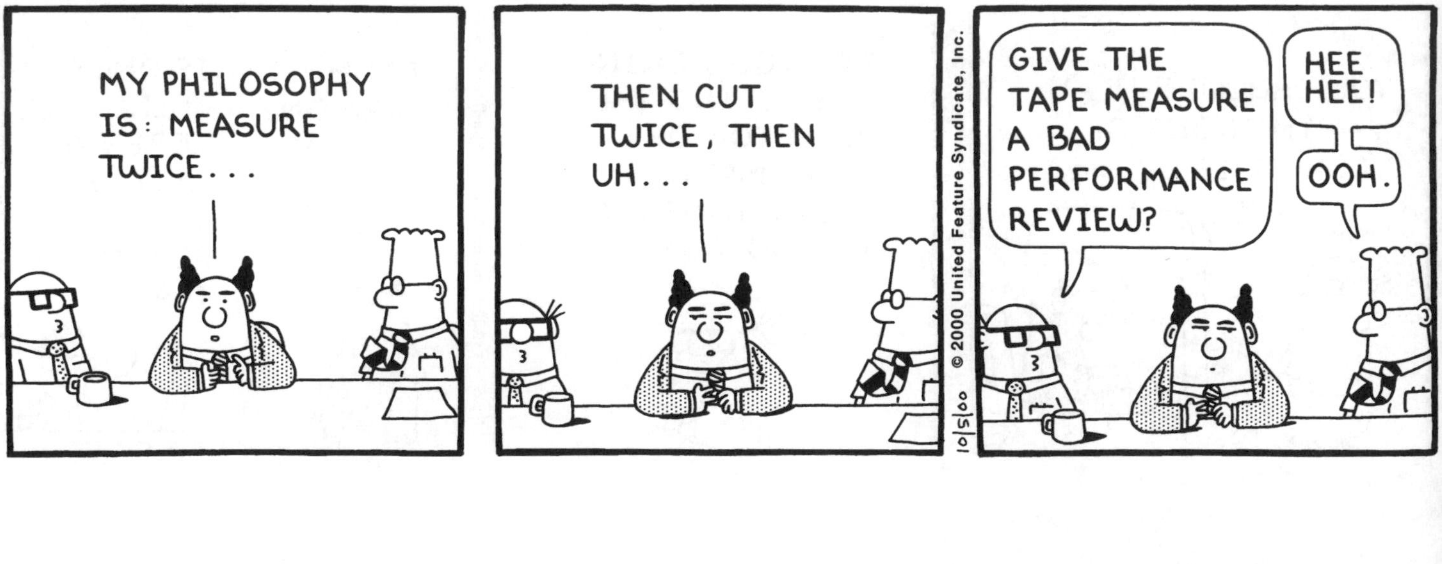
MY PHILOSOPHY IS: MEASURE TWICE...
THEN CUT TWICE, THEN UH...
10/5/00 © 2000 United Feature Syndicate, Inc.
GIVE THE TAPE MEASURE A BAD PERFORMANCE REVIEW?
HEE HEE!
OOH.

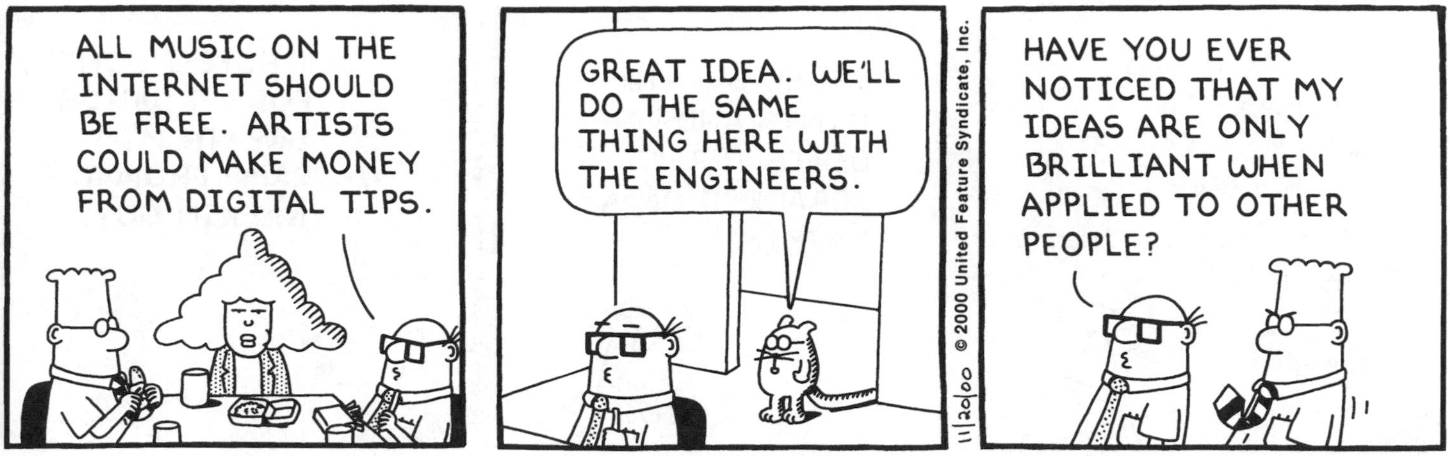
ALL MUSIC ON THE INTERNET SHOULD BE FREE. ARTISTS COULD MAKE MONEY FROM DIGITAL TIPS.
GREAT IDEA. WE'LL DO THE SAME THING HERE WITH THE ENGINEERS.
HAVE YOU EVER NOTICED THAT MY IDEAS ARE ONLY BRILLIANT WHEN APPLIED TO OTHER PEOPLE?

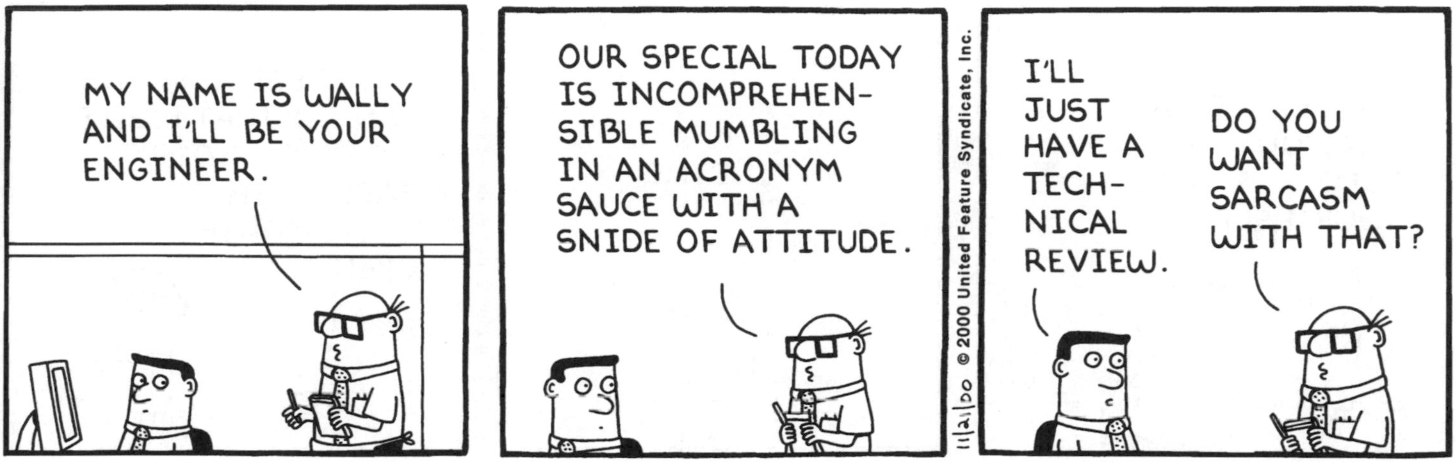
MY NAME IS WALLY AND I'LL BE YOUR ENGINEER.
OUR SPECIAL TODAY IS INCOMPREHEN-SIBLE MUMBLING IN AN ACRONYM SAUCE WITH A SNIDE OF ATTITUDE.
I'LL JUST HAVE A TECH-NICAL REVIEW.
DO YOU WANT SARCASM WITH THAT?

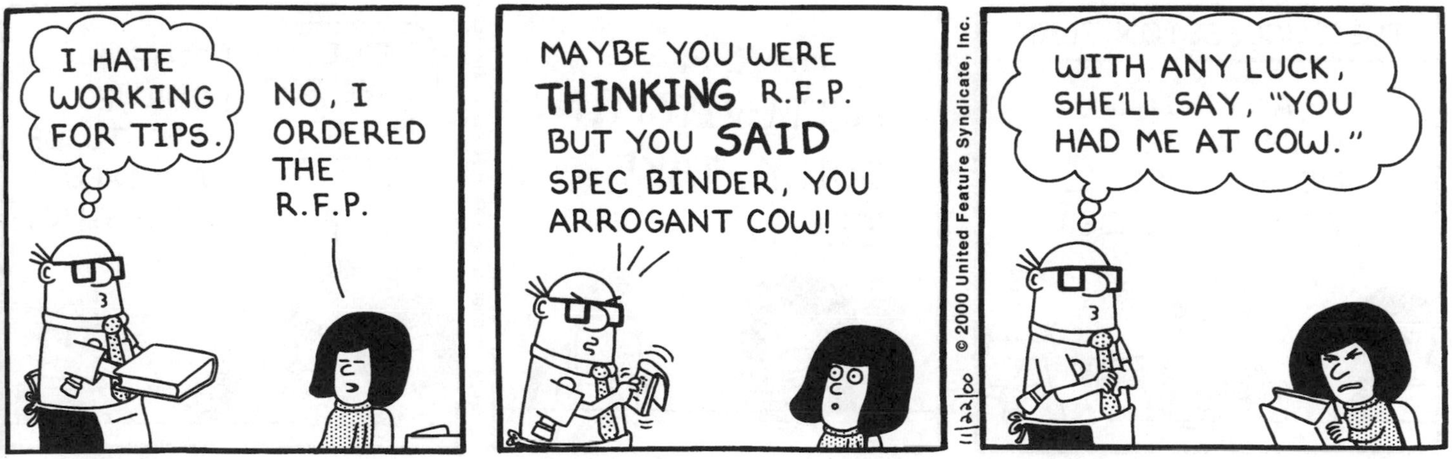
I HATE WORKING FOR TIPS.
NO, I ORDERED THE R.F.P.
MAYBE YOU WERE THINKING R.F.P. BUT YOU SAID SPEC BINDER, YOU ARROGANT COW!
WITH ANY LUCK, SHE'LL SAY, "YOU HAD ME AT COW."

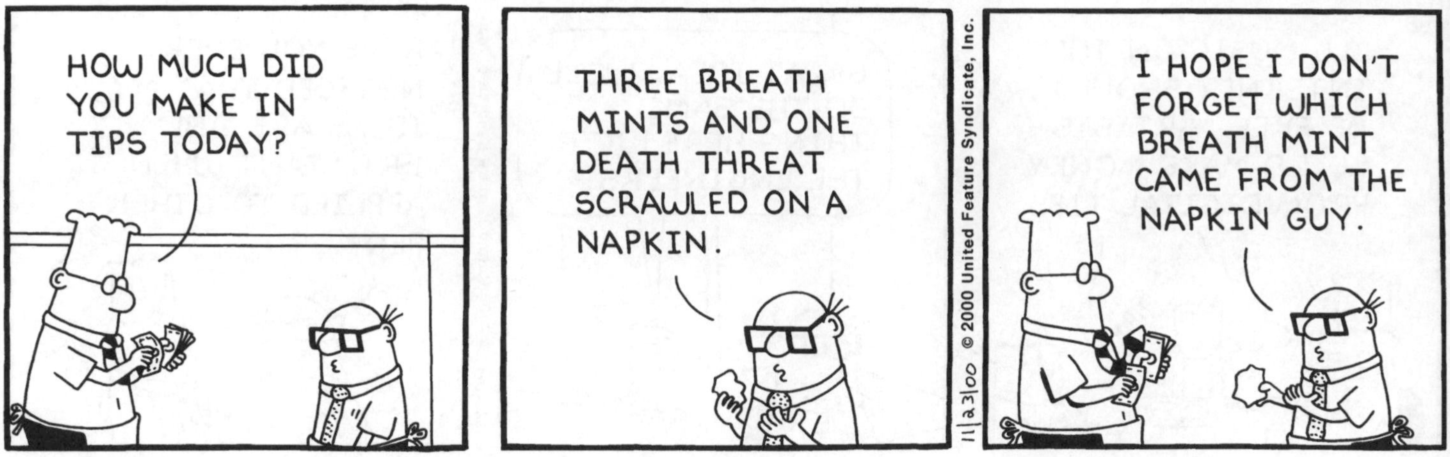
HOW MUCH DID YOU MAKE IN TIPS TODAY?
THREE BREATH MINTS AND ONE DEATH THREAT SCRAWLED ON A NAPKIN.
11/23/00 © 2000 United Feature Syndicate, Inc.
I HOPE I DON'T FORGET WHICH BREATH MINT CAME FROM THE NAPKIN GUY.

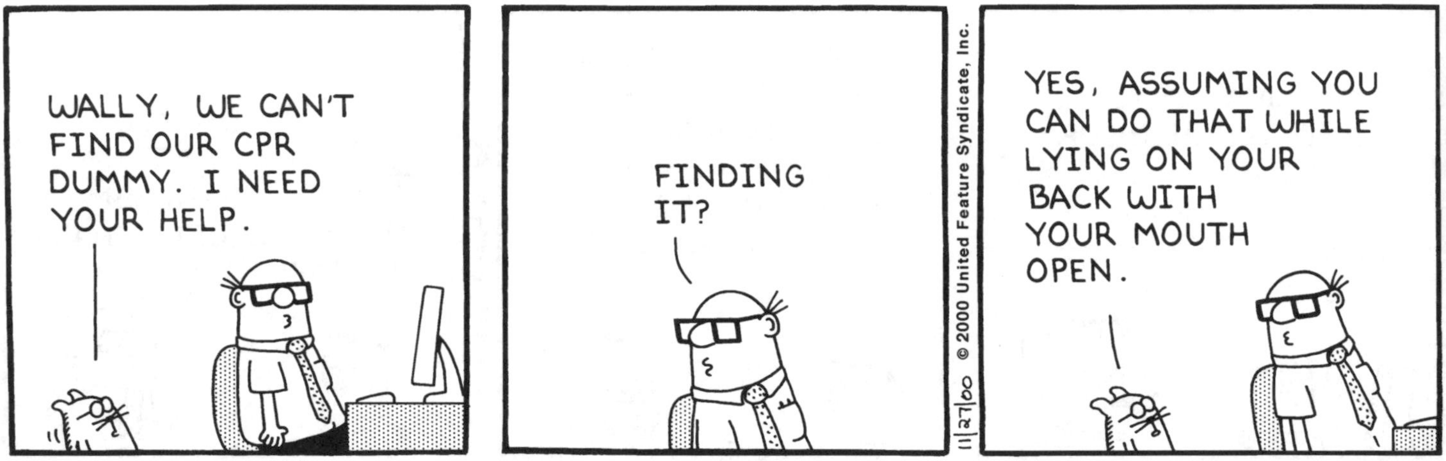
WALLY, WE CAN'T FIND OUR CPR DUMMY. I NEED YOUR HELP.
FINDING IT?
11/27/00 © 2000 United Feature Syndicate, Inc.
YES, ASSUMING YOU CAN DO THAT WHILE LYING ON YOUR BACK WITH YOUR MOUTH OPEN.

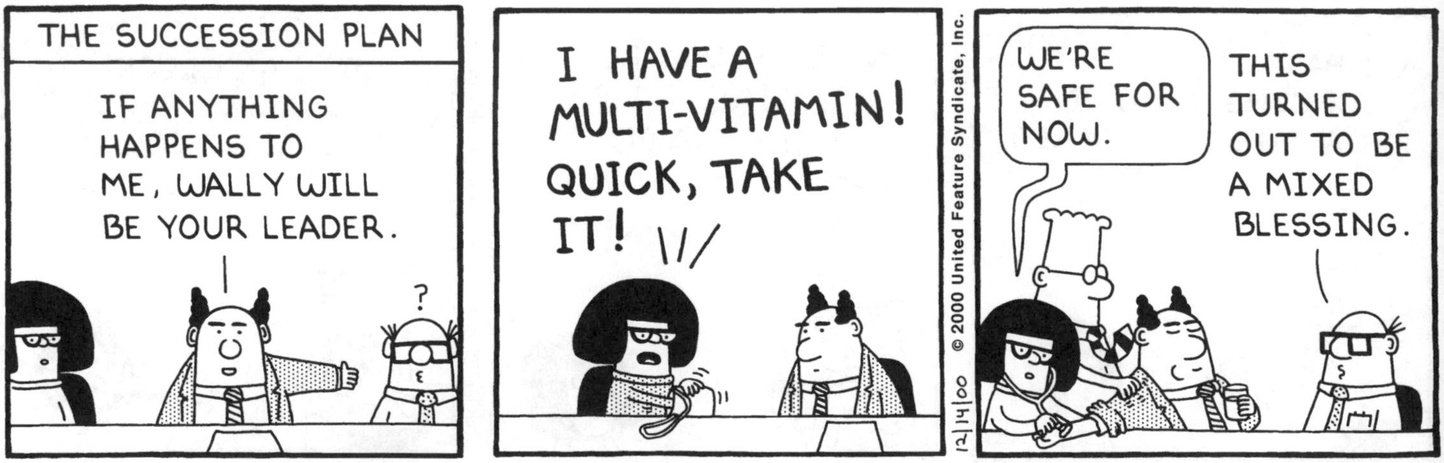
THE SUCCESSION PLAN
IF ANYTHING HAPPENS TO ME, WALLY WILL BE YOUR LEADER.
?
I HAVE A MULTI-VITAMIN! QUICK, TAKE IT!
12/14/00 © 2000 United Feature Syndicate, Inc.
WE'RE SAFE FOR NOW.
THIS TURNED OUT TO BE A MIXED BLESSING.

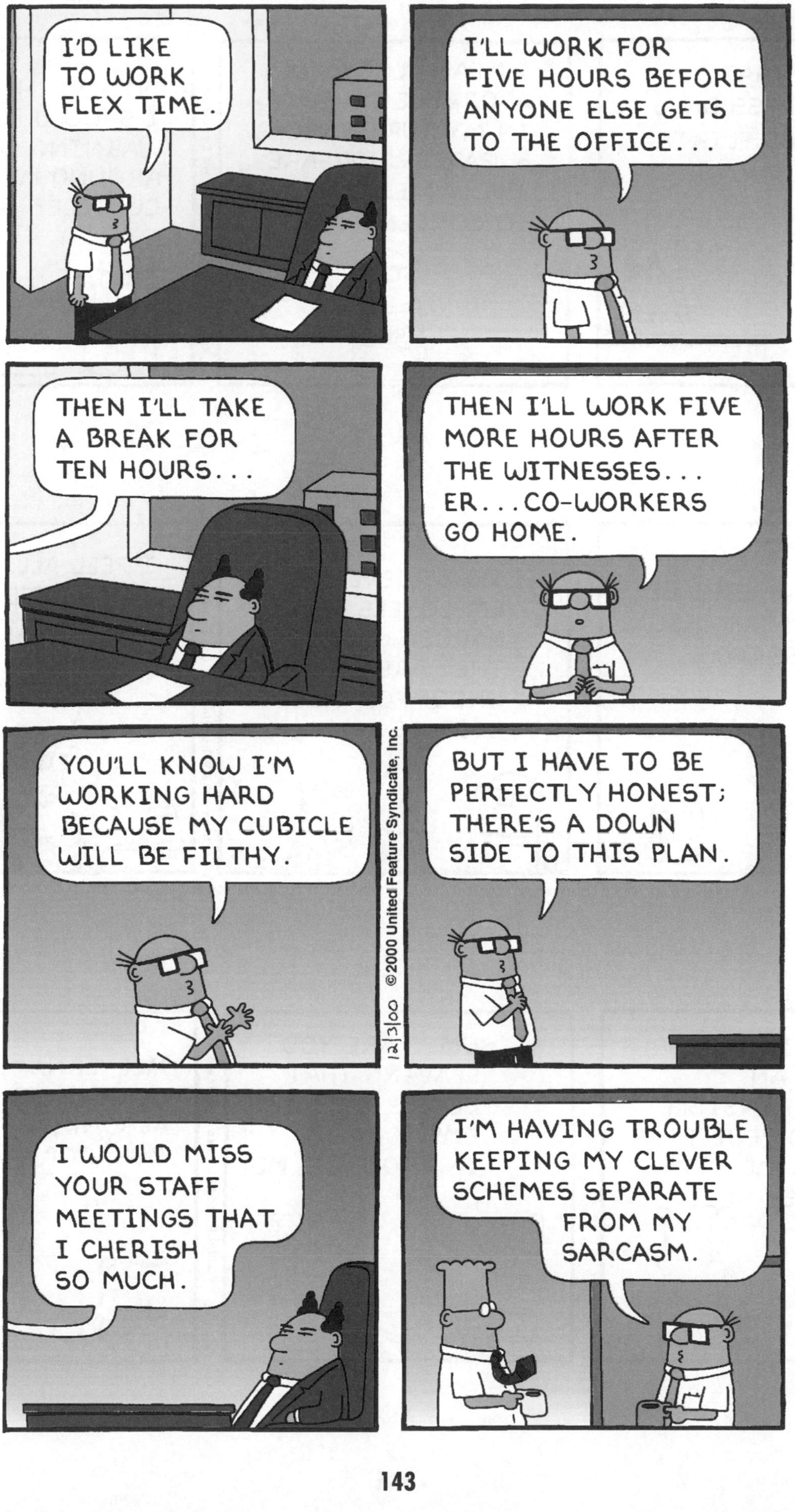
I'D LIKE TO WORK FLEX TIME.
I'LL WORK FOR FIVE HOURS BEFORE ANYONE ELSE GETS TO THE OFFICE...
THEN I'LL TAKE A BREAK FOR TEN HOURS...
THEN I'LL WORK FIVE MORE HOURS AFTER THE WITNESSES... ER...CO-WORKERS GO HOME.
YOU'LL KNOW I'M WORKING HARD BECAUSE MY CUBICLE WILL BE FILTHY.
12/3/00 ©2000 United Feature Syndicate, Inc.
BUT I HAVE TO BE PERFECTLY HONEST; THERE'S A DOWN SIDE TO THIS PLAN.
I WOULD MISS YOUR STAFF MEETINGS THAT I CHERISH SO MUCH.
I'M HAVING TROUBLE KEEPING MY CLEVER SCHEMES SEPARATE FROM MY SARCASM.

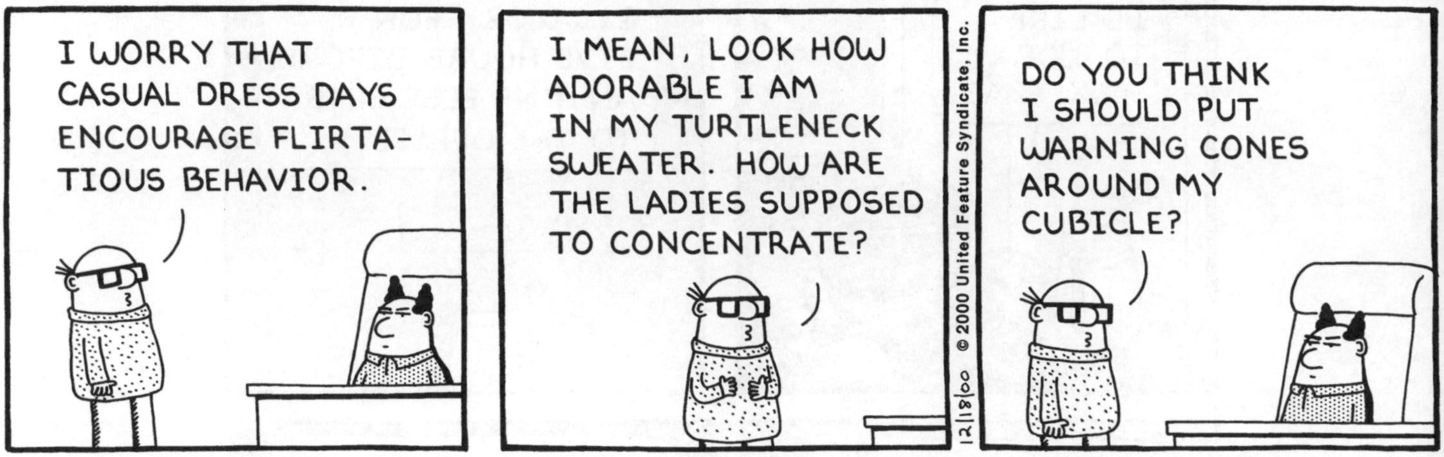
I WORRY THAT CASUAL DRESS DAYS ENCOURAGE FLIRTA-TIOUS BEHAVIOR.
I MEAN, LOOK HOW ADORABLE I AM IN MY TURTLENECK SWEATER. HOW ARE THE LADIES SUPPOSED TO CONCENTRATE?
12/18/00 © 2000 United Feature Syndicate, Inc.
DO YOU THINK I SHOULD PUT WARNING CONES AROUND MY CUBICLE?

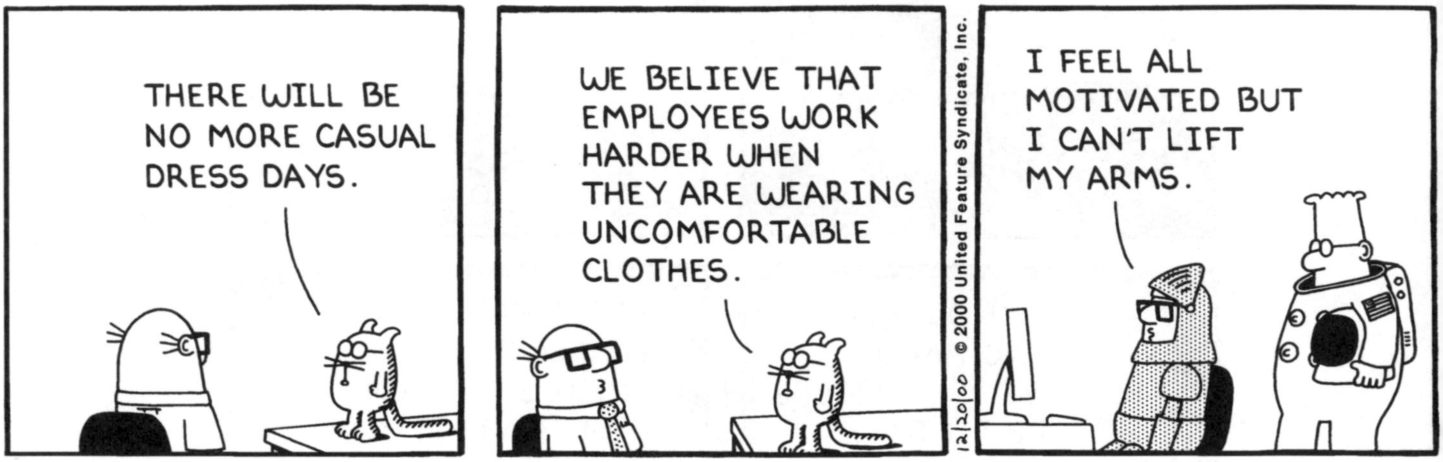
THERE WILL BE NO MORE CASUAL DRESS DAYS.
WE BELIEVE THAT EMPLOYEES WORK HARDER WHEN THEY ARE WEARING UNCOMFORTABLE CLOTHES.
12/20/00 © 2000 United Feature Syndicate, Inc.
I FEEL ALL MOTIVATED BUT I CAN'T LIFT MY ARMS.

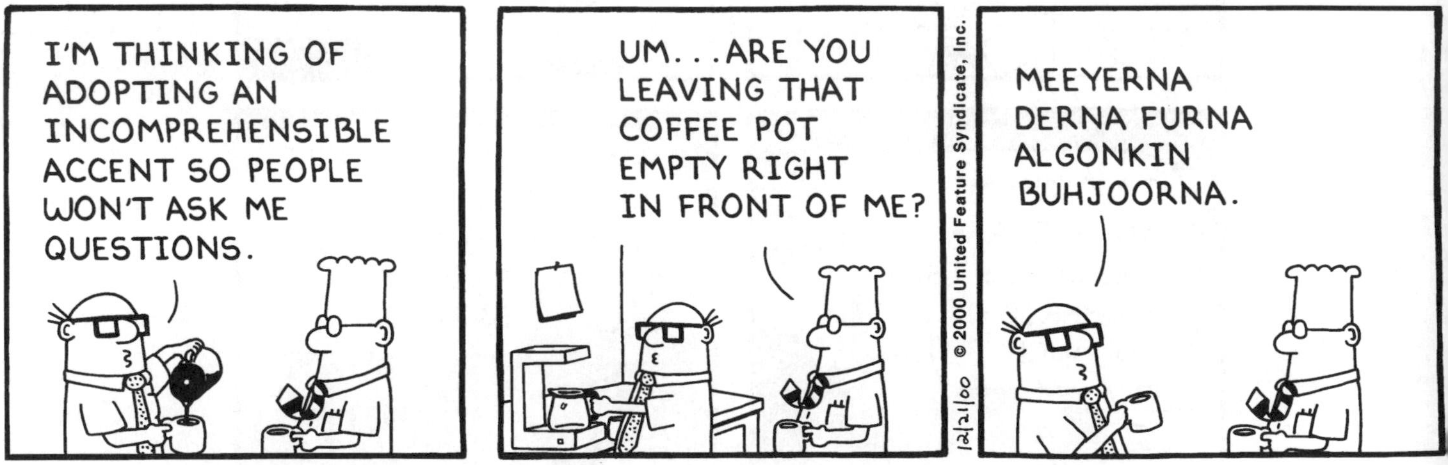
I'M THINKING OF ADOPTING AN INCOMPREHENSIBLE ACCENT SO PEOPLE WON'T ASK ME QUESTIONS.
UM...ARE YOU LEAVING THAT COFFEE POT EMPTY RIGHT IN FRONT OF ME?
12/21/00 © 2000 United Feature Syndicate, Inc.
MEEYERNA DERNA FURNA ALGONKIN BUHJOORNA.

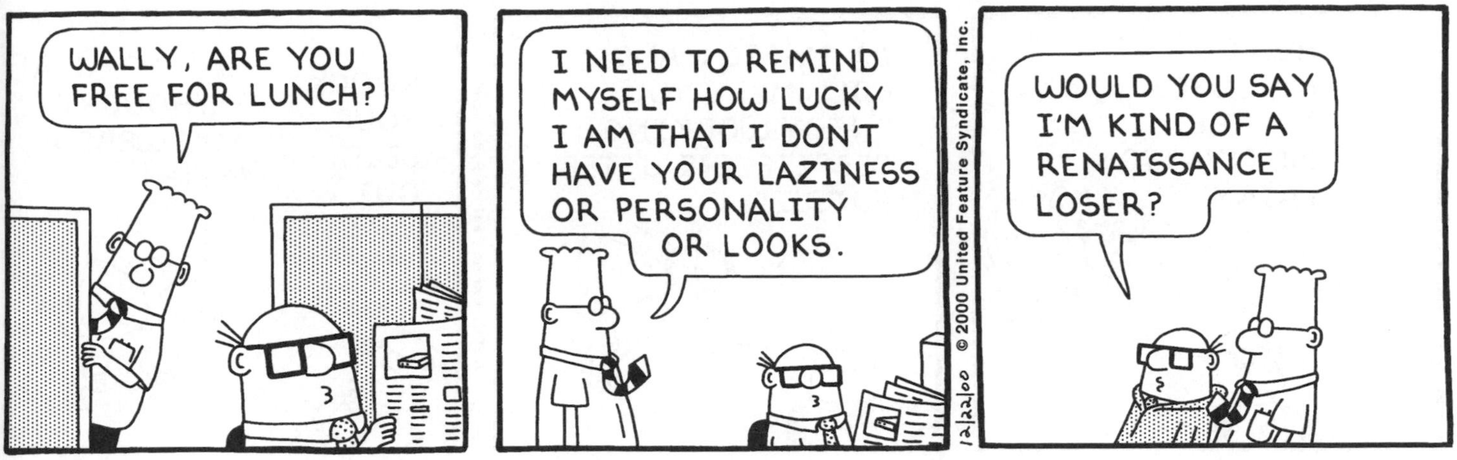
WALLY, ARE YOU FREE FOR LUNCH?
I NEED TO REMIND MYSELF HOW LUCKY I AM THAT I DON'T HAVE YOUR LAZINESS OR PERSONALITY OR LOOKS.
WOULD YOU SAY I'M KIND OF A RENAISSANCE LOSER?
© 2000 United Feature Syndicate, Inc.
12/22/00

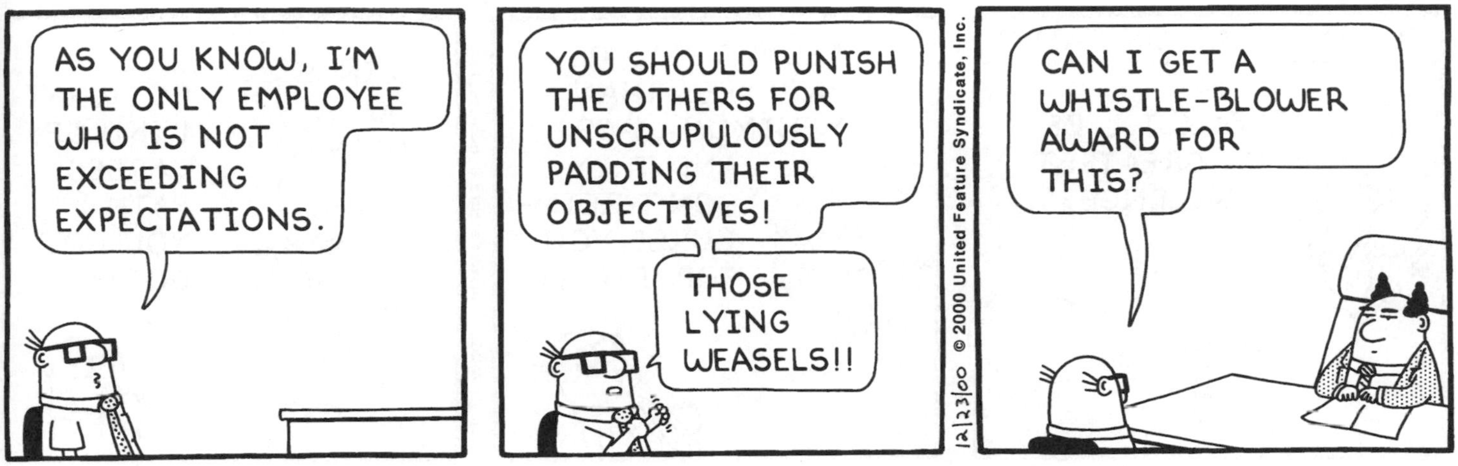
AS YOU KNOW, I'M THE ONLY EMPLOYEE WHO IS NOT EXCEEDING EXPECTATIONS.
YOU SHOULD PUNISH THE OTHERS FOR UNSCRUPULOUSLY PADDING THEIR OBJECTIVES!
THOSE LYING WEASELS!!
CAN I GET A WHISTLE-BLOWER AWARD FOR THIS?
© 2000 United Feature Syndicate, Inc.
12/23/00

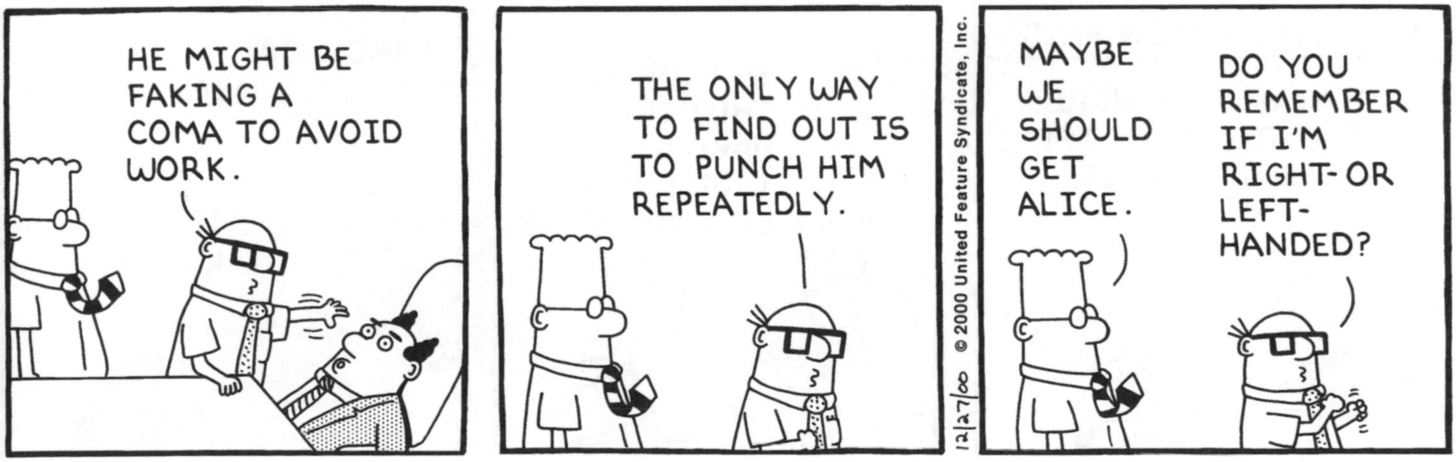
HE MIGHT BE FAKING A COMA TO AVOID WORK.
THE ONLY WAY TO FIND OUT IS TO PUNCH HIM REPEATEDLY.
MAYBE WE SHOULD GET ALICE.
DO YOU REMEMBER IF I'M RIGHT- OR LEFT-HANDED?
© 2000 United Feature Syndicate, Inc.
12/27/00

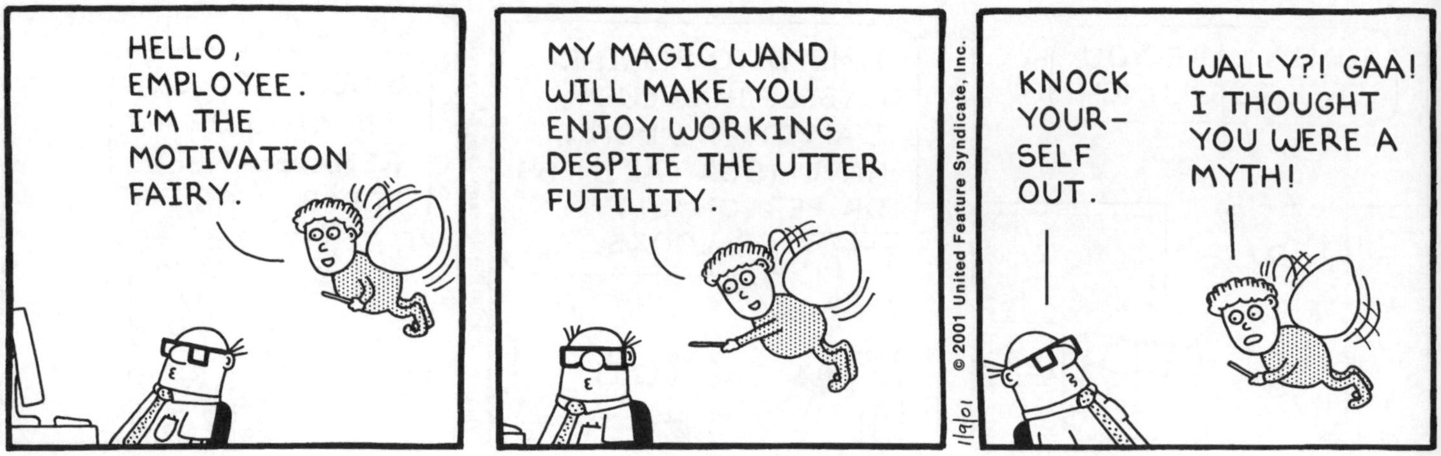
HELLO, EMPLOYEE. I'M THE MOTIVATION FAIRY.
MY MAGIC WAND WILL MAKE YOU ENJOY WORKING DESPITE THE UTTER FUTILITY.
1/9/01
© 2001 United Feature Syndicate, Inc.
KNOCK YOUR-SELF OUT.
WALLY?! GAA! I THOUGHT YOU WERE A MYTH!

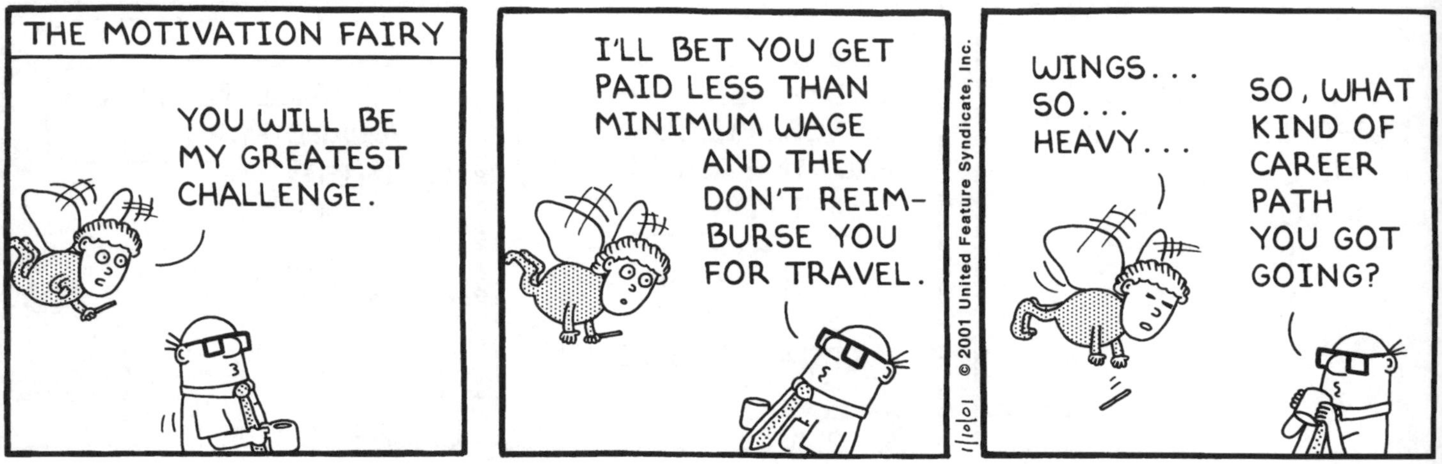
THE MOTIVATION FAIRY
YOU WILL BE MY GREATEST CHALLENGE.
I'LL BET YOU GET PAID LESS THAN MINIMUM WAGE
AND THEY DON'T REIM-BURSE YOU FOR TRAVEL.
1/10/01
© 2001 United Feature Syndicate, Inc.
WINGS... SO... HEAVY...
SO, WHAT KIND OF CAREER PATH YOU GOT GOING?

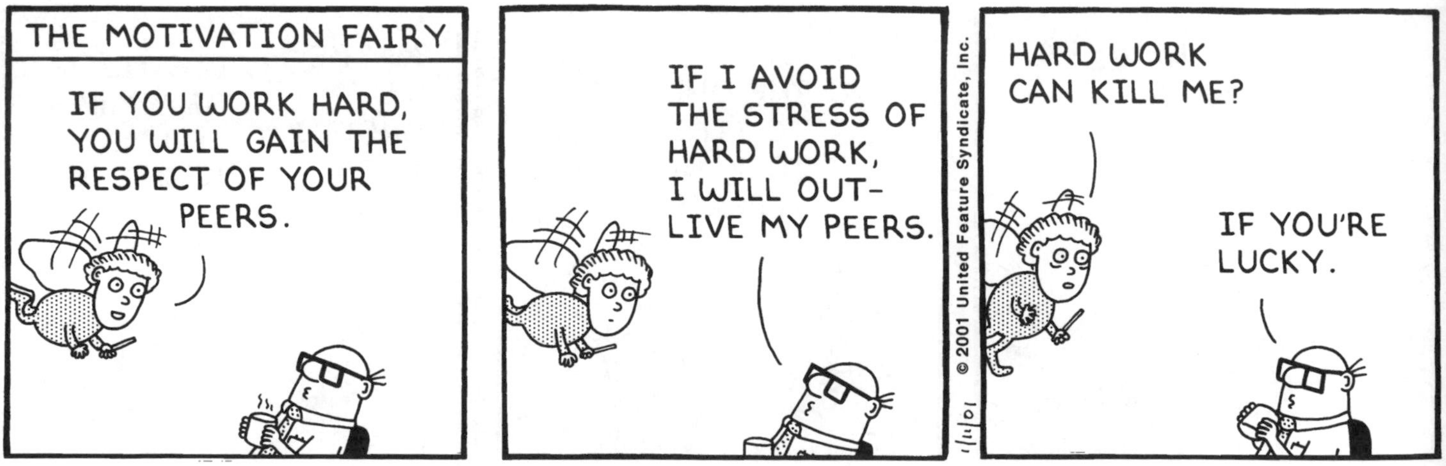
THE MOTIVATION FAIRY
IF YOU WORK HARD, YOU WILL GAIN THE RESPECT OF YOUR PEERS.
IF I AVOID THE STRESS OF HARD WORK, I WILL OUT-LIVE MY PEERS.
1/11/01
© 2001 United Feature Syndicate, Inc.
HARD WORK CAN KILL ME?
IF YOU'RE LUCKY.

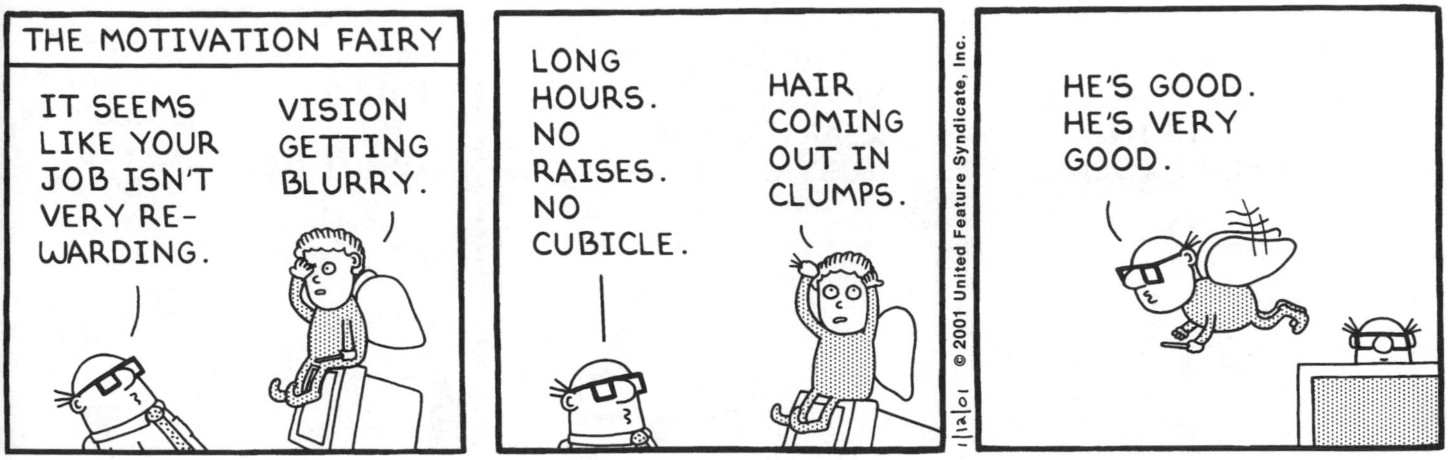
THE MOTIVATION FAIRY
IT SEEMS LIKE YOUR JOB ISN'T VERY RE-WARDING.
VISION GETTING BLURRY.
LONG HOURS. NO RAISES. NO CUBICLE.
HAIR COMING OUT IN CLUMPS.
HE'S GOOD. HE'S VERY GOOD.

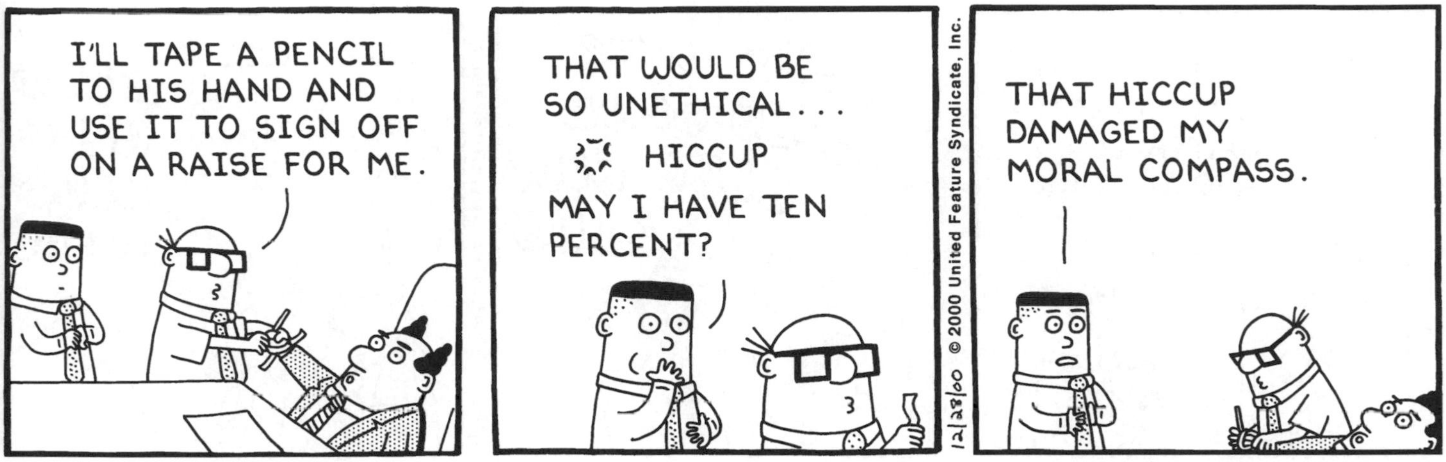
I'LL TAPE A PENCIL TO HIS HAND AND USE IT TO SIGN OFF ON A RAISE FOR ME.
THAT WOULD BE SO UNETHICAL...
HICCUP
MAY I HAVE TEN PERCENT?
THAT HICCUP DAMAGED MY MORAL COMPASS.

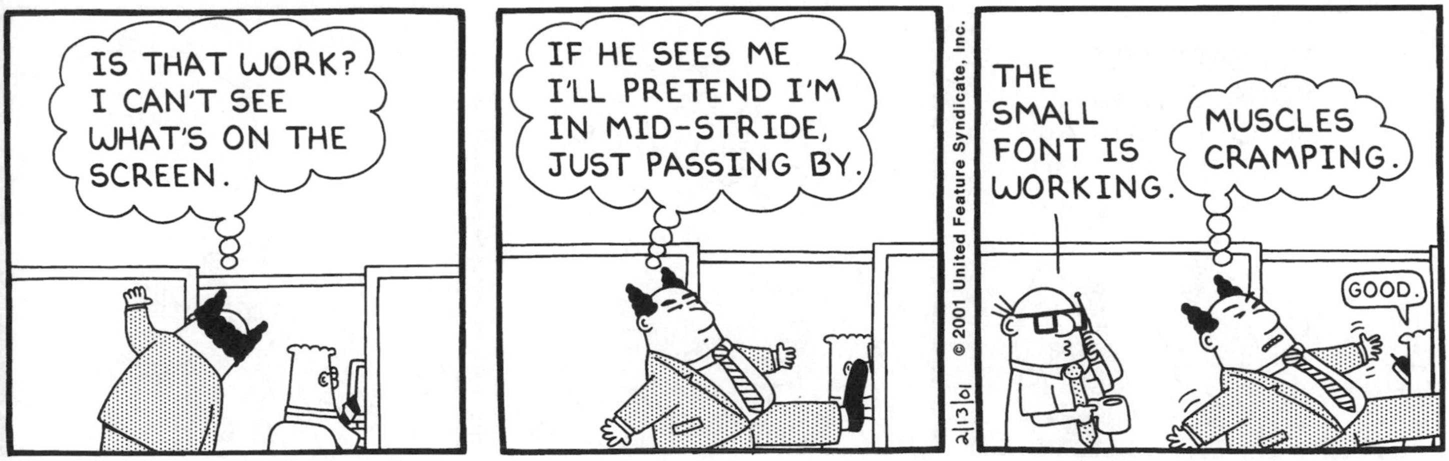
IS THAT WORK? I CAN'T SEE WHAT'S ON THE SCREEN.
IF HE SEES ME I'LL PRETEND I'M IN MID-STRIDE, JUST PASSING BY.
THE SMALL FONT IS WORKING.
MUSCLES CRAMPING.
GOOD.

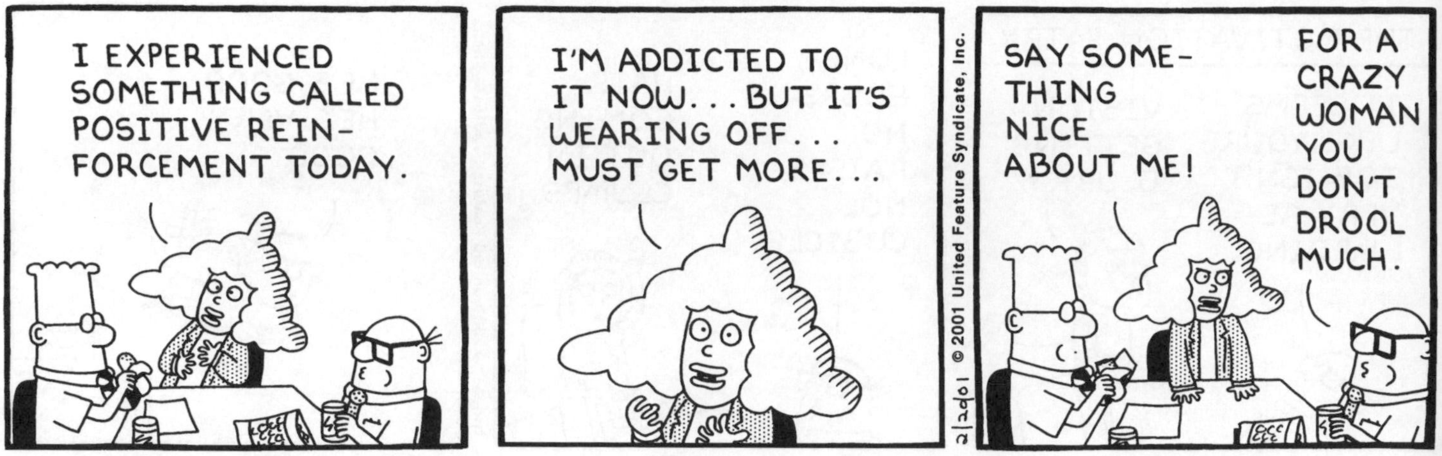
I EXPERIENCED SOMETHING CALLED POSITIVE REIN-FORCEMENT TODAY.
I'M ADDICTED TO IT NOW... BUT IT'S WEARING OFF... MUST GET MORE...
SAY SOME-THING NICE ABOUT ME!
FOR A CRAZY WOMAN YOU DON'T DROOL MUCH.
2/20/01 © 2001 United Feature Syndicate, Inc.

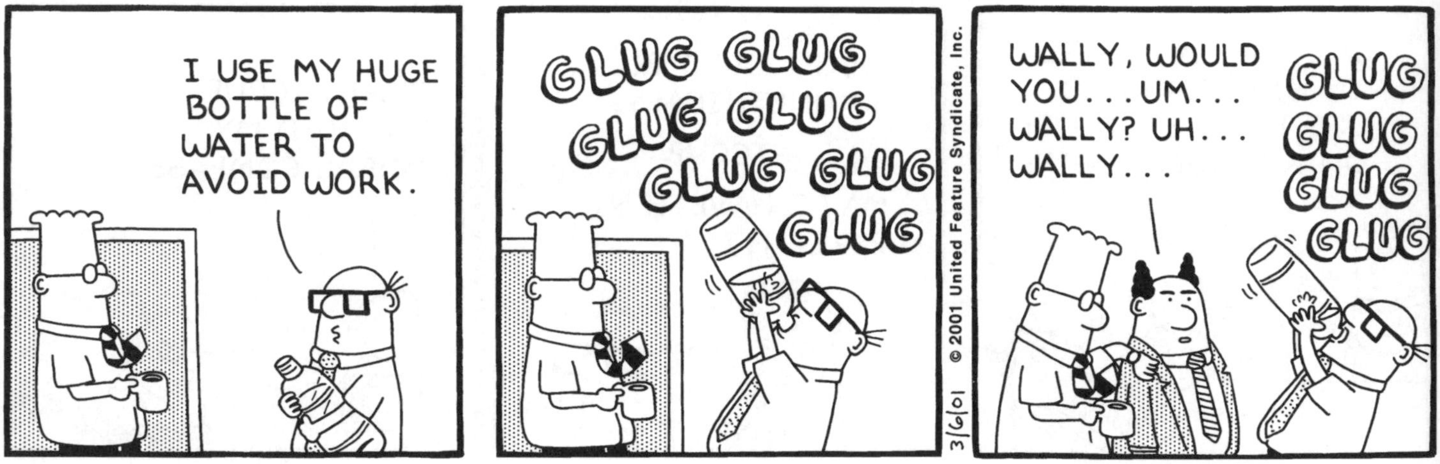
I USE MY HUGE BOTTLE OF WATER TO AVOID WORK.
GLUG GLUG GLUG GLUG GLUG GLUG GLUG
WALLY, WOULD YOU...UM... WALLY? UH... WALLY...
GLUG GLUG GLUG GLUG
3/6/01 © 2001 United Feature Syndicate, Inc.

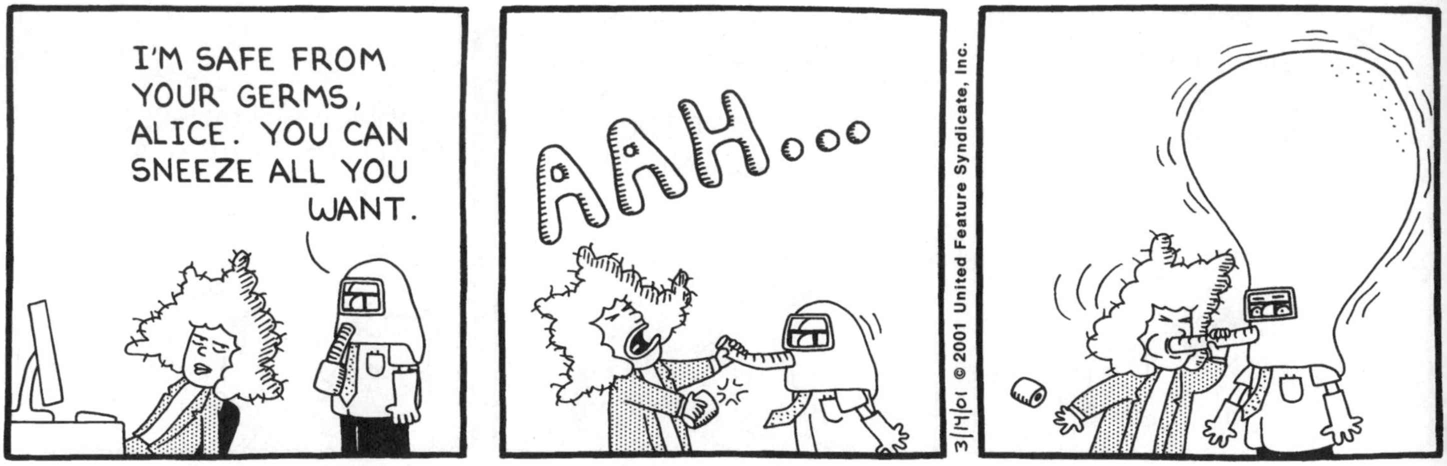
I'M SAFE FROM YOUR GERMS, ALICE. YOU CAN SNEEZE ALL YOU WANT.
AAH...
3/14/01 © 2001 United Feature Syndicate, Inc.

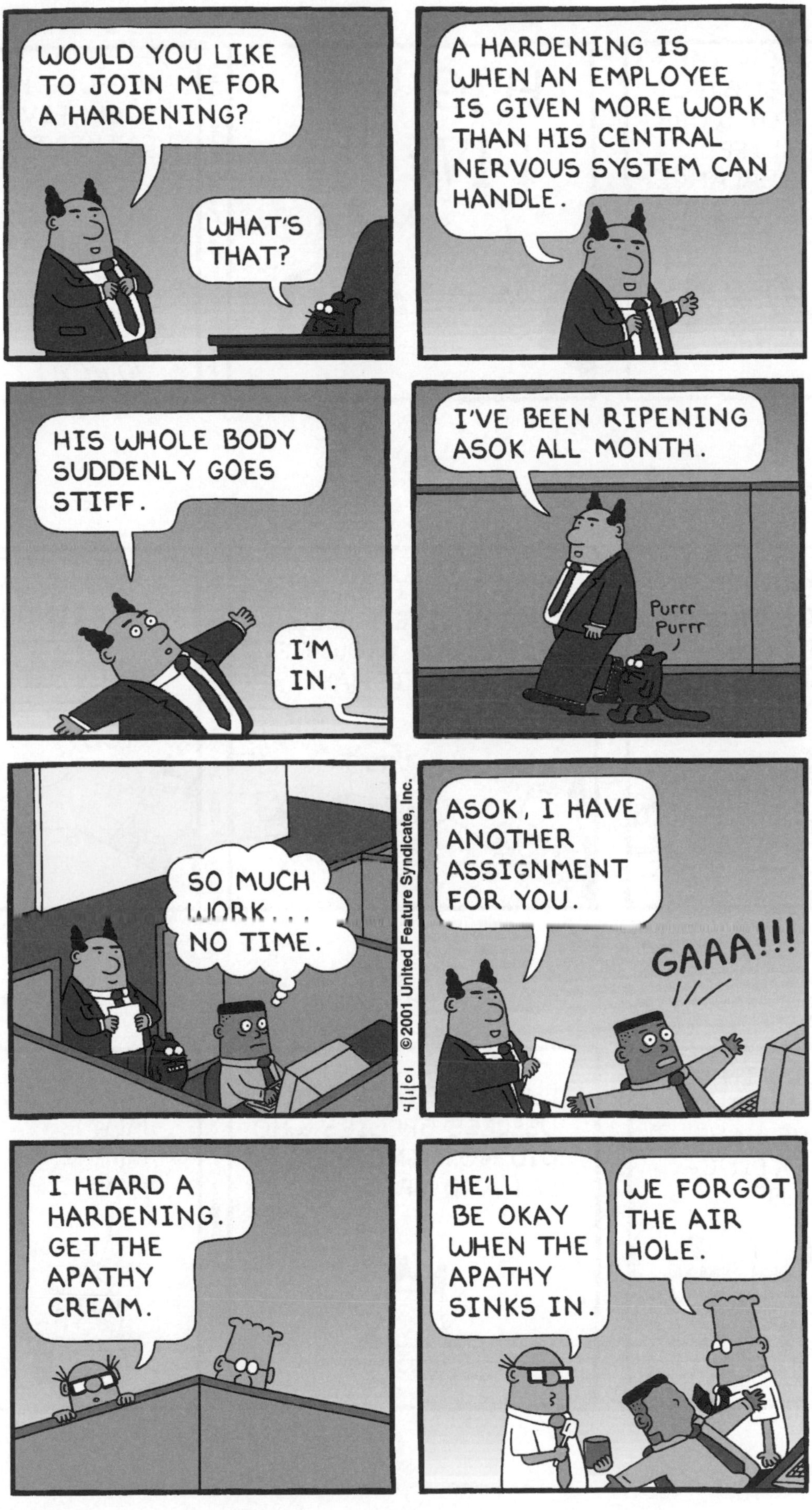

WOULD YOU LIKE TO JOIN ME FOR A HARDENING?
WHAT'S THAT?
A HARDENING IS WHEN AN EMPLOYEE IS GIVEN MORE WORK THAN HIS CENTRAL NERVOUS SYSTEM CAN HANDLE.
HIS WHOLE BODY SUDDENLY GOES STIFF.
I'M IN.
I'VE BEEN RIPENING ASOK ALL MONTH.
Purrr Purrr
SO MUCH WORK... NO TIME.
©2001 United Feature Syndicate, Inc.
4/1/01
ASOK, I HAVE ANOTHER ASSIGNMENT FOR YOU.
GAAA!!!
I HEARD A HARDENING. GET THE APATHY CREAM.
HE'LL BE OKAY WHEN THE APATHY SINKS IN.
WE FORGOT THE AIR HOLE.

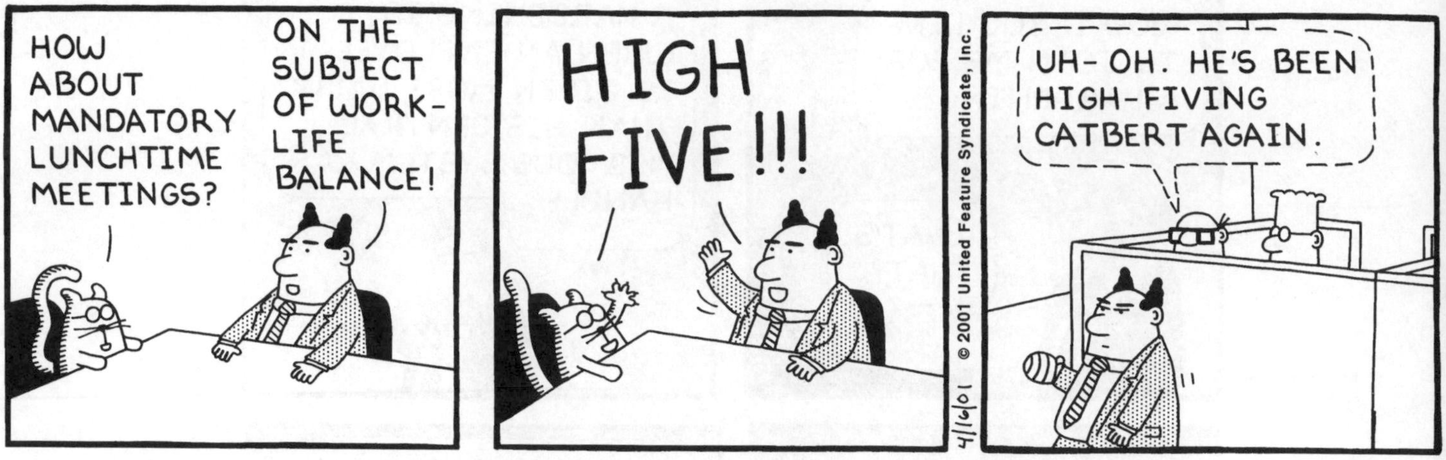
HOW ABOUT MANDATORY LUNCHTIME MEETINGS?
ON THE SUBJECT OF WORK-LIFE BALANCE!
HIGH FIVE!!!
UH-OH. HE'S BEEN HIGH-FIVING CATBERT AGAIN.
4/6/01 © 2001 United Feature Syndicate, Inc.

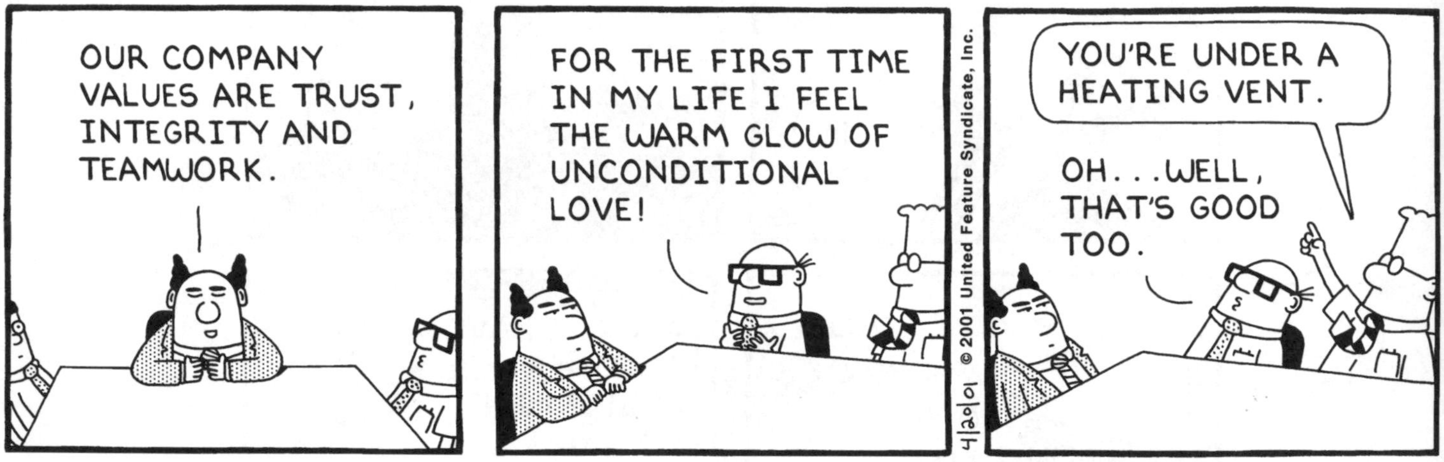
OUR COMPANY VALUES ARE TRUST, INTEGRITY AND TEAMWORK.
FOR THE FIRST TIME IN MY LIFE I FEEL THE WARM GLOW OF UNCONDITIONAL LOVE!
YOU'RE UNDER A HEATING VENT.
OH...WELL, THAT'S GOOD TOO.
4/20/01 © 2001 United Feature Syndicate, Inc.

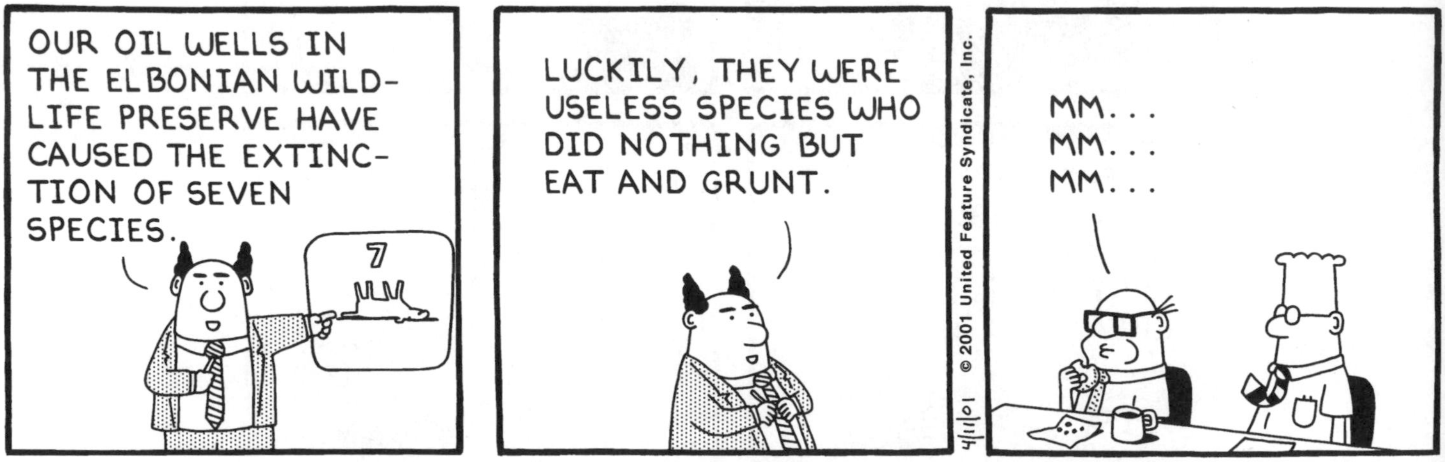
OUR OIL WELLS IN THE ELBONIAN WILD-LIFE PRESERVE HAVE CAUSED THE EXTINC-TION OF SEVEN SPECIES.
7
LUCKILY, THEY WERE USELESS SPECIES WHO DID NOTHING BUT EAT AND GRUNT.
MM... MM... MM...
4/11/01 © 2001 United Feature Syndicate, Inc.

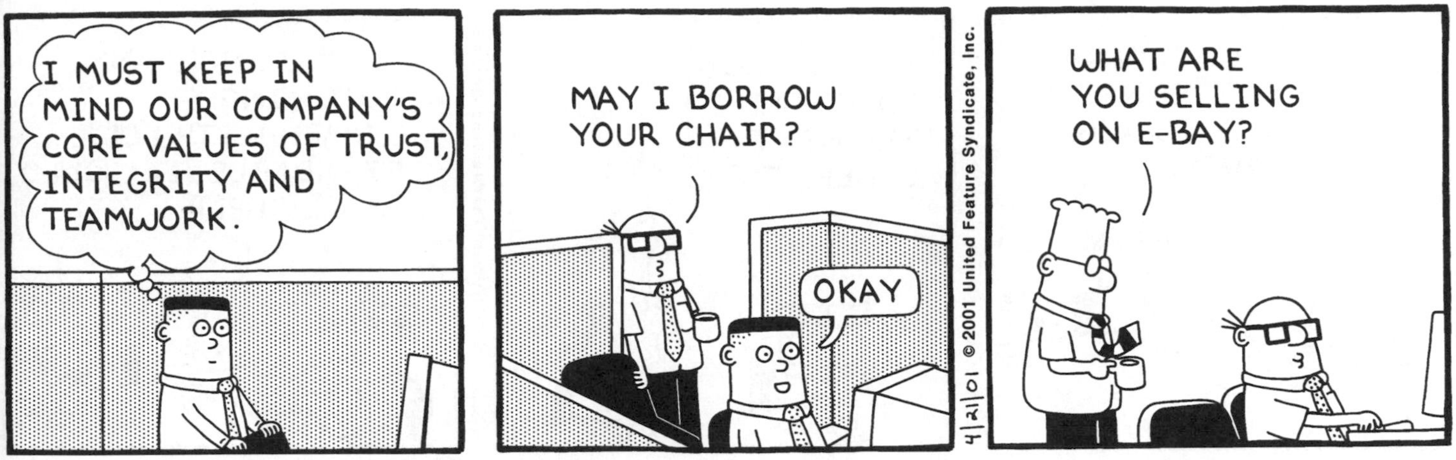
I MUST KEEP IN MIND OUR COMPANY'S CORE VALUES OF TRUST, INTEGRITY AND TEAMWORK.
MAY I BORROW YOUR CHAIR?
OKAY
4/21/01 © 2001 United Feature Syndicate, Inc.
WHAT ARE YOU SELLING ON E-BAY?

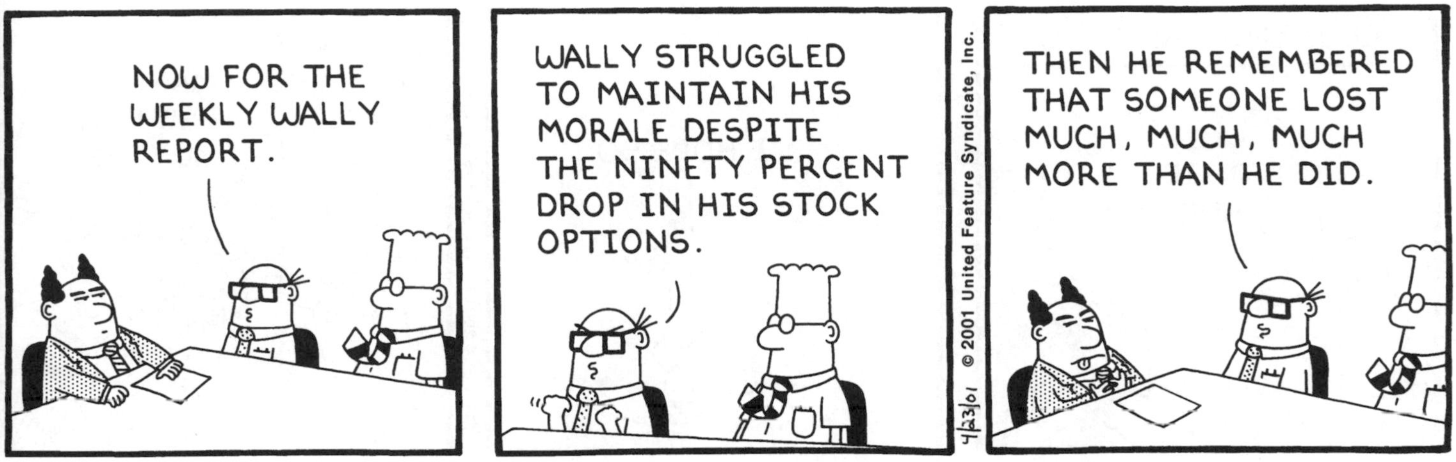
NOW FOR THE WEEKLY WALLY REPORT.
WALLY STRUGGLED TO MAINTAIN HIS MORALE DESPITE THE NINETY PERCENT DROP IN HIS STOCK OPTIONS.
4/23/01 © 2001 United Feature Syndicate, Inc.
THEN HE REMEMBERED THAT SOMEONE LOST MUCH, MUCH, MUCH MORE THAN HE DID.

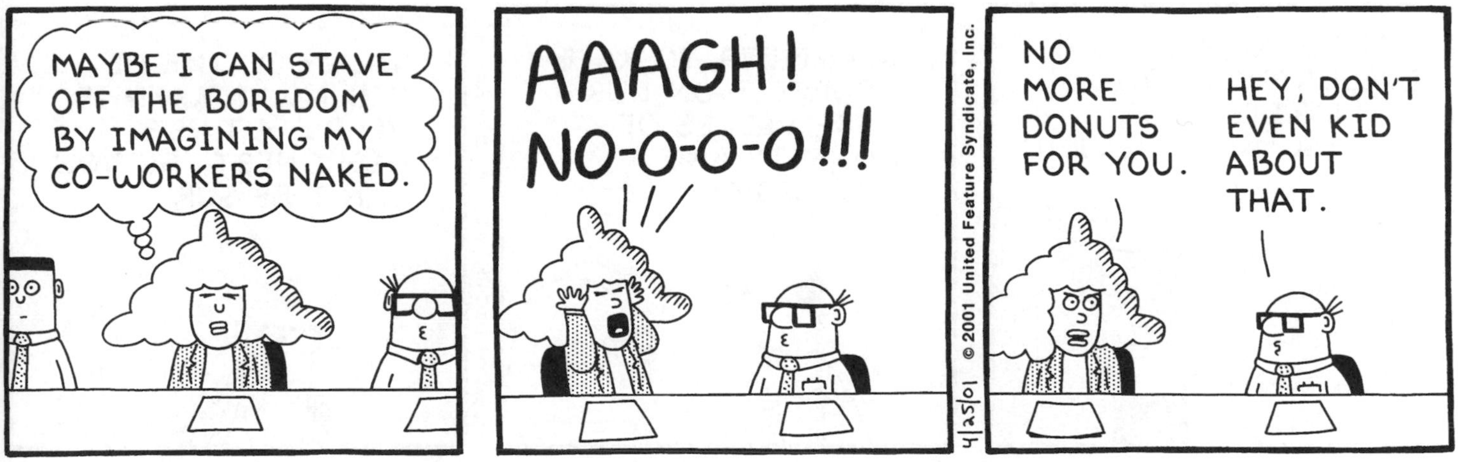
MAYBE I CAN STAVE OFF THE BOREDOM BY IMAGINING MY CO-WORKERS NAKED.
AAAGH! NO-O-O-O!!!
4/25/01 © 2001 United Feature Syndicate, Inc.
NO MORE DONUTS FOR YOU.
HEY, DON'T EVEN KID ABOUT THAT.

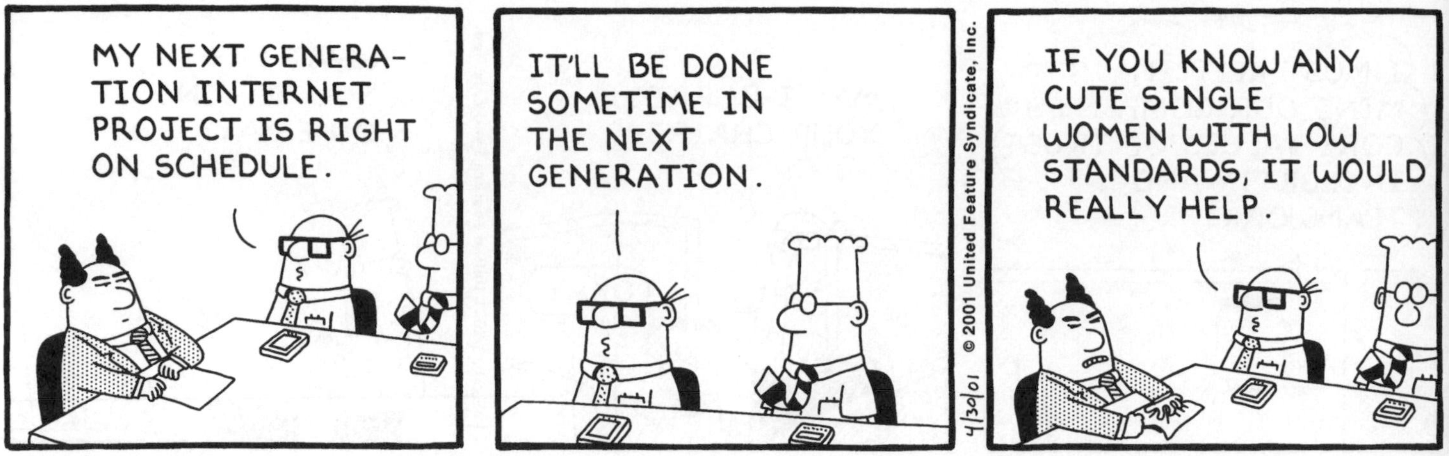
MY NEXT GENERATION INTERNET PROJECT IS RIGHT ON SCHEDULE.
IT'LL BE DONE SOMETIME IN THE NEXT GENERATION.
4/30/01 © 2001 United Feature Syndicate, Inc.
IF YOU KNOW ANY CUTE SINGLE WOMEN WITH LOW STANDARDS, IT WOULD REALLY HELP.

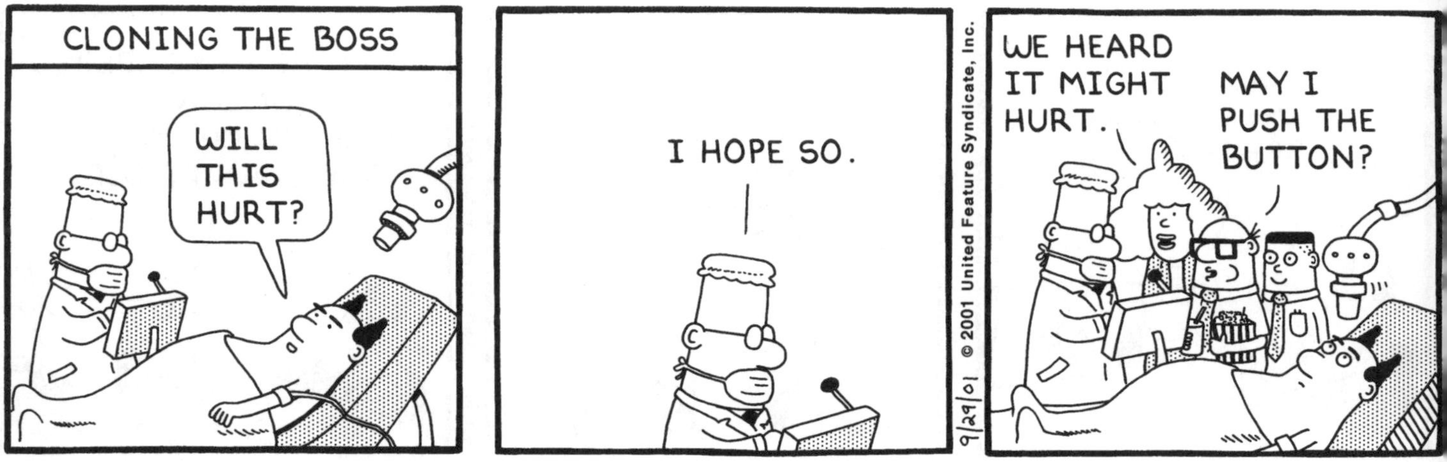
CLONING THE BOSS
WILL THIS HURT?
I HOPE SO.
9/29/01 © 2001 United Feature Syndicate, Inc.
WE HEARD IT MIGHT HURT.
MAY I PUSH THE BUTTON?

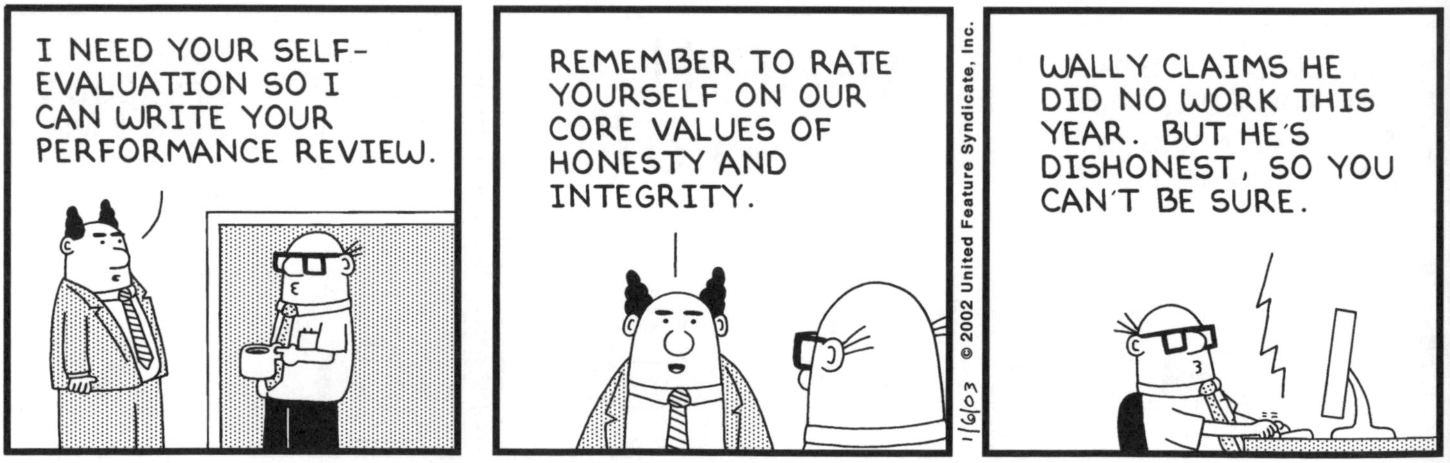
I NEED YOUR SELF-EVALUATION SO I CAN WRITE YOUR PERFORMANCE REVIEW.
REMEMBER TO RATE YOURSELF ON OUR CORE VALUES OF HONESTY AND INTEGRITY.
1/6/03 © 2002 United Feature Syndicate, Inc.
WALLY CLAIMS HE DID NO WORK THIS YEAR. BUT HE'S DISHONEST, SO YOU CAN'T BE SURE.

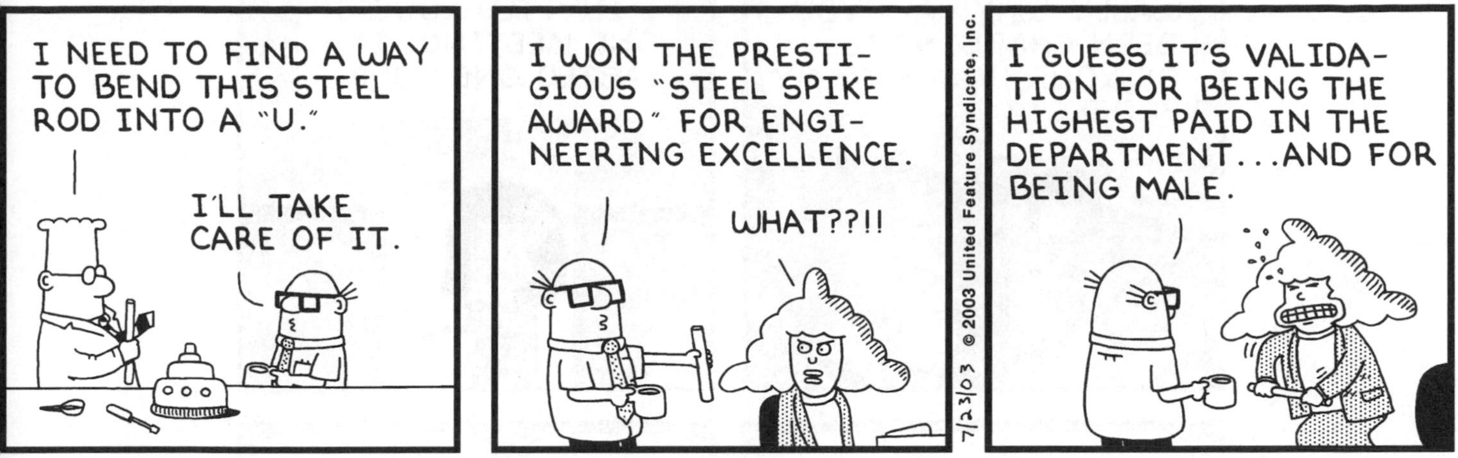
I NEED TO FIND A WAY TO BEND THIS STEEL ROD INTO A "U."
I'LL TAKE CARE OF IT.
I WON THE PRESTIGIOUS "STEEL SPIKE AWARD" FOR ENGINEERING EXCELLENCE.
WHAT??!!
7/23/03 © 2003 United Feature Syndicate, Inc.
I GUESS IT'S VALIDATION FOR BEING THE HIGHEST PAID IN THE DEPARTMENT...AND FOR BEING MALE.

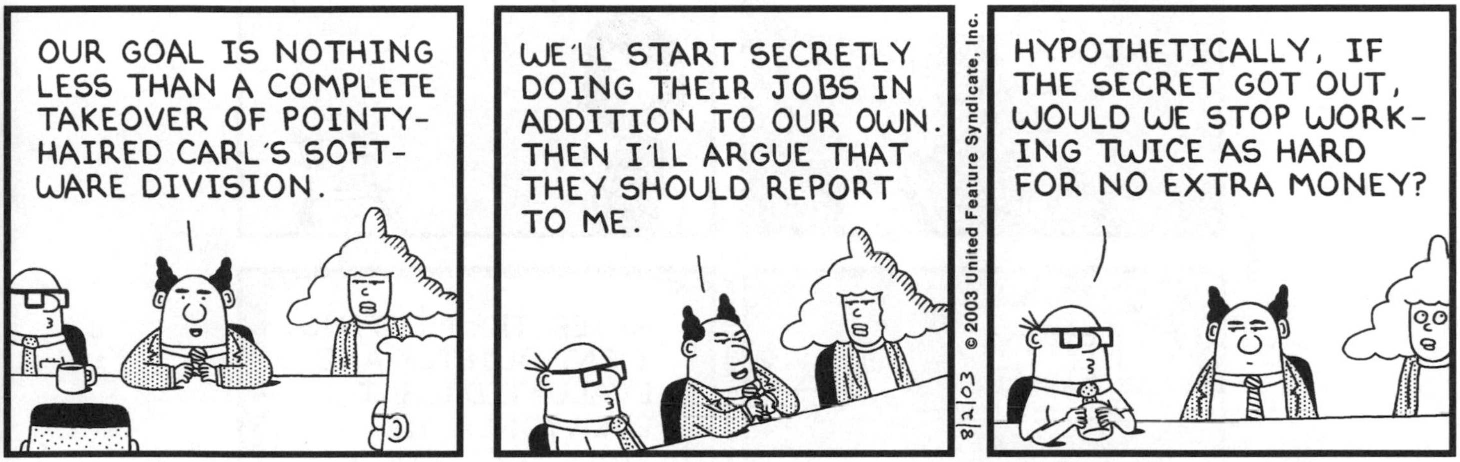
OUR GOAL IS NOTHING LESS THAN A COMPLETE TAKEOVER OF POINTY-HAIRED CARL'S SOFTWARE DIVISION.
WE'LL START SECRETLY DOING THEIR JOBS IN ADDITION TO OUR OWN. THEN I'LL ARGUE THAT THEY SHOULD REPORT TO ME.
8/2/03 © 2003 United Feature Syndicate, Inc.
HYPOTHETICALLY, IF THE SECRET GOT OUT, WOULD WE STOP WORKING TWICE AS HARD FOR NO EXTRA MONEY?

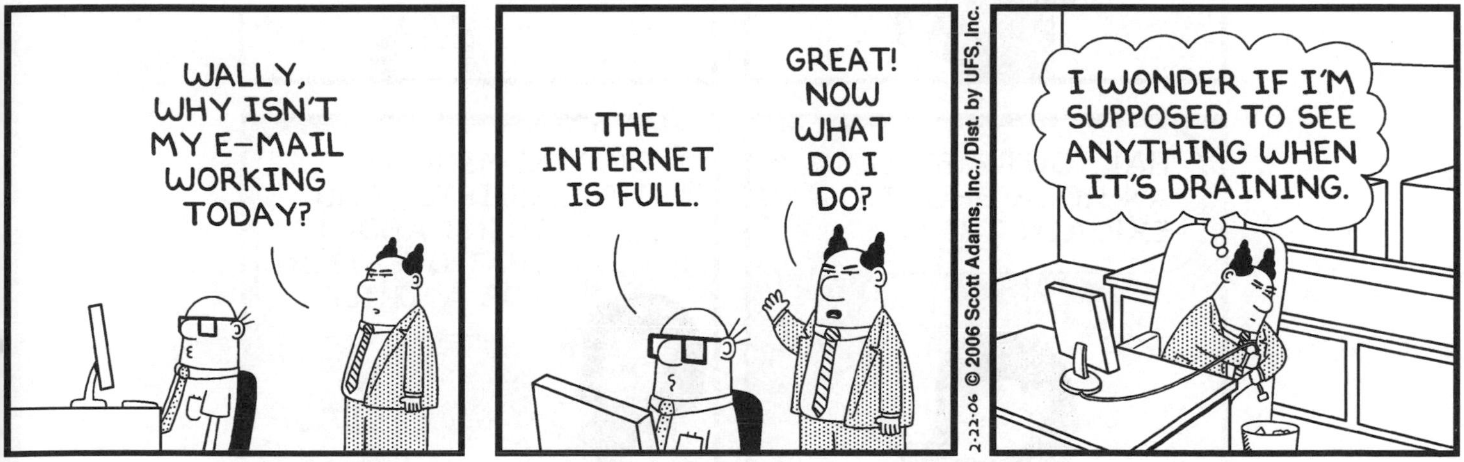
WALLY, WHY ISN'T MY E-MAIL WORKING TODAY?
THE INTERNET IS FULL.
GREAT! NOW WHAT DO I DO?
2-22-06 © 2006 Scott Adams, Inc./Dist. by UFS, Inc.
I WONDER IF I'M SUPPOSED TO SEE ANYTHING WHEN IT'S DRAINING.

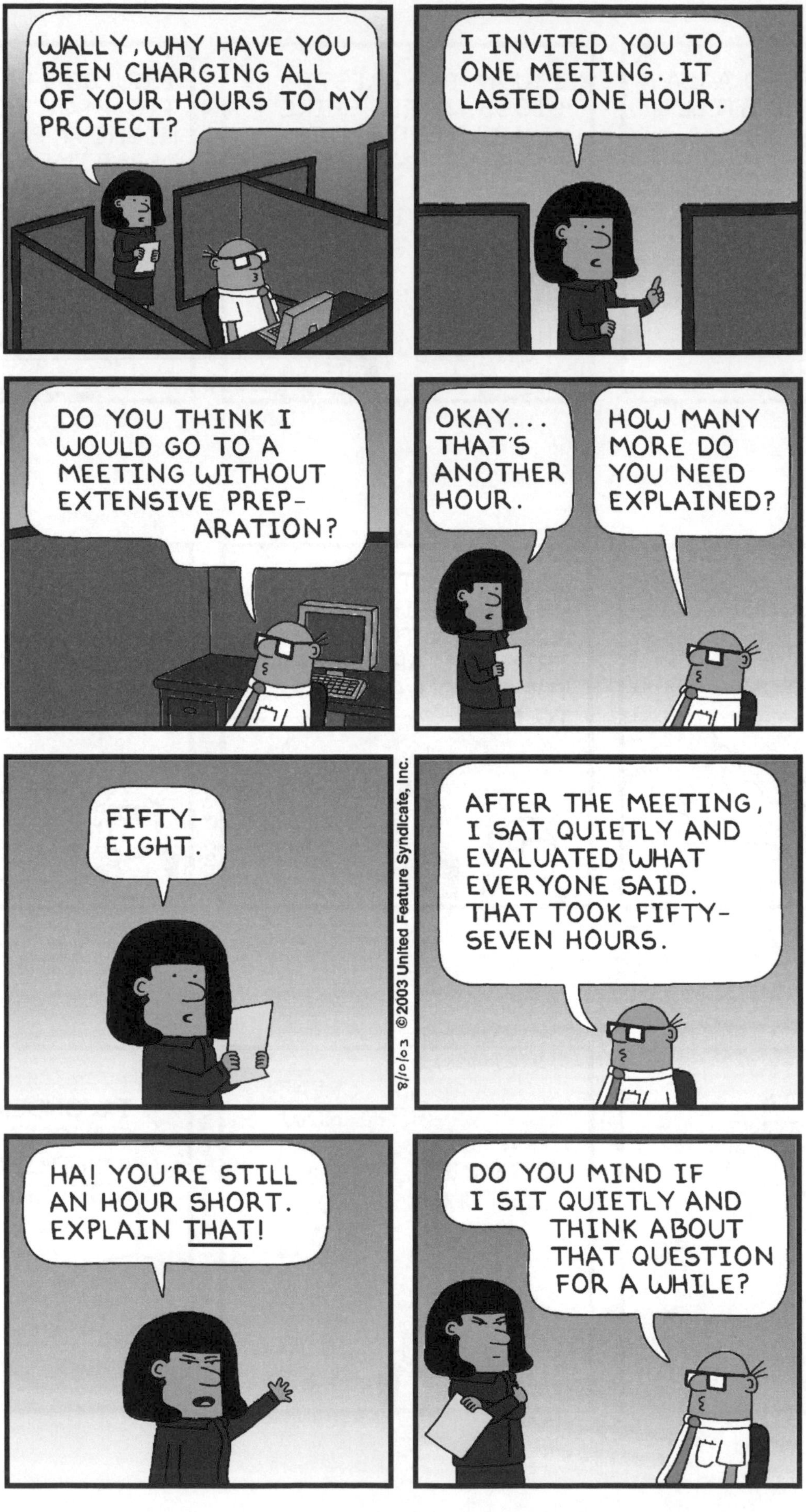
WALLY, WHY HAVE YOU BEEN CHARGING ALL OF YOUR HOURS TO MY PROJECT?
I INVITED YOU TO ONE MEETING. IT LASTED ONE HOUR.
DO YOU THINK I WOULD GO TO A MEETING WITHOUT EXTENSIVE PREP-ARATION?
OKAY... THAT'S ANOTHER HOUR.
HOW MANY MORE DO YOU NEED EXPLAINED?
FIFTY-EIGHT.
AFTER THE MEETING, I SAT QUIETLY AND EVALUATED WHAT EVERYONE SAID. THAT TOOK FIFTY-SEVEN HOURS.
HA! YOU'RE STILL AN HOUR SHORT. EXPLAIN THAT!
DO YOU MIND IF I SIT QUIETLY AND THINK ABOUT THAT QUESTION FOR A WHILE?
8/10/03

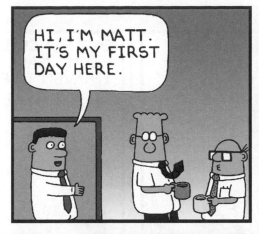

HI, I'M MATT. IT'S MY FIRST DAY HERE.

I'M DILBERT.

AND THIS IS...

I'D RATHER NOT SAY.

I PREFER TO REMAIN ANONYMOUS, SO YOU WON'T FEEL COMFORTABLE ASKING ME FOR ANYTHING LATER.

HERE'S MY CARD. IT'S BLANK.

THE PHRASE THAT YOU'RE LEAST LIKELY TO HEAR TODAY IS, "WE'RE JUST LIKE FAMILY."

ARE YOU WORRIED THAT HE'LL TURN OVER THE CARD AND SEE YOUR NAME?

NO.

WAS THAT MY CARD?

I'VE BEEN HANDING THEM OUT FOR YEARS.

8/31/03 © 2003 United Feature Syndicate, Inc.

155

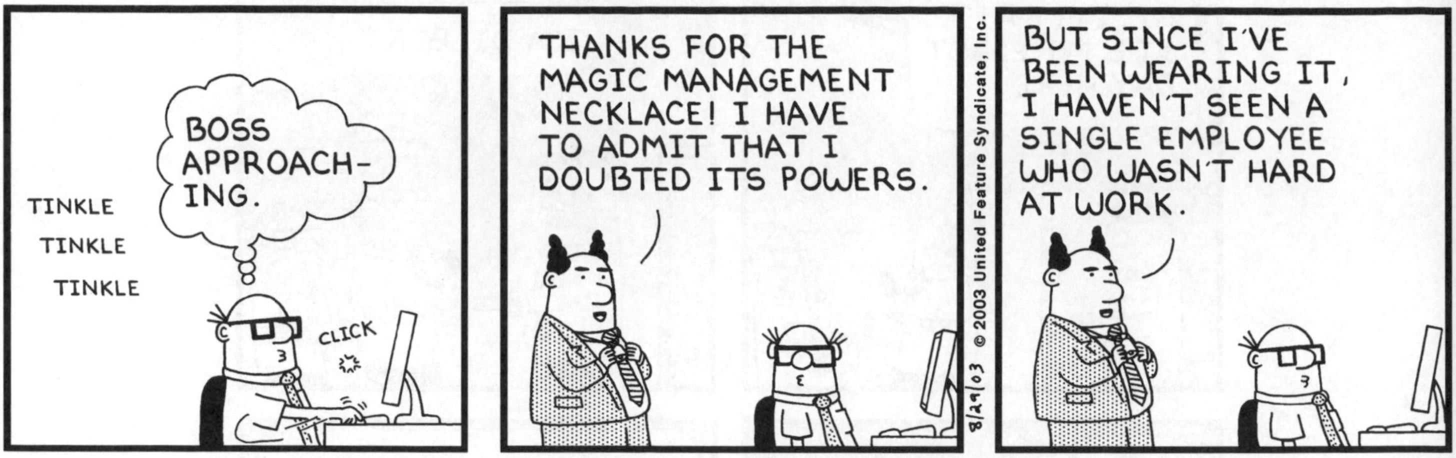
TINKLE
TINKLE
TINKLE
BOSS APPROACH-ING.
CLICK
THANKS FOR THE MAGIC MANAGEMENT NECKLACE! I HAVE TO ADMIT THAT I DOUBTED ITS POWERS.
8/29/03 © 2003 United Feature Syndicate, Inc.
BUT SINCE I'VE BEEN WEARING IT, I HAVEN'T SEEN A SINGLE EMPLOYEE WHO WASN'T HARD AT WORK.

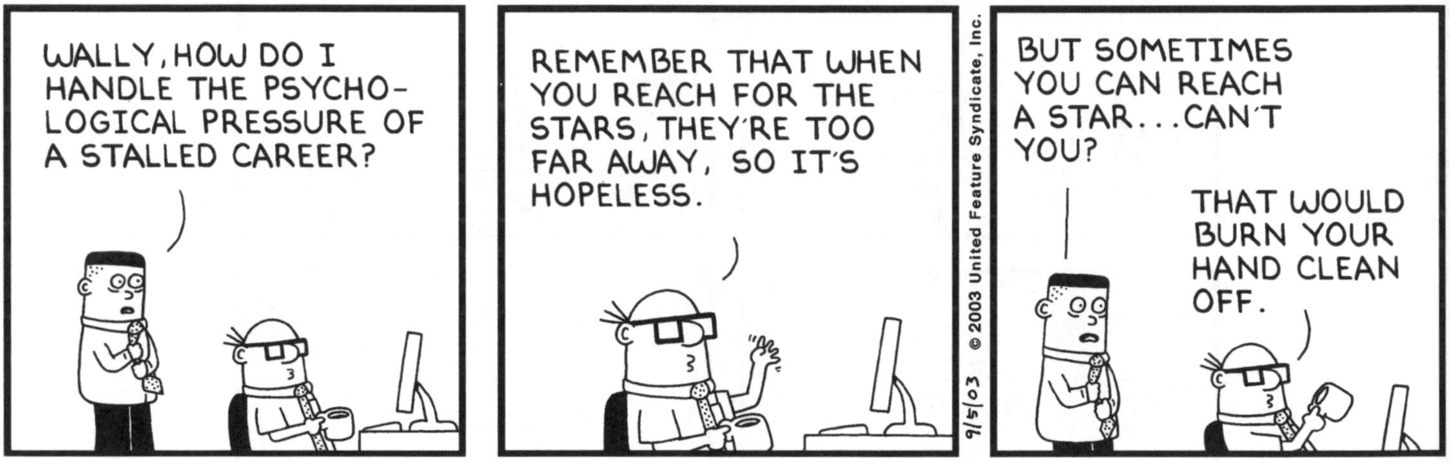
WALLY, HOW DO I HANDLE THE PSYCHO-LOGICAL PRESSURE OF A STALLED CAREER?
REMEMBER THAT WHEN YOU REACH FOR THE STARS, THEY'RE TOO FAR AWAY, SO IT'S HOPELESS.
9/5/03 © 2003 United Feature Syndicate, Inc.
BUT SOMETIMES YOU CAN REACH A STAR...CAN'T YOU?
THAT WOULD BURN YOUR HAND CLEAN OFF.

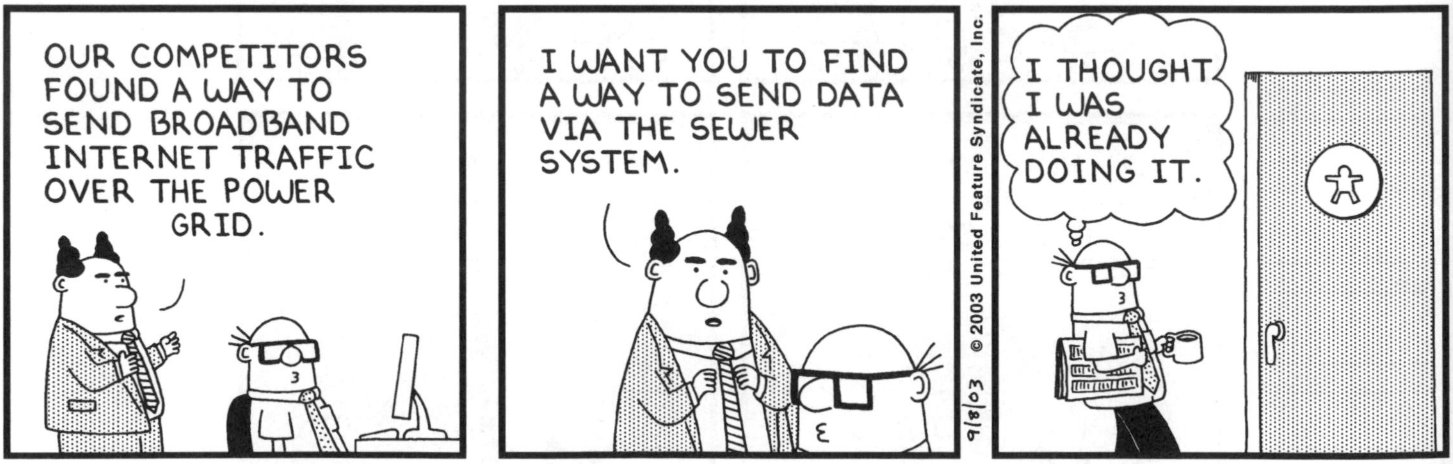
OUR COMPETITORS FOUND A WAY TO SEND BROADBAND INTERNET TRAFFIC OVER THE POWER GRID.
I WANT YOU TO FIND A WAY TO SEND DATA VIA THE SEWER SYSTEM.
9/8/03 © 2003 United Feature Syndicate, Inc.
I THOUGHT I WAS ALREADY DOING IT.

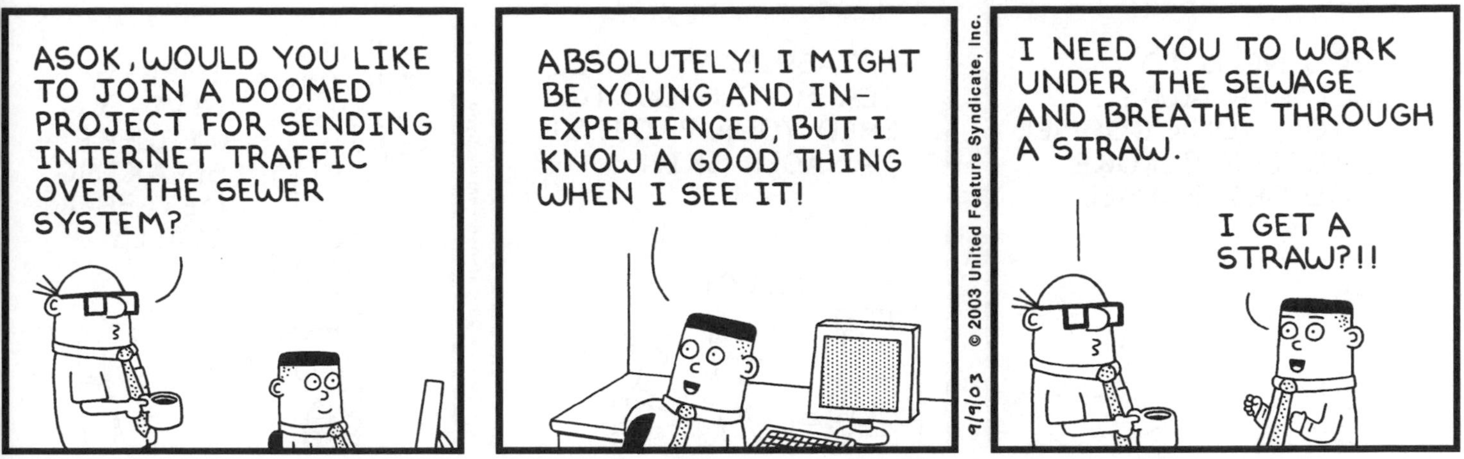
ASOK, WOULD YOU LIKE TO JOIN A DOOMED PROJECT FOR SENDING INTERNET TRAFFIC OVER THE SEWER SYSTEM?
ABSOLUTELY! I MIGHT BE YOUNG AND IN-EXPERIENCED, BUT I KNOW A GOOD THING WHEN I SEE IT!
9/9/03 © 2003 United Feature Syndicate, Inc.
I NEED YOU TO WORK UNDER THE SEWAGE AND BREATHE THROUGH A STRAW.
I GET A STRAW?!!

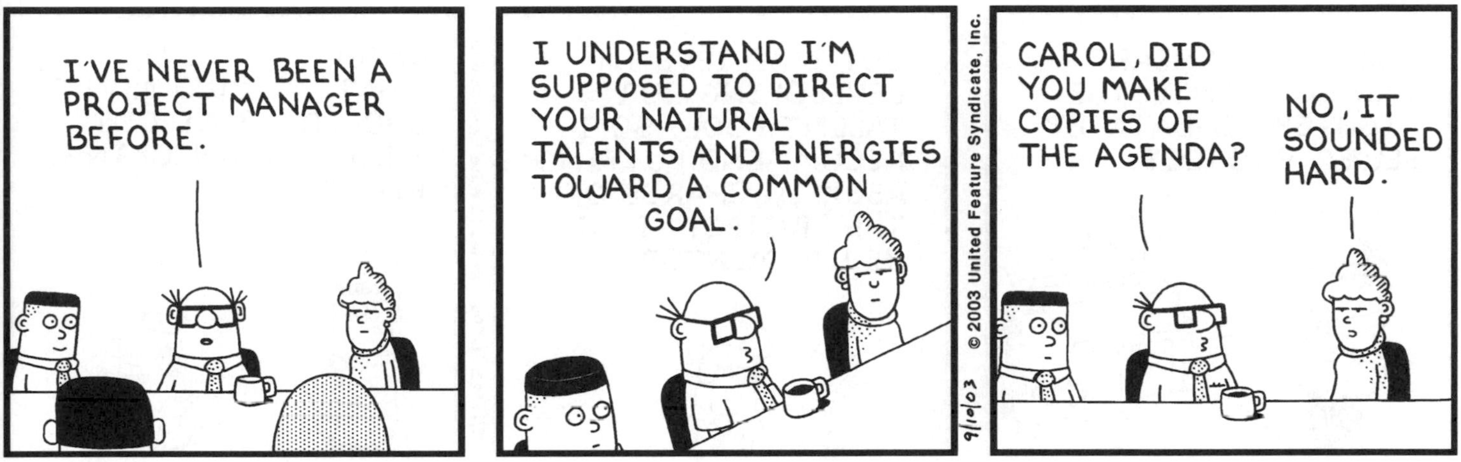
I'VE NEVER BEEN A PROJECT MANAGER BEFORE.
I UNDERSTAND I'M SUPPOSED TO DIRECT YOUR NATURAL TALENTS AND ENERGIES TOWARD A COMMON GOAL.
9/10/03 © 2003 United Feature Syndicate, Inc.
CAROL, DID YOU MAKE COPIES OF THE AGENDA?
NO, IT SOUNDED HARD.

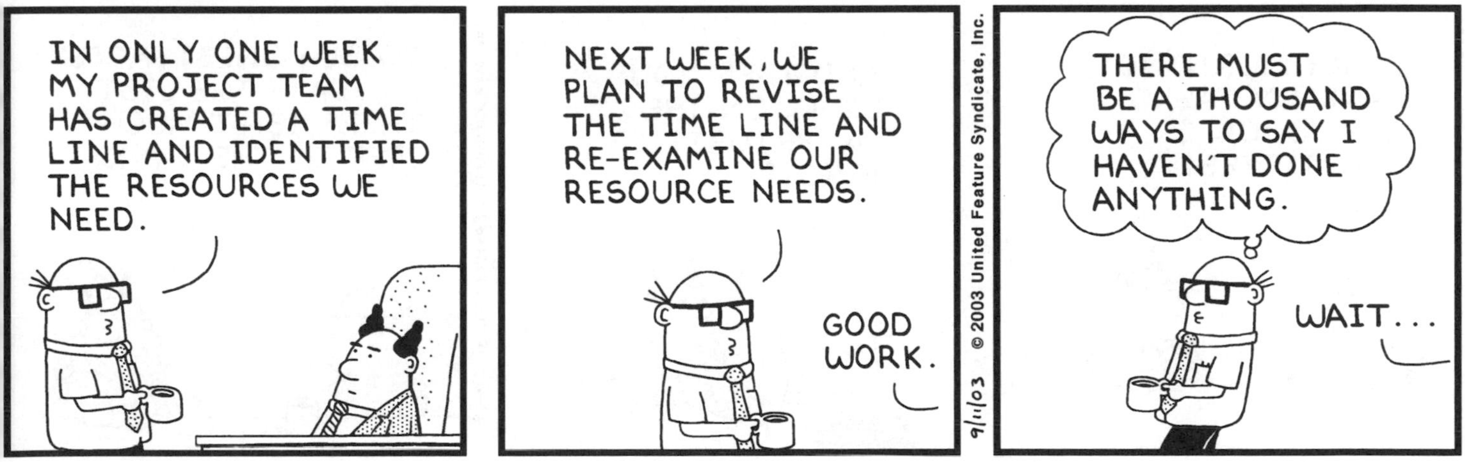
IN ONLY ONE WEEK MY PROJECT TEAM HAS CREATED A TIME LINE AND IDENTIFIED THE RESOURCES WE NEED.
NEXT WEEK, WE PLAN TO REVISE THE TIME LINE AND RE-EXAMINE OUR RESOURCE NEEDS.
GOOD WORK.
9/11/03 © 2003 United Feature Syndicate, Inc.
THERE MUST BE A THOUSAND WAYS TO SAY I HAVEN'T DONE ANYTHING.
WAIT...

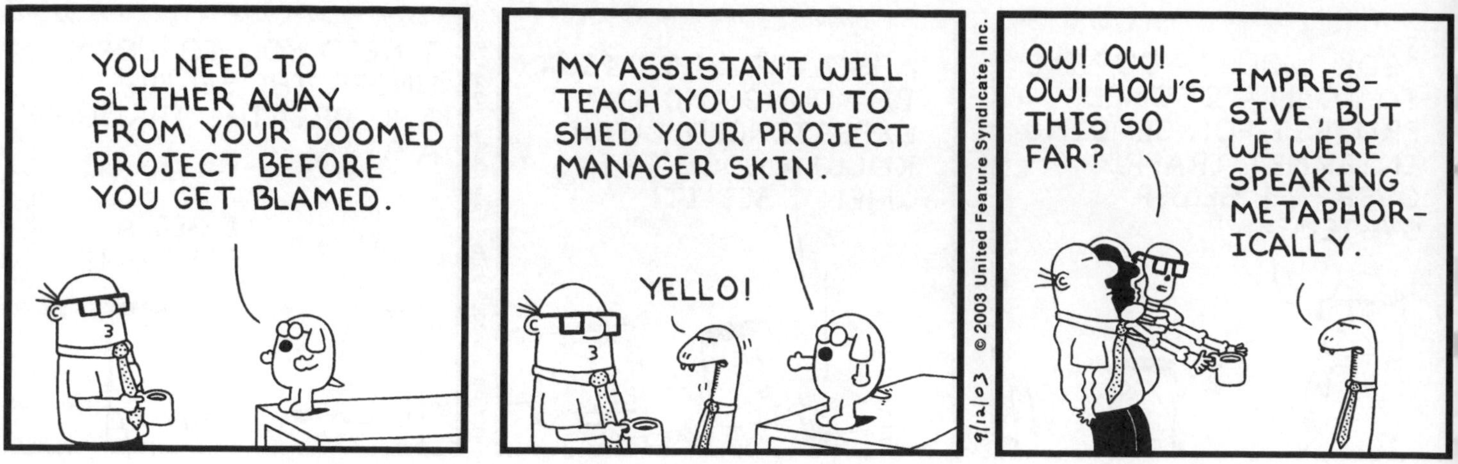
YOU NEED TO SLITHER AWAY FROM YOUR DOOMED PROJECT BEFORE YOU GET BLAMED.
MY ASSISTANT WILL TEACH YOU HOW TO SHED YOUR PROJECT MANAGER SKIN.
YELLO!
© 2003 United Feature Syndicate, Inc.
9/12/03
OW! OW! OW! HOW'S THIS SO FAR?
IMPRES-SIVE, BUT WE WERE SPEAKING METAPHOR-ICALLY.

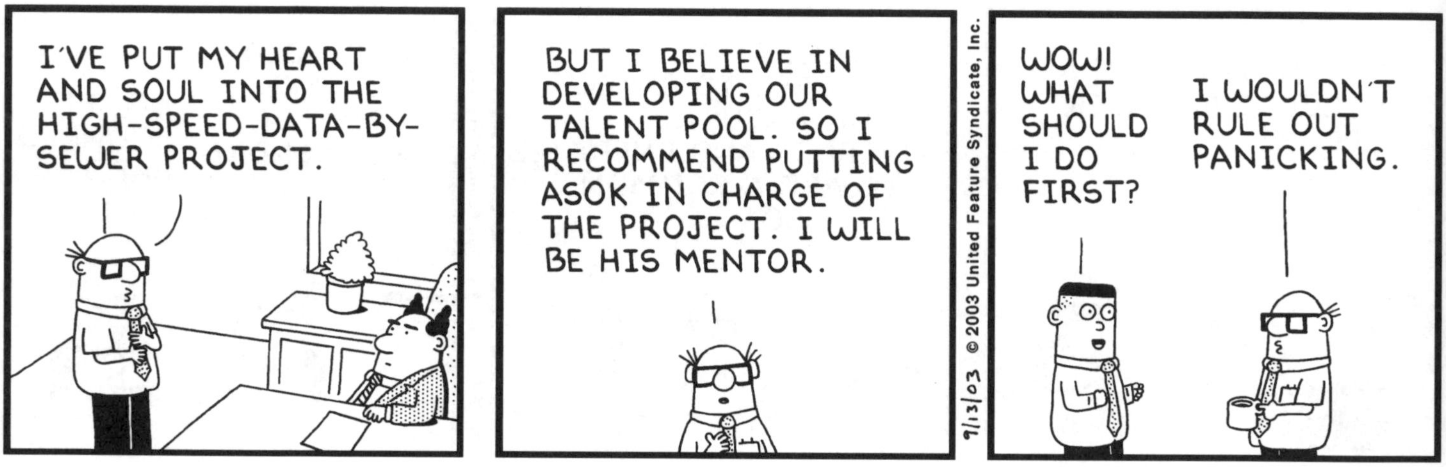
I'VE PUT MY HEART AND SOUL INTO THE HIGH-SPEED-DATA-BY-SEWER PROJECT.
BUT I BELIEVE IN DEVELOPING OUR TALENT POOL. SO I RECOMMEND PUTTING ASOK IN CHARGE OF THE PROJECT. I WILL BE HIS MENTOR.
© 2003 United Feature Syndicate, Inc.
9/13/03
WOW! WHAT SHOULD I DO FIRST?
I WOULDN'T RULE OUT PANICKING.

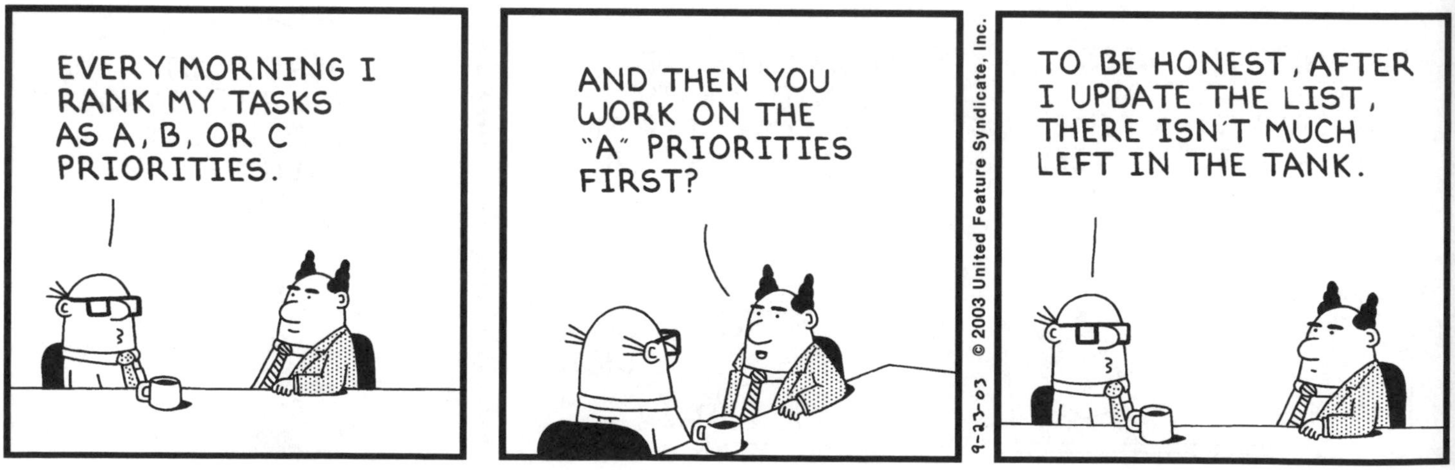
EVERY MORNING I RANK MY TASKS AS A, B, OR C PRIORITIES.
AND THEN YOU WORK ON THE "A" PRIORITIES FIRST?
© 2003 United Feature Syndicate, Inc.
9-23-03
TO BE HONEST, AFTER I UPDATE THE LIST, THERE ISN'T MUCH LEFT IN THE TANK.

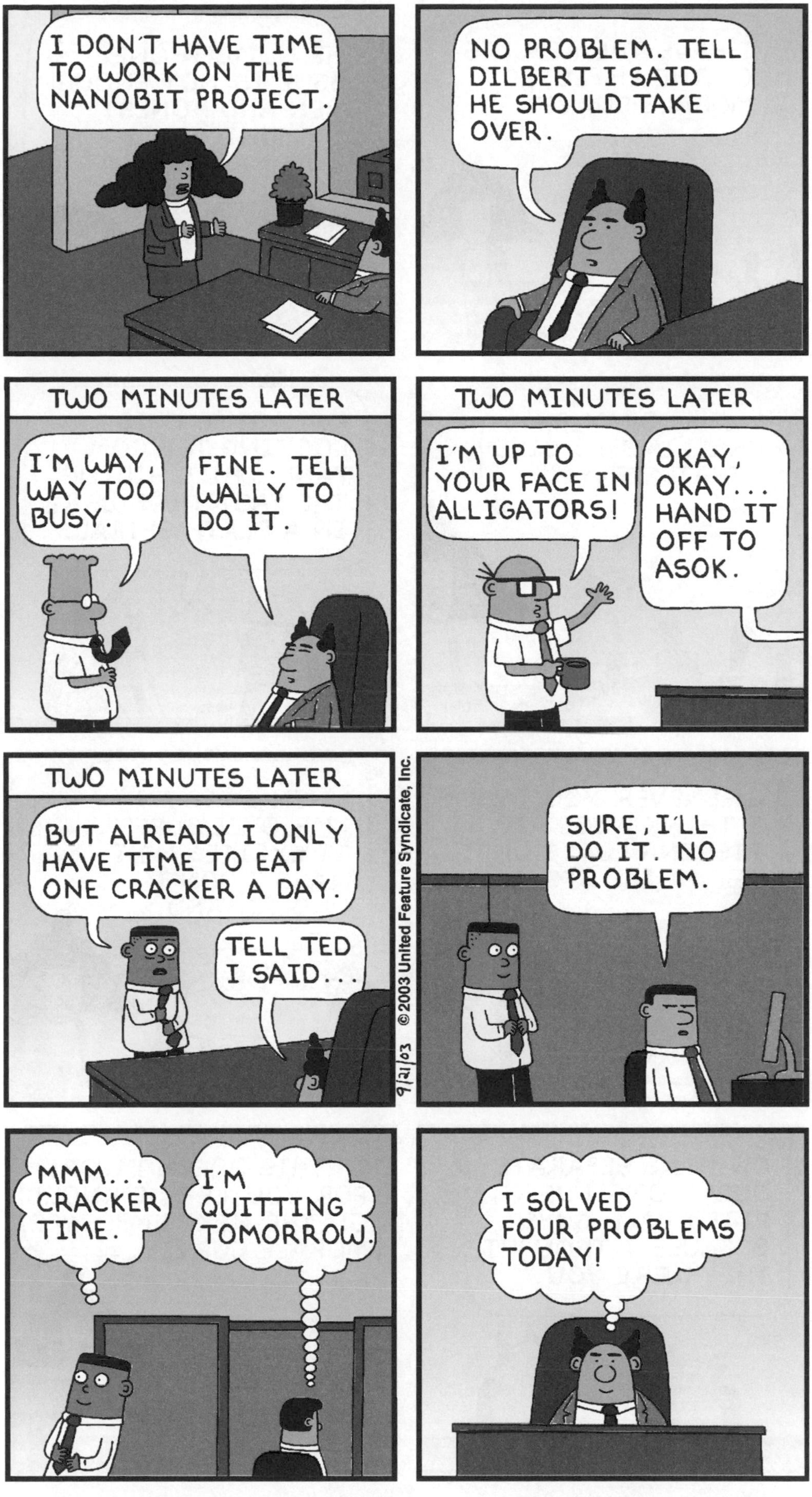
I DON'T HAVE TIME TO WORK ON THE NANOBIT PROJECT.
NO PROBLEM. TELL DILBERT I SAID HE SHOULD TAKE OVER.
TWO MINUTES LATER
I'M WAY, WAY TOO BUSY.
FINE. TELL WALLY TO DO IT.
TWO MINUTES LATER
I'M UP TO YOUR FACE IN ALLIGATORS!
OKAY, OKAY... HAND IT OFF TO ASOK.
TWO MINUTES LATER
BUT ALREADY I ONLY HAVE TIME TO EAT ONE CRACKER A DAY.
TELL TED I SAID...
SURE, I'LL DO IT. NO PROBLEM.
MMM... CRACKER TIME.
I'M QUITTING TOMORROW.
I SOLVED FOUR PROBLEMS TODAY!
©2003 United Feature Syndicate, Inc.
9/21/03

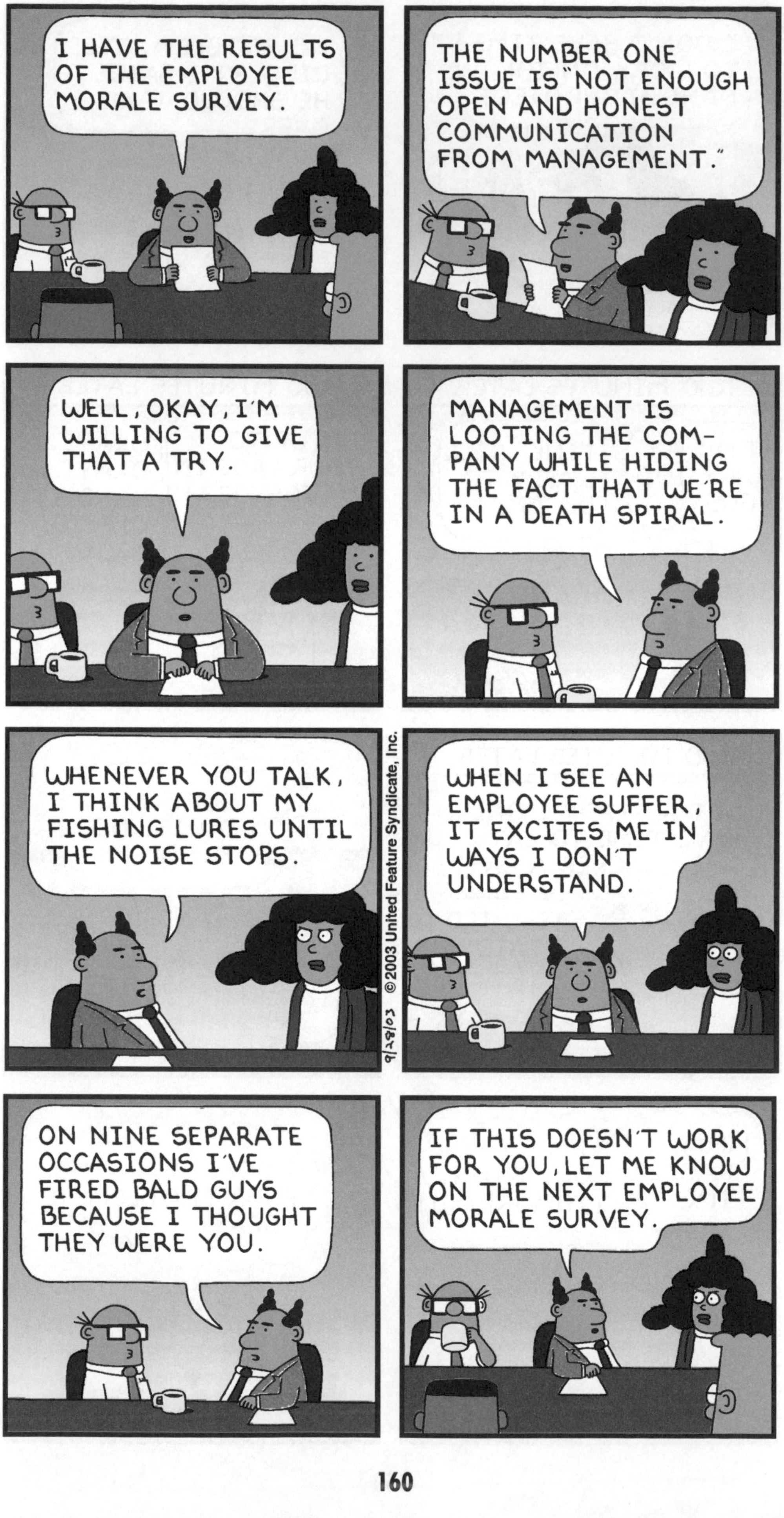
I HAVE THE RESULTS OF THE EMPLOYEE MORALE SURVEY.
THE NUMBER ONE ISSUE IS "NOT ENOUGH OPEN AND HONEST COMMUNICATION FROM MANAGEMENT."
WELL, OKAY, I'M WILLING TO GIVE THAT A TRY.
MANAGEMENT IS LOOTING THE COM-PANY WHILE HIDING THE FACT THAT WE'RE IN A DEATH SPIRAL.
WHENEVER YOU TALK, I THINK ABOUT MY FISHING LURES UNTIL THE NOISE STOPS.
WHEN I SEE AN EMPLOYEE SUFFER, IT EXCITES ME IN WAYS I DON'T UNDERSTAND.
ON NINE SEPARATE OCCASIONS I'VE FIRED BALD GUYS BECAUSE I THOUGHT THEY WERE YOU.
IF THIS DOESN'T WORK FOR YOU, LET ME KNOW ON THE NEXT EMPLOYEE MORALE SURVEY.
9/28/03
©2003 United Feature Syndicate, Inc.

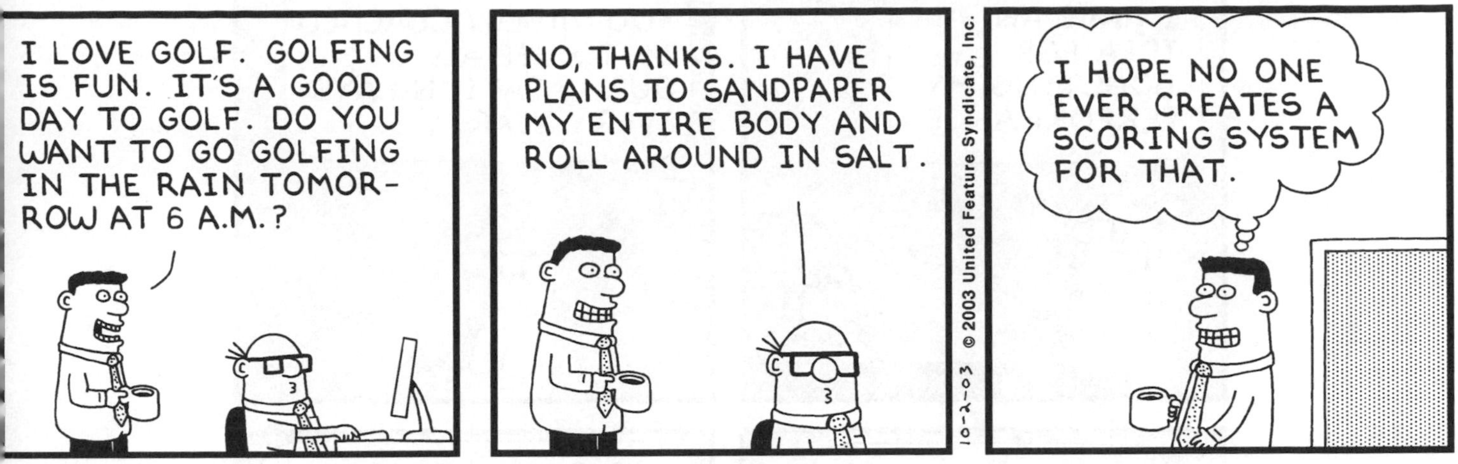
I LOVE GOLF. GOLFING IS FUN. IT'S A GOOD DAY TO GOLF. DO YOU WANT TO GO GOLFING IN THE RAIN TOMORROW AT 6 A.M.?
NO, THANKS. I HAVE PLANS TO SANDPAPER MY ENTIRE BODY AND ROLL AROUND IN SALT.
10-2-03 © 2003 United Feature Syndicate, Inc.
I HOPE NO ONE EVER CREATES A SCORING SYSTEM FOR THAT.

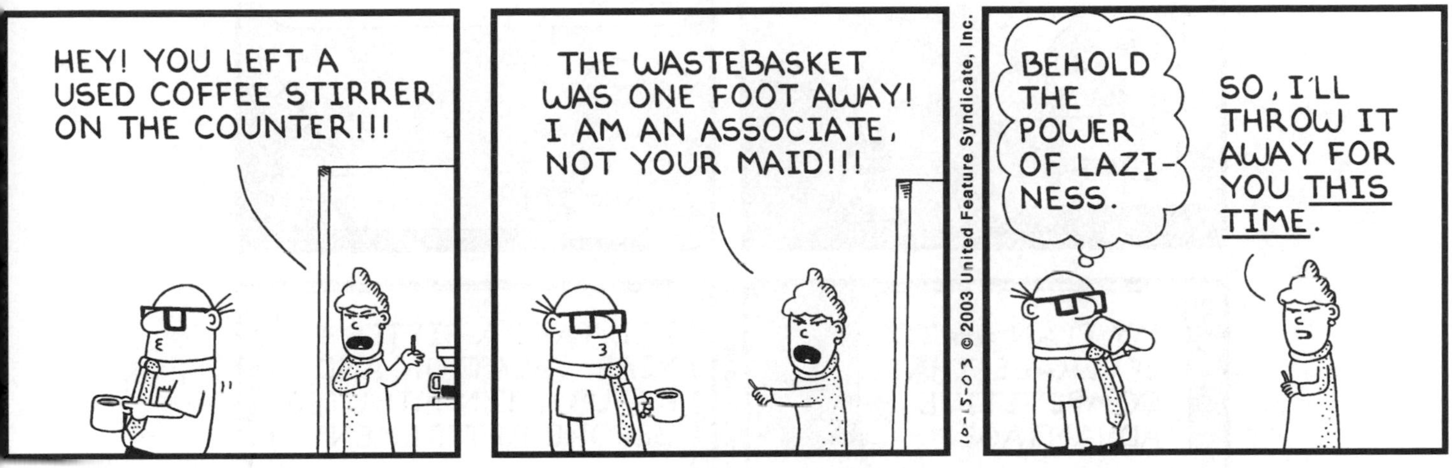
HEY! YOU LEFT A USED COFFEE STIRRER ON THE COUNTER!!!
THE WASTEBASKET WAS ONE FOOT AWAY! I AM AN ASSOCIATE, NOT YOUR MAID!!!
10-15-03 © 2003 United Feature Syndicate, Inc.
BEHOLD THE POWER OF LAZINESS.
SO, I'LL THROW IT AWAY FOR YOU THIS TIME.

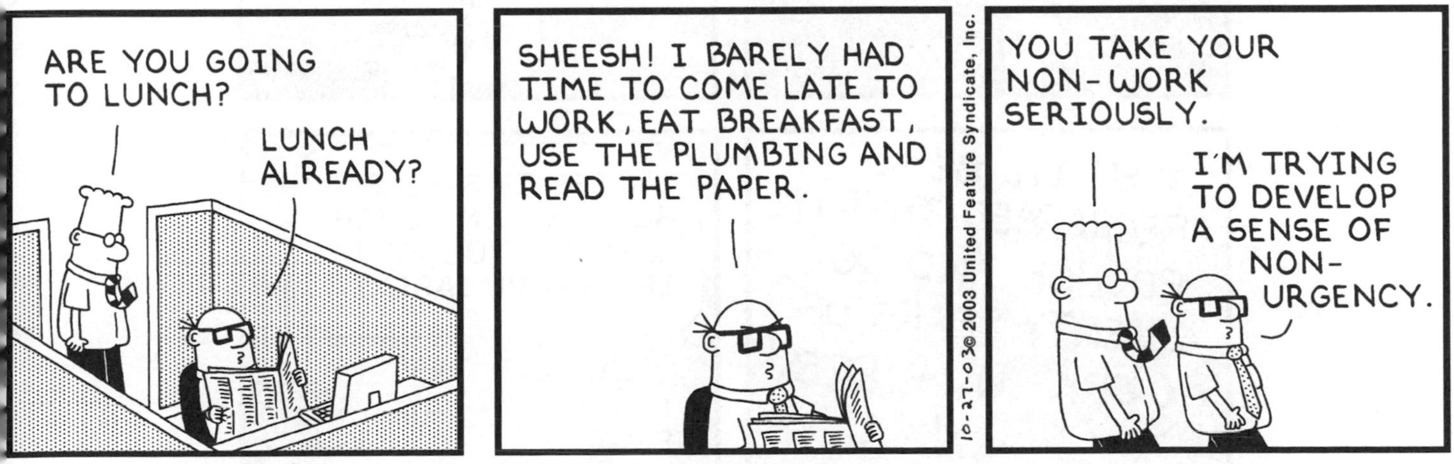
ARE YOU GOING TO LUNCH?
LUNCH ALREADY?
SHEESH! I BARELY HAD TIME TO COME LATE TO WORK, EAT BREAKFAST, USE THE PLUMBING AND READ THE PAPER.
10-27-03 © 2003 United Feature Syndicate, Inc.
YOU TAKE YOUR NON-WORK SERIOUSLY.
I'M TRYING TO DEVELOP A SENSE OF NON-URGENCY.

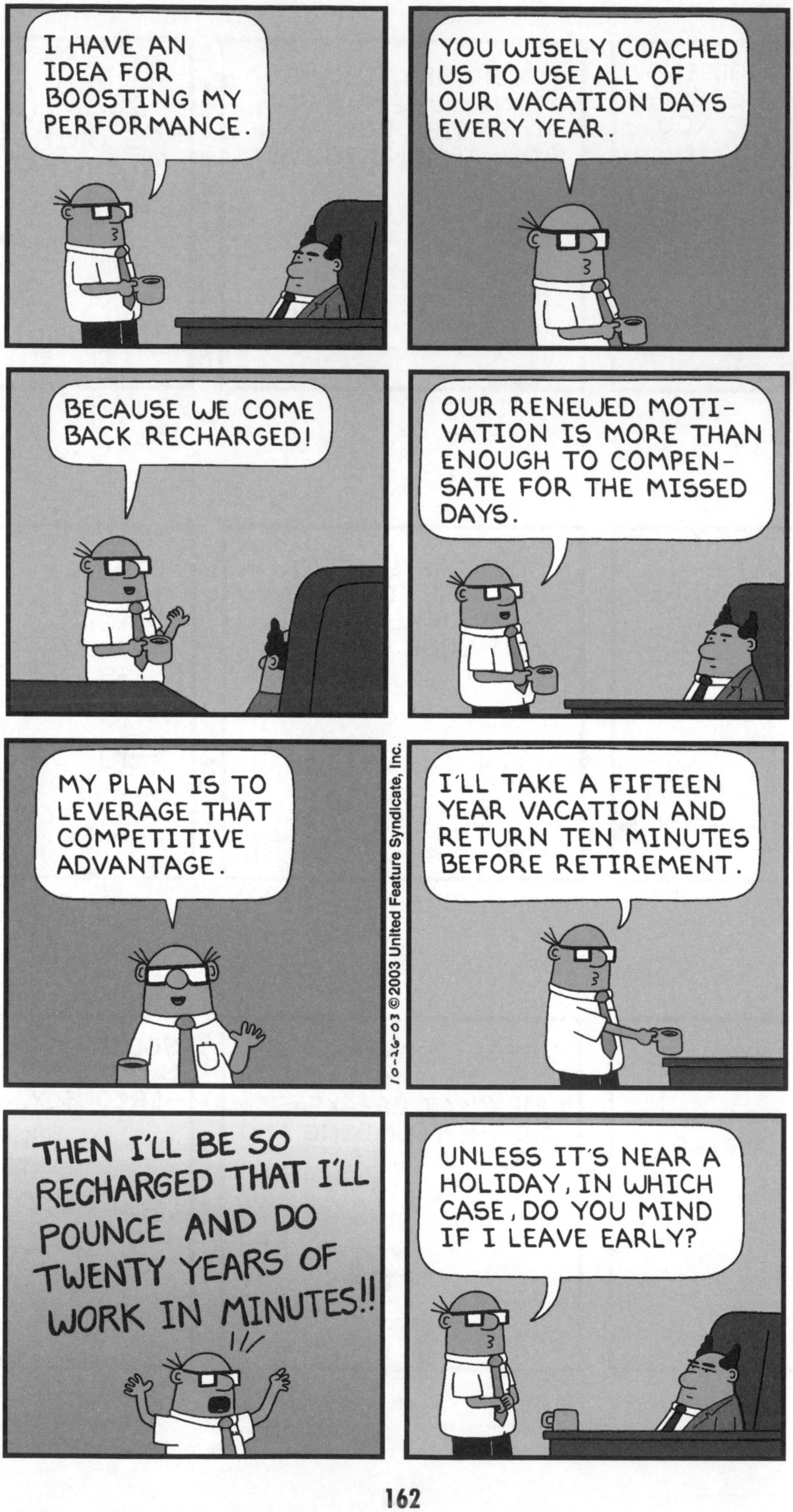
I HAVE AN IDEA FOR BOOSTING MY PERFORMANCE.
YOU WISELY COACHED US TO USE ALL OF OUR VACATION DAYS EVERY YEAR.
BECAUSE WE COME BACK RECHARGED!
OUR RENEWED MOTI- VATION IS MORE THAN ENOUGH TO COMPEN- SATE FOR THE MISSED DAYS.
MY PLAN IS TO LEVERAGE THAT COMPETITIVE ADVANTAGE.
I'LL TAKE A FIFTEEN YEAR VACATION AND RETURN TEN MINUTES BEFORE RETIREMENT.
THEN I'LL BE SO RECHARGED THAT I'LL POUNCE AND DO TWENTY YEARS OF WORK IN MINUTES!!
UNLESS IT'S NEAR A HOLIDAY, IN WHICH CASE, DO YOU MIND IF I LEAVE EARLY?
10-26-03 ©2003 United Feature Syndicate, Inc.

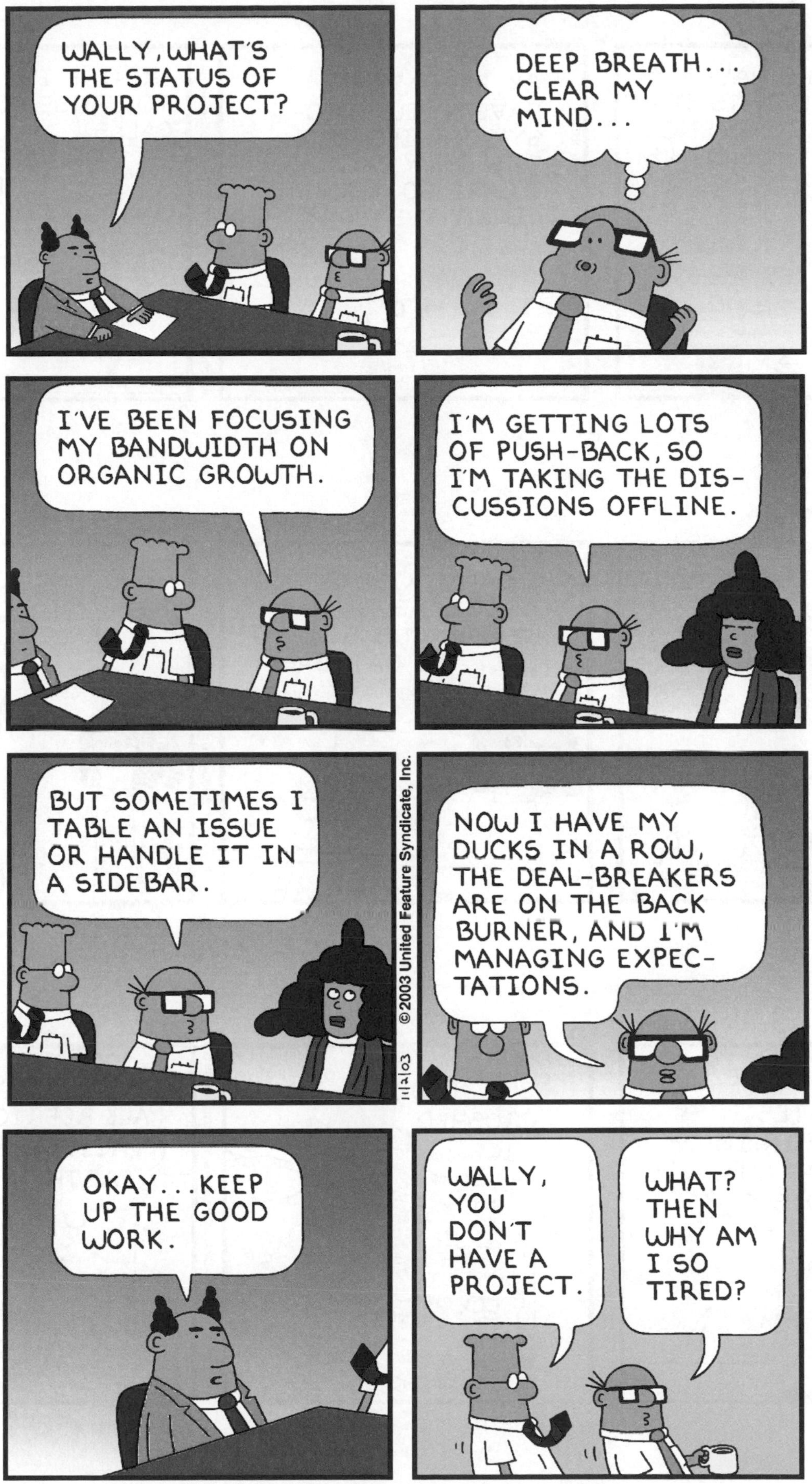
WALLY, WHAT'S THE STATUS OF YOUR PROJECT?
DEEP BREATH... CLEAR MY MIND...
I'VE BEEN FOCUSING MY BANDWIDTH ON ORGANIC GROWTH.
I'M GETTING LOTS OF PUSH-BACK, SO I'M TAKING THE DISCUSSIONS OFFLINE.
BUT SOMETIMES I TABLE AN ISSUE OR HANDLE IT IN A SIDEBAR.
©2003 United Feature Syndicate, Inc.
11/2/03
NOW I HAVE MY DUCKS IN A ROW, THE DEAL-BREAKERS ARE ON THE BACK BURNER, AND I'M MANAGING EXPECTATIONS.
OKAY...KEEP UP THE GOOD WORK.
WALLY, YOU DON'T HAVE A PROJECT.
WHAT? THEN WHY AM I SO TIRED?

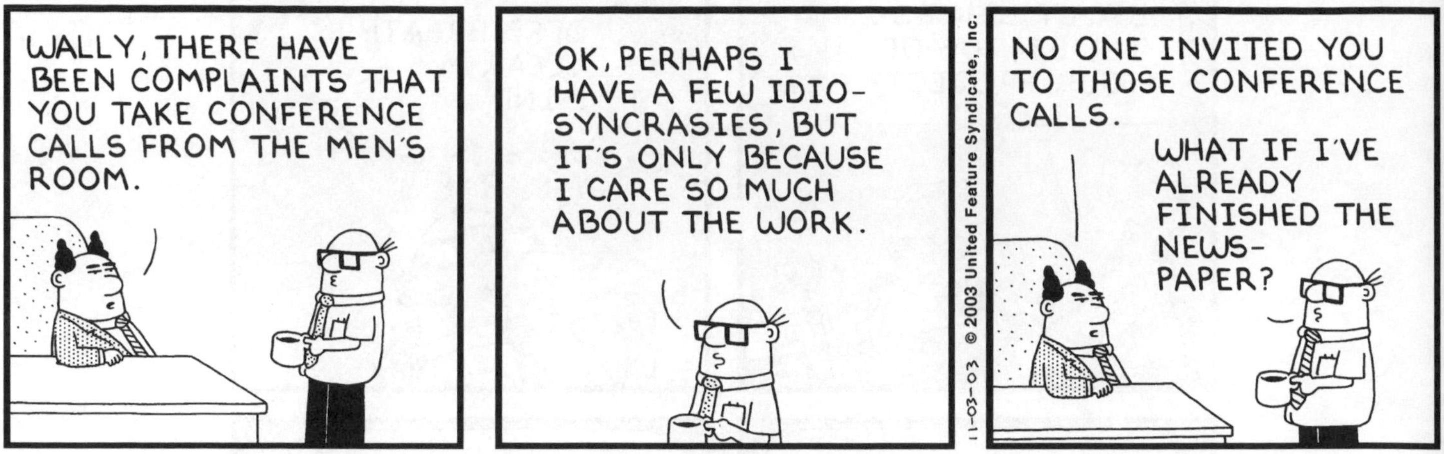
WALLY, THERE HAVE BEEN COMPLAINTS THAT YOU TAKE CONFERENCE CALLS FROM THE MEN'S ROOM.
OK, PERHAPS I HAVE A FEW IDIO-SYNCRASIES, BUT IT'S ONLY BECAUSE I CARE SO MUCH ABOUT THE WORK.
11-03-03 © 2003 United Feature Syndicate, Inc.
NO ONE INVITED YOU TO THOSE CONFERENCE CALLS.
WHAT IF I'VE ALREADY FINISHED THE NEWS-PAPER?

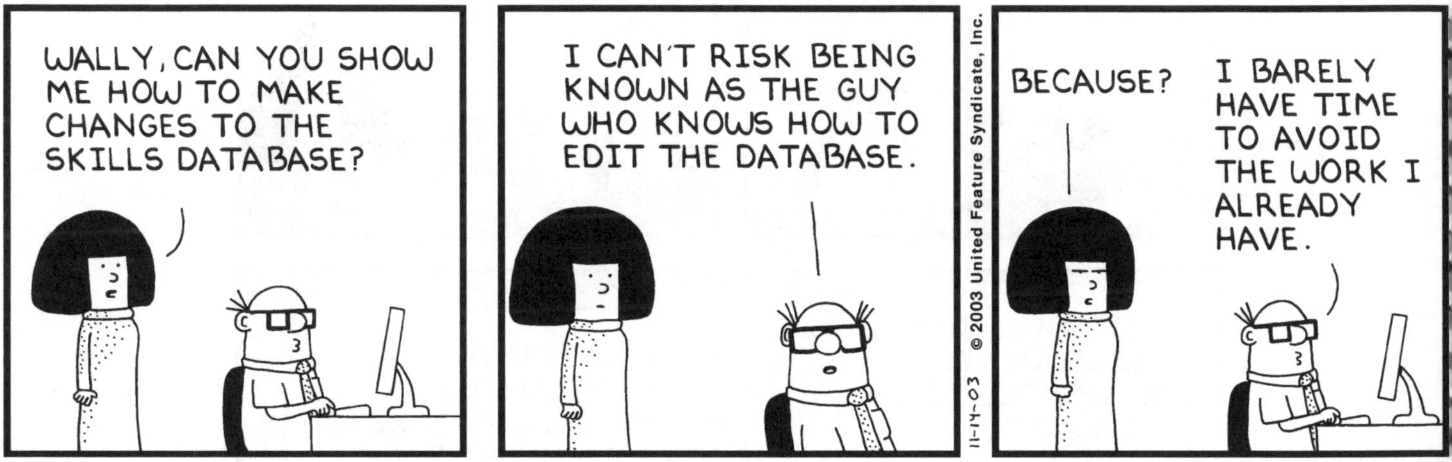
WALLY, CAN YOU SHOW ME HOW TO MAKE CHANGES TO THE SKILLS DATABASE?
I CAN'T RISK BEING KNOWN AS THE GUY WHO KNOWS HOW TO EDIT THE DATABASE.
11-14-03 © 2003 United Feature Syndicate, Inc.
BECAUSE?
I BARELY HAVE TIME TO AVOID THE WORK I ALREADY HAVE.

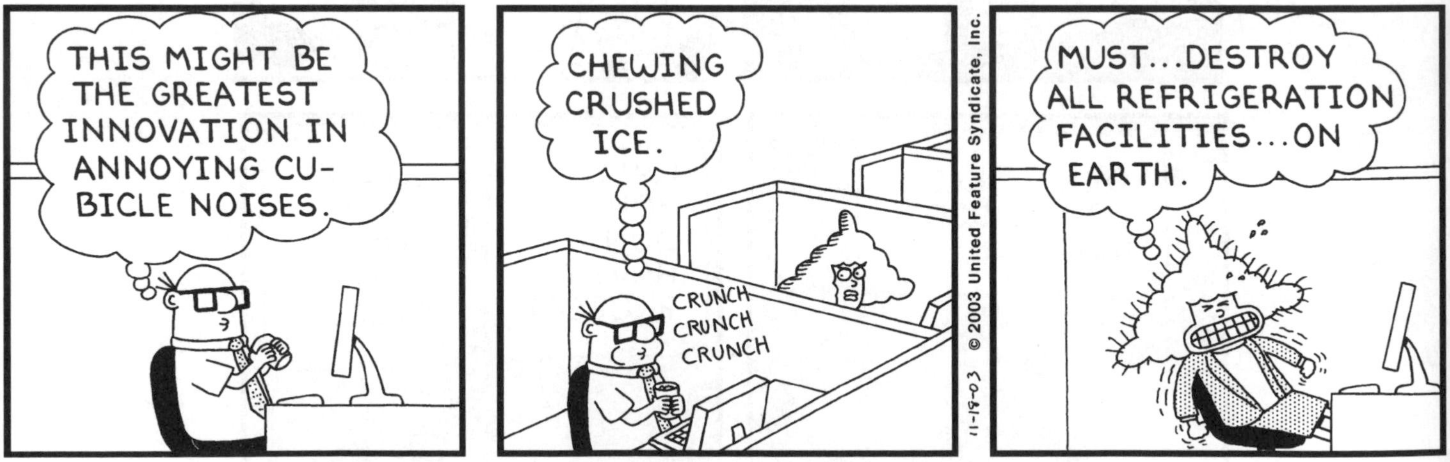
THIS MIGHT BE THE GREATEST INNOVATION IN ANNOYING CU-BICLE NOISES.
CHEWING CRUSHED ICE.
CRUNCH CRUNCH CRUNCH
11-19-03 © 2003 United Feature Syndicate, Inc.
MUST...DESTROY ALL REFRIGERATION FACILITIES...ON EARTH.

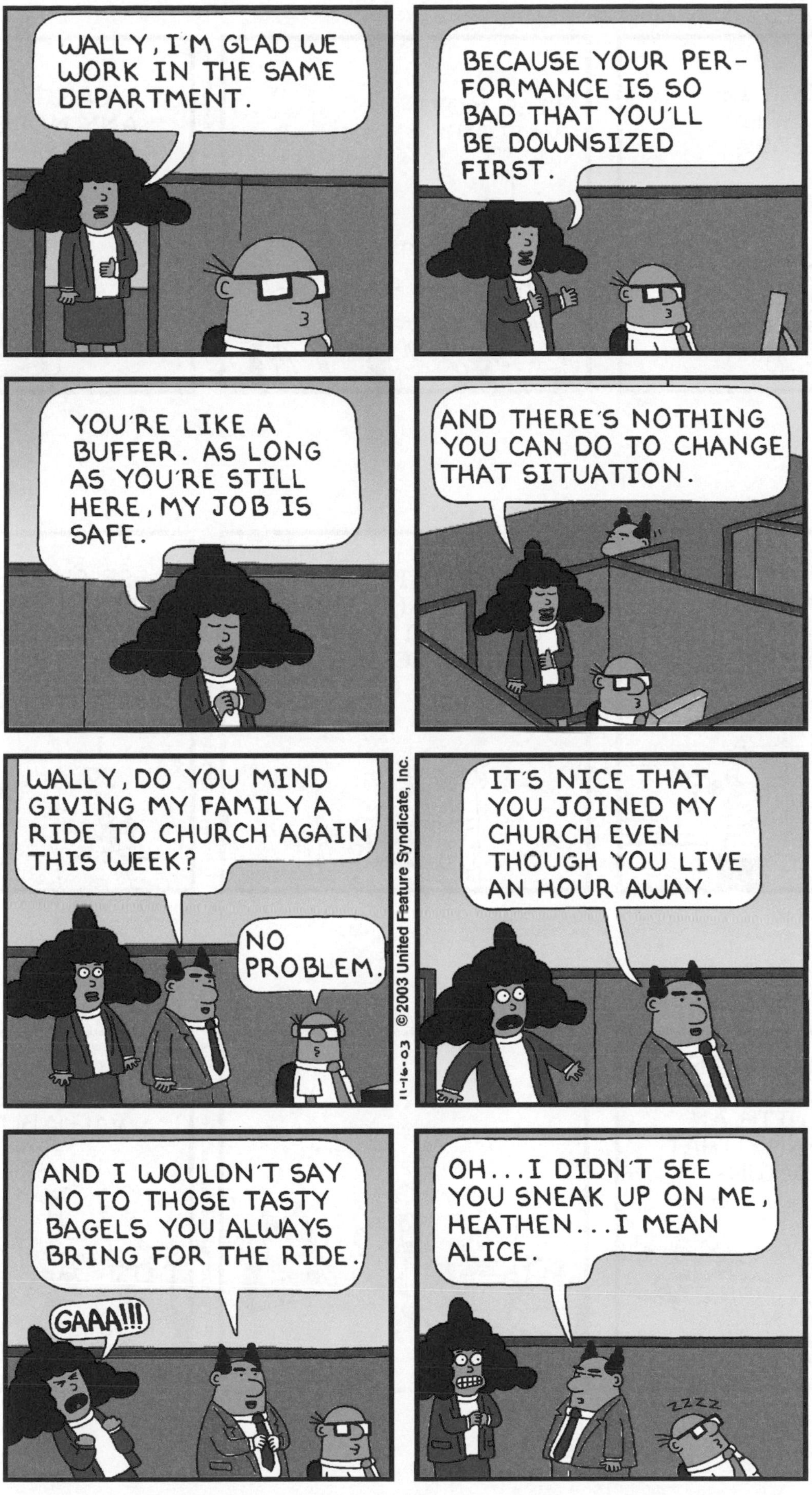
WALLY, I'M GLAD WE WORK IN THE SAME DEPARTMENT.
BECAUSE YOUR PERFORMANCE IS SO BAD THAT YOU'LL BE DOWNSIZED FIRST.
YOU'RE LIKE A BUFFER. AS LONG AS YOU'RE STILL HERE, MY JOB IS SAFE.
AND THERE'S NOTHING YOU CAN DO TO CHANGE THAT SITUATION.
WALLY, DO YOU MIND GIVING MY FAMILY A RIDE TO CHURCH AGAIN THIS WEEK?
NO PROBLEM.
©2003 United Feature Syndicate, Inc.
11-16-03
IT'S NICE THAT YOU JOINED MY CHURCH EVEN THOUGH YOU LIVE AN HOUR AWAY.
AND I WOULDN'T SAY NO TO THOSE TASTY BAGELS YOU ALWAYS BRING FOR THE RIDE.
GAAA!!!
OH...I DIDN'T SEE YOU SNEAK UP ON ME, HEATHEN...I MEAN ALICE.
ZZZZ

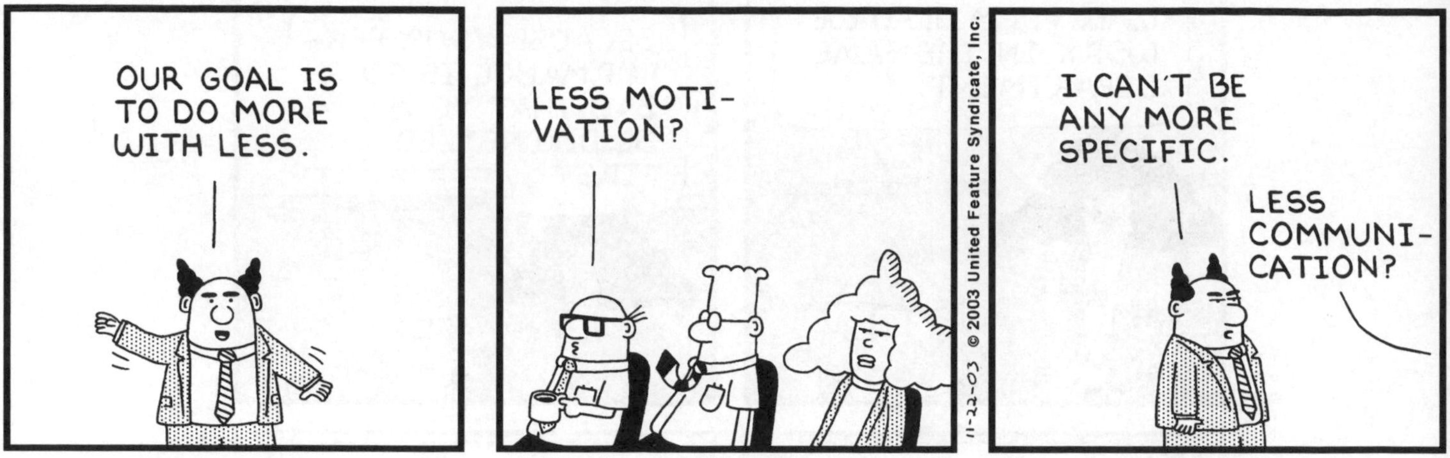
OUR GOAL IS TO DO MORE WITH LESS.
LESS MOTI-VATION?
11-22-03 © 2003 United Feature Syndicate, Inc.
I CAN'T BE ANY MORE SPECIFIC.
LESS COMMUNI-CATION?

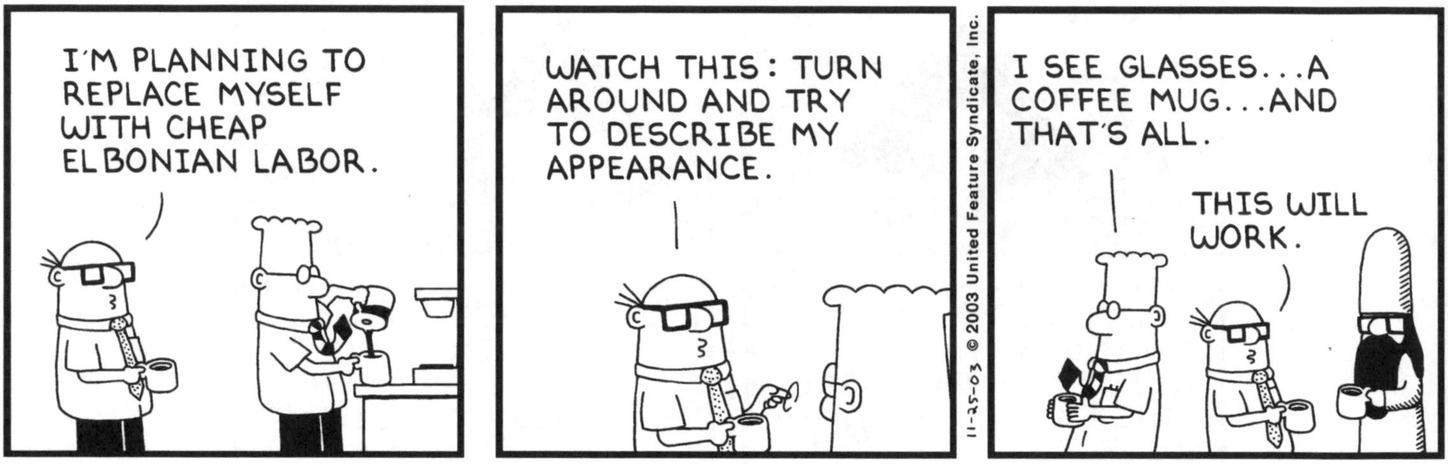
I'M PLANNING TO REPLACE MYSELF WITH CHEAP ELBONIAN LABOR.
WATCH THIS: TURN AROUND AND TRY TO DESCRIBE MY APPEARANCE.
11-25-03 © 2003 United Feature Syndicate, Inc.
I SEE GLASSES...A COFFEE MUG...AND THAT'S ALL.
THIS WILL WORK.

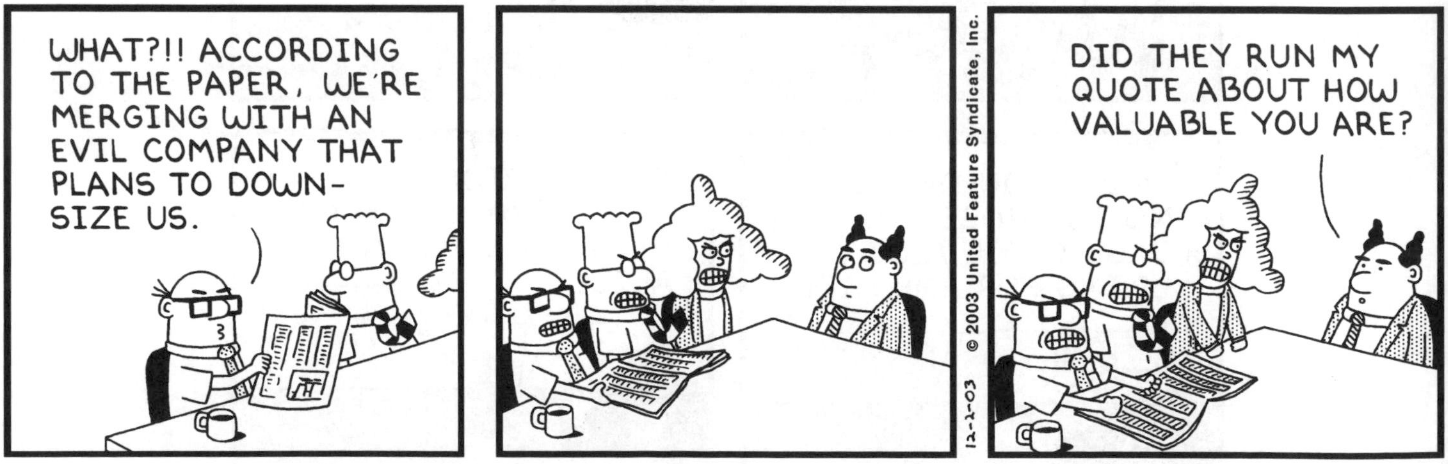
WHAT?!! ACCORDING TO THE PAPER, WE'RE MERGING WITH AN EVIL COMPANY THAT PLANS TO DOWN-SIZE US.
12-2-03 © 2003 United Feature Syndicate, Inc.
DID THEY RUN MY QUOTE ABOUT HOW VALUABLE YOU ARE?

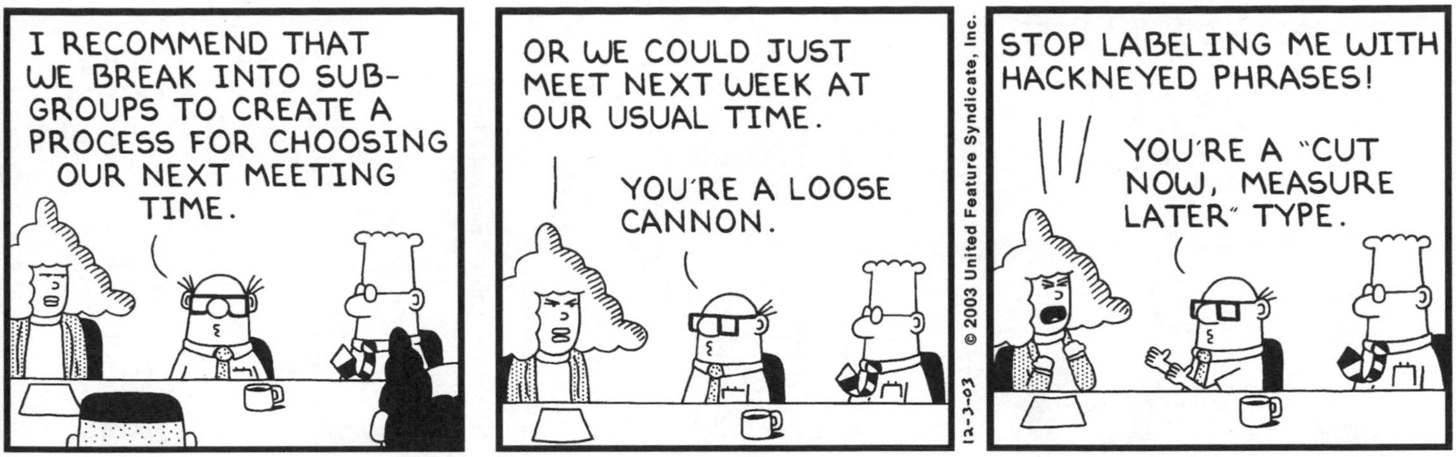
I RECOMMEND THAT WE BREAK INTO SUB-GROUPS TO CREATE A PROCESS FOR CHOOSING OUR NEXT MEETING TIME.
OR WE COULD JUST MEET NEXT WEEK AT OUR USUAL TIME.
YOU'RE A LOOSE CANNON.
© 2003 United Feature Syndicate, Inc.
12-3-03
STOP LABELING ME WITH HACKNEYED PHRASES!
YOU'RE A "CUT NOW, MEASURE LATER" TYPE.

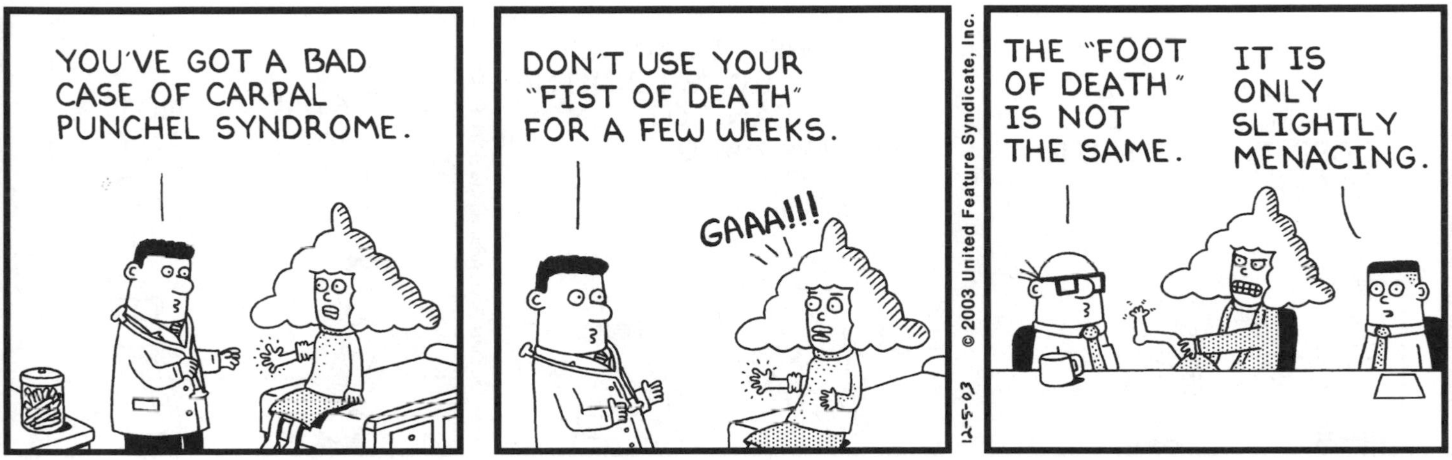
YOU'VE GOT A BAD CASE OF CARPAL PUNCHEL SYNDROME.
DON'T USE YOUR "FIST OF DEATH" FOR A FEW WEEKS.
GAAA!!!
© 2003 United Feature Syndicate, Inc.
12-5-03
THE "FOOT OF DEATH" IS NOT THE SAME.
IT IS ONLY SLIGHTLY MENACING.

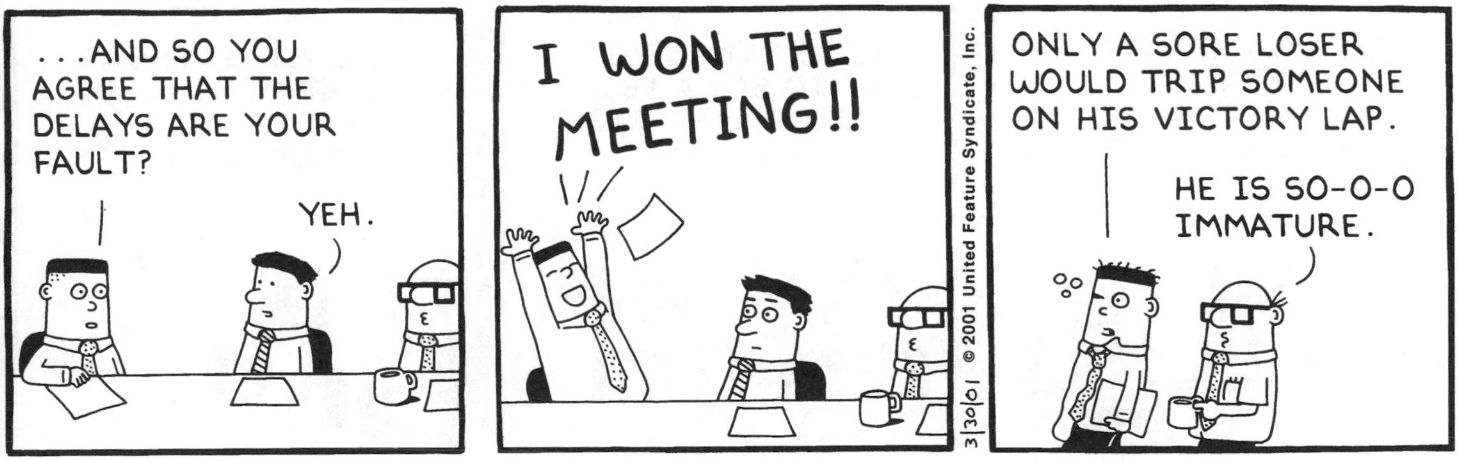
...AND SO YOU AGREE THAT THE DELAYS ARE YOUR FAULT?
YEH.
I WON THE MEETING!!
© 2001 United Feature Syndicate, Inc.
3/30/01
ONLY A SORE LOSER WOULD TRIP SOMEONE ON HIS VICTORY LAP.
HE IS SO-O-O IMMATURE.

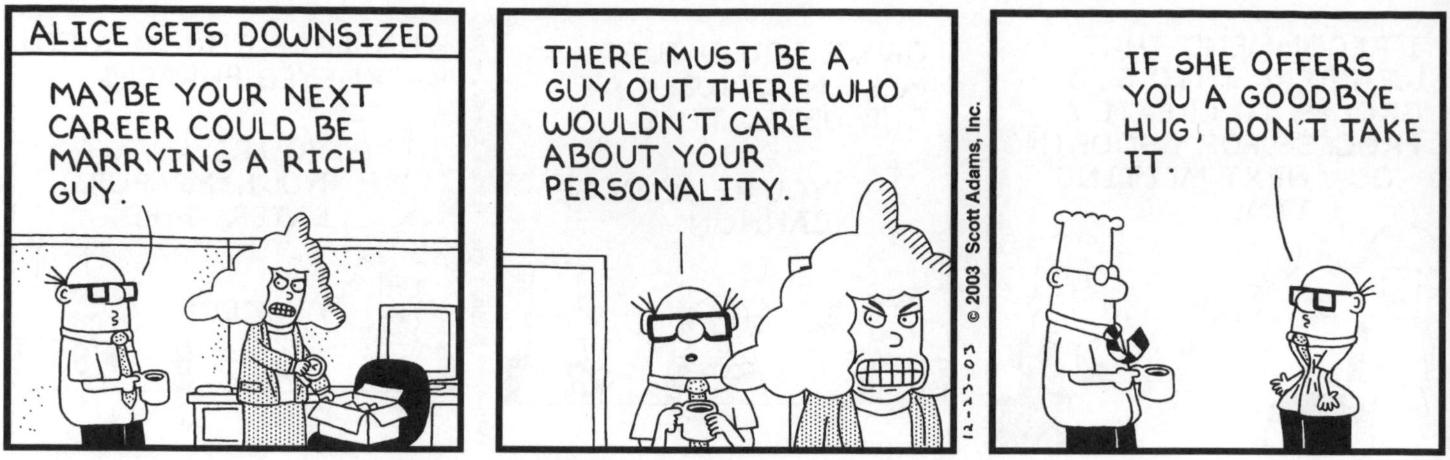
ALICE GETS DOWNSIZED
MAYBE YOUR NEXT CAREER COULD BE MARRYING A RICH GUY.
THERE MUST BE A GUY OUT THERE WHO WOULDN'T CARE ABOUT YOUR PERSONALITY.
12-23-03 © 2003 Scott Adams, Inc.
IF SHE OFFERS YOU A GOODBYE HUG, DON'T TAKE IT.

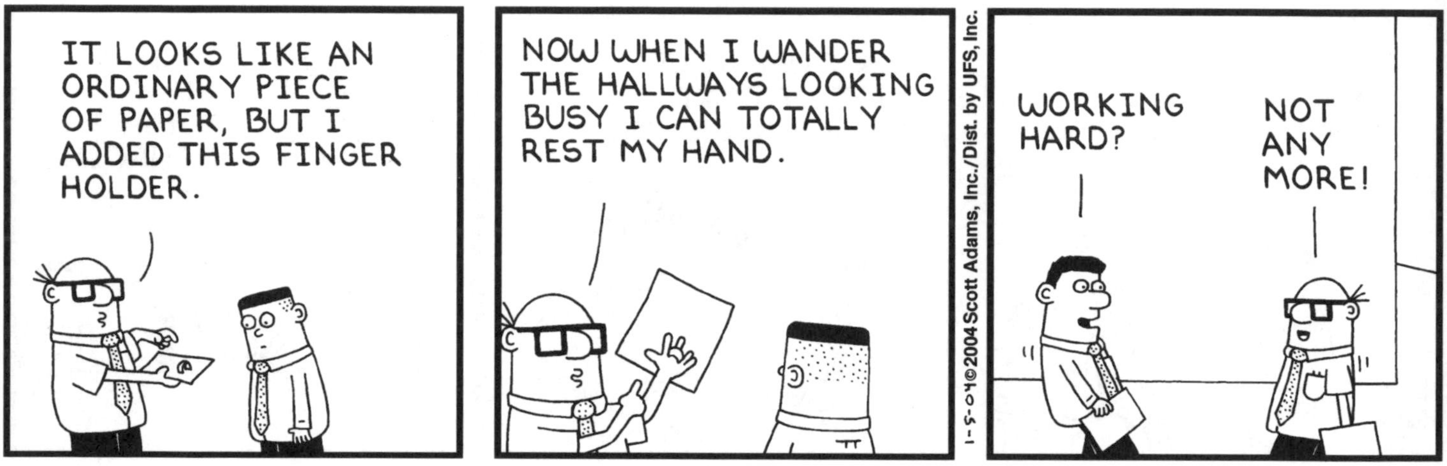
IT LOOKS LIKE AN ORDINARY PIECE OF PAPER, BUT I ADDED THIS FINGER HOLDER.
NOW WHEN I WANDER THE HALLWAYS LOOKING BUSY I CAN TOTALLY REST MY HAND.
1-5-04 © 2004 Scott Adams, Inc./Dist. by UFS, Inc.
WORKING HARD?
NOT ANY MORE!

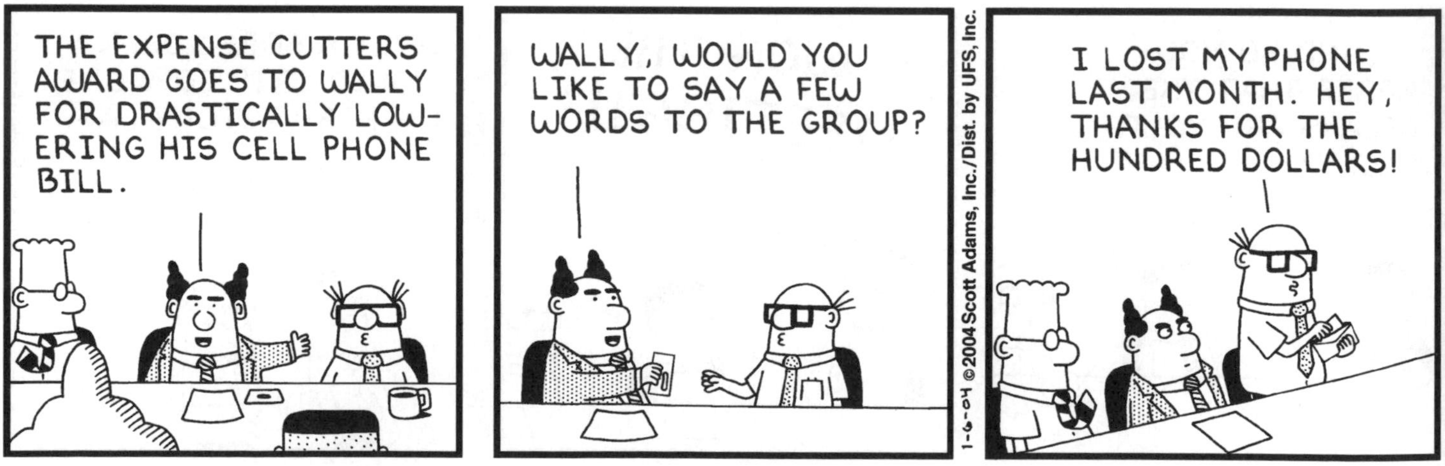
THE EXPENSE CUTTERS AWARD GOES TO WALLY FOR DRASTICALLY LOW-ERING HIS CELL PHONE BILL.
WALLY, WOULD YOU LIKE TO SAY A FEW WORDS TO THE GROUP?
1-6-04 © 2004 Scott Adams, Inc./Dist. by UFS, Inc.
I LOST MY PHONE LAST MONTH. HEY, THANKS FOR THE HUNDRED DOLLARS!

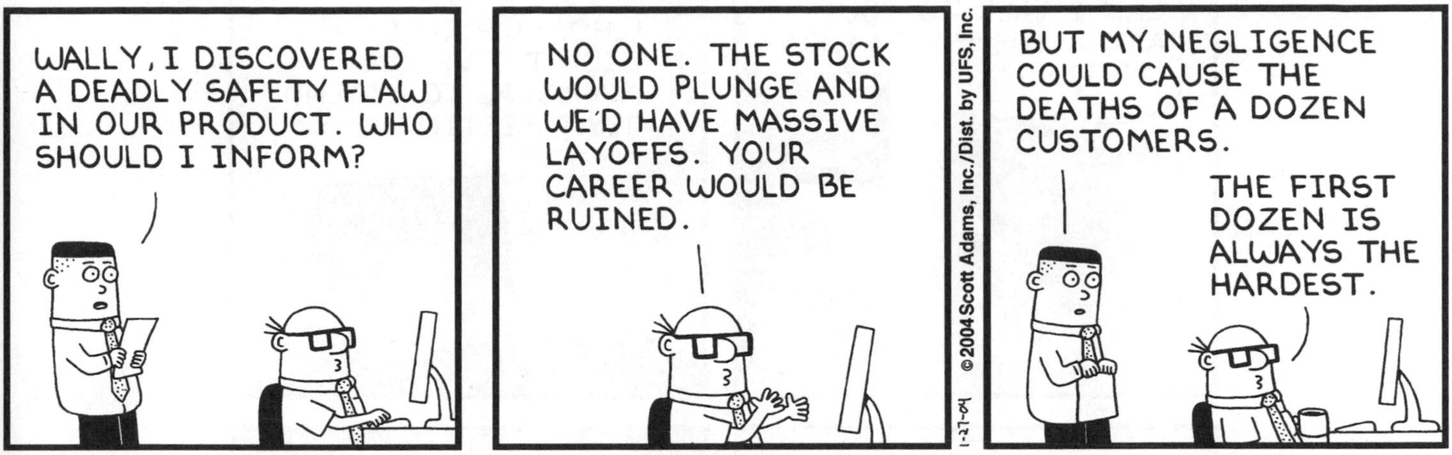

WALLY, I DISCOVERED A DEADLY SAFETY FLAW IN OUR PRODUCT. WHO SHOULD I INFORM?
NO ONE. THE STOCK WOULD PLUNGE AND WE'D HAVE MASSIVE LAYOFFS. YOUR CAREER WOULD BE RUINED.
1-27-04 © 2004 Scott Adams, Inc./Dist. by UFS, Inc.
BUT MY NEGLIGENCE COULD CAUSE THE DEATHS OF A DOZEN CUSTOMERS.
THE FIRST DOZEN IS ALWAYS THE HARDEST.

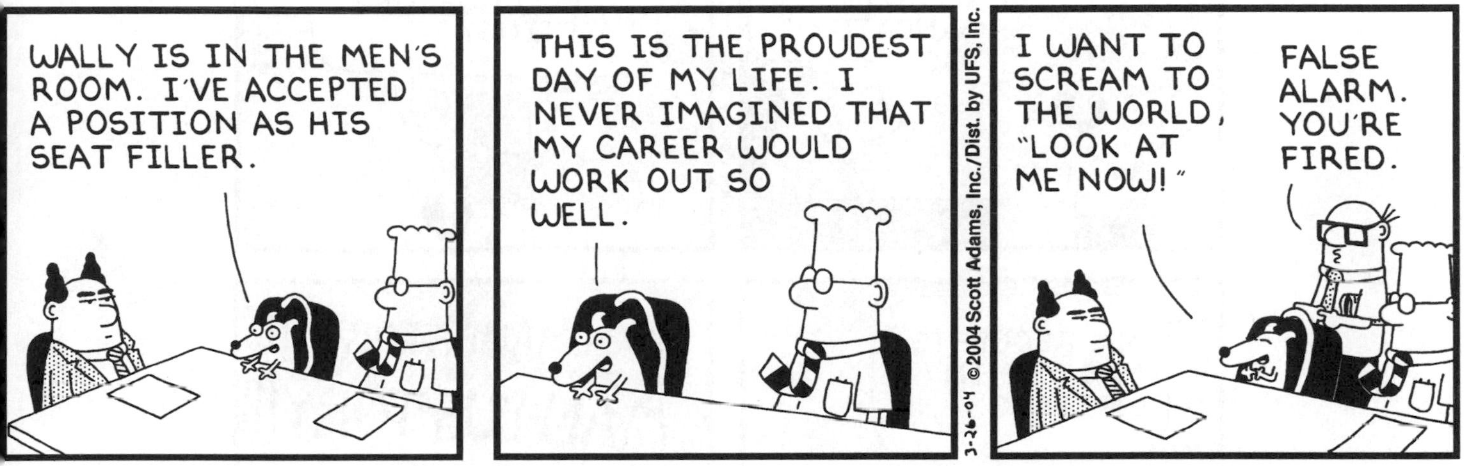

WALLY IS IN THE MEN'S ROOM. I'VE ACCEPTED A POSITION AS HIS SEAT FILLER.
THIS IS THE PROUDEST DAY OF MY LIFE. I NEVER IMAGINED THAT MY CAREER WOULD WORK OUT SO WELL.
3-26-04 © 2004 Scott Adams, Inc./Dist. by UFS, Inc.
I WANT TO SCREAM TO THE WORLD, "LOOK AT ME NOW!"
FALSE ALARM. YOU'RE FIRED.

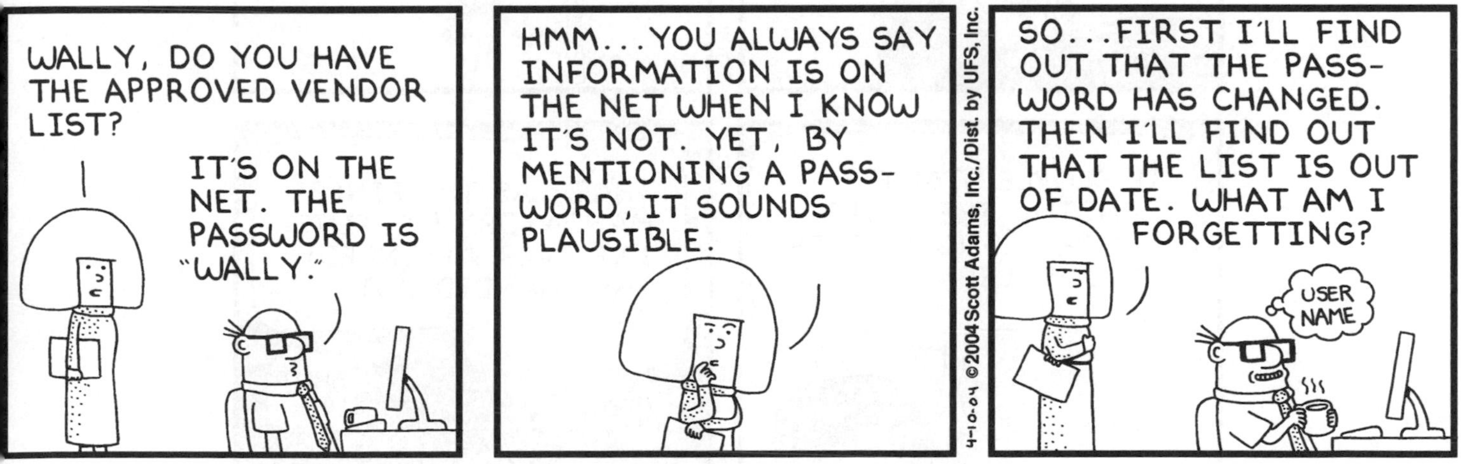

WALLY, DO YOU HAVE THE APPROVED VENDOR LIST?
IT'S ON THE NET. THE PASSWORD IS "WALLY."
HMM... YOU ALWAYS SAY INFORMATION IS ON THE NET WHEN I KNOW IT'S NOT. YET, BY MENTIONING A PASSWORD, IT SOUNDS PLAUSIBLE.
4-10-04 © 2004 Scott Adams, Inc./Dist. by UFS, Inc.
SO... FIRST I'LL FIND OUT THAT THE PASSWORD HAS CHANGED. THEN I'LL FIND OUT THAT THE LIST IS OUT OF DATE. WHAT AM I FORGETTING?
USER NAME

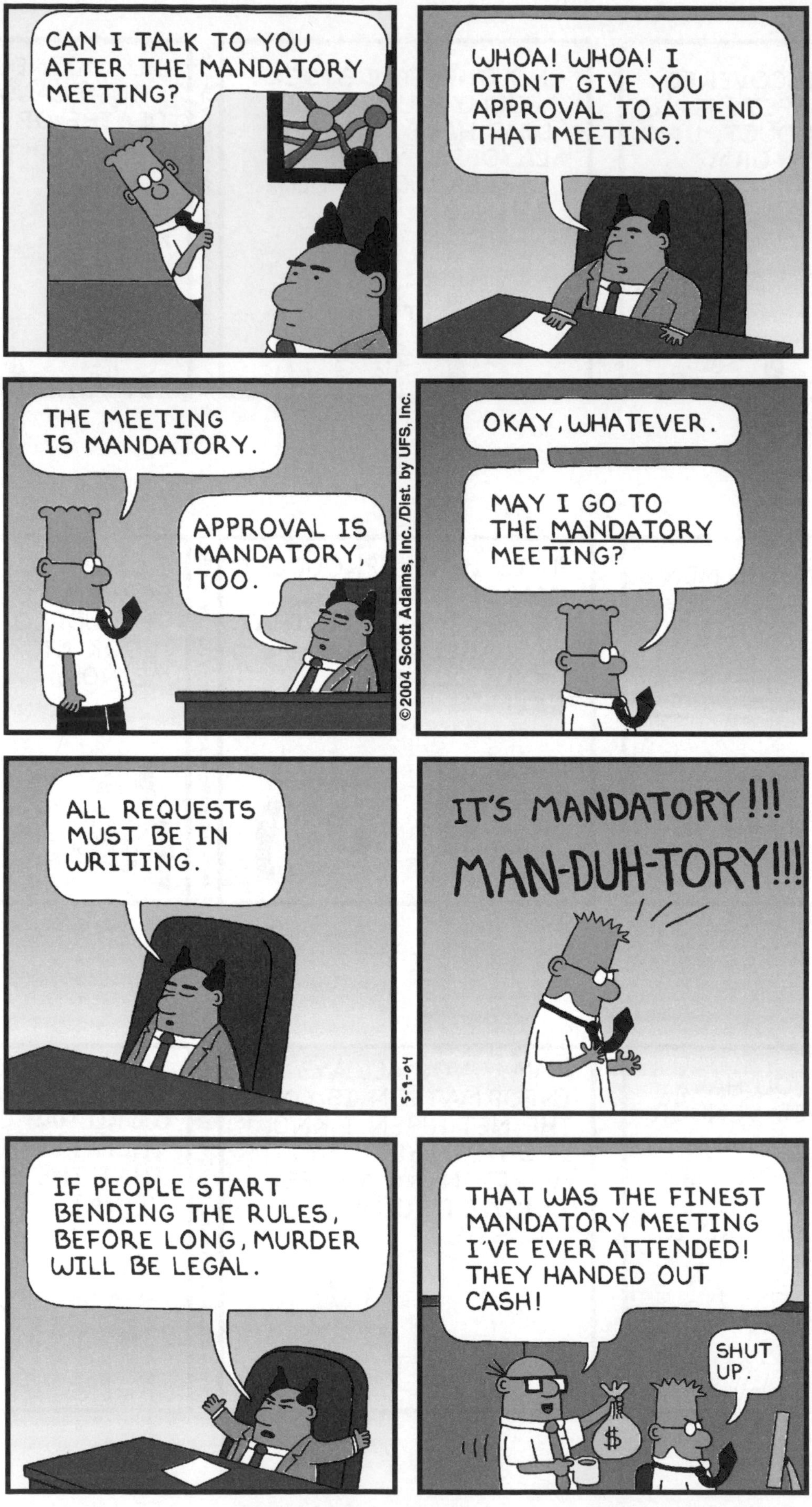
CAN I TALK TO YOU AFTER THE MANDATORY MEETING?
WHOA! WHOA! I DIDN'T GIVE YOU APPROVAL TO ATTEND THAT MEETING.
THE MEETING IS MANDATORY.
APPROVAL IS MANDATORY, TOO.
©2004 Scott Adams, Inc. /Dist. by UFS, Inc.
OKAY, WHATEVER.
MAY I GO TO THE MANDATORY MEETING?
ALL REQUESTS MUST BE IN WRITING.
5-9-04
IT'S MANDATORY!!!
MAN-DUH-TORY!!!
IF PEOPLE START BENDING THE RULES, BEFORE LONG, MURDER WILL BE LEGAL.
THAT WAS THE FINEST MANDATORY MEETING I'VE EVER ATTENDED! THEY HANDED OUT CASH!
SHUT UP.
$

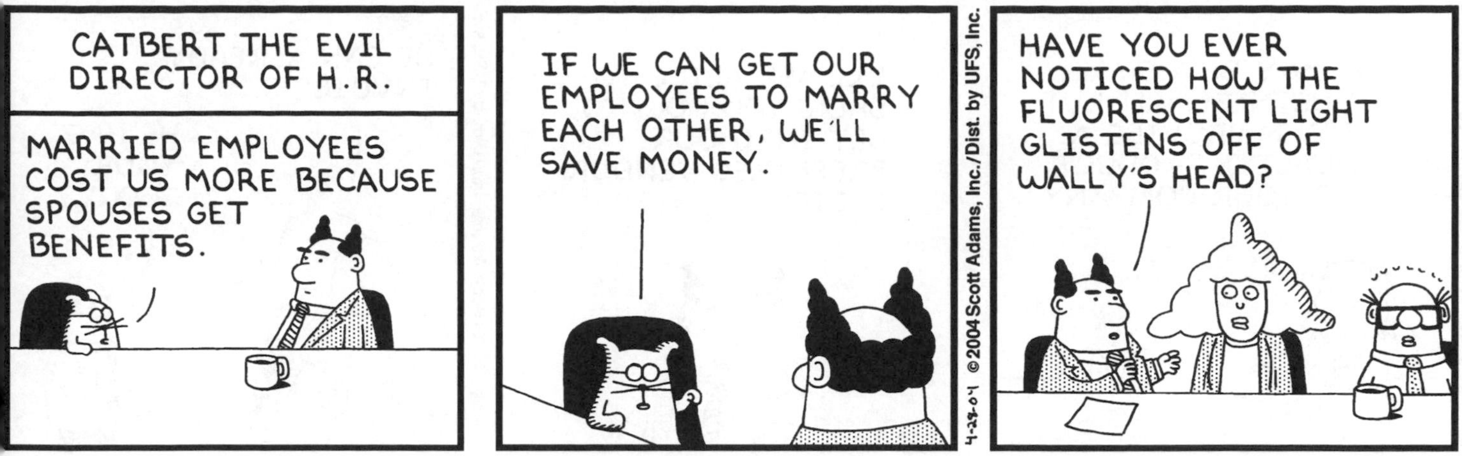
CATBERT THE EVIL DIRECTOR OF H.R.
MARRIED EMPLOYEES COST US MORE BECAUSE SPOUSES GET BENEFITS.
IF WE CAN GET OUR EMPLOYEES TO MARRY EACH OTHER, WE'LL SAVE MONEY.
4-23-04 ©2004 Scott Adams, Inc./Dist. by UFS, Inc.
HAVE YOU EVER NOTICED HOW THE FLUORESCENT LIGHT GLISTENS OFF OF WALLY'S HEAD?

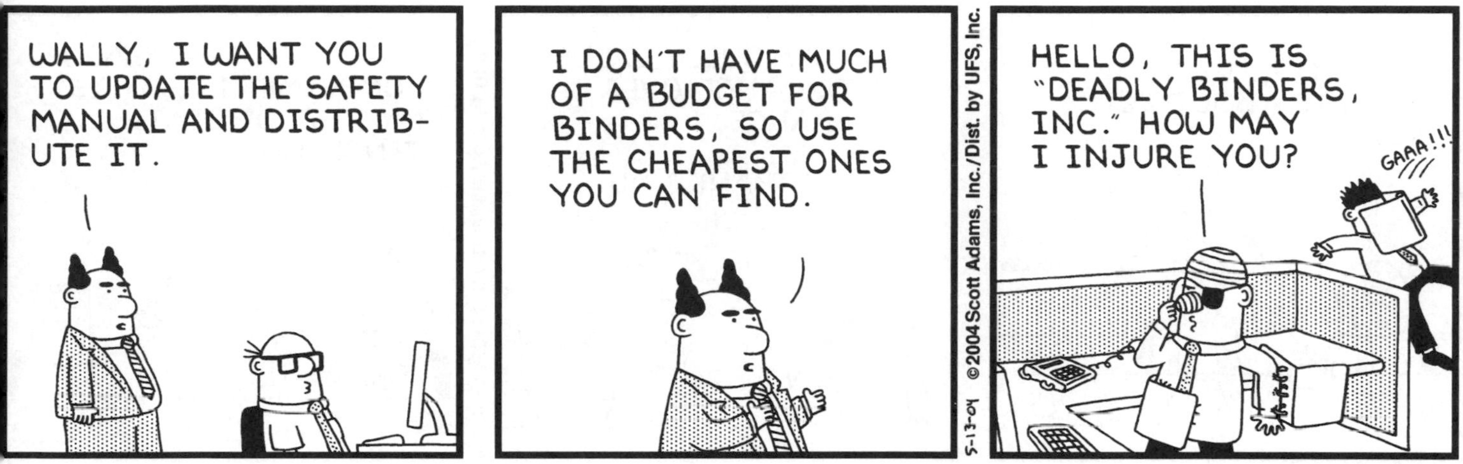
WALLY, I WANT YOU TO UPDATE THE SAFETY MANUAL AND DISTRIB-UTE IT.
I DON'T HAVE MUCH OF A BUDGET FOR BINDERS, SO USE THE CHEAPEST ONES YOU CAN FIND.
5-13-04 ©2004 Scott Adams, Inc./Dist. by UFS, Inc.
HELLO, THIS IS "DEADLY BINDERS, INC." HOW MAY I INJURE YOU?
GAAA!!!

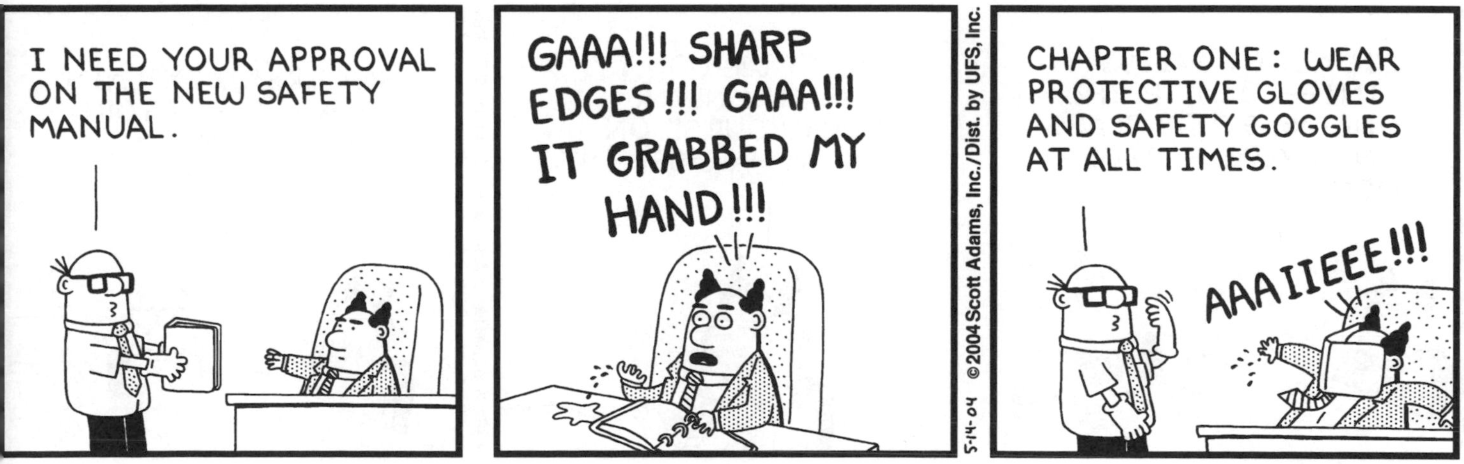
I NEED YOUR APPROVAL ON THE NEW SAFETY MANUAL.
GAAA!!! SHARP EDGES!!! GAAA!!! IT GRABBED MY HAND!!!
5-14-04 ©2004 Scott Adams, Inc./Dist. by UFS, Inc.
CHAPTER ONE: WEAR PROTECTIVE GLOVES AND SAFETY GOGGLES AT ALL TIMES.
AAAIIEEE!!!

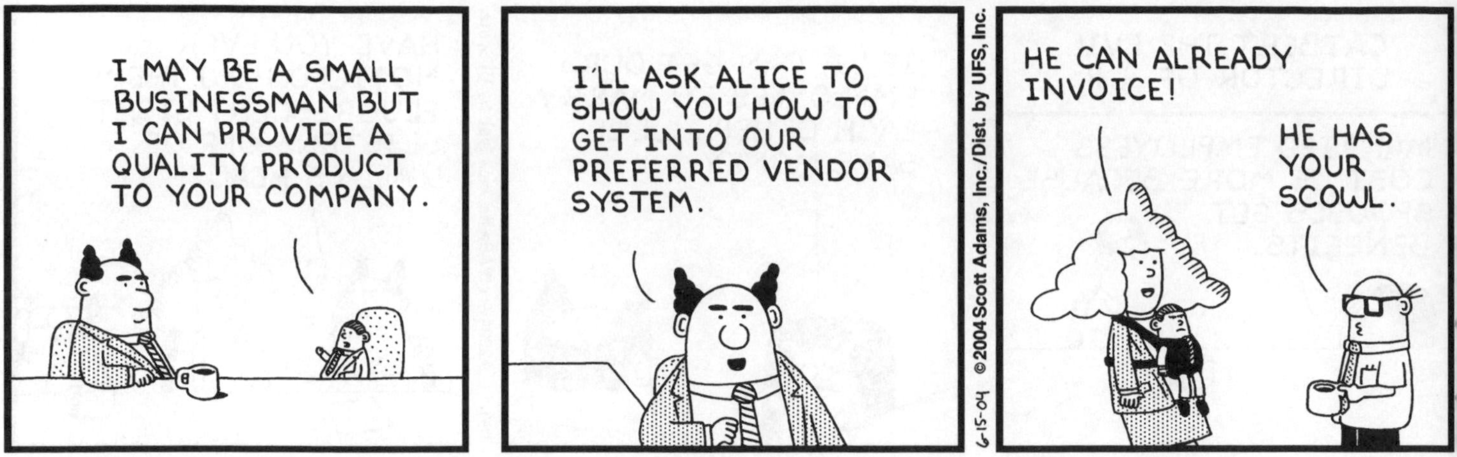
I MAY BE A SMALL BUSINESSMAN BUT I CAN PROVIDE A QUALITY PRODUCT TO YOUR COMPANY.
I'LL ASK ALICE TO SHOW YOU HOW TO GET INTO OUR PREFERRED VENDOR SYSTEM.
6-15-04 ©2004 Scott Adams, Inc./Dist. by UFS, Inc.
HE CAN ALREADY INVOICE!
HE HAS YOUR SCOWL.

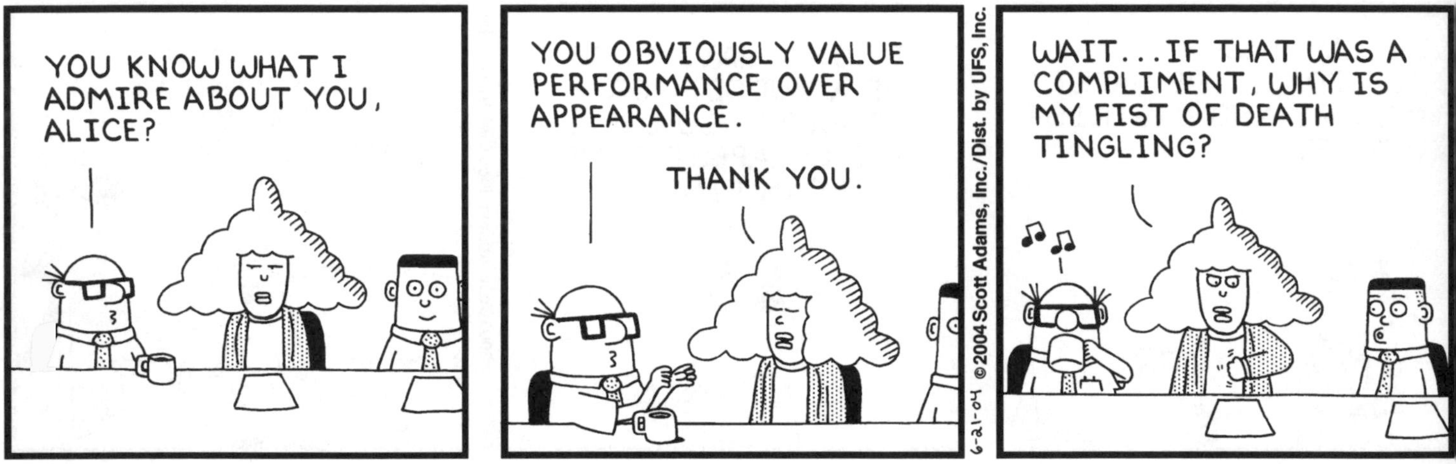
YOU KNOW WHAT I ADMIRE ABOUT YOU, ALICE?
YOU OBVIOUSLY VALUE PERFORMANCE OVER APPEARANCE.
THANK YOU.
6-21-04 ©2004 Scott Adams, Inc./Dist. by UFS, Inc.
WAIT...IF THAT WAS A COMPLIMENT, WHY IS MY FIST OF DEATH TINGLING?

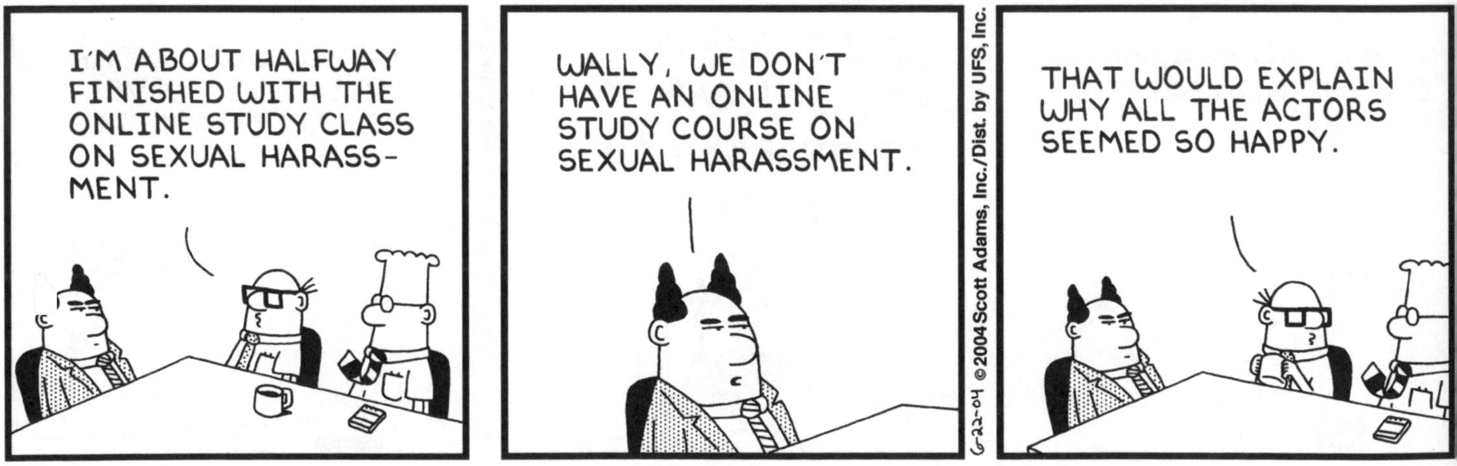
I'M ABOUT HALFWAY FINISHED WITH THE ONLINE STUDY CLASS ON SEXUAL HARASS-MENT.
WALLY, WE DON'T HAVE AN ONLINE STUDY COURSE ON SEXUAL HARASSMENT.
6-22-04 ©2004 Scott Adams, Inc./Dist. by UFS, Inc.
THAT WOULD EXPLAIN WHY ALL THE ACTORS SEEMED SO HAPPY.

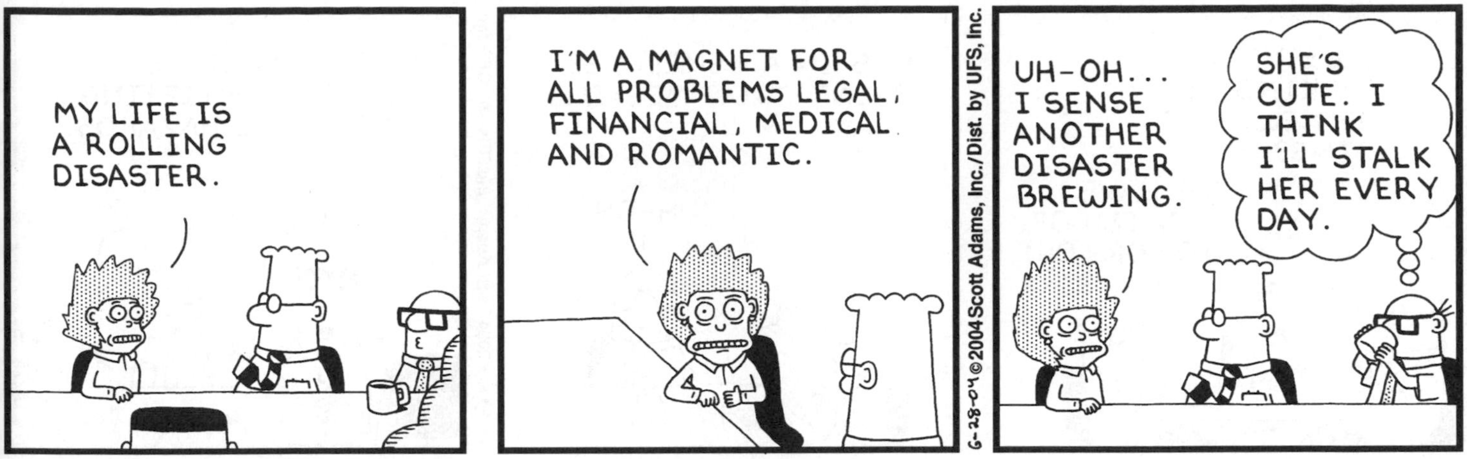
MY LIFE IS A ROLLING DISASTER.
I'M A MAGNET FOR ALL PROBLEMS LEGAL, FINANCIAL, MEDICAL AND ROMANTIC.
6-28-04 ©2004 Scott Adams, Inc./Dist. by UFS, Inc.
UH-OH... I SENSE ANOTHER DISASTER BREWING.
SHE'S CUTE. I THINK I'LL STALK HER EVERY DAY.

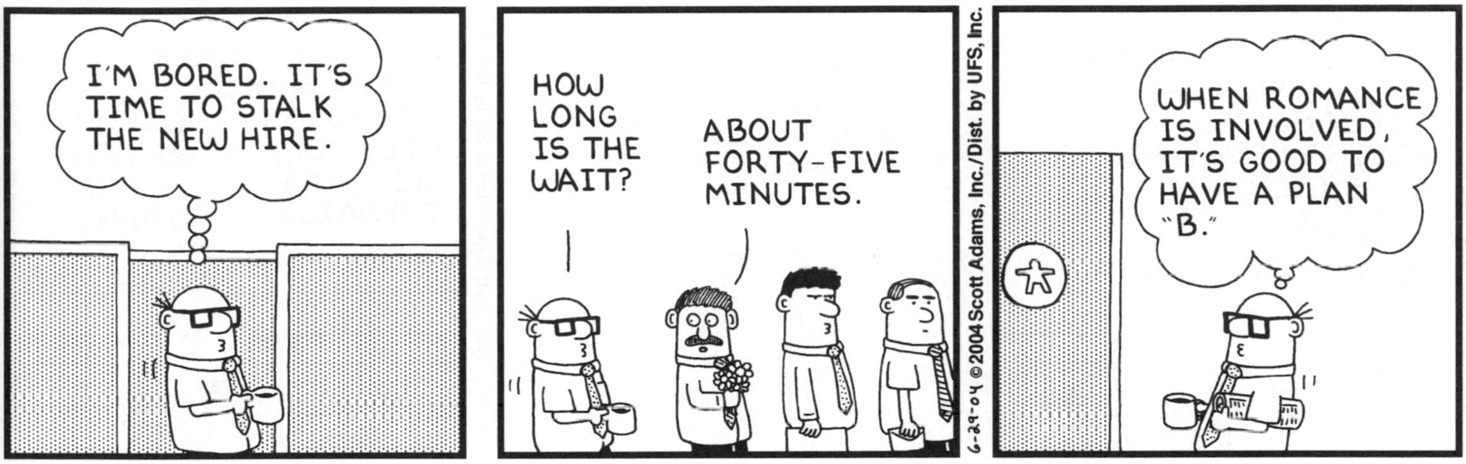
I'M BORED. IT'S TIME TO STALK THE NEW HIRE.
HOW LONG IS THE WAIT?
ABOUT FORTY-FIVE MINUTES.
6-29-04 ©2004 Scott Adams, Inc./Dist. by UFS, Inc.
WHEN ROMANCE IS INVOLVED, IT'S GOOD TO HAVE A PLAN "B."

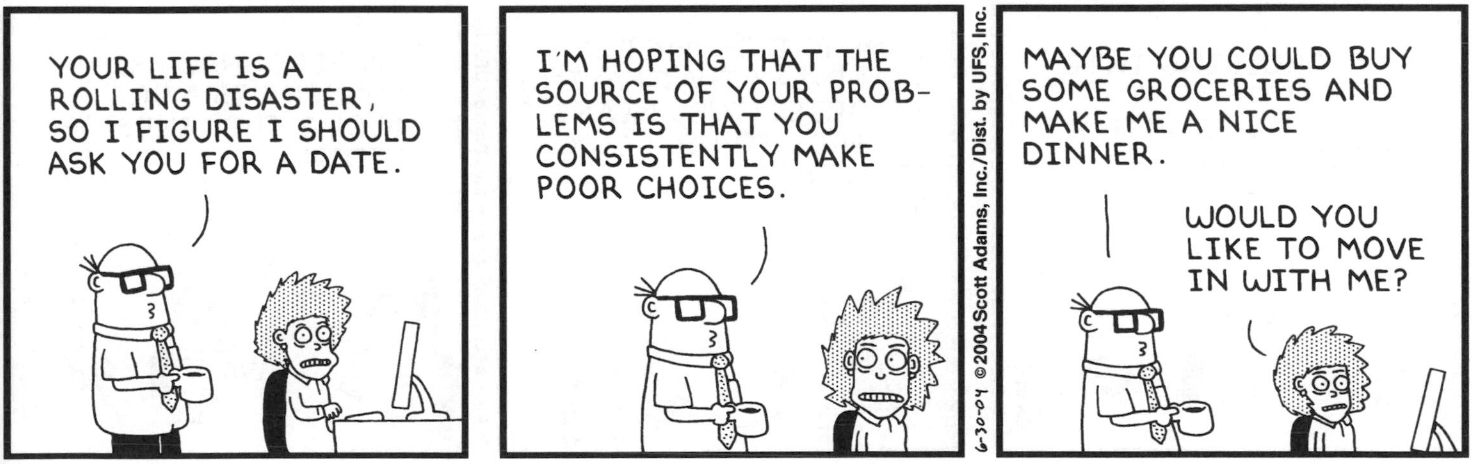
YOUR LIFE IS A ROLLING DISASTER, SO I FIGURE I SHOULD ASK YOU FOR A DATE.
I'M HOPING THAT THE SOURCE OF YOUR PROBLEMS IS THAT YOU CONSISTENTLY MAKE POOR CHOICES.
6-30-04 ©2004 Scott Adams, Inc./Dist. by UFS, Inc.
MAYBE YOU COULD BUY SOME GROCERIES AND MAKE ME A NICE DINNER.
WOULD YOU LIKE TO MOVE IN WITH ME?

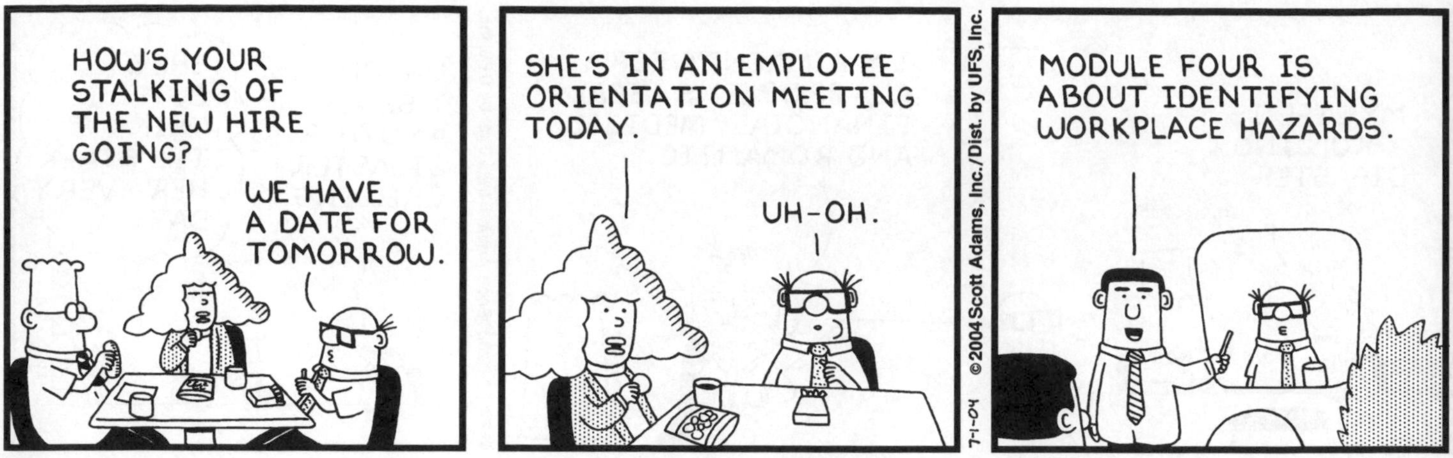
HOW'S YOUR STALKING OF THE NEW HIRE GOING?
WE HAVE A DATE FOR TOMORROW.
SHE'S IN AN EMPLOYEE ORIENTATION MEETING TODAY.
UH-OH.
7-1-04
© 2004 Scott Adams, Inc./Dist. by UFS, Inc.
MODULE FOUR IS ABOUT IDENTIFYING WORKPLACE HAZARDS.

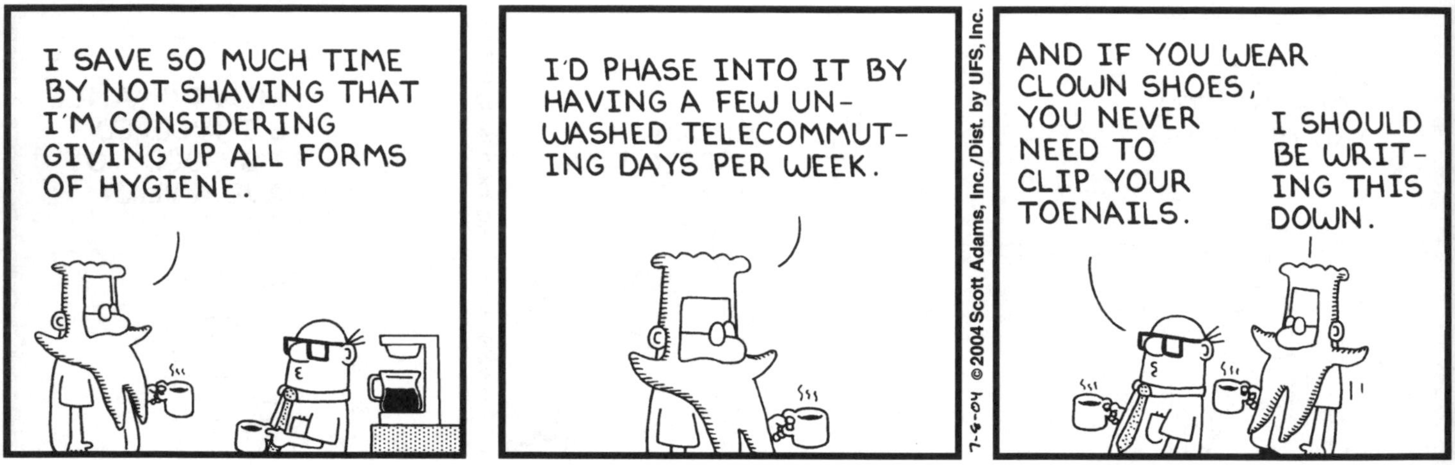
I SAVE SO MUCH TIME BY NOT SHAVING THAT I'M CONSIDERING GIVING UP ALL FORMS OF HYGIENE.
I'D PHASE INTO IT BY HAVING A FEW UN-WASHED TELECOMMUT-ING DAYS PER WEEK.
7-6-04
© 2004 Scott Adams, Inc./Dist. by UFS, Inc.
AND IF YOU WEAR CLOWN SHOES, YOU NEVER NEED TO CLIP YOUR TOENAILS.
I SHOULD BE WRIT-ING THIS DOWN.

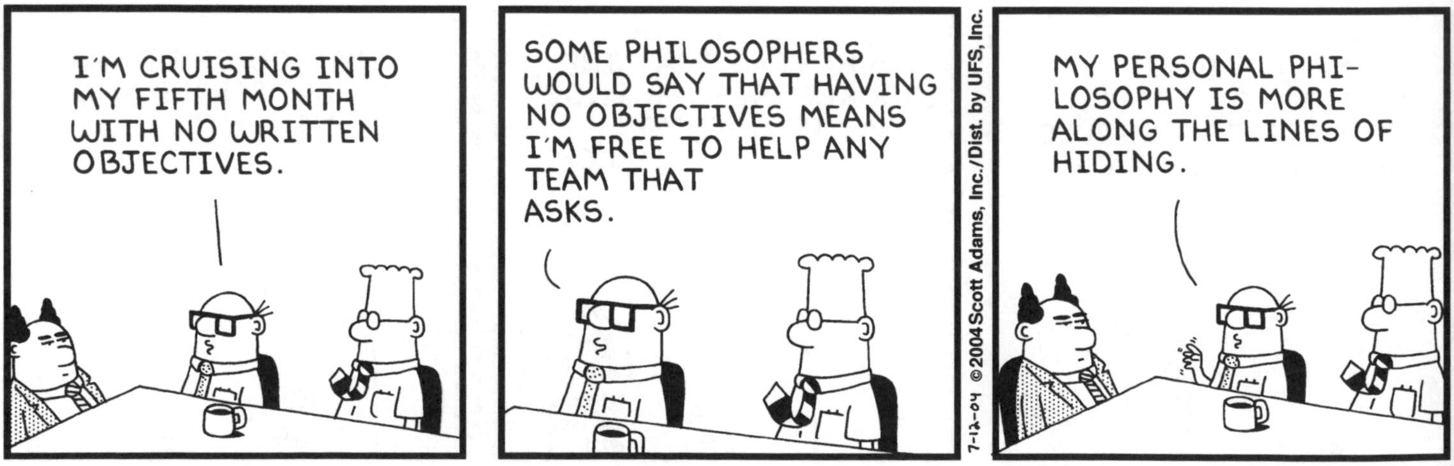
I'M CRUISING INTO MY FIFTH MONTH WITH NO WRITTEN OBJECTIVES.
SOME PHILOSOPHERS WOULD SAY THAT HAVING NO OBJECTIVES MEANS I'M FREE TO HELP ANY TEAM THAT ASKS.
7-12-04
© 2004 Scott Adams, Inc./Dist. by UFS, Inc.
MY PERSONAL PHI-LOSOPHY IS MORE ALONG THE LINES OF HIDING.

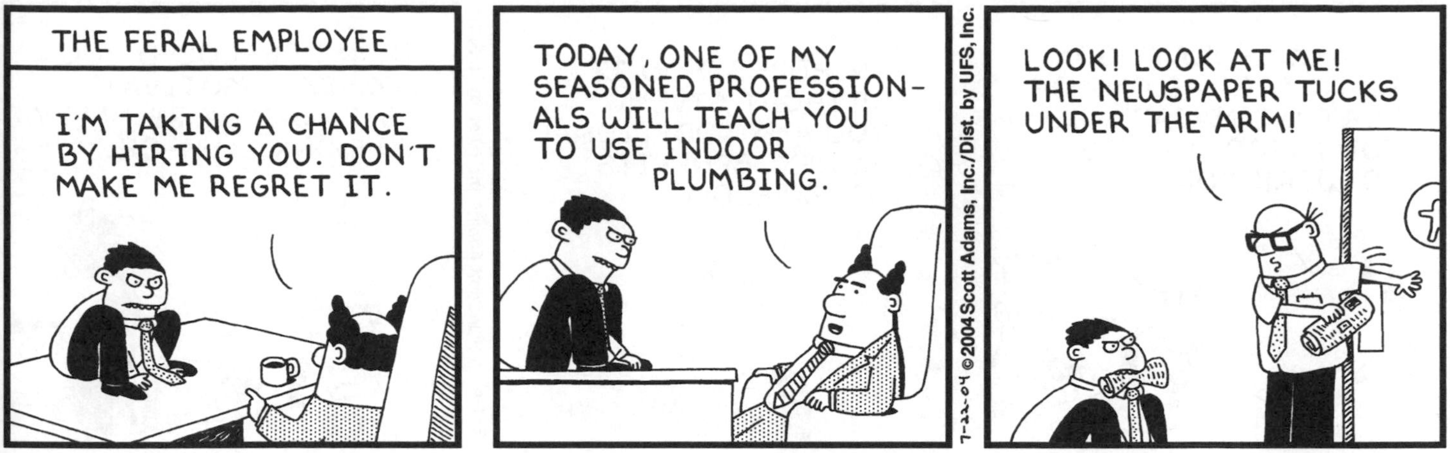
THE FERAL EMPLOYEE
I'M TAKING A CHANCE BY HIRING YOU. DON'T MAKE ME REGRET IT.
TODAY, ONE OF MY SEASONED PROFESSIONALS WILL TEACH YOU TO USE INDOOR PLUMBING.
7-22-04 ©2004 Scott Adams, Inc./Dist. by UFS, Inc.
LOOK! LOOK AT ME! THE NEWSPAPER TUCKS UNDER THE ARM!

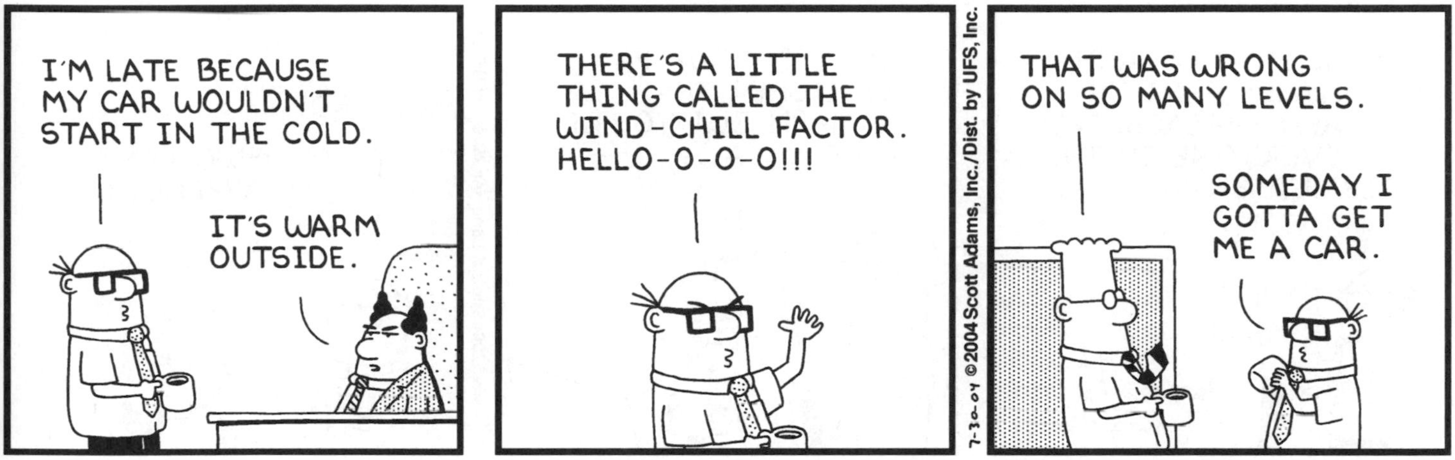
I'M LATE BECAUSE MY CAR WOULDN'T START IN THE COLD.
IT'S WARM OUTSIDE.
THERE'S A LITTLE THING CALLED THE WIND-CHILL FACTOR. HELLO-O-O-O!!!
7-30-04 ©2004 Scott Adams, Inc./Dist. by UFS, Inc.
THAT WAS WRONG ON SO MANY LEVELS.
SOMEDAY I GOTTA GET ME A CAR.

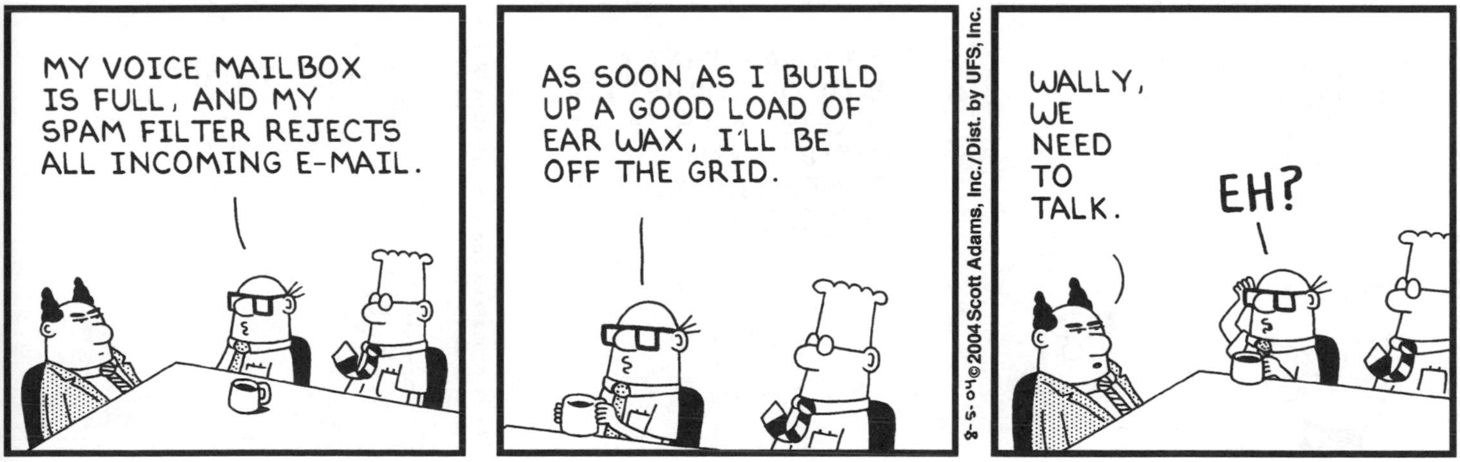
MY VOICE MAILBOX IS FULL, AND MY SPAM FILTER REJECTS ALL INCOMING E-MAIL.
AS SOON AS I BUILD UP A GOOD LOAD OF EAR WAX, I'LL BE OFF THE GRID.
8-5-04 ©2004 Scott Adams, Inc./Dist. by UFS, Inc.
WALLY, WE NEED TO TALK.
EH?

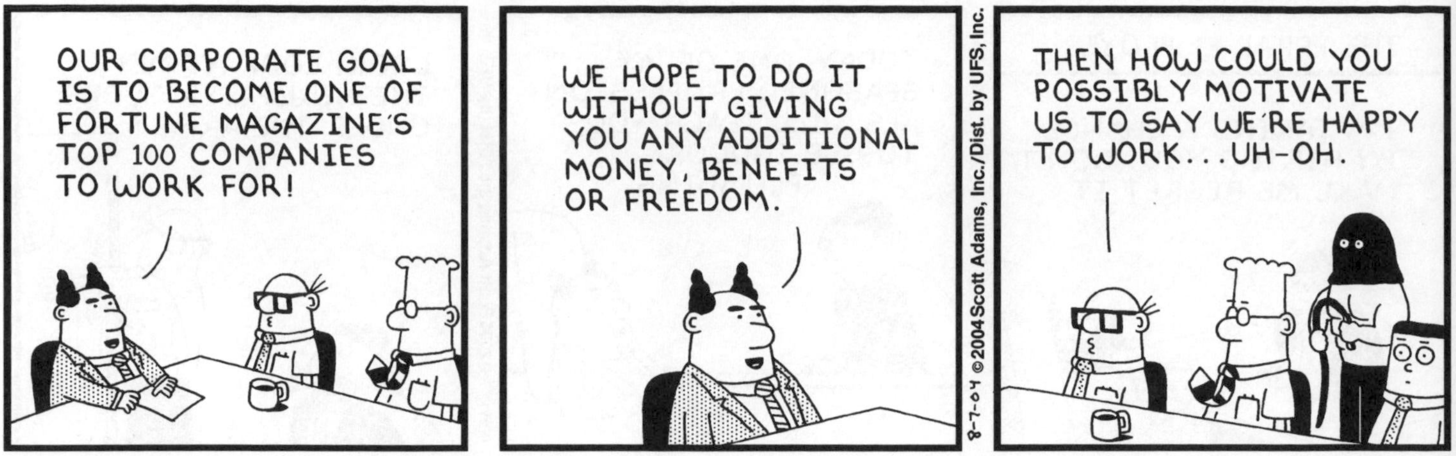
OUR CORPORATE GOAL IS TO BECOME ONE OF FORTUNE MAGAZINE'S TOP 100 COMPANIES TO WORK FOR!
WE HOPE TO DO IT WITHOUT GIVING YOU ANY ADDITIONAL MONEY, BENEFITS OR FREEDOM.
8-7-04 ©2004 Scott Adams, Inc./Dist. by UFS, Inc.
THEN HOW COULD YOU POSSIBLY MOTIVATE US TO SAY WE'RE HAPPY TO WORK...UH-OH.

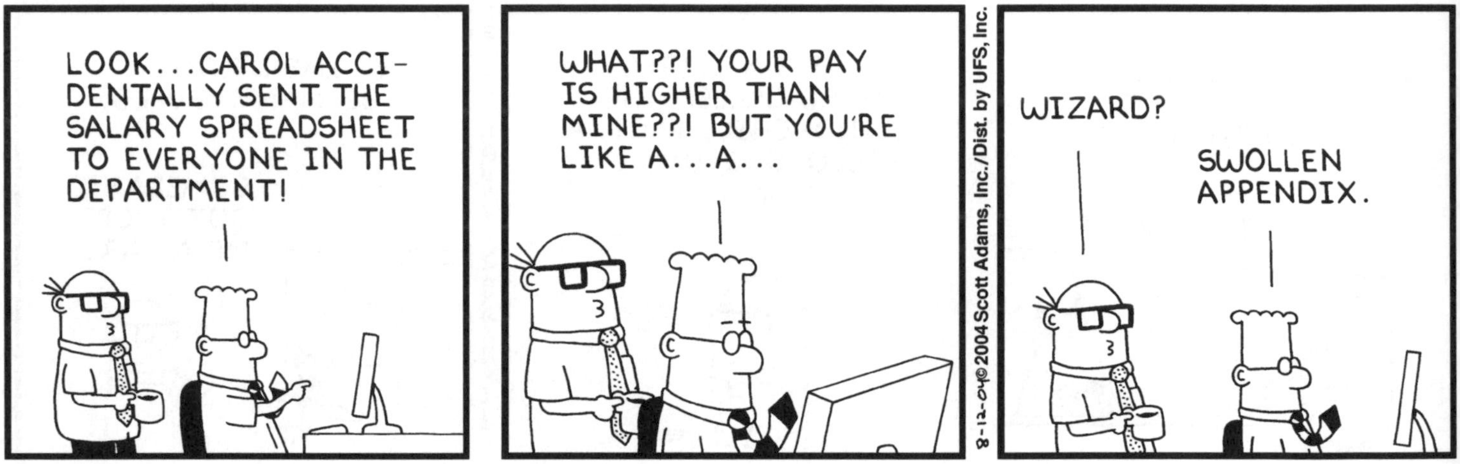
LOOK...CAROL ACCIDENTALLY SENT THE SALARY SPREADSHEET TO EVERYONE IN THE DEPARTMENT!
WHAT??! YOUR PAY IS HIGHER THAN MINE??! BUT YOU'RE LIKE A...A...
8-12-04 ©2004 Scott Adams, Inc./Dist. by UFS, Inc.
WIZARD?
SWOLLEN APPENDIX.

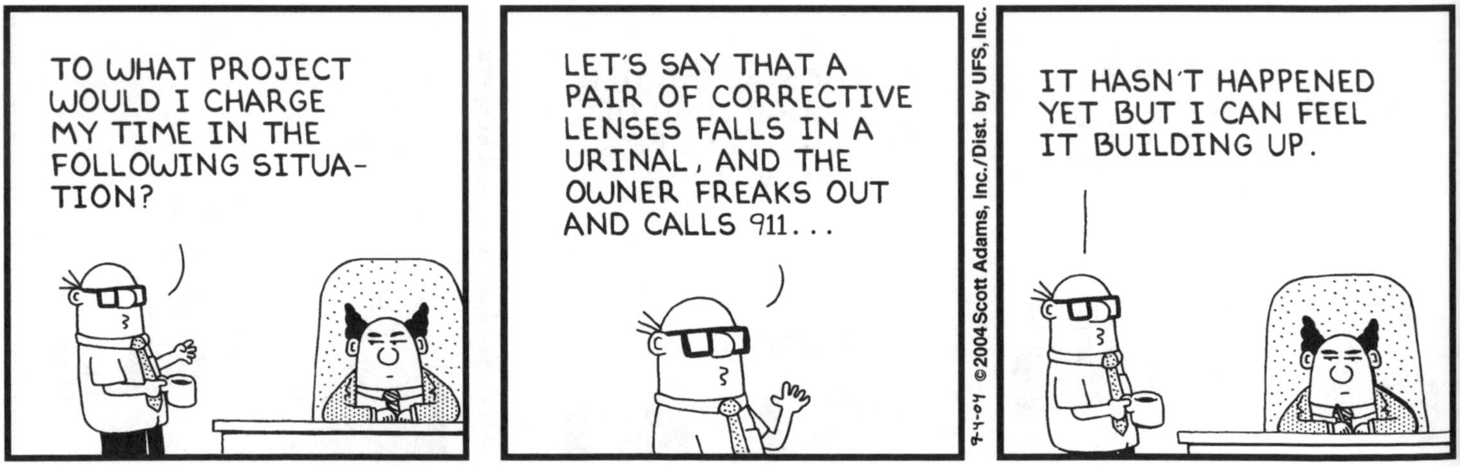
TO WHAT PROJECT WOULD I CHARGE MY TIME IN THE FOLLOWING SITUATION?
LET'S SAY THAT A PAIR OF CORRECTIVE LENSES FALLS IN A URINAL, AND THE OWNER FREAKS OUT AND CALLS 911...
9-4-04 ©2004 Scott Adams, Inc./Dist. by UFS, Inc.
IT HASN'T HAPPENED YET BUT I CAN FEEL IT BUILDING UP.

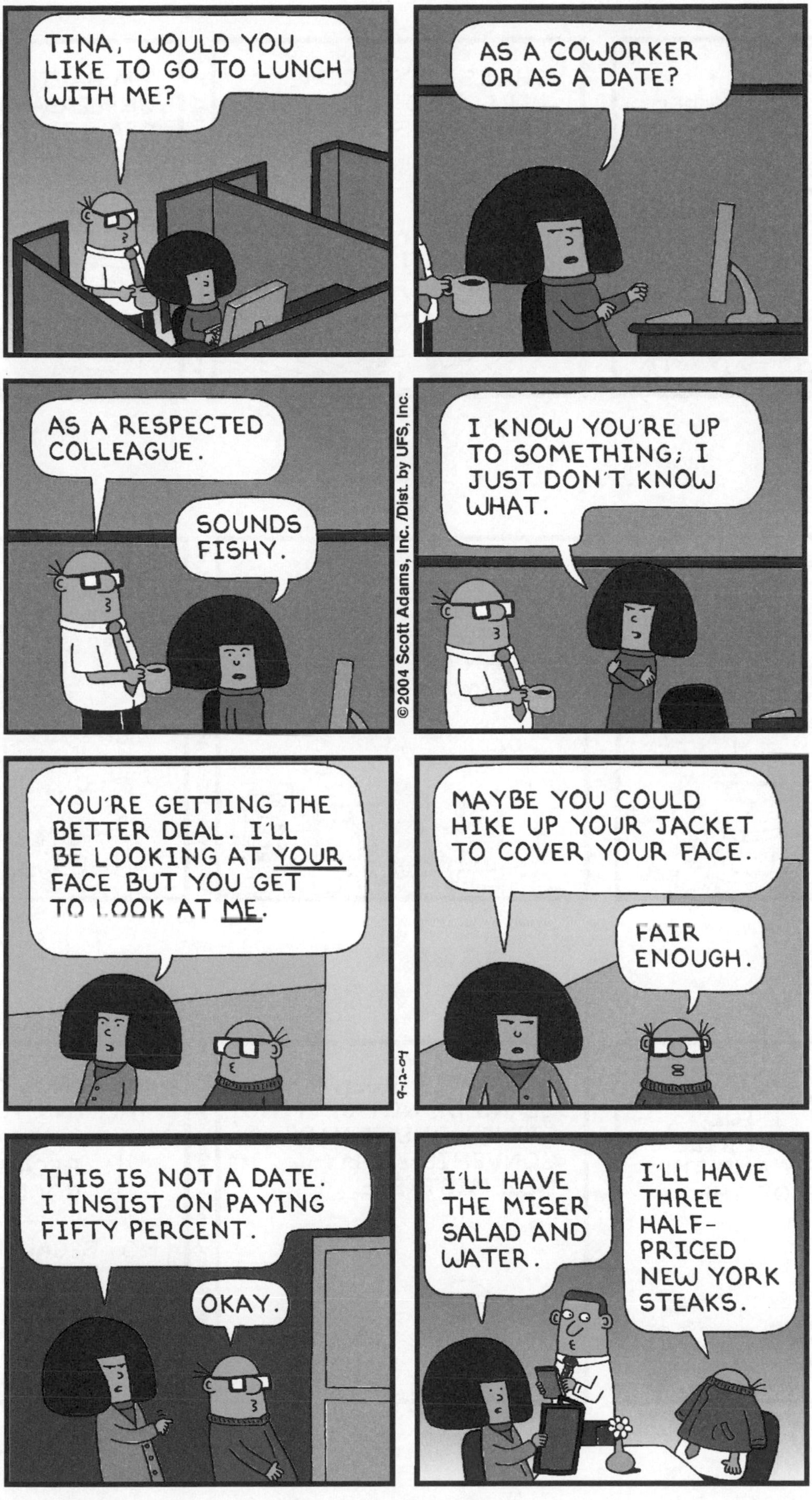
TINA, WOULD YOU LIKE TO GO TO LUNCH WITH ME?
AS A COWORKER OR AS A DATE?
AS A RESPECTED COLLEAGUE.
SOUNDS FISHY.
I KNOW YOU'RE UP TO SOMETHING; I JUST DON'T KNOW WHAT.
YOU'RE GETTING THE BETTER DEAL. I'LL BE LOOKING AT YOUR FACE BUT YOU GET TO LOOK AT ME.
MAYBE YOU COULD HIKE UP YOUR JACKET TO COVER YOUR FACE.
FAIR ENOUGH.
THIS IS NOT A DATE. I INSIST ON PAYING FIFTY PERCENT.
OKAY.
I'LL HAVE THE MISER SALAD AND WATER.
I'LL HAVE THREE HALF-PRICED NEW YORK STEAKS.
9-12-04

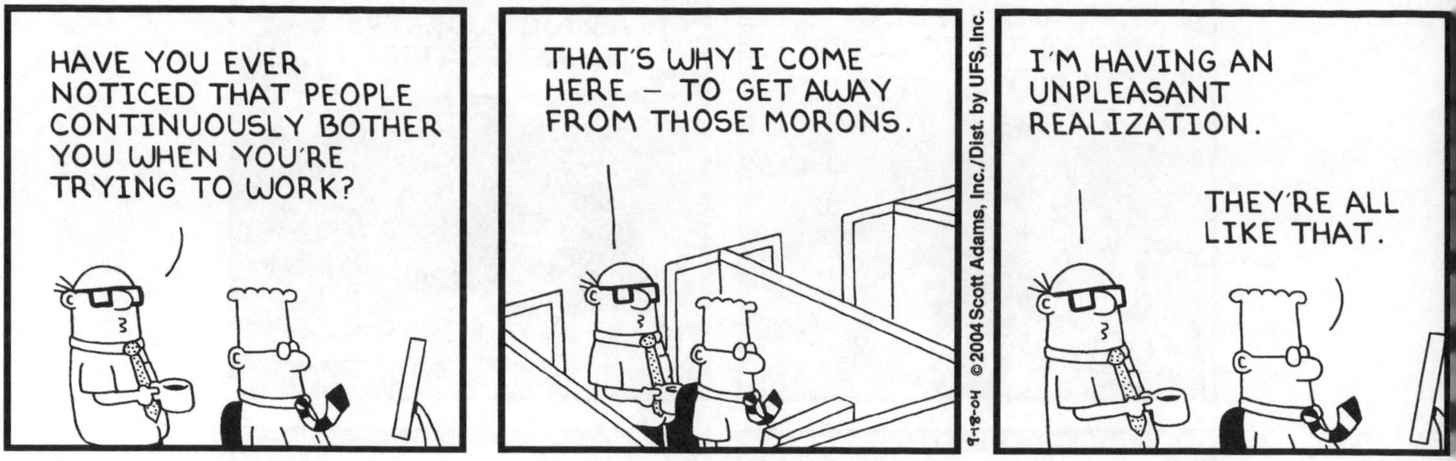
HAVE YOU EVER NOTICED THAT PEOPLE CONTINUOUSLY BOTHER YOU WHEN YOU'RE TRYING TO WORK?
THAT'S WHY I COME HERE – TO GET AWAY FROM THOSE MORONS.
9-8-04 © 2004 Scott Adams, Inc./Dist. by UFS, Inc.
I'M HAVING AN UNPLEASANT REALIZATION.
THEY'RE ALL LIKE THAT.

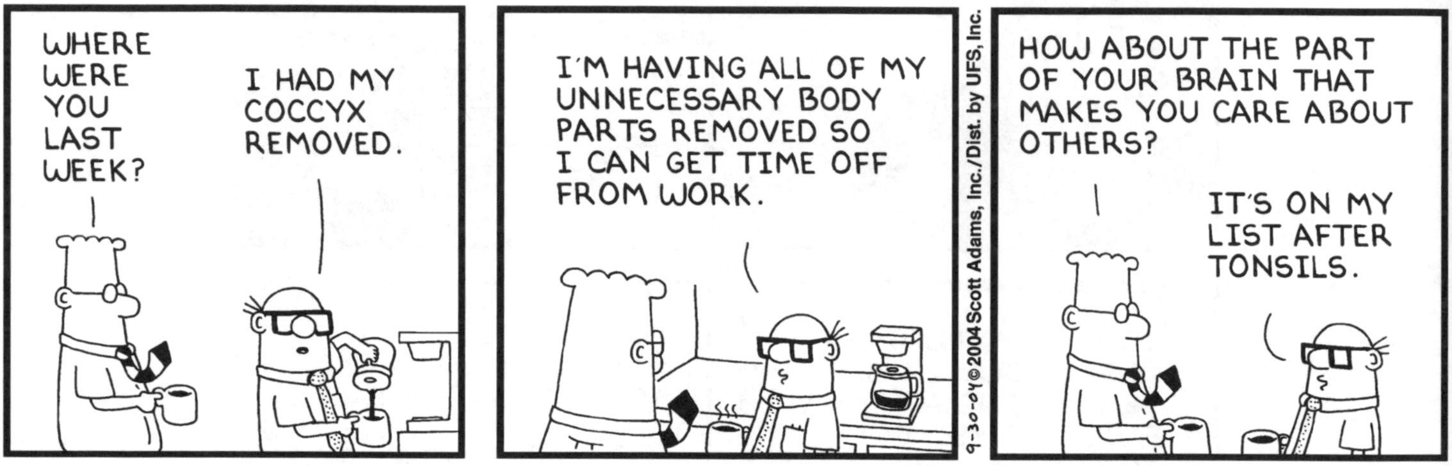
WHERE WERE YOU LAST WEEK?
I HAD MY COCCYX REMOVED.
I'M HAVING ALL OF MY UNNECESSARY BODY PARTS REMOVED SO I CAN GET TIME OFF FROM WORK.
9-30-04 © 2004 Scott Adams, Inc./Dist. by UFS, Inc.
HOW ABOUT THE PART OF YOUR BRAIN THAT MAKES YOU CARE ABOUT OTHERS?
IT'S ON MY LIST AFTER TONSILS.

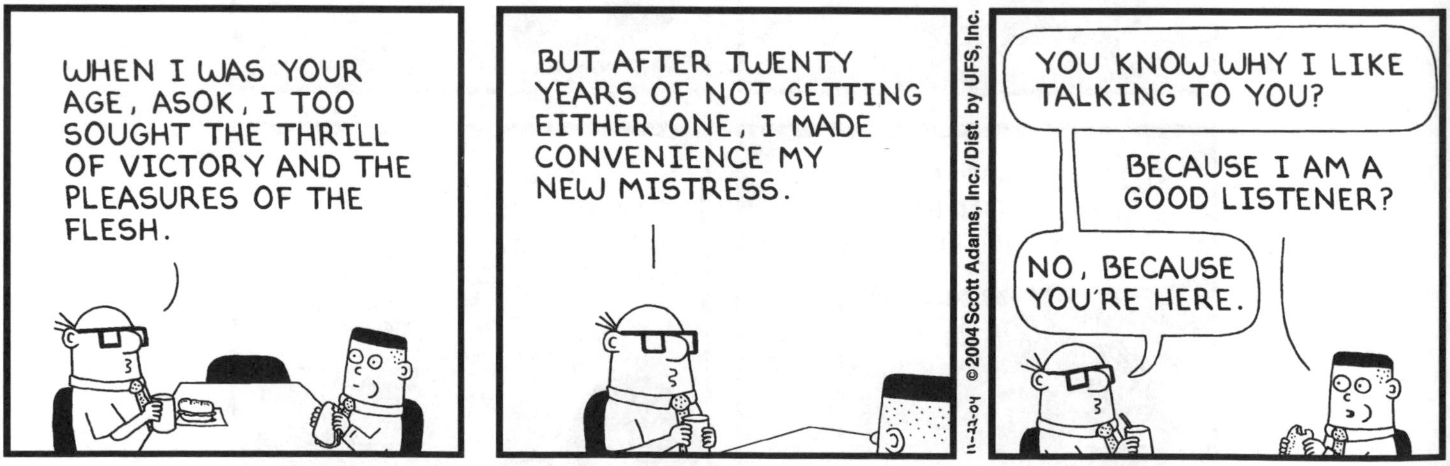
WHEN I WAS YOUR AGE, ASOK, I TOO SOUGHT THE THRILL OF VICTORY AND THE PLEASURES OF THE FLESH.
BUT AFTER TWENTY YEARS OF NOT GETTING EITHER ONE, I MADE CONVENIENCE MY NEW MISTRESS.
11-22-04 © 2004 Scott Adams, Inc./Dist. by UFS, Inc.
YOU KNOW WHY I LIKE TALKING TO YOU?
BECAUSE I AM A GOOD LISTENER?
NO, BECAUSE YOU'RE HERE.

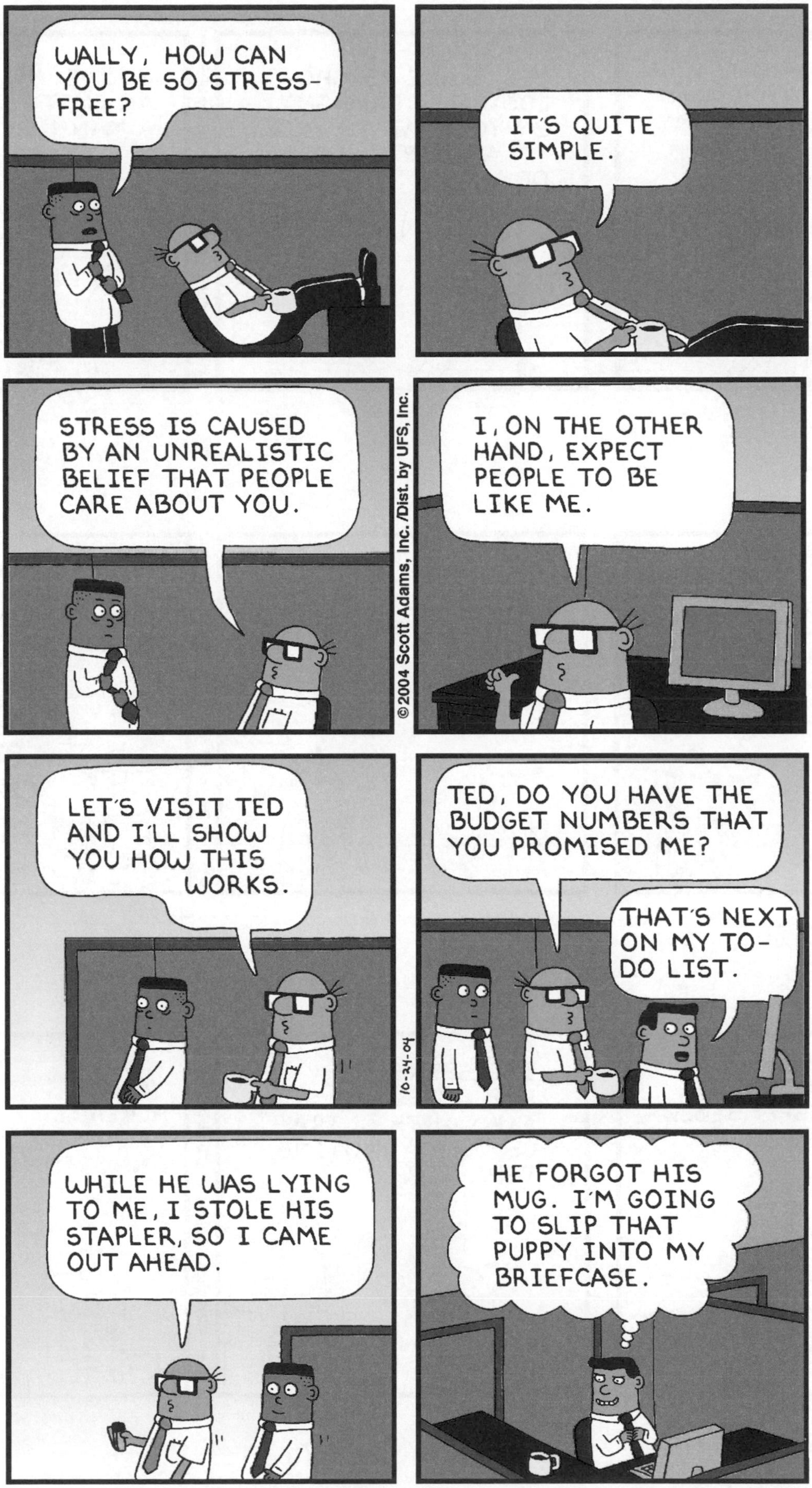
WALLY, HOW CAN YOU BE SO STRESS-FREE?
IT'S QUITE SIMPLE.
STRESS IS CAUSED BY AN UNREALISTIC BELIEF THAT PEOPLE CARE ABOUT YOU.
I, ON THE OTHER HAND, EXPECT PEOPLE TO BE LIKE ME.
LET'S VISIT TED AND I'LL SHOW YOU HOW THIS WORKS.
TED, DO YOU HAVE THE BUDGET NUMBERS THAT YOU PROMISED ME?
THAT'S NEXT ON MY TO-DO LIST.
WHILE HE WAS LYING TO ME, I STOLE HIS STAPLER, SO I CAME OUT AHEAD.
HE FORGOT HIS MUG. I'M GOING TO SLIP THAT PUPPY INTO MY BRIEFCASE.
©2004 Scott Adams, Inc./Dist. by UFS, Inc.
10-24-04

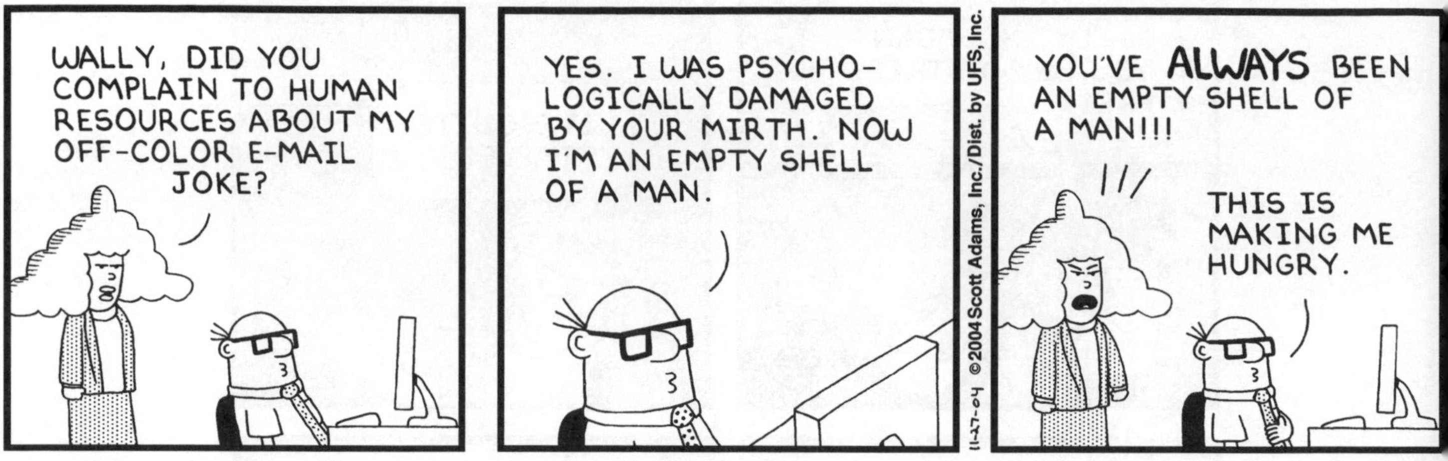
WALLY, DID YOU COMPLAIN TO HUMAN RESOURCES ABOUT MY OFF-COLOR E-MAIL JOKE?
YES. I WAS PSYCHO-LOGICALLY DAMAGED BY YOUR MIRTH. NOW I'M AN EMPTY SHELL OF A MAN.
11-27-04 ©2004 Scott Adams, Inc./Dist. by UFS, Inc.
YOU'VE ALWAYS BEEN AN EMPTY SHELL OF A MAN!!!
THIS IS MAKING ME HUNGRY.

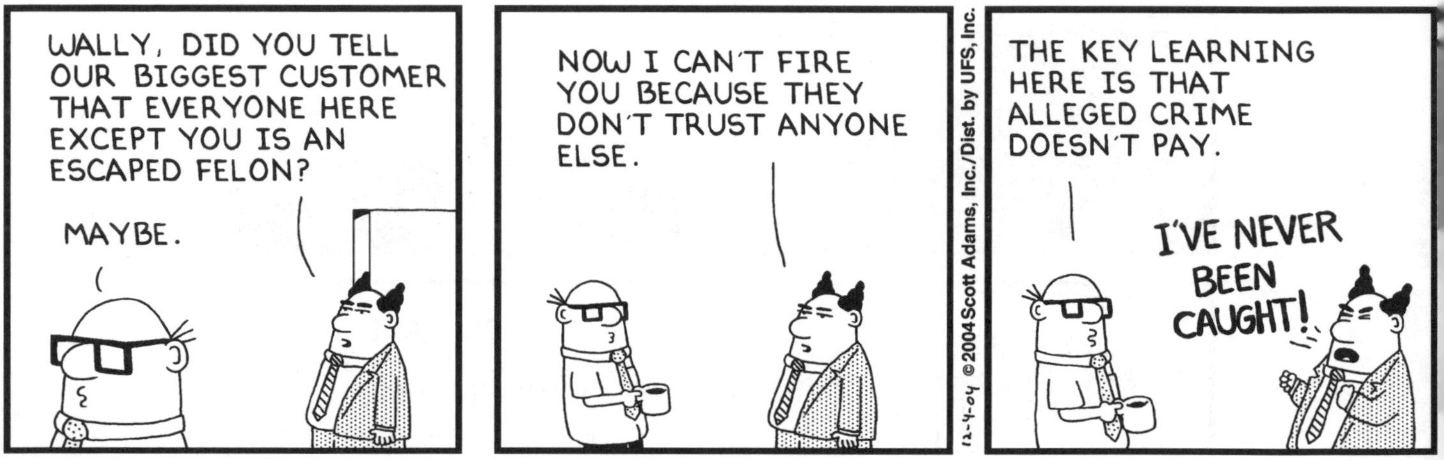
WALLY, DID YOU TELL OUR BIGGEST CUSTOMER THAT EVERYONE HERE EXCEPT YOU IS AN ESCAPED FELON?
MAYBE.
NOW I CAN'T FIRE YOU BECAUSE THEY DON'T TRUST ANYONE ELSE.
12-4-04 ©2004 Scott Adams, Inc./Dist. by UFS, Inc.
THE KEY LEARNING HERE IS THAT ALLEGED CRIME DOESN'T PAY.
I'VE NEVER BEEN CAUGHT!

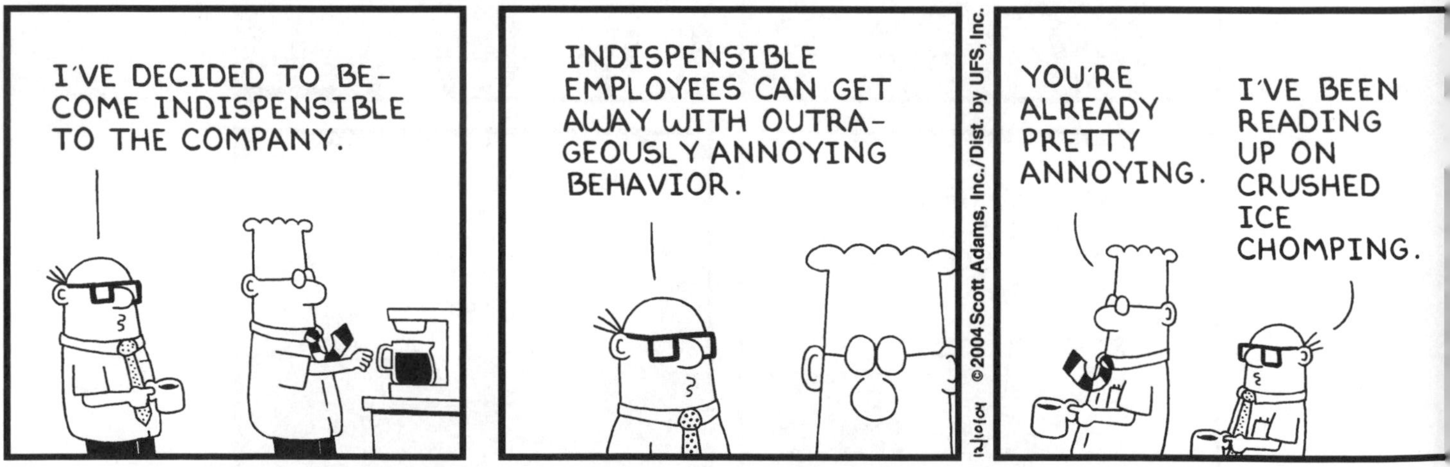
I'VE DECIDED TO BE-COME INDISPENSIBLE TO THE COMPANY.
INDISPENSIBLE EMPLOYEES CAN GET AWAY WITH OUTRA-GEOUSLY ANNOYING BEHAVIOR.
12/10/04 ©2004 Scott Adams, Inc./Dist. by UFS, Inc.
YOU'RE ALREADY PRETTY ANNOYING.
I'VE BEEN READING UP ON CRUSHED ICE CHOMPING.

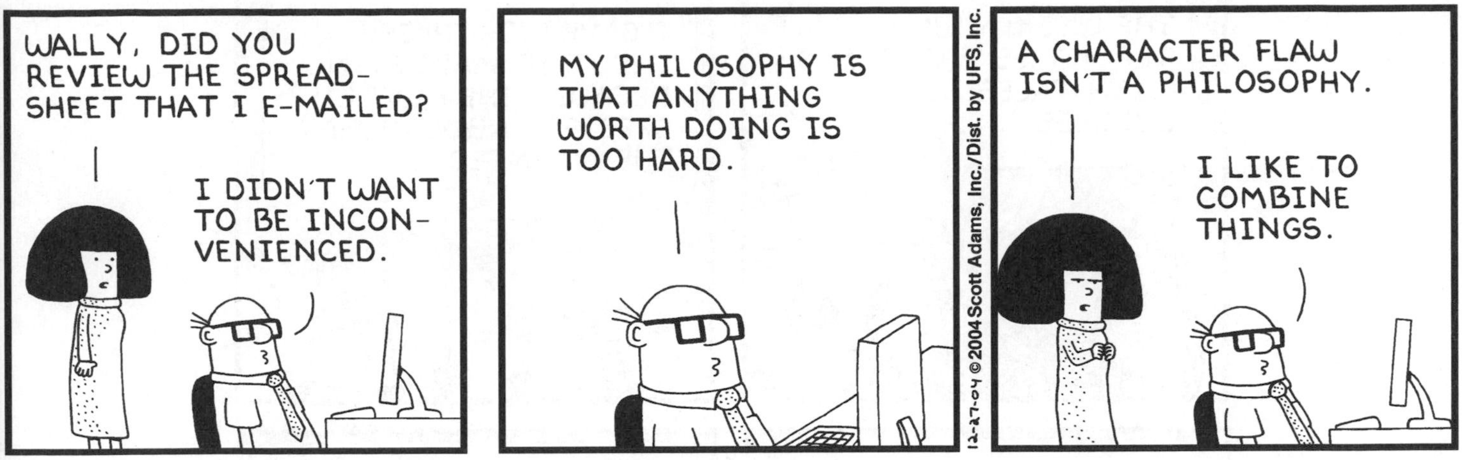
WALLY, DID YOU REVIEW THE SPREAD-SHEET THAT I E-MAILED?
I DIDN'T WANT TO BE INCON-VENIENCED.
MY PHILOSOPHY IS THAT ANYTHING WORTH DOING IS TOO HARD.
12-27-04 © 2004 Scott Adams, Inc./Dist. by UFS, Inc.
A CHARACTER FLAW ISN'T A PHILOSOPHY.
I LIKE TO COMBINE THINGS.

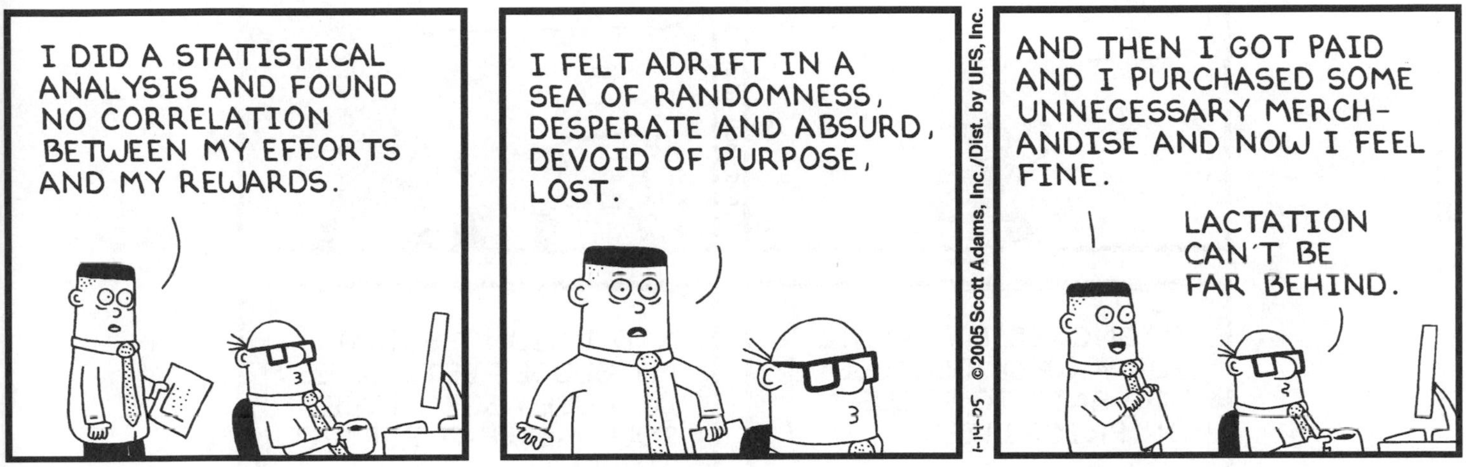
I DID A STATISTICAL ANALYSIS AND FOUND NO CORRELATION BETWEEN MY EFFORTS AND MY REWARDS.
I FELT ADRIFT IN A SEA OF RANDOMNESS, DESPERATE AND ABSURD, DEVOID OF PURPOSE, LOST.
1-14-05 © 2005 Scott Adams, Inc./Dist. by UFS, Inc.
AND THEN I GOT PAID AND I PURCHASED SOME UNNECESSARY MERCH-ANDISE AND NOW I FEEL FINE.
LACTATION CAN'T BE FAR BEHIND.

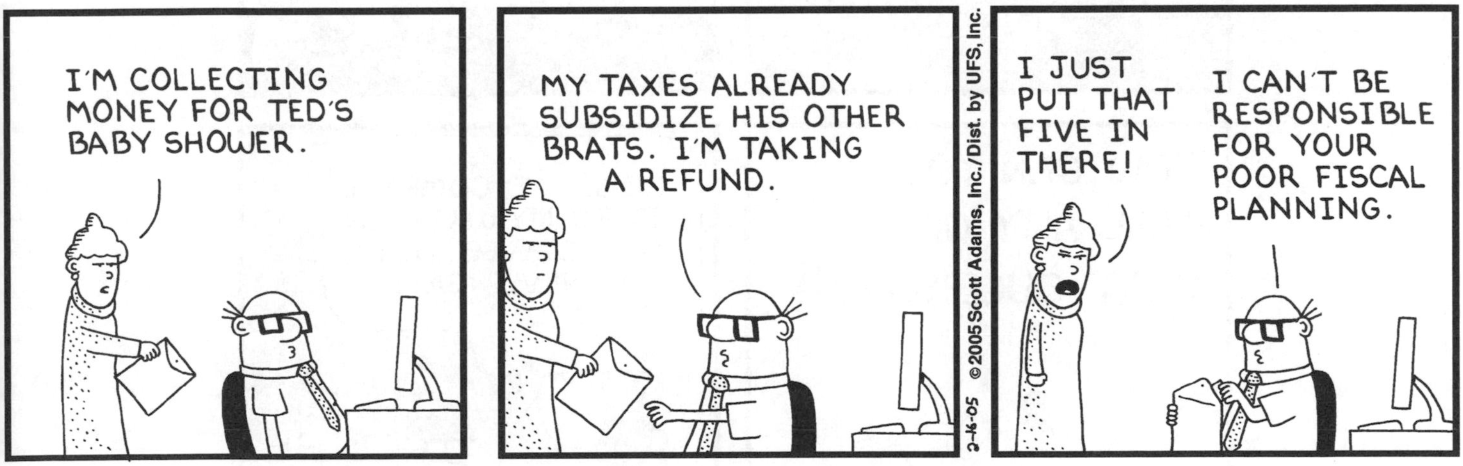
I'M COLLECTING MONEY FOR TED'S BABY SHOWER.
MY TAXES ALREADY SUBSIDIZE HIS OTHER BRATS. I'M TAKING A REFUND.
2-16-05 © 2005 Scott Adams, Inc./Dist. by UFS, Inc.
I JUST PUT THAT FIVE IN THERE!
I CAN'T BE RESPONSIBLE FOR YOUR POOR FISCAL PLANNING.

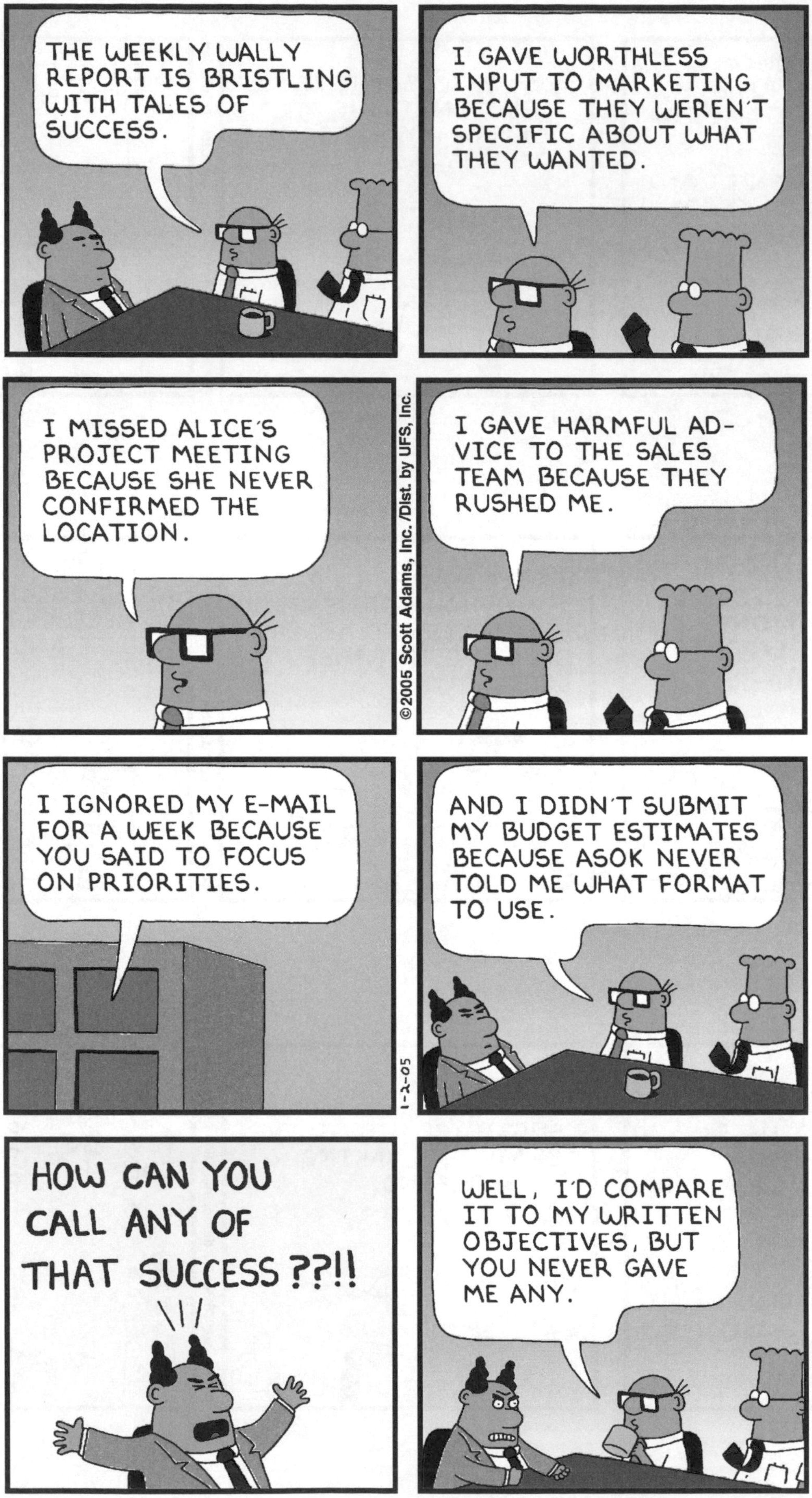
THE WEEKLY WALLY REPORT IS BRISTLING WITH TALES OF SUCCESS.
I GAVE WORTHLESS INPUT TO MARKETING BECAUSE THEY WEREN'T SPECIFIC ABOUT WHAT THEY WANTED.
I MISSED ALICE'S PROJECT MEETING BECAUSE SHE NEVER CONFIRMED THE LOCATION.
I GAVE HARMFUL AD-VICE TO THE SALES TEAM BECAUSE THEY RUSHED ME.
I IGNORED MY E-MAIL FOR A WEEK BECAUSE YOU SAID TO FOCUS ON PRIORITIES.
AND I DIDN'T SUBMIT MY BUDGET ESTIMATES BECAUSE ASOK NEVER TOLD ME WHAT FORMAT TO USE.
HOW CAN YOU CALL ANY OF THAT SUCCESS??!!
WELL, I'D COMPARE IT TO MY WRITTEN OBJECTIVES, BUT YOU NEVER GAVE ME ANY.
©2005 Scott Adams, Inc./Dist. by UFS, Inc.
1-2-05

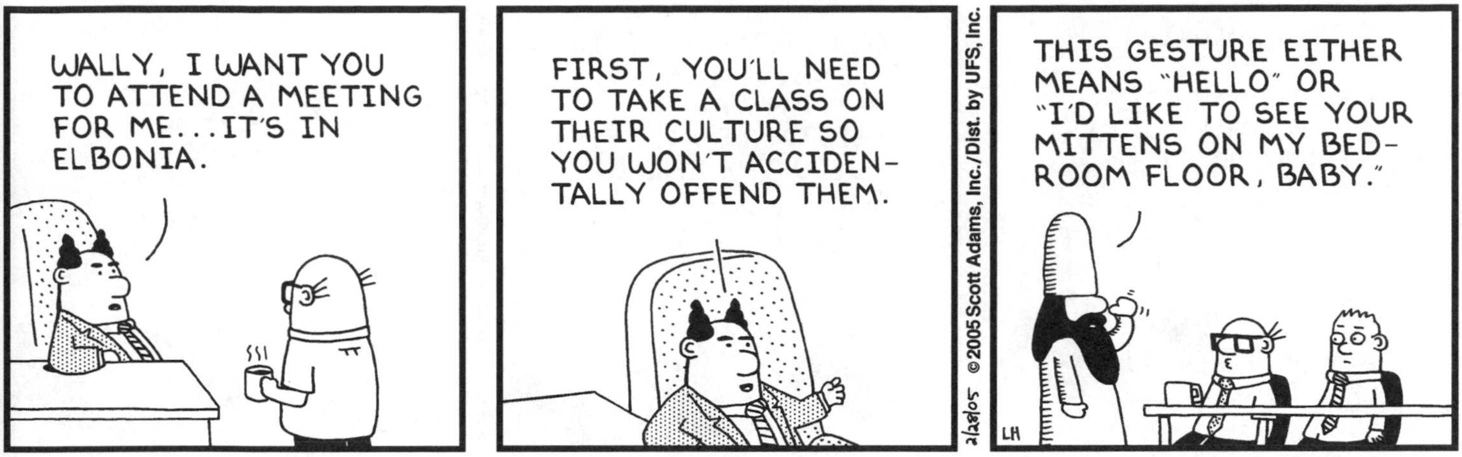
WALLY, I WANT YOU TO ATTEND A MEETING FOR ME...IT'S IN ELBONIA.
FIRST, YOU'LL NEED TO TAKE A CLASS ON THEIR CULTURE SO YOU WON'T ACCIDENTALLY OFFEND THEM.
2/28/05 © 2005 Scott Adams, Inc./Dist. by UFS, Inc.
THIS GESTURE EITHER MEANS "HELLO" OR "I'D LIKE TO SEE YOUR MITTENS ON MY BEDROOM FLOOR, BABY."

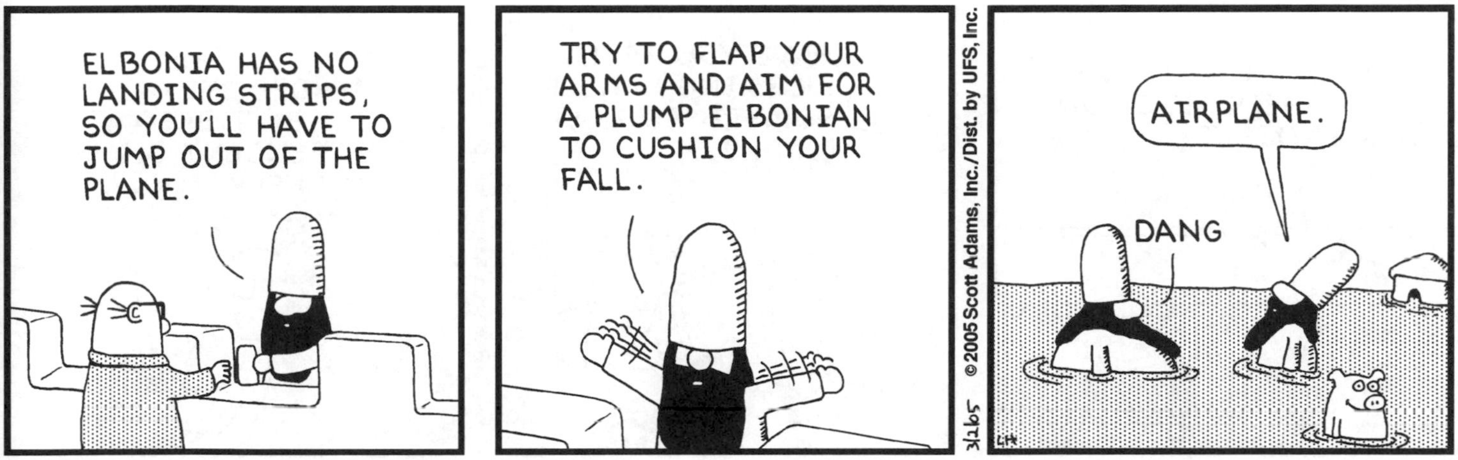
ELBONIA HAS NO LANDING STRIPS, SO YOU'LL HAVE TO JUMP OUT OF THE PLANE.
TRY TO FLAP YOUR ARMS AND AIM FOR A PLUMP ELBONIAN TO CUSHION YOUR FALL.
3/2/05 © 2005 Scott Adams, Inc./Dist. by UFS, Inc.
AIRPLANE.
DANG

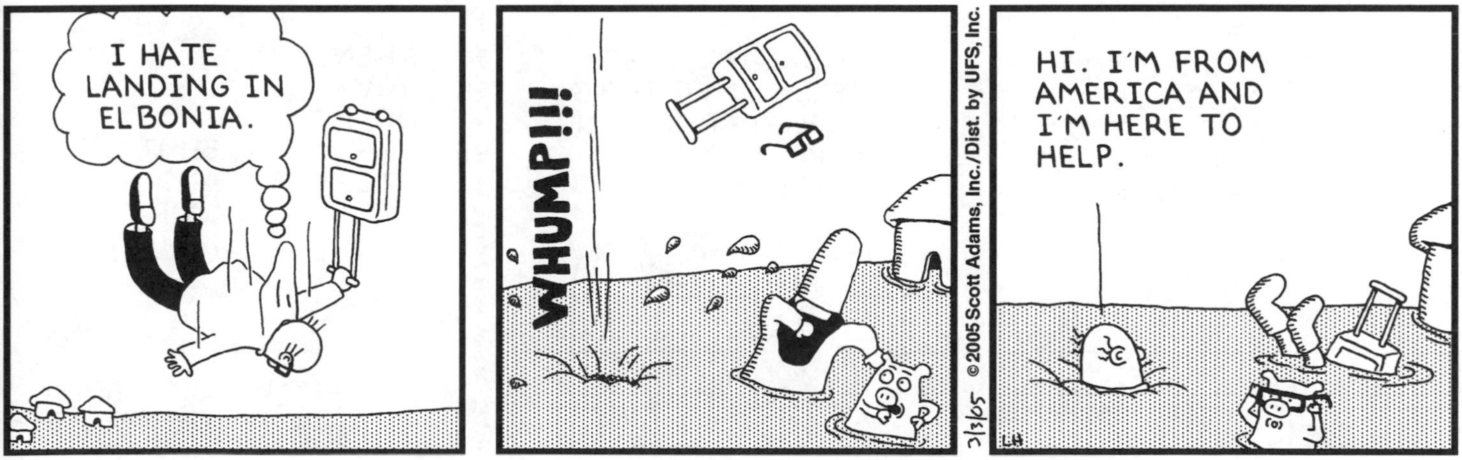
I HATE LANDING IN ELBONIA.
WHUMP!!!
3/3/05 © 2005 Scott Adams, Inc./Dist. by UFS, Inc.
HI. I'M FROM AMERICA AND I'M HERE TO HELP.

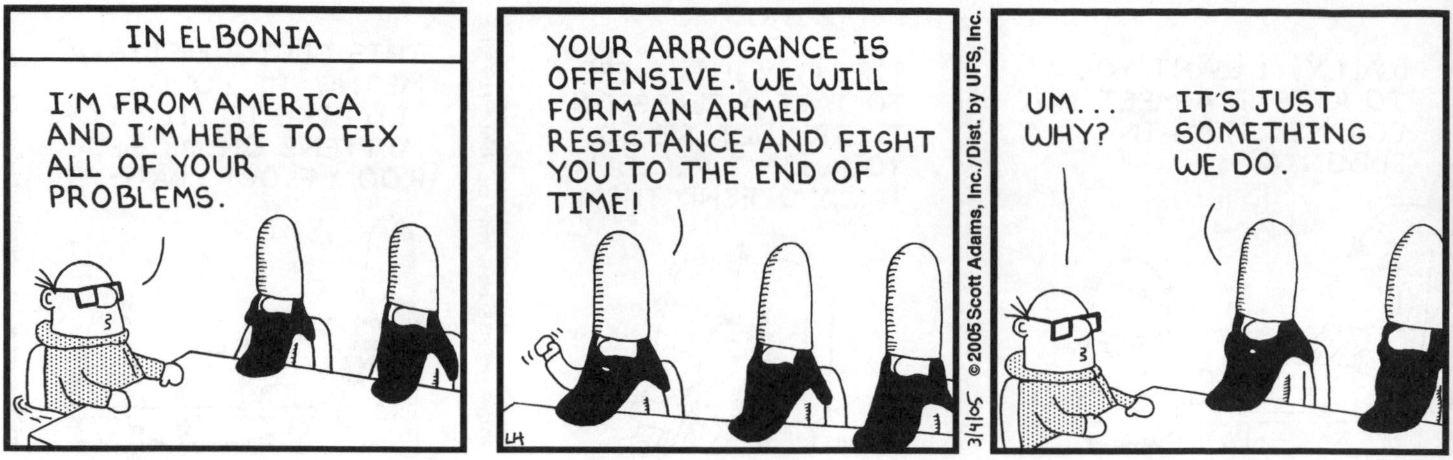
IN ELBONIA
I'M FROM AMERICA AND I'M HERE TO FIX ALL OF YOUR PROBLEMS.
YOUR ARROGANCE IS OFFENSIVE. WE WILL FORM AN ARMED RESISTANCE AND FIGHT YOU TO THE END OF TIME!
3/4/05 © 2005 Scott Adams, Inc./Dist. by UFS, Inc.
UM... WHY?
IT'S JUST SOMETHING WE DO.

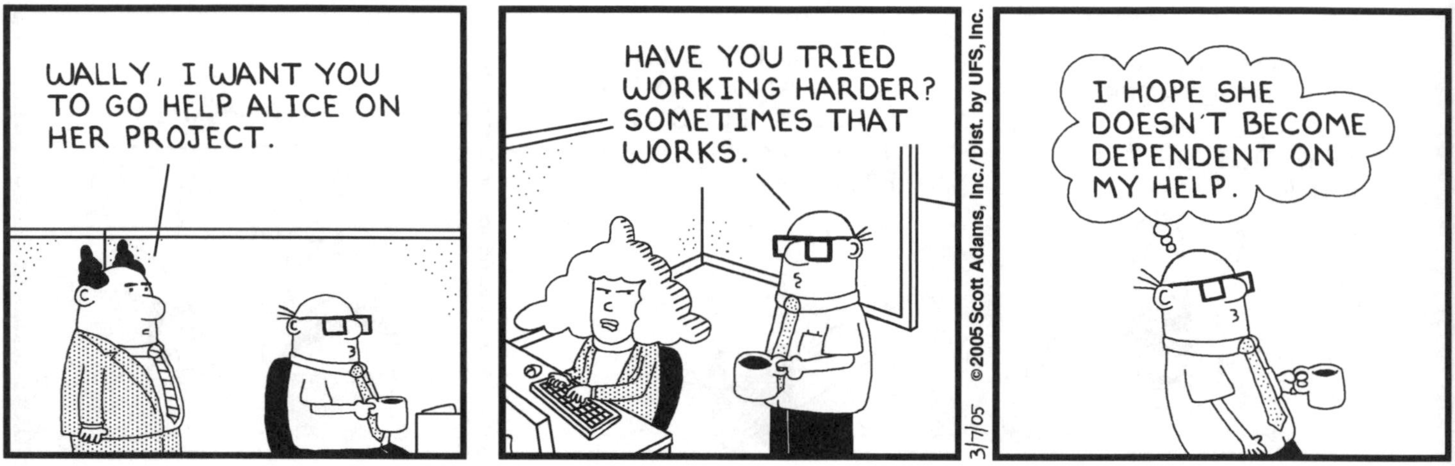
WALLY, I WANT YOU TO GO HELP ALICE ON HER PROJECT.
HAVE YOU TRIED WORKING HARDER? SOMETIMES THAT WORKS.
3/7/05 © 2005 Scott Adams, Inc./Dist. by UFS, Inc.
I HOPE SHE DOESN'T BECOME DEPENDENT ON MY HELP.

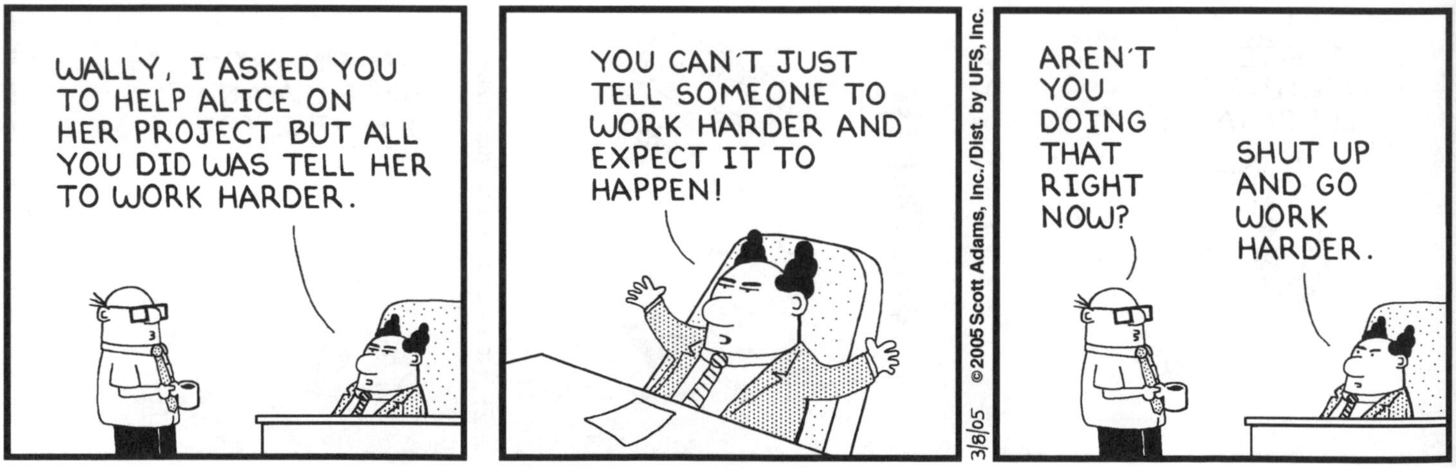
WALLY, I ASKED YOU TO HELP ALICE ON HER PROJECT BUT ALL YOU DID WAS TELL HER TO WORK HARDER.
YOU CAN'T JUST TELL SOMEONE TO WORK HARDER AND EXPECT IT TO HAPPEN!
3/8/05 © 2005 Scott Adams, Inc./Dist. by UFS, Inc.
AREN'T YOU DOING THAT RIGHT NOW?
SHUT UP AND GO WORK HARDER.

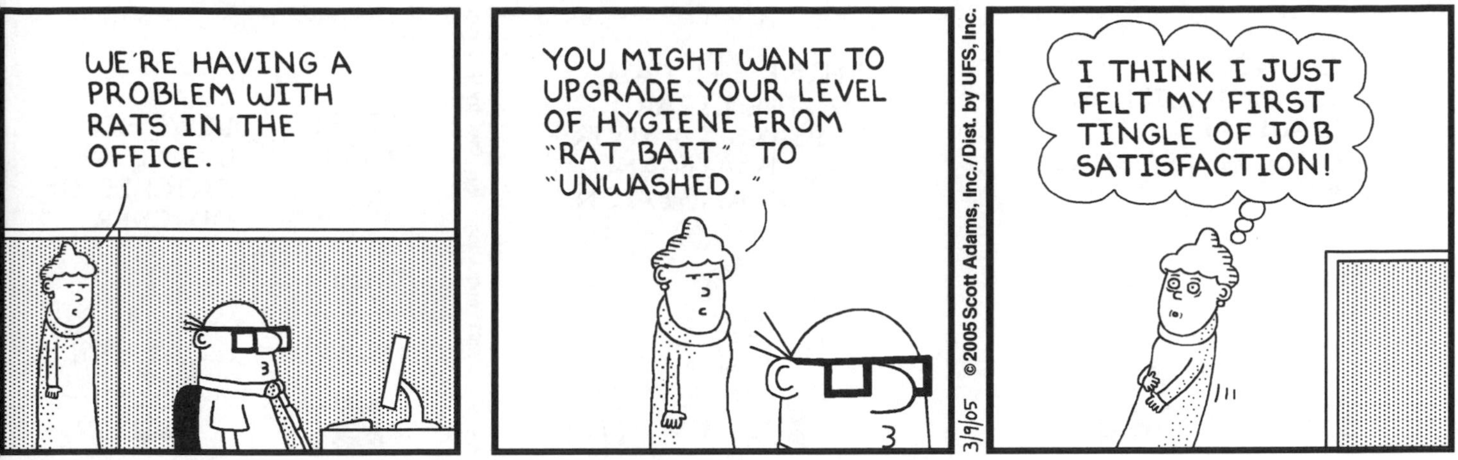
WE'RE HAVING A PROBLEM WITH RATS IN THE OFFICE.
YOU MIGHT WANT TO UPGRADE YOUR LEVEL OF HYGIENE FROM "RAT BAIT" TO "UNWASHED."
3/9/05 © 2005 Scott Adams, Inc./Dist. by UFS, Inc.
I THINK I JUST FELT MY FIRST TINGLE OF JOB SATISFACTION!

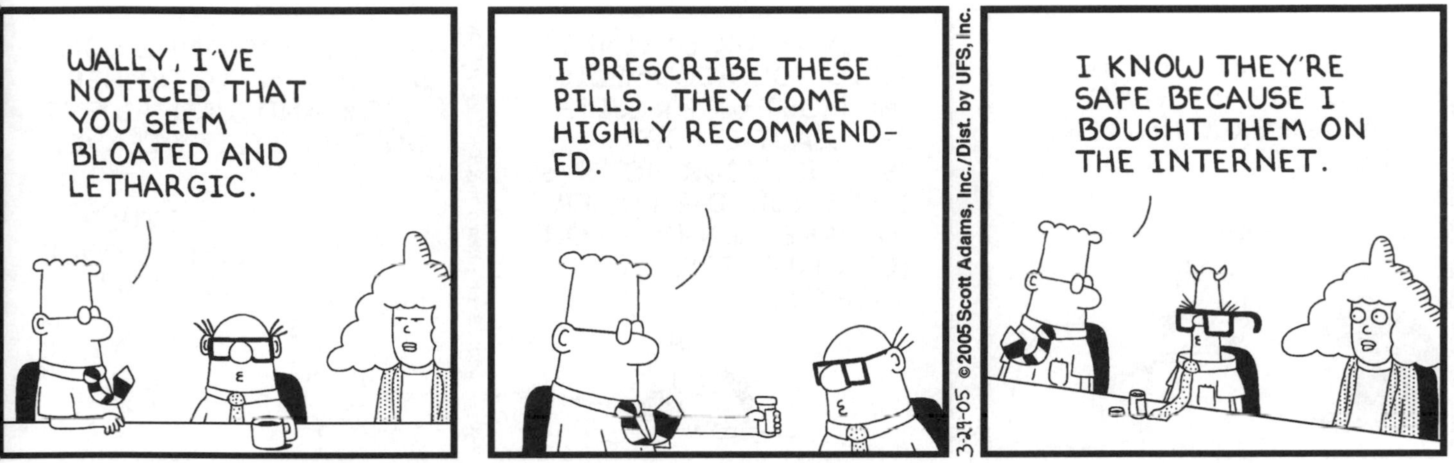
WALLY, I'VE NOTICED THAT YOU SEEM BLOATED AND LETHARGIC.
I PRESCRIBE THESE PILLS. THEY COME HIGHLY RECOMMEND-ED.
3-29-05 © 2005 Scott Adams, Inc./Dist. by UFS, Inc.
I KNOW THEY'RE SAFE BECAUSE I BOUGHT THEM ON THE INTERNET.

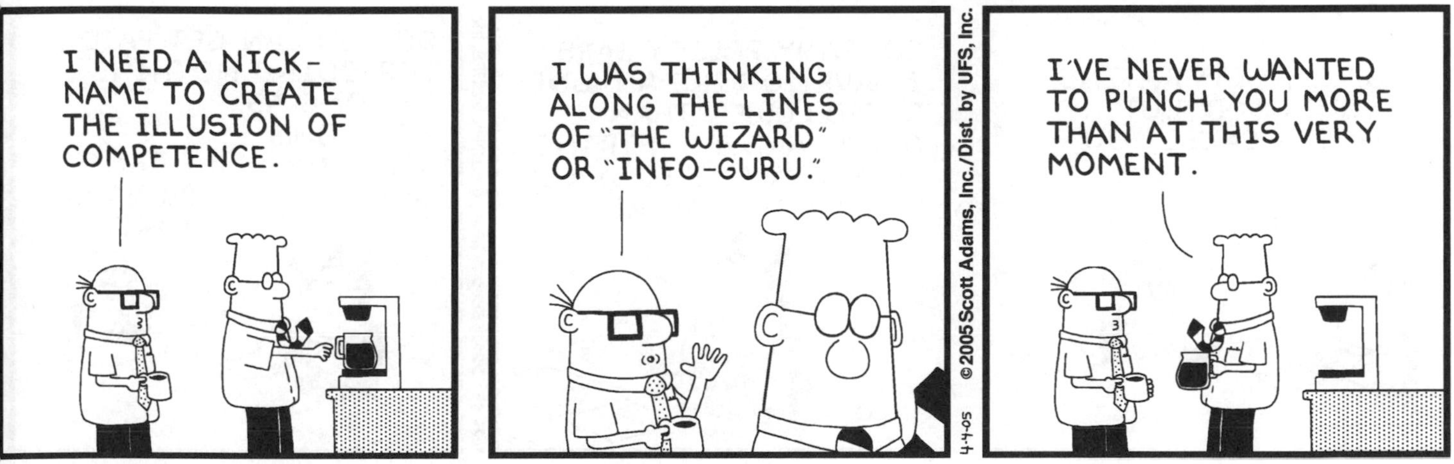
I NEED A NICK-NAME TO CREATE THE ILLUSION OF COMPETENCE.
I WAS THINKING ALONG THE LINES OF "THE WIZARD" OR "INFO-GURU."
4-4-05 © 2005 Scott Adams, Inc./Dist. by UFS, Inc.
I'VE NEVER WANTED TO PUNCH YOU MORE THAN AT THIS VERY MOMENT.

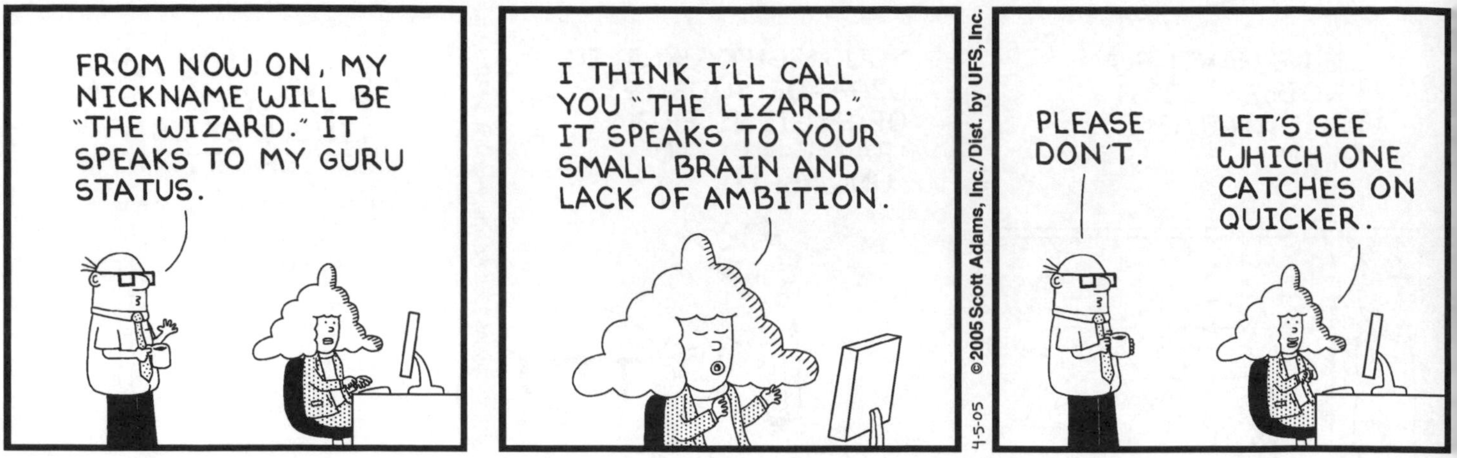
FROM NOW ON, MY NICKNAME WILL BE "THE WIZARD." IT SPEAKS TO MY GURU STATUS.
I THINK I'LL CALL YOU "THE LIZARD." IT SPEAKS TO YOUR SMALL BRAIN AND LACK OF AMBITION.
4-5-05 ©2005 Scott Adams, Inc./Dist. by UFS, Inc.
PLEASE DON'T.
LET'S SEE WHICH ONE CATCHES ON QUICKER.

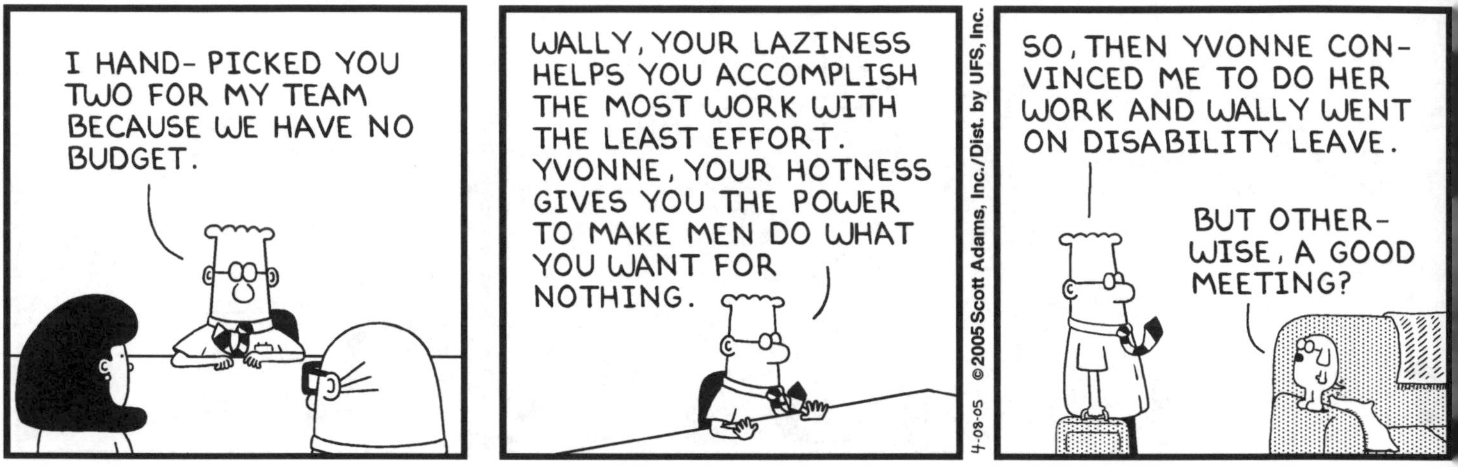
I HAND-PICKED YOU TWO FOR MY TEAM BECAUSE WE HAVE NO BUDGET.
WALLY, YOUR LAZINESS HELPS YOU ACCOMPLISH THE MOST WORK WITH THE LEAST EFFORT. YVONNE, YOUR HOTNESS GIVES YOU THE POWER TO MAKE MEN DO WHAT YOU WANT FOR NOTHING.
4-08-05 ©2005 Scott Adams, Inc./Dist. by UFS, Inc.
SO, THEN YVONNE CONVINCED ME TO DO HER WORK AND WALLY WENT ON DISABILITY LEAVE.
BUT OTHERWISE, A GOOD MEETING?

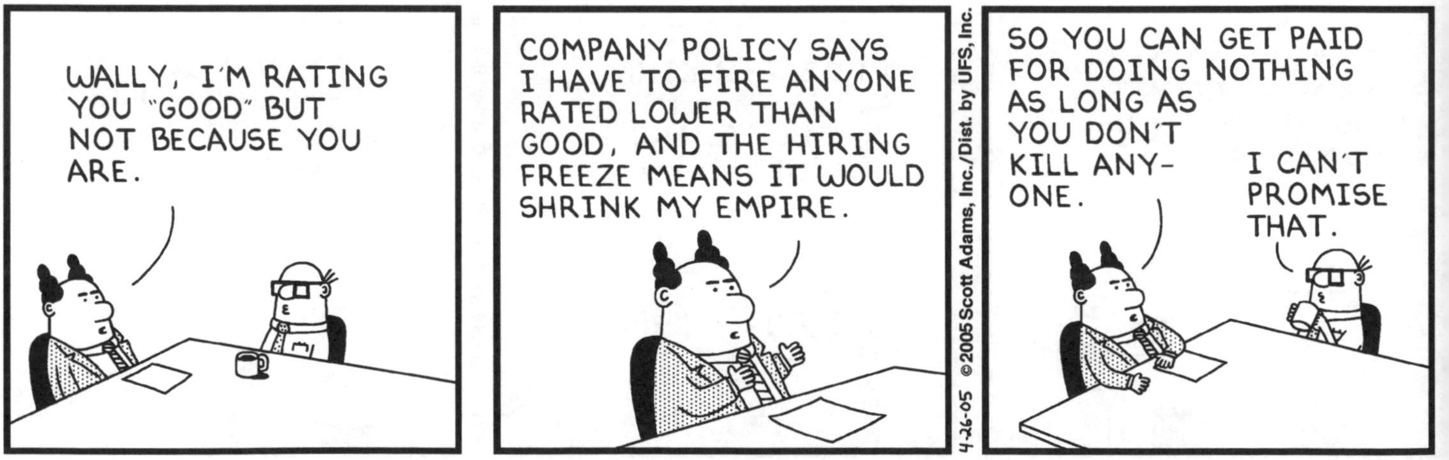
WALLY, I'M RATING YOU "GOOD" BUT NOT BECAUSE YOU ARE.
COMPANY POLICY SAYS I HAVE TO FIRE ANYONE RATED LOWER THAN GOOD, AND THE HIRING FREEZE MEANS IT WOULD SHRINK MY EMPIRE.
4-26-05 ©2005 Scott Adams, Inc./Dist. by UFS, Inc.
SO YOU CAN GET PAID FOR DOING NOTHING AS LONG AS YOU DON'T KILL ANYONE.
I CAN'T PROMISE THAT.

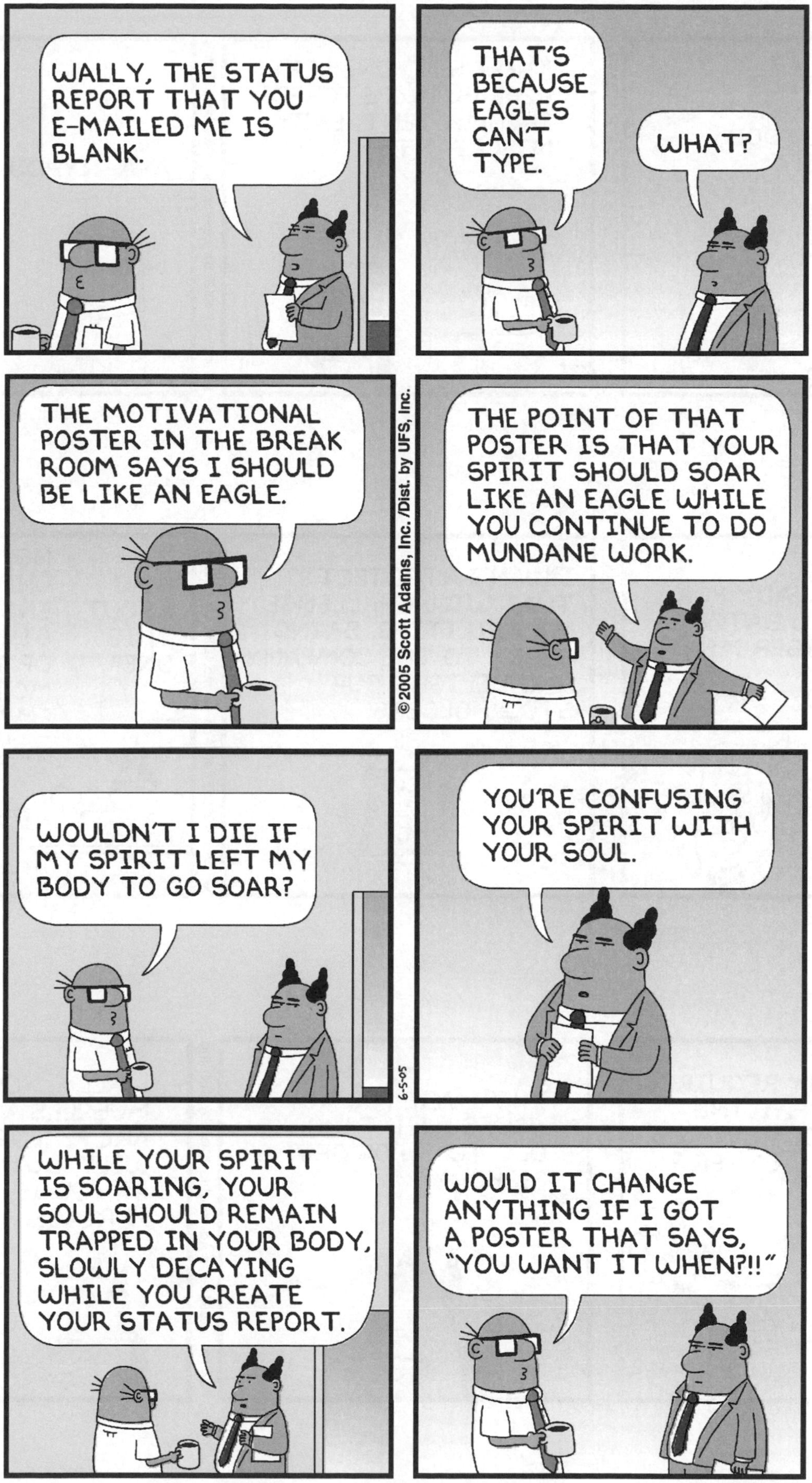

WALLY, THE STATUS REPORT THAT YOU E-MAILED ME IS BLANK.
THAT'S BECAUSE EAGLES CAN'T TYPE.
WHAT?
THE MOTIVATIONAL POSTER IN THE BREAK ROOM SAYS I SHOULD BE LIKE AN EAGLE.
THE POINT OF THAT POSTER IS THAT YOUR SPIRIT SHOULD SOAR LIKE AN EAGLE WHILE YOU CONTINUE TO DO MUNDANE WORK.
WOULDN'T I DIE IF MY SPIRIT LEFT MY BODY TO GO SOAR?
YOU'RE CONFUSING YOUR SPIRIT WITH YOUR SOUL.
WHILE YOUR SPIRIT IS SOARING, YOUR SOUL SHOULD REMAIN TRAPPED IN YOUR BODY, SLOWLY DECAYING WHILE YOU CREATE YOUR STATUS REPORT.
WOULD IT CHANGE ANYTHING IF I GOT A POSTER THAT SAYS, "YOU WANT IT WHEN?!!"
©2005 Scott Adams, Inc./Dist. by UFS, Inc.
6-5-05

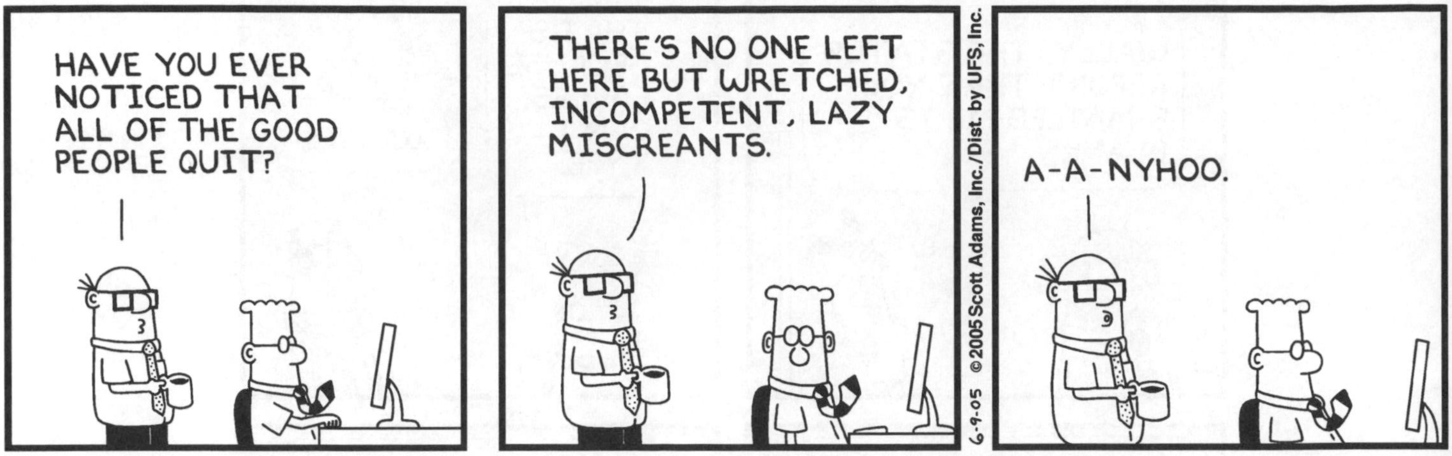
HAVE YOU EVER NOTICED THAT ALL OF THE GOOD PEOPLE QUIT?
THERE'S NO ONE LEFT HERE BUT WRETCHED, INCOMPETENT, LAZY MISCREANTS.
6-9-05 ©2005 Scott Adams, Inc./Dist. by UFS, Inc.
A-A-NYHOO.

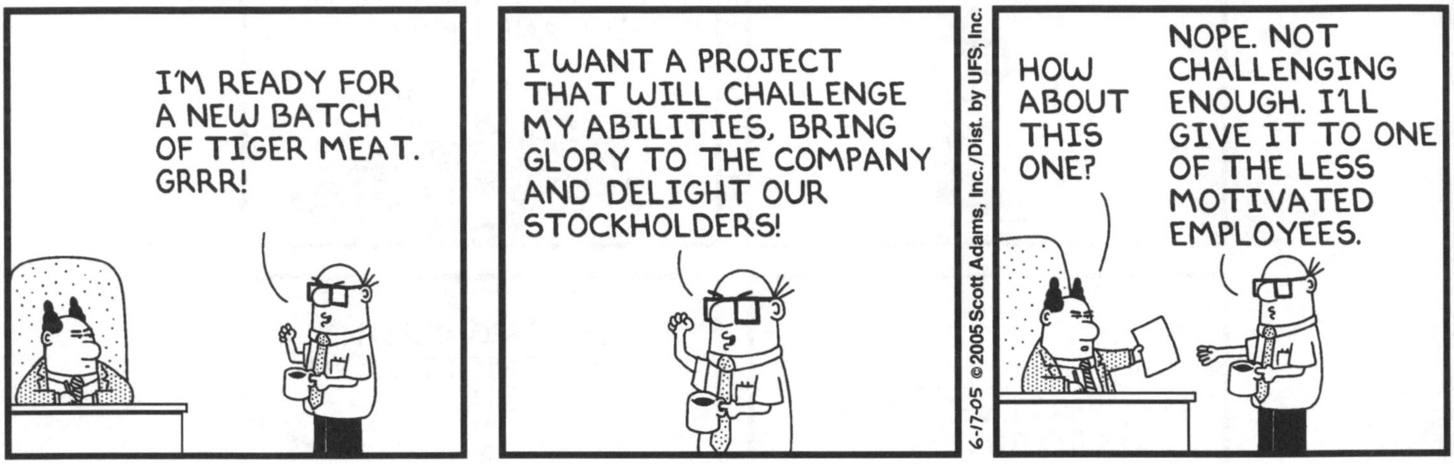
I'M READY FOR A NEW BATCH OF TIGER MEAT. GRRR!
I WANT A PROJECT THAT WILL CHALLENGE MY ABILITIES, BRING GLORY TO THE COMPANY AND DELIGHT OUR STOCKHOLDERS!
6-17-05 ©2005 Scott Adams, Inc./Dist. by UFS, Inc.
HOW ABOUT THIS ONE?
NOPE. NOT CHALLENGING ENOUGH. I'LL GIVE IT TO ONE OF THE LESS MOTIVATED EMPLOYEES.

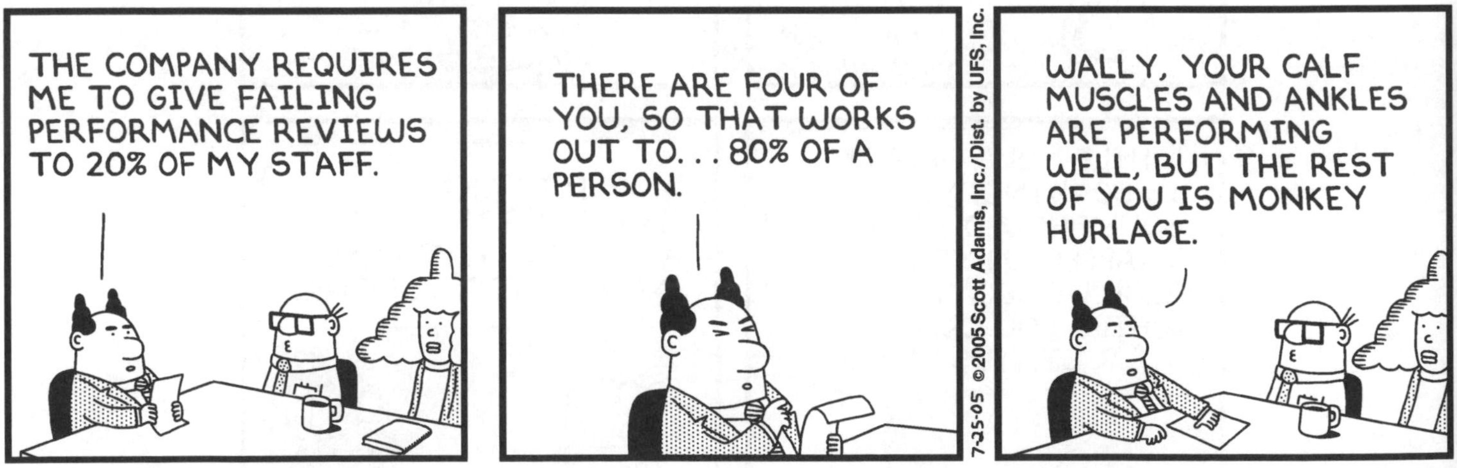
THE COMPANY REQUIRES ME TO GIVE FAILING PERFORMANCE REVIEWS TO 20% OF MY STAFF.
THERE ARE FOUR OF YOU, SO THAT WORKS OUT TO. . . 80% OF A PERSON.
7-25-05 ©2005 Scott Adams, Inc./Dist. by UFS, Inc.
WALLY, YOUR CALF MUSCLES AND ANKLES ARE PERFORMING WELL, BUT THE REST OF YOU IS MONKEY HURLAGE.

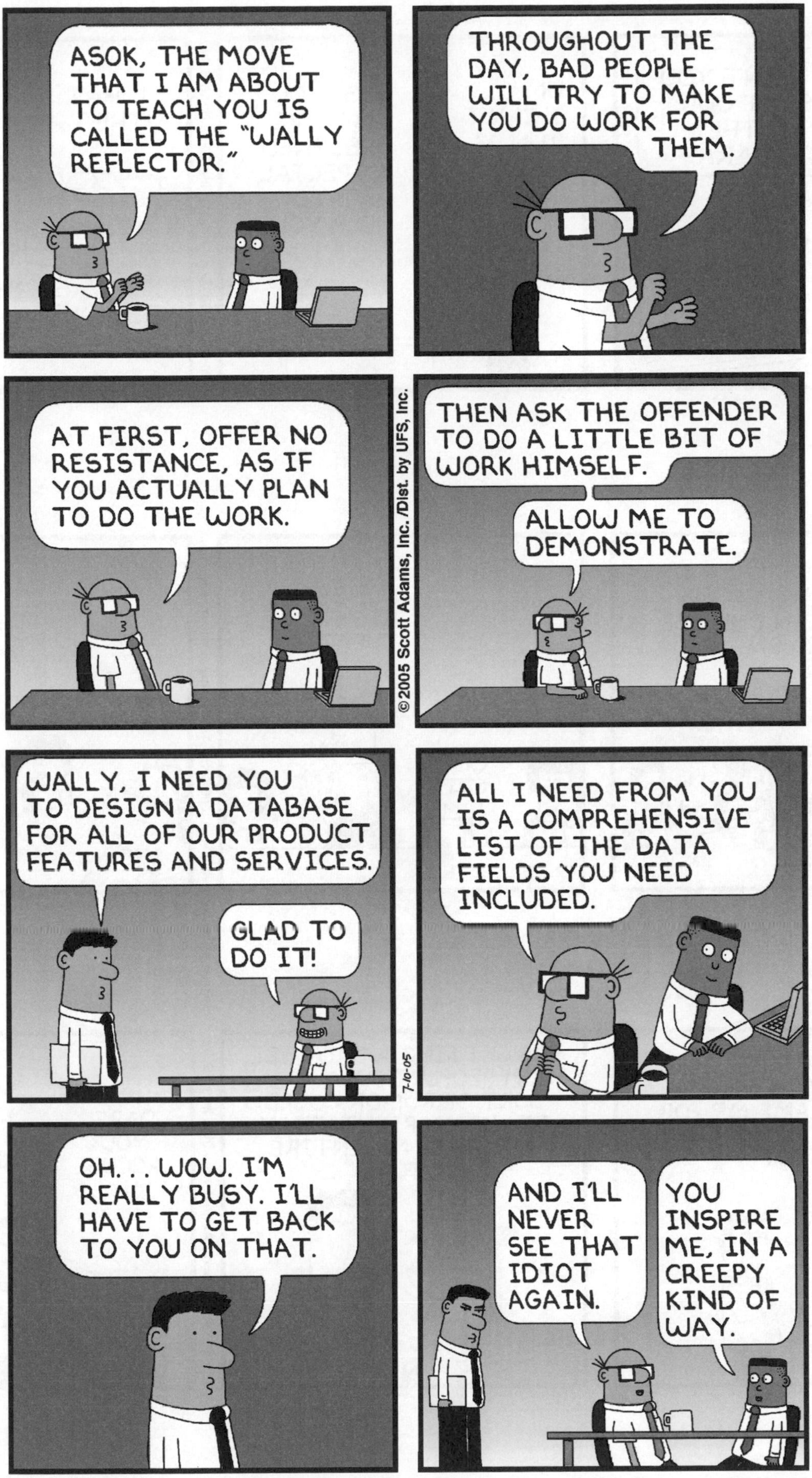
ASOK, THE MOVE THAT I AM ABOUT TO TEACH YOU IS CALLED THE "WALLY REFLECTOR."
THROUGHOUT THE DAY, BAD PEOPLE WILL TRY TO MAKE YOU DO WORK FOR THEM.
AT FIRST, OFFER NO RESISTANCE, AS IF YOU ACTUALLY PLAN TO DO THE WORK.
©2005 Scott Adams, Inc./Dist. by UFS, Inc.
THEN ASK THE OFFENDER TO DO A LITTLE BIT OF WORK HIMSELF.
ALLOW ME TO DEMONSTRATE.
WALLY, I NEED YOU TO DESIGN A DATABASE FOR ALL OF OUR PRODUCT FEATURES AND SERVICES.
GLAD TO DO IT!
7-10-05
ALL I NEED FROM YOU IS A COMPREHENSIVE LIST OF THE DATA FIELDS YOU NEED INCLUDED.
OH... WOW. I'M REALLY BUSY. I'LL HAVE TO GET BACK TO YOU ON THAT.
AND I'LL NEVER SEE THAT IDIOT AGAIN.
YOU INSPIRE ME, IN A CREEPY KIND OF WAY.

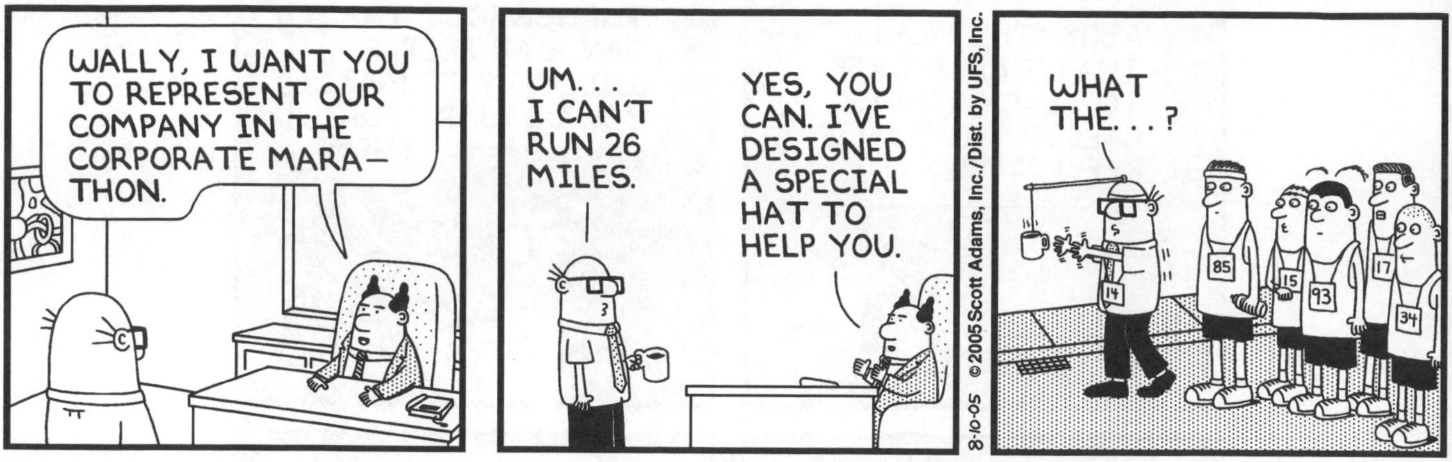
WALLY, I WANT YOU TO REPRESENT OUR COMPANY IN THE CORPORATE MARA-THON.
UM... I CAN'T RUN 26 MILES.
YES, YOU CAN. I'VE DESIGNED A SPECIAL HAT TO HELP YOU.
8-10-05 © 2005 Scott Adams, Inc./Dist. by UFS, Inc.
WHAT THE...?
85
14
15
93
17
34

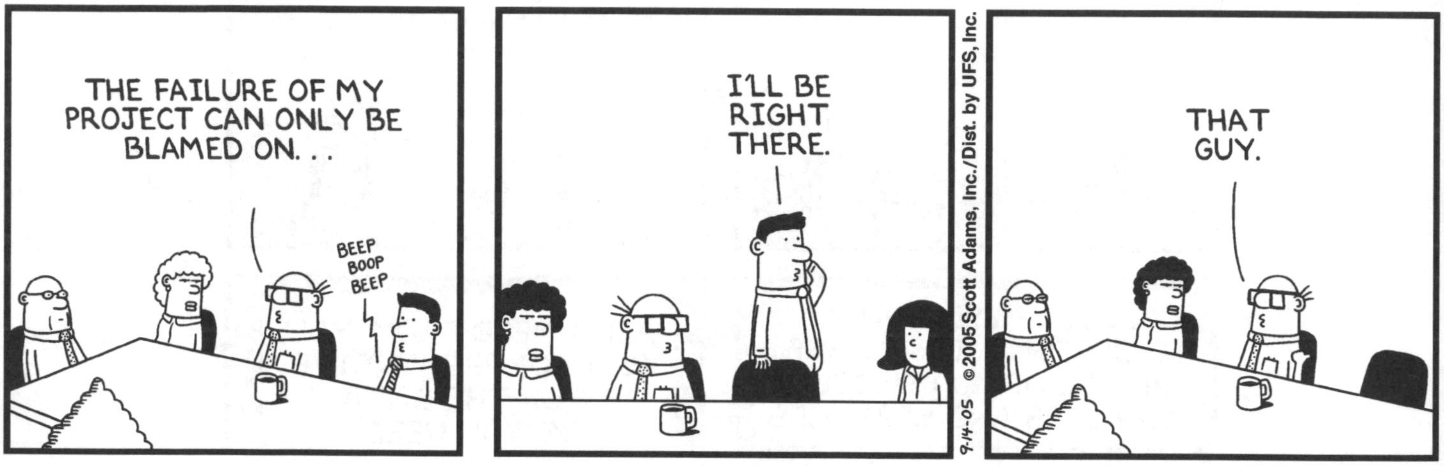
THE FAILURE OF MY PROJECT CAN ONLY BE BLAMED ON...
BEEP BOOP BEEP
I'LL BE RIGHT THERE.
9-14-05 © 2005 Scott Adams, Inc./Dist. by UFS, Inc.
THAT GUY.

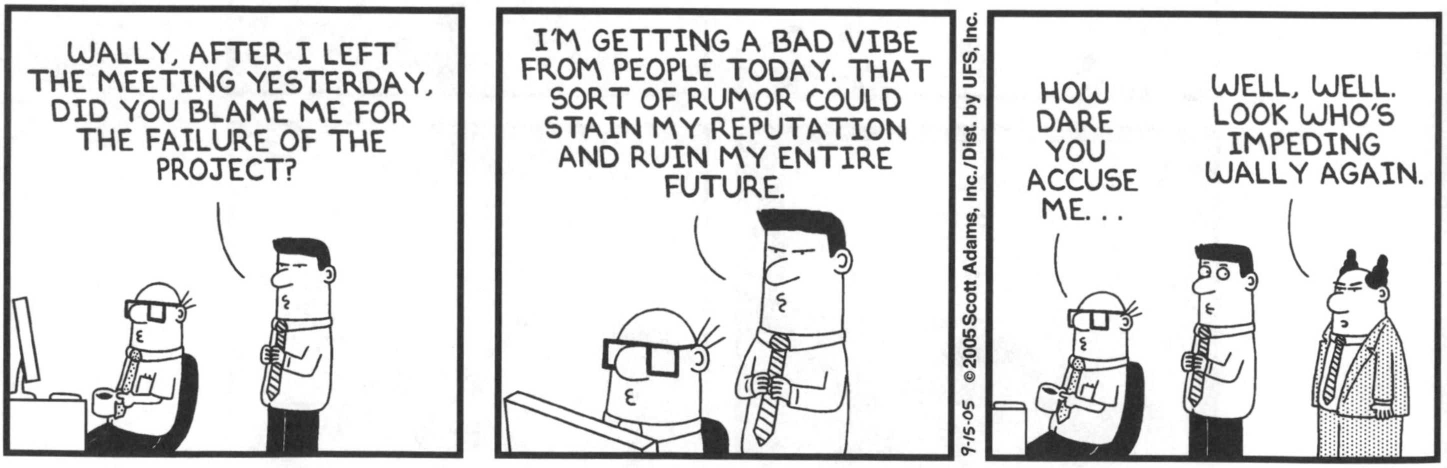
WALLY, AFTER I LEFT THE MEETING YESTERDAY, DID YOU BLAME ME FOR THE FAILURE OF THE PROJECT?
I'M GETTING A BAD VIBE FROM PEOPLE TODAY. THAT SORT OF RUMOR COULD STAIN MY REPUTATION AND RUIN MY ENTIRE FUTURE.
9-15-05 © 2005 Scott Adams, Inc./Dist. by UFS, Inc.
HOW DARE YOU ACCUSE ME...
WELL, WELL. LOOK WHO'S IMPEDING WALLY AGAIN.

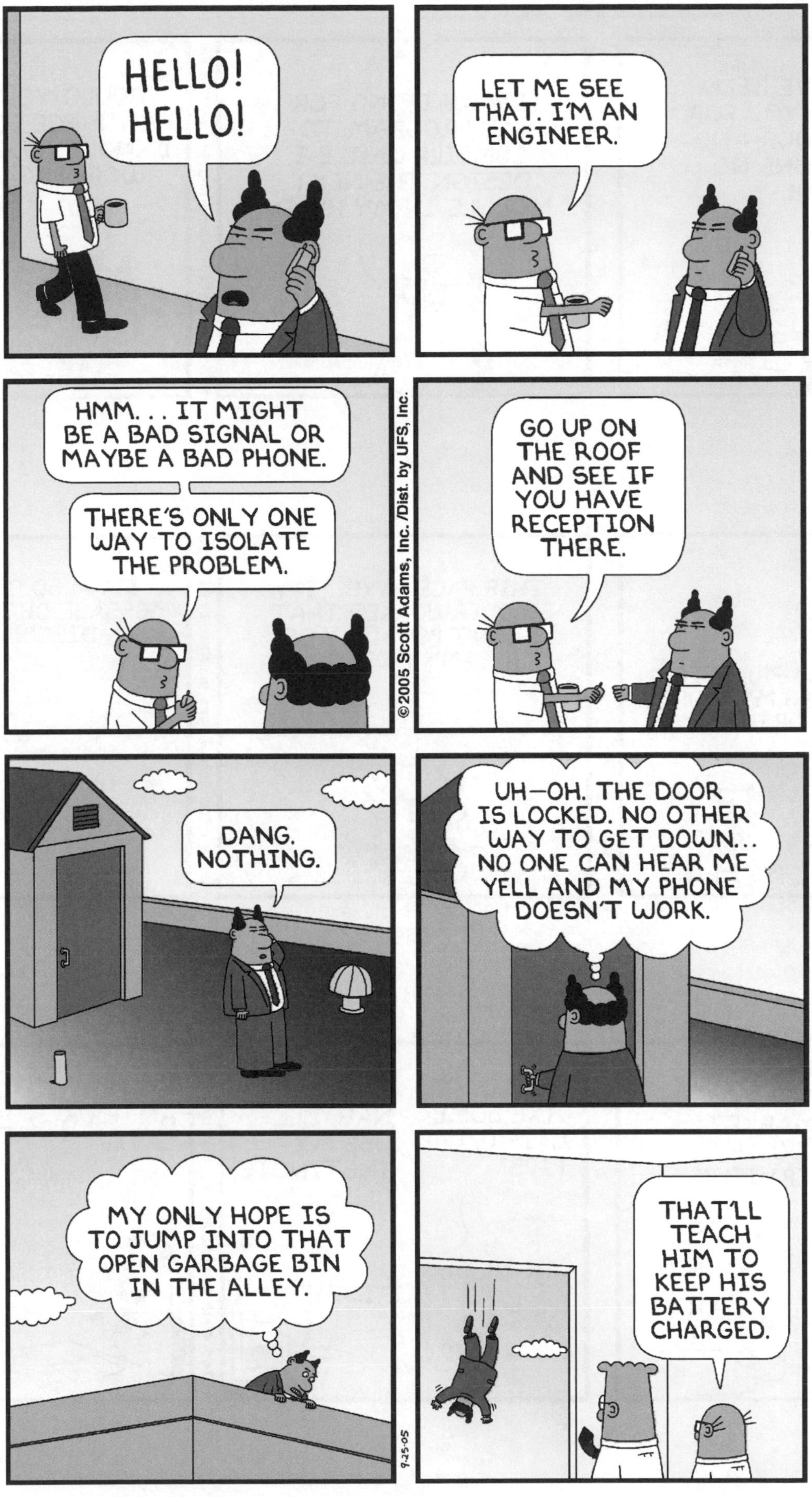
HELLO! HELLO!
LET ME SEE THAT. I'M AN ENGINEER.
HMM. . . IT MIGHT BE A BAD SIGNAL OR MAYBE A BAD PHONE.
THERE'S ONLY ONE WAY TO ISOLATE THE PROBLEM.
GO UP ON THE ROOF AND SEE IF YOU HAVE RECEPTION THERE.
DANG. NOTHING.
UH-OH. THE DOOR IS LOCKED. NO OTHER WAY TO GET DOWN... NO ONE CAN HEAR ME YELL AND MY PHONE DOESN'T WORK.
MY ONLY HOPE IS TO JUMP INTO THAT OPEN GARBAGE BIN IN THE ALLEY.
THAT'LL TEACH HIM TO KEEP HIS BATTERY CHARGED.
©2005 Scott Adams, Inc./Dist. by UFS, Inc.
9-25-05

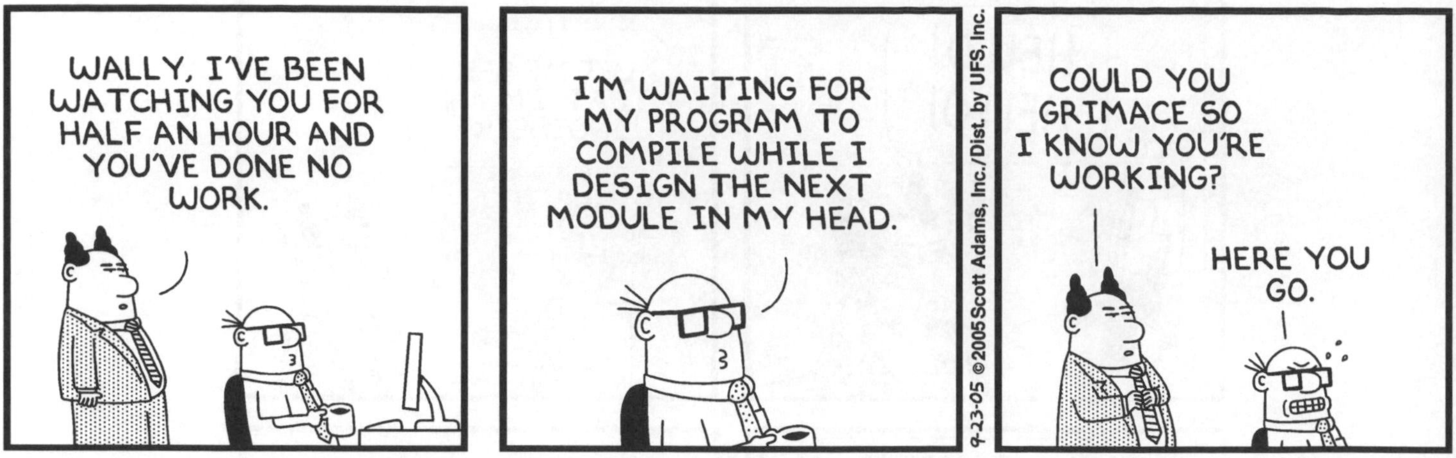
WALLY, I'VE BEEN WATCHING YOU FOR HALF AN HOUR AND YOU'VE DONE NO WORK.
I'M WAITING FOR MY PROGRAM TO COMPILE WHILE I DESIGN THE NEXT MODULE IN MY HEAD.
9-23-05 © 2005 Scott Adams, Inc./Dist. by UFS, Inc.
COULD YOU GRIMACE SO I KNOW YOU'RE WORKING?
HERE YOU GO.

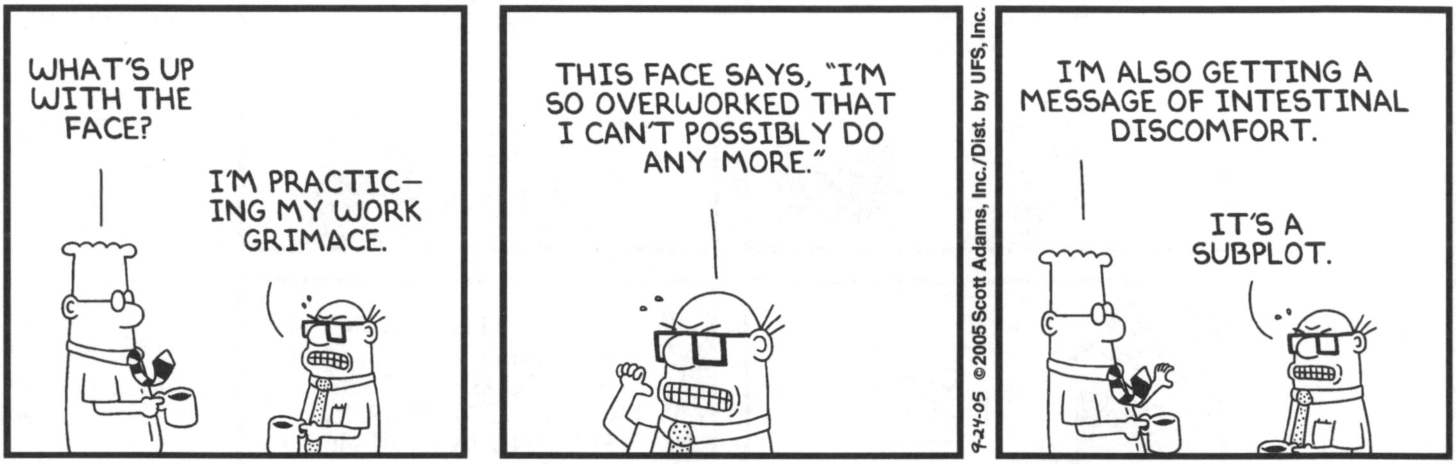
WHAT'S UP WITH THE FACE?
I'M PRACTIC-ING MY WORK GRIMACE.
THIS FACE SAYS, "I'M SO OVERWORKED THAT I CAN'T POSSIBLY DO ANY MORE."
9-24-05 © 2005 Scott Adams, Inc./Dist. by UFS, Inc.
I'M ALSO GETTING A MESSAGE OF INTESTINAL DISCOMFORT.
IT'S A SUBPLOT.

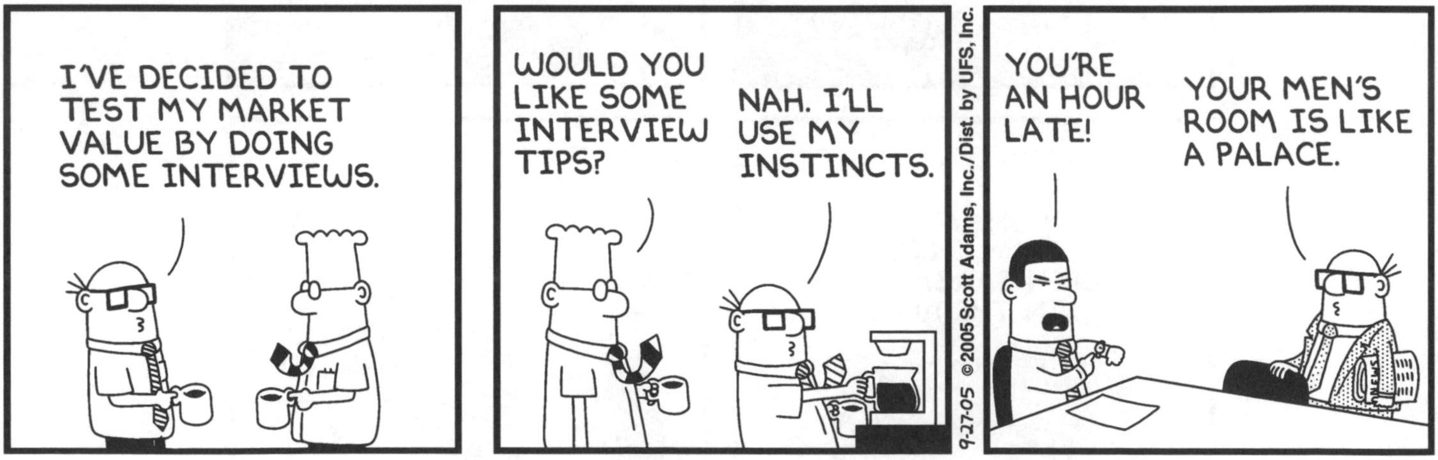
I'VE DECIDED TO TEST MY MARKET VALUE BY DOING SOME INTERVIEWS.
WOULD YOU LIKE SOME INTERVIEW TIPS?
NAH. I'LL USE MY INSTINCTS.
9-27-05 © 2005 Scott Adams, Inc./Dist. by UFS, Inc.
YOU'RE AN HOUR LATE!
YOUR MEN'S ROOM IS LIKE A PALACE.

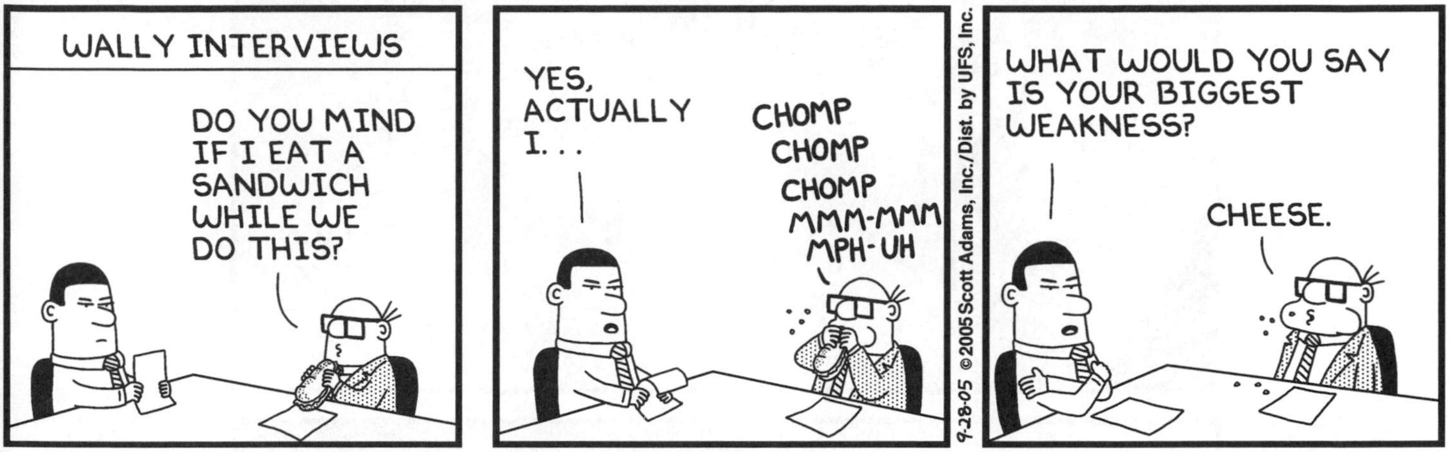
WALLY INTERVIEWS
DO YOU MIND IF I EAT A SANDWICH WHILE WE DO THIS?
YES, ACTUALLY I. . .
CHOMP CHOMP CHOMP MMM-MMM MPH-UH
9-28-05 © 2005 Scott Adams, Inc./Dist. by UFS, Inc.
WHAT WOULD YOU SAY IS YOUR BIGGEST WEAKNESS?
CHEESE.

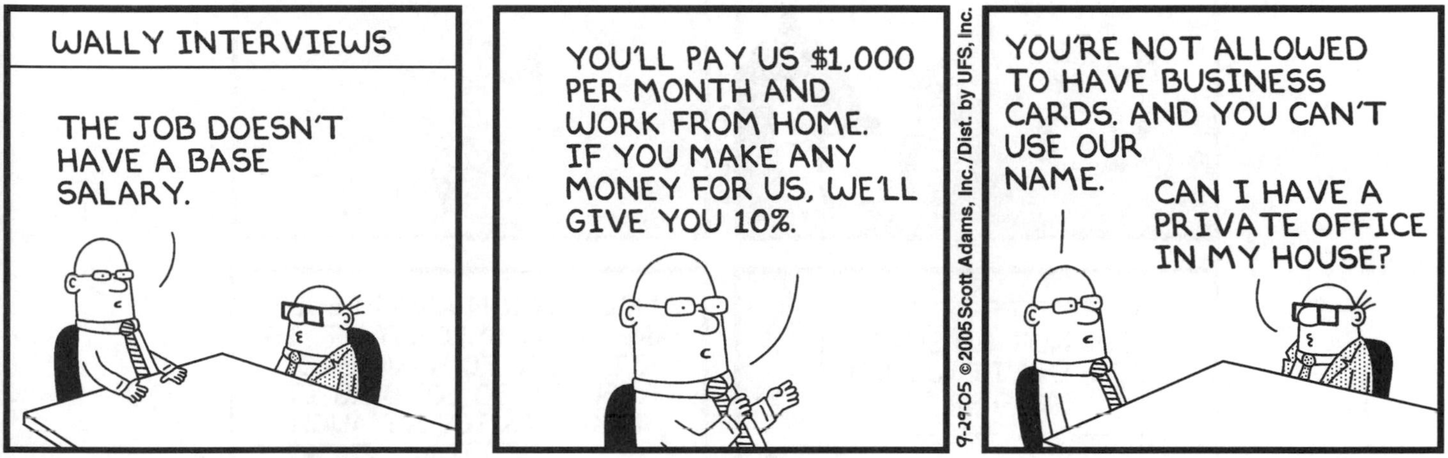
WALLY INTERVIEWS
THE JOB DOESN'T HAVE A BASE SALARY.
YOU'LL PAY US $1,000 PER MONTH AND WORK FROM HOME. IF YOU MAKE ANY MONEY FOR US, WE'LL GIVE YOU 10%.
9-29-05 © 2005 Scott Adams, Inc./Dist. by UFS, Inc.
YOU'RE NOT ALLOWED TO HAVE BUSINESS CARDS. AND YOU CAN'T USE OUR NAME.
CAN I HAVE A PRIVATE OFFICE IN MY HOUSE?

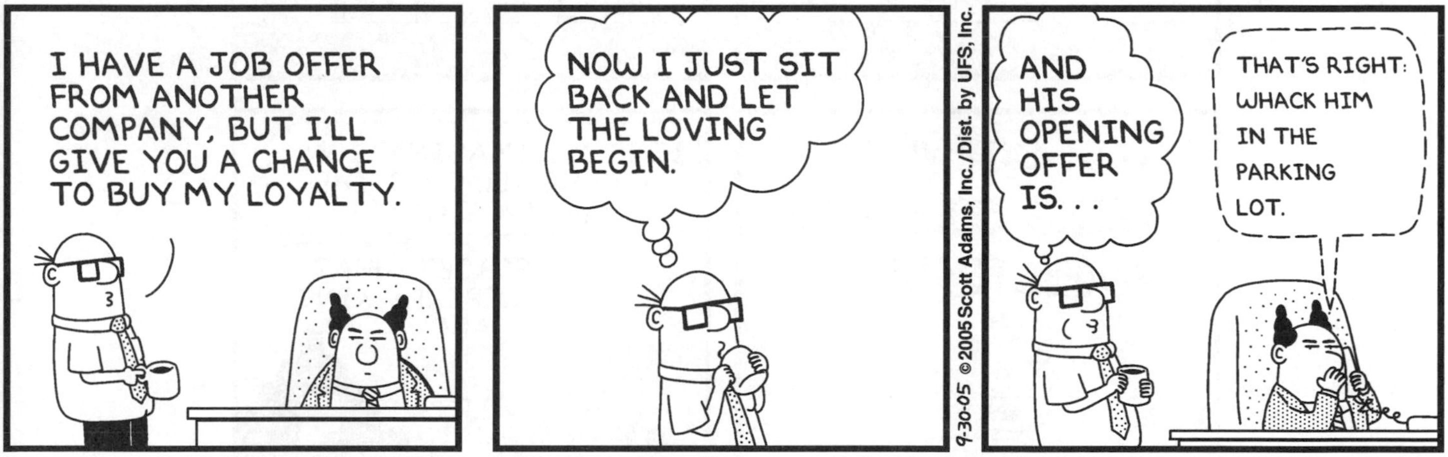
I HAVE A JOB OFFER FROM ANOTHER COMPANY, BUT I'LL GIVE YOU A CHANCE TO BUY MY LOYALTY.
NOW I JUST SIT BACK AND LET THE LOVING BEGIN.
9-30-05 © 2005 Scott Adams, Inc./Dist. by UFS, Inc.
AND HIS OPENING OFFER IS. . .
THAT'S RIGHT: WHACK HIM IN THE PARKING LOT.

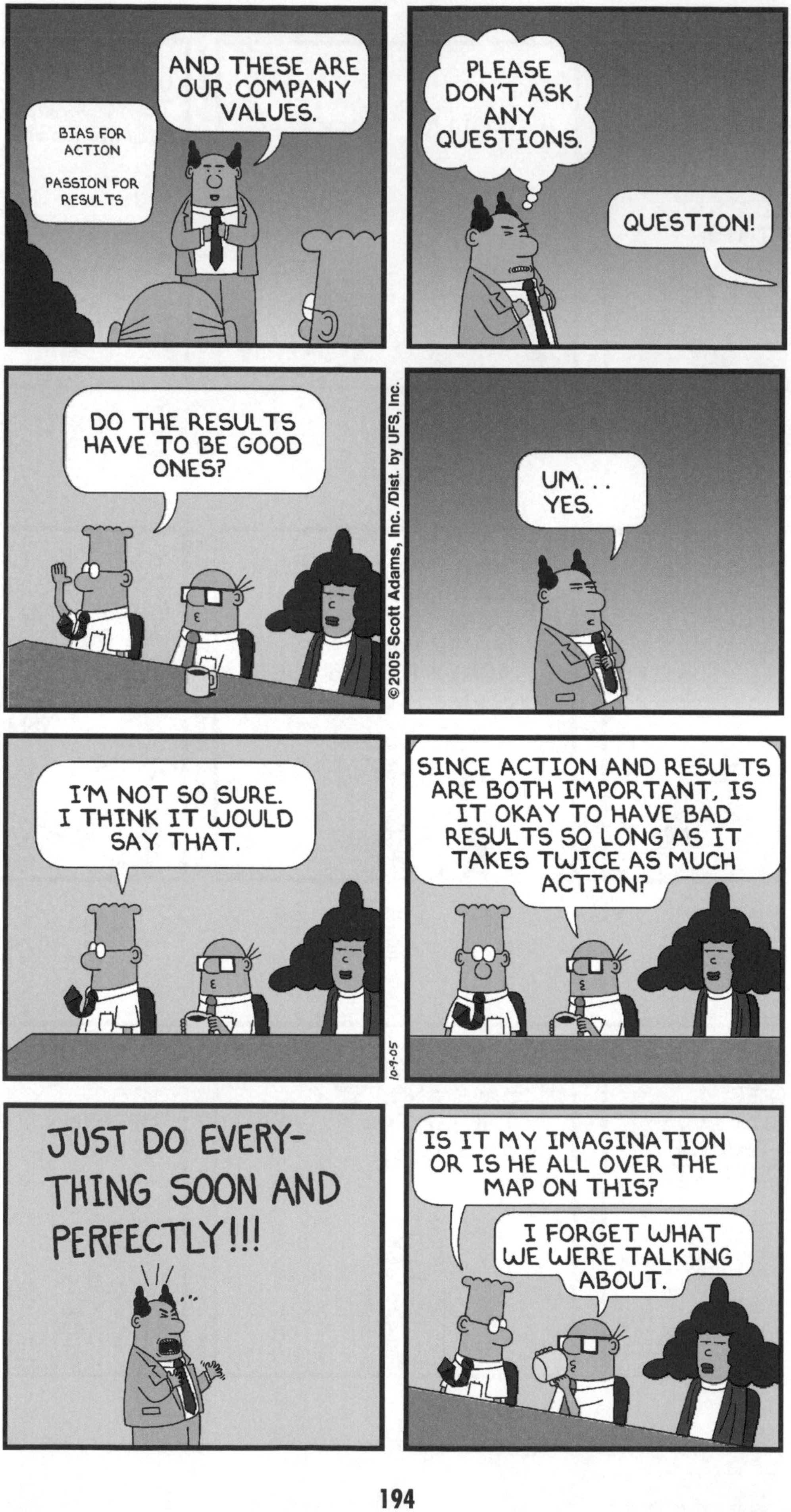
BIAS FOR ACTION
PASSION FOR RESULTS
AND THESE ARE OUR COMPANY VALUES.
PLEASE DON'T ASK ANY QUESTIONS.
QUESTION!
DO THE RESULTS HAVE TO BE GOOD ONES?
©2005 Scott Adams, Inc./Dist. by UFS, Inc.
UM. . . YES.
I'M NOT SO SURE. I THINK IT WOULD SAY THAT.
10-9-05
SINCE ACTION AND RESULTS ARE BOTH IMPORTANT, IS IT OKAY TO HAVE BAD RESULTS SO LONG AS IT TAKES TWICE AS MUCH ACTION?
JUST DO EVERY-THING SOON AND PERFECTLY!!!
IS IT MY IMAGINATION OR IS HE ALL OVER THE MAP ON THIS?
I FORGET WHAT WE WERE TALKING ABOUT.

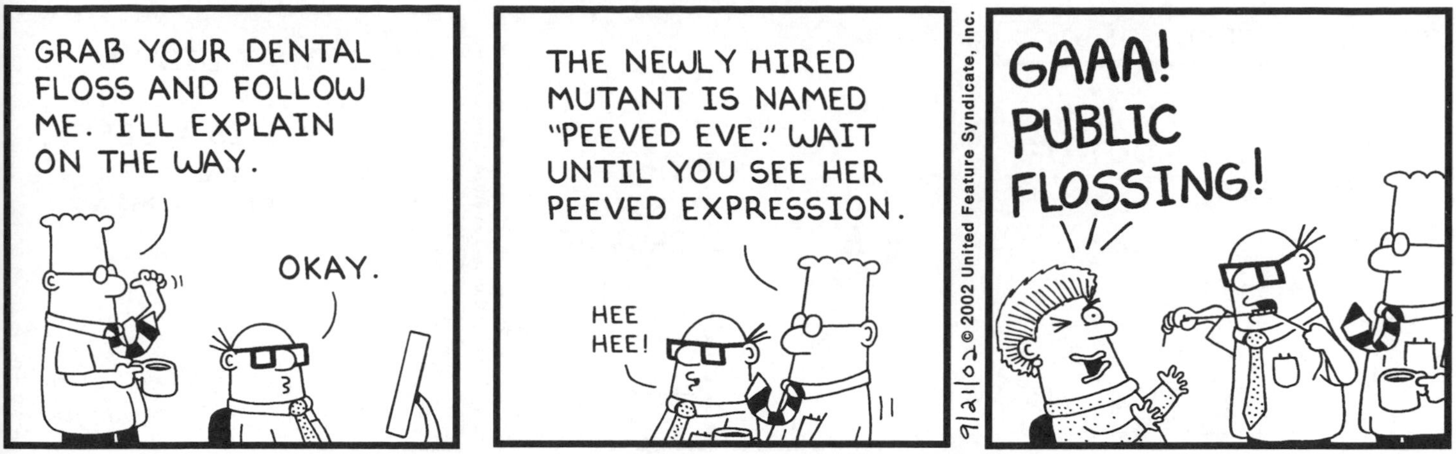
GRAB YOUR DENTAL FLOSS AND FOLLOW ME. I'LL EXPLAIN ON THE WAY.
OKAY.
THE NEWLY HIRED MUTANT IS NAMED "PEEVED EVE." WAIT UNTIL YOU SEE HER PEEVED EXPRESSION.
HEE HEE!
GAAA! PUBLIC FLOSSING!
9/21/02 © 2002 United Feature Syndicate, Inc.

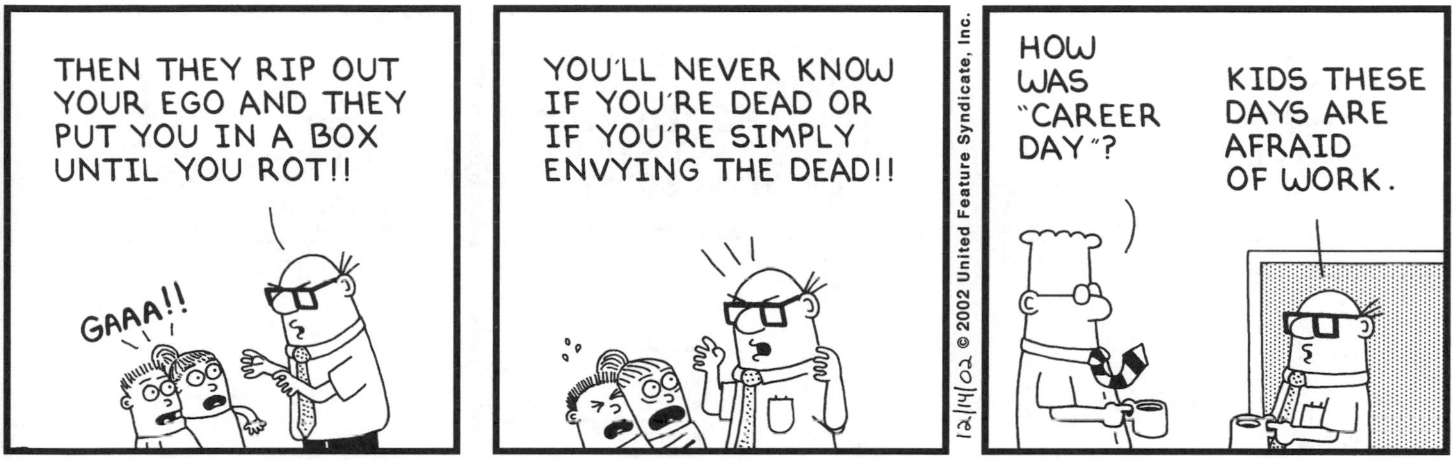
THEN THEY RIP OUT YOUR EGO AND THEY PUT YOU IN A BOX UNTIL YOU ROT!!
GAAA!!
YOU'LL NEVER KNOW IF YOU'RE DEAD OR IF YOU'RE SIMPLY ENVYING THE DEAD!!
HOW WAS "CAREER DAY"?
KIDS THESE DAYS ARE AFRAID OF WORK.
12/14/02 © 2002 United Feature Syndicate, Inc.

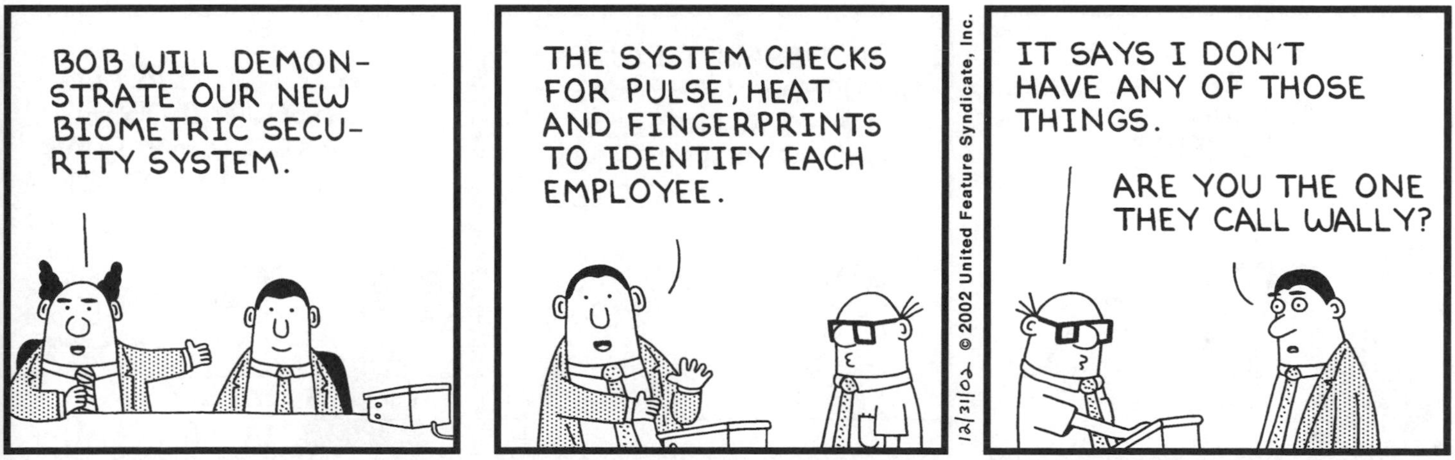
BOB WILL DEMON- STRATE OUR NEW BIOMETRIC SECU- RITY SYSTEM.
THE SYSTEM CHECKS FOR PULSE, HEAT AND FINGERPRINTS TO IDENTIFY EACH EMPLOYEE.
IT SAYS I DON'T HAVE ANY OF THOSE THINGS.
ARE YOU THE ONE THEY CALL WALLY?
12/31/02 © 2002 United Feature Syndicate, Inc.

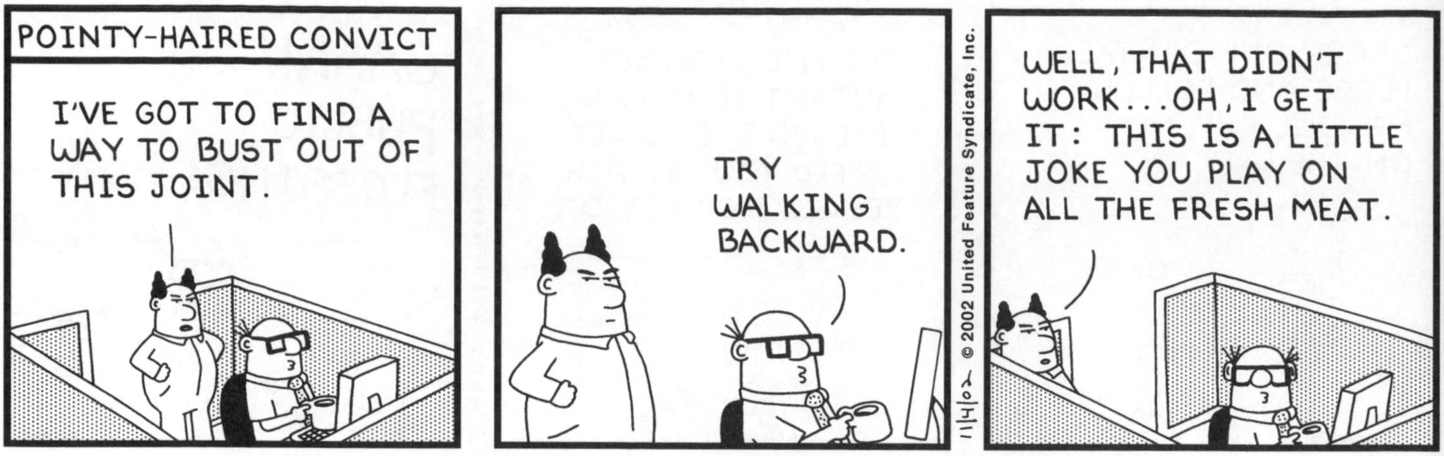
POINTY-HAIRED CONVICT
I'VE GOT TO FIND A WAY TO BUST OUT OF THIS JOINT.
TRY WALKING BACKWARD.
11/4/02 © 2002 United Feature Syndicate, Inc.
WELL, THAT DIDN'T WORK... OH, I GET IT: THIS IS A LITTLE JOKE YOU PLAY ON ALL THE FRESH MEAT.

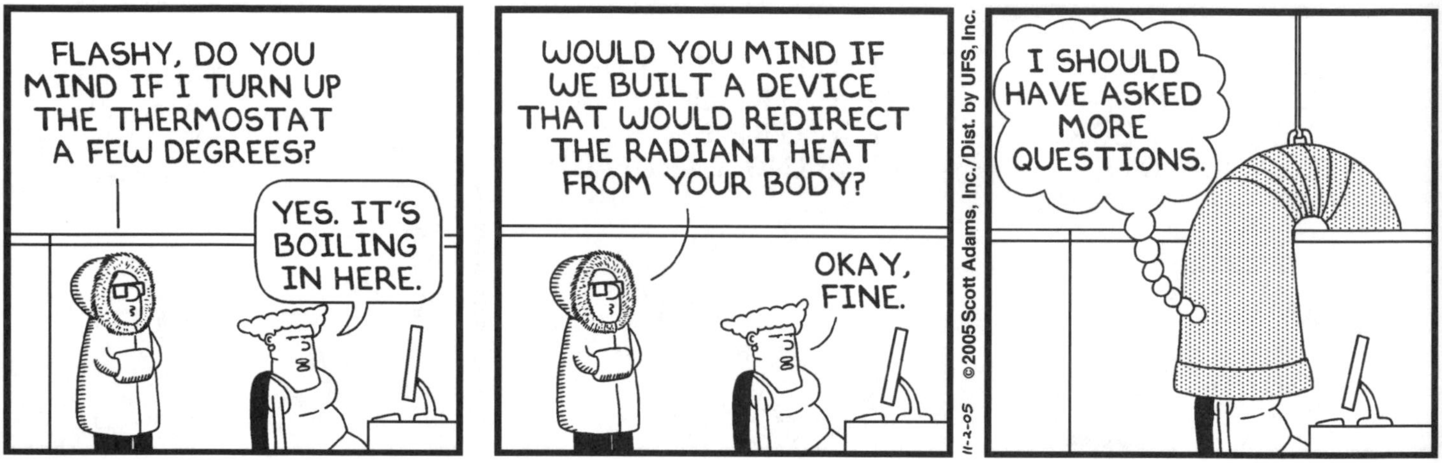
FLASHY, DO YOU MIND IF I TURN UP THE THERMOSTAT A FEW DEGREES?
YES. IT'S BOILING IN HERE.
WOULD YOU MIND IF WE BUILT A DEVICE THAT WOULD REDIRECT THE RADIANT HEAT FROM YOUR BODY?
OKAY, FINE.
11-2-05 © 2005 Scott Adams, Inc./Dist. by UFS, Inc.
I SHOULD HAVE ASKED MORE QUESTIONS.

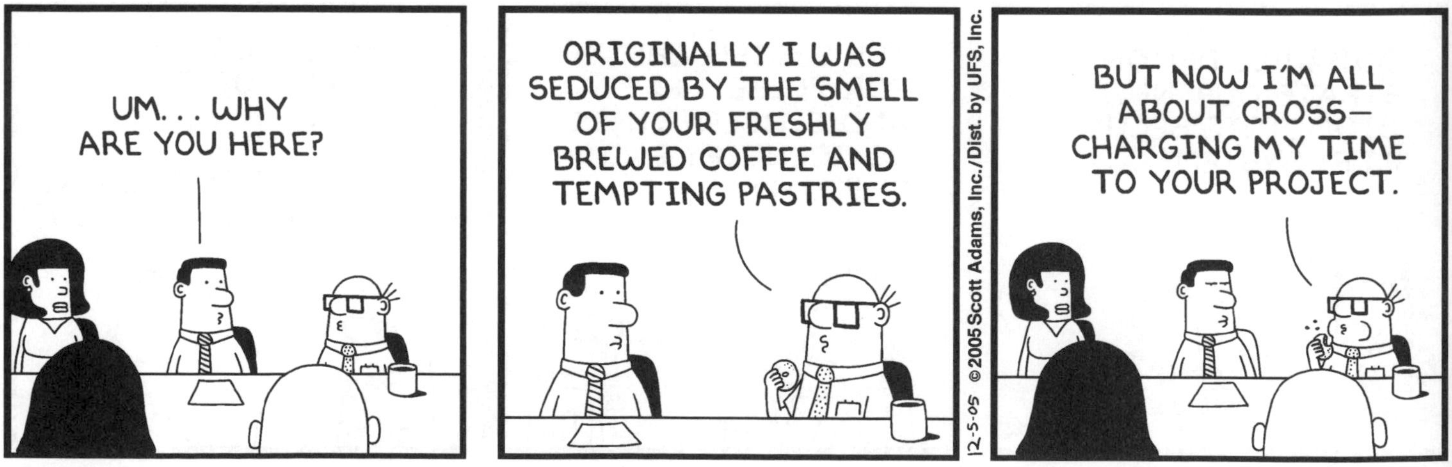
UM... WHY ARE YOU HERE?
ORIGINALLY I WAS SEDUCED BY THE SMELL OF YOUR FRESHLY BREWED COFFEE AND TEMPTING PASTRIES.
12-5-05 © 2005 Scott Adams, Inc./Dist. by UFS, Inc.
BUT NOW I'M ALL ABOUT CROSS-CHARGING MY TIME TO YOUR PROJECT.

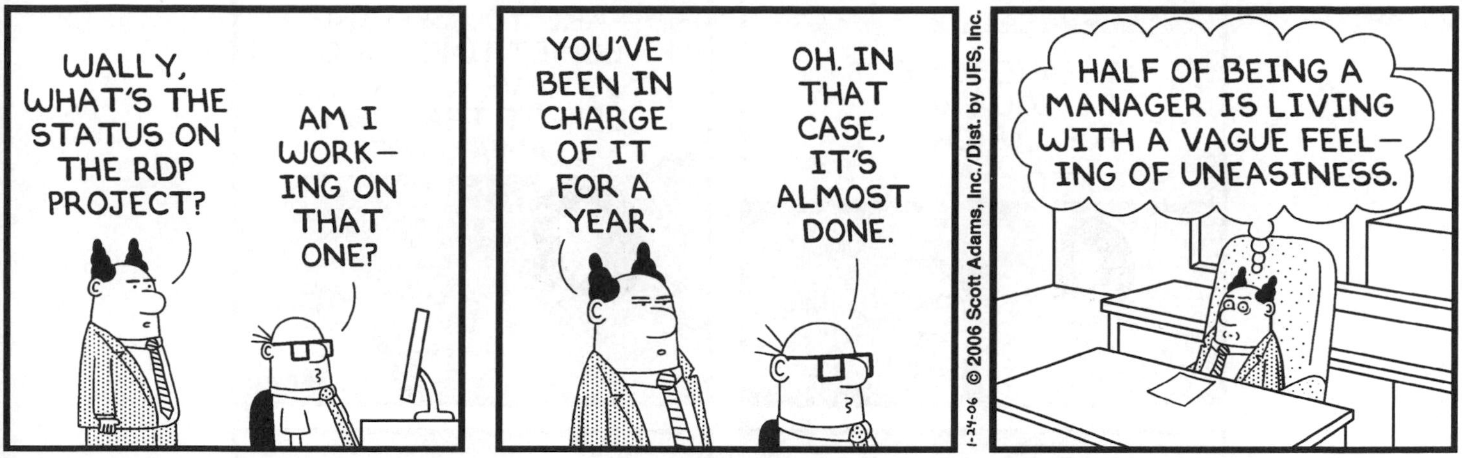
WALLY, WHAT'S THE STATUS ON THE RDP PROJECT?
AM I WORKING ON THAT ONE?
YOU'VE BEEN IN CHARGE OF IT FOR A YEAR.
OH. IN THAT CASE, IT'S ALMOST DONE.
1-24-06 © 2006 Scott Adams, Inc./Dist. by UFS, Inc.
HALF OF BEING A MANAGER IS LIVING WITH A VAGUE FEELING OF UNEASINESS.

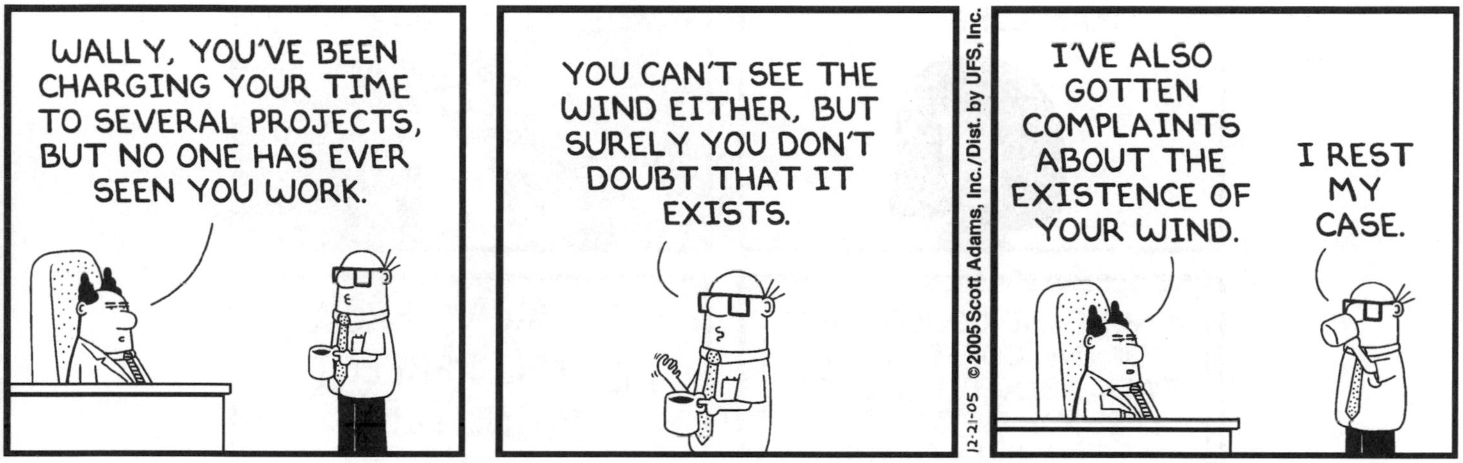
WALLY, YOU'VE BEEN CHARGING YOUR TIME TO SEVERAL PROJECTS, BUT NO ONE HAS EVER SEEN YOU WORK.
YOU CAN'T SEE THE WIND EITHER, BUT SURELY YOU DON'T DOUBT THAT IT EXISTS.
12-21-05 © 2005 Scott Adams, Inc./Dist. by UFS, Inc.
I'VE ALSO GOTTEN COMPLAINTS ABOUT THE EXISTENCE OF YOUR WIND.
I REST MY CASE.

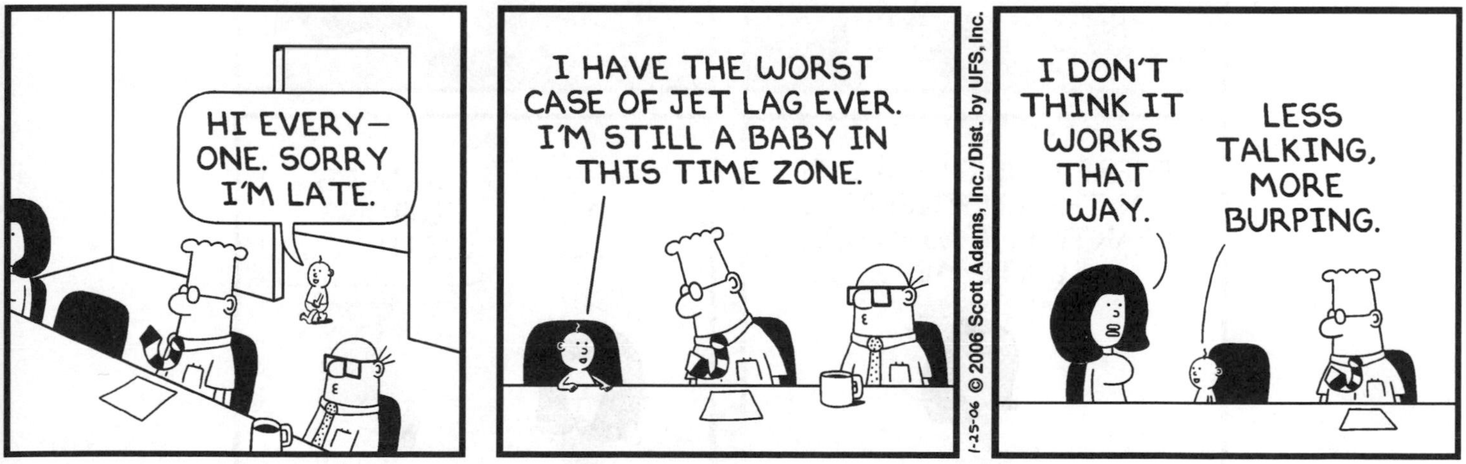
HI EVERYONE. SORRY I'M LATE.
I HAVE THE WORST CASE OF JET LAG EVER. I'M STILL A BABY IN THIS TIME ZONE.
1-25-06 © 2006 Scott Adams, Inc./Dist. by UFS, Inc.
I DON'T THINK IT WORKS THAT WAY.
LESS TALKING, MORE BURPING.

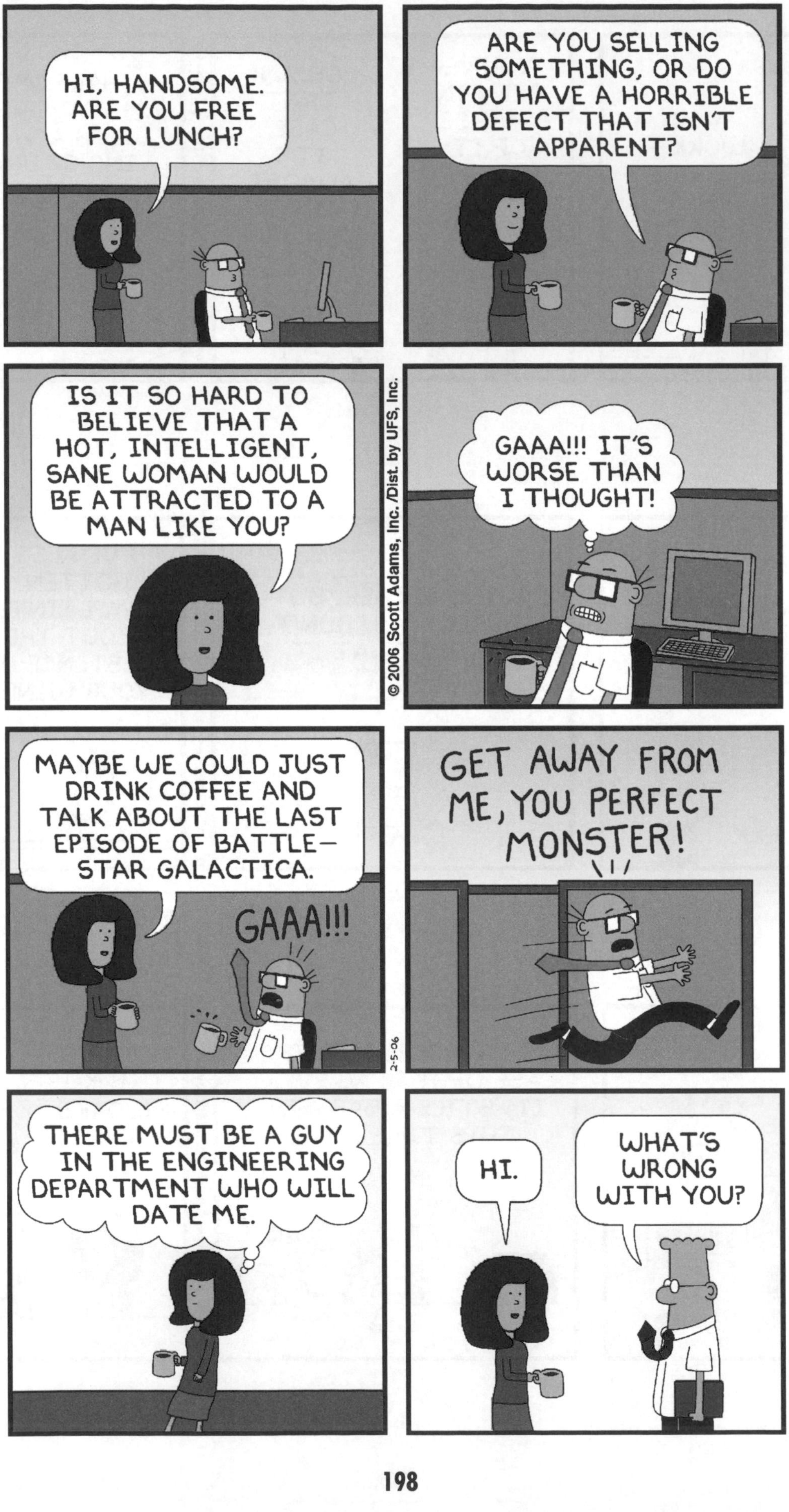
HI, HANDSOME. ARE YOU FREE FOR LUNCH?
ARE YOU SELLING SOMETHING, OR DO YOU HAVE A HORRIBLE DEFECT THAT ISN'T APPARENT?
IS IT SO HARD TO BELIEVE THAT A HOT, INTELLIGENT, SANE WOMAN WOULD BE ATTRACTED TO A MAN LIKE YOU?
GAAA!!! IT'S WORSE THAN I THOUGHT!
© 2006 Scott Adams, Inc. /Dist. by UFS, Inc.
MAYBE WE COULD JUST DRINK COFFEE AND TALK ABOUT THE LAST EPISODE OF BATTLE-STAR GALACTICA.
GAAA!!!
GET AWAY FROM ME, YOU PERFECT MONSTER!
2-5-06
THERE MUST BE A GUY IN THE ENGINEERING DEPARTMENT WHO WILL DATE ME.
HI.
WHAT'S WRONG WITH YOU?

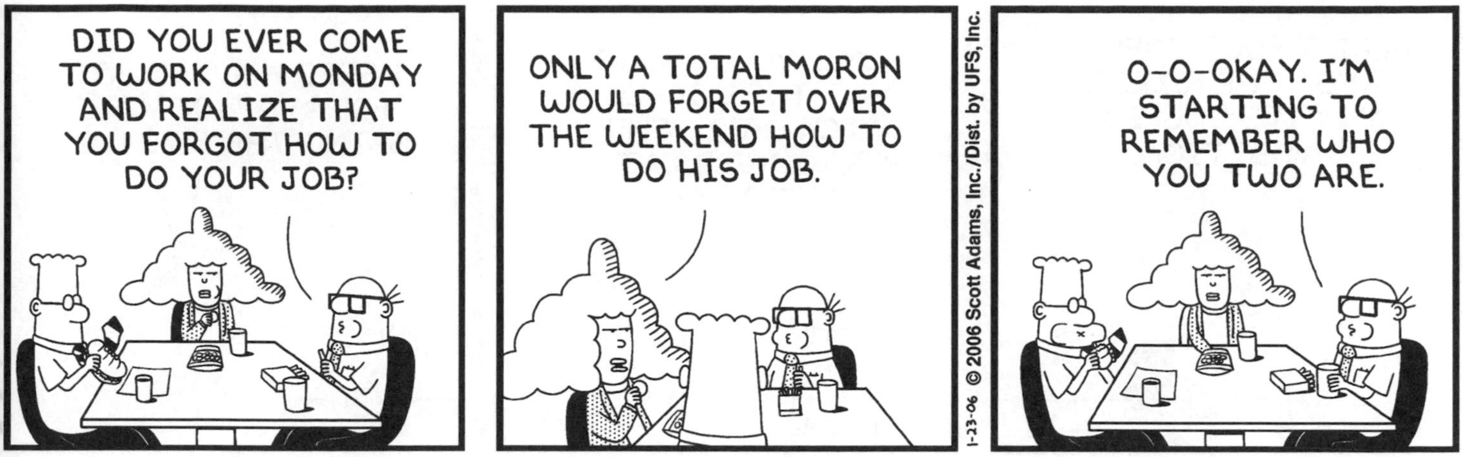

DID YOU EVER COME TO WORK ON MONDAY AND REALIZE THAT YOU FORGOT HOW TO DO YOUR JOB?
ONLY A TOTAL MORON WOULD FORGET OVER THE WEEKEND HOW TO DO HIS JOB.
1-23-06 © 2006 Scott Adams, Inc./Dist. by UFS, Inc.
O-O-OKAY. I'M STARTING TO REMEMBER WHO YOU TWO ARE.

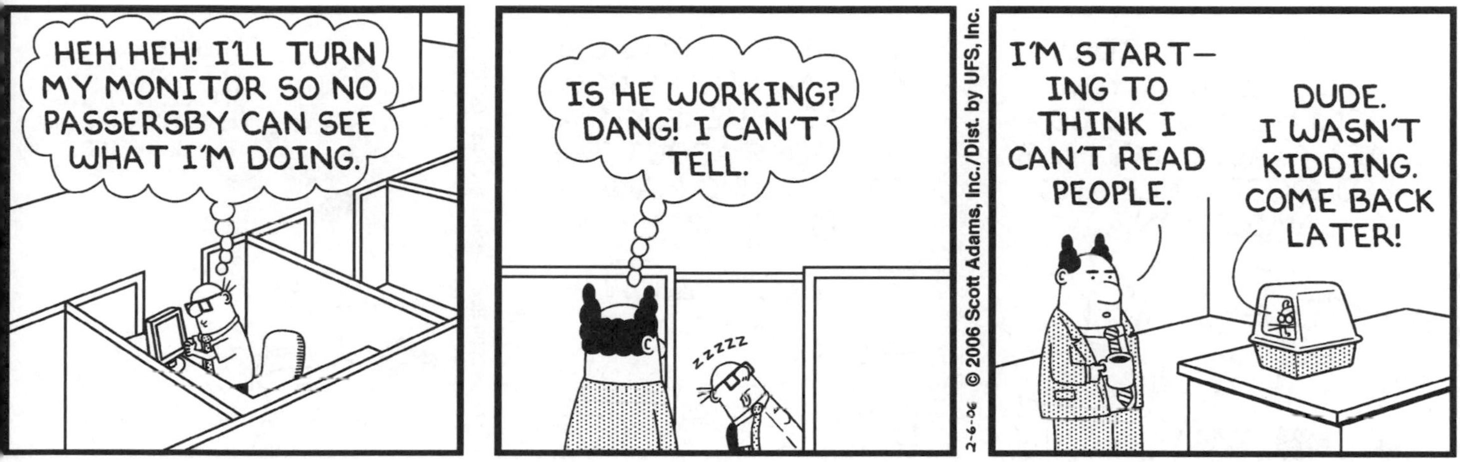

HEH HEH! I'LL TURN MY MONITOR SO NO PASSERSBY CAN SEE WHAT I'M DOING.
IS HE WORKING? DANG! I CAN'T TELL.
ZZZZZ
2-6-06 © 2006 Scott Adams, Inc./Dist. by UFS, Inc.
I'M START-ING TO THINK I CAN'T READ PEOPLE.
DUDE. I WASN'T KIDDING. COME BACK LATER!

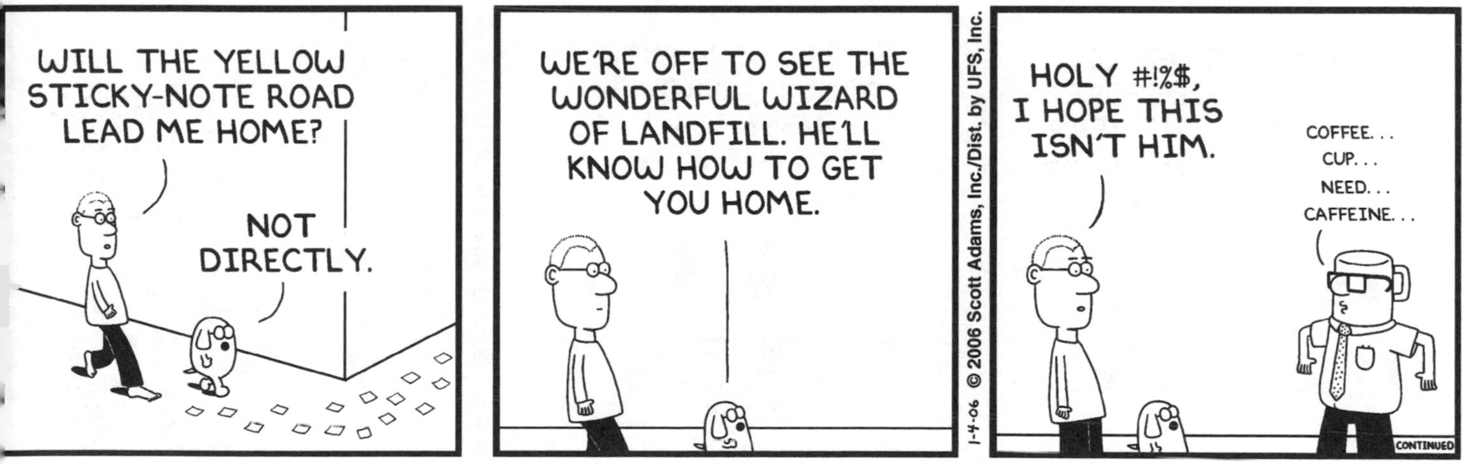

WILL THE YELLOW STICKY-NOTE ROAD LEAD ME HOME?
NOT DIRECTLY.
WE'RE OFF TO SEE THE WONDERFUL WIZARD OF LANDFILL. HE'LL KNOW HOW TO GET YOU HOME.
1-4-06 © 2006 Scott Adams, Inc./Dist. by UFS, Inc.
HOLY #!%$, I HOPE THIS ISN'T HIM.
COFFEE... CUP... NEED... CAFFEINE...
CONTINUED

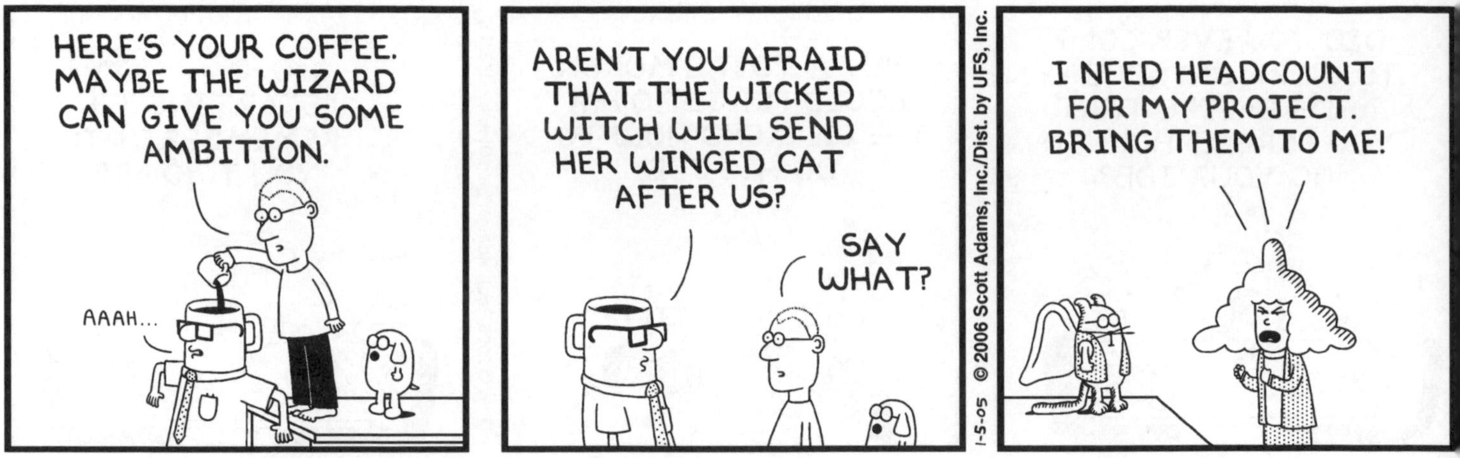
HERE'S YOUR COFFEE. MAYBE THE WIZARD CAN GIVE YOU SOME AMBITION.
AAAH...
AREN'T YOU AFRAID THAT THE WICKED WITCH WILL SEND HER WINGED CAT AFTER US?
SAY WHAT?
I NEED HEADCOUNT FOR MY PROJECT. BRING THEM TO ME!
1-5-05 © 2006 Scott Adams, Inc./Dist. by UFS, Inc.

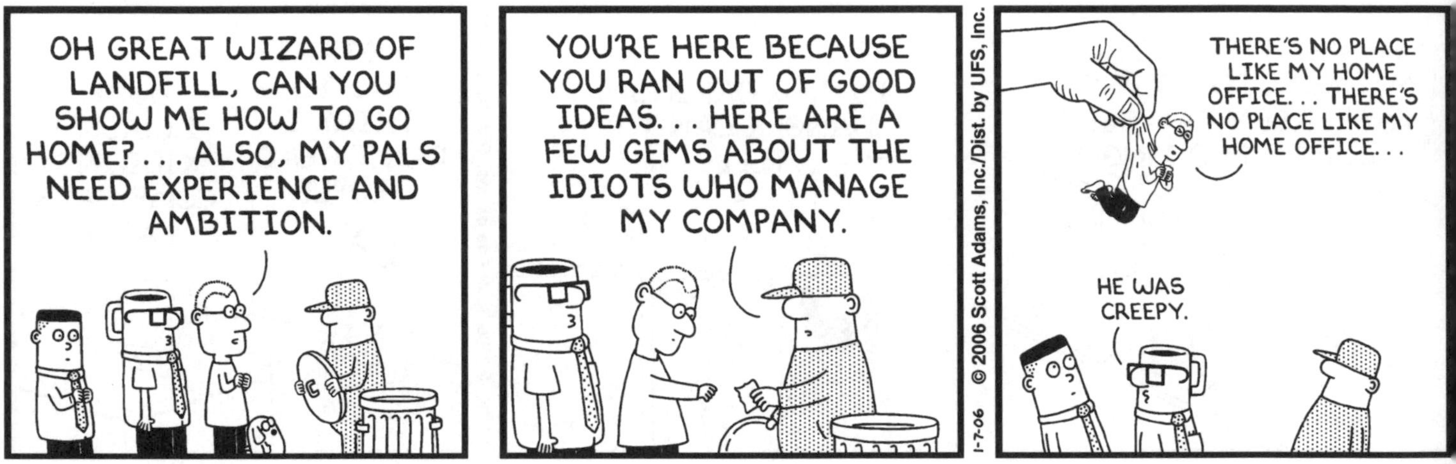
OH GREAT WIZARD OF LANDFILL, CAN YOU SHOW ME HOW TO GO HOME? . . . ALSO, MY PALS NEED EXPERIENCE AND AMBITION.
YOU'RE HERE BECAUSE YOU RAN OUT OF GOOD IDEAS. . . HERE ARE A FEW GEMS ABOUT THE IDIOTS WHO MANAGE MY COMPANY.
THERE'S NO PLACE LIKE MY HOME OFFICE. . . THERE'S NO PLACE LIKE MY HOME OFFICE. . .
HE WAS CREEPY.
1-7-06 © 2006 Scott Adams, Inc./Dist. by UFS, Inc.

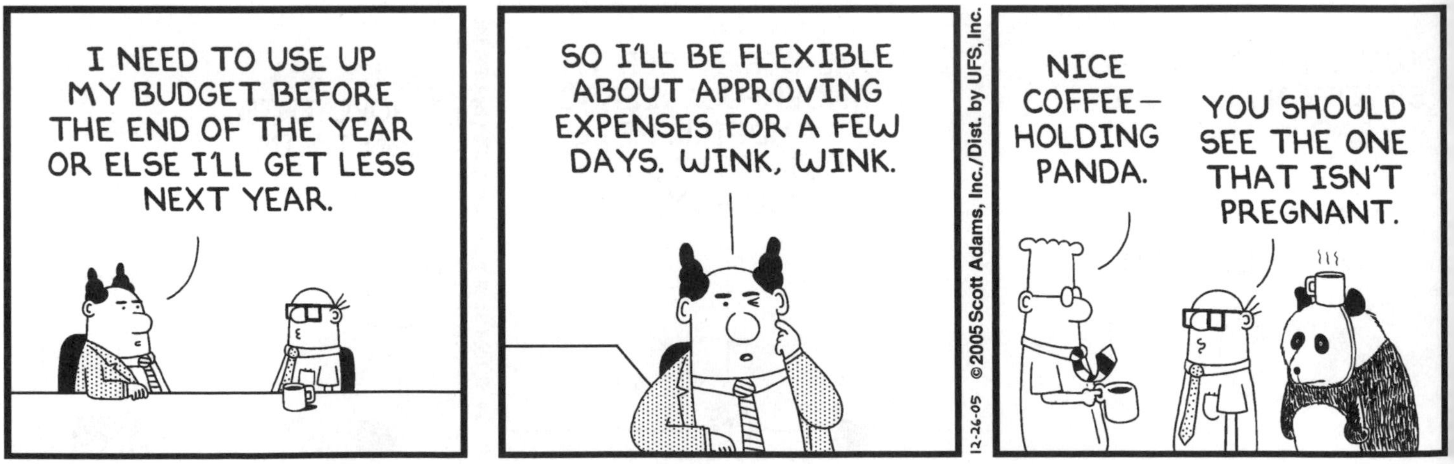
I NEED TO USE UP MY BUDGET BEFORE THE END OF THE YEAR OR ELSE I'LL GET LESS NEXT YEAR.
SO I'LL BE FLEXIBLE ABOUT APPROVING EXPENSES FOR A FEW DAYS. WINK, WINK.
NICE COFFEE-HOLDING PANDA.
YOU SHOULD SEE THE ONE THAT ISN'T PREGNANT.
12-26-05 © 2005 Scott Adams, Inc./Dist. by UFS, Inc.

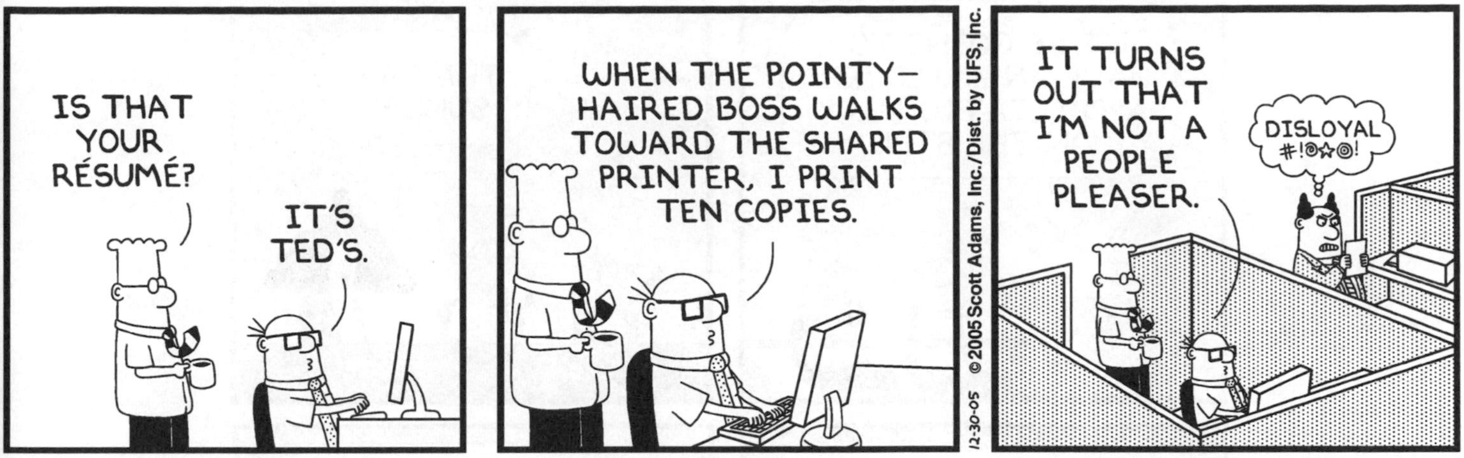
IS THAT YOUR RÉSUMÉ?
IT'S TED'S.
WHEN THE POINTY-HAIRED BOSS WALKS TOWARD THE SHARED PRINTER, I PRINT TEN COPIES.
IT TURNS OUT THAT I'M NOT A PEOPLE PLEASER.
DISLOYAL
12-30-05 © 2005 Scott Adams, Inc./Dist. by UFS, Inc.

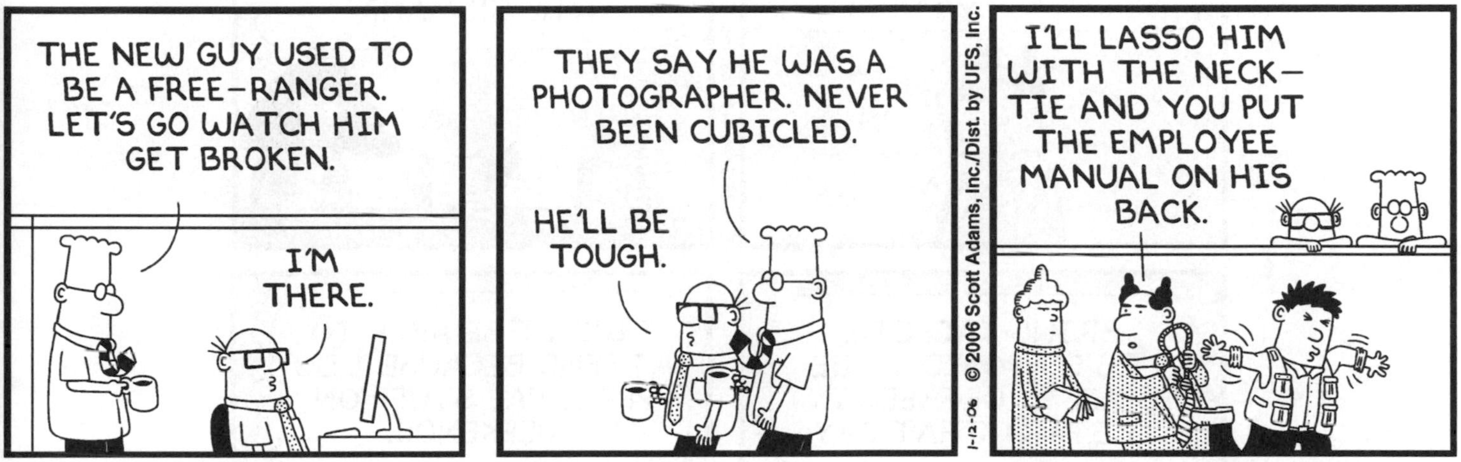
THE NEW GUY USED TO BE A FREE-RANGER. LET'S GO WATCH HIM GET BROKEN.
I'M THERE.
THEY SAY HE WAS A PHOTOGRAPHER. NEVER BEEN CUBICLED.
HE'LL BE TOUGH.
I'LL LASSO HIM WITH THE NECKTIE AND YOU PUT THE EMPLOYEE MANUAL ON HIS BACK.
1-12-06 © 2006 Scott Adams, Inc./Dist. by UFS, Inc.

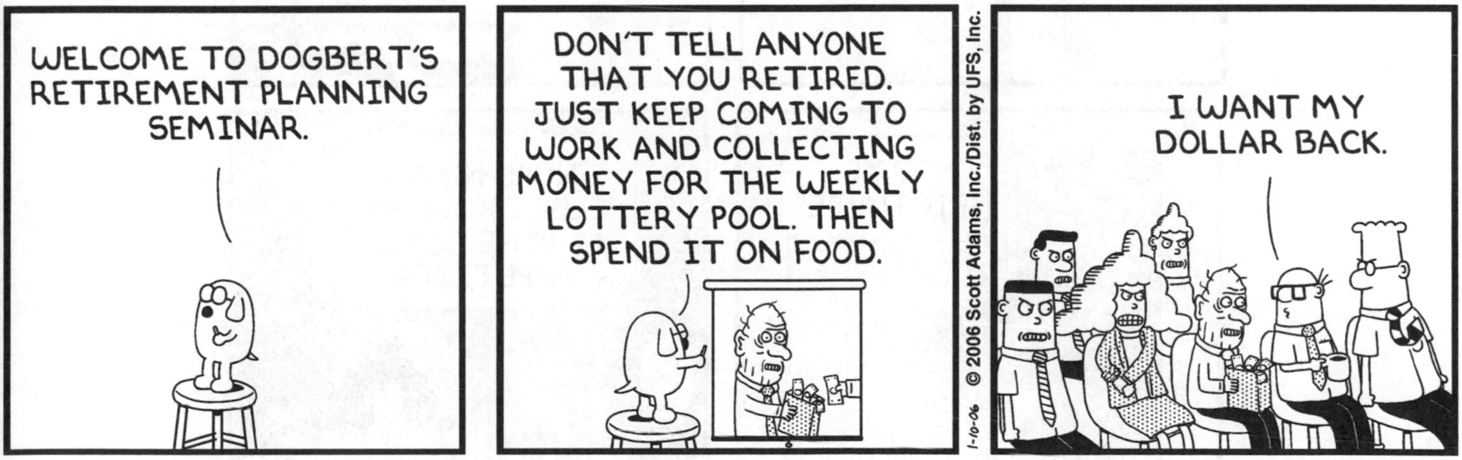
WELCOME TO DOGBERT'S RETIREMENT PLANNING SEMINAR.
DON'T TELL ANYONE THAT YOU RETIRED. JUST KEEP COMING TO WORK AND COLLECTING MONEY FOR THE WEEKLY LOTTERY POOL. THEN SPEND IT ON FOOD.
I WANT MY DOLLAR BACK.
1-10-06 © 2006 Scott Adams, Inc./Dist. by UFS, Inc.

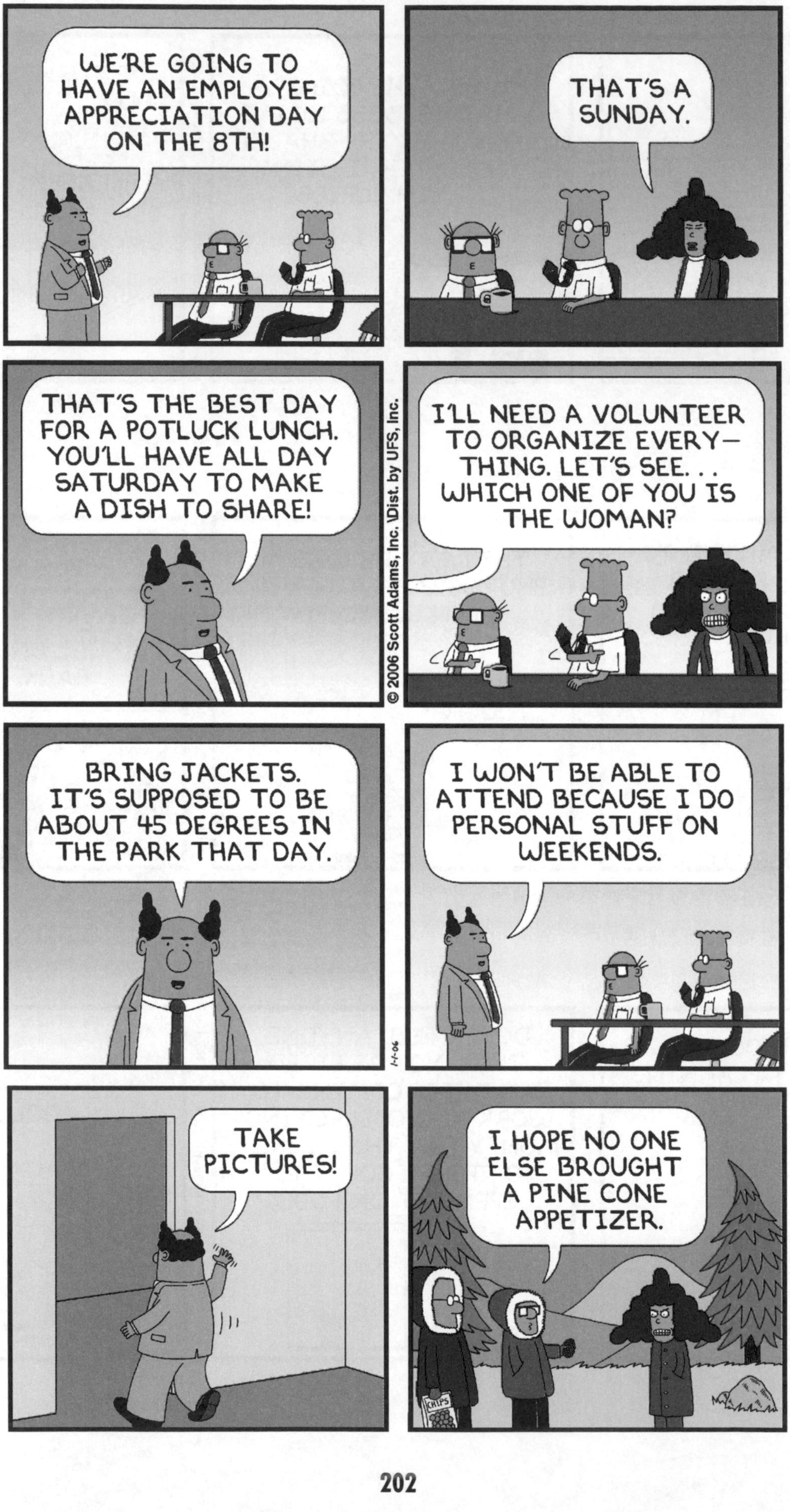
WE'RE GOING TO HAVE AN EMPLOYEE APPRECIATION DAY ON THE 8TH!
THAT'S A SUNDAY.
THAT'S THE BEST DAY FOR A POTLUCK LUNCH. YOU'LL HAVE ALL DAY SATURDAY TO MAKE A DISH TO SHARE!
I'LL NEED A VOLUNTEER TO ORGANIZE EVERY-THING. LET'S SEE. . . WHICH ONE OF YOU IS THE WOMAN?
BRING JACKETS. IT'S SUPPOSED TO BE ABOUT 45 DEGREES IN THE PARK THAT DAY.
I WON'T BE ABLE TO ATTEND BECAUSE I DO PERSONAL STUFF ON WEEKENDS.
TAKE PICTURES!
I HOPE NO ONE ELSE BROUGHT A PINE CONE APPETIZER.
CHIPS
© 2006 Scott Adams, Inc. \Dist. by UFS, Inc.
1-1-06

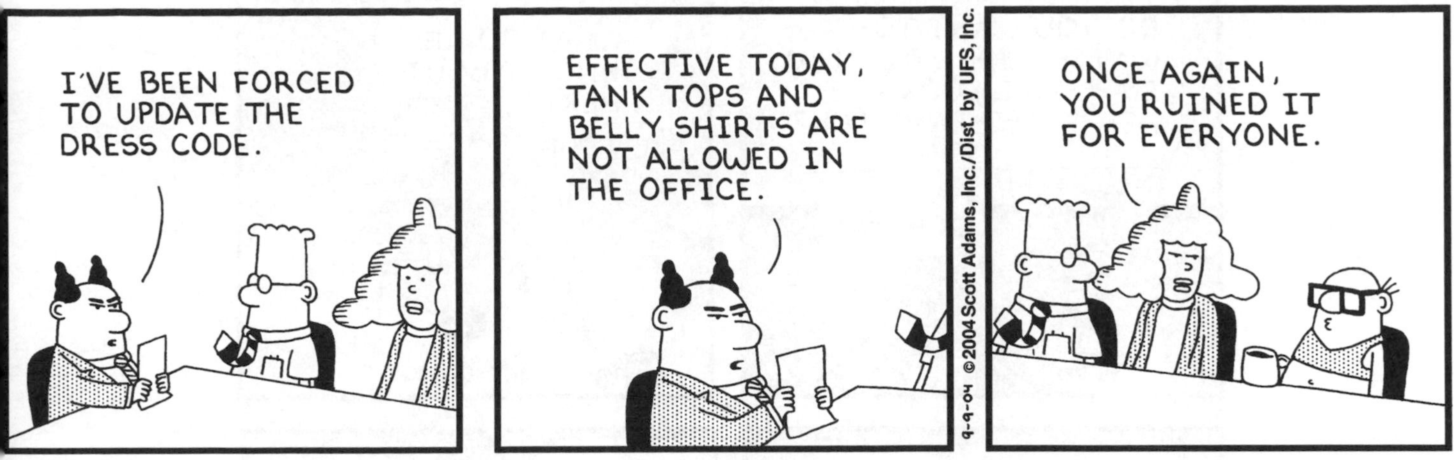
I'VE BEEN FORCED TO UPDATE THE DRESS CODE.
EFFECTIVE TODAY, TANK TOPS AND BELLY SHIRTS ARE NOT ALLOWED IN THE OFFICE.
9-9-04 ©2004 Scott Adams, Inc./Dist. by UFS, Inc.
ONCE AGAIN, YOU RUINED IT FOR EVERYONE.

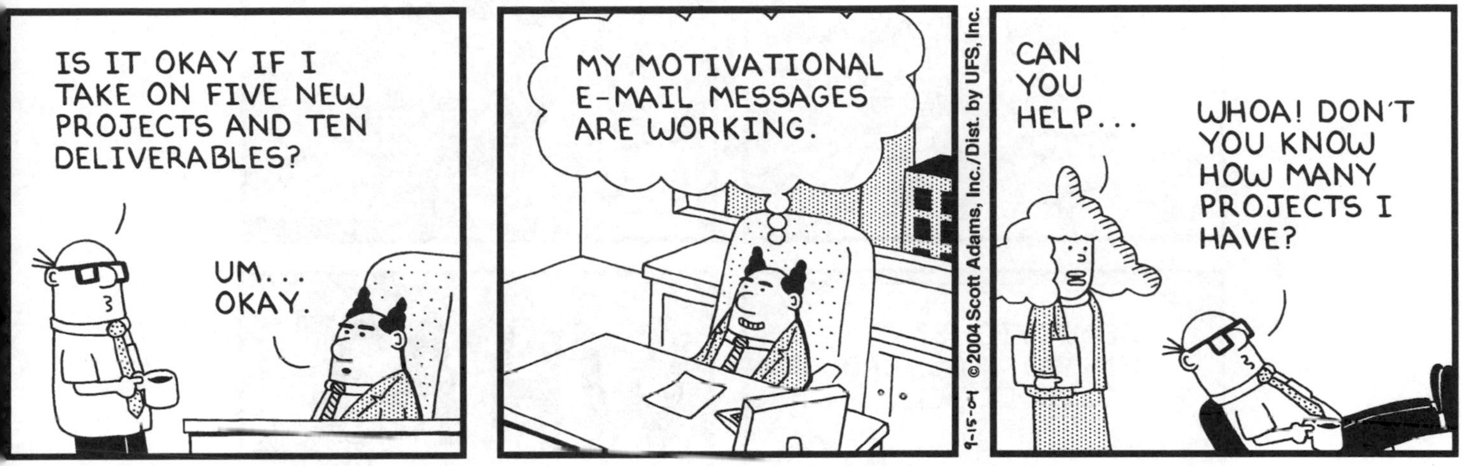
IS IT OKAY IF I TAKE ON FIVE NEW PROJECTS AND TEN DELIVERABLES?
UM... OKAY.
MY MOTIVATIONAL E-MAIL MESSAGES ARE WORKING.
9-15-04 ©2004 Scott Adams, Inc./Dist. by UFS, Inc.
CAN YOU HELP...
WHOA! DON'T YOU KNOW HOW MANY PROJECTS I HAVE?

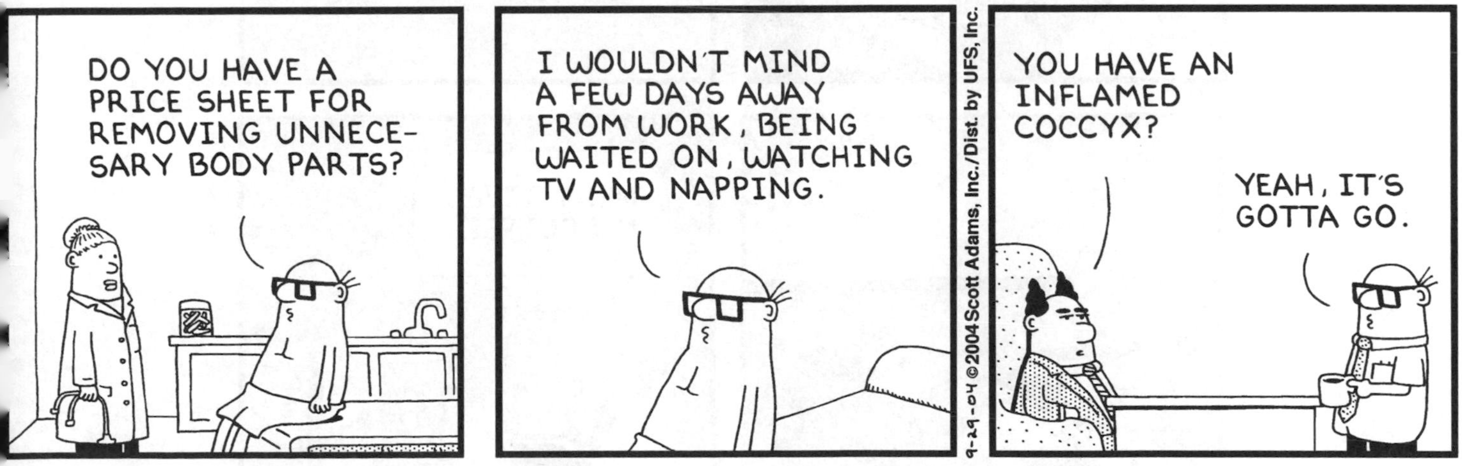
DO YOU HAVE A PRICE SHEET FOR REMOVING UNNECE-SARY BODY PARTS?
I WOULDN'T MIND A FEW DAYS AWAY FROM WORK, BEING WAITED ON, WATCHING TV AND NAPPING.
9-29-04 ©2004 Scott Adams, Inc./Dist. by UFS, Inc.
YOU HAVE AN INFLAMED COCCYX?
YEAH, IT'S GOTTA GO.

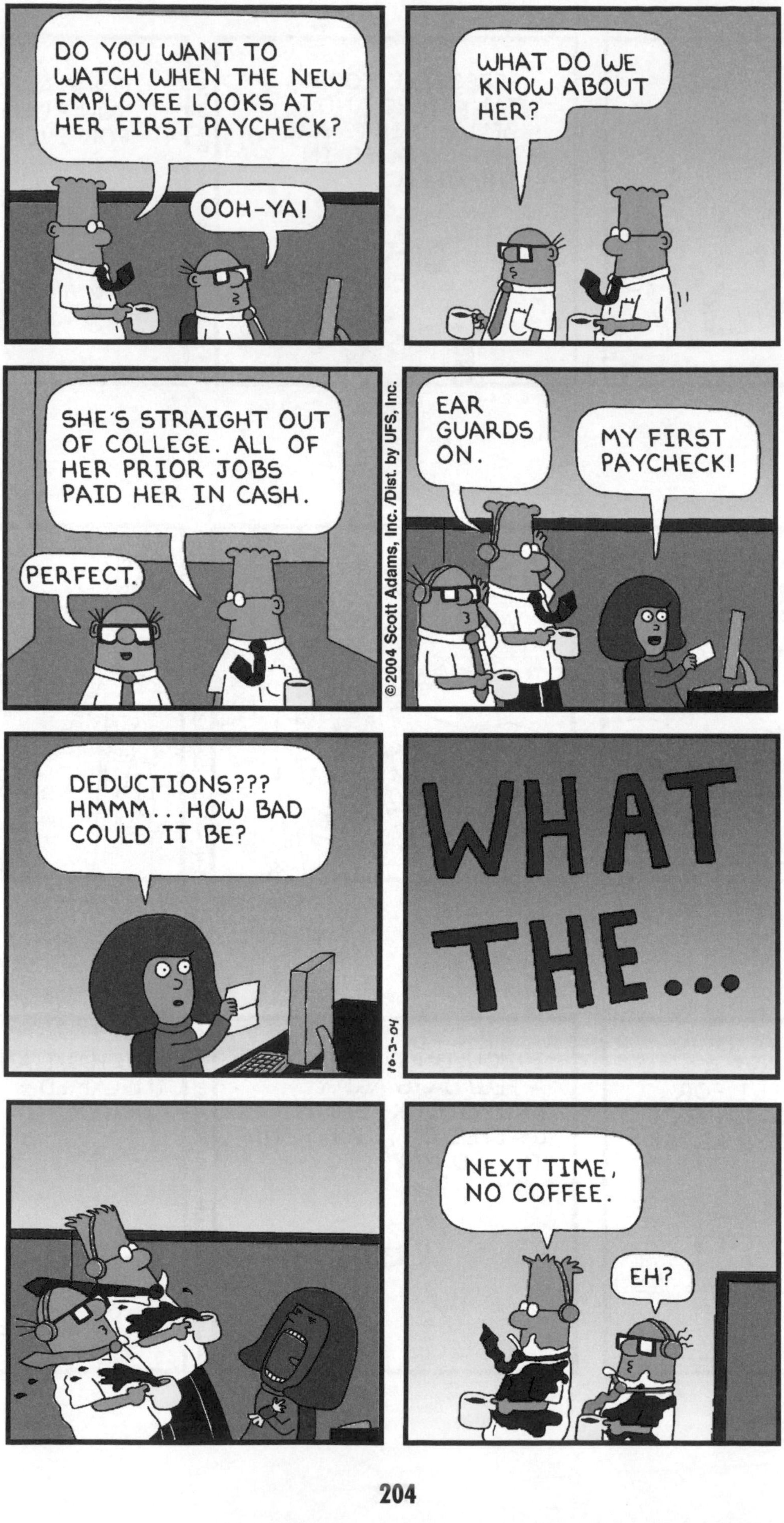
DO YOU WANT TO WATCH WHEN THE NEW EMPLOYEE LOOKS AT HER FIRST PAYCHECK?
OOH-YA!
WHAT DO WE KNOW ABOUT HER?
SHE'S STRAIGHT OUT OF COLLEGE. ALL OF HER PRIOR JOBS PAID HER IN CASH.
PERFECT.
EAR GUARDS ON.
MY FIRST PAYCHECK!
DEDUCTIONS??? HMMM...HOW BAD COULD IT BE?
WHAT THE...
NEXT TIME, NO COFFEE.
EH?
©2004 Scott Adams, Inc./Dist. by UFS, Inc.
10-3-04

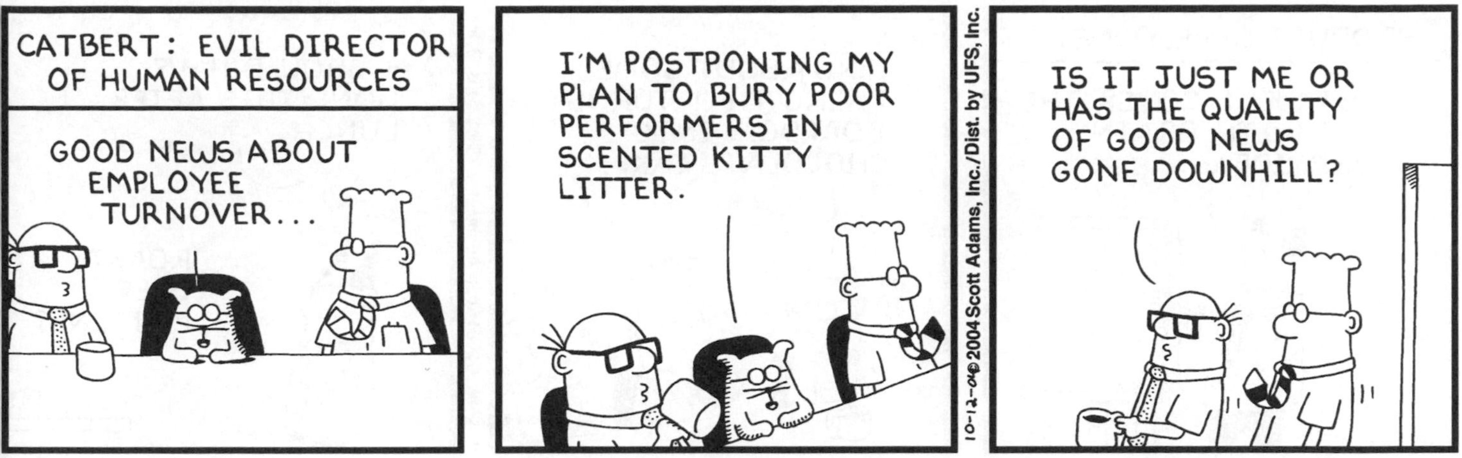
CATBERT: EVIL DIRECTOR OF HUMAN RESOURCES
GOOD NEWS ABOUT EMPLOYEE TURNOVER...
I'M POSTPONING MY PLAN TO BURY POOR PERFORMERS IN SCENTED KITTY LITTER.
10-12-04 © 2004 Scott Adams, Inc./Dist. by UFS, Inc.
IS IT JUST ME OR HAS THE QUALITY OF GOOD NEWS GONE DOWNHILL?

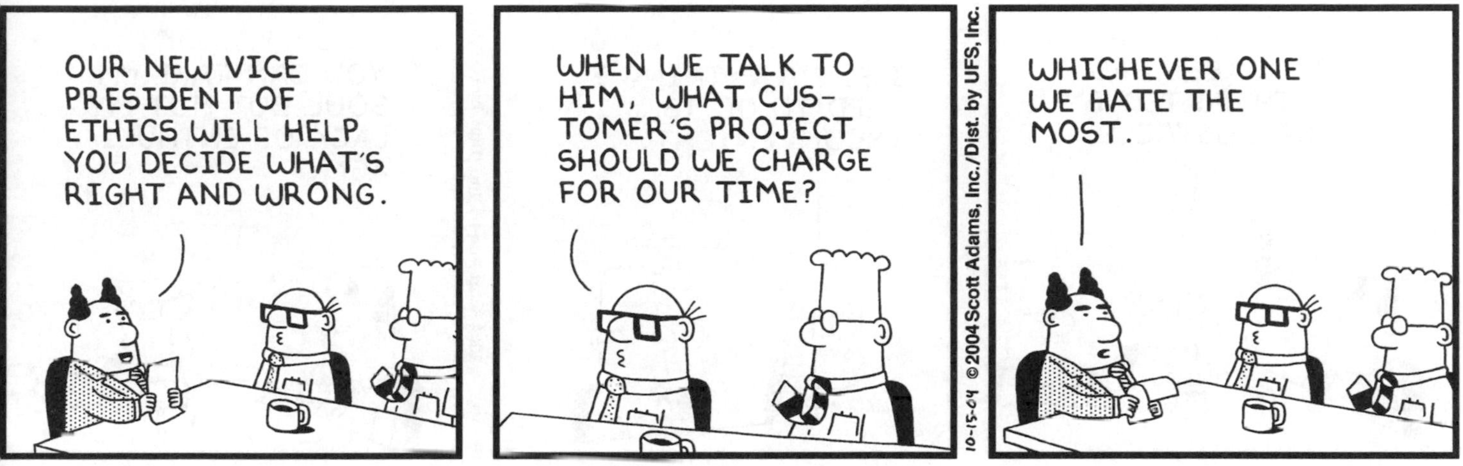
OUR NEW VICE PRESIDENT OF ETHICS WILL HELP YOU DECIDE WHAT'S RIGHT AND WRONG.
WHEN WE TALK TO HIM, WHAT CUS-TOMER'S PROJECT SHOULD WE CHARGE FOR OUR TIME?
10-15-04 © 2004 Scott Adams, Inc./Dist. by UFS, Inc.
WHICHEVER ONE WE HATE THE MOST.

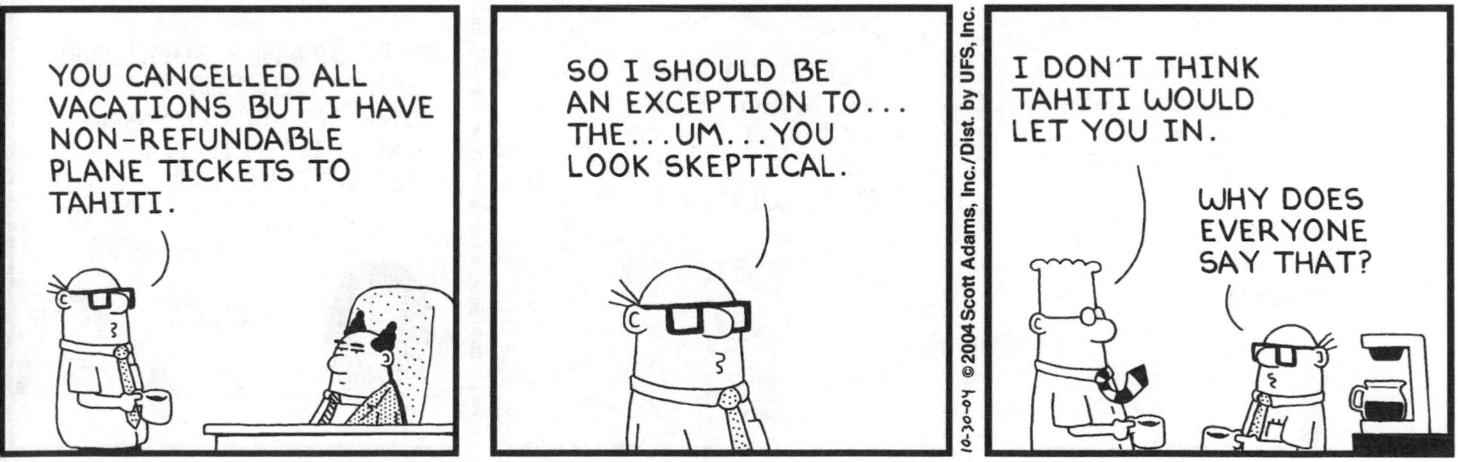
YOU CANCELLED ALL VACATIONS BUT I HAVE NON-REFUNDABLE PLANE TICKETS TO TAHITI.
SO I SHOULD BE AN EXCEPTION TO... THE...UM...YOU LOOK SKEPTICAL.
10-30-04 © 2004 Scott Adams, Inc./Dist. by UFS, Inc.
I DON'T THINK TAHITI WOULD LET YOU IN.
WHY DOES EVERYONE SAY THAT?

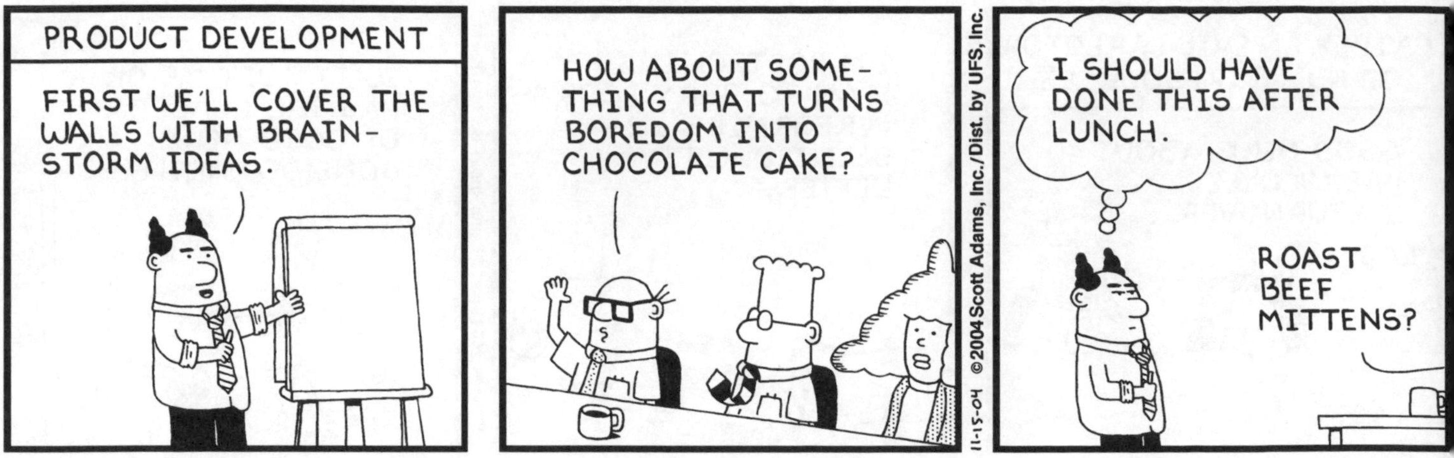
PRODUCT DEVELOPMENT
FIRST WE'LL COVER THE WALLS WITH BRAIN-STORM IDEAS.
HOW ABOUT SOME-THING THAT TURNS BOREDOM INTO CHOCOLATE CAKE?
11-15-04 © 2004 Scott Adams, Inc./Dist. by UFS, Inc.
I SHOULD HAVE DONE THIS AFTER LUNCH.
ROAST BEEF MITTENS?

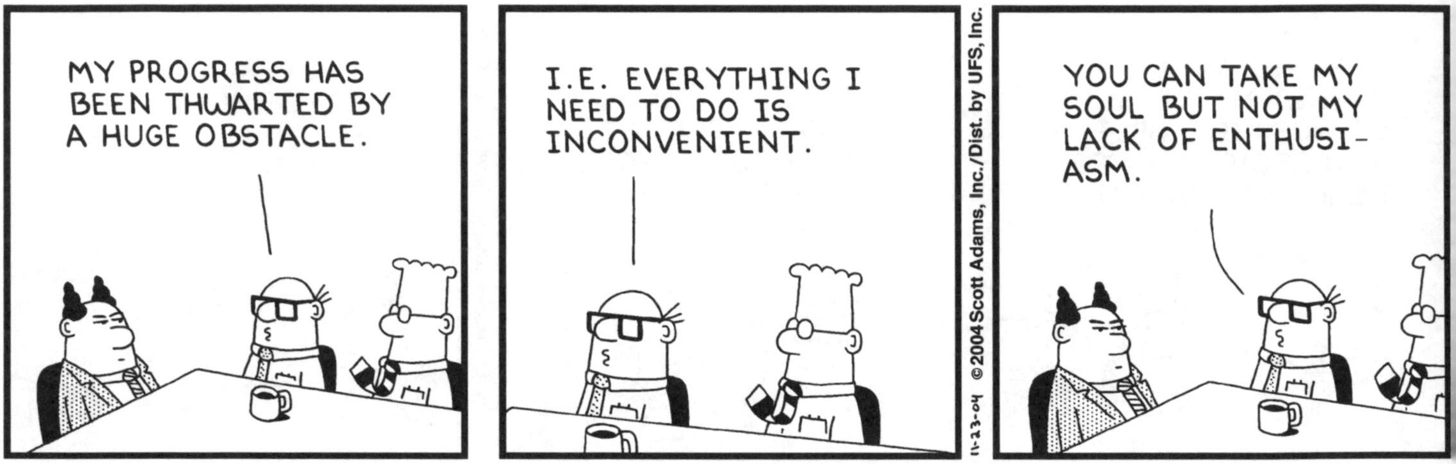
MY PROGRESS HAS BEEN THWARTED BY A HUGE OBSTACLE.
I.E. EVERYTHING I NEED TO DO IS INCONVENIENT.
11-23-04 © 2004 Scott Adams, Inc./Dist. by UFS, Inc.
YOU CAN TAKE MY SOUL BUT NOT MY LACK OF ENTHUSI-ASM.

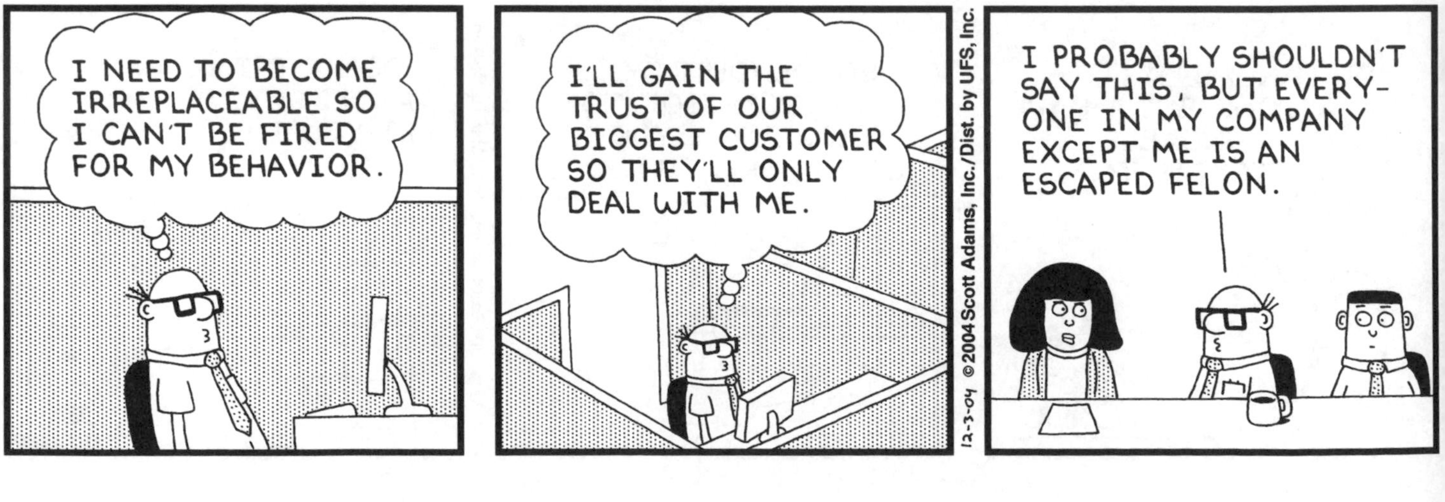
I NEED TO BECOME IRREPLACEABLE SO I CAN'T BE FIRED FOR MY BEHAVIOR.
I'LL GAIN THE TRUST OF OUR BIGGEST CUSTOMER SO THEY'LL ONLY DEAL WITH ME.
12-3-04 © 2004 Scott Adams, Inc./Dist. by UFS, Inc.
I PROBABLY SHOULDN'T SAY THIS, BUT EVERY-ONE IN MY COMPANY EXCEPT ME IS AN ESCAPED FELON.

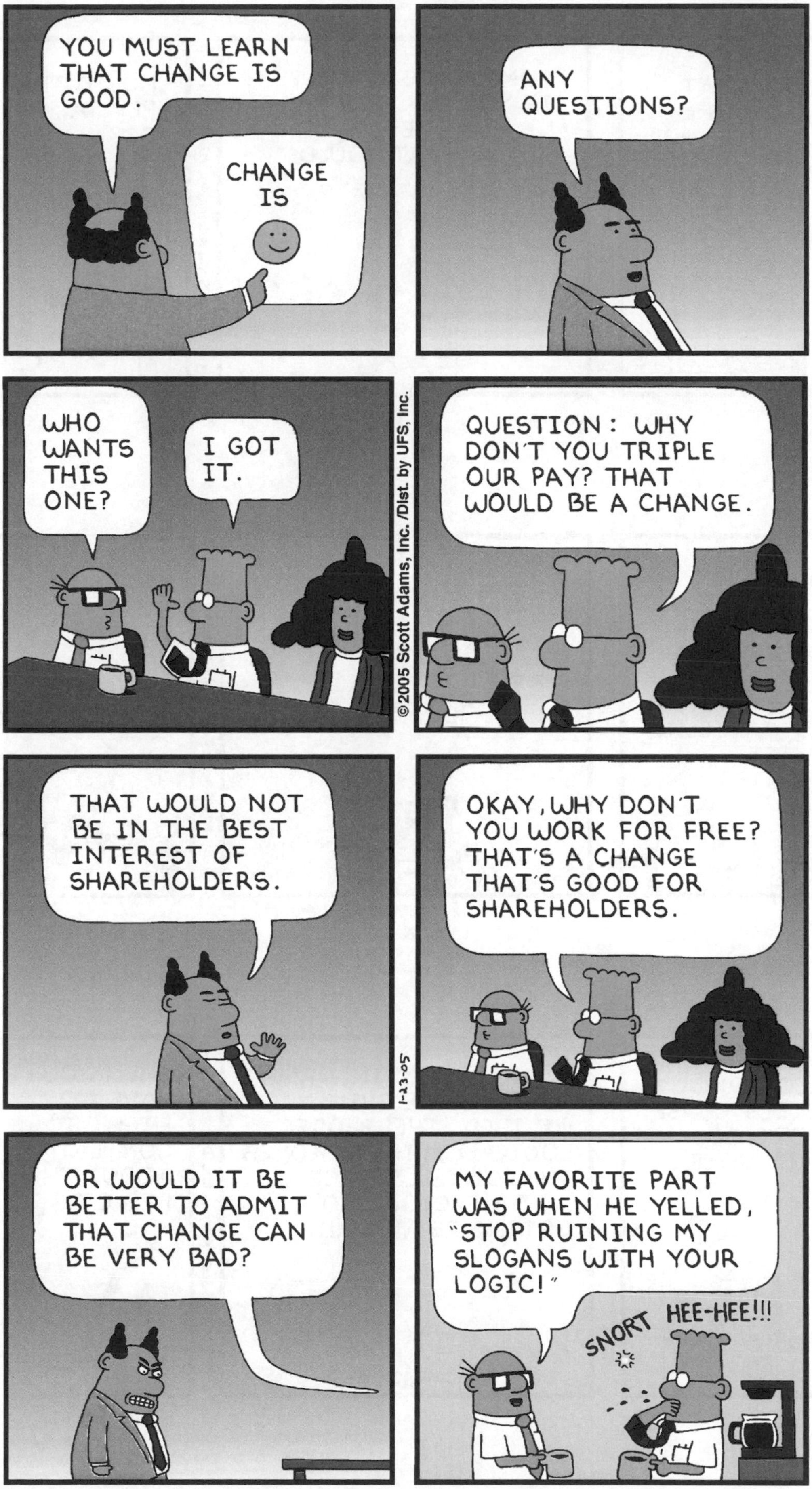
YOU MUST LEARN THAT CHANGE IS GOOD.
CHANGE IS
ANY QUESTIONS?
WHO WANTS THIS ONE?
I GOT IT.
QUESTION: WHY DON'T YOU TRIPLE OUR PAY? THAT WOULD BE A CHANGE.
©2005 Scott Adams, Inc. /Dist. by UFS, Inc.
THAT WOULD NOT BE IN THE BEST INTEREST OF SHAREHOLDERS.
OKAY, WHY DON'T YOU WORK FOR FREE? THAT'S A CHANGE THAT'S GOOD FOR SHAREHOLDERS.
1-23-05
OR WOULD IT BE BETTER TO ADMIT THAT CHANGE CAN BE VERY BAD?
MY FAVORITE PART WAS WHEN HE YELLED, "STOP RUINING MY SLOGANS WITH YOUR LOGIC!"
SNORT
HEE-HEE!!!

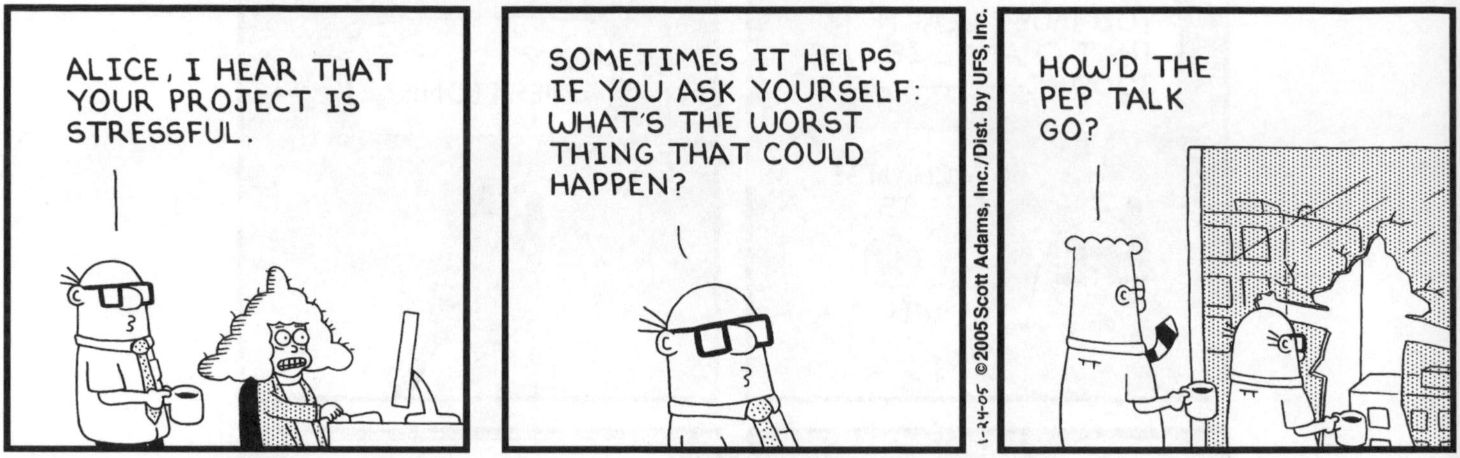
ALICE, I HEAR THAT YOUR PROJECT IS STRESSFUL.
SOMETIMES IT HELPS IF YOU ASK YOURSELF: WHAT'S THE WORST THING THAT COULD HAPPEN?
1-24-05 ©2005 Scott Adams, Inc./Dist. by UFS, Inc.
HOW'D THE PEP TALK GO?

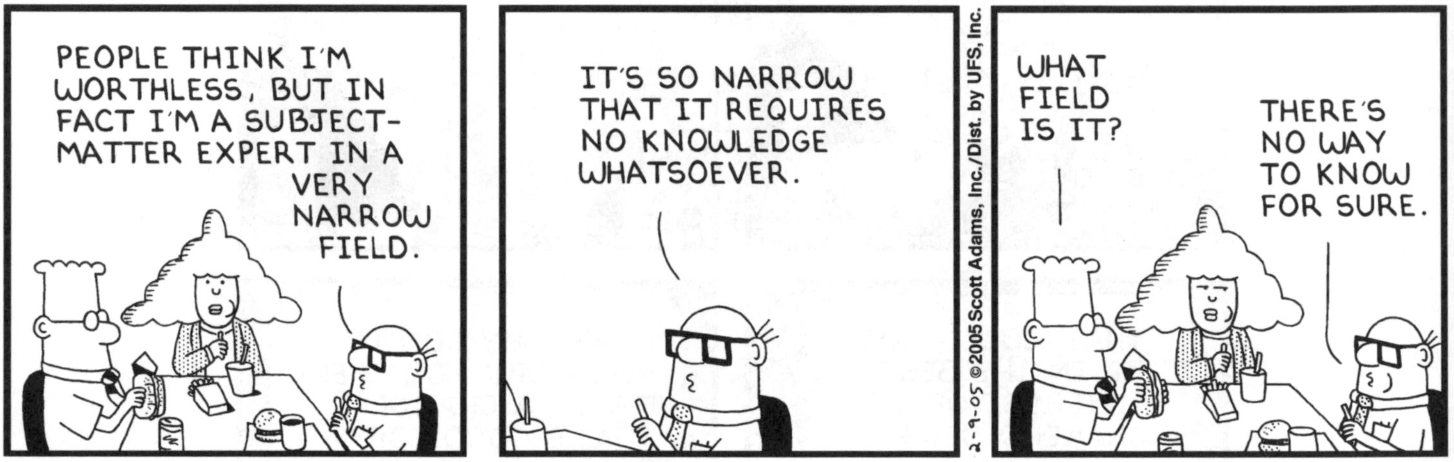
PEOPLE THINK I'M WORTHLESS, BUT IN FACT I'M A SUBJECT-MATTER EXPERT IN A VERY NARROW FIELD.
IT'S SO NARROW THAT IT REQUIRES NO KNOWLEDGE WHATSOEVER.
2-9-05 ©2005 Scott Adams, Inc./Dist. by UFS, Inc.
WHAT FIELD IS IT?
THERE'S NO WAY TO KNOW FOR SURE.

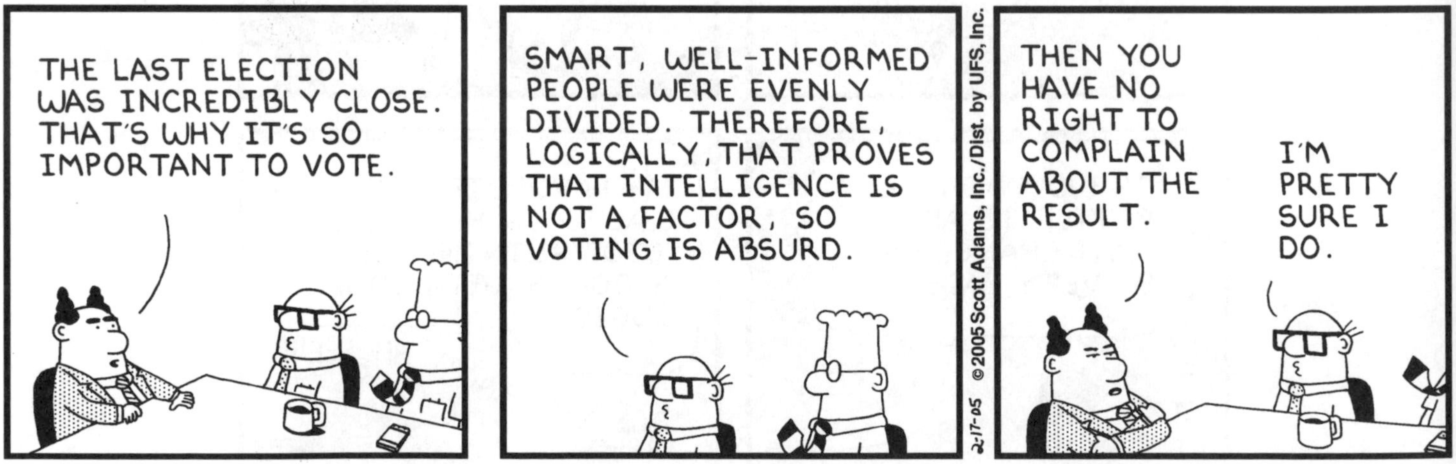
THE LAST ELECTION WAS INCREDIBLY CLOSE. THAT'S WHY IT'S SO IMPORTANT TO VOTE.
SMART, WELL-INFORMED PEOPLE WERE EVENLY DIVIDED. THEREFORE, LOGICALLY, THAT PROVES THAT INTELLIGENCE IS NOT A FACTOR, SO VOTING IS ABSURD.
2-17-05 ©2005 Scott Adams, Inc./Dist. by UFS, Inc.
THEN YOU HAVE NO RIGHT TO COMPLAIN ABOUT THE RESULT.
I'M PRETTY SURE I DO.

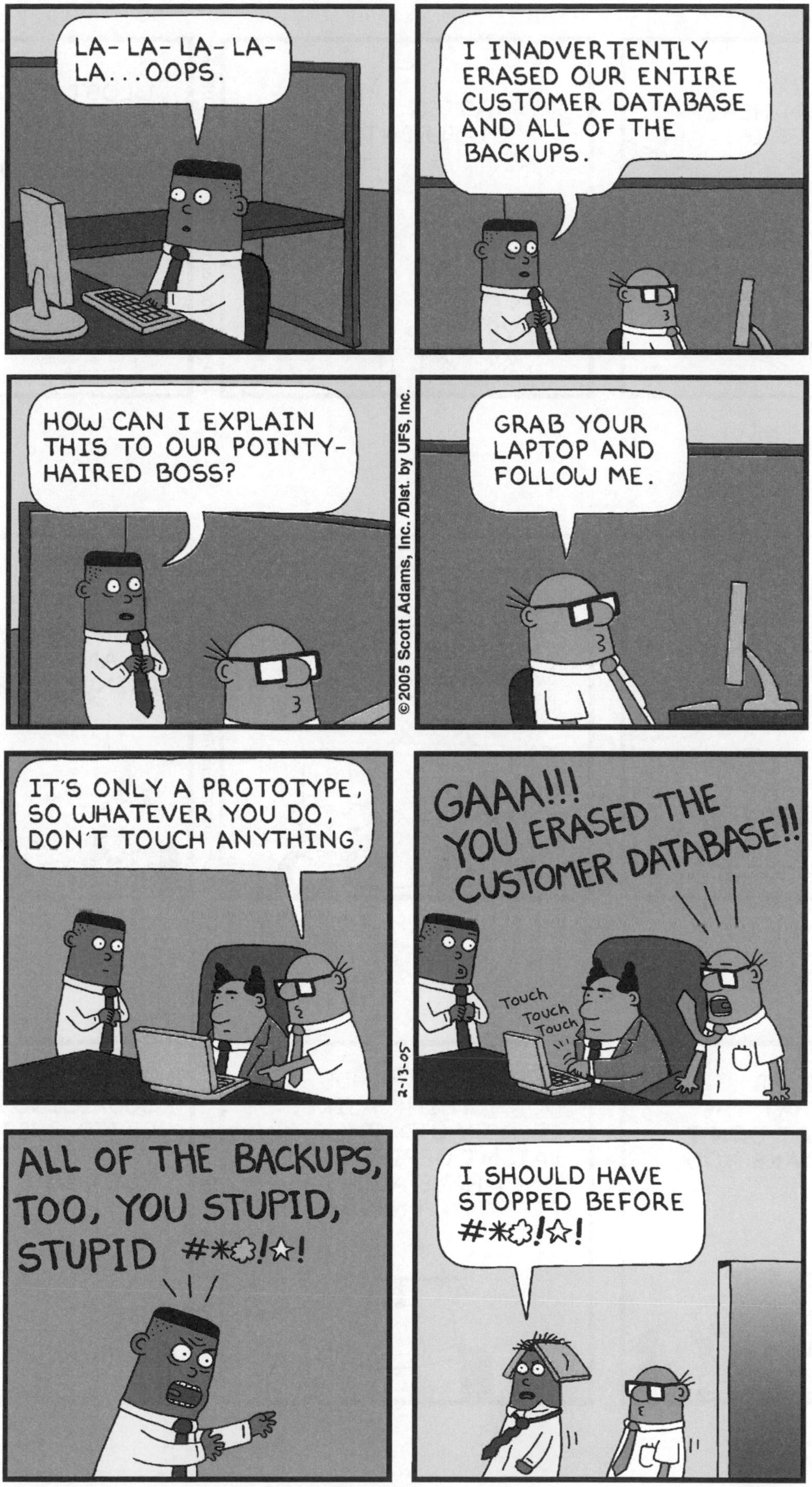
LA- LA- LA- LA- LA...OOPS.
I INADVERTENTLY ERASED OUR ENTIRE CUSTOMER DATABASE AND ALL OF THE BACKUPS.
HOW CAN I EXPLAIN THIS TO OUR POINTY-HAIRED BOSS?
©2005 Scott Adams, Inc./Dist. by UFS, Inc.
GRAB YOUR LAPTOP AND FOLLOW ME.
IT'S ONLY A PROTOTYPE, SO WHATEVER YOU DO, DON'T TOUCH ANYTHING.
2-13-05
GAAA!!! YOU ERASED THE CUSTOMER DATABASE!!
Touch Touch Touch
ALL OF THE BACKUPS, TOO, YOU STUPID, STUPID #*✿!☆!
I SHOULD HAVE STOPPED BEFORE #*✿!☆!

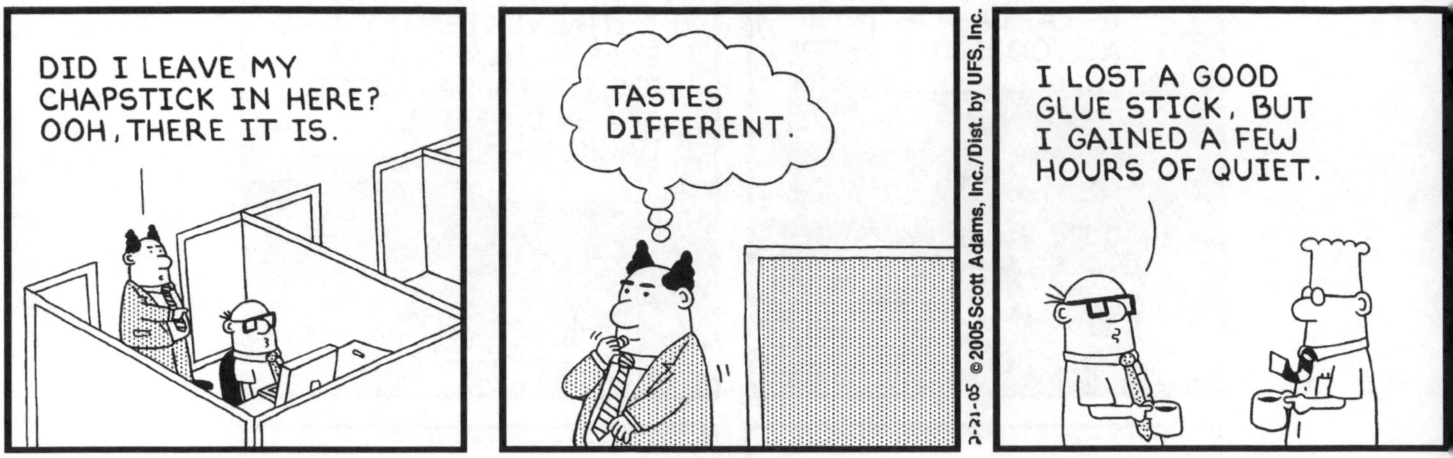
DID I LEAVE MY CHAPSTICK IN HERE? OOH, THERE IT IS.
TASTES DIFFERENT.
©2005 Scott Adams, Inc./Dist. by UFS, Inc.
I LOST A GOOD GLUE STICK, BUT I GAINED A FEW HOURS OF QUIET.

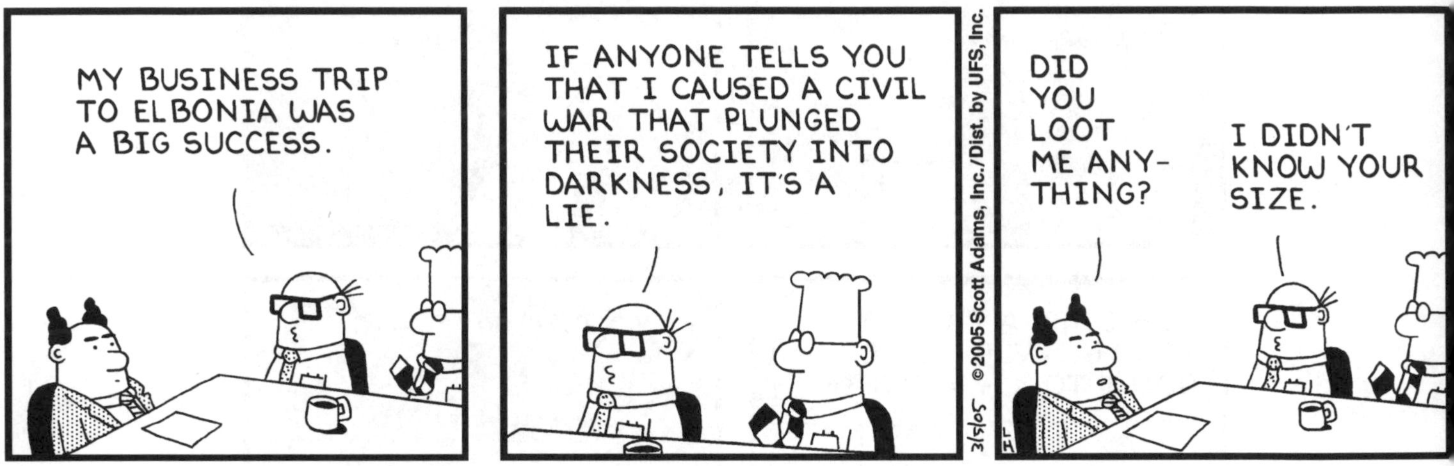
MY BUSINESS TRIP TO ELBONIA WAS A BIG SUCCESS.
IF ANYONE TELLS YOU THAT I CAUSED A CIVIL WAR THAT PLUNGED THEIR SOCIETY INTO DARKNESS, IT'S A LIE.
©2005 Scott Adams, Inc./Dist. by UFS, Inc.
DID YOU LOOT ME ANY-THING?
I DIDN'T KNOW YOUR SIZE.

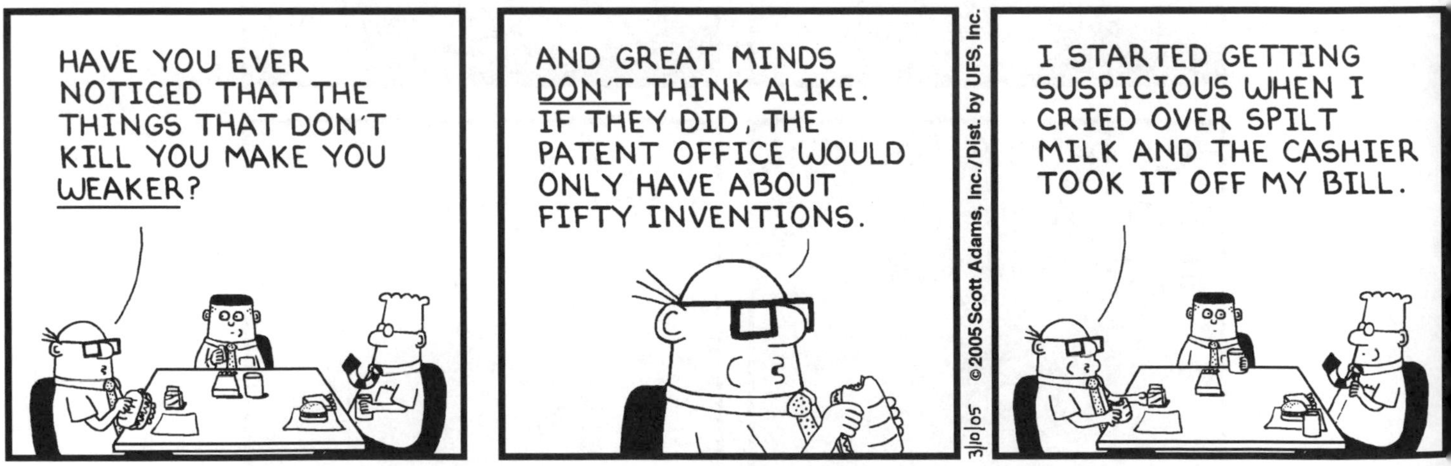
HAVE YOU EVER NOTICED THAT THE THINGS THAT DON'T KILL YOU MAKE YOU WEAKER?
AND GREAT MINDS DON'T THINK ALIKE. IF THEY DID, THE PATENT OFFICE WOULD ONLY HAVE ABOUT FIFTY INVENTIONS.
©2005 Scott Adams, Inc./Dist. by UFS, Inc.
I STARTED GETTING SUSPICIOUS WHEN I CRIED OVER SPILT MILK AND THE CASHIER TOOK IT OFF MY BILL.

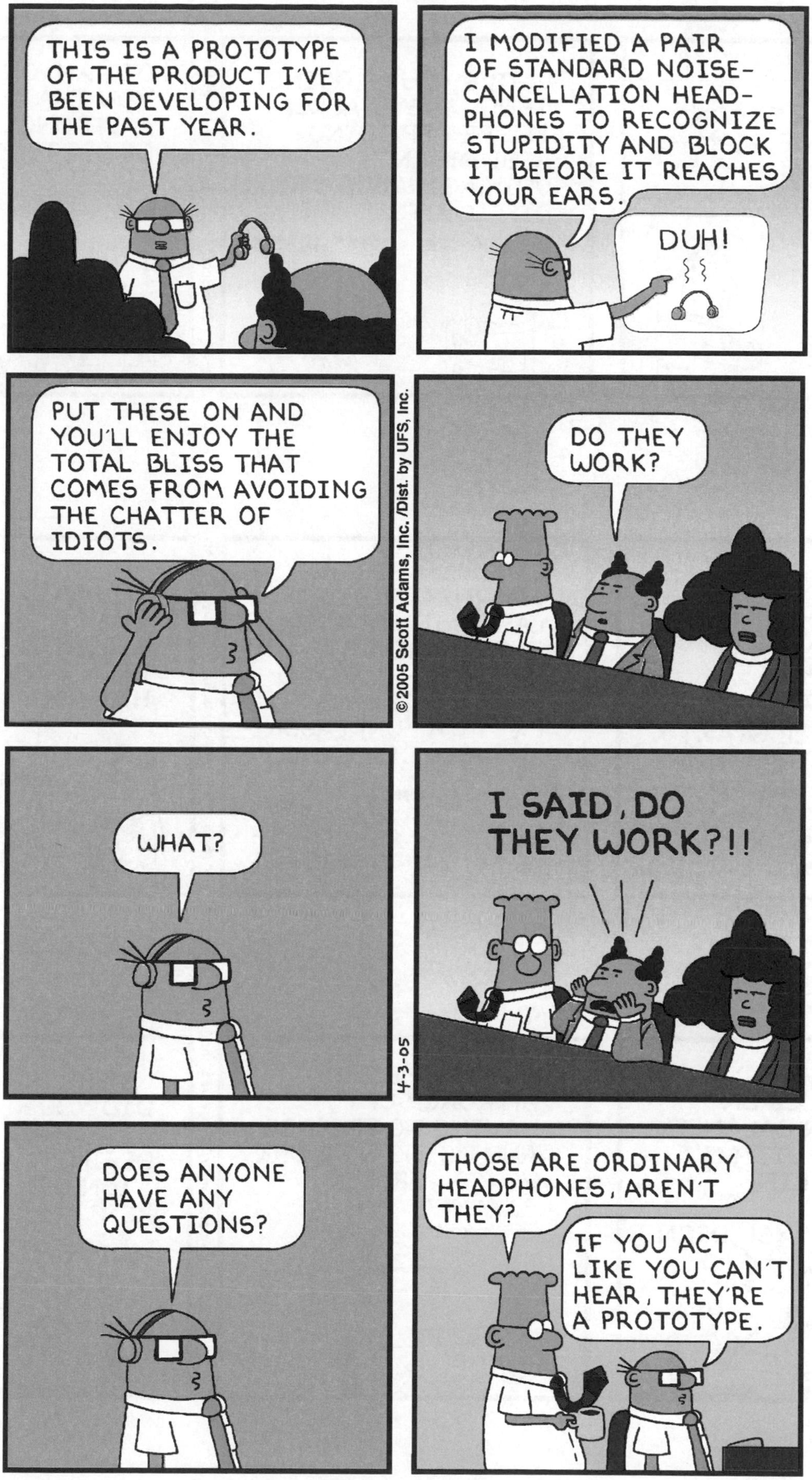

THIS IS A PROTOTYPE OF THE PRODUCT I'VE BEEN DEVELOPING FOR THE PAST YEAR.
I MODIFIED A PAIR OF STANDARD NOISE-CANCELLATION HEADPHONES TO RECOGNIZE STUPIDITY AND BLOCK IT BEFORE IT REACHES YOUR EARS.
DUH!
PUT THESE ON AND YOU'LL ENJOY THE TOTAL BLISS THAT COMES FROM AVOIDING THE CHATTER OF IDIOTS.
©2005 Scott Adams, Inc./Dist. by UFS, Inc.
DO THEY WORK?
WHAT?
4-3-05
I SAID, DO THEY WORK?!!
DOES ANYONE HAVE ANY QUESTIONS?
THOSE ARE ORDINARY HEADPHONES, AREN'T THEY?
IF YOU ACT LIKE YOU CAN'T HEAR, THEY'RE A PROTOTYPE.

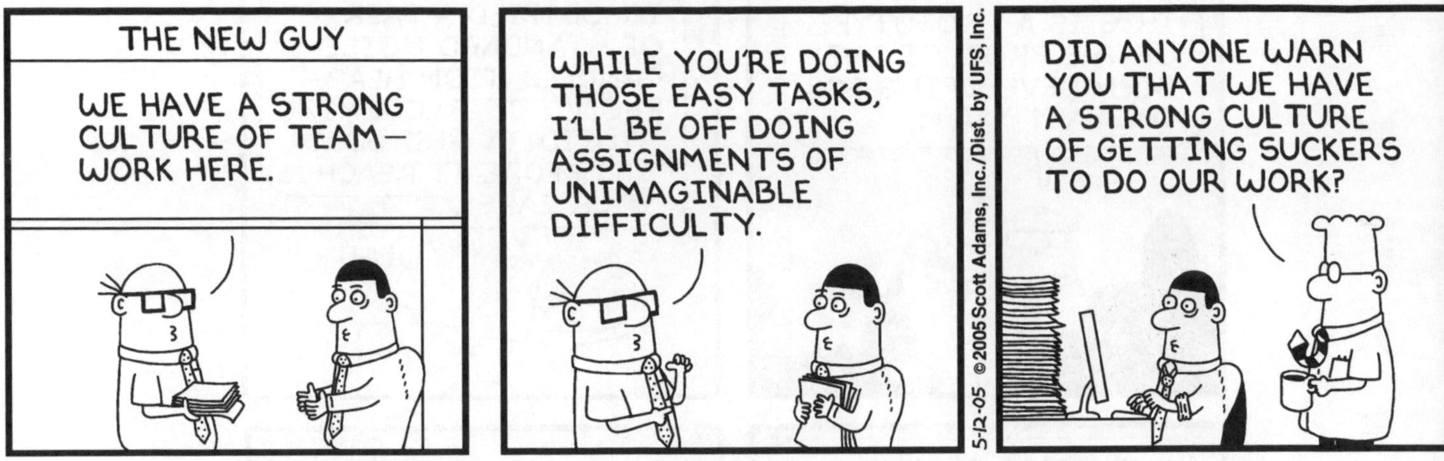
THE NEW GUY
WE HAVE A STRONG CULTURE OF TEAM-WORK HERE.
WHILE YOU'RE DOING THOSE EASY TASKS, I'LL BE OFF DOING ASSIGNMENTS OF UNIMAGINABLE DIFFICULTY.
5-12-05 © 2005 Scott Adams, Inc./Dist. by UFS, Inc.
DID ANYONE WARN YOU THAT WE HAVE A STRONG CULTURE OF GETTING SUCKERS TO DO OUR WORK?

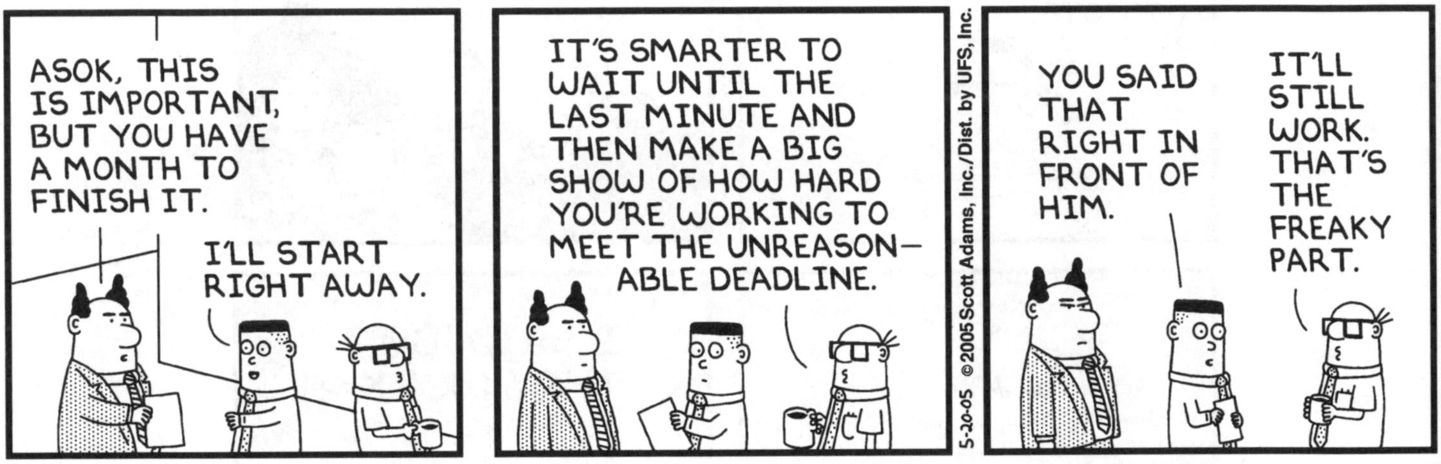
ASOK, THIS IS IMPORTANT, BUT YOU HAVE A MONTH TO FINISH IT.
I'LL START RIGHT AWAY.
IT'S SMARTER TO WAIT UNTIL THE LAST MINUTE AND THEN MAKE A BIG SHOW OF HOW HARD YOU'RE WORKING TO MEET THE UNREASON-ABLE DEADLINE.
5-20-05 © 2005 Scott Adams, Inc./Dist. by UFS, Inc.
YOU SAID THAT RIGHT IN FRONT OF HIM.
IT'LL STILL WORK. THAT'S THE FREAKY PART.

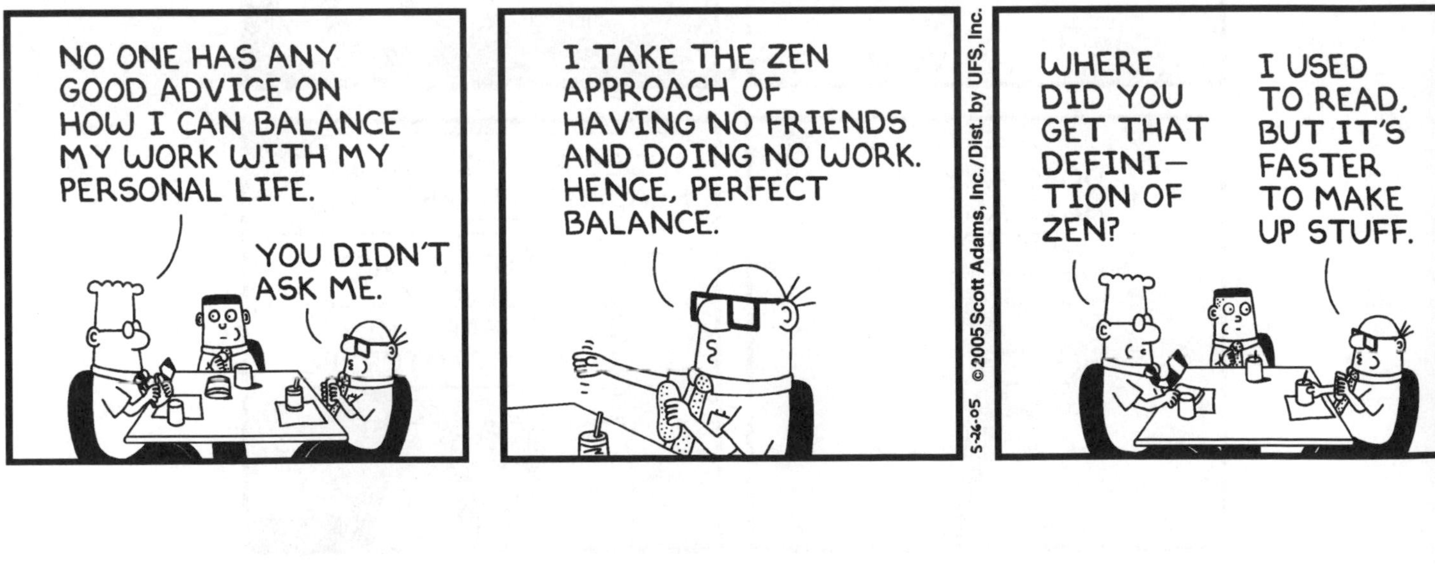
NO ONE HAS ANY GOOD ADVICE ON HOW I CAN BALANCE MY WORK WITH MY PERSONAL LIFE.
YOU DIDN'T ASK ME.
I TAKE THE ZEN APPROACH OF HAVING NO FRIENDS AND DOING NO WORK. HENCE, PERFECT BALANCE.
5-26-05 © 2005 Scott Adams, Inc./Dist. by UFS, Inc.
WHERE DID YOU GET THAT DEFINI-TION OF ZEN?
I USED TO READ, BUT IT'S FASTER TO MAKE UP STUFF.

MY ACCOMPLISHMENT THIS MONTH WAS OPENING A FILE THAT SOMEONE E-MAILED.
THAT TOOK AN ENTIRE MONTH?
IT WASN'T THAT EASY. I DIDN'T HAVE THE RIGHT SOFTWARE TO OPEN THE FILE.
I TRIED TO DOWN-LOAD THE VIEWER FROM THE INTERNET BUT THE WEB SITE DIDN'T SUPPORT MY BROWSER.
AND I COULDN'T UPGRADE MY BROWSER UNTIL I UPGRADED MY OPERATING SYSTEM!
THAT REQUIRED ME TO UPGRADE ALL OF MY APPLICATIONS SOFTWARE, TOO.
MY HARD DISK GOT MAXED OUT, SO I HAD TO UPGRADE MY COMPUTER AND TRANSFER ALL OF THE FILES.
SO, THEN YOU GOT TO VIEW THE FILE?
YEAH... IT WAS A FUNNY ONE ABOUT A CAT.
©2005 Scott Adams, Inc./Dist. by UFS, Inc.
4-24-05

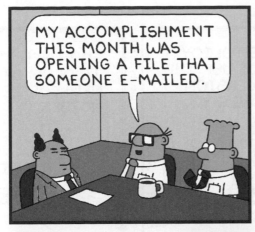

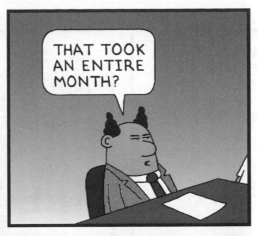

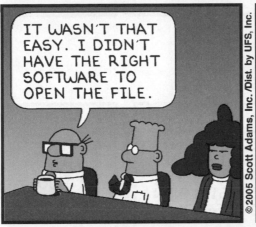

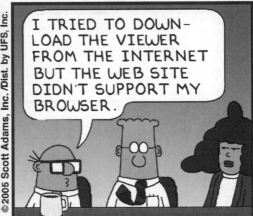

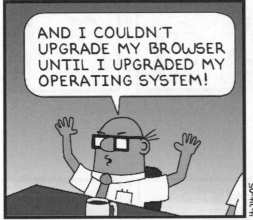

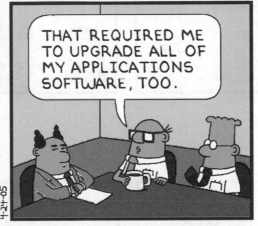

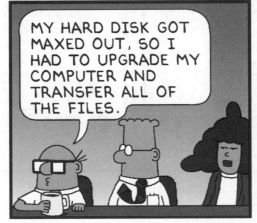

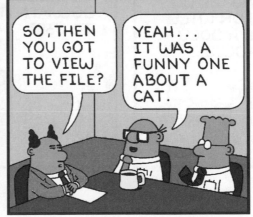

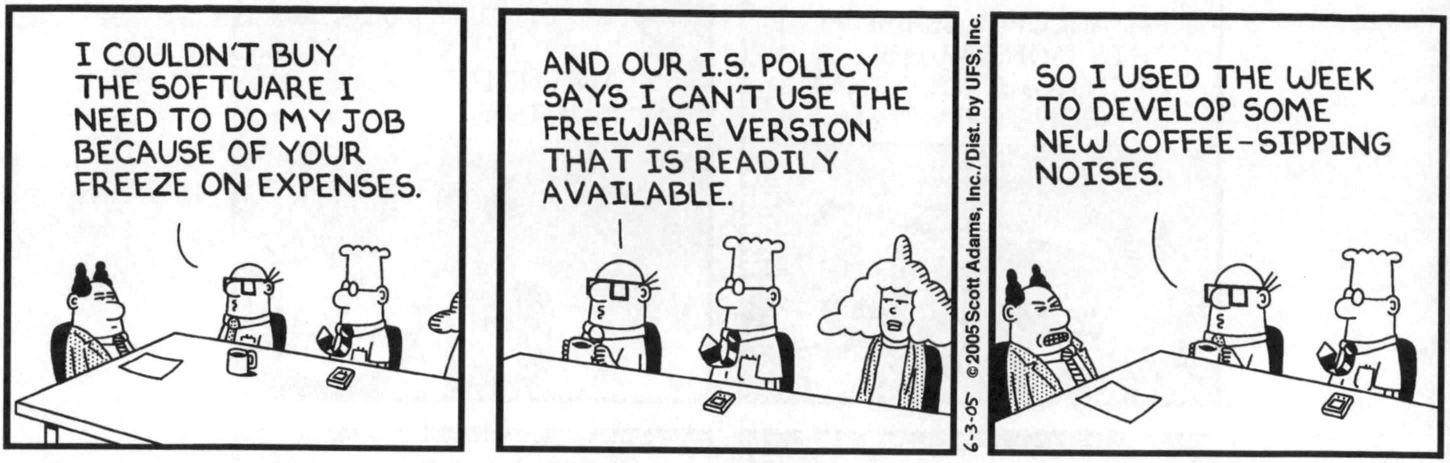
I COULDN'T BUY THE SOFTWARE I NEED TO DO MY JOB BECAUSE OF YOUR FREEZE ON EXPENSES.
AND OUR I.S. POLICY SAYS I CAN'T USE THE FREEWARE VERSION THAT IS READILY AVAILABLE.
SO I USED THE WEEK TO DEVELOP SOME NEW COFFEE-SIPPING NOISES.
6-3-05 © 2005 Scott Adams, Inc./Dist. by UFS, Inc.

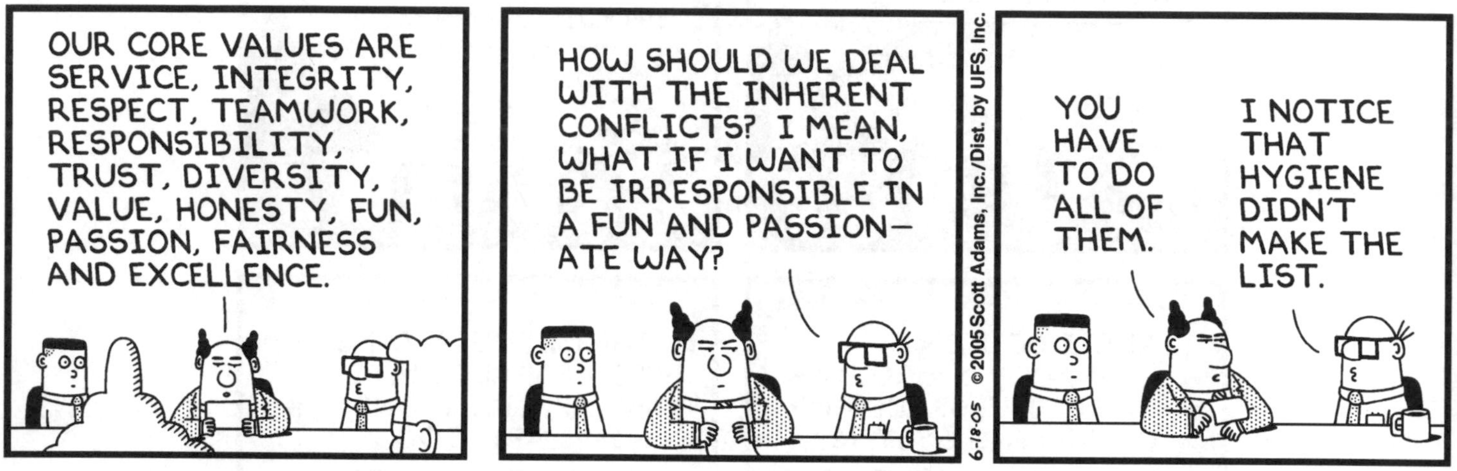
OUR CORE VALUES ARE SERVICE, INTEGRITY, RESPECT, TEAMWORK, RESPONSIBILITY, TRUST, DIVERSITY, VALUE, HONESTY, FUN, PASSION, FAIRNESS AND EXCELLENCE.
HOW SHOULD WE DEAL WITH THE INHERENT CONFLICTS? I MEAN, WHAT IF I WANT TO BE IRRESPONSIBLE IN A FUN AND PASSION-ATE WAY?
YOU HAVE TO DO ALL OF THEM.
I NOTICE THAT HYGIENE DIDN'T MAKE THE LIST.
6-18-05 © 2005 Scott Adams, Inc./Dist. by UFS, Inc.

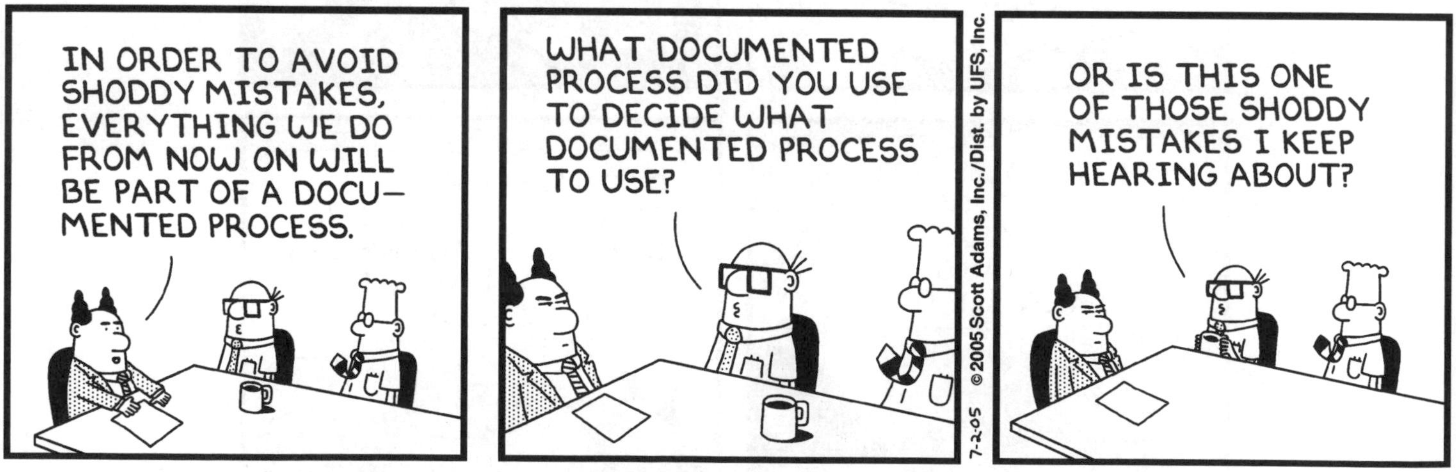
IN ORDER TO AVOID SHODDY MISTAKES, EVERYTHING WE DO FROM NOW ON WILL BE PART OF A DOCU-MENTED PROCESS.
WHAT DOCUMENTED PROCESS DID YOU USE TO DECIDE WHAT DOCUMENTED PROCESS TO USE?
OR IS THIS ONE OF THOSE SHODDY MISTAKES I KEEP HEARING ABOUT?
7-2-05 © 2005 Scott Adams, Inc./Dist. by UFS, Inc.

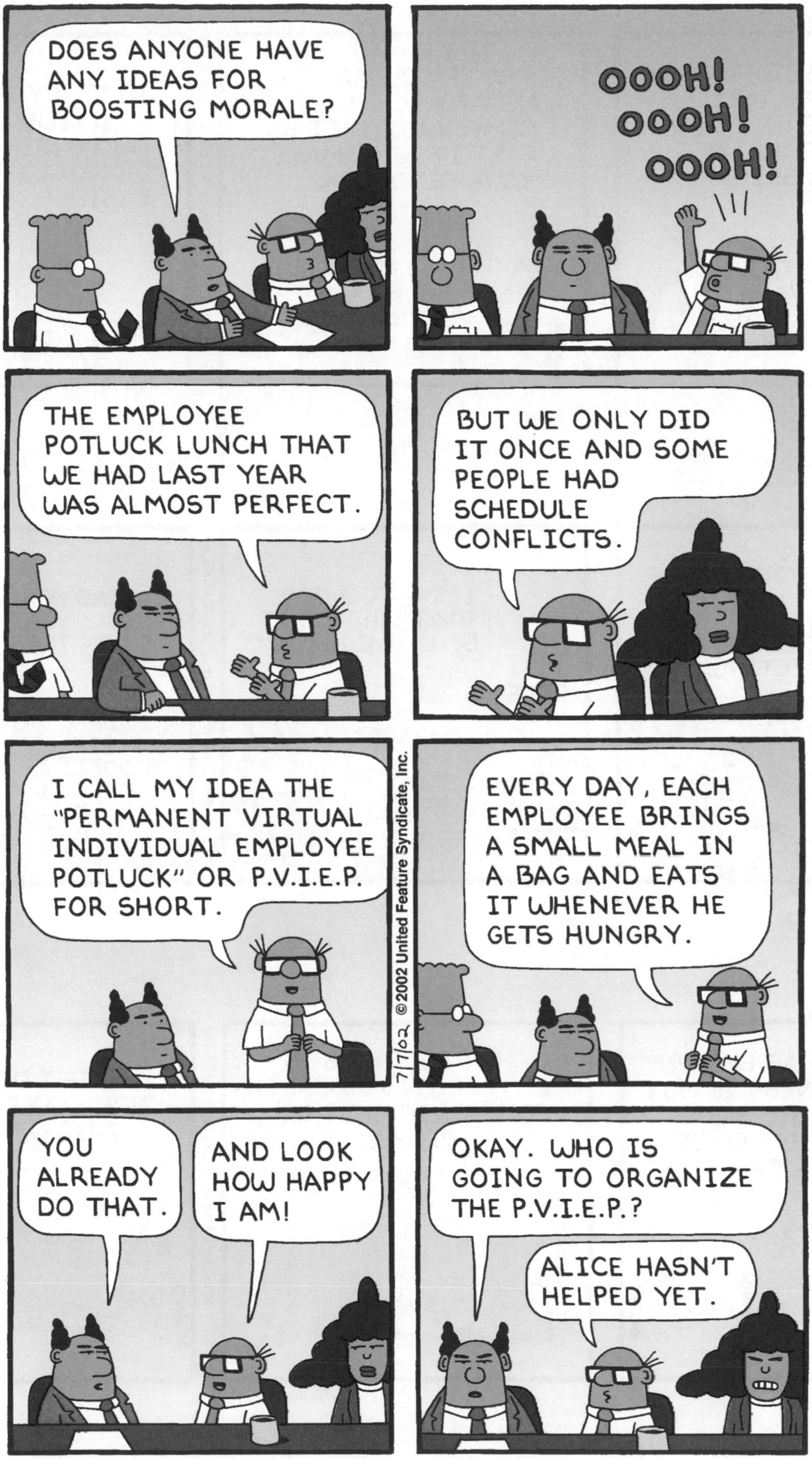

DOES ANYONE HAVE ANY IDEAS FOR BOOSTING MORALE?
OOOH! OOOH! OOOH!
THE EMPLOYEE POTLUCK LUNCH THAT WE HAD LAST YEAR WAS ALMOST PERFECT.
BUT WE ONLY DID IT ONCE AND SOME PEOPLE HAD SCHEDULE CONFLICTS.
I CALL MY IDEA THE "PERMANENT VIRTUAL INDIVIDUAL EMPLOYEE POTLUCK" OR P.V.I.E.P. FOR SHORT.
EVERY DAY, EACH EMPLOYEE BRINGS A SMALL MEAL IN A BAG AND EATS IT WHENEVER HE GETS HUNGRY.
YOU ALREADY DO THAT.
AND LOOK HOW HAPPY I AM!
OKAY. WHO IS GOING TO ORGANIZE THE P.V.I.E.P.?
ALICE HASN'T HELPED YET.
7/7/02 ©2002 United Feature Syndicate, Inc.

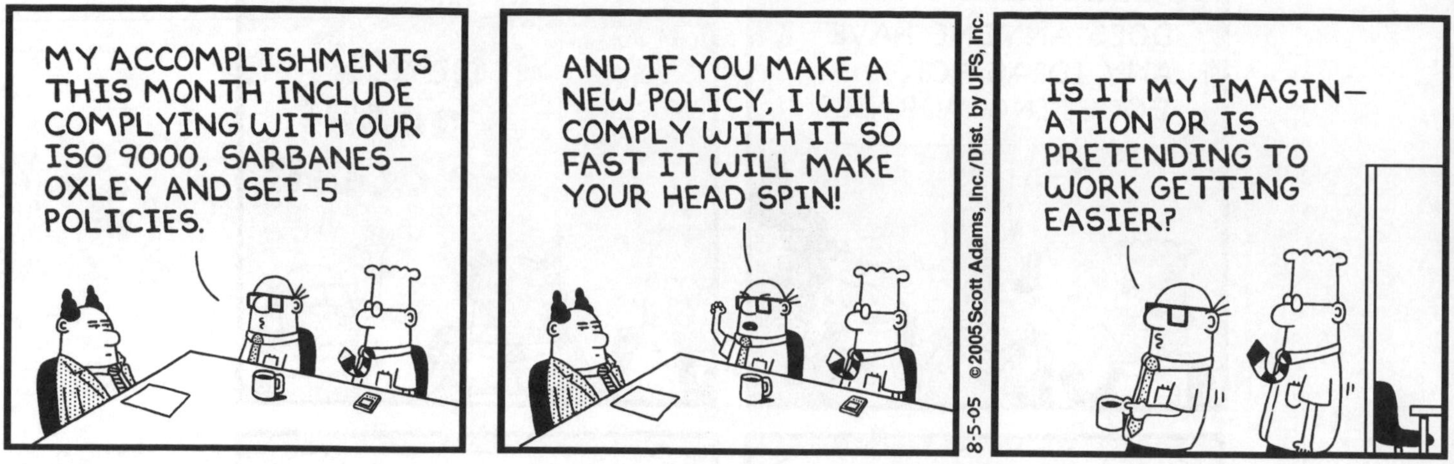
MY ACCOMPLISHMENTS THIS MONTH INCLUDE COMPLYING WITH OUR ISO 9000, SARBANES-OXLEY AND SEI-5 POLICIES.
AND IF YOU MAKE A NEW POLICY, I WILL COMPLY WITH IT SO FAST IT WILL MAKE YOUR HEAD SPIN!
8-5-05 © 2005 Scott Adams, Inc./Dist. by UFS, Inc.
IS IT MY IMAGINATION OR IS PRETENDING TO WORK GETTING EASIER?

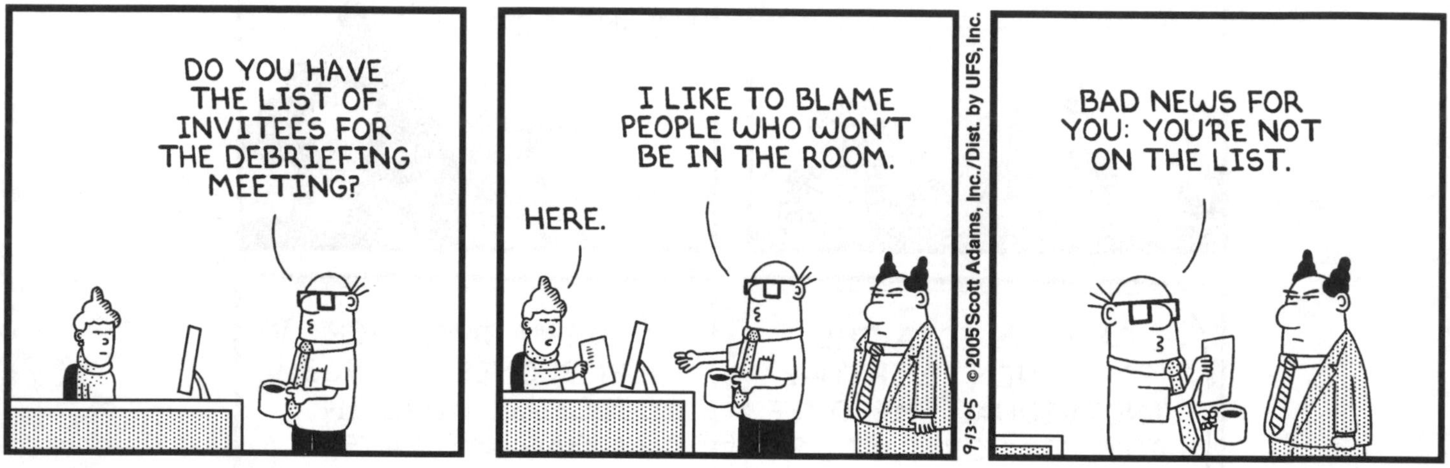
DO YOU HAVE THE LIST OF INVITEES FOR THE DEBRIEFING MEETING?
HERE.
I LIKE TO BLAME PEOPLE WHO WON'T BE IN THE ROOM.
9-13-05 © 2005 Scott Adams, Inc./Dist. by UFS, Inc.
BAD NEWS FOR YOU: YOU'RE NOT ON THE LIST.

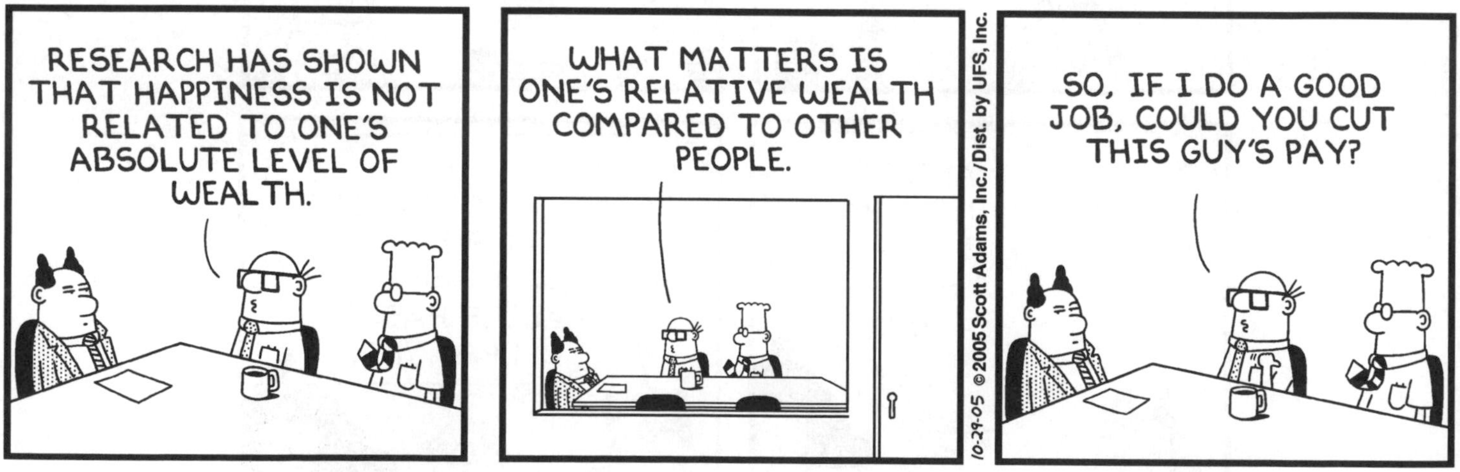
RESEARCH HAS SHOWN THAT HAPPINESS IS NOT RELATED TO ONE'S ABSOLUTE LEVEL OF WEALTH.
WHAT MATTERS IS ONE'S RELATIVE WEALTH COMPARED TO OTHER PEOPLE.
10-29-05 © 2005 Scott Adams, Inc./Dist. by UFS, Inc.
SO, IF I DO A GOOD JOB, COULD YOU CUT THIS GUY'S PAY?

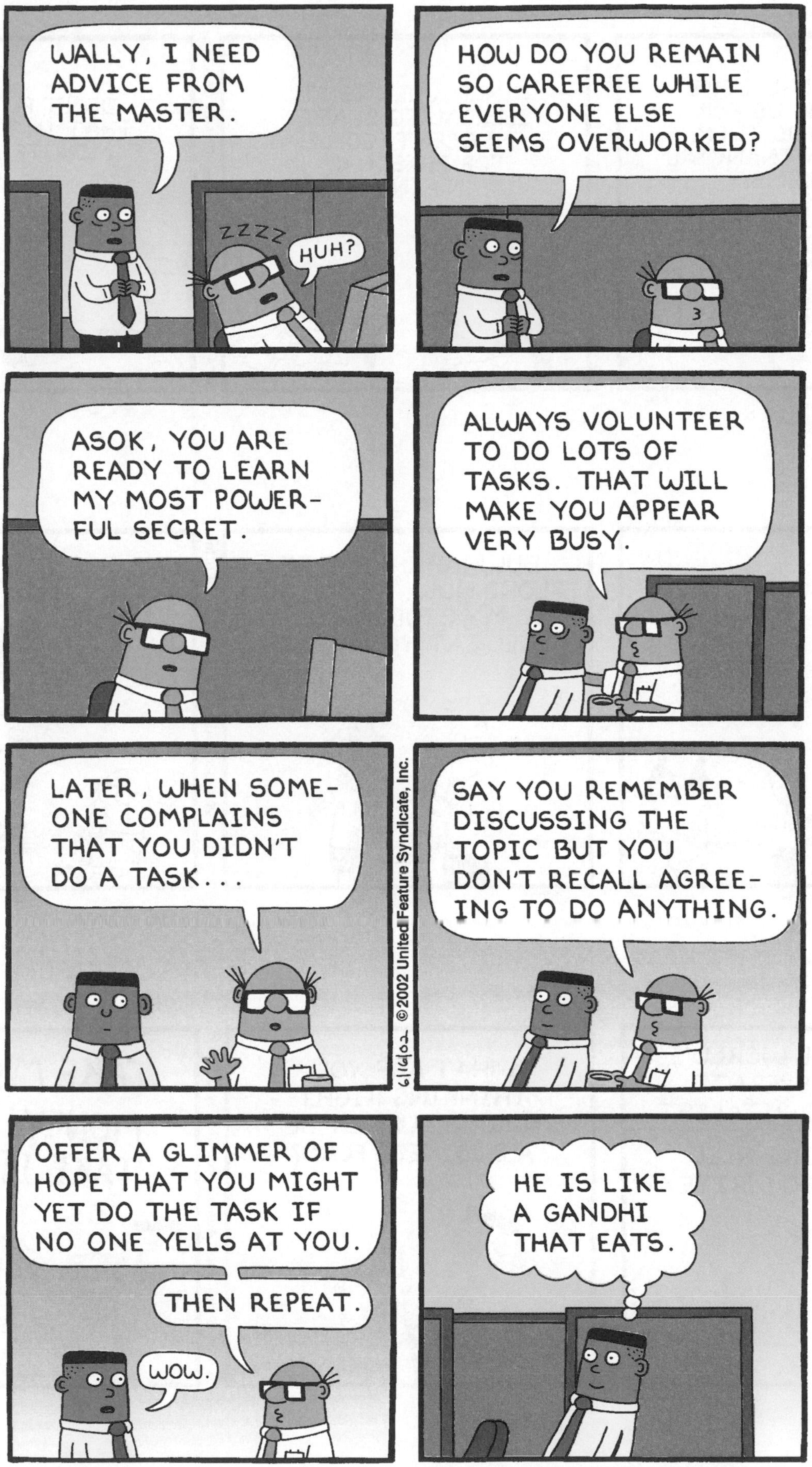
WALLY, I NEED ADVICE FROM THE MASTER.
ZZZZ
HUH?
HOW DO YOU REMAIN SO CAREFREE WHILE EVERYONE ELSE SEEMS OVERWORKED?
ASOK, YOU ARE READY TO LEARN MY MOST POWER-FUL SECRET.
ALWAYS VOLUNTEER TO DO LOTS OF TASKS. THAT WILL MAKE YOU APPEAR VERY BUSY.
LATER, WHEN SOME-ONE COMPLAINS THAT YOU DIDN'T DO A TASK...
6/16/02 © 2002 United Feature Syndicate, Inc.
SAY YOU REMEMBER DISCUSSING THE TOPIC BUT YOU DON'T RECALL AGREE-ING TO DO ANYTHING.
OFFER A GLIMMER OF HOPE THAT YOU MIGHT YET DO THE TASK IF NO ONE YELLS AT YOU.
THEN REPEAT.
WOW.
HE IS LIKE A GANDHI THAT EATS.

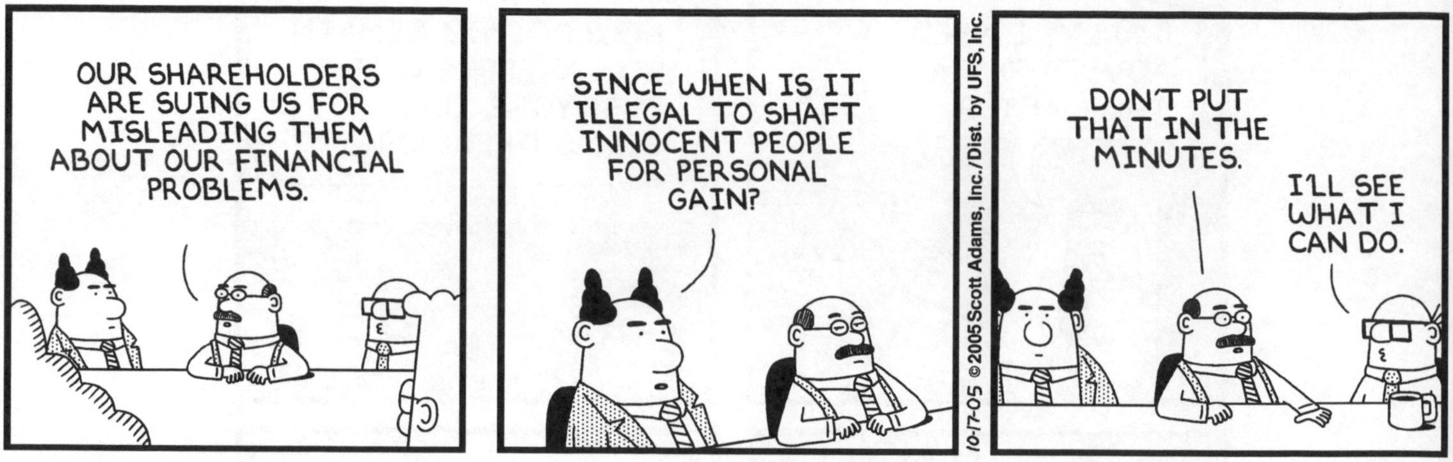
OUR SHAREHOLDERS ARE SUING US FOR MISLEADING THEM ABOUT OUR FINANCIAL PROBLEMS.
SINCE WHEN IS IT ILLEGAL TO SHAFT INNOCENT PEOPLE FOR PERSONAL GAIN?
10-17-05 © 2005 Scott Adams, Inc./Dist. by UFS, Inc.
DON'T PUT THAT IN THE MINUTES.
I'LL SEE WHAT I CAN DO.

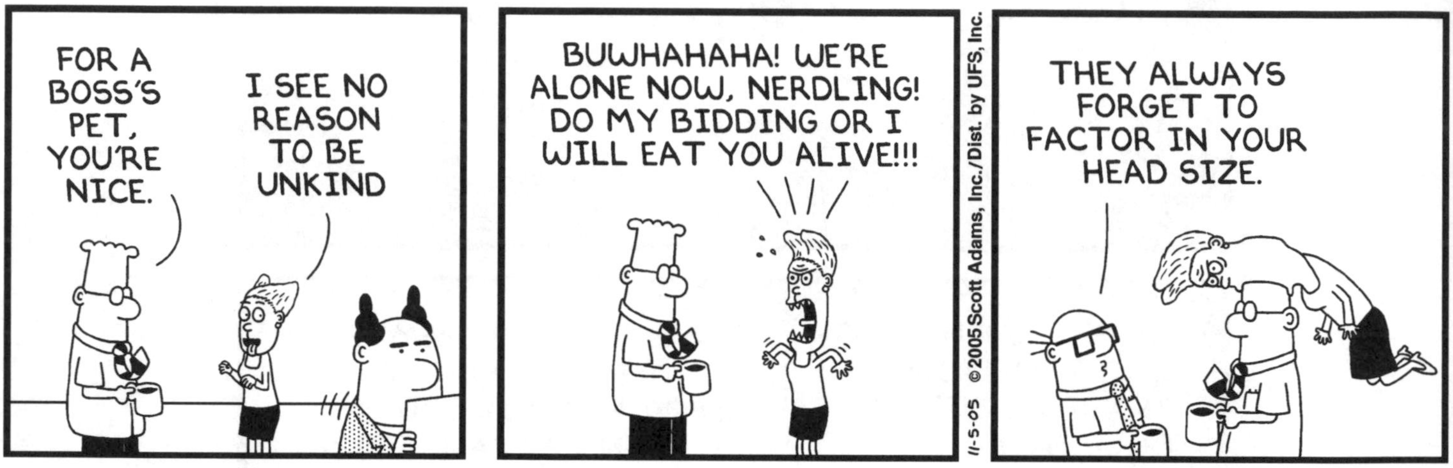
FOR A BOSS'S PET, YOU'RE NICE.
I SEE NO REASON TO BE UNKIND
BUWHAHAHA! WE'RE ALONE NOW, NERDLING! DO MY BIDDING OR I WILL EAT YOU ALIVE!!!
11-5-05 © 2005 Scott Adams, Inc./Dist. by UFS, Inc.
THEY ALWAYS FORGET TO FACTOR IN YOUR HEAD SIZE.

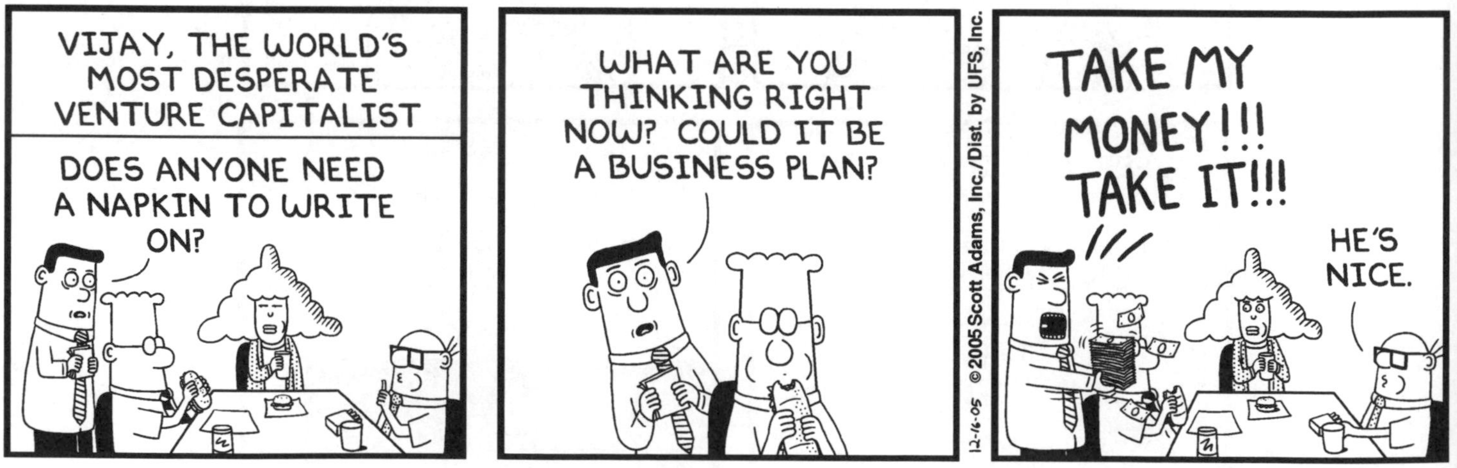
VIJAY, THE WORLD'S MOST DESPERATE VENTURE CAPITALIST
DOES ANYONE NEED A NAPKIN TO WRITE ON?
WHAT ARE YOU THINKING RIGHT NOW? COULD IT BE A BUSINESS PLAN?
12-6-05 © 2005 Scott Adams, Inc./Dist. by UFS, Inc.
TAKE MY MONEY!!! TAKE IT!!!
HE'S NICE.

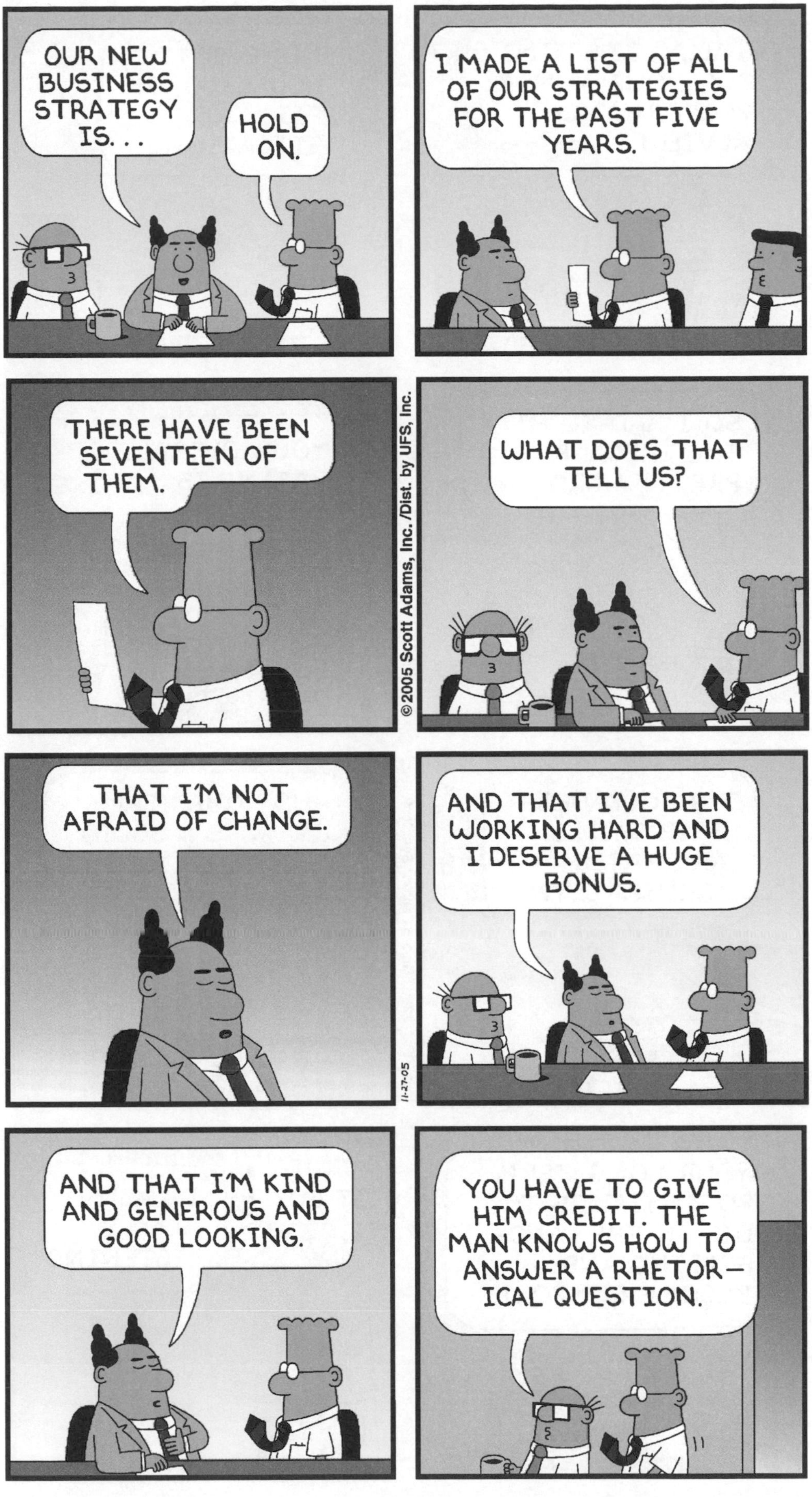
OUR NEW BUSINESS STRATEGY IS. . .
HOLD ON.
I MADE A LIST OF ALL OF OUR STRATEGIES FOR THE PAST FIVE YEARS.
THERE HAVE BEEN SEVENTEEN OF THEM.
©2005 Scott Adams, Inc./Dist. by UFS, Inc.
WHAT DOES THAT TELL US?
THAT I'M NOT AFRAID OF CHANGE.
11-27-05
AND THAT I'VE BEEN WORKING HARD AND I DESERVE A HUGE BONUS.
AND THAT I'M KIND AND GENEROUS AND GOOD LOOKING.
YOU HAVE TO GIVE HIM CREDIT. THE MAN KNOWS HOW TO ANSWER A RHETOR-ICAL QUESTION.

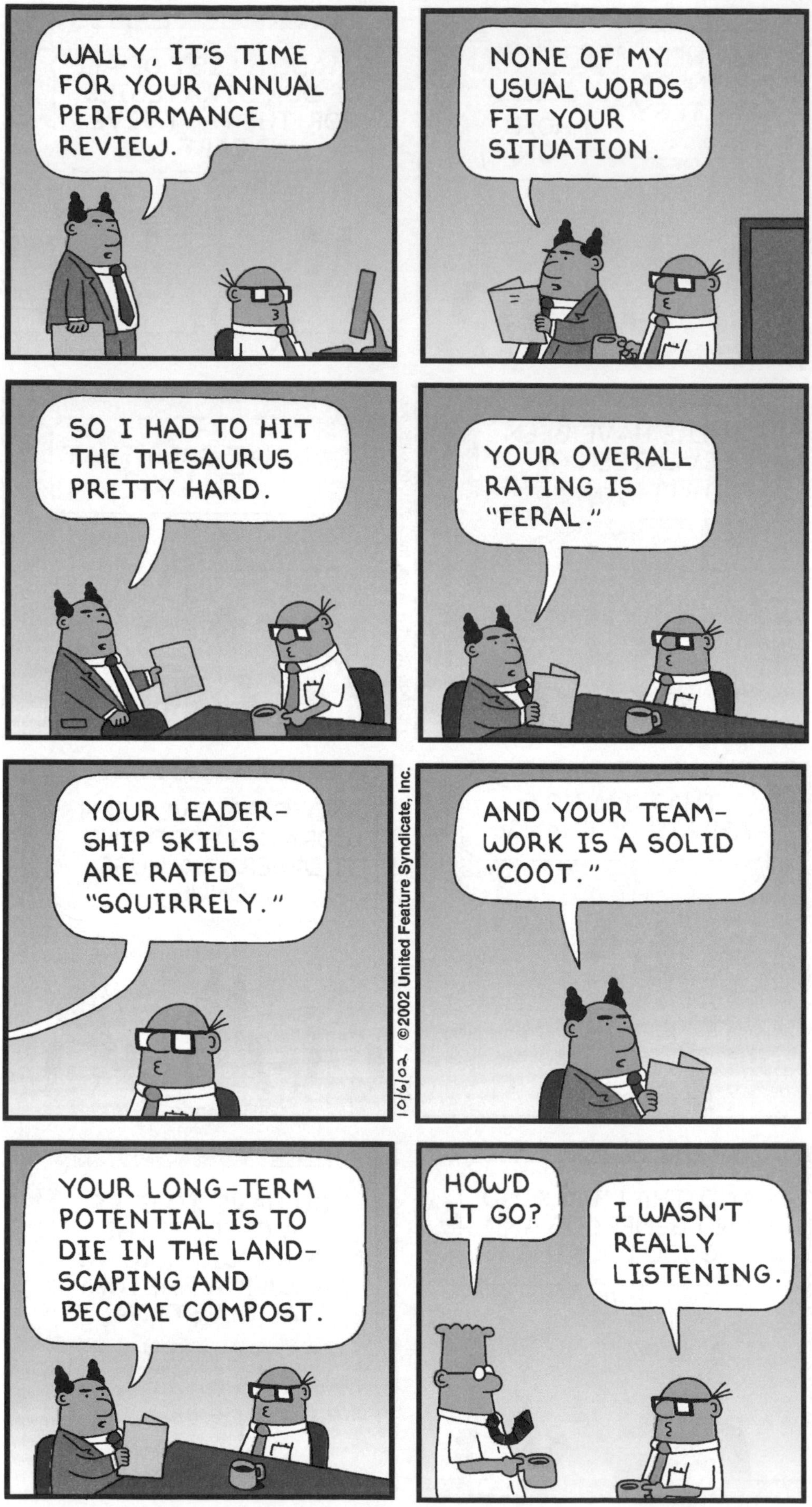
WALLY, IT'S TIME FOR YOUR ANNUAL PERFORMANCE REVIEW.
NONE OF MY USUAL WORDS FIT YOUR SITUATION.
SO I HAD TO HIT THE THESAURUS PRETTY HARD.
YOUR OVERALL RATING IS "FERAL."
YOUR LEADER-SHIP SKILLS ARE RATED "SQUIRRELY."
©2002 United Feature Syndicate, Inc.
10/6/02
AND YOUR TEAM-WORK IS A SOLID "COOT."
YOUR LONG-TERM POTENTIAL IS TO DIE IN THE LAND-SCAPING AND BECOME COMPOST.
HOW'D IT GO?
I WASN'T REALLY LISTENING.

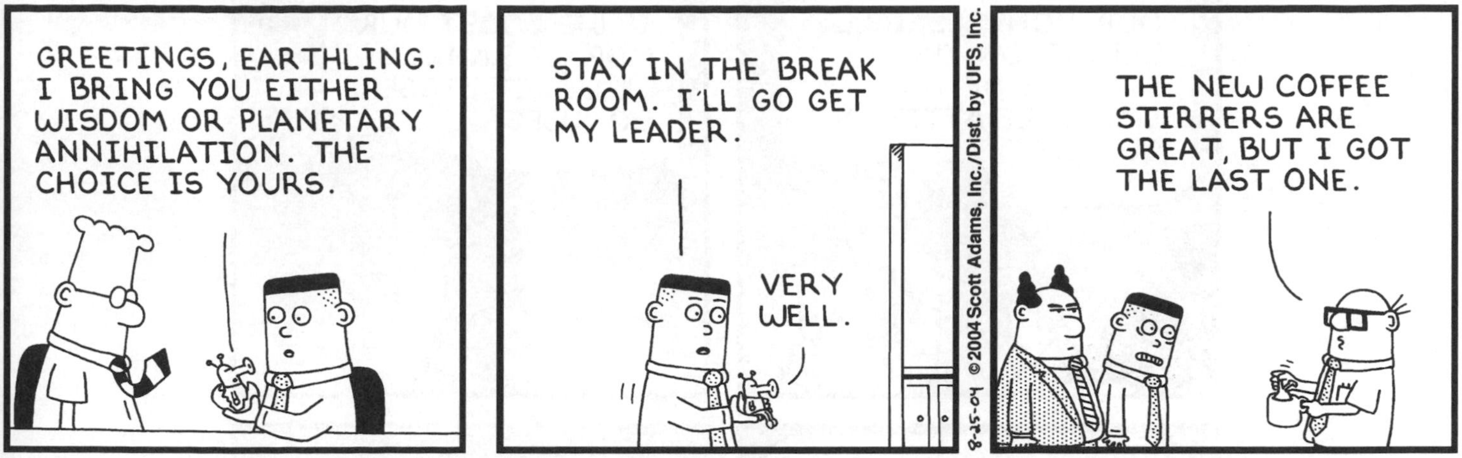
GREETINGS, EARTHLING. I BRING YOU EITHER WISDOM OR PLANETARY ANNIHILATION. THE CHOICE IS YOURS.
STAY IN THE BREAK ROOM. I'LL GO GET MY LEADER.
VERY WELL.
8-25-04 © 2004 Scott Adams, Inc./Dist. by UFS, Inc.
THE NEW COFFEE STIRRERS ARE GREAT, BUT I GOT THE LAST ONE.

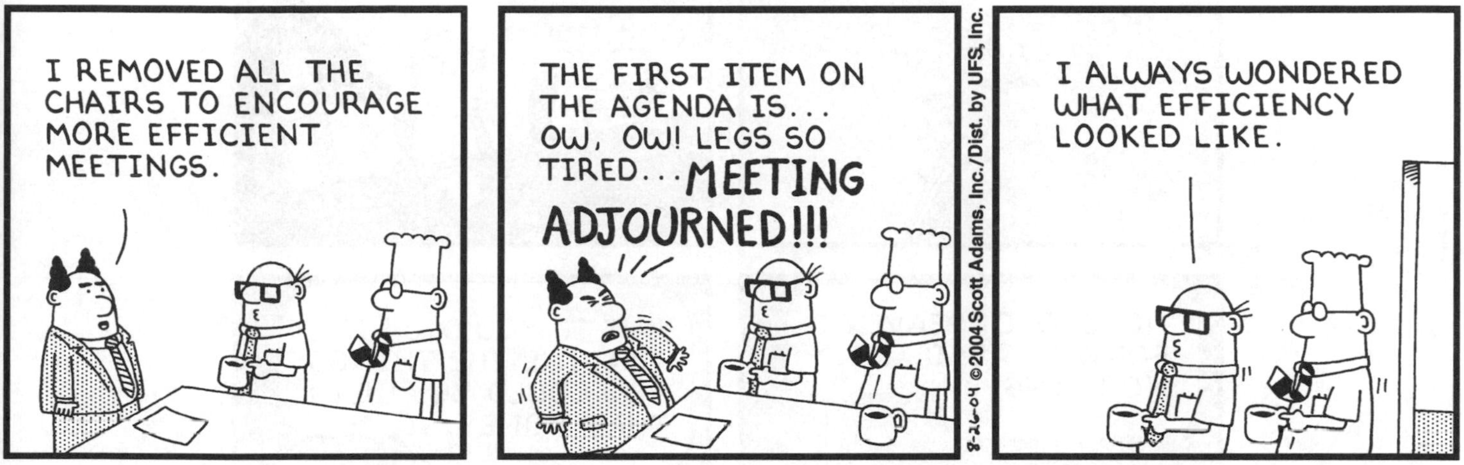
I REMOVED ALL THE CHAIRS TO ENCOURAGE MORE EFFICIENT MEETINGS.
THE FIRST ITEM ON THE AGENDA IS... OW, OW! LEGS SO TIRED... MEETING ADJOURNED!!!
8-26-04 © 2004 Scott Adams, Inc./Dist. by UFS, Inc.
I ALWAYS WONDERED WHAT EFFICIENCY LOOKED LIKE.

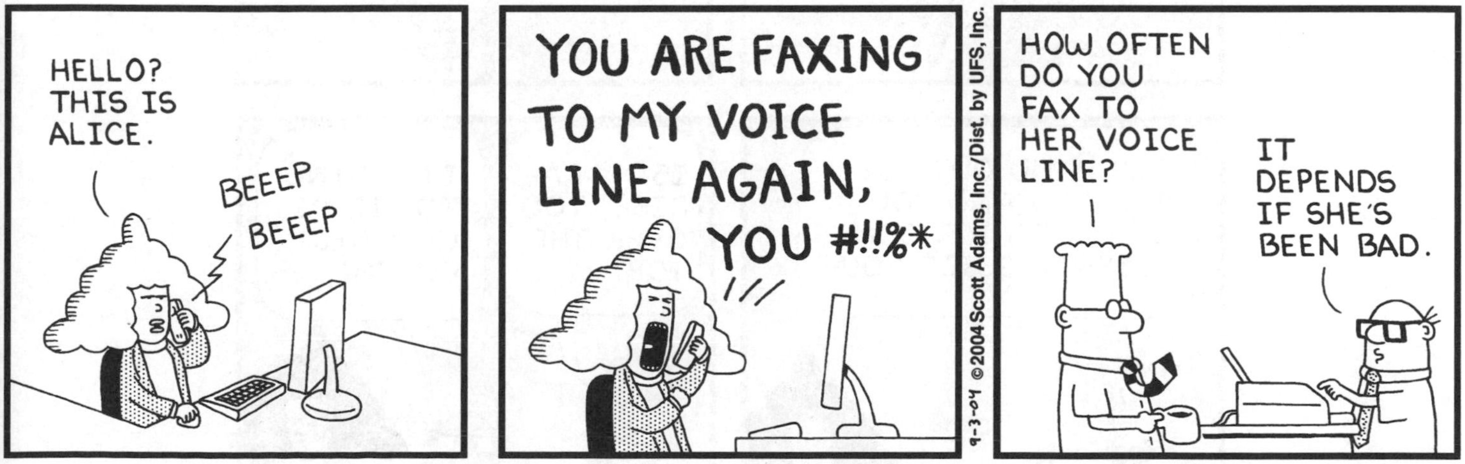
HELLO? THIS IS ALICE.
BEEEP BEEEP
YOU ARE FAXING TO MY VOICE LINE AGAIN, YOU #!!%*
9-3-04 © 2004 Scott Adams, Inc./Dist. by UFS, Inc.
HOW OFTEN DO YOU FAX TO HER VOICE LINE?
IT DEPENDS IF SHE'S BEEN BAD.

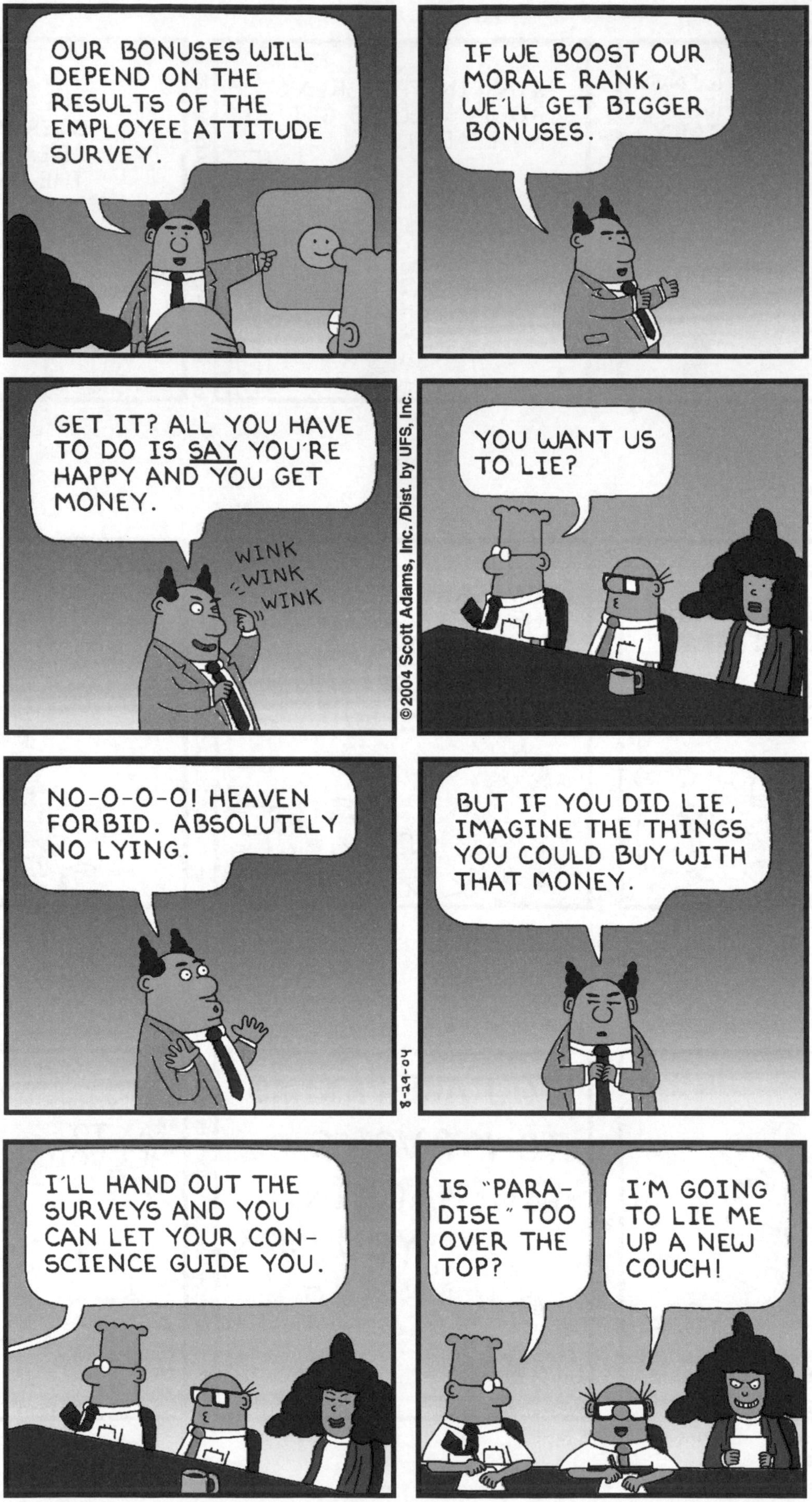
OUR BONUSES WILL DEPEND ON THE RESULTS OF THE EMPLOYEE ATTITUDE SURVEY.
IF WE BOOST OUR MORALE RANK, WE'LL GET BIGGER BONUSES.
GET IT? ALL YOU HAVE TO DO IS SAY YOU'RE HAPPY AND YOU GET MONEY.
WINK WINK WINK
YOU WANT US TO LIE?
NO-O-O-O! HEAVEN FORBID. ABSOLUTELY NO LYING.
BUT IF YOU DID LIE, IMAGINE THE THINGS YOU COULD BUY WITH THAT MONEY.
I'LL HAND OUT THE SURVEYS AND YOU CAN LET YOUR CON-SCIENCE GUIDE YOU.
IS "PARA-DISE" TOO OVER THE TOP?
I'M GOING TO LIE ME UP A NEW COUCH!
©2004 Scott Adams, Inc./Dist. by UFS, Inc.
8-29-04

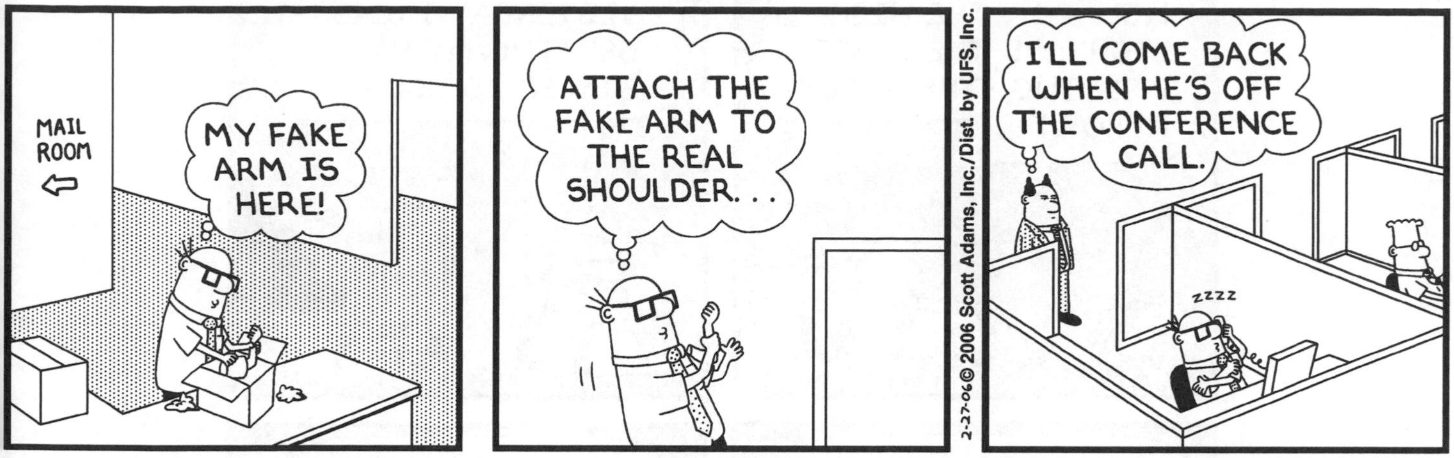
MAIL ROOM
MY FAKE ARM IS HERE!
ATTACH THE FAKE ARM TO THE REAL SHOULDER. . .
2-27-06 © 2006 Scott Adams, Inc./Dist. by UFS, Inc.
I'LL COME BACK WHEN HE'S OFF THE CONFERENCE CALL.
ZZZZ

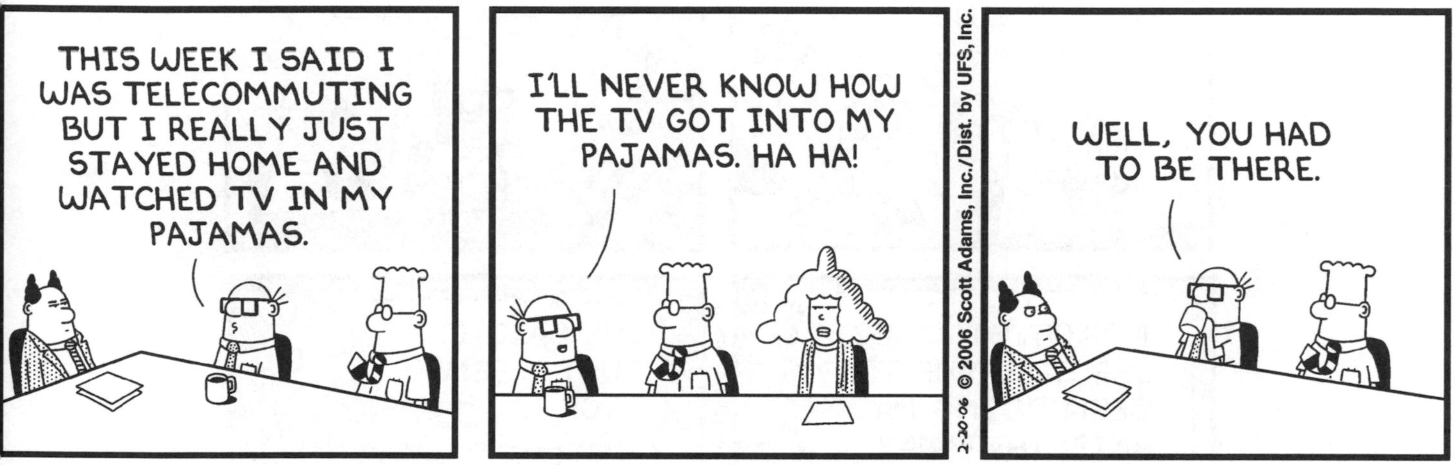
THIS WEEK I SAID I WAS TELECOMMUTING BUT I REALLY JUST STAYED HOME AND WATCHED TV IN MY PAJAMAS.
I'LL NEVER KNOW HOW THE TV GOT INTO MY PAJAMAS. HA HA!
2-20-06 © 2006 Scott Adams, Inc./Dist. by UFS, Inc.
WELL, YOU HAD TO BE THERE.

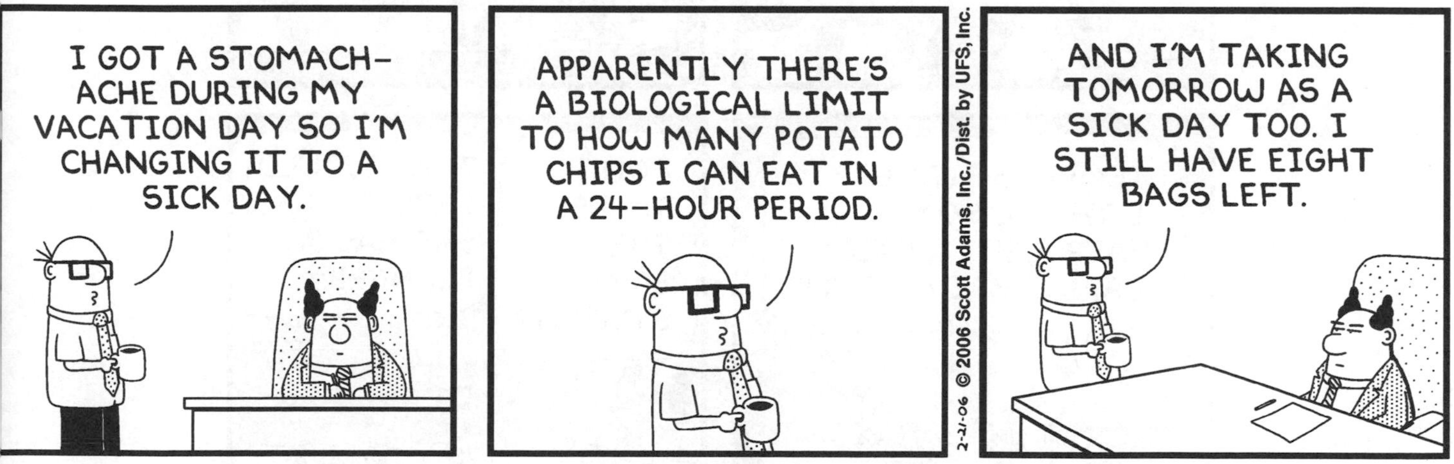
I GOT A STOMACH-ACHE DURING MY VACATION DAY SO I'M CHANGING IT TO A SICK DAY.
APPARENTLY THERE'S A BIOLOGICAL LIMIT TO HOW MANY POTATO CHIPS I CAN EAT IN A 24-HOUR PERIOD.
2-21-06 © 2006 Scott Adams, Inc./Dist. by UFS, Inc.
AND I'M TAKING TOMORROW AS A SICK DAY TOO. I STILL HAVE EIGHT BAGS LEFT.

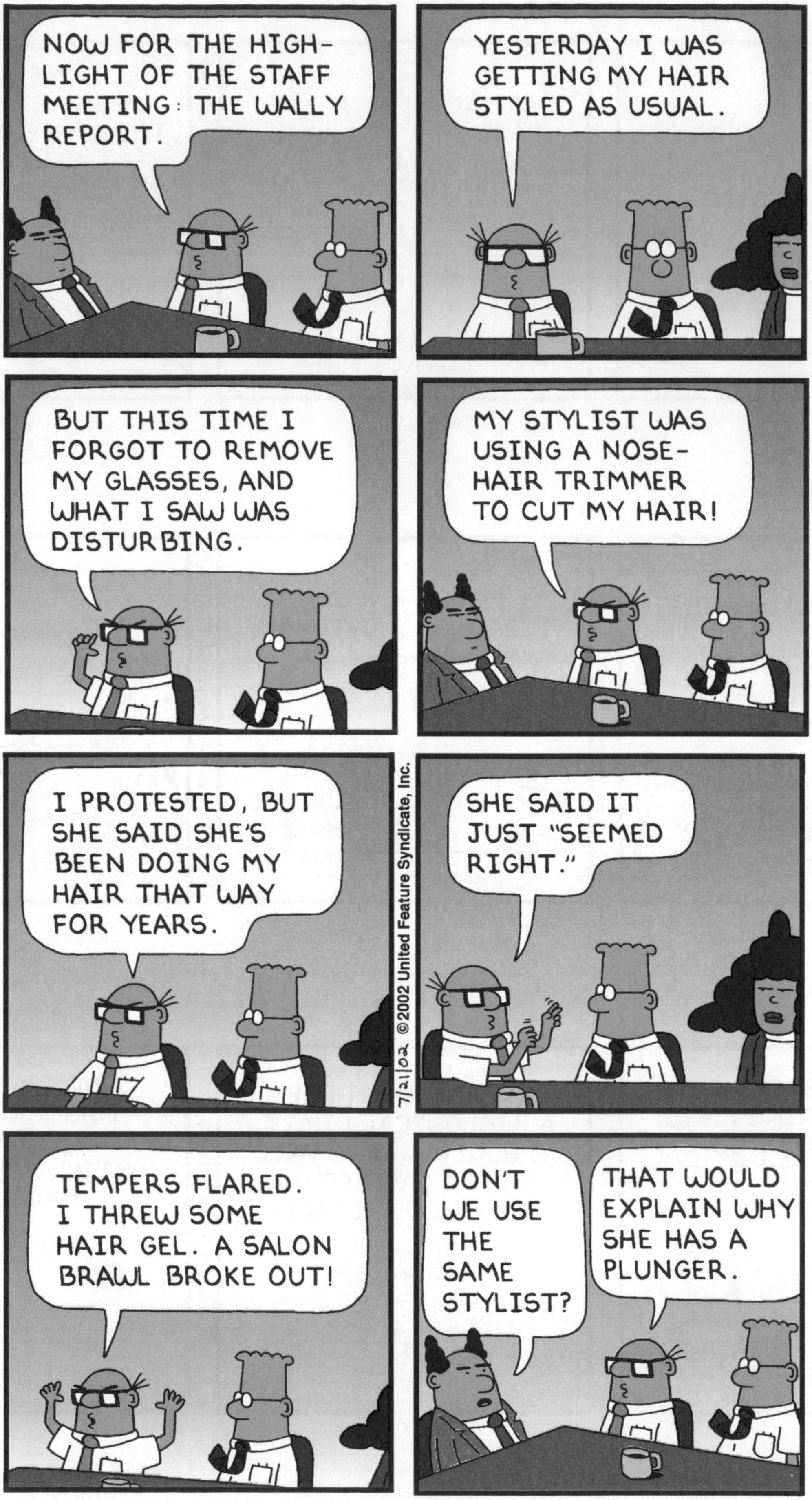
NOW FOR THE HIGH-LIGHT OF THE STAFF MEETING: THE WALLY REPORT.
YESTERDAY I WAS GETTING MY HAIR STYLED AS USUAL.
BUT THIS TIME I FORGOT TO REMOVE MY GLASSES, AND WHAT I SAW WAS DISTURBING.
MY STYLIST WAS USING A NOSE-HAIR TRIMMER TO CUT MY HAIR!
I PROTESTED, BUT SHE SAID SHE'S BEEN DOING MY HAIR THAT WAY FOR YEARS.
SHE SAID IT JUST "SEEMED RIGHT."
TEMPERS FLARED. I THREW SOME HAIR GEL. A SALON BRAWL BROKE OUT!
DON'T WE USE THE SAME STYLIST?
THAT WOULD EXPLAIN WHY SHE HAS A PLUNGER.
7/21/02 © 2002 United Feature Syndicate, Inc.